Women
and the
American Experience
A CONCISE HISTORY

SECOND EDITION

Women
and the
American
Experience

A CONCISE HISTORY

Nancy Woloch

Barnard College

Boston   Burr Ridge, IL   Dubuque, IA   Madison, WI   New York
San Francisco   St. Louis   Bangkok   Bogotá   Caracas   Kuala Lumpur
Lisbon   London   Madrid   Mexico City   Milan   Montreal   New Delhi
Santiago   Seoul   Singapore   Sydney   Taipei   Toronto

McGraw-Hill Higher Education

*A Division of The **McGraw-Hill** Companies*

WOMEN AND THE AMERICAN EXPERIENCE: A Concise History

Published by McGraw-Hill/Irwin, an imprint of The McGraw-Hill Companies, Inc. 1221 Avenue of the Americas, New York, NY, 10020. Copyright © 2002 and 1996, by The McGraw-Hill Companies, Inc. All rights reserved. No part of this publication may be reproduced or distributed in any form or by any means, or stored in a database or retrieval system, without the prior written consent of The McGraw-Hill Companies, Inc., including, but not limited to, in any network or other electronic storage or transmission, or broadcast for distance learning.

Some ancillaries, including electronic and print components, may not be available to customers outside the United States.

This book is printed on acid-free paper.

6 7 8 9 0 FGR/FGR 0 9 8 7 6 5

ISBN 0-07-241821-4

Publisher: *Jane Karpacz*
Sponsoring editor: *Lyn Uhl*
Developmental editor: *Kristen Mellitt*
Marketing manager: *Janise Fry*
Project manager: *Diane M. Folliard*
Production supervisor: *Rose Hepburn*
Coordinator freelance design: *Jennifer McQueen*
Cover designer: *JoAnne Schopler*
Cover Image: *© Christie's Images*
Photo research coordinator: *Jeremy Cheshareck*
Photo researcher: *Connie Gardner*
Compositor: *Interactive Composition Corporation*
Typeface: *Janson Text 10/12*
Printer: *Quebecor/Fairfield Graphics*

Library of Congress Cataloging-in-Publication Data

Woloch, Nancy
    Women and the American experience: a concise history / Nancy Woloch.--2nd ed.
        p. cm.
    Includes bibliographical references (p.) and index.
    ISBN 0-07-241821-4 (alk. paper)
        1. Women--United States--History. I. Title.

HQ1410.W642 2001
305,4'0973--dc21

2001030335

About the Author

 ancy Woloch teaches History and American Studies at Barnard College, Columbia University. She is the author of *Muller v. Oregon: A Brief History with Documents* (1996); editor of *Early American Women: A Documentary History, 1600–1900* (3d. ed., 2002); coauthor of *The American Century: A History of the United States since the 1890s* (5th. ed., 1998), with Walter Lafeber and Richard Polenberg; and coauthor of *The Enduring Vision: A History of the American People* (4th. ed., 2000).

Contents

5 Women at Work, 1860–1920

6 The Rise of the New Woman, 1860–1920

7 Feminism and Suffrage, 1860–1920

8 Cross-Currents: The 1920s

Preface

*I*N THE PAST three decades, the study of women's history has become a thriving academic enterprise. Spurred by feminist revival and the zeal of a new generation of scholars, courses in women's history have multiplied and publication has mushroomed. Collectively, since the late 1960s, historians of women have pursued a major revisionist mission. Not only have they made women historically visible but, by focusing on women's experience, they have uncovered a lost dimension—a distinctive world—of women's work, values, relationships, and politics. To recreate this world, historians have developed new types of data, new sets of concepts, and, above all, a new perspective.

This book is an introduction to the history of American women, based primarily on recent scholarship. It suggests the scope of the field, the types of questions that historians have asked, and the most important issues that have emerged. The focus is on women's experience in family life, economic life, and public life, with attention to diversity of class, race, and region. Of special concern are topics that give women's history its distinctive character. Recurrent themes include, for instance, women's movement into relatively empty or new areas of vocational space; the development of female association and the significance of women's institutions; and women's strategies, individual and collective, for acting as agents of change. Most important, these chapters suggest ways in which women's experience illuminates more general phenomena and thereby alters our interpretation of history as a whole.

NEW TO THE SECOND CONCISE EDITION

Since the first edition of *Women and the American Experience* appeared in 1984, women's history has held fast as the most rapidly growing sector of American history; the rate of productivity continues to accelerate. In subsequent editions, I have sought to keep pace with the continual torrent of research and publication. This revision of the concise edition reflects an ongoing effort to bring the contents of the book up to date. In the past decade, for example, extensive scholarship has offered new insight about woman suffrage. In this instance and many others, the text has been reshaped to include recent research. Second, this revision reflects increased attention to diversity and ethnicity. New or enlarged sections concern, for instance, Native American women in the eighteenth century, African American women under slavery and in Reconstruction, women's roles in Chinese communities in nineteenth-century California, Japanese American women in World War II, African American women and Mexican American women in the twentieth century, and women's recent experiences as immigrants. Third, the final chapter, Chapter 11, on women's history since

1975, now devotes more attention to women's impact on public policy and concludes with a new section on women and the law. Finally, the "Suggested Readings" that follow each chapter have been expanded to include recent publications. The book thus continues to offer readers the most comprehensive, up-to-date bibliography of American women's history available in print.

WEBSITE

Also new for this edition is an American women's history Website (www.mhhe.com/americanwomen), which provides quiz questions for students, links to relevant Websites, and more.

ACKNOWLEDGMENTS

During the years that this book was in progress, I have collected many debts. For the second edition of the concise version, I would like to thank the following reviewers: DeAnna E. Beachley, Community College of Southern Nevada; Sidney R. Bland, James Madison University; Virginia R. Boynton, Western Illinois University; Susan E. Gray, Arizona State University; Margaret A. Lowe, Bridgewater State College; Karen Pastorello, Tompkins Cortland Community College; Donna W. Sherwood, University of Tennessee; and Susan Thomas, Hollins University. My sincere gratitude to all of the reviewers for their constructive suggestions and their encouragement. My colleagues at Barnard College have been, as always, a fount of assistance. I would also like to thank project managers Diane Folliard and Brittney Corrigan-McElroy; copyeditor Kerry Beeaker; proofreader Stacey Corbin; and indexer Julie Nemer. Finally, I am most grateful to my editors at McGraw-Hill, Lyn Uhl and Kristen Mellitt. To all of the above, my immense appreciation.

NANCY WOLOCH

CHAPTER ONE

The Seventeenth Century: A Frontier Society

T HE SHIPS THAT brought the earliest settlers to Jamestown and Plymouth also carried a heavy load of social ideology. Along with their chests and trunks, cows and Bibles, English colonists imported firm ideas on how society should be ordered and authority distributed, in family, community, church, and state. Whatever their rank or sect, they knew that society was a living organism, its health dependent on that of its parts. They also knew that basic patterns of power, submission, and mutual obligation determined the nature of all relations, whether of child and parent, wife and husband, servant and master, subject and ruler, "inferiors" and "betters," or man and God. These patterns permeated their compacts, charters, contracts, sermons, statutes, and accounts of personal experience. Quickly incorporated in colonial institutions, they were used to impose a modicum of order on a shapeless terrain and to establish an English mode of life.

The position of women was a vital thread in the ideological cloth, so fundamental it was hardly conspicuous, so axiomatic it needed no defense. The Englishwoman had a subordinate place in the social scheme that could be defined only by deficiencies and limitations; she had no innate assets to distinguish her from a man. On the contrary, God and nature had made her weaker, in wit, will, and physical capacity. First in transgression and tainted by original sin, "the woman is a weak creature not endued with like strength and constancy of mind," as English parsons told their congregations. Inferior of brain and morally suspect, she depended on man to protect her interests, ensure her submission, and see that she did as little damage as possible. In England, as in every civilized state on the face of the earth, her passivity and powerlessness, divinely ordained, were bolstered by law, upheld by the church, and sanctioned by custom.

On a personal level, the Englishwoman was, ideally, meek and obedient. Tradition provided her with secondary status in the family, where she served her husband, cared for her children, and worked in the household. "We cannot but think that the woman was made before the Fall that man might rule over her," advised a manual of *Domesticall Duties* in the 1620s. In church as at home, her role was limited. According to a conservative reading of Paul, she was "not to teach, nor to hold authority over the man, but to be in silence." Her place in public life was similarly circumscribed. Common law, evaded only by those with class and clout, ensured the submergence of the married woman's identity under that of her husband. As a "feme covert," she was unable to own property, bring suit, make contracts, or act as a legal individual. Silent in church, subservient at home, and dependent on men, the seventeenth-century Englishwoman occupied a recessive space, an inconspicuous niche. She was part of the background scenery for a busy stage on which men made laws, wars, empires, and history.

If subordinate status was the common denominator of English womanhood, class provided variations. Upper-class women in England (aristocrats, gentry, or members of the mercantile elite) exerted authority over their inferiors and sometimes wielded power, especially when male relatives were absent or dead. Under such circumstances, they might inherit estates, run manorial courts, manage lands, and handle business affairs. Few were leisured or highly accomplished, but wealth and rank provided leverage. Propertied families could, for instance, arrange marriage contracts that preserved a daughter's property for her heirs or gave her control over it. The wives of "middling" people—small merchants, artisans, shopkeepers, and richer yeomen—had fewer options and more work. Their lives were devoted to housewifery, an all-encompassing realm of production soon familiar to colonial wives. If married to craftsmen or shopkeepers, they also helped out in shops and workshops or, if on the land, managed some aspects of family enterprise, such as poultry or dairy. Poor women in England might be part of the "excess" population, displaced by enclosure or tied down to tenancy. They worked in the fields or hired out their services as unskilled agricultural laborers or domestic servants, earning half as much as men. Some went into prostitution, begging, thieving, or the poorhouse, from which, if young, they might be released to enter servitude in some new and unpopulated colony.

While the contours of the English class structure were lost in transit across the Atlantic and gradually replaced by new ones, the ideology of female subordination, far more basic to the social order, was transported intact and easily replanted in colonial soil. The purpose of settlement was not to tamper with traditional roles and institutions but to re-create them as soon as possible. As a result, like their sisters in England, women in the seventeenth-century English colonies were excluded from positions of power and authority, such as government or ministry. Their lives centered around the household, and they rarely entered the foreground of events—nor had they any intention of doing so. The visible women of the seventeenth-century colonies were usually those brought briefly into center stage by catastrophe or deviance—such as Indian captivity or witchcraft charges.

But while the ideology of subordination remained intact, the hazards and needs of their new environment constantly affected women's roles. All colonists lived in a young society that bordered on the wilderness, an elongated frontier. Throughout the century, the English colonies had wealth of land, need for labor, paucity of women, and great dependence on the family as an agent of settlement. These frontier qualities affected the Anglo-American woman's options without revamping her basic status: as "weaker vessel," subordinate of man, and marginal member of society.

A NECESSARY GOOD

Anne Bradstreet, daughter of a prominent Puritan family, was the 18-year-old bride of a young colonist, an assistant of the Massachusetts Bay Company, when she landed in Boston harbor in 1630. Finding "a new world and new manners," she was initially overcome with dismay. "But after I was convinced that it was the will of God, I submitted to it." Whether women emigrated as family members or as indentured servants, they rarely controlled their own destiny. They were also in a minority. The vast majority of new arrivals were men.

The *Mayflower* arrived at Plymouth in 1620 with 102 passengers, 28 of them women. At Jamestown there were at first no women at all. In 1625, three-quarters of the white people of Virginia were men, and by midcentury there were six men to every woman. Maryland, by the 1650s, had about 600 men and fewer than 200 women. There, too, the proportion of men continued to increase. Throughout the colonies, of course, the balance—or imbalance—of the sexes was always in flux. More settlers constantly arrived, most of them men. New generations were born, which began to decrease the sexual disparities. Finally, colonists began to move off to the edge of settlement, which tended to drain some of the oversupply of men on the eastern seaboard. By 1700 or even earlier, in some parts of Massachusetts, the sex ratio started to approach equality. But as a rule during the first century of settlement, the balance of the sexes was always skewed and men outnumbered women—as they did not in England, where there were about 91 men to every one hundred women throughout the era of colonization.

Sexual disparity was greatest in the early Chesapeake, where it affected the process of settlement. Of the 75,000 white people who emigrated to Virginia and Maryland between 1630 and 1680, up to three-quarters were indentured servants who arrived as single individuals. Four out of five were men. Women were in such a minority that few male servants found wives, and those who did married relatively late, after their terms of indenture had expired. These marriages were brief; a harsh climate and rampant disease shortened life expectancy. Four out of 10 immigrants died within six years, often of malaria, typhoid, or dysentery. Chesapeake men might live to 48 and women to 44, about a decade less than in England. Under such circumstances, family life took on a tentative quality. Late in the seventeenth century, half of the spouses in one Maryland county became widows or widowers within seven years. Of the four children who might be born to such couples, two died in childhood. Survivors, if orphaned, were left in the care of neighbors or relatives or put out to service by special orphans courts.

From the outset, Chesapeake denizens recognized the dire implications of female scarcity. As soon as men arrive in Virginia, one colonist reported, "they grow very sensible of the Misfortune of Wanting Wives." Early Virginians attempted one remedy: importing shiploads of women. Between 1620 and 1622 about 150 "pure and spotless" women disembarked and were auctioned off for 80 pounds of tobacco apiece or more to future husbands. Recent research reveals the social origins of some of these prospective brides. Of the 57 women who arrived in 1621, median age 20, most were daughters of artisans, tradesmen, and gentry, mainly from the London area; they came with recommendations from their kinfolk and acquaintances attesting to their good character and domestic skills.

In some rare instances, unmarried women gained title to tracts of land. In Maryland in the 1630s, two English gentlewomen, Mary and Margaret Brent, each held large feudal estates. Subsequently, the southern colonies made efforts to attract men *with* wives. By basing the size of land grants given to household heads on the number of household members, the Virginia and Maryland legislatures attempted to spur the migration of families. Still, the preponderance of male newcomers continued; tobacco planters felt a greater need for men than women as indentured labor. Female scarcity and the frequency of early death prevented the early Chesapeake population from reproducing itself. To maintain a labor supply, the region became dependent on infusions of immigrants, primarily indentured servants and, later on, slaves.

The minority of women who arrived in the Chesapeake, almost all as indentured servants, derived several benefits from the region's unbalanced sex ratios. Because they were so vastly outnumbered, they had virtual certainty of marriage and far greater choice of spouse than did poor young women left behind in England. A female servant might even escape her full term of service by marrying a man who offered to buy out her contract and promote her to wife. Devastating death rates also affected women's opportunities. Chesapeake husbands who wrote wills often made their widows executors of their estates, a more liberal arrangement than practiced elsewhere. In the latter part of the seventeenth century, many husbands left their wives most or all of their property for life, despite the likelihood that these widows would remarry. But such gains for women reflected the region's serious problems—female scarcity and high mortality. Only at the end of the century, when a native-born population arose with higher immunity to disease and equal proportions of boys and girls, did life spans lengthen and sex ratios start to become more balanced. The Chesapeake population soon began to grow primarily through natural increase.

New England settlement provided a startling contrast. Indeed, the Puritan colonists held demographic advantages over both their southern neighbors and kinfolk left in England. Unlike new arrivals in the Chesapeake, who were mainly single individuals, most immigrants to New England arrived in family units. A salubrious climate extended life expectancy to 65 for men and slightly less for women. Marriages might last a quarter-century or more, and large families abounded. Although the seventeenth-century New England wife did not have the 10 or 12 children once thought to be the typical colonial brood, she might have six or seven—more than the four or five children in the average English family. About 80 percent of infants survived to maturity. Reproducing themselves at a prodigious rate, New Englanders created their own labor force and never depended on servants or slaves. Unlike seventeenth-century southerners, they achieved a fairly balanced sex ratio quite quickly, which facilitated their population boom.

Dependent on the family as an agent of settlement, Puritan authorities took steps to see that all women married. In Salem, Massachusetts, unmarried women at first received their own land parcels. But this procedure soon ended. No woman was expected to remain unmarried for long, nor did Puritan authorities wish to encourage the single state. "It would be a bad president [sic]," the Massachusetts governor told one applicant, Deborah Holmes, "to keep hous alone." The colonies needed productive families, not propertied spinsters. Women, moreover, were clearly "without which there is no comfortable living for men," as Puritan minister John Cotton proclaimed. "It is true of them what is wont to be said of governments, *That bad ones are better than none."* According to Cotton, woman was not a necessary evil but "a necessary Good, such as it was not good that man should be without."

It is tempting to debate the relative advantages of Chesapeake women, who seemed to profit from their low numbers, and New England women, with their longer life expectancy and greater chance of stable family life. But as historian Mary Beth Norton points out, the contrast between these two modes of seventeenth-century settlement obscure the commonality of female experience throughout the colonies. North or South, immigrant or native-born, virtually all white women in the English colonies married. Consequently much of a woman's life would be spent as the mistress of a family unit on a family farm.

In the colonies, as in England, lines of authority and submission within the family were clearly drawn—most clearly by Puritans, who constantly examined social theories. But the basic prerequisite for a happy home, wifely obedience, applied everywhere. "A true wife accounts her subjection [as] her honor and freedom," John Winthrop, Massachusetts Bay's governor, explained in 1645, "and would not think her condition safe and free, but in subjection to her husband's authority." Among Chesapeake residents, the same ideal prevailed, though authorities interfered less frequently to impose it in practice. The head of the family, in all colonies, North or South, was expected to control its members. He wielded authority over wife and children, supervised finances, made family decisions, served as intermediary between family and community, and in more pious circles, provided the conduit through which God's blessings flowed.

The preoccupation of seventeenth-century authorities with the "Well Ordered Family"—the title of a 1712 sermon by New England minister Benjamin Wadsworth—appealed to colonists for several reasons. In seventeenth-century England, patriarchy was not only a domestic habit but a political and religious one; the family was a model for church and state. Every institution had its own hierarchy, with authority residing in the "head." The English Reformation, especially the rise of Puritanism, had increased the importance of the patriarchal family. Colonization did so even more. In the colonies, where the family served as an agent of settlement and a source of population, where the economy depended on the family farm, and where other institutions were new and precarious, domestic order was especially crucial. The colonial family was the very foundation of social cohesion and far too valuable to be ripped apart by internal discord.

Accordingly, colonial authorities frequently reiterated the principle of male authority and wifely submission. But for the same reason, colonial wives were protected within marriage to a greater degree than English counterparts and beyond the dictates of common law. Because domestic unity was viewed as a public good, all colonies devised measures that encroached on the home. Such laws were intended to keep families intact, to protect family members from one another, and to prevent dependents from being thrown on public welfare as community charges. This was not a coherent, systematic policy, intended to enhance the status of women, but rather an amalgam of statutes and practices intended to maintain social order. Still, wives sometimes benefited.

Throughout the colonies, marriage was recognized as a civil contract based on the mutual consent of both parties. Husbands were compelled to support, and cohabit with, their wives; deserters could be hounded or errant husbands hauled into court for adultery or failing to provide. In New England, where authorities kept an especially "watchfulle eye" over the home, "disorderly carriage" within it was likely to evoke reprimands. Statutes outlawed or limited physical abuse of wives. The Massachusetts Body of Liberties in 1641 prohibited wife-beating, "unless it be in his own defense upon her assault." A New England husband might be fined for "abusing his wife by kiking her of from a stoole into the fier," as was a man in Plymouth. Law enforcement did not end desertion, which was common, or eliminate domestic disorder. The violence that pervaded seventeenth-century life tended to flare up within the home as well as outside it. In the southern colonies, moreover, the law prevented husbands only from inflicting permanent injury or death on wives—one of many factors that distinguished the lot of a southern woman colonist from that of a New England woman. Still, the colonial wife gained, in principle, some legal protection that her English counterpart lacked.

Colonial wives might also benefit from antenuptial and postnuptial contracts, which mitigated common law and were used in England only by the rich. The antenuptial contract enabled a woman to retain control over her own property; for example, that signed by a Plymouth woman in 1667 entitled her "to enjoy all her house and lands, goods and cattle, that she is now possessed of, to dispose of them at her own free will." Typically, widows who remarried signed antenuptial contracts. The postnuptial contract reconciled a couple who had disputes or enabled them to separate but compelled the husband to support his family. Acceptance of such contracts, or equity practices, helped to preserve domestic peace and public order. They also served to keep wives and children off the public dole.

In New England, some wives had a last resort. The Puritans, in their zeal to promote domestic unity, granted absolute divorce, with the right to wed again (divorce *a vinculo matrimonii*). The rationale was that once an unstable marriage was dissolved, the aggrieved spouse, usually a woman, would be free to remarry and establish a stable, harmonious family. This policy was a major innovation. In England, where marriage was a sacrament and indissoluble, only the wealthy, mainly men, were able to terminate their unions, through special acts of Parliament or ecclesiastical annulments. Elsewhere in the colonies, legal separations with property settlements (divorce *a mensa et thoro*) might be arranged, but absolute divorce was rare, and in the southern colonies, nonexistent. In New England, however, divorce with remarriage was possible. Divorces were granted most frequently for such causes as desertion, bigamy, failure to provide, and adultery. They were granted more often to women than to men. Nevertheless, far more women petitioned for divorces than received them. Overall, there were few such divorces. Massachusetts granted 27 divorces between 1639 and 1692. Connecticut granted nine between 1665 and 1678, all for desertion. Women were petitioners in eight of the nine cases.

Women, however, were not the only beneficiaries of the colonies' concern with maintaining harmonious homes. Seventeenth-century laws and decisions also protected husbands from wives who ran up debts, waged attacks, or engaged in adultery, a crime against husband and community. The most common offense committed by wives was verbal abuse. If seventeenth-century women were silent in church, they were verbally assertive outside it—at least according to court records. Apparently keen on local gossip, they were liable to scold their husbands, slander their neighbors, and curse their enemies, thereby threatening the stability of home and community. Reports of women's verbal aggression were not peculiar to colonial America; such aggression was noted frequently in English villages too. The hostile harangue may have been the Englishwoman's response to a world controlled by men, in which women had no formal power. In her study of Maryland slander cases, historian Mary Beth Norton points out that gossip, which could lead to defamation, was for the seventeenth-century woman a means of affecting the social order and "perhaps the most valuable and reliable means of advocating or protecting her own interests." But colonial courts made efforts to check verbal aggression.

Massachusetts women might be sanctioned for persisting in "scurrilous language and bad speeches," as was Bridget Oliver, hauled into the Essex County Court in 1678 for calling her husband "opproprious" names on a Sunday. In New Haven, one-third of seventeenth-century slander cases involved women as complainants or alleged slanderers. In New Netherland, where Dutch law permitted married women a wide array of independent action, wives were sued for defamation and on a few occasions sued others for the same. A Virginia statute of 1662 provided ducking as a penalty for "brabling women [who] often slander and scandalize their neighbors," to relieve their spouses of "vexatious suits." Public order and domestic peace, it seemed, were too valuable to be ruined by a loud-mouthed wife. The ideal of marriage, as expressed in a Virginia postnuptial contract reconciling an especially disputatious couple, was "to live lovingly together and behave themselves to each other as a good wife and husband ought to do." In this case, the wife had to promise to stop running off with the husband's money and to forswear "vile names."

Whatever legal improvements the seventeenth-century colonial wife might enjoy, moreover, did not revise the structure of the family or provide her with a power base within it. The "well-ordered" home was a patriarchy; the wife's role was always subordinate. Her obligation, as Benjamin Wadsworth explained, was to devote herself to husband and household, "to keep at home, educating her children, keeping and improving what is got by the industry of man." Although expected to be obedient, the wife was not a servant or child but more of a junior partner, with partial control over children and servants. But her clout as a parent was limited. Children were legally a father's possession. More to the point, he was likely to work in or around the home and was therefore an active participant in child rearing. Parenthood was a joint occupation, in which mothers had more responsibility but fathers had more authority. It was also an increasingly important one.

In these new colonies, with their scarcity of population and paucity of labor, child rearing took on new significance. Children formed a larger part of the population than in England, exceeding half the inhabitants in some colonies, and there were more of them per household. With the exception of the early Chesapeake, colonial reproduction was impressive. The colonial wife, who married several years younger than her English counterpart at age 20 to 23 instead of 25 or 26, spent up to two decades of her life bearing children and most if not all of her adult life raising them. In addition, she might have several pregnancies that ended in miscarriage or stillbirth. Despite the frequency of infant deaths (slightly over half of colonial infants could expect to reach adulthood), the mortality of children was lower than in England. A higher colonial survival rate may have fostered greater emotional investment in children on the part of parents. Still, as early death occurred regularly, seventeenth-century family life had an aura of risk, loss, and impermanence.

In two-thirds of colonial marriages, one of the partners could be expected to die within 10 years. The seventeenth-century mother who had her last child in her late 30s might well be dead or widowed before that child left home. Or she might die much earlier. One-fifth of adult deaths among women occurred during childbirth. When preparing the equipment for lying-in, as a 1663 pamphlet of advice for "teeming American women" counseled, "she might perchance need no other linen than a winding sheet." The drama of childbirth, the pivotal event of women's lives, was clearly a perilous one. It was also a public event, an all-female ritual, at which a group of women relatives and neighbors congregated, along with the ubiquitous midwife. On no other commonplace public occasion were women in control and men excluded or relegated to the sidelines.

Once the risks of childbirth were survived, seventeenth-century motherhood was neither a power preserve nor an outlet for specific gender-linked abilities. Women were not believed to be endowed with any specific feminine attributes, such as a gift for passing on moral precepts to the young. Most seventeenth-century records of family life, such as the diary of Samuel Sewall, exemplary Puritan, give the impression that the father was the focal figure in child rearing. Sewall, for instance, actively prepared his children for the possibility of early death or eternal damnation, a prospect that threw his daughter Betty into fits of weeping and months of melancholia. Still, wives had a special realm of control as parents: the socialization of girls. Almost all education took place in the home, and the major thrust of this education was character formation and vocational training. Girls were supposed to absorb the personality traits valued in women, such as obedience, industry, piety, and the habit of silence—although the last may have been a fond hope. They were also supposed to learn the arts of housewifery, as were young servants and apprentices who lived in the household for extended terms.

The relations of seventeenth-century mothers and daughters remain murky. But because daughterhood was primarily a long apprenticeship in housewifery, one can assume that daughters, like young apprentices, faced a disadvantage. After surviving early childhood, a period devoted to breaking the will and eradicating aggression, girls had to spend most of their time in the home, listening to, working for, and emulating the parent or mistress, who herself held a subservient role even while in charge of children, apprentices, and servants. Although conflict between mothers and daughters rarely surfaced in colonial records, the status of servitude was rarely trouble-free for either mistress or young servant. When Mary Dudley begged her stepmother, Margaret Winthrop, in 1636, to send her "a good lusty servant that hath skill in a dairy," the girl turned out to be "a great affliction," "insolent in carriage," and "insufferable," who abused her mistress with "reviling speeches and filthie language"—the standard weapon of female discontent.

The tiny size of the seventeenth-century house made such discord (whether between mistress and servant, parent and child, or husband and wife) especially intolerable. The Winthrop home in the 1630s, with its six rooms, lofts, and garrets, was relatively large. But the ordinary dwelling in the new colonies was more likely to be one room—"the hall," which served for sleeping, eating, cooking, and working—or possibly two, plus whatever lean-tos and sleeping lofts were later added on. This limited space, inhabited by parents, children, and sometimes apprentices or servants, offered little privacy; but the modern concept of privacy was alien to the seventeenth-century. Private life, moreover, was difficult to distinguish from public life, especially as living and working were not separated. The seventeenth-century home was not removed from the family enterprise, usually a farm. Nor was it a haven from labor but rather its fulcrum. The household, for women, was an arena of production. The seventeenth-century wife was a "necessary good" not only as a wife and parent but also as a worker.

HOUSEWIFERY AND TRADE

Household labor, like the ideology of subordination, shaped women's lives. The seventeenth-century housewife, in her confined living space, might be encumbered with equipment—cast-iron pots, enormous cauldrons, kettles, mortars, pestles, candle molds, salt barrels, and possibly a butter churn or spinning wheel. "Housewifery" meant the lifelong production of food, clothing, and household items; the newer the region, the more rugged the job.

Commonly, the wife cooked and washed clothes over open fires. She planted vegetable gardens, milked cows, operated dairies, produced hard cider, pickled and preserved food, and smoked and salted meat. When not feeding hens, pigs, children, and servants, or stitching shirts or knitting stockings, she made lye out of ashes, soap out of lye and animal fat, wax out of bayberries, tallow out of wax, candles out of tallow, and medicines out of weeds and herbs. Often she exchanged labor with neighbors, if she had any, to complete a job, such as berrying, or a product, such as a skein of thread. Spinning was the colonial housewife's prized vocation, as well as an important skill to be passed on to daughters and apprentices. Not every housewife possessed such a skill. In mid-eighteenth-century Massachusetts, for instance, only about half of households contained dairy equipment or spinning wheels. The seventeenth-century household was typically more primitive, and the woman who ran it was unlikely to have such special skills.

In addition to the basic tasks of housewifery, the colonial wife helped out in the family enterprise, whether shop, plantation, or frontier farm—a type of labor that merged into whatever she did at home. If married to a craftsman or shopkeeper, she assisted in shop or workshop. If married to a farmer, she might help in the fields, although outdoor work was increasingly relegated, if possible, to servants and slaves. Still, on the perimeter of settlement, as William Byrd discovered when exploring the North Carolina–Virginia frontier, a woman might "carry a gun in the woods, and kill deer, turkeys etc. and shoot down wild cattle, catch and tye hogs . . . and perform most exercises as well as men." Whatever the locale, her responsibilities were fairly well defined—especially in the case of the Maryland bride who was obliged by contract in 1681 to "Dresse the victuals, milk the Cowes, wash for the servants and Doe all the things necessary for a woman to doe upon the . . . plantation."

The necessity of work was easily absorbed into ideals of womanhood, which reflected the needs of family and community. If obedience was the prerequisite for a harmonious home, industry was vital to a productive one. For women as for men, idleness was frowned upon, hard work was a virtue, and physical labor was not seen as a degradation, as so much of it was involved in housewifery. In New England, "idleness and scottish carriage" resulted in a summons to court and a fine or worse. Moreover, the work women did at home in the English colonies was familiar enough to wives of "middling" means in England. The economic value of housewifery, however, did not enlarge a wife's authority or enhance her status. Wives lacked control over the distribution of family resources and, in most cases, as common law applied, had no control over their own possessions. Still, seventeenth-century roles had a certain fluidity. When a husband was absent, historian Laurel Thatcher Ulrich points out, the wife was expected to take over his position as household head and defender of family interests. Hiring hands, keeping accounts, or managing a farm, the spouse of an absentee husband assumed full authority as his surrogate.

Industry, moreover, was a passport to active roles beyond the home, where women filled a wide variety of economic loopholes left by men. The colonies were so land-rich, labor-scarce, and sparsely inhabited that economic space was not yet firmly divided between the sexes, and woman's "place" easily expanded to fill up whatever vacancies existed. This meant there was opportunity to earn income, by producing goods, providing services, or running a commercial venture. Again, this was not a coherent policy but a pragmatic, haphazard one, appropriate in a young economy with few skilled workers. Women in the colonies, as in England, were a marginal work force; their options contracted and expanded as the economy warranted. In seventeenth-century England, women's roles were contracting. There, too, women had commonly filled the interstices of economic space, as "spinsters" and "brewsters," healers and midwives, even carpenters and printers. But by the end of the century, the most profitable of these spaces had vanished and women were forced out of them by men's craft organizations and guilds. Specialization of labor eroded their economic options. In the relatively empty colonies, however, where men could easily acquire land, there was plenty of space in trades and services for women.

The colonial housewife had an eye for exchange. If she was a skilled worker, she could turn homemade goods into income. Housewives sold whatever surplus items they baked, brewed, preserved, spun, wove, or sewed, as well as such products as medicines or cosmetics. This type of trading was an easy extension of household industry, domestic enterprise enlarged. A housewife might also run a small shop out of her home, to supply her neighbors with hardware, needles, cloth, or thread. Married women often sold their services as nurses, midwives, and medical practitioners. These services, too, were extensions of their domestic roles and involved some facet of household skills. Finally, widows might replace their husbands—again an extension of their work in the family as helpers and assistants in family enterprise.

As a result, throughout the colonial era, widows could be found in a wide range of occupations and trades. Indeed, seventeenth-century propertied men often left their estates to the charge of their wives—a practice that declined in the eighteenth century. Widows, therefore, managed lands they had inherited, ran small businesses, and invested in large ones. They took over enterprises their husbands had started (sometimes temporarily until sons could replace them); widows commonly worked as shopkeepers, grocers, booksellers, tavernkeepers, or even, on occasion, as blacksmiths, butchers, or gunsmiths. A dead husband could provide legitimate entrée to commerce, trades, and managerial roles.

The widow, as a single woman, or feme sole, had many rights under common law. Unlike the wife, or feme covert, whose legal identity was "covered" by that of her husband, the feme sole, whether spinster or widow, was a legal individual. She could own, buy, and sell property, sue and be sued, make contracts, administer estates, and hold power of attorney. The spinster was a rarity in the seventeenth century, and the propertied spinster even more so. One was Margaret Brent, a wealthy Catholic who arrived in Maryland in 1638 with her sister and two brothers. Maryland then offered 1,000-acre manors to anyone who transported and provided for able male workers, so each of the Brents received huge land grants, run on the pattern of feudal estates. As a proprietor, Margaret Brent reigned over a manorial court, speculated in land, sponsored the migration of other settlers, and served as agent and attorney for her brothers. She also spent much of her time in the Maryland courts, suing for debts that were owed her and acting on behalf of others as well. (There were only a few hundred people in Maryland at this time.) Before Governor Leonard Calvert died in 1647, he named Margaret Brent executrix of his will, and in this capacity she took over his affairs and settled his estate. To facilitate her task, she applied to the Maryland assembly for two votes, one as proprietor and the other as executrix. When the assembly denied her request, she contested its authority by protesting "against all proceedings in this present assembly unless she may be present and have vote afores'd."

Brent's status as landed proprietor in a new colony was unusual. But other seventeenth-century women occasionally served in court, representing themselves, their absent husbands, and others. Although Maryland ended women's right to represent clients a decade after Margaret Brent's protest, other colonies permitted the practice. In New Amsterdam, where Dutch law allowed great latitude, the wife whose husband was away on a voyage could manage his land and serve as his attorney. She could also be licensed as a "feme sole trader," to keep his affairs alive in his absence or even, on occasion, during his presence. Not every colony distributed feme sole privileges with such largesse, but colonial assemblies liberally granted permission to unmarried or widowed women to run businesses. When the Massachusetts General Court, in 1692, provided that any single woman of good repute be permitted "exercise of any lawful trade or employment for a livelihood," with the permission of the selectmen, it confirmed a practice of long standing.

This latitude, of course, was in the community interest. A destitute spinster or widow could be a drain on a locale's resources. Enterprise on the part of the feme sole kept her off the public dole and enabled her to keep her family unit intact. It also provided the community with useful trades and services. The wealthy widow was especially welcome, because she would be able to invest her funds in local enterprises. In the seventeenth-century Chesapeake region, where women were so scarce, widows who outlived a succession of husbands, acquiring property with each marriage, created what has been called a "widowarchy."

The loss of a husband and the opportunity to enter the world of trade and commerce were hardly prospects women welcomed. Dinah Nuthead, one of the first women to run a print shop, inherited the business in 1695 at the death of her husband, the public printer of Maryland. Nuthead had left her with the press, shop, and—although this was usually a profitable post—a great many debts. With the assembly's consent, Dinah Nuthead continued the business, which must have been a difficult task, as she was illiterate. She remarried as quickly as possible, a year later. Maria Van Rensselaer, widowed in Holland in 1674, came to New York to administer the huge patroonship of Rensselaerwyck, which covered 700,000 acres on both sides of the Hudson, because there was no available man in her family to take charge. Despite her gristmill, sawmill, and sales of wheat and furs to Dutch buyers, Maria had to struggle to keep the estate afloat. "Consider, dear brother," she wrote to her uncooperative brother-in-law in Holland, who was long on criticism but short on assistance, "whether to lose my health and in addition to lose my property and my dearest partner and to be left with six children and such an encumbered estate is not hard on me either." Still, she remained in control of the estate and dealt with its problems until her oldest son was able to take over.

The access of widows to trade and commerce might present problems for local authorities, especially in the case of taverns. New England towns were stringent about who received a liquor license and for what purpose, as taverns in busy seaports rarely catered to a genteel clientele. Usually permission to run a tavern or brew or sell liquor was encumbered with a proviso, such as that a man be hired to work on the premises, or that a woman "sell to none but housekeepers." Or a woman might be licensed to distill and retail liquor, "provided shee did not sell to any of the inhabitants of the town to drinke in her house." But some enterprising women—among them Alice Thomas, Boston tavernkeeper—evaded the rules. In the 1670s, Widow Thomas was accused of selling liquor without a license, receiving stolen goods, profaning the Sabbath, and sponsoring "frequent secret and unseasonable entertainment in her house to Lewd Lascivious and notorious persons of both sexes, giving them opportunity to commit Carnale Wickedness." Although Widow Thomas was fined, whipped, and imprisoned, she pacified the authorities by giving Boston funds for the construction of a sea wall—and presumably returned to her tavern.

Not surprisingly, a high concentration of tradeswomen appeared in New Amsterdam, where liberal Dutch law permitted grants of feme sole trader privileges to married women. Here, Margaret Philipse, merchant and shipowner, pursued her vocation through several marriages. Born in Holland, she had arrived in New Netherlands in the 1650s as the sister of an indentured servant and soon married a wealthy trader. Before his death, she worked as an agent for Dutch merchants; and after she was widowed in 1661, she became a merchant and trader herself, shipping furs to Holland and selling the merchandise she received in New York. After marriage to another rich New Yorker in 1662 and the signing of an antenuptial agreement that left her part of her inheritance, Margaret Philipse continued her business as a feme sole trader. In this capacity, she established a shipping line between Amsterdam and New York and personally supervised her ship in transit—to the discomfort of those who worked on it, according to passengers who reported her "avarice" and "covetesnous."

The energy and enterprise of memorable femes soles, such as Margaret Brent and Margaret Philipse, however, are misleading clues to the status of women in the seventeenth-century colonies. Femes soles were able to engage in profitable activities because their services and self-support were good for the community, because there were few skilled workers and no guilds of craftsmen or professionals, and because economic space was expanding, not contracting. Most widows did not run estates or shipping lines but survived on small dower rights or scratched out a living. Indeed, most colonists, male or female, had little wealth. The number of femes soles in commerce and trade, moreover, was far less than that of another type of single woman, the indentured servant, whose options and rights were minimal.

SERVANTS AND SLAVES

The condition of servitude was familiar to anyone who had grown up in England or its colonies. During the seventeenth century, servitude was a common status. One-third of colonial households included indentured servants who worked for the family and were considered part of it. Colonial servitude was a temporary status, not a lifelong one. Indentured servants were a distinctive underclass of the young. All were single, or allegedly so, and about a third were women, aged 18 to 25. Their labor was sold for four or five years or longer, in return for transportation to America and maintenance and support during their terms of indenture. Perhaps as many as half of women newcomers arrived in that status; the vast majority went at first to the southern colonies and later to the middle colonies.

Servitude was also a mode of upbringing and vocational training for native-born children, under the apprenticeship system. A colonial daughter could be apprenticed at 11, 12, or 13 for a lengthy term—some indentures lasted up to 10 years—during which time she provided her master and mistress with help and acquired useful skills. Orphans and the children of poor widows were similarly "bound out," sometimes at very young ages, to be reared and to work in other homes until age 21. The families who took in such children were legally responsible for bringing them up and teaching them trades. Indeed, the term of service repaid the expense of child rearing. (Parents expected similar service from their own children.) While boy apprentices might learn cordwaining, tanning, or other trades, girls were trained in domestic work. Like daughters, female apprentices were supposed to acquire such useful skills as "spining, sewing, knitting, or any other manner of housewifery," and sometimes basic literacy ("to read the English tongue").

Indentured servitude, for the emigrant, lay somewhere between voluntary and forced labor. Even when a woman signed a contract of indenture voluntarily in England, promising "to oblige myself as a faithful and obedient servant . . . according to the Laws and Customs . . . in the said place," as did one young woman before embarking for Carolina in 1669, she ended up an ocean away, working under conditions far more harsh than domestic servitude in England. Subject to physical abuse and a high mortality rate, she was also required to endure a long period of celibacy, as marriage was prohibited. Not all women servants volunteered for such an experience. Some were kidnapped, some were pardoned felons, and some were convicts, such as the "fifty lewd women out of the house of correction" who were shipped off to Virginia in 1692, along with "thirty others who walked the streets." The promotional literature that lured young women to the southern colonies (such as Maryland, where 85 percent of newcomers and almost all of the women among them were servants) promised that they would not have to do field work. But once installed on a remote farm in a far-off colony, servants had no control over the nature of their labor. Even domestic work in a newly settled region would have to be done under the most primitive conditions. In addition, the "Laws and Customes" regulating servitude were severe.

Servants who ran away or otherwise violated their terms of indenture were penalized by an extension of the term of service. The most common violation of which women were accused was pregnancy. Servants were not free to marry until the indenture term ended because they literally did not own themselves. Although all servants were enjoined to avoid sexual relations, the brunt of the prohibition fell upon women; child bearing would deprive their masters of their services. In Maryland, one-fifth of women servants were hauled into court for "bastardy." In Pennsylvania, Carolina, and Virginia, pregnancy was penalized with an extension of the period of servitude. In Massachusetts, servants who had been "unfaithful, negligent, or unprofitable" were saddled with extended terms; and in cases of "bastardy," the alleged father (determined by questioning the woman servant in labor) was forced to support the illegitimate child. Such children might themselves be put into service for the entire period of their youth—as was young Hannah Woolery, a New Englander bound out at the age of two until she was 21.

A recurrent problem, as a Virginia statute of 1692 suggests, was that "some dissolute masters have gotten their maids with child, and yet claim the benefit of their service." Although the guilt of the servant was not absolved in such cases, the law provided that the woman's extra term of service be sold to another master, with the profits of the sale going to the local parish. The term of extra service was too valuable to discard when it could be of use to the labor-scarce community. So was the labor of the Maryland servant whose master claimed that she had been absent for short periods over the years amounting, in sum, to 113 days. He was awarded 1,130 days of extra service. Legislation increasingly regulated conditions of servitude. Some laws limited servants, by prohibiting fornication and miscegenation, for instance. Other laws restrained masters and mistresses from excessive abuse. "Cruel Mistress prevent'd from having servants" a Virginia Court injected tersely in its records of 1680.

Once a term of indenture was up, a young woman servant was available for marriage and virtually assured of it in the southern colonies, where women were so greatly outnumbered. Indeed, because she had no property or family, marriage was her only option. She was likely to become the wife of a farmer on a small, perhaps new, plantation, probably marrying at an older age than a free counterpart and therefore having fewer children—as was the case in seventeenth-century Maryland. But once the spouse of a landowner, she might herself become the mistress of servants. This leap in status would have been far less likely in England, where land was unavailable, men in a minority, and servitude usually a lifelong condition. The seventeenth-century colonial servant could at least look forward to upward mobility.

The same could not be said for the black woman servant or slave; even in the early seventeenth century, before slavery became a legal institution, race was a more crucial determinant of status than gender. Hostile to blacks and short of capital, Virginians far preferred indentured servants to slaves; no more than 5,000 slaves lived in the North American colonies by 1675, compared to 100,000 in the British

West Indies. Still, as early as the 1640s in Virginia, when many blacks were indentured servants, albeit serving longer terms than whites, court records began to mention sales for life and the inheritance by black children of the status of "perpetual servant." The value of black women as producers of more "servants for life" was suggested in the record of the sale of "one Negro girl named Jowan, aged about ten years" made to a Virginian in 1652, as he acquired "her issue and produce during her . . . Life tyme and their successors forever."

Even before slavery was established by law, black women servants were distinguished from white women servants in another way: They were used without qualm in field work. Once colonies drew up slave codes, the distinction between black and white female labor was clear-cut. "A white woman is rarely or never put to work in the ground if she is good for anything else," Robert Beverly reported from Virginia in 1705, but "It is a common thing to work a woman slave out of doors." Moreover, while the white servant was forced to be celibate, or penalized if she was not, slavery introduced a different set of standards. Only in New England, where slaves were few and slavery mainly a domestic institution, were slave marriages legal and sexual mores required of slaves. Elsewhere, criminal codes for slaves provided no barrier to fornication or adultery, for which whites could be prosecuted, because slave marriages were not recognized in law. The most important issue in law was *who* was a slave. This was settled in Virginia in the 1660s, and, as historian Kathleen M. Brown shows, gender affected the legal origins of slavery. As early as the 1640s, legal distinctions between African and English women emerged. A 1643 Virginia law categorized African women as "tithable" (individuals who performed taxable labor) as were all able-bodied male persons. English women, in contrast, were classified as dependents (as were children "and other unservicable people," as the Governor and Council stated in one edict). The 1643 law "stigmatized female African labor that would have been valued in a West African context," Brown contends. It distinguished English from African women and "revealed different expectations for their roles in the colony." Subsequent laws, over the course of the seventeenth century, extended tithability to white women servants who worked "in the ground," to black women who were free, and to wives of "Negroes, mulattoes, or Indians," regardless of race. Meanwhile, a double-barreled law of 1662 defined slavery. The law provided, first, that all blacks would inherit the mother's condition and, second, that if "any Christian shall commit fornication with a Negro man or woman, he or she offending shall pay double the fines imposed." The 1662 law reversed the practice by which English children took the condition of the father, Brown points out, and made the paternity of children or slave women legally irrelevant. It also made black women servants more valuable than white ones. Overall, it "represented a bold attempt to naturalize the condition of slavery by making it inheritable and embedding it in a concept of race." Henceforth, "servant" and "slave" were terms with different meanings. Thus, as Brown shows, gender played a crucial role in the creation of a slave system based on race. "Racial slavery, in turn," she contends, "breathed new life into patriarchal social relations."

Imbalanced sex ratios affected the lives of southern black women. According to historian Ira Berlin, the sex ratio among Chesapeake slaves may have at first been more evenly balanced than that of the white population. Although some early arrivals came directly from Africa, in boatloads that were predominantly male, most black arrivals in the early Chesapeake were Atlantic Creoles—persons of mixed ancestry—European, African, Latin American, and Caribbean. These newcomers had some experience in the new world as well as some immunity to disease. As Chesapeake society matured, however, "A society with slaves gave way to a slave society," Berlin writes. From the 1660s on, "slaves slowly but steadily replaced white indentured servants as the main source of plantation labor." At the end of the seventeenth century, as more slaves came directly from Africa, slave sex ratios became more imbalanced. Chesapeake planters imported twice as men many as women. In Virginia, male slave arrivals outnumbered female arrivals at least two to one. Southern Maryland's sex ratio (the number of men per hundred women) was 125 in 1650; it reached 180 by 1730. In some of the older, more densely populated eastern counties, slave sex ratios began to reach parity in the 1720s and 1730s. But in general, sexual imbalance in the Maryland and Virginia slave populations dwindled only in the late eighteenth century, when imports dropped and were exceeded by natural increase.

"Africanization," as Ira Berlin calls it, marked a deterioration in the condition of slave life. It became difficult to establish families, birth rates fell, and mortality rose. Whether sent from a plantation in the Caribbean or severed from African relatives, the black woman slave had little to gain from her minority status. Most southern plantations were small—few had more than 20 slaves and a majority of slaveowners had less than five—so she was unlikely to form any type of permanent union. The black population, moreover, was thinly spread over large areas, which made finding a partner especially difficult. Nor did the excess of men in the slave population create circumstances conducive to family life. This was only part of the slave woman's plight. Her life expectancy, like that of all southern immigrants, white and black, was short; lack of immunity to new diseases caused chronic ill health and early death. Few slaves could expect to reach old age (more than 50 years), although among those who did, at least in Maryland, women seemed to predominate, despite the larger male population. Finally, the child-bearing rate of immigrant slave women was extremely low. Indeed, seventeenth-century southern slave populations experienced a natural decline rather than an increase. In part, this is attributable to such factors as high adult mortality, poor health, and the relatively old age of female slave immigrants in terms of childbearing. But low black fertility in the early South has also been attributed to the desperate condition of new women slaves; their inability to adjust to slavery; and their alienation, depression, and morbid state of mind. Under such circumstances, presumably, the first woman slaves were reluctant to reproduce.

The northern slave was more likely to be a woman, because the most promising and desirable slaves were sold in the South. She was more likely than a southern slave to do domestic work rather than field work; to live in a town or village, which meant greater autonomy; to be hired out, which brought certain perquisites; and even to hold personal property—as was the custom in New York, where slavery was a less stringent institution. Such regional distinctions in the nature of slavery affected the status of the woman slave as much as those imposed by gender.

Finally, North or South, the woman slave, like the woman servant, played a vital part in the colonial economy through her labor. So, indeed, did the average colonial housewife and her daughters. The Native American woman played a similarly vital part in the Indian economy. Like the seventeenth-century colonial housewife, she had multiple roles—as family member, community member, and productive worker.

NATIVE AMERICAN WOMEN

When minister's wife Mary Rowlandson spent 11 weeks as a captive of the Narragansett Indians in 1676, during King Philip's War, she saw her captors as an alien race of "murtherous wretches" with diabolic motives. She was also, inadvertently, an acute observer of Native American life—including the roles of Indian women as food gatherers, traders, and raft builders. Such data hardly served the same function as an anthropologist's field report. Mary Rowlandson's observations were filtered through a Puritan prism and, like those of other seventeenth-century colonists who had contacts with Native Americans, were colored by her English assumptions. Still, colonial records, along with ethnographic evidence, have been used to reconstruct the role of Indian women during the first century of colonization.

By the time of King Philip's War, a conflict between New England colonists and local Indian tribes, interaction with Europeans had drastically affected the life of coastal Indians in the Algonquian language group. Members of the group ranged from New England bands such as the Wampanoag and Narragansett down to the Powhatan in Chesapeake Bay. New England tribes, for instance, had almost been wiped out by epidemics of plague and smallpox by the 1630s. The remnant that survived, estimated at only about 10 percent of the original population, had been further affected by half a century of contact with colonists. By 1676, as Mary Rowlandson's captivity narrative suggests, local Indians were long accustomed to communicating and trading with the English, as well as to acquiring English weapons, clothing, and money. The process of colonization, which steadily eroded and weakened the position of all coastal Indians, also affected the roles of women in Indian society, roles that had been traditional for centuries.

The coastal Algonquians, an agricultural people, engaged in hunting and fishing, farming and gathering. As in English society, gender determined roles in Indian society; this was evident in the sexual division of labor. Men were active in hunting, war, and diplomacy—or "international" relations, both among tribes and with the colonists. Women did almost all of the farming. They planted and harvested crops, work that centered around family garden plots and could be most easily combined with child rearing. In general, coastal Indians created a division of work roles not unlike that of the colonists, in which women engaged in domestic production or work that took place near where they lived, while men's work ranged farther afield, involved more danger, and required their absence from the village.

By the seventeenth century, however, at least in some places, women's work had become more vital to subsistence. In southern New England, for instance, agriculture had replaced hunting as the primary source of food. Native American women, who developed the wide variety of crops that evoked the interest of colonists, produced 90 percent of their tribes' food supplies. Much of their time was spent tending fields and in complex tasks of food processing—such as the pounding, drying, packing, and storing that made cornmeal available in the winter. Indian women also fished, gathered wild plants, produced household items, and participated in some stages of the hunting process, such as lugging the game home. They were, in addition, responsible for specific tasks in their village, such as setting up and dismantling camp.

The increased importance of women's agricultural work during the era of colonization did not necessarily generate higher status within the community. European colonization may well have increased the significance of the male sphere, because once settlement of coastal areas began, the realms of trade, diplomacy, and war became still more important. In any case, when seventeenth-century Englishmen observed Native American life, they not only described a sexual division of labor but painted a picture of female drudgery and male idleness. "The men bestow their times in fishing, hunting, warres, and such man-like exercises," wrote John Smith in 1607,

> scorning to be seen in any woman-like exercise, which is the cause that the women be very painefull, and the men often idle. The women and children doe the rest of the worke. They make mats, baskets, pots, mortars, pound their corne, make their bread, prepare their victuals, plante their corne, gather their corne, bear all kinds of burdens, and such like.

An unequal division of labor continued to pervade colonists' accounts, down to William Byrd, a century later. "The little work that is done among the Indians is done by the poor women," said Byrd, "while the men are quite idle, or at most employ'd only in the Gentlemanly diversion of hunting and fishing." In colonial eyes, the Indian concept of gender roles was at best peculiar and in general unjust, and the status of Indian women a degraded one.

But the description of female degradation by such men as Smith and Byrd was probably unjust as well. Other accounts suggest more cooperation between the sexes as well as some crossing over of occupational lines. Roger Williams, an unusually acute observer, reported that Indian men and women often joined together for special tasks, such as breaking up a field, and older people of both sexes engaged in agricultural work, as did children. At least one group of Englishwomen, who had extensive opportunities to assess Indian life, also had a different reaction to the roles of women. While seventeenth-century captives—among them Mary Rowlandson and her children—were taken for ransom, in the mid-eighteenth century, some New England tribes attempted to adopt captive women and children and transform them into band members. Many such "white Indians" preferred to remain with their tribes, or at least were returned only under force, and these women voiced special reasons for appreciating Native American life. Indian women's work was "not so severe," said one famous captive, Mary Jemison, their tasks "probably not harder than [those of] white women." In particular, Indian women were spared the labor of housewifery ("no spinning, weaving, sewing, stocking knitting"). In addition, they worked together, in village units not nuclear family units, and had control of their own realm of work, village agriculture.

Cooperative crop raising and food production were not the only activities of coastal Indian women. Even in wartime, they remained involved in trade. Like

The first English colonist to depict coastal Native American women was artist John White, who arrived on Roanoke Island in 1585. In the many paintings and drawings that he brought back to England, White presented an extremely favorable impression of villages, rituals, and everyday life, because his purpose was to attract settlers to Roanoke. He also attempted to dispel English visions of naked and immoral savages, as did the expedition's chronicler, Thomas Hariot. Indian women, Hariot reported, "cover themselves before the behynde, from the naval unto the midds of their thighes . . . with a deered skynne handsomely dressed and fringed." And unmarried women, dignified and virtuous, "lay their hands often uppon their shoulders, and cover their breasts in token of maydenlike modesty." Two years later, in 1587, John White led an ill-fated contingent of 120 settlers to Roanoke and went back to England for supplies. When he returned in 1590, all of the colonists, including his daughter, had vanished, and to this day their fate is unknown. Above, a John White watercolor of an Indian woman and child, holding a doll in English dress, 1585–1587. *(The British Museum)*

colonial housewives, Native American women were always engaged in internal trade—indeed, it was a staple of their day-to-day existence. Incessant exchange of crops and goods was a basic part of tribal social life and part of a tradition of reciprocity. When Philip, the leader of the Narragansetts, met captive Mary Rowlandson, for instance, he at once proposed an exchange of clothing items for a dinner. Rowlandson, moreover, was already enmeshed in the Indians' system of barter and exchange. Although external trade, with English colonists, was dominated by men, colonial observers throughout the century mentioned women traders who sold skins to the colonists or English goods to the various tribes. By the end of the century, coastal Indian women were themselves interested in acquiring English products, from needles and cloth to kettles and tea. Like the women Mary Rowlandson met during her captivity, they became customers for English clothing items—caps, aprons, handkerchiefs, stockings, and occasionally shoes.

Native American women were also as conscious of kinship relations as were the colonists. Within Indian villages, the clan was the primary unit of social and political organization. Coastal Indians lived in extended lineal families and formed exogamous marriages—that is, marriages to members of other clans or bands. As a result, New England tribes were linked by intermarriage. Patrilineal kinship reckoning and patrilocal residence were customary among coastal Indians, as they were among the Narragansetts. But in some bands outside southern New England, kinship was determined through the mother's heritage, property descended through the female line, and married couples lived with the wife's family. These matrilineal, matrilocal arrangements, adopted by such tribes as the Iroquois and Delaware in the east and the Creek and Seminole in the south, increased female influence in family and village life. Even without them, Indian women commonly exerted a large degree of authority within the clan, where they supervised affairs of domestic life, such as marriage choices, and regulated the arrangements for farming.

Indian women's daily lives, unlike those of Englishwomen, were affected by a pattern of sexual segregation. Women of the New England tribes, for instance, customarily ate separately from men and during menstruation inhabited separate menstrual huts. In Indian culture, a tradition of female modesty and male sexual restraint prevailed. Colonists continued to be surprised, as was Mary Rowlandson, at the lack of vulgar behavior among the Indians, and even more so by the absence of sexual assault. Most seventeenth-century English captives held for ransom were women and children, whose reports confirmed Mary Rowlandson's observations and revealed as much about English expectations as they did about Indian men. One explanation for male sexual restraint, as historian James Axtell points out, was that Indian warriors had a tradition of continence in times of conflict, fearing that indulgence would bring misfortune. In addition, members of tribes, usually related to one another, had stringent incest taboos. Captives may have been regarded as temporary band members, protected by the same customs that applied to Indian women. This was certainly true in the case of the mid-eighteenth-century captives studied by Axtell, who were adopted as band members. Finally, the Indians may have regarded rape as an abhorrent crime under any circumstances, because it was the only capital offense punishable by the band as a whole, whereas murder, for instance, might be avenged by the victim's immediate family.

If the Native American custom of sexual restraint surprised the colonists, so did Indian women's occasional roles as tribal leaders or sachems. Throughout the seventeenth century, colonial accounts mentioned various women sachems among the coastal tribes—for example, the "Massachusetts queen" who in 1620 sold land to the English. Succession to a sachem's role was based on primogeniture (inheritance by the firstborn), but retention of that role depended on performance—that is, the ability to gain a band's respect. While the vast majority of sachems were men, some women, like captive Mary Rowlandson's "mistress," Weetamoo, inherited tribal office; others replaced deceased male relatives who had been sachems. Conventionally, sachems were supported by food contributions made by their followers and were expected to give gifts of some sort to those followers in return. Weetamoo, as Mary Rowlandson observed, worked at making belts, rather than at food collecting, the work in which other Indian women were occupied.

By the time of King Philip's War, female band leaders had appeared in profusion. The Narragansett sachem Quaiapan, whose warriors had attacked Nipmuck villages in the 1660s, was later drawn into King Philip's War, during which she was killed. Another war leader was Awashunks, a Rhode Island sachem who joined Philip's cause for about a year and then negotiated a separate peace. A third was Weetamoo, who before Mary Rowlandson's captivity had commanded more than 300 Pocasset male warriors. By the summer of 1676, however, their numbers had dropped to 30, all of whom were soon captured or killed, as was Weetamoo. Significantly, the three female sachems were at first reluctant to join the conflict and became involved either when their villages were attacked or, in Weetamoo's case, at Philip's insistence.

Access of Native American women to tribal office distinguished their roles from those of European women, and so did their authority in religious life. Among the Indians, women sometimes assumed roles as shamans, or priests, which meant that they ran medical practices, specializing either in natural cures, as herbalists, or in supernatural cures. To be sure, women practitioners were most active in those bands that lacked an established male priesthood. Also, many of these religious/medical practitioners were older people of both sexes. Nonetheless, in some cases women served as both shamans and warleaders, a powerful combination. To colonists, the supernatural influence of a religious practitioner held the greatest fascination. Among the Wampanoag and Delaware, for instance, shamans could communicate with the dead, find missing persons or things, and predict future events. Not surprisingly, one colonial observer, Daniel Gookin, described Wampanoag shamans as part physician and part witch or wizard, because the powers they claimed were like those the English attributed to the devil's servants.

Many aspects of women's roles among coastal Algonquian bands were later encountered among inland tribes, such as the Seneca and Iroquois, as well as among western plains Indians in the nineteenth century. Though Indian societies were typically characterized by male dominance and a sexual division of labor, women exerted varying degrees of authority, formal and informal, within their clans and tribes. Those seventeenth-century colonists who observed Indian life were most impressed with aspects of women's roles that seemed unusual or even bizarre, whether their extensive agricultural work or their leadership roles as sachems or shamans. Although Englishwomen never filled any public offices, they were hardly excluded from involvement in religious life. This involvement was greatest in the northern colonies, where sectarianism was rampant.

PROPHETS AND SAINTS

The cutting edge of change in seventeenth-century women's history, blunt as it may have been, was somewhere along the northern seaboard, in towns, in trade, and especially in church—the sole institution beyond the family in which women might become "members." For women, church membership was the only formal affiliation outside the home, their only title beyond that of daughter, sister, wife, and mother. Church membership also provided entrée into a religious community, which at Sunday sermons and weekly meetings offered a degree of respite from the patriarchal family. In women's experience, therefore, the church was something of a halfway house between domestic life and public life. Indeed, among English sects such as the Puritans or the Friends (Quakers) whose emigration had been spurred by religious motives, religion was a form of political life. To the extent that it was, portions of seventeenth-century Puritan and Quaker women were highly politicized.

The growth of dissenting sects such as Puritanism in seventeenth-century England had a twofold impact on women's lives in colonial America. First, sectarianism put new focus on the family as a vehicle for the transmission of religious values. The Puritan, Quaker, or Separatist home in the colonies, as in England, became an arena for indoctrination and character formation, which placed further demands on parents and children. Second, sectarianism contained an expansive dimension for women as individuals. By recognizing their souls, it raised their expectations. Even if subordinate in family and community, women could enjoy equal access to intimacy with God, or equality of souls.

This sense of personal contact with divinity, whether based on "inner light," revelation, or simply faith, had further ramifications. It helped women endure bad experiences—such as the trials of emigration, for Anne Bradstreet, or the period of captivity, for Mary Rowlandson, or the commonplace deaths of infants and children. It also contained an inspirational impulse, a sense of spiritual individualism, that was pregnant with potential. Such spiritual individualism was usually difficult to transfer to "worldly" affairs, as equality of souls was at odds with the English belief in woman's inferiority and the need for her subordination. There was, however, one exception: the unique role of the woman Quaker.

The Society of Friends was a minority sect whose singular customs affected only its own communities, primarily in Pennsylvania and New Jersey, starting in the 1650s. But the egalitarian precedent of Quakers was significant, not least because it aroused such hostility among outsiders. The Friends provided a model of alternative roles for women that was, in the context of the seventeenth century, revolutionary. By discarding a professional ministry, Friends provided reprieve from clerical domination. By insisting on the equality of souls, they opened the field of prophecy, or ministerial roles, to women. Finally, Quaker women created their own organizational structure, a groundwork for collective action, through which they exerted authority within the community.

According to the Friends, the restrictions on women imposed by Paul for "silence in church" did not apply to those who had established contact with God or found their "inner light." Spiritual rebirth entailed the power of prophecy, or access to the calling of lay minister or "public" Friend. As the founder of the sect, George Fox, had explained in England, the spirit of Christ could "speak in the female as well as in the male." A goal of the Friends, moreover, was "to liberate for the service of the Church the gifts of government which lay dormant and barren in both men and women." This radical view had profound implications for women.

Of the 59 public Friends who arrived in the colonies at the start of the Quaker migration, from 1656 to 1663, nearly half were women. Active proselytizers, these women traveled throughout the colonies, supported by their "meetings," to spread the word and make new converts. Believing that God protected them with an "armour of light," they challenged more orthodox sects such as the Puritans. Female militancy was even carried to martyrdom by an avid proselytiser, Mary Dyer, in the late 1650s. Banned from Boston and New Haven, and repeatedly expelled, Mary Dyer returned to Boston four times and was finally executed by the exasperated Puritans, because she refused to end her crusade. Several Quaker men had been hanged before her for the same reason.

Although most Quaker women were not public Friends, the society's organizational structure also provided singular opportunities. Women played a major part in Quaker "government" through women's meetings, which began in 1681 and emerged in all locales where Friends settled. Here, women conducted discussions, drew up rules, kept records, managed finances, trained younger members, and contributed to Friends' regional meetings. In no other formal institution in the seventeenth-century colonies did women play such roles. One special function of the women's meetings was to keep in touch with sister Friends through circular letters that passed from one meeting to another. Another function, as expressed in a letter from English sisters, was "to prevent our Children from running into the world [the non-Quaker community] for husbands, or for wives." Through their meetings, Quaker women supervised the realm of Quaker marriage, exerted authority over family life, and transformed "equality of souls" into collective influence within the community of Friends.

In the view of Puritans, however, the Friends had carried reformation to an ungodly extreme, especially by supporting female prophecy. Giving women access to religious leadership, the Puritans believed, could only upset the natural order of society, sabotage domestic life, subvert government, and lead to chaos. Even the most pious of Puritan women never gained access to the ministry or to collective influence over the community. Rather, Puritan goals of social cohesion and domestic order made the submission of women, at home and outside it, especially vital. But in New England, Puritan women achieved a limited version of "equality of souls" because they could be accepted as nonvoting church members, or saints. The tension in the roles of these female saints, an elite group, lay in their dual status, as saints and women.

Sainthood was an asexual status, even if women's temporal lives were subordinate. It required of women and men the same attitudes toward God—submission, obedience, meekness, humility—the very postures required of women by men in worldly affairs. Indeed, these same postures were required of *men* toward men of higher status; seventeenth-century society was hierarchical, and most men were utterly in control only within their own families. Accordingly, Puritans valued many of the same virtues in both men and women. Even the character traits recommended by Cotton Mather, a leading exponent of womanhood at the end of the century, in his "Ornaments of the Daughters of Zion"—modesty, silence, obedience, industriousness, humility, thrift, and discretion—were not overwhelmingly gender-specific. (Silence and modesty, admittedly, were not constraints that Puritan men imposed on themselves.) Mourners praised departed women saints at their funerals for prudence, industry, piety, and charity, as well as for poring over the Scriptures, taking notes at sermons, and "pious society and discourse."

These studious attributes were significant. New England women were more likely to be literate than were women in England or elsewhere in the colonies. As late as the mid-eighteenth century, only one out of three Englishwomen was able to sign her name in the marriage register, and even fewer could do so in the seventeenth century. In the colonies, under half of seventeenth-century women were able to read at all, and far fewer were able to write. But Puritan women were at an advantage. Although most of their training was in housewifery, they might learn to read at home. A modicum of learning was desirable to promote piety and facilitate study of the Bible. Unlike obedience and submissiveness, however, learning had its limits.

Puritan authorities believed that women were innately weaker of brain and easily seduced by bad influences, especially if they strained their minds beyond reasonable limits and crossed the line between private piety and critical thought. The learned, illustrious woman, a phenomenon rare elsewhere in the colonies, might be most admired if she devoted her efforts to pious matters and kept her learning to herself, or at least confined it to the home. Women's writings were preferably private documents, not to be exposed to public view but to be read by themselves and family members. Anne Bradstreet, whose poems were published anonymously and not at her instigation in England, provided a model of such private writings in her "Religious Experiences," intended to convey "spiritual advantages" to her eight children. This personal narrative was written not for self-glorification but in humility, "not to sett forth myself but the Glory of God." It was never published in her lifetime. Mary Rowlandson's captivity narrative, published in 1682, contained a similar disclaimer. Like Anne Bradstreet's poems, it was published anonymously.

Both Bradstreet and Rowlandson used their learning for private benefit, not for public troublemaking or "medling" in the affairs of men. "Medling" was the crucial word. Conveying a sense of incompetence and illegitimacy, it was frequently used to describe the sort of intrusive, aggressive female behavior to which seventeenth-century men objected. The epitome of such behavior was the disruptive example set by Anne Hutchinson in the 1630s, at the outset of the Puritan experiment. Described by John Winthrop as "a woman of fierce and haughty carriage," Hutchinson had been not merely a "medler" but an insurgent. Her intellectual power led to extreme assertiveness, insubordinate action, and, worst of all, charismatic power over others.

Anne Hutchinson was a woman of status, the middle-aged wife of a landowner, merchant, and public official. She was also a fervent Puritan saint. Since her arrival in Massachusetts Bay in 1634 with her husband and 14 of her children, she had created

THE

NARRATIVE

OF THE

CAPTIVITY and RESTORATION

OF

Mrs. *Mary Rowlandſon,*

Who was taken Priſoner by the INDIANS with ſeveral others, and treated in the moſt barbarous and cruel Manner by thoſe vile Savages : With many other remarkable Events during her TRAVELS.

Written by her own Hand, for her private Uſe, and now made public at the earneſt Deſire of ſome Friends, and for the Benefit of the afflicted.

The title page of a 1773 edition of Mary Rowlandson's captivity narrative. First published in Cambridge, Massachusetts, in 1682, the book appeared in scores of subsequent editions.
(From Frederick L. Weis, ed., The Narrative of the Capitivity and Restoration of Mrs. Mary Rowlandson, *Boston, 1930)*

a base of support in Boston. While her services as a midwife gave her entrée into many homes, her talents as a theologian attracted yet more attention. Soon 60 or 80 townsfolk, at first mainly women but later men as well, were gathering in the Hutchinson home to hear Anne Hutchinson's learned discussions of weekly sermons. Here, her "medling" became apparent. Anne Hutchinson attacked the pivot on which Puritanism uneasily rested by throwing her weight toward the Covenant of Grace (a conviction that redemption came solely through God's grace, regardless of an individual's efforts) and away from the Covenant of Works (the belief that good behavior, a righteous life, was a sign of salvation).

This was not a small or harmless error, as Anne Hutchinson compounded it by challenging the sanctity of ministers who opposed her. Worse yet, she held a powerful sway over her followers, a "potent party" of Bostonians who were people of substance—merchants, landowners, and their wives. After inquisition by the leading ministers and a trial for sedition before the General Court, Anne Hutchinson was convicted, excommunicated, and banished. At the end of her trial, she admitted divine revelation, which proved her undoing. Even a man to whom God spoke directly would have been in trouble. But Anne Hutchinson had long been a triple threat, as her judges informed her, to home, church, and state. She had assumed male postures—by dominating her husband and exerting authority over her supporters, by attacking the sanctity of ministers and usurping their roles, and by having no respect for the "fathers" of the community. Anne Hutchinson was guilty not only of heresy and sedition but of role reversal. As she was told at her trial, "You have rather bine a Husband than a Wife, and a Preacher than a Hearer, and a Magistrate than a subject."

Anne Hutchinson's career after her expulsion from Massachusetts in 1637 confirmed the suspicions of her judges. Moving to Rhode Island with her husband, younger children, and a contingent of followers, she continued to get into political squabbles. In Rhode Island, she attacked the magistracy by questioning its authority. The family next moved on to New York, where Anne Hutchinson and her younger children, except for one, were killed by Indians in 1643. Puritans viewed this massacre only as divine retribution for her errors. Even four decades later, during King Philip's War, when one of Anne Hutchinson's nephews was killed, Increase Mather concluded that the demise of the Hutchinsons was an "observable work of Providence."

But Anne Hutchinson's cause had great appeal for women, who formed a vocal part of the "potent party" that supported her. In the eyes of such women, dependence on God alone may have seemed preferable to dependence on intermediaries, whether ministers, magistrates, or husbands. Not surprisingly, Anne Hutchinson's example remained more than an unpleasant memory in New England. Some of her supporters, such as Mary Dyer, followed her to Rhode Island. Dyer, whom Winthrop described as "notoriously infected with error" and "very censorious and troublesome," later embarked on her career as a Quaker proselytizer. Other women supporters, who remained in Boston, fell under suspicion—among them Mary Oliver, who criticized ministers and magistrates and ended up in the stocks.

In the decade that followed, other women of status paid the price for "persistence in error" or pernicious "medling." Ann Eaton, the governor's wife in New Haven, who disavowed infant baptism, was excommunicated in 1644 for lying and stubbornness. Her daughter, Ann Hopkins, another governor's wife as well as a delver into theological matters, bore God's wrath more directly. She was driven mad, as John Winthrop explained, by too much reading and writing and attempting "to meddle in such things as are proper for men, whose minds are stronger, etc." Assertive behavior continued to be regarded as a threat, as illustrated in the contentious case of Ann Hibbens, wife of a prominent Boston merchant and former official. Brought to trial in 1641 for lying and slander, and excommunicated, Ann Hibbens was denounced for usurping the authority of her husband, "whom she should have obeyed and unto whom God put her into subjection." Female dissent or aggressiveness remained evils to be suppressed before they got out of hand.

New England Puritans differed little from other Englishmen, at home or in the colonies, in their low opinion of women's capacities or their belief in the need for female subordination. Nor did New England Puritans differ from those left behind in England, who followed a divergent path but experienced some of the same problems with women. In the English Civil War (1642–1660), women of the more radical Puritan sects, carried away by their sense of equality in the eyes of God, held demonstrations, petitioned Parliament, and "medled" collectively in men's affairs. At the same time, during the years when Puritanism was on the rise, epidemics of witchcraft struck the areas in which English Puritans lived. Women's alleged defects—of wit, will, and moral fiber—had dual ramifications in seventeenth-century society. First, female interference in men's affairs, such as theology and government, was considered dangerous and subversive, as the Anne Hutchinson episode in Boston suggested. Second, due to their supposed moral weakness, women were seen as ready prey for seduction by fiends and likely candidates for careers in witchcraft, a low and malevolent form of assertiveness.

INVISIBLE FURIES

Witches were not unknown in the colonies, although there had never been large numbers of them. Still, seventeenth-century society was rural, agrarian, traditional, and superstitious. And witches had been found—mainly in New England, where villagers kept a close watch on one another and the devil's works were more easily recognized. By the end of the century, some 40 towns had discovered several hundred witches in their midst.

As in England, accused witches were usually women (only one out of four was a man) of eccentric and cantankerous disposition who went about harming their neighbors, invariably after a quarrel or dispute. Or rather, their curses, threats, or unwelcome visits were followed by a variety of misfortunes, such as a cow's death or a child's illness. Margaret James, for example, was executed in 1648 for a malignant touch, suspicious medicines, and (at her trial) intemperate behavior and notorious lying. Ann Hibbens, long known for her "crabbedness" of nature, was executed in 1656 after an exceptionally contentious career. Susanna Martin was accused in 1669 of bewitching a neighbor, although not tried until 1692. The famous witch Glover, who caused fits in children, was one of several witches executed in the 1680s. Of diverse social origins, women charged with witchcraft were usually middle-aged women with long histories of abrasive relations and involvement in community squabbles. Relatively few accused witches were executed; most were exonerated of the charges against them and returned to their places in the community. Moreover, convictions for witchcraft, and then even accusations, seemed to fall in the 1650s and 1660s. But the "invisible furies" of witchcraft reappeared in force in New England at the end of the century. Their arrival coincided with a period of unusual stress in eastern Massachusetts and the rebellion of a small group of teenage girls.

According to seventeenth-century beliefs, witches engaged in pacts with Satan, night rides, and nocturnal meetings, where they mocked propriety and abandoned restraint. In this woodcut from *The King of Darkness* (London, 1688), popular in England and the colonies, witches cavort with devils. "Such representations," writes historian Elizabeth Reis, "both reflected and encouraged the idea of woman as witches." *(Connecticut Historical Society)*

By the 1690s, coastal New England had undergone many changes, including transformation of Massachusetts from a Bible commonwealth to a royal colony. Less tangible changes had also occurred, such as a falling off of religious interest among men. In the early days of settlement, men and women became church members in family units and in roughly equal numbers. At midcentury, when the sex ratio in eastern towns first showed signs of evening out, the proportion of women saints began to rise; and it continued to do so after church admissions were liberalized in 1662. By the time of King Philip's War, more than two-thirds of new church members in

Massachusetts and Connecticut were women; and women continued to join in disproportionate numbers. While ministers bemoaned a communal loss of piety, to an increasingly feminized flock, young men in New England turned to other pursuits.

One was land, which led them farther away from the seaboard villages where earlier settlers had congregated. By the end of the century, the loss of men in more densely settled areas, where land was unavailable, probably left fewer men than women in some places. Another source of diversion was trade and commerce, which led men away from more pious concerns. By the late seventeenth century, enterprising New England men were either losing faith or else eastern New England was losing them. Both "worldliness" and expansion affected the eastern town of Salem, which had divided into Salem Village, a rural, farming backwater, and Salem Town, where those who had profited from trade and commerce were concentrated. In 1692, animosity between village and town, farmers and merchants, old values and new profits, erupted in a confrontation between two marginal groups of women. One was the "accusors" or "afflicted"—a dozen or so young women and girls, including some servants. The other group was the accused witches, the majority of them older women, sometimes tainted by a degree of deviance or peculiarity, and some of their husbands and children.

During a single year, 115 local people were accused of witchcraft, three-quarters of them women, and 20 were put to death. Throughout the episode, women occupied center stage, from meetinghouse to courtroom to gallows. They played almost all the leading roles in the witchcraft trials—except those of the judges and a second string of witnesses, mainly men, who testified against the accused. What occurred in Salem was a role reversal of unique dimensions, in which the "afflicted" girls exerted authority over everyone else—ministers and magistrates, masters and mistresses, neighbors and enemies. With tales of sucking birds and barking dogs, and with perverse behavior that ordinarily would have led directly to the stocks, they gained attention routinely denied them and an outlet for aggressiveness that was impermissible in normal times. By describing specters that flew around the area biting and tormenting their victim or, alternatively, offering them land, goods, clothes, and wealth if they would sign the devil's book, the girls gave shape and voice to widely shared antagonisms and resentments. By identifying the specters, they directed retribution toward the most susceptible of villagers—ranging from suspicious neighborhood hags such as pipe-smoking, muttering Sarah Good or the already discredited Susanna Martin to the pious and respectable, if somewhat deaf, Rebecca Nurse.

It was no surprise that middle-aged women were the prime targets of witchcraft charges, as this had been the case in earlier episodes. Nor were the accusations hurled against them unusual. The youth of their accusors, finally, was not unique either. Many previous witches had also been identified by young, unmarried women, indeed teenage girls, one generation younger than the women they accused. The history of New England witchcraft, historian John Demos suggests, seems to reveal a hidden theme in the lives of seventeenth-century women: intense hostility of younger women toward the power and control of older women. Or, as also has been suggested, middle-aged women, often slightly deviant, may well have been merely the most vulnerable scapegoats—or stand-ins for the less assailable male authority figures. Or, as historian Carol F. Karlson contends, inheritance patterns may have played a role in witchcraft accusations. Most New Englanders accused of witchcraft, Karlson points out, were middle-aged or old women who, lacking brothers or sons, stood to inherit; such women impeded "the orderly transition of property from one generation to another." In any case, what distinguished the 1692 episode was its large scope, and the way it spread beyond the bounds of Salem to neighboring areas. Another distinctive feature was the unity, and consequent influence, of the young accusors.

Under ordinary circumstances, young women were the weakest and most marginal of community members, always under the domination of others. Only two of the Salem accusors lived in homes with fathers present. The rest, subject to the directives of mothers, uncles, masters, and mistresses, may have felt particularly powerless. Once their witchcraft accusations held, however, these otherwise insignificant young women were able to exert life-and-death power over the entire community. Before the trials were over, they had gone beyond indicting immediate neighbors, traditionally the bulk of the "accused," to charge more distant and prominent citizens, including some ministers. Only after accusations reached outlandish proportions was "spectral evidence" called into question. By then the witchcraft trials had provided an unprecedented outlet for personal grievances and community tensions. They also brought the common mode of female aggression—the squabble, harangue, and verbal assault—out of the home and into the historical record.

In the wake of the trials, New Englanders attempted to guess the cause of the unprecedented outbreak of witchcraft—as historians have done ever since. Two decades later, when the Massachusetts legislature exonerated those accused of witchcraft, it reversed the charges, contending that "evil spirits" had in fact been behind the accusers. But in 1692, attention turned toward evil influences outside the community. Cotton Mather, a prominent minister, was quick to spot the similarity between witchcraft practice and Indian religious/medical practice. A well-known authority on possession and captivity, Mather suggested a link between heathen diabolism and "the prodigious war made by the spirits of the invisible world upon the people of New England." The inexplicable attack of witchcraft in Salem, he thought, "might well have some of its origins among the Indians whose chief sagamores . . . have been horried sorcerers and hellish conjurors and such as conversed with demons." Mather's example was loud-mouthed Mercy Short, aged 17 in 1692. In the Salem trials, Mercy had been an effective "accusor," notably of unfortunate Sarah Good, with whom she had quarreled. Her "affliction" by specters continued afterward while Mather subjected her to a period of extensive examination.

Mercy Short had been captured in 1690, when living with her family at the edge of settlement, in New Hampshire near the Maine border. She had seen her parents and much of her family killed before being carried off on a long "remove" to Canada with several of her brothers and sisters. Mercy was finally ransomed; but release from captivity did not bring her praise, glory, or a grand reception as it had Mary Rowlandson, the wife of an important man. Instead, now orphaned, Mercy Short became a household servant, a lowly position alleviated only by her notoriety at the witchcraft trials. Her testimony afterward, which Mather recorded, revealed an imagination, as he observed, that was "strangely disordered." It also revealed intense hostility, and not only toward Indians. Mercy Short objected to her servile condition, "Fatherless" status, and lack of options. Her remarks, while arguing with the specters of unseen witches, suggested a lack of submission to divine will.

What Mercy wanted, as the specters guessed, was security, status, wealth, and power. The marital prospects for an orphaned servant were poor, so they offered her a husband. "Fine Promises! You'l bestow a husband on me, if I' bee your Servant," Mercy responded. "An Husband! What? A Divel! I shall then bee finely fitted with an Husband: No I hope the Blessed Lord Jesus Christ will marry my Soul to Himself yett before Hee has done with me, as poor a Wretch as I am!" The specters also offered clothes, just as they had tempted other villagers with silks and leisure and other accoutrements of wealth. But Mercy turned them down. "Fine Clothes! What? Such as Your Friend Sarah Good had, who hardly had rags to cover her!" After offering, next, eternal life, the specters turned to intimidation, and in response, Mercy voiced her objection, not uncommon to the teenage servant, to the authority exerted by older women:

> What's that? Must the Younger Women, do yee say, hearken to the Elder?—They must bee another Sort of Elder Woman than You then! they must not bee Elder witches, I am sure. Pray, do you for once Hearken to me—What a dreadful Sight are you! An Old Woman, an Old Servant of the Divel! You, that should instruct such poor, young Foolish Creatures as I am, to serve the Lord Jesus Christ come and urge me to serve the Divel!

Mercy's responses, while "insolent" and "abusive," Matter observed, were never "profane." Like any good dramatist, too, she based her performance on the situation with which she was most familiar: the domestic squabble.

Neither the experience of possession nor the attention it attracted brought to the "afflicted" girls the wealth, security, and status for which Mercy Short expressed a desire. Nor did their accusations bring them permanent reprieve from the control of the older generation. What the Salem episode provided was a rare, brief instance in which seventeenth-century women of any age acted in unison in public for any purpose. The witchcraft trials also threw a spotlight on "invisible" conflicts within the female community and on the "afflictions" of some of its younger members. The epidemic had struck at a time of stress, when the customary availability of land and excess of men had vanished, leaving young women, such as the "accusors," with limited options and negligible marital possibilities. By 1692, they had decreasing chances of escaping from the insignificant positions they already held, in their own homes, in other people's homes, and in the community. Fatherless Mercy Short, deserted by God in New Hampshire and tormented by shapes in Massachusetts, could well expect to be husbandless, landless, and powerless at home and outside it—a prospect that had not been faced by women colonists at the start of the century.

During the early decades of settlement, between the first voyages to New England and Virginia and the witchcraft trials of 1692, colonial women benefited from an unusual set of frontier circumstances. These circumstances improved their options, at least in comparison to their English counterparts of "middling" rank and below, without altering their subordinate status. In the eighteenth century, women's status remained subordinate. But modern impulses began to permeate their insular, traditional, backwoods world.

SUGGESTED READINGS AND SOURCES

For women's place in English society during the era of colonization, see Sara Mendelson and Patricia Crawford, *Women in Early Modern England* (New York, 1998). Lawrence Stone, *The Family, Sex and Marriage in England, 1500–1800* (New York, 1979), is a gold mine of revelations about domestic life and women's roles.

For an overview of women's history in the seventeenth and eighteenth centuries, see Carol Berkin, *First Generations: Women in Colonial America* (New York, 1996). Mary Beth Norton explores the lives of seventeenth-century New England and Chesapeake women in *Founding Mothers and Fathers: Gendered Power and the Forming of American Society* (New York, 1996). See also Norton, "The Evolution of White Women's Experience in Early America," *American Historical Review*, 89 (June 1984), 593–619. Paula A. Treckel's survey, *"To Comfort the Heart": Women in Seventeenth-Century America* (New York, 1996) suggests the scope of recent research. For documents on the seventeenth and eighteenth centuries, see Carol Berkin and Leslie Horowitz, eds., *Women's Voices, Women's Lives: Documents in Early American History* (Boston, 1998).

For New England family life, see Edmund Morgan, *The Puritan Family: Religion and Domestic Relations in Seventeenth-Century New England* (New York, 1966), and John Demos, *A Little Commonwealth: Family Life in Plymouth Colony* (New York, 1970). Two contrasting studies of women's roles are Laurel Thatcher Ulrich, *Good Wives: Image and Reality in the Lives of Women of Northern New England 1650–1750* (New York, 1982), and Lyle Koehler, *A Search for Power: The Weaker Sex in Seventeenth-Century New England* (Urbana, Ill., 1980). For the experience of the first women colonists in the Chesapeake region, see David R. Ransome, "Wives for Virginia, 1621," *William and Mary Quarterly*, 3d series, 48 (January 1991), 3–18; Virginia Bernhard, "'Men, Women and Children' at Jamestown: Population and Gender in Early Virginia, 1607–1610," *Journal of Southern History*, 58 (November 1992), 599–618; Lois Greene Carr and Lorena Walsh, "The Planter's Wife: The Experience of White Women in Seventeenth-Century Maryland," *William and Mary Quarterly*, 3d series, 34 (1977), 542–571; and Lorena S. Walsh, "'Till Death Do Us Part': Marriage and Family in Seventeenth-Century Maryland," in Thad W. Tate and David Ammerman, eds., *The Chesapeake in the Seventeenth Century: Essays on Anglo-American Society* (Chapel Hill, N.C., 1979), pp. 126–152. Allan Kulikoff examines the lives of early southerners in *Tobacco and Slaves: The Development of Southern Cultures in the Chesapeake, 1680–1800* (Chapel Hill, N.C., 1986). Kathleen M. Brown analyzes the origins of southern patriarchy in *Good Wives, Nasty Wenches, and Anxious Patriarchs: Gender, Race, and Power in Colonial Virginia* (Chapel Hill, N.C., 1996). For scholarship on the early Chesapeake, see Tate and Ammerman, eds., *The Chesapeake*, cited above, and Lois G. Carr, Philip Morgan, and Jean B. Russo, eds., *Colonial Chesapeake Society* (Chapel Hill, N.C., 1988). For women's verbal assaults, see Mary Beth Norton, "Gender and Defamation in Seventeenth-Century Maryland," *William and Mary Quarterly*, 3d series, 44 (January 1987), 3–39, and Jane Kamensky, *Governing the Tongue: The Politics of Speech in Early New England* (New York, 1997).

For the roles of Dutch and English women in early New York, see Joyce D. Goodfriend, *Before the Melting Pot: Society and Culture and Colonial New York City, 1664–1730* (Princeton, N.J., 1992), chs. 5 and 8 on the marriage patterns of Dutch women, and Linda Biemer, *Women and Property in Colonial New York: the Transition from Dutch to English Law, 1643–1727* (Ann Arbor, Mich., 1983). Women's experience in Quaker communities from the 1680s to the mid-eighteenth century is discussed in Barry Levy, *Quakers and the American Family: British Settlement in the Delaware Valley* (New York, 1988), ch. 6. For family life, see Seven Mintz and Susan Kellogg, *Domestic Revolutions: A Social History of American Family Life* (New York, 1988), chs. 1 and 2, and Helena M. Wall, *Fierce Communion: Family and Community in Early America* (Cambridge, Mass., 1990). Carole Shammas explores the exercise of authority in colonial families in "Anglo-American Household Government in Comparative Perspective," *William and Mary Quarterly*, 3d series, 52 (January 1995), 104–161, with comments by Daniel Scott Smith, Richard White, and Patricia Seed. For childbirth, see Catherine M. Scholten, *Childbearing in American Society, 1650–1850* (New York, 1985).

A classic study of women's legal status in the English colonies is Richard B. Morris, "Women's Rights in Early American Law," *Studies in the History of American Law with Special Reference to the Seventeenth and Eighteenth Century Colonies*, 2d ed. (Philadelphia, 1959), pp. 126–300. Puritan divorce policy is examined in D. Kelly Weisberg, "'Under Greet Temptations Heer': Women and Divorce in Colonial Massachusetts," *Feminist Studies*, 2 (1975), 183–184. For recent scholarship on sexual attitudes and behavior, see Merril D. Smith, ed., *Sex and Sexuality in Colonial America* (New York, 1998). Roger Thompson discusses sexual crimes in *Sex in Middlesex: Popular Mores in a Massachusetts County, 1649–1699* (Amherst, Mass., 1986). N.E.H. Hull examines women criminals in *Female Felons: Women and Serious Crime in Colonial Massachusetts* (Champaign, Ill., 1987). Cornelia Hughes Dayton examines women's roles in early New England courts in *Women Before the Bar: Gender, Law, and Society in Connecticut, 1639–1789* (Chapel Hill, N.C., 1995).

For household production and other aspects of women's work, see Alice Morse Earle, *Home Life in Colonial Days* (New York, 1898); Alice Clark, *Working Life of Women in the Seventeenth Century* (New York, 1919); and Ulrich, *Good Wives*, part 1. The standard work on indentured servitude is Abbott Smith, *Colonists in Bondage: White Servitude and Convict Labor in Colonial America, 1607–1776*, 2d ed. (New York, 1971). For slavery in the colonial era, see Ira Berlin, *Many Thousands Gone: The First Two Centuries of Slavery in North America* (Cambridge, Mass., 1998). For the experience of the first generations of women slaves, see also Winthrop D. Jordan, *White Over Black: American Attitudes Toward the Negro, 1550–1812* (Baltimore, 1973); Allan Kulikoff, *Tobacco and Slaves*, part III; Russell Menard, "The Maryland Slave Population, 1658–1730: A Demographic Profile of Blacks in Four Counties," *William and Mary Quarterly*, 3d series, 32 (1975), 29–54; Carole Shammas, "Black Women's Work and the Evolution of Plantation Society in Virginia," *Labor History*, 26 (Winter 1985), 5–28, and, for the legal origins of slavery, Kathleen M. Brown, *Good Wives, Nasty Wenches*, cited above, part 2. For a comparative perspective, see Marietta Morrissey, *Slave Women in the New World: Gender Stratification in the Caribbean* (Lawrence, Kan., 1989), which covers the West Indies from 1600 to the nineteenth century.

For the impact of European colonization on Native American women, see two suggestive, though contradictory, views of women's roles among Algonquian-speaking coastal tribes: Neal Salisbury, *Manitou and Providence: Indians, Europeans, and the Making of New England,*

1500–1643 (New York, 1982), ch. 1, and Robert Steven Grumet, "Sunksquaws, Shamans, and Tradeswomen: Middle Atlantic Coastal Algonquian Women during the 17th and 18th Centuries," in Mona Etienne and Eleanor Leacock, eds., *Women and Colonization: Anthropological Perspectives* (New York, 1980), pp. 43–62. See also Grumet, *Historic Contact: Indian People and Colonists in Today's Northeastern United States in the Sixteenth through the Eighteenth Centuries* (Norman, Okla., 1995), and Ann Marie Plant's article on Awashunkes in Grumet, ed., *Northeastern Indian Lives, 1632–1816* (Amherst, Mass., 1996), pp. 140–165. A splendid collection of primary sources on gender roles among Native Americans in the colonial era is James Axtell, ed., *The Indian Peoples of Eastern America: A Documentary History of the Sexes* (New York, 1981). For recent scholarship, see Nancy Shoemaker, ed., *Negotiators of Change: Historical Perspectives on Native American Women* (New York, 1995); Laura F. Klein and Lillian A. Ackerman, eds., *Women and Power in Native North America* (Norman, Okla., 1995); and Theda Perdue, ed., *Sifters: Native American Women's Lives* (New York, 2001), a collection of biographical essays covering four centuries. For anthropological sources, see Rayna Green's review essay, "Native American Women," *Signs*, 6 (Winter 1980), 248–267. For more sources on Native American women in the colonial era, see the "Suggested Readings" in ch. 2.

A growing literature on captivity offers insights about women's roles in the colonial era. For Mary Rowlandson's famous captivity narrative, which first appeared in 1682, see Alden T. Vaughan and Edward C. Clark, eds., *Puritans Among the Indians, Accounts of Captivity and Redemption 1676–1724* (Cambridge, Mass., 1981), pp. 29–75, and Neal Salisbury, ed., *The Sovereignty and Goodness of God by Mary Rowlandson* (Boston, 1997). Scholarship on Rowlandson includes Douglas Edward Leach, "The 'Whens' of Mary Rowlandson's Captivity," *New England Quarterly*, 34 (September 1961), 352–362; David L. Greene, "New Light on Mary Rowlandson," *Early American Literature*, 20 (Spring 1985), 24–38; and Mitchell Robert Breitwieser, *American Puritanism and the Defense of Mourning: Religion, Grief, and Ethnology in Mary Rowlandson's Captivity Narrative* (Madison, Wisc., 1990). For the genre of captivity accounts, see R. H. Pearce, "The Tradition of the Captivity Narrative," *American Literature*, 19 (March 1947), 1–20; Vaughan and Clark, *Puritans Among the Indians*, pp. 1–27; and Kathryn Zabelle Derounian-Stodola and James Arthur Levernier, *The Indian Captivity Narrative, 1550–1900* (New York, 1993). Captivity experiences in the eighteenth century are explored in James Axtell, "The White Indians of Colonial America," *William and Mary Quarterly*, 3d series, 32 (January 1975), 55–88; June Namias, *White Captives: Gender and Ethnicity on the American Frontier* (Chapel Hill, N. C., 1993); and John Demos, *The Unredeemed Captive: A Family Story from Early America* (New York, 1994). For a major conflict between colonists and Native Americans, see Jill Lepore, *The Name of War: King Philip's War and the Origins of American Identity* (New York, 1999), which analyzes contemporary accounts of the war.

Mary Maples Dunn describes the unique role of Quaker women in "Women of Light," in Carol Ruth Berkin and Mary Beth Norton, eds., *Women of America: A History* (Boston, 1979), pp. 114–136, and Dunn, "Saints and Sisters: Congregational and Quaker Women in the Early Colonial Period," *American Quarterly*, 30 (Winter 1978), 582–601. See also Elisabeth Potts Brown and Susan Mosher Stuart, eds., *Witnesses for Change: Quaker Women over Three Centuries* (New Brunswick, N.J., 1989), and Jean R. Soderlund, "Women's Authority in Pennsylvania and New Jersey Quaker Meetings, 1680–1760," *William and Mary Quarterly*, 3d series, 44 (October 1987), 722–749. Qualities valued in Puritan women are suggested in Laurel Thatcher Ulrich, "Vertuous Woman Found: New England Ministerial Literature, 1668–1735," *American Quarterly*, 28 (Spring 1976), 19–40. Charles Lloyd Cohen describes female conversion relations in *God's Caress: The Psychology of Puritan Religious Experience* (New York, 1986). Amanda Porterfield considers Puritanism's appeal to women in *Female Piety in Puritan New England: The Emergence of Religious Humanism* (New Haven, Conn., 1992). For a darker view, see Elizabeth Reis, *Damned Women: Sinners and Witches in Puritan New England* (New Haven, Conn., 1997). For Anne Hutchinson, see Emery Battis, *Saints and Sectaries: Anne Hutchinson and the Antinomian Controversy in the Massachusetts Bay Colony* (Chapel Hill, N.C., 1962); Amy Shrager Lang, *Prophetic Women: Anne Hutchinson and the Problem of Dissent in the Literature of New England* (Berkeley, Cal., 1987); and David D. Hall, ed., *The Antinomian Controversy, 1636–1638: A Documentary History*, 2d ed. (Durham, N.C., 1990). Hutchinson's role is also discussed in Koehler, *A Search for Power*, ch. 8; Norton, *Founding Mothers and Fathers*, ch. 8; Porterfield, *Female Piety*, ch. 3; and Kamensky, *Governing the Tongue*, ch. 1. Marilyn J. Westerkamp surveys women's religious history in *Women and Religion in Early America, 1600–1850: The Puritan and Evangelical Traditions* (New York, 1999). For colonial women's writings, many on religion, see Sharon M. Harris, ed., *American Women Writers to 1800* (New York, 1996).

Studies of witchcraft present vivid pictures of women's roles in seventeenth-century New England society. In *Entertaining Satan: Witchcraft and the Culture of Early New England* (New York, 1982), John Demos uses social science methods, psychological theory, and collective biography to analyze several decades of witchcraft accusations. See also Demos, "Underlying Themes in the Witchcraft Trials of Seventeenth-century New England," *American Historical Review*, 85 (June 1970), 1311–1326. Carol F. Karlson, who also examines witchcraft charges, suggests a link between accusations of women and inheritance patterns; see *The Devil in the Shape of a Woman: Witchcraft in Colonial New England* (New York, 1987). Attention often centers on the witchcraft trials of 1692. Three different approaches are Paul Boyer and Stephen Nissenbaum, *Salem Possessed: The Social Origins of Witchcraft* (Cambridge, Mass., 1974), which analyzes social and political tensions in Salem; Chadwick Hansen, *Witchcraft at Salem* (New York, 1969), which contends that witchcraft induced psychosomatic effects in its victims; and Marion Starkey, *The Devil in Massachusetts* (New York, 1949), which points to hysteria among the young "accusors." Recent studies include Bernard Rosenthal, *Salem Story: Reading the Witch Trials of 1692* (New York, 1993); Peter Charles Hoffer, *The Devil's Disciples: Makers of the Salem Witchcraft Trials* (Baltimore, 1996); and Laurie Winn Carlson, *A Fever in Salem: A New Interpretation of the New England Witch Trials* (Chicago, 1999), which suggests that a form of sleeping sickness, encephalitis lethargica, afflicted the "possessed." Elaine Breslau, *Tituba, Reluctant Witch of Salem: Devilish Indians and Puritan Fantasies* (New York, 1996), offers another perspective on the trials. For primary sources on witchcraft, see David D. Hall, ed., *Witch-Hunting in Seventeenth-Century New England: A Documentary History, 1638–1692*, 2nd. ed. (Boston, 1999); Paul Boyer and Stephen Nissenbaum, eds., *Salem-Village Witchcraft: A Documentary Record of Local Conflict in Colonial New England* (Boston, 1993); and Elizabeth Reis, ed., *Spellbound: Women and Witchcraft in America* (Wilmington, Del., 1998).

⊗ For quizzes and additional resources related to American women's history, visit the book's Website at *www.mhhe.com/americanwomen*.

CHAPTER TWO

The Eighteenth Century:
The Eve of Modernity

N THE EIGHTEENTH century, a network of changes slowly transformed the remote, insular, and traditional colonial world and thereby affected women's lives. The inroads made by modern trends were gradual, selective, and uneven. Traditional roles, for men and women, re-emerged along the shifting frontier, in the rural backwater, and on the family farm, where more than 90 percent of Americans lived. Modernity encroached in cities and towns on the eastern seaboard, spurred by the rise of a mercantile, propertied elite. This privileged class served as a vanguard of innovation. After 1750, and especially in the post-Revolutionary decades, many of the values and ideals it transmitted began to gain a larger audience.

The rise of class was only one way in which eighteenth-century society became more settled, stable, and in many ways more like England. As the seventeenth-century garrison mentality grew obsolete, enterprising colonists shifted their energies from mere survival to commercial profit. By the end of the century, the communal ethos of the earliest settlements gave way to a competitive one. The expanding population was also in flux. Unbalanced sex ratios, characteristic of the early frontier, began to fade or even vanish in the east, though they reappeared in more remote regions, where new communities were carved out. Like class distinctions, economic change and shifting sex ratios impinged on women's lives by altering, for instance, their domestic work and marital options.

For much of the century, however, Anglo-American women remained in a traditional world of their own, relatively insulated from their changing environment. As dependent family members, most women had little opportunity to function in either family or society as autonomous individuals. Typically, they had little control over their own destinies and few contacts beyond the household. Whereas men might gather in informal institutions such as taverns and formal ones such as colonial assemblies, women lacked institutional involvements beyond family and church. They were rarely able to adopt "modern" attitudes—such as ambition, achievement, risk—as did those men who negotiated transatlantic shipments of lumber, tobacco, and slaves; or cut the salaries of royal governors in provincial legislatures; or surveyed tracts in remote woodlands for future speculation. Not all men were able to adopt such attitudes either. But women were still in a world apart. Home-based, child-bound, and limited by law, they remained subordinate in private life and marginal in public life.

The era of the American Revolution provided a turning point in women's history. The Revolution did not destroy women's separate realm of life but, rather, threw it into convulsions. In wartime, women became involved, unavoidably, in the turmoil and conflict of public events. Called on to provide public services as well as to handle enlarged domestic responsibilities, women began to express themselves politically, in groups and as individuals. Wives and housekeepers became boycotters and camp followers, petitioners and fund raisers, loyalists and patriots. Whether women were capable of taking a political stance, however, remained a moot point throughout the war. They could, of course, be convicted of treason. But even if praised for patriotism, a woman was not a full citizen. The newly independent states recognized that married women were femes coverts, not autonomous beings, and therefore unable to voice any political will.

After the Revolution, women were only indirect beneficiaries of "independence." They gained no new legal codes, save in the area of divorce, or access to political life. By increasing men's political rights, the Revolution increased the extent of female exclusion. But in the first decades of nationhood, social changes that had been filtering into colonial society, especially into its upper echelons, emerged on a larger scale. The patriarchal family of the seventeenth century, with absolute power residing in the male "head," started to be replaced by a new type of family that was more private, more affectionate, and less authoritarian. Within the family, women and children began to assume enhanced roles as distinctive individuals. In the early days of the new republic, finally, elite women began to profit from a new image, a change in the way they regarded themselves and were regarded by others. The "new woman" of the turn of the century was no longer considered morally suspect, mentally dim, or potentially dangerous to those around her. Rather, she might now be considered a rational individual and even a quasi-autonomous one—within the family circle. At home, she had been promoted from a "necessary good" to a custodian of values. In this role, she was capable of transmitting ideas, having a positive influence on her children, and playing a role in society at large.

WIVES AND WIDOWS

For most of the eighteenth century, while modern impulses made selective inroads in colonial society, the role of women—like that of most farmers, backwoodsmen, servants, slaves, and artisans—lagged behind, locked into a traditional mold. Whatever her locale or station in society, the contours of a woman's life were defined by her dependent role within the family. Her wealth and status depended on that of the men to whom she was related. Although she might be, through birth or marriage, the beneficiary of extensive property—as was plantation mistress Eliza Lucas Pinckney of South Carolina, who assumed a prominent role in her family and community—she was far more likely to belong to a family of modest means and to spend her life on a family farm. Here her labor remained vital, although not necessarily highly valued in her own view or that of others. In either case, her career was most likely to be shaped not by her own achievements but by her relations to men and by the changing shape of her family, as its members were born, married, and died.

These were circumstances over which she had no control, with one major exception: her own marriage—a step so momentous it was rarely made without the advice and consent of parents, relatives, and friends. Acceptance of a proposal was the most significant decision to which she would ever contribute, perhaps the sole instance in which her judgment carried weight, and often the only occasion on which modern attitudes—such as risk or individualism—came within grasp. In the eighteenth century, daughters' leverage over their own marriage arrangements increased. Beyond this decisive moment, however, autonomy—the ability to shape her own destiny— usually remained beyond a woman's reach.

She had no control over the family locale, status, or property. Nor, in most cases, could she control the property she had brought with her to the marriage—as wives of loyalists such as Grace Galloway discovered during the Revolution, when property they had inherited was confiscated because of their husbands' political views. Although the eighteenth-century woman commonly expected to spend most if not all of her adult life bearing children and taking care of them, she had no legal control over her children—a disadvantage in the event that her marriage failed. Even under the most favorable circumstances, she lacked control over the number of children she bore, except by prolonging the nursing of one, which was likely to delay the arrival of the next, or by extended stays at a relative's home. Nor could she regulate the amount of her time involved in her children's care. "When I had but one child my hands were tied," confided Esther Burr, wife of the president of the College of New Jersey to her friend Sally Prince in 1756, after the birth of her second child, Aaron, "but now that I am tied hand and foot how I shall get along when I have 1/2 dozen or 10 children I can't devise."

If inability to control fertility helped to lock women into traditional roles, so did lack of literacy. A small minority, the daughters of propertied families, might have the advantage of a few years in school, but such experiences were atypical. Throughout the century, women's ability to read, and especially to write, consistently lagged behind that of men. Reading and writing, when taught at all, were taught separately; even women who learned to read, usually at home, did not necessarily learn how to write. Only a portion of late-eighteenth-century women could write their names on wills, for instance, and still fewer could write a coherent letter. Among New Englanders, whose literacy exceeded that of other colonists, gender limited transmission of skills. Viewed as a craft and a vocational skill, writing was taught primarily by men and required mainly of boys. In Massachusetts in 1789, less than half of the women were minimally literate, as opposed to about 90 percent of the men. Women elsewhere fared no better. As communication through the written word became steadily more important, women's lagging literacy put them at a disadvantage. Women were also confined to traditional roles, as men were not, by their common vocation, domestic work.

Whether the eighteenth-century woman lived in a bustling seaport or in the backwoods, whether she was married to a merchant or a farmer, she managed a household, where she was likely to labor for all of her life. Traditionally, the household work of wives and daughters comprised repetitive tasks, which though varied were continual. Washing, ironing, cooking, baking, sewing, knitting, preserving food, preparing food, whitewashing walls—the housekeeper spent her days on a sequence of responsibilities, some seasonal, most perpetual. Her daughters were in training for the same role. When Abigail Foote, a Connecticut girl, recounted a day's activity in 1775, she captured both the tedium and the timelessness of household work in its typical locale, the family farm:

> Fix'd gown for Prude—mend Mother's Riding-hood—Spun short thread . . . carded two—spun linen—Worked on Cheesebasket, Hatchel'd flax with Hannah . . . Pleated and ironed—Read Sermon of Dodridge's—Spooled a piece—Milked the cows— Spun linen, did 50 knots—Made a Broom of Guinea wheat straw,—Spun thread to whiten—Set a Red dye . . . corded two pounds of white wool. . . . Spun Harness twine—scoured the pewter.

But domestic work began to change in some ways too. The eighteenth century brought new distinctions in the types of work women did at home, and the types of homes within which they worked. The frontier of housewifery was a new brick house in an eastern town, rather than a two-room cabin in a newly carved-out settlement.

By midcentury, the urban housewife had more opportunity to buy some of the things her family needed—notably cloth and clothing items—than did her rural counterpart or less prosperous neighbor. In seaport cities and thriving market towns, a new dynamic was at work within the home: where goods were available for purchase, household production decreased as wealth and privilege rose. Specifically, buying might replace spinning. The housewife's new role as purchaser was evident in the diary of Mary Vial Holyoke, a well-off Boston woman, in the 1760s. Like all housekeepers, Mary Holyoke was constantly busy with domestic routines. She preserved food, produced soap, stitched clothes, scoured rooms, maintained a garden, and even raised hens, ducks, and pigs. But she did not spin. And she was able to buy tea, milk, butter, candles, sheets, cloth, coats, and gowns.

Once urban women such as Mary Holyoke could purchase such items, the seventeenth-century mode of housewifery symbolized by the wheel became increasingly a badge of lower status. In rural areas, however, wives and daughters continued to be surrounded by reels, spools, and knots of flax. Comparable distinctions appeared in the South. Mistresses of large plantations assumed managerial roles, supervising the slaves who did household tasks—sometimes a large work force—and directing food and clothing production for the whole plantation. Slaveless neighbors, meanwhile, continued to milk cows, tend churns, and spin thread themselves.

Just as women could not control the encroachment of class distinctions or determine the nature of their domestic work, they lacked control over the way their status might suddenly change, most commonly through a husband's death. The eighteenth-century widow, who gained legal rights her married sister lacked, was also affected by changes in the class structure and economy. Although many widows may have felt, when bereaved, like "a walking Ghost"—as Eliza Pinckney did—few could assume the managerial roles filled by widows of means. In all the colonies, a growing number of widows lived off holdings they inherited, but this was hardly the typical situation.

Needlework provided an artistic outlet for eighteenth-century
women in the English colonies. Mary Swett Bulman of
York, Maine, designed and produced this floral coverlet, with
wool crewel embroidery on unbleached linen homespun,
around 1745. *(Old York Historical Society, York, Maine)*

By midcentury in eastern Massachusetts, always in the forefront of social change,
the widow was likely to inherit, by will or dower right, a third of her husband's estate.
This meant, in most cases, a corner of the farmhouse in which she lived (perhaps now
occupied by one of her grown children), the use of a well, a few cows, and a small plot
of land, from which it was difficult or impossible to reap an income. She was also
likely to remain single, not necessarily out of choice. The age of widows was rising;
Massachusetts widows now tended to be middle-aged or older and therefore less
marriageable. In addition, more densely settled eastern regions continually lost
younger men who wanted land and moved away. These regions were likely to have
an oversupply of unmarried women. Shifting sex ratios made the marriage market
more competitive even for younger women, and the option of remarriage for middle-
aged widows quite remote. For instance, in one Massachusetts town, Hingham,
about 14 percent of women who were widowed in their 40s and 50s had remarried in
the decades before 1760, but only 5 percent afterward. Younger women, widowed
in their 20s and 30s, fared somewhat better in the marriage market, 57 percent re-
marrying before 1760 and 35 percent afterward. Still, in both cases chances of finding a new husband dwindled decade by decade. The widow was therefore likely to fall

into the category of family or community dependent. Or if young enough, she might enter the ranks of working women, especially if she lived in a town or city or was able to move to one.

Although the proportion of self-supporting working widows (and, increasingly, spinsters) in the eighteenth century never exceeded 10 percent of the adult female population and was in most cases far less, they congregated in towns and cities. In Boston, as early as the 1740s, 13 percent of the 16,000 residents were widows, "almost all of them poor," according to the town's records. As in other cities, these femes soles were likely to be active in business and trade. Such activism was a by-product of a labor-scarce society. But it also reflected, on a limited scale, the commercial spirit that pervaded eighteenth-century life; this was clear in the newspaper advertisements that proffered the services of seamstresses and starchmakers, boardinghouses and food shops.

As in the seventeenth century, some working widows managed trades inherited from their husbands, at least until sons could replace them, and were therefore found in many occupations—including that of mortician, blacksmith, and carpenter. But most working women labored in trades connected to household production and in ventures they started themselves, usually catering to women clients. In Baltimore, 8 percent of the city's households were headed by women in 1796, and two-thirds of these women were widows, less than half of whom worked to support themselves. The rest were spinsters, almost all of whom worked. Although their number included the occasional printer, mill owner, and land speculator—vocations invariably inherited by widows—most of Baltimore's working women, like those elsewhere, entered the wide array of trades stemming from domestic work. These became more specialized. Women were not only seamstresses and laundresses but dyers, starchers, lacemakers, and mantua makers. As shop proprietresses, they dealt in china, groceries, pastries, dry goods, millinery, and hardware. As in other cities, they ran inns, boardinghouses, coffeehouses, and taverns. By now, in most towns, women held most of the liquor licenses. No licenses were needed to run "dame schools," attended by small children, or small boarding schools, where girls could learn drawing, writing, and needlework, or to sell homemade cosmetics or medicines, or to offer one's services as midwife, wet-nurse, or domestic worker. Married women who pursued vocations, like busy midwife Martha Ballard of Maine, may have depended on a retinue of female assistants. Ballard, who delivered 30 to 40 babies a year, used the services of her teenage daughters and later a succession of hired girls to help her with household tasks.

Two Boston shopkeepers of the late eighteenth century illustrate contrasting approaches, traditional and modern, to careers in trade. Benjamin Franklin's younger sister, Jane Mecom, was the last of her mother's 10 children and the seventeenth of her father's, a soap and candle maker. Wed to a saddler at 15, she gave birth to 12 children, most of whom died before maturity and the rest soon thereafter. After her husband became an invalid, unable to support the remnants of their brood, Jane Mecom took in boarders, a move of desperation more than enterprise. "Sorrows," she told Franklin, "roll upon me like the waters of the sea." When widowed, Jane Mecom opened a small millinery shop, with assistance from her brother, and imported fabric, ribbon, laces, and caps until imports were cut off by the Revolution. As none of her children survived her, she spent her old age in relatives' homes, feeling like a "vagrant."

While Jane Mecom fell victim to successive disasters, domestic and commercial, Elizabeth Murray experienced increasing autonomy, influence, and an ability to manipulate her environment. An English emigrant, widowed when young, Elizabeth Murray ran a profitable millinery and cloth business and converted her economic success into what she called "a spirit of independence." This was revealed in the increasingly stringent antenuptial contracts she signed with the last two of her three husbands and in the disposition of her estate, which she left to nieces whose upbringing and education she had supervised.

Elizabeth Murray's achievement was more the exception than the rule in the eighteenth century. A series of barriers circumscribed most women's lives. Autonomy was precluded not only by a dependent role at home but by limited notions of women's capacities. Before the Revolution, the ideology of woman's "place" was rarely discussed. As it was uncontroversial and unchallenged, there was little need to define or defend its perimeters. Rather, it rested on common assumptions that were widely shared by men and women alike.

CHARACTER AND CAPACITY

In the eighteenth century, no one would deny that gender affected character or that being female encompassed a spectrum of distinctive characteristics. A crucial distinction between the sexes was that "rationality" was believed to be in short supply among women. This belief emerged even in the rhetoric of the day, which was loaded in favor of men. Like her contemporaries, Eliza Pinckney viewed "reason" as a masculine quality, although clearly one to which women might aspire; as a rational person, Eliza laid claim to what was called a "masculine mind," which meant intelligence. Similarly, she deplored activities, in men or women, that tended to "effeminate" the mind—that is, to make one vain, capricious, fickle, foolish, frivolous, or extravagant.

For most of the century, in language and in life, femininity connoted inherent defects and disabilities. These defects appeared in popular advice tracts, published in England but reprinted in the colonies. The role of reason as a dividing line between the sexes was clearly set forth in Lord Halifax's *Advice to a Daughter* (1688), an English import with colonial sales throughout the century. Halifax conveyed a harsh view of women's capacities. "There is inequality in the sexes," he posited. "[T]he men who were to be the law givers, had the larger share of reason bestowed upon them, by which means your sex is better prepared for the compliance that is necessary for the better performance of those duties which appear to be most properly assigned to it." In Halifax's view of women's roles, "compliance"—a corollary of defective reason—was the crucial word. The woman who was pliable, flexible, patient, submissive, and resigned would be able to adapt to whatever type of husband she happened to get. Aptitude for "compliance" was at once an innate trait and one that daughters and wives would do well to develop. By midcentury, an array of compensatory virtues joined the basic list of female disabilities. In *A Father's Legacy to his Daughter*, a popular tract of the 1770s, Dr. John Gregory attributed to women "softness and sensibility of heart." He also urged cultivation of qualities that would gain men's affection and protection. Toward this end, a woman ought to be modest, cheerful, timid, delicate, tender, affectionate, graceful, and sympathetic. Innate or acquired, the "virtues" recommended in prescriptive literature were those that appealed to men.

Such imported advice tracts were no doubt inaccessible to the average colonial housewife, who would most likely have been unable to read them. Rather, they were manuals of upward mobility, destined for an audience of means and ambition who aspired to a high social status or the lifestyle of English counterparts. But the assumptions on which they were based—that women were weak and helpless, defective of reason, and dependent on men—were commonplace in the colonies. Women shared such assumptions, as is suggested in the journals and letters of the literate elite. In the second half of the century, women extolled the "softer" virtues in their private papers, but they also admitted to a medley of "foibles" and deficiencies.

One Virginia housewife, Elizabeth Foote Washington, left her unborn daughter a "legacy" in the form of a diary; here she tried to describe her dual role, as competent mistress and deferential wife. But had a daughter survived to read the legacy (none did), she would have met the spirit of resignation and inadequacy that pervaded it. "I am totally at a loss, in many respects," wrote Elizabeth, when her husband was sick and she had to deal with plantation accounts. "Indeed, I scarce know anything that goes on." A similar inability to grasp, cope, or control pervaded women's self-assessments. In her survey of the diaries and correspondence of late-eighteenth-century women, historian Mary Beth Norton finds that women habitually referred to themselves in self-deprecating and negative ways, as "weaker vessels," "imperfect," and "helpless." Bemoaning their lack of confidence and inarticulateness, they often belittled their domestic work, apologized for failings, and even referred to their own imbecility. Even literate eighteenth-century women, Norton reveals, tended to express low self-esteem.

This inferior self-image, like the negative assumptions that infiltrated language, reflected social reality. Women's roles *were* dependent, circumscribed, and, barring distinctions of class or race, interchangeable. What one woman did might just as well be done by another, whatever their capacities. Although motherhood offered personal gratification, along with social esteem and security, neither child rearing nor housewifery provided a sense of individuality within the home or outside it. There were two loopholes in these general rules, however, one traditional and one innovative; and some women took advantage of them, especially in the second half of the century.

The traditional loophole was piety. Although women's capacity for rational thought was questioned, their piety was never in doubt. It had been effectively internalized, along with other passive qualities such as helplessness and resignation. But piety also had an activist facet. Churches remained the sole institution outside the home to which women had access; indeed, they often constituted a majority of congregants. Moreover, the liberating mood of the Great Awakening of the 1740s expanded their participation. Spates of revivals and multiplication of sects spawned a diffusion of authority and a climate of excitement in which women were more likely to assert themselves. In some congregations, women influenced the admission of members and selection of ministers. On some occasions, female practitioners, however irregular, assumed leadership roles on the fringes of religious life. In the 1760s, for instance, Sarah Osborn of Newport held religious meetings in her home for more than 300 persons in the course of a week. Several women promoted new sects—as did Shaker leader Mother Ann Lee in the 1770s—or attracted large numbers of followers—as did revivalist Jemima Wilkinson in the 1780s. Finally, female energy pervaded the Society of Friends, now a large and prominent sect. Between 1700 and 1775, historian Rebecca Larson reveals, at least 1,300 Quaker women served as preachers in the transatlantic world that comprised England and its colonies.

Such activist roles might induce anxiety, even among public Friends, who traveled widely to prophesy in other communities. Quaker convert Elizabeth Ashbridge, an indentured servant in New York who later became a public Friend, was at first thrown into shock when she heard a woman preach. Public Friend Rebecca Jones was reduced "to the brink of the grave" when she felt the call to prophesy but finally, "in fear and trembling," gave herself up "to the Lord's will." Other activists voiced reluctance to invade the public sphere. Although Sarah Osborn achieved an influential position in Newport, she was deferential to ministerial authority and "greatly distress'd" lest she "Move beyond my Line." Still she supervised the conversions of marginal community members, such as local blacks and young unmarried women, "who were awakened to a concern for their souls and desired my assistance and advice." Indeed, the Revolutionary era saw a surge of evangelical fervor and religious rebellion among women. Toward the end of the century, some female dissidents challenged their ministers; women members of newer sects, such as the Baptists or Methodists, became prophets and lay preachers; and rampant enthusiasm disrupted long-established sects. In Philadelphia, Quaker matron Elizabeth Drinker reported that so many zealous women crowded the Yearly Women's Meeting of 1803 that some had to be turned away. But the peak of female activism had passed. Among Baptists, the largest of the evangelical sects, according to historian Susan Juster, male clergy used the revolutionary moment to support independence, increase their own authority, and devalue female activism. By the first decade of the nineteenth century, Juster contends, women had been silenced in evangelical sects.

While piety provided women, on occasion, with an avenue of access to public influence, "friendship" served a different function. An innovative relationship, friendship enhanced private influence and self-esteem. In the eighteenth century, the meaning of the word "friend" was in transition. Traditionally, a "friend" meant an ally or connection, usually a family member. But by mid-century, the meaning had started to shift. As a friend, a woman could establish an effective link, as an autonomous individual, with someone who was not a family member, indeed, with a peer or equal. Often involving extensive visiting and lifelong correspondence, friendship differed from traditional modes of social connection among the loose coalitions of relatives and neighbors typical of the seventeenth-century village. Indeed, it provided an escape hatch from authoritarian relationships within the traditional family. Friendship was a modern connection and, in the context of women's history, a political one. It also was a defiant connection, or at least one that required defense. Esther Burr of New Jersey defended friendship in the 1750s when she took issue with an obnoxious college tutor, Mr. Ewing, who had "mean thoughts of women." Ewing revealed his colors when he contended that "he did not think women knew what friendship was, they were hardly capable of anything so cool and rational as friendship," as Esther reported in the journal she kept to send to her best friend, Sally Prince.

The long-term Burr-Prince correspondence, however, was hardly "cool and rational." Rather, it was warm and affectionate. So was the four-decade correspondence between Susanna Anthony and Sarah Osborn. "O, my dear, my bosom-friend," wrote Susanna, "I feel my love to you to be without dissimulation." In the late eighteenth century, letters between woman friends adopted the same affectionate tone. Eunice Callender of Boston, for instance, addressed her cousin Sally Ripley as "the dearest Friend of my heart" throughout their three-decade correspondence. "I never knew how much I loved you," wrote Martha Lauren of Charleston in the 1770s to her friend Elizabeth Brailsford. "You have . . . imprinted on my soul your beloved image, in character so indelible that neither time nor absence can erase it." Nor would marriage end their relationships, young women announced. Matrimony, declared Lucy Orr of Virginia to friend Polly in the 1780s, "is, I fear the bane of Female Friendship. Let it not be with ours, my Polly, if we should ever Marry."

Evidence of female friendship, concentrated at the end of the century, appears connected to the development of a literate female elite; similar bonds no doubt existed between women with less ability to express them in writing. In either case, friendship provided an independent, egalitarian connection, as well as a loophole of escape from traditional roles. The law, however, reinforced traditional roles, just as it reflected the negative assumptions about women's character and capacity so widely shared in the eighteenth century. On those occasions when a woman had to resort to law, as a feme sole or a feme covert, she was likely to find that the law demanded dependence on men.

LEGAL INSTITUTIONS

The legal status of eighteenth-century women derived from a combination of common law, equity practices, and provincial statutes, which varied from colony to colony, providing release from some common-law limitations and upholding others. As in the seventeenth century, policies diverged among the colonies, though practices were fairly similar. The statutes enacted by provincial legislatures were not intended to enhance the position of women, or of men, but rather to protect community interests—by reducing public welfare obligations, for instance, or by increasing the ease of business transactions. Colonial laws often protected women's interests—by facilitating a woman's self-support if she were destitute, for example. But they rarely promoted her autonomy or independence. Almost inevitably, the approval of men—husband, judge, or legislature—was needed for the exercise of any legal "right."

All colonies, for instance, accepted antenuptial contracts; such acceptance apparently gave colonial women an advantage that most Englishwomen lacked. But only a minority of couples signed these contracts and very rarely in a woman's first marriage. Through an antenuptial contract, parents of means might insist on keeping property in trust for a daughter and her heirs, thereby preventing the new husband from gaining control of it but not giving control to the daughter either. Wealthy widows, however, the more frequent beneficiaries of antenuptial contracts, might bargain for and insist on control over property they had inherited or acquired. In either case, the new husband's approval was needed. A married woman's control of property was not so much a legal option as it was a concession from a future spouse—and one not commonly given or requested.

Without benefit of special contracts, the real property a woman brought to her marriage, if any, went under her husband's control or management, just as her personal property, earnings, children, and person belonged to him. A wife could bequeath her personal property, such as jewelry or clothing, to her heirs; but she needed her husband's consent to do so. Real property was another matter. Most colonies (Connecticut was an exception) prohibited a husband from alienating property that his wife brought to the marriage, without the latter's consent. But the wife was at a disadvantage. She could be coerced into giving consent—for the sale of land, for instance. Or in the event that a scheming husband sold off her property without such consent, she would have to resort to law to fight the transaction, which was not a simple matter. Her position was yet more difficult if her husband was abusive or unfaithful or merely unable or unwilling to live with and support her, as he was obliged to do under common law.

Although common law clearly set forth the rights and obligations of husbands and wives, it provided no machinery for enforcement—which meant, in practice, that a married woman's fate depended much more on luck than on law. In most cases, if her marriage failed, her luck ran out. Absolute divorce, with the right to remarry, was available in the New England colonies. It was granted to only a small proportion of those who petitioned for it, to men more often than women and never to women for the cause of adultery until the era of the Revolution. Other colonies sometimes permitted divorce by individual legislative acts. But such grants could be, and often were, disallowed by the English Privy Council as "improper and unconstitutional." Most important, to obtain even a legal separation from an adulterer or criminal, a woman would have to muster support from others and exert much initiative. But men found it far easier to terminate an unsatisfactory marriage by desertion—a mode of escape used by wives, too, but less often. Of the 229 petitions for divorce submitted in Massachusetts between 1692 and 1786, the majority came from wives, and 65 percent of these were based on desertion or nonsupport. Only 37 percent of husbands cited desertion as a cause for divorce. In all colonies, when a husband vanished through desertion, long-term absence, or death, the courts and legislature replaced him as the final arbiter of the woman's "rights."

The deserted wife was a special but not uncommon case; she had no legal rights or property but was still unable to support herself as a feme sole in trade. Colonies might grant feme sole trader rights to such women, if requested, through private legislative acts. In 1718, Pennsylvania enacted a feme sole trader statute to cover such cases. But, as historian Marylynn Salmon shows, legislators shaped the law with caution and with more concern for creditors than for wives. The statute made feme sole status available to wives of men who were absent for long terms (such as sailors) or who had deserted or gone bankrupt. It enabled them to engage in trade, support themselves, feed their children, and even assume liability for the debts their husbands had incurred. Deserted wives could thereby keep themselves off the public dole and, if need be, satisfy their husbands' creditors. South Carolina recognized feme sole trader status through two more liberal laws, in 1712 and 1744, that made married businesswomen liable for their own debts and enabled them to sue for debt.

Although widows, unlike deserted wives, automatically gained feme sole rights and could own property, sign contracts, and sue and be sued, their autonomy was also curtailed by law. Most colonies provided that a widow was assured of her dower right—a life estate in one-third of her husband's real property and a similar proportion of his personal property—if he died intestate. (If he wrote a will, he could leave her more.) The real property could not be sold or bequeathed by the widow without special permission from a court or legislature. In Pennsylvania, a widow could lose even her dower right if her husband was in debt—an innovation unknown to common law. In any colony, a husband in his will could make retention of the dower right or whatever his wife was to inherit, whether much or little, contingent on her remaining single. In no case did the dower right provide the widow with control over the property; she received only a life interest in it, which might or might not be enough to sustain her, depending on the size of the estate. The legal system stood between the widow and autonomy, just as it did for the wife.

Colonial women's limited ability to own property or control capital severely limited their economic power. According to a study of probate records by historian Carole Shammas, men held at least 90 percent of colonial wealth. The increasingly commercial economy, moreover, distanced women from the law. The late eighteenth-century courtroom, where women's presence had been drastically reduced, historian Cornelia Hughes Dayton contends, became a forum primarily for men involved in trade, credit, and business transactions. Nor did the Revolution radically alter the status of women under law. During the war, when states confiscated Tory property, new problems arose involving dower rights and married women's property rights. Such problems were often solved with consideration for women's predicaments, though not by any alteration of law. Still, the Revolutionary era brought the beginning of change. Abolition of primogeniture, for instance, made all offspring equal to the eldest son as heirs—though all that daughters inherited still fell under their husbands' control. More important, in the post-Revolutionary years, most states enacted laws to provide for absolute divorce in limited instances. But jurists discarded neither the doctrine of coverture nor insistence on female dependence. After the war, as before, English common law remained in effect.

Lawyers continued to rely on Sir William Blackstone's *Commentaries* on English common law, published in 1765, which provided a guide to the status of the feme covert. As Blackstone explained, "The very being or legal existence of the woman is suspended during the course of marriage, or at least is incorporated and consolidated into that of the husband; under whose wing, protection, and cover she performs every thing." Blackstone's list of the feme covert's limitations served not only eighteenth-century lawyers but their successors. Only in the mid-nineteenth century, when states began to grant married women the right to possess inherited property, did the doctrine of coverture start to crack—and the proportion of total wealth held by men begin to decline.

Subordination of women was peculiar to neither the English legal system nor to Anglo-American society on the eastern seaboard. Patterns of sex hierarchy also characterized non-English communities, such as those of Hispanic settlers in the southwest, Indian tribes in the east, and slave societies, north and south. In each case, however, as in English society, elements of change impinged.

DIVERSITY OF CULTURES

Distinctive social customs emerged in the non-English communities of North America, such as the Spanish settlements in the Rio Grande valley. By the start of the eighteenth century, about 3,000 Spanish settlers lived in towns like Santa Fe and Albuquerque, and on small ranches on the Rio Grande, along with some 15,000 Pueblo Indians. Until 1770, these remote northern settlements, linked to Mexico City only by yearly mule train, remained isolated from the rest of Spanish society. Within Spanish settlements, a complex status system prevailed. At the top, a tiny Spanish aristocracy that intermarried owned most of the land. A peasantry of *mestizo* (mixed race) origins also considered itself Spanish; *mestizos* held small land plots and worked as wage laborers. At the bottom of Spanish society, a large labor force of *genizaros*, or detribalized Indians (often prisoners of war) performed most of the physical labor, as household servants or farm workers.

Among the small group of Spanish aristocrats, historian Ramon A. Gutierrez contends, sex roles were sharply delineated. Men embodied the virtue of "honor" and exerted authority over family members and subordinates. Women embodied the equivalent virtue of "shame" *(verguena)*. Expected to be shy and retiring, they were ideally pure before marriage and faithful afterward. This concept of feminine virtue applied only in aristocratic households, where women led isolated existences. *Mestizo* women, who worked on farms, had less secluded lives. *Genizaro* women, some of them slaves, were left out of the Spanish value system. One friar complained in 1734 that "an Indian does not care if you fornicate with his wife because she has no shame." On the Spanish frontier, as throughout the Spanish empire, historian David J. Weber confirms, a formal class system discriminated against the non-Spanish. But on the frontier, Weber contends, *mestizos*, mulattoes, and Hispanicized Indians "found ample opportunity to transcend their official racial categories." In particular, scarcity of Spanish women promoted the intermarriage of Spaniards and Indians. Demographic patterns also made women's roles in Spanish frontier communities distinctive, Weber points out. High death rates (mainly of men) offset high birth rates; consequently, Spanish settlements contained large numbers of orphans, widows, remarried widows, and widows who served as heads of families.

In the last quarter of the century, the isolation of northern "New Spain" diminished. Other European powers encroached in Texas, New Mexico, and California. Commerce with Mexico increased, the populations of Spanish settlements expanded, the authority of the church dwindled, and the rules that governed Spanish society loosened. Among aristocrats, according to Gutierrez, marriage for love and free choice of partners gained sway over arranged marriages, a change that was under way in Anglo-American society as well.

Native American women on the eastern seaboard, such as the Cherokee and Iroquois, may well have experienced a decline in status in the eighteenth century. Among southern Cherokees, for instance, contact with white settlers seemed to spur a process of female devaluation that continued into the 1800s. Originally, the Cherokees had been a matrilineal, matrilocal tribe that favored farming over hunting. The agrarian rhythms of women's lives determined tribal routines. But the disruption of war and trade with white settlers, historian Theda Perdue shows, made hunting (traditionally men's work) more important than farming (women's work). As early as 1725, Cherokees had become dependent on the deerskin trade with the English and accustomed to such items as European garments, guns, and brass kettles. Women stopped making tools and utensils, deerskins became the currency, and men, empowered by the importance of trade, assumed dominant roles as household heads.

The deerskin trade dismantled the former balance in Cherokee culture. Hunting, no longer limited to the winter months, became a year-round activity. Trade encouraged acquisition of material goods, increased exploitation of the natural world, and diminished the value of women's agrarian roles. As hierarchy replaced harmony, an ethos of individualism replaced one of cooperation. Women also lost political powers they had formerly enjoyed, such as deciding the fate of captives (death or adoption into families). Local leadership councils, in which women had participated, declined in importance. Only Cherokee men met with colonial officials, and women lost their role in decision-making. In the second half of the century, conflict among Europeans completed the transformation that the deerskin trade had begun. The Seven Years' War (1756–1763) took a severe toll on the old Cherokee lifestyle; the invasion of Indian fields led to devastation and starvation. In the Revolution, some 30 Cherokee towns were destroyed, crops ruined, and Indian children sold into slavery.

By the end of the century, the Cherokee community had been permanently transformed. Cherokees now lived in isolated homesteads, not cooperative villages, and the nuclear family replaced the clan. Intermarriage of traders and Indians introduced class divisions. Female status became linked to family wealth, not clan well-being. Overall, once European values impinged, women's influence and prestige shrank; decades of gradual anglicization took their toll. Well before Cherokee removal in the 1830s, according to Perdue, women had lost most of their power in the community.

Women's roles in Iroquois society also changed over the course of the eighteenth century. Traditionally, among the Iroquois, women enjoyed exceptionally high economic and political status. "All real authority is vested in them," declared French explorer and missionary Joseph François Lafitau in 1724. "The land, the fields, their harvest all belong to them. They are . . . the arbiters of peace and war. . . . They have charge of the public treasury. . . . The children are their domain." Moreover, women wielded political leverage through their all-woman councils. "The women are always the first to deliberate a private or community battle," Lafitau wrote. "They hold their councils apart and . . . advise the chiefs." Lafitau may have exaggerated the degree of female political power, which resided in matrons, widows, and older female heads of households. Still, on a day-to-day basis, Iroquois women controlled community life. "An Iroquois town was largely a female world," writes historian Daniel K. Richter. Under the sexual division of labor that prevailed, men concerned themselves mainly with external affairs; women "took primary responsibility not only for their children but the village as whole—its homes, food supplies, and surrounding fields." During the Revolution, the Iroquois Confederation—the Seneca, Cayuga, Onondaga, Oneida, Tuscarora, and Mohawk tribes—supported the British, whose defeat left Iroquois towns in ruins. Many left their tribal lands for Canada or the West; acre-hungry speculators besieged those who remained. When white farmers claimed tribal hunting territories, the customary division of work roles dissolved. Iroquois men lost their traditional roles in trade, diplomacy, and politics, and became agriculturalists; women gave up farming, took responsibility solely for household labor, and lost status in their community. Both sexes had to adjust to Anglo-American ways, which in women's case meant patriarchal households, weakened kinship ties, loss of autonomy, and dependent roles.

The changes experienced by Cherokee women in the South and Iroquois women in the North culminated two centuries of interaction between Native Americans and Europeans, a confrontation that affected gender roles, though not necessarily in uniform ways. Trade with Europeans in many cases made Native American tribes less self-sufficient. The demands generated by the fur trade, for instance, transformed stable agricultural communities into nomadic ones, altered village life, weakened family organization, and redefined women's work. By the end of eighteenth century, European influences had impinged on Algonquian lifestyles in other ways as well. First, "Women's participation in public affairs sometimes declined," historian Colin G. Calloway points out, "since Europeans insisted on dealing with men." Second, Calloway contends, Europeans disparaged egalitarian gender relations among Native Americans and sought to restructure Indian societies "along European lines"; such restructuring involved female subordination: "men, not clan mothers, must dominate society." Finally, endemic warfare took a toll. Continual conflict with Europeans and other tribes from the 1750s through the Revolution reduced economic productivity, upset diplomacy, caused political upheaval, and disrupted normal patterns of life. Yet the impact on women varied. "In some societies, the influence of women declined as Europeans dealt exclusively with males as the hunters and warriors," Calloway concludes. "In others, women's traditional role escaped relatively undisturbed and provided a much-needed source of stability."

While the numbers of eastern Native Americans fell in the eighteenth century, the institution of slavery enjoyed a period of phenomenal growth. Slave codes, the most innovative of provincial statutes, created a black subculture with different rules from those that applied in white society. Still, some of the factors that altered white women's experience—such as increasing parity of sex ratios and the development of a southern plantation aristocracy—affected slave women, too.

Slave women on large plantations in stable areas, such as the Chesapeake or the Tidewater, had many advantages that new arrivals, frontier slaves, or women slaves with less privileged owners lacked. By the 1720s and 1730s, these older, wealthier regions had dense black populations, a high proportion of native-born slaves, and more balanced sex ratios. Women were able to find marital partners, establish family lives, and develop networks of relatives on the same plantation or a neighboring one. Women stranded on small isolated farms—north or south—had less chance of finding appropriate marital partners or any at all. Moreover, despite the continued skewing of southern slave ratios in favor of men, a far larger proportion of slave women than white women lacked partners. Still, despite the precarious conditions of slavery and lack of legal marriage, others managed to maintain long-term unions.

They also began to have more children. As slave society became more stable in Maryland and Virginia, and as a native-born slave population developed, child-bearing rates rose. Slave women in these settled regions now had almost as many children as white women, beginning in their late teens—a contrast to the low fertility of immigrant slave women in the seventeenth century. By the early eighteenth century, as slavery became a self-perpetuating institution, the slave family became its distinguishing feature. Women served as the major bastions of slave family life—as reflected in plantation records, where slave genealogy was traced through mothers.

The rise of a plantation aristocracy in older, stable areas also affected the work roles of women slaves. Most women on large plantations worked in the fields, as they invariably did on small ones. But on sizable estates, women might occupy preferable posts—such as dairymaid, poultry maid, nurse, laundress, seamstress, or midwife, a pivotal job. These specialized vocations, which involved working in or around the house, not in the fields, were likely to be handed down from mother to daughter. But the woman slave's prospects of escaping field work remained limited. Only about 10 or 15 percent of slaves did so, and the majority were men, who might work not only as house servants but as artisans in a variety of trades or as slave overseers. After 1760, the percentage of slaves of both sexes engaged in non-field work rose, and by the end of the century, on large Virginia estates, one-third or more of slave women labored in house service. Still, a higher proportion of women than men worked in the fields. Some performed housework or other jobs only when too young or too old for field work, and others held alternate assignments according to plantation needs. "A stout able field wench and an exceedingly good washer and ironer," was the way a late-eighteenth-century Virginian evaluated a favored slave.

If the development of large plantations brought advantages to some women slaves, so did the era of the Revolution. The proximity of the British army encouraged slaves to escape, and they did so in large groups that included family units and therefore women and children. Of the 23 slaves who departed from Thomas Jefferson's Virginia lands during the war, for instance, more than half were women and girls, all but two leaving in family groups. In British-occupied New York City, similarly, a large proportion of fugitives who sought the protection of the British army when the city was evacuated were women and girls in family groups. In some instances, women led groups of fugitives to liberty. The *Royal Georgia Gazette* in 1781 reported an escape from the plantation of one Mary Thomas led by Old Ross, described as an Ibo woman, age 56. The runaways included Old Ross's daughter, Celia, 36; Celia's husband, Cato, 61; another daughter, Country Sue, 32; a son, Dick, 22; Elsie, a "thick and chubbed" granddaughter; and several non-family members. Such group escapes of families and friends from the same plantation, contends historian Sylvia R. Frey, suggests the significance of community bonds and kinship ties and the depth of commitment to the dream of freedom. Women who remained enslaved, however, may well have faced harder times. A new hiring-out system in the Chesapeake decreased family stability. Expanding cotton production in the lower South depressed living conditions and increased work demands.

The Revolutionary era, finally, underlined the contrast between colonial de-mands for self-determination and the slaves' lack of it. A particular grievance was the inability of slaves to establish the type of family life that whites enjoyed. When a group of Massachusetts slaves in 1774 petitioned the state legislature for freedom, they stressed the incompatibility of slavery with family life. "How can a slave perform the duties of husband to wife or a parent to a child?" asked the Massachusetts petition. "How can a husband leave [his] master to work and cleave to his wife. How can the wife submit to her husband in all things?" The upheavals of the Revolution-ary years improved the lives of a minority of slaves, including the Massachusetts petitioners, when northern states abolished slavery. In the upper South, a spate of voluntary emancipation created a large free black population, a majority of which was female and mulatto. The Revolution left the legal status of most slaves, as of white women, untouched. But during the Revolutionary War, women were suddenly caught up in the turmoil of public events and drawn into new activities.

THE CRADLE OF THE REVOLUTION

The era of the American Revolution, which epitomized shifts of power and author-ity, altered white women's relations to public life and, on occasion, expanded men's views of women's capacities. The conflicts that began in the 1760s drew attention to women's household work and upgraded the value of their domestic contributions—as producers of homespun, boycotters of imports, and enthusiasts of the cause. The disruption of war, which shifted families to new locales and often removed men from the home, enabled or forced women to assume new authority. Finally, the war at home compelled women to become concerned about public affairs—a concern that was hard to avoid if one's town, for instance, was under siege. Most important, under the stress of the first modern revolution, women were suddenly assumed to be capa-ble of sharing a highly valued and rational political sentiment: patriotism.

Expressions of patriotism were novel and varied. In some rare instances women entered battle—for example, male impersonator Deborah Sampson Gannett, who enlisted in the fourth Massachusetts Regiment and eventually received a pension for her service. (After her death, the pension was passed on to her husband, a curious ex-ample of role reversal.) But Gannett's role as a soldier reflected the primitive nature of the rebel army more than any new option open to women. In the Revolution, as in other eighteenth-century wars, women played a traditional role as camp followers. To Washington, who desperately tried to create a professional army, the presence of female camp followers was a liability. "The Multitudes of women," he contended in 1777, "especially those who are pregnant or have children, are a clog upon every movement." Washington appreciated, however, one of the most modern roles women adopted during the war: raising money for the cause. In 1781, he congratu-lated the Ladies Association of Philadelphia (a more elite group than the camp followers) on their fund gathering, and awarded its members a tribute for "female patriotism." The Philadelphia ladies, Washington asserted, proved "that the love of country is blended with those softer domestic virtues, which have always been allowed to be more peculiarly *your own*."

Not only did the war throw a spotlight on "domestic virtue," but it imbued household work with political content. Once boycotts of English goods began in the 1760s, the spinning and weaving of cloth—activities usually relegated to less prosperous and rural homes—became patriotic acts. "I carded two pounds of whole wool and felt Nationaly," wrote Abigail Foote in her diary. Urban wives and daughters began making clothes out of homespun. Later, during the war, they made blankets and shirts for the rebel army. Southern mistresses too turned to the wheel, once imports of English cloth ended. Women slaves were affected as well. Starting in the 1760s, some were reassigned to spinning. The stimulus to home manufacture provided by colonial boycotts opened up a vocation. In urban areas and especially in New England households, women (and children) began producing cloth for income under the putting-out system; manufacturers paid them by the piece. Finally, the boycotts of the 1760s drew attention to the role of urban women as family purchasing agents, when they refused to buy British goods.

Besides affecting women's household roles, the rebel cause sanctioned group activities for women. For over a decade, the gatherings of rebel women received publicity in the patriot press. Sometimes, women in groups created mob scenes—as did the 500 women who, Abigail Adams reported, harassed and hounded a Massachusetts merchant for hoarding coffee in 1777. Indeed, women conducted almost one-third of 30 food riots in the late 1770s. Housewives and tradeswomen joined forces to confront merchants, intimidate shopkeepers, and seize scarce commodities, among them tea, coffee, sugar, salt, and bread. More commonly, "association" took the form of sewing circles. Groups as large as 60 or 70 women or more convened to spin, weave, and sew. Women in association also passed resolutions not to patronize merchants who broke nonimportation agreements, took oaths renouncing marriage with men who did not support the patriot cause, and professed supportive sentiments. "We cannot be indifferent," declared a group of 51 North Carolina women, "on any occasion that appears to affect the peace and happiness of our country."

The chaos produced by war at home precluded indifference. It disrupted the livelihood of self-supporting women such as the small shopkeepers of Boston, many of whom had been put out of business when importation ceased. It created hardship for property owners such as Eliza Pinckney, whose income fell when rents were not paid and slaves refused to work. "They all do now what they please every where," she complained to her son Thomas in 1779. Most of all, the war disrupted families, with mixed effects. In the absence of men, women sometimes assumed new authority—for example, by taking over and managing farms and businesses. Many were unprepared for such responsibility, as was the case with those loyalist wives who, when pressing claims after the war, revealed that they knew little of their husbands' business affairs, earnings, debts, or even what property they owned. However, for patriots such as Abigail Adams, a master of egalitarian rhetoric, responsibility provided opportunity. "I find it necessary to be the directress of our husbandry," she wrote to her husband in 1776. "I hope in time to have the reputation of being as good a farmer as my partner has of being a good statesman."

Women's competent management of the home front, historian Mary Beth Norton suggests, made some men pay more attention to their wives' roles—a new tack, as household work was customarily regarded as trivial and inconsequential. The

A British cartoon of "a society of patriotic ladies" determined
to boycott British goods. Society members, depicted as either
ferocious or simple-minded, are signing a petition not to buy
tea or use British cloth "until such time that all acts which
tend to Enslave this our Native Country shall be repealed."
An attentive slave holds the inkwell, a child is forgotten under
the table, and a dog desecrates the scenery. *(Mezzotint by
Philip Dawes, 1775. Library of Congress)*

war also inspired collective activity and philanthropy, as exemplified by the Ladies
Association of Philadelphia. Formed in 1780, the association attracted a core of
prominent, well-off local women; they planned to collect from women and girls the
money that would no longer be spent on extravagant clothes and to donate this sum
to the rebel army. Dividing the city into districts, the women visited every home, in
pairs, and amassed a substantial sum for the cause. ("People were obliged to give
them something to get rid of them," complained loyalist Anna Rawle to her friend
Rebecca Shoemaker.) They also spurred women in four more states to similar
attempts. Proud of the "favor and affection found in this effort," according to one
participant, the Philadelphia women offered proof that women could share the
rational sentiment of patriotism and act effectively on it.

Patriot women with less local clout may have had less opportunity for formal association, and loyalist women, who often felt isolated, still less. But all could engage in the discussion of politics—with husbands, relatives, visitors, and each other, sometimes in correspondence. Women voiced ambivalence about entering the arena of political discussion, a male preserve, and even apologized for going beyond their "province." Others apologized as a matter of form. "I've transgress'd the line . . . by dipping into politicks," wrote Sarah Jay, daughter and wife of politicians, in a letter to her family, although "politicks" were her preoccupation. Some women, such as Abigail Adams and Mercy Warren, wrote to each other constantly about politics, without apology. One New England woman, who later described the excitement she had felt "while rocked in the cradle of revolution," contended that the war era had inspired a lifelong interest in public affairs. Outspoken Eliza Wilkinson of South Carolina insisted to a friend in 1782 that political interest was within her province. Women had enough "sense" to voice opinions, she asserted, without being told that spinning and domestic affairs were "the only matters we are capable of thinking or speaking of with justness and propriety."

Even for those as politicized as Eliza Wilkinson, the Revolution brought only negligible gains. Women did not receive new legal status or independence from coverture. On the contrary, after the Revolution, colonial equity practices such as antenuptial contracts or dower rights, which tended to mitigate common law to women's advantage, fell increasingly into disuse. Nor did women receive (or demand) the vote. Property ownership remained the basis for suffrage, and as married women owned no property, they had no free political will. Unmarried women were excluded too. The sole exception was in New Jersey, where for three decades an aberration in the suffrage law enabled unmarried women property owners to vote. This privilege came to an end in 1807, when women, boys, blacks, and other "irregulars" were finally excluded from the polls. The New Jersey precedent, ignored elsewhere, was unique. After the Revolution as before, as historian Linda Kerber points out, the family circle remained a woman's "state." From a legal and political point of view, the Revolution was a "conservative" one for American women.

But the apolitical status of women was not unique; not all white men had access to voting or public office, either. In most states, those who owned little or no property (as did most women) were unable to vote. More important, most men who had the franchise had little interest in using it, rarely bothered to do so, and cultivated a grand indifference to politics. Few could afford to leave private concerns for public office, and those who did were constantly torn between civic obligation and the desire to return to farms and plantations, family life, and provincial retreats. For women, as for the majority of men, the raised expectations incurred by "independence" existed more at a personal level than a political one.

In the postwar decades, these expectations started to surface in a private context, within the family. It would be rash to assume that a modern mode of marriage suddenly replaced the traditional one, or that an enhanced notion of womanhood immediately supplanted widespread convictions of female inferiority. Shifts within the private sphere were always far more gradual and less visible than authority shifts in political life. Some of the changes within the family, minimizing paternal power and giving more "liberty" to other family members, began before the Revolutionary era and accompanied rather than followed it. Other changes in domestic habits, despite the democratic rhetoric of the late eighteenth century, tended to start at the top of the social scale and only slowly filter downward. Still, in the last two decades of the century, new ideals of family life at least began to encroach and impinge. In the process, women's status in the family began to rise.

THE PURSUIT OF HAPPINESS

During the eighteenth century, the analogy between the family and the state, an Anglo-American favorite, began to provoke new questions. In the wake of the English Revolution of 1688, when absolute monarchy fell out of favor, domestic patriarchy was also open to assault. "If absolute sovereignty be not necessary in a state, how comes it to be so in a family?" asked the English writer Mary Astell in 1706. "Is it not then partial in men to the last degree to contend for and practise that arbitrary dominion in their families which they abhor and exclaim against in the state?" In the era of the American Revolution, women of political bent asked the same question and applied republican theory to domestic politics. "Emancipating all nations, you insist upon retaining absolute power over Wives," Abigail Adams wrote to her husband in 1776. "Do not put such unlimited powers into the hands of the husbands," she told John Adams while he was serving in the Continental Congress. "Remember all men would be tyrants if they could."

What Abigail Adams advocated was a redistribution of authority within the family, a curb on "absolute power over Wives," and the elevation of women to the status of partners and companions in marriage. In the 1780s and 1790s, when postwar exuberance peaked, such ideals emerged in the new nation's magazines and journals, which flourished in cities such as Boston and Philadelphia. The new, companionate ideal of marriage was one based on sympathy, affection, esteem, friendship, and mutual obligation, as opposed to the hierarchical mode of traditional marriage. Husband and wife were to be not only "the first and dearest friends of their partners," as described in a marriage guide, but interdependent ones. The tyranny of the domineering patriarch and the obedience of the servile wife gave way to complementarity, mutuality, and "reciprocal union of interest," as set forth in Philadelphia's newly founded *Lady's Magazine* by a writer who identified herself as a "Matrimonial Republican." According to the Massachusetts essayist Judith Sargent Murray, in an anonymous article of the 1790s, the ideal marriage was an egalitarian one requiring "mutual esteem, mutual friendship, mutual confidence, *begirt about by mutual forbearance.*" In less egalitarian publications, such as Boston's *Gentleman's and Lady's Town and Country Magazine* in the 1780s, husband and wife engaged in a minuet of deference and good manners: "Acknowledging his superior judgement, [the wife] complies with all his reasonable desires, whilst he attempts to suit his requests to her inclinations."

The new ideal of companionate marriage was not mere wishful thinking on the part of "matrimonial republicans." A less authoritarian type of marriage already prevailed among the propertied classes in England and was therefore familiar to members of the colonial elite. It was more likely to be found in the prosperous urban home than in the backwoods outpost; its beneficiary was more likely to be the wife relieved of incessant domestic drudgery than the wife bound to reels, spools, churns, cows, and chickens. The pursuit of domestic happiness had been customarily a privilege of the family of means. In the prosperous post-Revolutionary decades, in the glow of independence, the companionate ideal of marriage began to find a wider audience. Moreover, it had important corollaries for the role of women in the new nation.

In the late-eighteenth-century version of companionate marriage, the wife enjoyed a higher status within the home. She could now be considered a rational being rather than a mental incompetent; an amicable companion rather than a shrew; a virtuous partner rather than a servile drudge. Her individualism was also enhanced. The replacement of compulsory obedience with voluntary affection made the "happiness" of the partners a vital component of marriage rather than merely a fortuitous by-product. The new stress on "affection" and "happiness" appealed to young women at the end of the century. Precocious Eliza Southgate, a Maine teenager, for instance, decided at first that marriage was not "absolutely essential to my happiness" but later chose a husband "calculated to promote my happiness." In private papers as in public journals, the language used to describe marriage changed.

The ideal of happiness endorsed by Eliza Southgate had further ramifications. It seemed to be recognized in divorce proceedings in Massachusetts, where "loss of affection" sufficed in several instances as cause for divorce. Although divorce remained a limited option until the century's end, since the 1760s more people had applied for it in Massachusetts and Connecticut. Many Massachusetts applicants were women, and their petitions increasingly succeeded; these petitioners promoted their own "independence." After the Revolution, significantly, divorce became more accessible. By 1799, historian Norma Basch points out, 12 states and the Northwest territory had recognized the legal right of divorce. Divorce statutes varied widely, with southern states more resistant to change and western ones on the cutting edge. Absolute divorce remained rare; in most instances, the courts and state legislatures that ended marriages did so by granting separations and property settlements. Still, increased access to divorce was the major legal advantage that women gained in the new republic; "the impress of the Revolution was unmistakable," Basch contends. Diverging from English precedent, American states offered far more liberal arrangements to terminate marriages. Divorce in the new nation, Basch concludes, "was light years beyond its English equivalent."

Integration of the companionate ideal with traditional marriage caused confusion in Massachusetts divorce proceedings. This was reflected in the petition for divorce of one young man in 1781 who complained that he wanted his wife to be his "friend" and "in Subjection to me." He probably used the term "friend" in its older sense, but still he pointed to a real problem. The crux of companionate marriage was the replacement of patriarchal tyranny by benevolent leadership. Clearly, any shift in domestic politics limited the power of men. But men were still afflicted by what Abigail Adams called "the natural propensity in human nature to domination." The interweaving of authority and affection could be achieved only if wives adopted an attitude of deference; it was incumbent on wives to defer to their spouses in order to preserve a companionate tone. "The happiness of your life depends now on continuing to please a single person," Jefferson told his daughter Martha on her marriage. "To this all objects must be secondary, even your love for me." Elizabeth Foote Washington was even more specific in her diary of the 1790s. She had resolved never to argue with her husband, she revealed, as "husbands cannot bear to be thought in the wrong. . . . It was ever more pleasing to have my husband's opinion coincide with mine."

If the substitution of voluntarism for compulsion, deference for submission, and affection for obedience began to change the status of women in the post-Revolutionary family, it did even more for children. The parent-child relationship had been especially important in rebel rhetoric, which often conjured up the image of an adolescent society struggling to assert its independence from parental domination. In the new nation, children, like women, began to be viewed as individuals with distinctive characteristics and the capacity for reason. The late-eighteenth-century parent–child relationship was characterized by a decrease in paternal power, a rise in attention to child-rearing, and the substitution of suasion for domination. The modern parent hoped to inculcate values that would prepare the child for independence and, in this interest, to provide the proper combination of guidance and indulgence, love and restraint. The new mode of child-rearing enhanced the authority of mothers, who were as capable as fathers of providing or withholding affection (as opposed to property, which remained under men's control). The messages imparted by notable parents of the late eighteenth century strove to elicit a combination of love and deference. "I have placed my happiness on your being good and accomplished," Jefferson told his 11-year-old daughter in the 1780s, "and no distress which this world can now bring me could equal that of your disappointing my hopes." Abigail Adams, a memorable mother, was just as demanding with teenage John Quincy, at school in England. "I would rather see you find a grave in the ocean you have crossed," she wrote, "than see you an immoral, profligate or graceless child."

The altered parent–child relationship was even more marked in diminishing parental control over children's marriages, another tilt in the family power structure, and one that had been in progress since midcentury. By the late eighteenth century, children were marrying when they wanted. Daughters might marry ahead of their older sisters, a new development; sons might marry before or without inheriting property from their fathers. Children also married whom they wanted. As marriages would now, ideally, rest on personal preference and compatibility, they were more likely to be arranged by the partners themselves, subject to parental objections, rather than arranged by parents, subject to the veto of the child. Eliza Lucas Pinckney's experience in the 1740s had included both patterns: in 1741 she had strongly opposed her father's nominees; and three years later, confident of his approval, she had informed him of her own choice. By the end of the century, such freedom in selecting partners was far more widespread than at the beginning. But it was likely to have a different impact on daughters than on sons.

Daughters could no longer depend on parents to act on their behalf, by initiating negotiations or bargaining over arrangements. They now had to rely on their own discretion and aptitude in a more competitive market. Although an excess of men in the American population continued throughout the eighteenth century, western emigration, a man's option, threw sex ratios askew in the east. A steady exodus of young men, unable to obtain land in more densely settled areas, to more remote ones, left a diminished pool of suitors behind. In Massachusetts, the bellwether of social change, there were only about 90 adult white men to every 100 white women as early as 1765. The scarcity of men was most pronounced in eastern towns and less evident, if it existed at all, in more sparsely populated western counties. Still, by the last decades of the century, the age of marriage in New England had risen, as had the numbers of never-married women. The proportion of spinsters in the female population, small until now, would continue to grow for much of the nineteenth century.

In the colonial era, remaining a spinster had been a mark of opprobrium; it usually meant a dismal life of quasi-dependence, living in relatives' homes. But in the 1780s and 1790s, spinsterhood became an option—or at least more of a likelihood. The increase of spinsters in eastern regions may have reflected a rise in the autonomy of daughters, who had gained the right to refuse proposals, or a paucity of eligible candidates, or, most likely, a combination of both factors. Women's rising independence on the marriage market, however, was an ambivalent gain. It coincided with new demands of compatibility, fewer available men, less geographic mobility than men, and less leverage than men—who could choose whom to court. American daughters had little "liberty" to choose a husband, as 18-year-old Eliza Southgate observed in 1800, as they were unable to take the initiative. "It is true we have the liberty of refusing those we dont like," said Eliza, "but not of selecting those we do." In the marriage market, as in the commercial one, deregulation fostered competition, individualism, and high expectations. But it also brought a new set of risks and liabilities.

Under these more competitive circumstances, emphasis fell on the personal qualifications and discretion of the candidate herself. A well-informed woman, "conscious of her nature and dignity," Abigail Adams pointed out, would be more capable of "engaging and retaining the affection of a man of understanding." Such considerations, among others, fostered an interest in girls' education in the 1780s and 1790s and the emergence of innovative "female academies"—schools that offered academic programs. The new academies reflected an image of women as rational individuals, capable of absorbing and transmitting ideas. They also reflected the new prosperity of ambitious Americans. A daughter's education, though not exorbitant, was nonetheless an investment—possibly one that served as a substitute for a dowry. "Independence," in the postwar decades, probably affected daughters more directly than wives and, especially, a small core of privileged daughters from eastern propertied families.

FATHERS AND DAUGHTERS, MOTHERS AND SONS

Rationales for women's education had been utilitarian since 1692, when Cotton Mather described his feminine ideals in a sermon, "Ornaments for the Daughters of Zion." Education, said Mather, would enable a woman to better serve her husband and family and, by the same token, would prevent the degeneration of her character into what, it was feared, was its natural state: wickedness. The opening of female academies a century later elicited an equally utilitarian rationale. But it was based on a broader vision of women's roles, one that accepted female rationality and incorporated women into the ideology of the new republic.

Until the last half of the eighteenth century, girls' education, when available at all, was rudimentary and limited to the well-to-do. Few families were able to provide much schooling for any of their children, and those who could educated their sons. Young children in towns and cities might attend "dame schools" run by local widows or impoverished wives. Here, girls learned some reading and spelling. By the 1750s and 1760s, well-off daughters might have a few more years at boarding or "adventure" schools that offered instruction in the "ornamentals," such as French, embroidery, drawing, and harpsichord; such schools might also teach writing or "cyphering," the rudiments of arithmetic. As a rule, whatever learning daughters acquired, they were likely to acquire at home.

The first years of nationhood, however, accelerated change in female education. Opportunities for primary schooling increased, and some opportunities for girls' secondary education emerged along the eastern seaboard, catering to the daughters of families who could afford them. In several instances, New England boys' academies held special sessions for girls. More significant were the novel female academies. The Philadelphia Young Ladies Academy, born with the nation in 1787, was the leading example—probably a unique example, in fact, as few schools of the time could measure up to it. The academy provided a complete academic program. Classes, taught by men, included spelling, reading, writing, arithmetic, geography, rhetoric, and composition—that is, all subjects except the classics, a male preserve, and the sciences, although a series of lectures was held in this area. Over the next few decades, other ambitious institutions, some run by women, appeared in towns and cities. In the 1790s, northern girls could attend a roster of academies in Philadelphia or Boston or small schools in New England towns, such as Sarah Pierce's Litchfield Academy. By the first decade of the new century, planters' daughters might be sent to board at northern schools or at female academies in Georgia or North Carolina. "You know how anxious I am that you should be Clever as well as good," a Virginia mother urged her daughter in 1801. "Take every advantage to improve your mind that falls in your way."

Ideally, the new schools were not only academic institutions but permanent ones, rather than temporary means of support for schoolmistresses, like the adventure schools. This meant that they needed financial support from men in the community. Fathers paid the bills, served as trustees, and raised funds for school buildings. The Philadelphia Academy, significantly, was founded by prominent local men active in commerce, government, and the professions, many of them college graduates. The school's goals reflected the ideals of these well-off fathers. Academy education, according to one eminent trustee, was intended to inculcate neither pedantry nor frivolity, neither "excessive refinement nor extreme erudition," but rather the quality essential to republican womanhood— "a rational, well-informed piety."

Such moderate goals held large but not universal appeal. The prospect of educated women was controversial; the most powerful eighteenth-century argument against education was not that girls were ineducable but rather that education would make them repulsive to men. Critics contended that learning would limit a girl's marital opportunities, unsuit her for domestic work, and turn her into an unfeminine monster. Such sentiments had been voiced in the 1750s by Esther Burr's unwelcome guest, the college tutor Mr. Ewing, who contended that education would make a woman "disgussful to all her acquaintance." Masculine minds and manners, as a minister confirmed in an 1801 Boston magazine, would not "inspire the tender passion." Female education, moreover, said its foes, might even destroy family life. But defenders of women's education argued that the new nation needed educated women as wives and mothers; they sought to fuse the modern notion of female rationality with women's traditional family roles.

Benjamin Rush presented this defense in his "Thoughts on Female Education," offered to the Philadelphia Academy on its opening. Education, Rush explained, would prepare a student to fulfill the role of wife in a companionate marriage, "to be an agreeable companion for a sensible man." It would enable her to assume responsibility for the home, even if servants were unavailable. Educated wives could take charge of family business, purchases, accounts, and upkeep. They could serve as "stewards and guardians of their husbands' property" and liberate men for profit-making ventures. Not only did family success depend on women's ability in household management, but in times of adversity, such as widowhood, the educated woman would have survival skills. She would also be able, in all circumstances, to assume responsibility for the training of her children—an argument that carried increasing weight in the new republic.

This argument had both private and public facets. It occurred to Jefferson as a father in the 1780s when supervising, from France, his daughter Martha's course of study. Jefferson's logic was unassailable: "The chance that in marriage she will draw a blockhead I calculate at about fourteen to one, and . . . the education of her family will probably rest on her own ideas and direction without assistance." (He was right, as Martha had 12 children, by a husband who was mad part of the time and in debt most of it.) But Rush argued that educated mothers would also fill a civic role. As every man now had an "equal share" in the country's liberty, it was necessary "that our ladies should be qualified to a certain degree, by a peculiar and suitable education, to concur in instructing their sons in the principles of liberty and government." Well-trained mothers, in Rush's vision, would be responsible not only for instructing daughters, whose upbringing had customarily been in their hands, but for shaping the values of their sons, who were likely to have a direct impact on the nation's success.

The address made by Benjamin Rush in 1787 revealed an ideal of "republican motherhood," a term coined by historian Linda K. Kerber in the 1970s. The ideal had a dual thrust. It included women in the new nation, at least on the periphery of political life. As value transmitters, women could serve as a link between founding fathers and republican sons and provide the country with patriotic men. At the same time, the republican motherhood ideal confirmed female exclusion from public life, because it limited women to familial roles. Above all, it bolstered the social significance of mothers, who had gained an enlarged sphere of influence at home. Academy heads argued that virtue could be inculcated only by mothers. The goal of female education, the founder of a Georgia Academy announced, was "to nurture and fix the principle of virtue." Only mothers, contended the head of a Connecticut academy, could "plant the seeds of vice or virtue in their offspring." "Let the ladies of a country be educated properly," as Rush told his Philadelphia audience, "and they will form its manner and character."

Female education also served as a crux of raised expectations. After the Revolution, a rhetoric of female self-esteem emerged, along with a new contention: Education could remedy female inequality. Author Judith Sargent Murray, who celebrated "excellency in our sex," expounded this view in a series of articles under the pseudonym "Constantia." Education, she contended, would eradicate women's sense of inferiority. An anonymous "aged matron of Connecticut," who published her own *Female Advocate*, continued the argument in 1801. Women, she asserted, had been deprived of education in order to keep them inferior and subject. A similar claim appeared in the salutatory address of a 1793 Philadelphia Academy graduate who launched an attack on "despotic man." Men, said Priscilla Mason, had "doomed the sex to servile or frivolous employment on purpose to degrade their minds, that they themselves might hold unrivalled the power and preemptions they usurped." For much of the eighteenth century, women had described themselves with reference to female weakness and foibles. The new assault on male power and the celebration of "excellency in our sex" represented a significant departure.

Idealized in portraiture, the republican mother imbued her offspring with virtue, piety, and patriotism. A Charles Willson Peale painting of Mrs. Richard Tilghman of Maryland and her sons, 1789. *(Maryland Historical Society, Baltimore)*

Education's role as a remedy for inequality was not solely an American theme. It was also the gist of Englishwoman Mary Wollstonecraft's *Vindication of the Rights of Women*, which appeared in 1792. Like Benjamin Rush, Wollstonecraft contended that education would produce superior wives and mothers. She also decried the "false system of education" that prepared women only to appeal to men and left them in a "state of perpetual childhood." Her book, however, won little praise from American women. Even when readers accepted Wollstonecraft's conclusions, they usually condemned her lifestyle, deplored her premarital liaisons, or felt she denigrated feminine character. Still, several readers voiced appreciation. "In very many of her sentiments, she . . . *speaks my mind*," Philadelphia Quaker Elizabeth Drinker wrote in her diary in 1796. Young Eliza Southgate of Maine, in 1801, conceded to her diary that she admired the English author's sentiments, "prejudice set aside."

Wollstonecraft's ideas echoed those set forth by Judith Sargent Murray, whose essays appeared in Massachusetts journals in the 1780s and 1790s. Murray, too, endorsed pragmatic arguments for women's education. "Felicity of families," she contended, depended on competent wives who could manage their time and accounts. But women's education, Murray asserted, would benefit self as well as society. Development of women's rational faculties would inculcate self-respect, self-confidence, and aspiration. The daughter addressed as a "rational being," Murray wrote in 1784, would develop "reverence of self . . . the glow of virtue . . . that elevation of soul, that dignity, which is ever attendant upon self-approbation." Such a daughter would not throw herself away on the first suitor who proposed; nor should girls be trained solely for marriage. Rather, "the art of economical independence should be placed within their grasp." To Judith Sargent Murray, women's education held the key to the future. As she wrote in 1798, "I expect to see our young women forming a new era in female history."

The graduates of the early academies did not fulfill all of the goals set forth for women in the heady 1790s. For many students, the experience of independence provided by a few years of academy training was a finite one. But academy graduates soon became prominent among those women who entered teaching, missionary work, and reform in the early nineteenth century. Expansion of primary schooling, meanwhile, affected women's status in the new nation. After the Revolution, female literacy began to rise; sometime between 1790 and 1830, the substantial literacy gap between men and women closed. Although academy training involved only a small group, increased literacy brought far greater numbers of women a step a farther into the modern world.

Major signs of a post-Revolutionary change in women's status, therefore, included a new ideal of companionate marriage, the new legitimacy of women's education, a new rhetoric of female self-esteem, and an enhanced regard for motherhood. These signs were class-based. Republican womanhood, as historian Robert Gross observes, was a concept that "essentially served the interests of the emerging elite" and helped to "consolidate a middle-class gentry." The early years of nationhood also brought the claim that women might serve a civic function. The role of the "republican mother," Linda Kerber points out, was limited. It provided a context in which "female virtues might comfortably coexist with civic virtue," and it appeared to reconcile politics and domesticity. But it was a role played solely in the home. Before the Revolution, women had been excluded from political life; afterward, they remained "on the periphery of the political community." It is possible, writes Kerber, "to read the subsequent political history of women in America as the story of women's efforts to accomplish for themselves what the Revolution failed to do."

Such accomplishments were a long way off. But by the end of the eighteenth century other omens of change in women's roles emerged. One was the start of female association; church-sponsored benevolent societies, which first appeared in eastern cities around 1800, multiplied in the following decades. Another augury was periodical literature and fiction catering to women readers. A popular novel of 1794, Susanna Rowson's *Charlotte Temple*, exemplified the genre. A morality tale written by the founder of a prominent Massachusetts female academy, the book concerned, significantly, the evil consequences of seduction. Like female societies, women's publications would increase in number in the years to come. A less visible sign of impending change was the beginning of a drop in family size, at least in some Quaker and New England communities, that had taken place between the Revolution and 1800; a steady decline in the birth rate would characterize the nineteenth century. A final preview of coming events was Samuel Slater's cotton mill in Pawtucket, Rhode Island. Started in 1791, the mill employed as its first operatives nine children under the age of 12. In the next half-century, American manufacturing would draw thousands of women into paid employment.

If these omens were hardly noticed at the end of the century, another trend in American society caught the attention of two relentless commentators, Abigail Adams and Mercy Warren. "I deprecate that restless spirit, and that baneful pride, ambition, and thirst for power which will finally make us as wretched as our neighbors," Abigail Adams wrote to her sister, Elizabeth Shaw, in 1787. On the other side of the political fence, her longtime friend Mercy Warren, who became a Jeffersonian Republican, reacted similarly to post-Revolutionary prosperity. According to Mercy Warren, changing standards of wealth and class had taken their toll on American values and virtues. "A sudden accumulation of property by privateering, by speculation, by accident or by fraud, placed many in the lap of affluence, who were without principle, education, or family," she recorded in her *History of the Revolution*, published in 1805. This sudden elevation in wealth, Mercy Warren contended, fostered immoderation, avarice, tastelessness, and extravagance. Instead of the simplicity and elegance that had briefly characterized the new republic, the rising generation had acquired "a thirst for the accumulation of wealth, unknown to their ancestors." In the next half-century, republican motherhood, too, took on proportions that would have surprised its early proponents.

SUGGESTED READINGS AND SOURCES

For overviews of eighteenth-century women's lives, see Mary Beth Norton, *Liberty's Daughters: The Revolutionary Experience of American Women, 1750–1800* (Boston, 1980); Linda K. Kerber, *Women of the Republic: Intellect and Ideology in Revolutionary America* (Chapel Hill, N.C., 1980); Ronald Hoffman and Peter J. Albert, eds., *Women in the Age of the American Revolution* (Charlottesville, Va., 1989); and Carol Berkin, *First Generations: Women in Colonial America* (New York, 1996).

Until recently, the major sources of information on eighteenth-century women were the works of historians of the 1920s and 1930s. See Elizabeth Dexter, *Colonial Women of Affairs* (Boston, 1931; first published 1924); Mary Sumner Benson, *Women in Eighteenth Century America: A Study of Opinion and Social Usage* (Port Washington, N.Y., 1966; first published 1935); and Julia Cherry Spruill, *Women's Life and Work in the Southern Colonies* (New York, 1938).

Much work on eighteenth-century women lies in the realm of family history, often in local studies. On marriage and family life, suggestive articles include Daniel Scott Smith, "Parental Power and Marriage Patterns: An Analysis of Historical Trends in Higham, Massachusetts," *Journal of Marriage and the Family*, 35 (August 1973), 419–428; Robert V. Wells, "Quaker Marriage Patterns in a Colonial Perspective," *William and Mary Quarterly*, 3d series, 29 (July 1972), 415–442; Nancy F. Cott, "Divorce and the Changing Status of Women in Eighteenth-Century Massachusetts," *William and Mary Quarterly*, 3d series, 33 (October 1976), 586–614; and Cott, "Eighteenth-Century Family and Social Life Revealed in Massachusetts Divorce Records," *Journal of Social History*, 10 (1976–1977), 20–43. Elaine Forman Crane compares the impact of skewed sex ratios in New England and the Caribbean in "The Socioeconomics of a Female Majority in Eighteenth-Century Bermuda," *Signs* 15 (Winter 1990), 231–258, and explores the feminization of New England seaports in *Ebb Tide in New England: Women, Seaports, and Social Change, 1630–1800* (Boston, 1998). For southern women's roles, see Daniel Blake Smith, *Inside the Big House: Planter Family Life in Eighteenth-Century Chesapeake Society* (Ithaca, N.Y., 1980); Allan Kulikoff, *Tobacco and Slaves: The Development of Southern Cultures in the Chesapeake, 1680–1800* (Chapel Hill, N.C., 1986); Jan Lewis, *The Pursuit of Happiness: Family and Values in Jefferson's Virginia* (New York, 1983); Kathleen M. Brown, *Good Wives, Nasty Wenches, and Anxious Patriarchs: Gender Race and Power in Colonial Virginia* (Chapel Hill, N.C., 1996), chs. 8–10; and Cynthia A. Kierner, *Beyond the Household: Women's Place in the Early South, 1700–1835* (Ithaca, N.Y., 1998).

Philip Greven examines child-rearing attitudes and practices in *The Protestant Temperament: Patterns of Child-rearing, Religious Experience, and the Self* (New York, 1977). For widows, see Alexander Keysser's study of Woburn, Massachusetts, "Widowhood in Eighteenth-Century Massachusetts: A Problem in the History of the Family," *Perspectives in American History*, 8 (1974), 83–119, and Lisa Wilson, *Life After Death: Widows in Pennsylvania, 1750–1850* (Philadelphia, 1992). Cornelia Hughes Dayton discusses sexual attitudes and social relations in "Taking the Trade: Abortion and Gender Relations in an Eighteenth-Century New England Village," *William and Mary Quarterly*, 3d series, 48 (January 1991), 19–49. For comparisons of male and female educational skills, see Kenneth Lockridge, *Literacy in Colonial New England* (New York, 1974); Linda Auwers, "Reading the Marks of the Past: Exploring Female Literacy in Colonial Windsor, Connecticut," *Historical Methods*, 13 (1980); E. Jennifer Monaghan, "Literacy Instruction and Gender in Colonial New England," *American Quarterly*, 40 (March 1988), 18–41; Joel Perlman and Dennis Shirley, "When Did New England Women Acquire Literacy?" *William and Mary Quarterly*, 3d series, 48 (January 1991), 50–67; and Patricia Cline Cohen, *A Calculating People: Numeracy in Early America* (Chicago, 1982).

For the experience of an exceptional eighteenth-century woman, see Elise Pinckney and Marvin R. Zahniser, eds., *The Letterbook of Eliza Lucas Pinckney 1739–1762* (Chapel Hill, N.C., 1972). For Elizabeth Murray's career, see Mary Beth Norton's article "A Cherished Spirit of Independence: The Life of an Eighteenth-Century Boston Businesswoman," in Carol Ruth Berkin and Mary Beth Norton, eds., *Women of America: A History* (Boston, 1979), pp. 37–67;

and Patricia Cleary, *Elizabeth Murray: A Woman's Pursuit of Independence in Eighteenth-Century America* (Amherst, Mass., 2000). Katherine A. Jacobs examines women's roles in trade in "The 'Second Sex' in Baltimore," *Maryland Historical Magazine*, 71 (Fall 1976), 283–295. See also Gloria T. Main, "Gender, Work, and Wages in Colonial New England," *William and Mary Quarterly*, 3d series, 51 (January 1994), 39–66, which explores the impact of market changes on family members' labor; and, for household manufacture, Laurel Thatcher Ulrich, "Wheels, Looms, and the Gender Division of Labor in Eighteenth-Century New England," *William and Mary Quarterly*, 3d series, 55 (January 1998), 13–38. Ulrich explores a midwife's experience in "Martha Ballard and Her Girls: Women's Work in Eighteenth-Century Maine," in Stephen Innes, ed., *Work and Labor in Early America* (Chapel Hill, N.C., 1988), pp. 70–105; "'The Living Mother of a Living Child': Midwifery and Mortality in Post-Revolutionary New England," *William and Mary Quarterly*, 3d series, 46 (January 1989), 27–48; and *A Midwife's Tale: The Life of Martha Ballard, Based on her Diary, 1785–1812* (New York, 1990). An impressive film, *The Midwife's Tale* (1997) dramatizes Ballard's experience. Ballard's diary, which she kept from 1785–1812, and other primary sources are available at www.dohistory.org. Joan M. Jensen considers the work roles of rural women in the Philadelphia hinterland in the late colonial and early national periods in *Loosening the Bonds: Mid-Atlantic Farm Women 1750–1850* (New Haven, Conn., 1986).

   The economic roles of single women are discussed in Karin Wulf, *Not All Wives: Women of Colonial Philadelphia* (Ithaca, N.Y., 2000). For women's participation in the economy at the end of the century, see Susan Branson, "The Invisible Woman: The Female Economy in the Early Republic—The Case of Elizabeth Meredith," *Journal of the Early Republic*, 16 (Spring 1996), 47–71; Jeanne Boydston, "The Woman Who Wasn't There: Women's Market Labor and the Transition to Capitalism in the United States," *Journal of the Early Republic*, 16 (Summer 1996), 183–206; and Boydston, *Home and Work: Housework, Wages, and the Ideology of Labor in the Early Republic* (New York, 1990), ch. 2. Carole Shammas draws connections between household furnishings and women's domestic roles in "The Domestic Environment in Early Modern England and America," *Journal of Social History*, 14 (1980), 3–24. See also Shammas, "Early American Women and Control Over Capital," in Hoffman and Albert, eds., *Women in the Age of the American Revolution*, pp. 134–154, and *The Pre-Industrial Consumer in England and America* (Oxford, 1990).

   Marylynn Salmon assesses women's legal disabilities in *Women and the Law of Property in Early America* (Chapel Hill, N.C., 1986), and "Equality or Submersion? Feme Covert Status in Early Pennsylvania," in Berkin and Norton, eds., *Women of America*, pp. 92–111. Cornelia Hughes Dayton traces women's dwindling roles in courtroom proceedings in *Women Before the Bar: Gender, Law, and Society in Connecticut, 1639–1789* (Chapel Hill, N.C., 1995). Deborah A. Rosen discusses women's economic marginalization in *Courts and Commerce: Gender, Law, and the Market Economy in Colonial New York* (Columbus, Ohio, 1997), part 3. For inheritance law, see Toby L. Ditz, *Property and Kinship: Inheritance in Early Connecticut, 1750–1820* (Princeton, N.J., 1986), and Carole Shammas, Marylynn Salmon, and Michel Dahlin, *Inheritance in America: Colonial Times to the Present* (New Brunswick, N.J., 1977). Joan R. Gunderson and Gwen Victor Gampel stress practices benefiting women that differed from English practices in "Married Women's Legal Status in Eighteenth-Century New York and Virginia," *William and Mary Quarterly*, 3d series, 39 (January 1982), 114–134. Informative articles on inheritance law and women's legal rights appear in Hoffman and Albert, eds., *Women in the Age of the American Revolution*, cited previously, parts 1 and 4.

Aspects of female religious experience are examined in Mary Beth Norton, "'My Resting Reaping Times': Sarah Osborn's Defense of her Unfeminine Activities, 1767," *Signs 2* (Winter 1976), 515–529; Louis Billington, "Female Laborers in the Church: Women Preachers in the Northeastern United States, 1790–1840," *Journal of American Studies* 19 (1985), 369–394; Ann Taves, ed., *Religion and Domestic Violence in Early New England: The Memoir of Abigail Abbot Bailey* (Bloomington, Ind., 1989); and Catherine A. Brekus, *Strangers and Pilgrims: Female Preaching in America, 1740–1845* (Chapel Hill, N.C., 1998). For the link between religious experience and female friendship, see Carol F. Karlsen and Laurie Crumpackers, eds., *The Journal of Esther Edwards Burr: 1754–1757* (New Haven, Conn., 1984). For Ann Lee's followers, see Stephen J. Stein, *The Shaker Experience in America* (New Haven, Conn., 1992). For the Society of Friends, see Jean Soderlund, "Women's Authority in Pennsylvania and New Jersey Quaker Meetings, 1680–1760," *William and Mary Quarterly*, 3d series, 44 (October 1987), 722–749; Elaine Forman Crane et al., eds., *The Diary of Elizabeth Drinker*, 3 vols. (Boston, 1991), also available in an abridged version (Boston, 1994); Christine Levenduski, *Peculiar Power: A Quaker Woman Preacher in Eighteenth-Century America* (Washington, D.C., 1996); and Rebecca Larson, *Daughters of Light: Quaker Women Preaching and Prophesying in the Colonies and Abroad, 1700–1775* (New York, 2000). See also William L. Andrews, ed., *Journeys in New Worlds: Early American Women's Narratives* (Madison, Wisc., 1990), which includes the narrative of Quaker convert Elizabeth Ashbridge, ed. by Daniel B. Shea, pp. 117–180. For women and religion in the Revolutionary era, see Laurel Thatcher Ulrich, "Daughters of Liberty: Religious Women in Revolutionary New England," in Hoffman and Albert, eds., *Women in the Age of the American Revolution*, cited previously, pp. 211–243; Elaine Forman Crane, "Religion and Rebellion: Women of Faith in the American War for Independence," in Ronald Hoffman and Peter J. Albert, eds., *Religion in a Revolutionary Age* (Charlottesville, Va., 1994), pp. 52–86; and Susan Juster, *Disorderly Women: Sexual Politics in Revolutionary New England* (Ithaca, N.Y., 1995), which explores evangelical women's loss of power between the first and second Great Awakenings. See also Susan Juster and Lisa McFarland, eds., *A Mighty Baptism: Race, Gender, and the Creation of American Protestantism* (Ithaca, N.Y., 1996). Marilyn J. Westerkamp surveys women's religious history in *Women and Religion in Early America, 1600–1850: The Puritan and Evangelical Traditions* (New York, 1999).

For women's roles in Spanish settlements, see Ramon A. Gutierrez, "Honor Ideology, Marriage Negotiations, and Class-Gender Domination in New Mexico, 1690–1846," *Latin American Perspectives*, 12 (Winter 1985), 81–104; Gutierrez, *When Jesus Came, the Corn Mothers Went Away: Marriage, Sexuality, and Power in New Mexico, 1500–1846* (Stanford, 1992); David J. Weber, *The Spanish Frontier in North America* (New Haven, 1992), ch. 11, which discusses class systems and lifestyles in the eighteenth century; and Albert L. Hurtado, *Intimate Frontiers: Sex, Gender, and Culture in Old California* (Albuquerque, N.M., 1999), which covers the 1760s to the 1850s. Gary B. Nash, "The Hidden History of Mextizo America," *Journal of American History*, 82 (December 1995), 941–962, explores the theme of intermarriage among Native Americans, African Americans, and European Americans. The Nash essay is reprinted on pp. 10–32 of Martha Hodes, ed., *Sex, Love, Race: Crossing Boundaries in North American History* (New York, 1999), part 1 of which examines interracial sexual relations in colonial America.

Theda Perdue assesses the impact of white settlement on eighteenth-century Indian women in *Cherokee Women: Gender and Culture Change, 1700–1835* (Lincoln, Neb., 1998) and "Women, Men, and American Indian Policy: The Cherokee Response to 'Civilization,'" in

Nancy Shoemaker, ed., *Negotiators of Change: Historical Perspectives on Native American Women* (New York, 1995), pp. 90–114. See also Judith K. Brown, "Economic Organization and the Position of Women Among the Iroquois," *Ethnohistory*, 17 (Summer–Fall 1970), 151–167; Joan Jensen, "Native American Women and Agriculture: A Seneca Case Study," *Sex Roles*, 3 (1977), 432–441; Elisabeth Tooker, "Women in Iroquois Society," in Michael K. Foster, Jack Campisi, and Marianne Mithun, eds., *Extending the Rafters: Interdisciplinary Approaches to Iroquoian Studies* (Albany, N.Y., 1984), pp. 109–123; Nancy Shoemaker, "The Rise or Fall of Iroquois Women," *Journal of Women's History*, 2 (Winter 1991), 39–67; and Kathryn E. Holland Braund, "Guardians of Tradition and Handmaidens to Change: Women's Roles in Creek Economic and Social Life During the Eighteenth Century," *American Indian Quarterly*, 14 (1990), 239–258.

Aspects of Native American women's changing roles are discussed in J. Leitch Wright, Jr., *Creeks and Seminoles: The Destruction and Regeneration of the Muscogulge People* (Lincoln, Neb., 1986); James H. Merrell, *The Indians' New World: Catawbas and their Neighbors from European Contact Through the Era of Removal* (Chapel Hill, N.C., 1989); Richard White, *The Middle Ground: Indians, Empires, and Republicans in the Great Lakes Region, 1650–1815* (New York, 1991); Daniel K. Richter, *The Ordeal of the Longhouse: The Peoples of the Iroquois League in the Era of European Colonization* (Chapel Hill, N.C., 1992); James Axtell, *The Indians' New South: Cultural Change in the Colonial Southeast* (Baton Rouge, La., 1997); Colin G. Calloway, *New World for All: Indians, Europeans, and the Remaking of Colonial America* (Boston, 1997); and Jean M. O'Brien, *Dispossession By Degrees: Indian Land and Identity in Natick, Massachusetts, 1650–1790* (New York, 1997). For the impact of the Revolution, see also Colin G. Calloway, *The American Revolution in Indian Country: Crisis and Diversity in Native American Communities* (New York, 1995) and Paula Gunn Allen, *The Sacred Hoop: Recovering the Feminine in the American Indian Tradition* (Boston, 1986), pp. 32–41. For the experience of Native American women in North America beyond the English colonies, see Sylvia Van Kirk, *Many Tender Ties: Women in Fur Trade Society in Western Canada, 1670–1870* (Winnepeg, Man., 1980); Karen Anderson, *Chain Her By One Foot: The Subjugation of Women in Seventeenth Century New France* (London, 1991); and Carol Devens, *Countering Colonization: Native American Women and Great Lakes Missions, 1630–1900* (Berkeley, 1992).

African American women's experience in the eighteenth century is discussed in Carole Shammas, "Black Women's Work and the Evolution of Plantation Society in Virginia," *Labor History*, 26 (Winter 1985), 5–28; Mary Beth Norton, Herbert G. Gutman, and Ira Berlin, "The Afro-American Family in the Age of Revolution," in Ira Berlin and Ronald Hoffman, eds., *Slavery and Freedom in the Era of the American Revolution* (Evanston, Ill., 1983), pp. 175–191; Jacqueline Jones, "Race, Sex, and Self-Evident Truths: The Status of Slave Women During the Era of the American Revolution," in Hoffman and Albert, eds., *Women in the Era of the American Revolution*, cited previously pp. 293–337; Sylvia R. Frey, *Water From the Rock: Black Resistance in a Revolutionary Age* (Princeton, 1991); and David Barry Gaspar and Darlene Clark Hine, eds., *More Than Chattel: Black Women and Slavery in the Americas* (Bloomington, Ind., 1996), which covers the eighteenth century and after. For interracial sex, see Peter W. Bardaglio, "'Shameful Matches': The Regulation of Interracial Sex and Marriage in the South before 1900," in Martha Hodes, ed., *Sex, Love, Race*, cited previously, pp. 112–138. For the conflict among historians over one interracial relationship, see Annette Gordon Reid, *Thomas Jefferson and Sally Hemings: An American Controversy*, 2nd ed. (Charlottesville, Va., 1999), and Jan Lewis and Peter Onuf, eds., *Sally Hemings and Thomas Jefferson* (Charlottesville, Va., 1999). Much information on gender appears in Ira Berlin, *Many Thousands Gone: The First Two Centuries of Slavery in North America* (Cambridge, Mass., 1998) and Philip D. Morgan, *Slave Counterpoint: Black Culture in the Eighteenth-Century Chesapeake and Low Country* (Chapel Hill, N.C., 1998).

The Revolution's impact on Anglo-American women is a subject of debate. In *Liberty's Daughters*, Mary Beth Norton offers an account of women's everyday lives and stresses the positive impact of the Revolutionary era. Linda K. Kerber, in *Women of the Republic*, concentrates on women's legal status and presents a more muted view of the Revolution's impact, which she sees as uneven. For a negative view, see Joan Hoff Wilson's argument that the Revolution bypassed women in "The Illusion of Change: Women and the American Revolution," in Alfred E. Young, ed., *The American Revolution: Explorations in the History of American Radicalism* (DeKalb, Ill., 1976), pp. 385–415. Joan R. Gundersen examines women's place in revolutionary rhetoric in "Independence, Citizenship, and the American Revolution," *Signs* 13 (Autumn 1987), 59–77. For southern women, see Cynthia A. Kierner, ed., *Southern Women in Revolution, 1776–1800: Personal and Political Narratives* (Columbia, S.C., 1998). Barbara Clark Smith explores an activist facet of women's roles in "Food Rioters and the American Revolution," *William and Mary Quarterly*, 3d series, 51 (January 1994), 3–38. Norma Basch assesses the impact of the revolutionary era on divorce law in *Framing American Divorce: From the Revolutionary Generation to the Victorians* (Berkeley, Calif. 1999), ch. 1. The 1976 bicentennial spurred the publication of many books about women during the war, among them Linda Grant DePauw, *Founding Mothers: Women of the Revolutionary Era* (Chicago, 1975); Paul Engle, *Women in the American Revolution* (Chicago, 1976); and Elizabeth Evans, ed., *Weathering the Storm: Women of the American Revolution* (New York, 1975). For more recent interpretations, see the relevant essays in Hoffman and Albert, eds., *Women in the Era of the American Revolution*, cited previously, and Harriet B. Applewhite and Darline G. Levy, *Women and Politics in the Age of the Democratic Revolution* (Ann Arbor, Mich., 1990).

For Abigail Adams, see Lynne Withey, *Dearest Friend: A Life of Abigail Adams* (New York, 1981); Paul C. Nagle, *The Adams Women: Abigail and Louisa Adams, Their Sisters and Daughters* (New York, 1987); Edith B. Gelles, "The Abigail Industry," *William and Mary Quarterly*, 3d series, 45 (October 1988), 657–683; and Gelles, *Portia: The World of Abigail Adams* (Bloomington, Ind., 1992). Another biography of interest is Rosemary Zagarri, *A Woman's Dilemma: Mercy Otis Warren and the American Revolution* (Wheeling, Ill., 1995). For the wartime experience of a Connecticut woman, see Joy Day Buel and Richard Buel, Jr., *The Way of Duty: A Woman and Her Family in Revolutionary America* (New York, 1989) and the excellent film based on that book, *Mary Silliman's War* (1995).

For new attitudes toward women's education at the end of the eighteenth century, see Linda K. Kerber, "Daughters of Columbia: Educating Women for the Republic, 1787–1805," in Stanley Elkins and Eric McKitrick, eds., *The Hofstadter Aegis: A Memorial* (New York, 1974), and Ann D. Gordon, "The Young Ladies Academy of Philadelphia," in Berkin and Norton, eds., *Women of America*, pp. 68–91. Changes in women's status during the postrevolutionary decades are examined in Linda K Kerber, "The Republican Mother: Women and the Enlightenment, an American Perspective," *American Quarterly*, 28 (Summer 1976), 187–205; Kerber, "The Paradox of Women's Citizenship in the Early Republic: The Case of Martin *v.* Massachusetts, 1805," *American Historical Review*, 97 (April 1992), 349–378; Patricia M. Alexander, "The Creation of the American Eve: The Cultural Dialogue on the Nature and Role of Women in Late Eighteenth-Century America," *Early American Literature*, 9 (1975), 252–266; Ruth H. Bloch, "American Feminine Ideals in Transition: The Rise of the Moral

Mother, 1785–1815," *Feminist Studies*, 4 (June 1978), 101–126; Bloch, "The Gendered Meanings of Virtue in Revolutionary America," *Signs* 13 (Autumn 1987), 37–58; Jan Lewis, "The Republican Wife: Virtue and Seduction in the Early Republic," *William and Mary Quarterly*, 3d series, 44 (October 1987), 689–721; Linda Kerber et al., "Beyond Roles, Beyond Spheres: Thinking About Gender in the Early Republic," *William and Mary Quarterly*, 3d series, 46 (July 1989), 565–585; and, for recent commentary on the concept of republican motherhood, Margaret A. Nash, "Rethinking Republican Motherhood: Benjamin Rush and the Young Ladies' Academy of Philadelphia," *Journal of the Early Republic*, 17 (Summer 1997), 171–191. Linda K. Kerber's essays on women in the revolutionary and post-revolutionary eras are available in Kerber, *Toward an Intellectual History of Women* (Chapel Hill, N.C., 1997). For Mary Wollstonecraft and the language of "rights," see Rosemarie Zagarri, "The Rights of Men and Women in Post-Revolutionary America," *William and Mary Quarterly*, 3rd series (April 1998), 203–230. Chandos Michael Brown examines the decline in Wollstonecraft's reputation after 1800 in "Mary Wollstonecraft, or the Female Illuminati: The Campaign Against Women and 'Modern Philosophy' in the Early Republic," *Journal of the Early Republic* 15 (Fall 1995), 395–424. For new ideals of women's roles, see also Sharon Harris, ed., *Selected Writings of Judith Sargent Murray* (New York, 1995) and Sheila L. Skemp, *Judith Sargent Murray: A Brief Biography with Documents* (Boston, 1998). For changes in childbirth rates, see Susan E. Klepp, "Revolutionary Bodies: Women and the Fertility Transition in the Mid-Atlantic Region, 1760–1820," *Journal of American History*, 85 (December 1998), 910–945. For changing trends in marriage and in its dissolution, see Merril D. Smith, *Breaking the Bonds: Marital Discord in Pennsylvania, 1730–1830* (New York, 1991).

Jane Rendall provides a comparative perspective in *The Origins of Modern Feminism: Women in Britain, France, and the United States, 1780–1860* (Chicago, 1985). For links between material culture and social mobility, see Richard L. Bushman, *The Refinement of America: Persons, Houses, Cities* (New York, 1992), chs. 1–6, and Cary Carson, Ronald Hoffman, and Peter J. Albert, eds., *Of Consuming Interests: The Style of Life in the Eighteenth Century* (Charlottesville, Va., 1994). Richard D. Brown provides an overview of changes in eighteenth-century society and attitudes in *Modernization: The Transformation of American Life, 1600–1865* (New York, 1976), chs. 3–5. Lawrence Stone describes the rise of "companionate marriage" in eighteenth-century England in *The Family, Sex, and Marriage in England 1500–1800* (New York, 1979), ch. 8. For the emergence of the modern American family, see Carl Degler, *At Odds: Women and the Family in America from the Revolution to the Present* (New York, 1980), ch. 1.

🌐 For quizzes and additional resources related to American women's history, visit the book's Website at *www.mhhe.com/americanwomen*.

CHAPTER THREE

Promoting Woman's Sphere, 1800–1860

I N THE FIRST half of the nineteenth century, economic growth transformed the nation. As America started to industrialize, home production shifted to workshop and then to factory. Productivity, trade, and commerce increased. Transportation improved, markets grew, income rose, and the urban population tripled. By midcentury, almost a fifth of Americans lived in towns and cities, many of them recent migrants. The nation's inhabitants seemed to be in constant motion. While more and more joined the swirl of population around urban areas, others filled up vacant land, east and west, transforming wilderness into territories, territories into states, and by the 1840s, crossing the continent to settle the Pacific coast.

The great mobility of early-nineteenth-century Americans was social as well as geographic. Economic expansion opened new avenues of advancement. Income beckoned in land speculation, business investment, and the professions. Opportunity to rise in the world was accompanied by the extension of suffrage to virtually all free white men, by the development of common schools, and by outbursts of evangelism that democratized even prospects for salvation. New attitudes arose to suit these expanding options. Americans now lived by an ethos in which ambition, initiative, and achievement counted for more than social origin. The new egalitarian order, observers agreed, was one in which wealth and status were always in flux, where change and risk were the only constants.

Under such shifting, precarious circumstances, a new middle class began to emerge, first in the urban and industrializing Northeast. Always expanding, the new middle class had no fixed boundaries or stable membership. Americans could fall out of it as rapidly as they rose into it. But it did have some recognizable characteristics. Middle-class Americans had rising incomes, expectations, and living standards. They provided a market for consumer goods—for clothing, furniture, books, and magazines. They supported churches, schools, and voluntary associations. Most of all, the middle class had a new type of family life. The doctrine of "woman's sphere," as promoted by author and editor Sarah Josepha Hale in the *Ladies Magazine* and *Godey's Lady's Book*, reflected changes in the middle-class home.

THE HOME AND THE WORLD

When the first issue of the *Ladies Magazine* appeared in 1828 in Boston, a change in domestic life was well underway, at least in the commercial, urbanizing Northeast. In colonial days, when most families lived on farms, the household was a productive unit. All family members engaged in work to sustain it, work that was done in or near the home. As part of the family labor force, women and children were subordinate to paternal authority. But in the early nineteenth century, as a market economy developed, old patterns of life waned. Some men who once would have been farmers or craftsmen now worked outside the home to earn the income that supported it. Their homes were no longer centers of production, nor did family members work together for family sustenance. Within the emerging middle class, "home" became a private enclave, a retreat from the "world" and a refuge from commercial life; within the home, women assumed a distinctive role.

The middle-class wife, like the *Ladies Magazine* reader of 1828, remained at home while her income-earning husband went to work outside it, in office or store, business or profession. While the man ventured forth into the world, the woman at home gained an independent realm of her own, one no longer under constant male domination. Domestic life now fell under female control. Nor was the wife tied down to wheel and loom, hearth and dairy. Once home manufacture shifted to workplace, the woman at home took responsibility for housekeeping, child rearing, and moral and religious life. In her own domestic space, she gained both a new degree of autonomy and a new degree of authority over others.

The doctrine of sphere, as expounded in the *Ladies Magazine* and other publications, celebrated the new status of the middle-class woman, along with her distinctive vocation, values, and character. It also described an unspoken bargain between middle-class women and men. While men remained heads of families, their real domain was now in the world—a world of business, professions, politics, and money-making. Family status depended on their earned income and public roles. Women were expected to devote themselves entirely to private life, to the "chaste circle of the fireside," and to maintain an alternate world with separate values. But their domestic roles also helped to define family status. Moreover, at home, they had gained new clout and respect. The unspoken bargain was based on mutual gain. If men had the opportunity to rise in the world, women had the opportunity to rise in the home.

The middle-class woman's role was a dependent one. Her authority expanded only as the family's productive functions contracted, and those functions contracted only when family income went up. Rising income was at the center of woman's sphere. Only with substantial support could a married woman adopt the nonproductive role once reserved for the wealthy; few women could completely escape either home production or physical work. Middle-class women and those who aspired to that status remained active albeit unpaid contributors to the family economy through household labor. Indeed, unpaid labor, historian Jeanne Boydston points out, was now largely, though not exclusively, "the province of women." Most women, moreover, were only remote beneficiaries of or untouched by the middle-class bargain. In rural areas, on farms North and South, and on the frontier, traditional ways of life persisted. Household production continued, women and children remained part of the family labor force, and paternal authority as head of that labor force remained in effect. A woman's influence did not increase if a family was poor or if she was not attached to a dependable, income-producing man. In many cases, the perquisites of woman's sphere—influence, autonomy, and authority—were little more than shared aspirations.

Nor were women of any class able to ignore worldly concerns: woman's sphere was as precarious an ideal as its counterpart for men—the opportunity to rise in the world. The early-nineteenth-century family was likely to be in financial and geographical motion. Income rose or fell according to personal fate and twists and turns of the economy such as the depression that diminished *Ladies Magazine* subscriptions in 1834. Buffeted by panics or elevated by good fortune, Americans faced the possibility of downward mobility at every turn. The "vicissitudes" were precarious for women, who lacked control over family finances. When a husband died or a father failed in business, consequences could be dire. Shifts in family fortune were usually linked to shifts in locale, to constant waves of internal migration—from rural areas to towns and cities, or from crowded areas to vacant land. Hardly insulated by sphere, early-nineteenth-century women continually adapted to new homes, communities, associations, and economic situations. The very concept of "woman's sphere," many historians contend, is misleading and must be modified or qualified, if not discarded. The shared experience of men and women, some argue, invalidates the stress on gender distinctions.

But in important ways, many antebellum women could identify with woman's sphere because their everyday patterns of life and work differed from those of men. Even on the family farm, men were now attuned to the market economy while women's responsibilities remained tied to the household economy. In towns and cities, differences between male and female work patterns were more marked. In colonial times, historian Nancy Cott points out, the work of both men and women was closely tied to the land. It was seasonal, discontinuous, and task-oriented. But in the early nineteenth century, as wage labor replaced family labor, male work patterns became oriented to time, not task. Whatever a man did for a living—laborer, businessman, tradesman, or clerk—he now had a clearly defined working day. His work became separated from the rest of life. Household work, however, remained in a time warp of task orientation. Women's workday expanded and contracted to fit the jobs at hand, whether the washing of clothes, baking of bread, or care of children—activities that merged into life. In short, women's work and homebound world remained premodern, whereas men's was changing. A distinctive rhythm of labor and lifestyle also defined woman's sphere.

Finally, a broad spectrum of women could hope to benefit from the new importance now attributed to their shared vocation. In traditional society, household work and child care had never drawn much acclaim. In the early nineteenth century, however, they gained social significance. Woman's sphere was a new social space, one that had not been recognized before. On the one hand, it was an enclosed, limited, private space. On the other, it was an improvement over having no space at all. Woman's sphere, according to popular literature, encompassed a now important social institution, the home. It linked all women together in a valuable vocation—domesticity and child rearing. It fostered a positive consciousness of gender, one that had not existed in the colonial era. Finally, it impelled a redefinition of female character, one appropriate to the middle-class woman's elevated domestic status.

In the early nineteenth century, the home took on new significance, material and emotional. By midcentury, the middle-class home had become a substantial place, with pantries and drawing rooms, mirrors and pianos, and at least some of the items featured in *Godey's Lady's Book*—upholstered sofas, elaborate furniture, carpets, and draperies. The center of the home was no longer the hearth, where colonial women did much of their work, but the parlor, where the family assembled. Middle-class Americans had not only far more possessions but rising standards of neatness and cleanliness, so "housework" quickly replaced "housewifery." Even with hired help, the middle-class woman remained industrious; home maintenance was now a more elaborate procedure.

The middle-class home was also viewed as an emotional space, a refuge from the competitive world, and a source of stability and order in a society that seemed to be losing both. It was now under feminine sway. The home was idealized as a bastion of feminine values, of piety, morality, affection, and self-sacrifice—commodities in short supply outside it. Literature directed at women, especially, defined the home as a feminine fief. "The family state . . . is the aptest earthly illustration of the heavenly kingdom and woman is its chief minister," educator Catharine Beecher declared in her *Treatise on Domestic Economy* in the 1840s. "Our homes—what is their corner-stone but the virtue of a woman, and on what does social well-being rest but in our homes?" asked *Godey's Lady's Book* in 1856. "Must we not trace all other blessings of civilized life to the doors of our private dwellings? Are not our hearthstones . . . the corner-stone of church and state, more sacred than either, more necessary than both? . . . Oh! spare our homes."

While the middle-class home expanded in size and significance, the family grew smaller. Americans were having fewer children. In 1800, the national birthrate had been the highest in the world; but in the next few decades it rapidly fell, a process that would continue for the rest of the century. The mother of 7.04 in 1800 became the mother of 5.92 in 1850 and 3.56 by 1900. The decline was national, but uneven. In the early nineteenth century, large families were still the rule in most agricultural regions, along the newly settled frontier, and among immigrants and blacks. Rural fertility also fell, but urban fertility was consistently lower. The most precipitous drop was among the new middle class in towns and cities.

As the family began to shrink, the value attached to motherhood rose. Though post-Revolutionary rhetoric had suggested such mounting significance, it increased dramatically. Once household production waned, child raising became the family's central focus and purpose. In the middle-class home, children were no longer family workers but rather *what* the family produced. More time was devoted to their upbringing, more resources to their education, more effort to instilling the values and traits that would keep them in the middle class. The increased importance of child rearing contributed to an authority shift in the family. Paternal power dropped a notch as maternal affection became the main psychological force at home. The mother was now the primary child rearer, the crucial dispenser of values and former of character. She could "generate those moral tendencies which cover the whole of existence," as a minister wrote in the *Ladies Magazine*. "Her character is felt throughout

A metaphor for the privacy of family life, "woman's sphere"
was depicted in popular literature as a calm and isolated
retreat. Here, the middle-class homemaker devoted herself to
an endless circle of domestic tasks and cultural pursuits,
centering around child care. The floral motif was ubiquitous.
Frontispiece from Caroline Howard Gilman, *The Housekeeper's
Annual and Lady's Register (1844)*. *(Library of Congress)*

the intricate workings of society." In the 1830s, when the publishing industry began
an era of rapid expansion, the mother's significance received extensive publicity.

Innumerable tracts and stories paid tribute to the mother of Washington. In
prints and etchings, a new iconography of motherhood emerged. Magazines featured
scenes of mothers at home, surrounded by children, in affectionate poses. Literature
directed at women celebrated motherhood as the ultimate opportunity for self-
sacrifice and, simultaneously, the epitome of female power. "How entire and perfect
is this dominion over the unformed character of your infant," *Ladies Magazine* author

Lydia Sigourney exuded in her *Letters to Mothers* (1838). It was mothers, as Lydia Maria Child declared in her popular *Mother's Book* (1831), "on whose intelligence and discretion the safety and prosperity of our nation so much depend." Nor was the expansion of maternal influence just rhetorical. By midcentury, it was recognized even in law. Northern states started to alter the tradition of paternal custody in cases of separation and divorce. Courts began to consider the "good of the child" and "parental fitness." "The father's custodial right is not an absolute one," stated an 1852 treatise on marriage law, "and is usually made to yield when the good of the child . . . is the chief matter to be regarded." Southern courts, too, began to award custody to mothers of young children. Women did not gain equal custody rights, to say nothing of preference, until the end of the century. But adulation of motherhood still had some legal ramifications.

While celebrations of woman's sphere stressed the significance of domestic roles and maternal influence, they also suggested a new and positive consciousness of gender. The polarity of spheres that segregated middle-class men and women offered an emotional bonus. As women shared a common vocation and values, they had more in common with one another than with men, Sarah Hale contended in the *Ladies Magazine*. They profited from long-term, intense relationships with other women—relationships that continued for decades, despite marriage and geographical separation, often in the form of lengthy visits and correspondence. Such correspondence, historian Carroll Smith Rosenberg contends, reveals that "Women's sphere had an essential dignity and integrity that grew out of women's shared experiences and mutual affection." Within their self-contained female world—noncompetitive, empathetic, and supportive—women valued one another and thereby gained a sense of security and self-esteem. "Women, who had little status and power in the larger world of male concerns, possessed status and power in the lives of other women."

Historians disagree as to whether an intimate mother–daughter relationship lay at the heart of this female world, or whether the peer relationship was more important. In either case, early-nineteenth-century middle-class women assumed centrality in one another's lives, depended emotionally on one another, and appreciated their same-sex connections and friendships. The role of friendship as an outlet for shared "sentiments" emerges in the New England letters and diaries analyzed by historian Nancy Cott. Men, in these documents, were usually remote, distant figures, often nameless. Or they might be referred to, with muted sarcasm, as "the Lords of Creation," an expression favored by Sarah Hale in the *Ladies Magazine*. But affection among women was explicit. Friendship provided an opportunity to exchange "reciprocal views and feelings," wrote Eliza Chaplin to Laura Lovell in 1820. "To you I unfold my whole heart without apology." "I do not believe that men can ever feel so pure an enthusiasm for women as we can feel for one another," *Ladies Magazine* author Catharine Sedgwick revealed to her diary in 1834. "Ours is nearest to the love of angels."

The positive consciousness of gender suggested by personal documents reflected a new assessment of female character. Men were expected to be competitive, assertive, individualistic, and materialistic; the woman at home needed a compensatory set of character traits. Dependent and affectionate, she was pious, pure, gentle, nurturant, benevolent, and sacrificing. Such "softer" virtues had been filtering in throughout the eighteenth century, especially in advice tracts aimed at the upwardly mobile, but now became accepted as innate. Compared to men, women were believed to have a firmer grip on religion and morals, a stronger claim to piety and purity, and, overall, a sense of moral superiority. In traditional society, women were not viewed as superior to men in any way. Now, piety and purity provided some leverage. They also led to a new set of bargains between women and men.

PIETY AND PURITY

Early-nineteenth-century ministers bolstered the doctrine of woman's sphere. They opposed those forces antithetical to women's interests—materialism, immorality, intemperance, and licentiousness—and helped to formulate a new definition of female character. Christian virtues—such as humility, submission, piety, and charity—were now primarily female virtues. Most important, ministers confirmed female moral superiority. Women might be the weaker members of society, but, said clerics, they exceeded men in spiritual fervor and moral strength.

Religion was also one of the few activities beyond the home in which women might indulge without abdicating their sphere. Their participation in the churches was in fact vital. Women formed the majority of congregants. Accordingly, female piety, and even activism, won ministerial applause. "We look to you, ladies, to raise the standard of character in our own sex," announced New England clergyman Joseph Buckminster in an 1810 sermon. "We look to you for the continuance of domestick purity, for the revival of domestick religion, for the increase of our charities, and the support of what remains of religion in our private habits and publick institutions." Under such circumstances, a mutually dependent relationship developed between Protestant clerics and their middle-class female parishioners. Both saw themselves as outsiders in a society devoted to the pursuit of wealth, as allies who strove for morality in a competitive world. It was no accident that women's publications counted on ministers for articles exalting female character. Ministers in turn depended on women for their loyal support.

Despite clergymen's fears of dwindling authority, Protestantism flourished. The Second Great Awakening of the first quarter of the nineteenth century led to the great evangelical crusades of the second. Presbyterians and Congregationalists attracted members in New England, fiery waves of revivals swept over New York State, westerners flocked to camp meetings on the frontier, and Baptists and Methodists made gains nationwide. According to some estimates, church membership tripled. Throughout this fervor, women remained prominent. Their affinity for piety emerged at the start of the century. The Second Great Awakening marked the beginning of the new alliance between women and ministers as well as of their unstated bargain: clerical endorsement of female moral superiority in exchange for women's support and activism.

Female converts outnumbered male converts three to two in the Second Great Awakening in New England, and women formed the bulk of congregations thereafter. They played an equally active role in revival-swept western New York. By 1814, for instance, women outnumbered men in the churches and religious societies of bustling Utica, and they could be relied on to urge the conversion of family members. A mother's conversion, ministers learned, could lead to those of her children and husband; a daughter's conversion might soon create a pious family. The most zealous activists of these early revivals, significantly, were women of the new middle class—the wives and daughters of men who worked outside the home. Church membership boosted upward mobility. But female religiosity also moved down the social scale, to wives of artisans and farmers, just as it spread to other regions. On the midwestern frontier, women formed congregations, joined religious societies, and demanded Sabbath observance. Piety had become female property. When Englishwoman Frances Trollope investigated American society in the 1830s, she claimed that she had never seen a country "where religion had so strong a hold upon the women, or a slighter hold upon the men."

If religion had a hold on women, however, they in turn had a hold on the clergy. Through weight of numbers, women gained influence in Protestant churches that they lacked elsewhere. They contributed, for instance, to a softening of doctrine: the old idea of infant damnation had little appeal to American mothers. Ministers, accordingly, granted that Christian nurture could outweigh original sin. Discarding predestination as an axiom, clergymen now suggested that mothers, not God, were responsible for their children's souls. "Feminization" of religion and of child rearing went hand in hand. Ministers bolstered the authority not only of the pious mother but of any pious woman, even the once insignificant daughter. Evangelical magazines, for instance, celebrated female influence in tales of dying daughters who, to the end, sought the conversion of relatives and friends. Fatal illness was no obstacle to spiritual strength.

Religious commitment offered other advantages: it provided a community of peers outside the home, among like-minded women in church-related associations. The passivity of the convert, once united with her sisters, could become activist zeal. Early-nineteenth-century women provided the constituency for a multitude of societies formed under clerical auspices. They joined Bible and tract societies, which distributed pious literature, Sabbath school unions, and missionary societies, which raised funds for pious endeavors. They formed charitable associations to aid the indigent and maternal associations to foster Christian motherhood. Through voluntary religious groups, women gained one another's company, new routes to collective ventures, and clerical approval. "While the pious female . . . does not aspire after things too great for her," a minister told a women's charitable society in 1815, "she discovers that there is wide field opened for the exercise of all her active powers."

In many ways, the evangelical Protestant experience held potential for women. Conversion encouraged introspection and self-attention. Cooperative efforts in church groups inspired a sense of sisterhood and mutual interest. Clerical assurance of moral superiority supported a new degree of authority over others. But religious activism also had built-in boundaries; clerical support meant clerical control. In the heat of revivals, as female piety assumed new import, ministers warned women to avoid leadership roles as, for example, revivalists. Their piety was to be confined to the private role of personal persuasion; "influence" was contingent on acceptance of limits. As long as a woman kept to her "proper place," a tract society pamphlet explained in 1823, she might exert "almost any degree of influence she pleases." This was part of the implicit bargain between clergymen and women parishioners.

If piety became a vital component of female character, so did purity, a word with several meanings. One was passionlessness, or lack of sexual feeling. According to the doctrine of sphere, lust and carnality were male characteristics, or liabilities. Women, less physical, more spiritual, and morally superior, were indeed closer to "angels." This was a new development. In traditional society, women, like men, were assumed to be sexual beings. Weaker of will, they were seen as more lustful, licentious, and insatiable than men. But around the time of the Second Great Awakening, purity became a female bargaining point and a prerequisite for influence. "Let her lay aside delicacy," a minister held in 1837, "and her influence over our sex is gone."

By midcentury, the medical profession confirmed that passionlessness was an innate and commendable female characteristic. "The majority of women (happily for them)," physician William Acton stated in a much-quoted medical treatise, "are not much troubled with sexual feeling of any kind." Some doctors dissented. But in medical manuals aimed at the middle class, midcentury physicians usually emphasized the debilitating effects of sexual indulgence, recommended infrequent intercourse, opposed contraception, and confirmed female asexuality. They also assured women that their physical health, and social roles, were determined by their reproductive organs. Doctors explained that the uterus was linked to the female nervous system, and that any malfunction affected the entire body, causing a gamut of ailments—headaches, backaches, indigestion, insomnia, and nervous disorders. Woman's unusual physiology, indeed, determined her emotions, character, and vocation. "Mentally, socially, spiritually, [woman] is more interior than a man," a Philadelphia physician concluded in the 1860s. "The house, the chamber, the closet, are the centers of her social life and power."

Like other components of woman's sphere, purity encompassed sanctions and benefits. Advice literature, aimed at middle-class women, stressed sanctions; etiquette manuals counseled prudent behavior that would deter male advances. Magazine fiction offered tales about girls who lacked discretion, became victims of male predators, and ended up ruined, impoverished, ostracized, or dead. Such proscriptions reflected changes in courtship customs: the incidence of premarital pregnancy sharply declined, from a high of almost 30 percent of first births in the late eighteenth century to a new low of under 10 percent in the mid-nineteenth century. This precipitous drop, historians contend, suggests the acceptance by both young men and women of a new ideology of sexual restraint. Convictions about female purity imposed limitations not only on women but on men as well.

Purity was also a code word for a new degree of female sexual control within marriage. As the fertility of white women began to decline, the shrinking family became a hallmark of the new middle class. It may also have represented the new clout of wives within middle-class homes. Now imbued with moral superiority, wives gained a right of refusal, an escape from "submission," and power to limit the frequency of sexual relations. They also gained more control over the number of children they had. Methods of family limitation (beyond folk remedies and patent medicines) included abstinence, as recommended in medical literature, and withdrawal, which was condemned; abortion was also a possible last resort, at least until later in the century when it was outlawed. Although abstinence was not the sole effective means of curbing births, it probably was in widespread use. Female purity was probably an ideal on which middle-class men and women agreed, an asset for the family that wanted to rise in the world—a family in which children were no longer economic assets but, rather, liabilities. Sexual restraint thus seemed to serve family goals and to enhance women's autonomy within the home.

Convictions about female purity affected women's relation to the medical profession, which took shape only after the turn of the century. By the 1820s, all states except three had laws requiring medical practitioners to be licensed, and most licensing laws required graduation from medical college. As a result, medical practice excluded women, and midwifery, once a female monopoly, began a slow decline. In rural areas and on the frontier, and also among the urban poor, midwives continued to deliver babies. The rural midwife remained in business into the twentieth century. But the urbanizing East set the trend for the future. In the early nineteenth century, middle-class mothers in towns and cities turned to physicians. No longer a public female ritual, childbirth became a private event with two main participants, a woman and a male professional. The physician's new role in childbirth brought both loss and gain. The entourage of women relatives and friends who had once played a supportive part gradually vanished. But middle-class women seemed to appreciate the use of the forceps (the physician's prerogative) as the means of a faster delivery with less pain. Mothers became the doctor's prime constituency; a successful obstetric practice paved the way for a profitable family practice.

With the rise of the medical profession, female ill health assumed new visibility. Middle-class women of the early nineteenth century endured debilitating illnesses—nervousness, anemia, hysteria, headaches, backaches. The marked rise in female illness may have been connected to physical causes—such as the spread of venereal disease—or psychological ones. Women's dependent status could have had ill effects on their health. Sickness might also have had a positive function, providing reprieve from domestic work. In any case, physical fragility became a female liability. When Catharine Beecher surveyed women's health across the nation in the 1850s, she concluded that sick women outnumbered the healthy three to one. If all the facts and details of women's diseases were known, Beecher claimed, "It would send a groan of terror and horror over the land."

Even when chronically ill, women did not completely trust their doctors. The professionalization of medicine did not ensure its competence. At midcentury, as historian Regina Morantz explains, medicine was in a state of crisis. "Heroic" medicine—bleeding and enormous doses of dangerous substances—was on the wane, but it had not yet been replaced by anything better. Well-trained doctors were unlikely to be very effective, and few were well trained. In the 1830s, any profit-minded doctor could open a medical college and, however lax its standards, produce hundreds of graduates to be licensed. Not surprisingly, middle-class women sought alternatives. One set of alternatives were nonmedical remedies or fads—Grahamism (diet reform), water cures, animal magnetism, or phrenology. Middle-class women also took refuge at spas and joined ladies' physiological societies, where health and medicine were discussed. Health reformers promoted preventive measures that would preclude the need to resort to physicians—such as exercise, fresh air, baths, and cereals. Women also turned to irregular practitioners—unlicensed dispensers of remedies and advice, who might well be women. Dr. Harriot Hunt, for instance, went into practice in Boston with her sister in the 1830s, after an apprenticeship with other irregulars. Opposed to the "heroic" methods of the licensed profession, which rejected her, she prescribed homeopathic, preventive measures and became interested in the psychological causes of women's ailments. An even less regular practitioner, Mary Gove Nichols, became a water cure therapist and health reformer, catering, like Hunt, to a female clientele. Although not committed to the idea of female passionlessness, these leading irregulars urged the protection of women from male depravity.

Another response to the professionalization of medicine appeared in *Godey's Lady's Book*. Women, wrote Sarah Hale, should enter the medical profession to minister to women and children. Hale's argument rested on the sanctity of sphere: propriety and morality dictated that women should be examined by women. The woman physician, moreover, would raise the moral tone of the profession and open to women new avenues for practicing their altruism, benevolence, and sympathy. The entry of women into medicine would preserve, not destroy woman's sphere. Hale lent support to Elizabeth Blackwell, the first woman medical college graduate and licensed woman physician. Blackwell did not subscribe to the doctrine of female asexuality, but did crusade against prostitution and obscenity and supported the moral purity movement.

The doctrine of woman's sphere, and its redefinition of female character, could therefore be used as a bargaining tool. Piety, purity, and moral superiority could be mobilized to increase women's authority at home and seek influence outside it. The doctrine of sphere could also bolster other demands, such as that for "advanced" education. Although only a small proportion of Americans had any education beyond the primary level, a growing number of them were women.

ACADEMY AND COMMON SCHOOL

By 1828, when the *Ladies Magazine* first appeared, rapid development of female literacy was closing a great divide between the sexes. The movement for common schools, starting in the 1820s, accelerated this process. By midcentury, more than half the nation's school-age white youth were enrolled in schools, 90 percent of them in primary school. Even where common schools existed, education was often sporadic, with short terms and irregular attendance. Regional variations were profound. In New England, more than 75 percent of school-age boys and girls attended school, and in the South, less than half of this percentage. In all regions, girls were slightly less likely than boys to be enrolled in school at all. But by 1850, at least half the nation's women could read and write—a great advance over the eighteenth century. In New England, always ahead of the rest of the nation economically and culturally, literacy was almost universal. In the early decades of the century, New England women took the lead in expanding opportunities for women's education.

Since the late eighteenth century, daughters of well-off families might be sent to female academies, although such schools did not always fulfill academic criteria. Their offerings often stressed those "ornamentals" that were supposed to enhance girls' chances for matrimony. Benjamin Rush's vision of a "peculiar and suitable education" remained elusive. By 1820, however, an outgrowth of female academies or "seminaries" appeared in New England, and between 1830 and 1860 such schools spread to other regions. Clearly connected to the rising income and ambitions of middle-class families, academies and seminaries also signified a rise in women's status, especially to advocates of "female improvement."

Some early New England schools had been founded in the late eighteenth century—such as Sarah Pierce's Litchfield Academy, begun in her home in 1792 and incorporated in 1827. Most were new ventures. Often ministers ran schools for young women. Other schools were administered by women, such as Emma Willard, whose Middlebury Female Seminary opened in 1814; Catharine Beecher, who started a female seminary at Hartford in the 1820s; or Zilpah Grant, invited to run a female academy at Ipswich in 1828. These pioneer educators wanted to establish and endow academic institutions that went beyond the ornamentals but, at the same time, provided a type of secondary education appropriate to woman's separate sphere and special destiny. Advanced education, they contended, would improve women's performance as housekeepers and mothers, enlarge their moral influence in society, and increase their social utility by preparing them to teach.

When Emma Willard appealed to the New York legislature in 1819 for the endowment of a female institution of advanced study, she summarized this pragmatic rationale. The classes offered at a female academy, Willard assured the legislators, would be "as different from those appropriated to the other sex, as the female character and duties are from the male." Suitable instruction for young women, she contended, would be "First, moral and religious; second, literary; third, domestic; and fourth, ornamental." Such a curriculum, Willard explained, would make graduates better homemakers. It would equip future mothers for the upbringing of sons who would later govern. Finally, if "women were properly fitted by instruction, they would be likely to teach children better than the other sex." Unlike "Constantia" (Judith Sargent Murray) in the 1780s and 1790s, Willard did not promote education as a remedy for inequality or a route toward "reverence of self." Instead, she posed a utilitarian argument. Advanced education, crafted to women's needs, would enable them to be "the greatest possible use to themselves and to others."

Although Willard failed to win funds from the New York legislature, she fared better with the citizens of Troy, New York, who contributed enough to open a female seminary in 1821. The first endowed institution for women, the Troy seminary became a model of the new type of women's school. Within a decade, it had 300 students and provided an enormous range of instruction. Besides the required female courses—moral philosophy and domestic science—and the ornamentals, which were optional, the school taught science, mathematics, history, and languages. Like similar institutions that followed, the Troy seminary catered to a special clientele—the daughters of the ambitious middle class. It also became a model teacher training institute, whose graduates fanned out to staff other schools.

Like Emma Willard, Mary Lyon capitalized on the new regard for women's sphere. A teacher at the Ipswich Academy, Lyon began a campaign in 1833 to found an endowed institution of higher learning for women, one that would rescue young women from "empty gentility" and prepare them for enlarged social roles. "Our future statesmen and rulers, ministers and missionaries must come inevitably under the moulding hand of the female," Lyon declared. When Mount Holyoke Seminary opened in 1837, Lyon introduced high academic standards, a selective admissions policy, and curricular offerings similar to those at men's colleges. But the seminary also promoted specifically feminine roles. Students performed domestic chores, contributing at once to the school's support and to their own preparation for domesticity. Most important, Mount Holyoke fostered an emphasis on piety; Mary Lyon conducted regular revivals among her students. A graduate, according to the 1839 catalogue, was expected to be "a handmaid to the Gospel and an efficient auxiliary in the great task of renovating the world." Not only did the school train hundreds of missionaries, but it also produced a corps of what Mary Lyon called "self-denying female teachers," who staffed other seminaries and common schools.

Many of the ambitious schools established in the 1820s and 1830s, unlike the Troy seminary and Mount Holyoke, failed to secure permanent endowments. Catharine Beecher's Hartford Female Seminary, where domestic economy replaced the ornamentals, failed for lack of funds within a decade. The respected Ipswich Academy, known for its religious piety and teacher training, capsized. Nor did most

Envisioned by Mary Lyon as a "residential seminary to be founded and sustained by the Christian public," Mount Holyoke Female Seminary was chartered in 1836 and opened its doors to 80 students the following year. Funds to erect the red brick Georgian building were raised by Lyon, who solicited her first donations from Massachusetts housewives. N. Currier lithograph, 1836. *(Culver Pictures)*

institutions meet Willard's and Lyon's high academic standards. Nearly any type of school for girls could proclaim itself an "academy" or "seminary" and bid for paying clientele. Critics assailed female academies for their superficial curricula. Still, by midcentury, no state lacked at least a small cluster of women's institutions for "advanced" study. The female academy provided a crucial experience in the lives of its middle-class students, an interlude in which they spent a few years in the company of peers. "The union which subsisted among us bound our hearts with no feeble ties," a New England alumna wrote to a classmate in 1822. It also became a spawning ground for women teachers.

The seminary's goal of teacher preparation was timely. Expansion of common schooling created a national teacher shortage. Few men wanted low-paid, low-status teaching posts in common schools but, as school boards discovered, young women were anxious to teach and would do the same work for half of men's salaries or less. After 1830, the young woman teacher made inroads into primary education. In New England, women began to teach common school summer sessions, attended only by girls, in the 1820s. By the 1830s, they had begun to replace men in winter sessions at the common schools, teaching both boys and girls. In the next two decades, women teachers extended their domain through the East and Midwest. "As the business of teaching is made more respectable," an Ohio school superintendent observed, "more females engage in it and wages are reduced."

Advocates of women's education always cited low cost when explaining the virtues of the female teacher. Emma Willard had stressed this point when she appealed to the New York legislature in 1819, and Sarah Hale reiterated it in the *Ladies Magazine*. When Catharine Beecher appealed to Congress in the 1850s for appropriations for women's teacher training, she put the case concisely: "To make education universal, it must be at moderate expense, and women can afford to teach for one-half, or even less, the salary which men would ask," Beecher declared. "The female teacher has only to sustain herself; she does not look forward to the duty of supporting a family, should she marry, nor has she the ambition to amass a fortune." According to women educators, women would make superior teachers. "Nature designated our sex for the care of children," Emma Willard claimed. "If men have more knowledge, they have less talent at communicating it," argued Harriet Beecher Stowe, once a teacher at her sister's Hartford Seminary. "Nor have they the patience, the long-suffering, and gentleness necessary to superintend the formation of character." By midcentury, such arguments, plus the powerful factor of low cost, had made an impact. "It is the *manner* and the very weakness of the teacher that constitutes her strength," a New York State committee of educators concluded. Also, unlike men, women teachers were "much more apt to be content with, and continue in, the occupation of teaching."

The woman teacher faced many hurdles. A woman moving to a new post in a rural area usually boarded with the families of her pupils. In the classroom, she confronted all ages of children, including unruly teenage boys. School boards worried about her competence, but her low cost outweighed any reservations; the teaching profession was rapidly feminized, at least in the East. By 1860, one-quarter of the nation's teachers were women but in Massachusetts, a harbinger of future trends, almost four-fifths of the teaching force was female. "It seems as if the daughters of New England have a peculiar faculty and love for this occupation," observed traveler

Frederica Bremer in the 1850s. "Whole crowds go hence to the western and southern states where schools are daily established and placed under their direction."

Since the 1830s, New England educators had placed seminary graduates in teaching jobs in other states. In the 1840s, Catharine Beecher transformed teacher training and placement into a crusade. She led a campaign to raise funds for the recruitment and training of teachers who would be sent west to staff the common schools, and for the establishment of teacher training schools around the nation. Beecher's goal was "the elevation of my sex by the opening of a profession for them in the education of the young." She envisioned a distinguished profession for women, a profession equivalent to the vocation of motherhood but, at the same time, comparable to the male professions of law, medicine, and ministry. For those who must earn a living, teaching surpassed exploitation in the textile mills. It was preferable as well to the frivolity of the wealthy, which served no function. For those thrown into financial straits, it provided a respectable means of self-support. If only a temporary vocation, it prepared young women for "happy superintendence of a family." According to her biographer, Kathryn Sklar, Catharine Beecher viewed the teaching profession as a national benevolent movement, similar to the missionary movement—a crusade that would extend female influence across the continent.

Catharine Beecher threw her energies into this crusade with assertiveness. Under the auspices of two groups she created, the Board of Popular Education and the American Women's Educational Association, she began a round of speaking tours and fund raising. Crossing the country, Beecher coopted male collaborators, selected sites for western training schools, sought recruits for "missionary teachers," and cultivated the influential. Mobilizing the work force of a voluntary benevolent association, she rounded up boards of managers, supportive clergymen, and committees for teacher recruitment. Sarah Hale, for instance, lent her support by serving on the board of the American Women's Educational Association and giving it publicity in *Godey's Lady's Book.* In 1847, 70 New England women were sent west, after a month of training with Beecher, to meet the challenge of frontier schools. Almost 400 soon followed. Catharine Beecher also managed to establish a group of western training schools, although few survived the era. By the Civil War, she had done much to convince the nation that woman was "the best as well as the cheapest guardian and teacher of children in the school as well as in the nursery."

Like Sarah Hale, Catharine Beecher campaigned for "the elevation of my sex" and female influence. Like Hale, she promoted the values of woman's sphere. Like Hale, finally, she used the medium of print to wage her campaign and earn an income. Although Beecher and Hale had unusual success in the book market, they were not alone. Early nineteenth-century women rose to prominence as the authors of popular literature. They also became the major part of the American reading public.

READERS AND AUTHORS

From the 1820s a barrage of printed matter conveyed the values of woman's sphere to a growing female audience. Periodicals such as the *Ladies Magazine, Godey's Lady's Book,* and their competitors were only one facet of this outpouring. Sermons and religious tracts provided tributes to female piety. Didactic manuals on housekeeping, marriage, manners, and child rearing confirmed the significance of domesticity. Gift books filled with stories and poems catered to feminine sentimentality. A mass of popular novels written by women for women readers showed the force of female influence. In the antebellum decades, in short, an unprecedented amount of literature was directed at and bought by women. Never before had so vast a literate female audience existed, nor had women authors ever been so welcome in the literary marketplace. Never before had the technology existed to mass produce what they wrote.

By 1830, a major transformation in publishing was underway. The wooden hand press of colonial days was replaced by an iron press, a machine press, and then a steam press. The rest of the publishing business, from paper-making to typecasting and typesetting, became mechanized as well. Stereotyping and electrotyping improved the mass production of text and engravings. By the 1850s, the assembly line had been adapted to publishing, and the work place had shifted to the urban factory in New York, Boston, and Philadelphia. The nation's annual book production, more than 12 million volumes at midcentury, was five times as much as it had been in 1820. The transformation of the industry was symbolized in 1853 when Harper and Brothers built two seven-story buildings in which thousands of books a year could be produced.

While technology provided for the mass production of books and magazines, prosperity and literacy created an enormous middle-class female market. Women readers bought gift books at the rate of 60 new titles a year. By the 1850s, *Harper's Magazine* estimated that four-fifths of the reading public were women—to whom culture had been relegated, along with religion, morality, child care, and other nonprofit activities. Vast profits were available, however, to those who could capitalize on the female market, as did the Harper brothers. Successful authors profited as well. Publishing was a field in the "bank-note world" in which women's talents were in demand and in which female influence was tangible.

In the 1830s and 1840s, when "home" and "mother" became central themes in popular culture, a steady stream of publications explained the role of the middle-class woman, her conduct, character, and new significance. Figures of authority such as ministers had always defined ideal roles and continued to do so. Antebellum clerics, historian Karen Halttunen points out, directed many conduct manuals at young men who left rural homes to work in cities. Professional men also produced much of the advice directed at women. Marriage guides such as physician William Alcott's *The Young Wife* (1836) gave directions in every area from "submission" to "moral influence on the husband." Ministers produced guides to wifehood and child-rearing, and contributed steadily to women's periodicals. But professional men were no longer the sole authorities. Women assumed a prominent place among the advice givers in the periodical press and in manuals for wives, mothers, homemakers.

Especially prominent were a group of New England authors who had contributed, usually anonymously, to Sarah Hale's *Ladies Magazine* in the 1830s and later developed their own followings. Like Hale, they combined cautionary injunctions with celebrations of female influence. In *Home* (1835), for instance, Catharine Sedgwick offered fictionalized tracts on domestic life that idealized the new middle-class family. In a succession of parlor scenes, father and mother joined together to surmount domestic crises and demonstrate wise, compassionate modes of child-rearing. Caroline Gilman, another *Ladies Magazine* contributor, established a reputation with her fictionalized *Recollections of a House-keeper* (1834)—a trough of advice on all responsibilities from managing servants to pacifying husbands ("Reverence his *wishes* even when you do not his *opinions*"). Enterprising Lydia Sigourney produced a steady stream of conduct guides such as *Letters to Young Ladies* (1835) and *Letters to Mothers* (1838). Counseling stoicism, patience, and "passive" virtue, Sigourney celebrated power and control. "You have . . . taken a higher place in the scale of being," she informed mothers. "You have gained an increase in power." But while women authors had to share the advice field with professional men, they had a monopoly over the realm of housekeeping manuals.

The first housekeeping manual was probably Hannah Barnard's *Dialogues on Domestic and Rural Economy* (1820). Directing her advice at farm women, Barnard used fictional characters such as "Lady Homespun" and "Uncle Thrifty" to impart techniques of household production. Lydia Maria Child reached a far wider audience with *The Frugal Housewife* (1829), which went through 33 editions before its last printing in 1870. Throughout the antebellum decades, it made its way to New England farms and remote frontier cabins, providing household hints, recipes, and above all, advice on thrift. "How to Endure Poverty" was a particularly useful chapter for women thrown into financial distress by the vagaries of economic life. In this "land of precarious fortunes," they might suddenly have to do all their own housework on a minimal budget. This was indeed Lydia Maria Child's predicament, because her husband, a sometime lawyer, editor, reformer, and farmer, was downwardly mobile and she had to become a "frugal housewife" herself.

If Lydia Maria Child failed to connect housework and influence, Catharine Beecher made up for it. Beecher's monumental *Treatise on Domestic Economy*, first published in Boston in 1841, was reprinted annually through 1856 and revised and republished thereafter, with supplements written by the author and her sister Harriet. Catharine Beecher created a new profession: the domestic economist. The encyclopedic *Treatise* covered every conceivable aspect of domestic activity, from infant care to kitchen plumbing. The homemaker could learn about health and hygiene, basic physiology, suitable meal hours, appropriate home furnishings, the importance of regular domestic routines, and even the appropriate design of an eight-room house, complete with physical plans. In Beecher's hands, the role played by women at home became a highly skilled and multifaceted vocation. Domestic responsibility, Beecher contended, united all women, whatever they did, in a great and glorious mission. Mother, teacher, seamstress, or servant—"each and all may be animated by the consciousness, that they are agents in accomplishing the greatest work that was ever committed to human responsibility."

Antebellum women readers were also the major audience for novels. Fiction had long had a female following. Since the late eighteenth century, women readers had been warned against its corruptive influence, but such warnings had little impact. Men might assume the major roles in government, politics, and business; but in the realm of popular fiction, women assumed important roles, which appealed to women readers. Through the pages of long, sentimental novels, fictional heroines, often orphaned and impoverished, rose from obscurity to authority through talent, ingenuity, virtue, and benevolence. Defying adversity, they overcame the perils created by defective men—deserters, philanderers, gamblers, drinkers, profligates, inept speculators, or financial failures. In the world of the popular novel, heroines exerted influence. So did their authors. As early as the 1820s, women wrote a third of American novels; by midcentury, women authors had captured the market.

In the 1850s, an insatiable female reading audience kept sentimental fiction selling in huge editions. While Melville went out of print and Thoreau's library filled up with his own books, all returned unsold by his publisher, women dominated the literary market. Susan Warner's *Wide, Wide World* (1850) went through 14 editions in two years, and Elizabeth Stuart Phelps's *The Sunny Side* (1851) sold 100,000 copies. Novels by Sarah Payson Willis (Fanny Fern) and Elizabeth Oakes Smith went through dozens of printings, while Mrs. E.D.E.N. Southworth, a prolific hack, earned more than $10,000 a year from serial publication of her melodramatic Gothic romances. Harriet Beecher Stowe broke all records in 1852, when *Uncle Tom's Cabin* kept eight presses working day and night; 300,000 copies sold within the first year. Stowe adhered to many of the rules for feminine fiction. She presented an array of domestic scenes, and featured an innocent, virtuous, dying child-heroine. But she violated a tradition of noncontroversy by delving into "politics." Women authors, as Sarah Hale once contended in the *Ladies Magazine*, could not choose their themes at will, as could "the Lords of Creation." In fiction as in life, they were obliged to avoid "the agitation of political questions" and depict instead "domestic scenes and deep emotions." Most best-selling authors followed these precepts; they also celebrated feminine values, character, and influence.

Susan Warner's overwhelmingly popular *Wide, Wide World*, for instance, elaborated on female aversion to the crass, mundane world beyond the home. Ellen Montgomery, a pious, heroic little girl, is forced to confront the base domain of commercial life when her father loses a lawsuit and collapses financially. Interested only in the Bible and good deeds, virtuous Ellen rejects the values of the world and after innumerable risks and rebuffs is adopted by rich relatives. Elizabeth Oakes Smith's *Bertha and Lily* (1854) celebrated female moral superiority. Since childhood, talented Bertha has served as the "conscience" for her neighborhood and has been revered by all. In later life, however, she runs into difficulties. Rejecting Nathan Underhill, the repentant father of her long-lost illegitimate daughter—the saintly child Lily, now a foundling in an almshouse—she marries an adoring young minister. But Bertha is superior to her spouse and soon usurps *his* role as spiritual guide for the entire town. Woman is "closer to the spiritual manifestations of being," Bertha proclaims. "She will live in nearer relation with the divine."

Not all women's novels satisfied the criteria posited for feminine fiction. Sarah Payson Willis wrote a best-seller of 1855, *Ruth Hall*, that violated the rules. Orphaned, widowed, impoverished, and victimized, Ruth is an ambitious woman writer who triumphs over adversity by discarding conventional virtues. On the contrary, she becomes aggressive and shrewd and finally achieves overwhelming literary success, spurred on by a desire for fame and financial rewards. Although *Ruth Hall* enjoyed sensational sales, most reviewers accused her creator of defiling the "sacredness" of the home "for the sake of profit." The woman author, in fiction as in life, was expected to be a defender of sphere, not an interloper in the male world of ambition and financial success.

Like Ruth Hall, women who achieved success in literary sales were assertive entrepreneurs who needed income. If single, like Catharine Sedgwick, they supported themselves. If widowed, like Sarah Hale, they supported their families. If married, they earned the bulk of their families' incomes, as was the case with Harriet Beecher Stowe, Lydia Maria Child, Elizabeth Oakes Smith, and Lydia Sigourney. However, most women authors denied their role in the marketplace and affirmed, instead, their femininity. They contended variously that their work was divinely inspired, that creative and domestic urges were inextricably linked, or both. Far from harboring ambition, they only gradually became inured to seeing their work in print. Caroline Gilman's first published lines made her feel "as alarmed as if I had been detected in man's apparel." Sarah Hale assumed her role as editor only with "trembling" and later assured her readers that "The Mother, not the Author has been successful." Susan Warner, according to her sister, wrote her best-selling novel "on her knees." While denying that they had invaded the male preserve of commerce, women authors succeeded in popularizing feminine values, celebrating domestic influence, and feminizing the literary marketplace.

They were also able to earn income without appearing to leave the home, to adhere to the limits of woman's sphere while capitalizing on it. As literary critic Ann Douglas points out, publishing enabled women authors "to be unobtrusive and everywhere at the same time." But authors were not the only women involved in the "bank-note world." The same long-term changes that created the publishing industry also provided new roles for women in manufacturing.

FACTORY AND MILL

"You want to know what I am doing," wrote sixteen-year-old Mary Paul from Lowell, Massachusetts, to her widowed father in Claremont, New Hampshire, in 1846.

> I am at work in a spinning room tending four sides of warp which is one girl's work. The overseer tells me that he never had a girl get along better than I do. . . . I have a very good boarding place, have enough to eat. . . . The girls are all kind and obliging. The girls that I room with are all from Vermont and good girls too. . . . I get along very well with my work. . . . The usual time allowed for learning is six months but I think I shall have frames before I have been in there as I get along so fast. I think that the factory is the best place for me and if any girl wants employment, I advise them to come to Lowell.

Before entering the mills, Mary Paul had worked as a domestic in Bridgewater, Vermont, near where she had grown up. During the next four years, she moved in and out of mill work at Lowell. After leaving the mills, Mary Paul cared for her father in New Hampshire, started a coat-making business with another woman in Vermont, worked at an associationist community in New Jersey, and found a job as a housekeeper in New Hampshire. Finally, after 12 years of self-support, she married the son of her former boardinghouse keeper at Lowell and settled down in Lynn, Massachusetts. By the late 1850s, Mary Paul was a New England housewife. But by working a few years at the Lowell mills, like thousands of other young New England women, she had participated in a major development, the shift of production from household to workplace.

This shift affected only a minority of women who worked for pay. The largest numbers of women wage earners in the early nineteenth century labored as domestic servants, laundresses, and seamstresses—work that was low-status and "invisible," because it was performed either in one's own home or in someone else's. Moreover, it was usually work performed for other women. Domestic service was in transition, as historian Faye Dudden has shown. Early in the century, the typical domestic worker was the "hired girl," a neighbor's daughter who worked for and lived with a local family, as did Mary Paul before she turned to factory work. The hired girl helped with household chores and home production, working along with her mistress. By midcentury, the hired girl had been replaced by a domestic servant, often an immigrant woman, whose work was more specialized and whose relationship with her employer was more formal, distant, and decidedly unequal. Free black women in northern and southern cities also did domestic work. Some earned livings by providing services for other women, such as hairdressing or dressmaking; more often, they took in work at home, such as washing, ironing, or sewing.

Many farm wives were also drawn into the commercial economy. Rural Pennsylvania women, for instance, processed milk into butter to be sold to the Philadelphia market. Middle-class women, too, when thrown into need, might engage in paid work at home, by taking in boarders, by sewing, or by selling goods they made to other women. Most manufacturing work was also done at home. Under the putting-out system, entrepreneurs distributed work on garments, hats, books, and other items to women at home who were paid by the piece. The women who colored *Godey's Lady's Book* fashion plates in the 1830s, for instance, were home workers, as were young New England women who made straw hats and seamstresses in the urban garment industry. But the factory hand such as Mary Paul, although hardly the typical female wage earner, was the most novel. By 1828, nine out of 10 New England textile workers were women.

As thread and cloth had once been produced in self-sufficient households, it is often assumed that women who became mill hands followed their "natural" productive work outside the home. To an extent this is true. Once textile work moved to the factory, it became more difficult for New England farm girls to contribute to family income by spinning or weaving at home. Prices paid for homemade cloth fell, and the amount of homemade goods dropped accordingly. However, it was not solely an affinity for making thread or cloth—or beer, cigars, or shoes—that lured women into factory work. Employers too had an affinity—for cheap, tractable labor. They hired women only when other labor was scarce and when there was no competition from men for the jobs they did. In the printing trades, for instance, which mechanized and unionized early, women were quickly excluded from the best jobs and hired only at the bottom rung. At Harper's big New York factory, a few hundred young women worked as binders, gatherers, stitchers, gilders, letterers, and folders; but only men worked as printers. Manufacturing was not a wide-open field.

The rationale for hiring women workers was not that they were cheap, tractable, and available, but that manufacturing work was good for them and good for the country. In the new nation, land-rich and labor-scarce, the employment of women in manufacturing would free men for farming and, later, for business, while saving women "from poverty and idleness," as mill owners contended in the 1820s. Champions of women's welfare such as Mathew Carey, Sarah Hale's Philadelphia publisher, agreed. An advocate of women's employment in manufacturing, Carey contended that such work prevented young women from spending their time perniciously or burdening their parents. It taught them "habits of order, regularity, and industry, which pave a broad and deep foundation of public and private usefulness." Female employment, in the mouths of advocates, became a combination of social welfare, poor relief, and education.

American industry had been stirred into life during the War of 1812, when imports of manufactured goods were curtailed. According to government reports of 1822 and 1832, women worked in more than 100 industries, from beer and nails to gunpowder and lumber. By midcentury, when only about 10 percent of adult women worked for pay, women formed one-quarter of the labor force in manufacturing, with the largest numbers employed in the cotton textile, men's clothing, and shoe industries. Each had been transformed over the past half-century. Tasks became more specialized, machinery was introduced, and production shifted from household to factory. But in each industry, these changes had a different impact on women workers.

The urban garment industry, centered in New York, Boston, and Philadelphia, customarily used the putting-out system. Seamstresses employed in the manufacture of cheap, ready-made men's clothing worked at home and in small tailor shops, hand-stitching garments cut by skilled tailors. The labor market for seamstresses was crowded. Cities overflowed with women in need of income—married, unmarried, widowed, and deserted—who competed for piece work. If regularly employed, they earned half the income of female factory operatives; the going wage for piece work was that offered by the almshouse. Irregular, ill-paid employment made their condition precarious. "The wages paid to seamstresses who work in their own apartments . . . are utterly inadequate to their support, even if fully employed," Mathew Carey observed in Philadelphia in 1829. The introduction of the sewing machine in the 1840s transformed the garment industry, but not to the advantage of homebound seamstresses. As the scale of production increased, the need for workers declined, and much of the labor shifted to factories, where it was done by men. The homebound seamstress now had to buy or rent a machine as well as to compete with skilled tailors.

The sewing machine also affected the shoe industry of eastern Massachusetts, where women had long been employed. Even before mechanization, shoemakers had divided the craft between men and women. One part of the process, the sewing of uppers, was turned over to wives, widows, and children, who labored at home as stitchers and binders. By the 1830s, 15,000 New England women worked in boot and shoe production at home. When sewing machinery arrived in the 1850s, work shifted to factories, but the sexual division of labor continued. This proved an advantage for many women employees, historian Mary Blewett contends. Not only did they profit from their group experience in central shops, but their virtual monopoly over the stitching process meant increased leverage in the industry. Sexual division of labor in shoemaking, Blewett concludes, "rewarded the skills and experience of some female industrial workers, which they used to control the work process."

The textile industry followed another pattern. Textiles were first manufactured under the putting-out system, with spinning and weaving done in the household. After the power loom was introduced in 1814, more and more work shifted to mills, which soon peppered the New England countryside. Half the textile labor force worked under the "family system," introduced in the original cotton "manufactury" founded by Samuel Slater in Pawtucket, Rhode Island, in 1791. Slater hired entire families, often English immigrants, under annual contracts. His system was used in New England, the middle Atlantic states, the Midwest, and part of the South. But the "boardinghouse" system, introduced by Francis Cabot Lowell in Massachusetts in 1821, employed only women and gave the New England mills a new image.

In five years, Lowell transformed a farm town into an industrial center of six mills, and he attracted a unique labor force. Young, unmarried farm girls from all over New England flocked to Lowell and other mill towns. Like Mary Paul, they moved into and out of mill work, some staying a few months, some a few years, and some longer. All weighed the attractions of mill work against the alternatives—teaching, sewing, and domestic work—which paid less. "There are very many young ladies at work in the factories that have given up milinary dressmaking and school-keeping for to work in the mill," mill worker Malenda Edwards wrote to her cousin Sabrina Bennett from Nashua, Massachusetts, in 1839. The mill workers lived in company-run boardinghouses under the supervision of widowed matrons. Here they were subject to elaborate codes of company rules, such as curfews, room cleaning, and compulsory church attendance. But Lowell's paternalistic system provided an unusual combination of opportunities: income, independence, and community.

"At five o'clock in the morning the bell rings for the folks to get up," Mary Paul told her father. "At seven they are called to the mill. At half past twelve we have dinner, are called back again at one and stay until half past seven." The twelve- to thirteen-hour workday may not have been longer than the workday on a farm, although it seemed so at the outset. "I was so sick of it, at first, I wished the factory had never been thought of," Malenda Edwards wrote to Sabrina Bennett. "But the longer I stay, the better I like [it]." Mill workers appreciated their female community. They engrafted friends made at Lowell or Nashua onto networks of friends and relatives from home. They also organized a great array of activities: lending libraries, benevolent associations, debating clubs, missionary societies, Sabbath school unions, and the company-sponsored *Lowell Offering*, where their writings were published. According to Harriet Robinson, a "graduate" of the mills, the workers discussed dress reform, phrenology, Grahamism, and the Mexican War. They subscribed to *Godey's Lady's Book* and brought Lydia Maria Child's *Frugal Housewife* back to their farm-bound mothers.

Most important, the mill girls enjoyed their autonomy. Whether banking their wages, supporting their parents, or paying off family mortgages, they had become independent wage earners. "Don't I feel independent!" wrote Anne Appleton to her sister Sarah in the 1840s. "The thought that I am living on no one is a happy one indeed to me." "It was like a young man's pleasure in entering upon business for himself," concluded former mill worker Lucy Larcom. "Girls had never tried that experiment before and they liked it." Finally, mill work was usually temporary. The time spent as an operative was, ideally, a profitable interlude between a rural past and a middle-class future—as wife, mother, student, or teacher. Lowell's "boardinghouse" system and the labor force it attracted fused factory work and respectability.

Lucy Larcom and Harriet Robinson, who immortalized their Lowell experiences in vivid memoirs, celebrated this fusion. Daughters of widows who worked as dormitory supervisors, both had spent their youth in the mills as "bobbin girls," and both went on to careers. Larcom moved west, attended college, taught school, and returned to New England as an author. Robinson, who married, became an advocate of antislavery and woman suffrage. For both, the mills had provided advantages without the odium of working-class identification. "Lowell might well have been looked upon as a rather selective industrial school for young people," Larcom claimed. "We were happy in the knowledge that, at the longest, our employment was only temporary." For Robinson, mill work was a "preparatory school" for life. In *Loom and Spindle*, she too celebrated income, independence, and impermanence. The best part of the factory experience, Robinson explained, were the workers themselves: industrious, moral, religious, frugal, mutually supportive, and capable of "self-cultivation." Above all, they were economically liberated. "For the first time in this country, woman's labor had a money value," Robinson declared. "She had become not only an earner and a producer, but also a spender of money, a recognized factor in the political economy of her time."

The unique opportunity provided by the mills was short-lived. By the 1840s, the operatives complained of long hours, wage cuts, and speed-ups, as well as of a decline in housing conditions. "I never worked so hard in my life," Mary Paul wrote to her father in 1848. "The company pretends they are losing immense sums every day and therefore they are obliged to lessen the wages, but this seems perfectly absurd to me."

An engraving of workers at power looms in a New England textile
mill in 1839. By the late 1830s, real wages in the mills declined,
the workday was lengthened, and mill hands were urged
to increase productivity. The operative who once tended
one or two looms might now be tending
five or six. *(Culver Pictures)*

Although the women at Lowell had organized earlier, in 1834, when their Factory Girls Association protested wage cuts and blacklists, the panic of 1837 wiped out their efforts. In 1845, however, the Lowell workers organized a Female Labor Reform Association led by energetic Sarah Bagley, who had worked in the mills for a decade. The labor reformers agitated for a ten-hour day, allied themselves with the New England Workingmen's Association, and petitioned the state legislature to investigate mill conditions. Dismissing the *Offering* as a company organ, they stated their grievances in a new publication, the *Voice of Industry*. Mill operatives, complained the *Voice*, now had to "tend three or four looms, where they used to tend but two . . . the pay is not increased to them, while the increase to the owners is very great." In 1846, the *Voice* issued ominous warnings:

> [T]he time is not far distant when those who labor in the mills will (as is the case with many now) earn barely enough to purchase the necessities of life by working hard thirteen hours a day; recollect that those who worked here before you, did less work and were better paid for it than you are, and there are others to come after you.

The militant rumblings of the *Voice* did not sit well with the new generation of manufacturers, whose predecessors had wanted, two decades before, to "save respectable women from poverty and idleness." By now, mill owners had discovered a more tractable labor force—Irish immigrants, both men and women. Throughout the 1840s, the number of native New England women in the mills dwindled, and the lure of temporary industrial work as an avenue to upward mobility soon faded. But for those who had worked in the mills at their peak, the experience was a transforming one. Mill operatives married later and had fewer children than peers left behind on the farm. They also tended to settle in towns and cities. Like Mary Paul, they became middle-class housewives.

New England textile workers were not the only early-nineteenth-century women to leave the countryside for towns and cities. Between 1800 and 1860, the number of "urban" places—with residents numbering a few thousand or more—multiplied tenfold, and waves of newcomers swelled the populations of older cities. Simultaneously, the pace of westward expansion increased. The lure of land had led settlers west for decades, beyond the Appalachians and then beyond the Mississippi. At midcentury, families embarked on the long overland trip across the Great Plains to Oregon and California. For many women in transient circumstances—migrants, immigrants, pioneers—the middle-class notion of woman's sphere was likely to be a remote ideal or irrelevant. Similarly, for the majority of women who lived in rural areas, the perquisites of woman's sphere were minimal.

CITY AND FRONTIER

Most antebellum urban migrants were fairly poor people forced into motion by changing conditions. Young folk from farming communities, artisans whose crafts were vanishing, day laborers in need of jobs, widows seeking self-support, all settled in the working-class neighborhoods of eastern cities. So did immigrant families, primarily from England, Ireland, and Germany. These new city residents faced chronic insecurity. For working-class people, employment was precarious. Only a narrow line separated the "respectable" or "worthy" poor from the destitute. Women faced a special insecurity, for they might well descend into abject poverty if deprived of male support. Destitute female heads of household, like those observed by Mathew Carey in Philadelphia, often became pieceworkers and seamstresses in tenements, laboring for less-than-subsistence wages and facing frequent bouts of unemployment. Under such deprived conditions, the experience of many urban women had little connection with middle-class visions of domesticity.

The identity of antebellum working-class women, historian Christine Stansell contends, was rooted not in the home but in the city neighborhood. For the New York women whom Stansell examines, "home" was likely to be a piece of an attic, basement, stable, or shed. Domestic furnishings were few, private space unimportant, and physical labor arduous. Indeed, "the poorer the family, the heavier was women's work." Coping with clogged chimneys, smoking stoves, and flooded cellars, working-class wives' labored to obtain water, fuel, and food. To survive, they spent much of their time on errands outside the home, in a bustling population of neighbors, lodgers, peddlers, and shopkeepers; scavenging children also contributed to family upkeep. "Laboring women made their lives as wives and mothers on the streets as much as by the hearthside," Stansell points out. Working-class women's life in the tenements and on the street drew them into a community of women. Heavily involved in the lives of neighbors and acquaintances, they were usually gossiping, borrowing, lending, providing services, or seeking them. Women's involvement with one another ranged from solicitude and cooperation to disputes, fracases, and other outbursts of hostility. When visiting working-class neighborhoods, representatives of charitable organizations cited "conditions which others of refinement would find intolerable" and strove to impose middle-class values, which working-class women tended to resist.

Region, too, diluted the impact of woman's sphere. The sense of community shared by poor women in city neighborhoods became more rare in rural outposts. On southern farms as on the western frontier, homes were likely to be remote if not isolated; traditional forms of household production continued; and contact with other women was difficult to maintain. For women, the family farm was never the frontier of opportunity, especially when it had been removed to some remote place. Not surprisingly, women's attitudes toward their experience as pioneers often reflected more deprivation than advantage.

Westward-bound women in the early nineteenth century were the wives and daughters of farmers, tradesmen, army men, Mormons, and missionaries. Their numbers included some unattached women, ranging from the schoolteachers Catharine Beecher sent west to the prostitutes in California mining camps. For the most part, women moved west as members of families, not of their own volition. Westward treks, initiated by men in search of economic advancement, often struck women family members, in the words of one diarist, as a "wild goose chase." Migrating families usually covered long distances, ensuring separation from prior connections. Women migrants lost their friends and relatives, churches and homes; comfort, companionship, and community vanished. They also lost the benefits of eastern society, where women were held in higher esteem, enjoyed one another's company, and had more influence within the family. For the woman migrant, moving west seemed to mean moving backward in time, away from the benefits of modern life and into a harsh frontier world, where they would have to play traditional roles.

Such sentiments appeared in the diaries and letters of women who crossed the Great Plains in the 1840s and 1850s. The overland trek to Oregon and California, in women's eyes, seemed a double battle. A struggle against hardships and hazards—storms, insects, snakes, cholera, dysentery—it was also a struggle to maintain the higher status that women had achieved in middle-class homes. Wives and daughters on the overland trail, historians John Faragher and Christine Stansell contend, did not view their westward journey as an opportunity for equality but as an all-male enterprise; along the trail, male dominance reigned and female influence dwindled. "Men on the plains . . . were not so accommodating, nor so ready to wait upon women, as they were in the most civilized communities," observed Lavinia Porter, who traveled by ox team to California.

Although the traditional sexual division of labor often broke down en route, women's access to men's work, such as driving wagons or livestock, in addition to their traditional jobs of laundering and cooking, hardly seemed a step forward. Rather it seemed a violation of feminine roles. In addition, women on the trail experienced an overwhelming sense of loss. They missed their homes and all that went with them—personal possessions, domestic routines, and female companionship. When they were able to enjoy the company of other women along the trail, such relationships were treasured. When wagon trains separated and newfound friends disappeared, desolation increased. Women migrants were often left with the sense that they had lost the benefits of "civilization" itself. After crossing the Missouri, Margaret Chambers felt "as if we had left all civilization behind us." To Phoebe Judson, "each doomed step . . . carried us farther and farther into a desolate, barren country."

When they arrived at their destinations, women migrants confronted trying circumstances. Home, on the frontier, was not a model cottage but rather, at first, a hut, tent, or gravel-floored cabin. Everyday life resembled that of colonial times. In midwestern farming communities, the family was the basic work unit; wives and children formed part of the labor force. Midwestern farm wives tended animals, raised gardens, ran dairies, and produced most of their families' food, cloth, and clothing. In the frontier farming community, men dominated both private and public life. But women struggled to maintain kinship and friendship networks and to re-create familiar institutions—home, school, church, and association. Sabbath observance took on crucial significance. "What opportunities these days of rest a home present to the wife and mother," Sarah Hale once exclaimed in an etiquette book. Sharing such views, frontier women united to form congregations and demand Sabbath observance, though sometimes in vain. "The Sabbath is little regarded and is more a day for diversion than devotion," one of Catharine Beecher's teachers reported from the Midwest. "Those days of social communion and prayer at Hartford I shall never forget."

The battle grew more difficult in the Far West. Here the proportion of women dropped sharply—for instance, only 8 percent of the California population was female in 1850. But the challenge to female moral superiority increased. Women complained of Sabbath desecration and lack of female companionship; of lawlessness and vice; and of unkempt characters. Full of transitory miners, adventurers, and malefactors, the Far West of the 1850s seemed masculinized beyond redemption. "There is little in California society . . . to engage the higher order of female intelligence," Eliza Farnham warned eastern women. Overall, the commentary of many women pioneers supports a recent, critical interpretation of western history. Far from being a triumphant achievement, some historians contend, the conquest of the West represented a moral failure and a white man's adventure, one that exploited the environment, native peoples, and members of pioneer families. For women migrants, westward expansion frequently meant lives of isolation, exhaustion, and endurance.

The experience of Hispanic women on the Mexican borderland suggests that frontier conditions could have different impacts on different female populations. The western frontier for antebellum Americans overlapped the northern frontier for Mexicans, who in 1821 declared their independence from Spain and established a republic. Until the late 1840s, when the United States claimed New Mexico, Arizona, California, and parts of Texas, these territories formed the northern edge of Mexico. Here, frontier conditions may have mitigated the tradition of female subjugation that characterized Spanish society in more settled areas to the south, and also altered the traditional sexual division of labor. Hispanic frontierswomen, historians point out, engaged in a wide variety of paid occupations, as bakers, weavers, venders, craftswomen, farmers, and ranchers. Some gender barriers that existed in central Mexico vanished. A number of California women, for instance, received land grants in their own names, and New Mexico women commonly ran business establishments.

Hispanic women also inherited a legal tradition that enabled wives to maintain property separate from that of their husbands, as well as their maiden names, and that gave them easy access to court, where they could sue and be sued. Unlike American frontier communities, where men outnumbered women, in Mexican communities such as Santa Fe and San Antonio, and in other Texas and New Mexico towns, women slightly outnumbered men—probably because the latter often met violent deaths. Living conditions hardly exceeded those of American frontier people. In California, the well-off might have adobe homes of three or four rooms, but most families lived in single rooms, sparsely furnished; cooking was done outdoors. At midcentury, growing affluence brought the well-off more possessions, such as mirrors, clocks, and pianos, and improvements such as glass windows, planked floors, and indoor fireplaces. But as Americans penetrated and then occupied the Hispanic borderland, women lost the independent lifestyle they had created during the era of the Mexican frontier.

Westward expansion, finally, affected the lives of Native American women. Some were involuntary migrants, such as those dispossessed from tribal lands in the South and removed to reservations in Indian territory, or what would become Oklahoma. Displacement and resettlement disrupted tribal life, as among the Mississippi Choctaws, most of whom reluctantly left for Indian territory in 1831–1832. The minority that stayed in Mississippi, historian Clara Sue Kidwell shows, retained aspects of their traditional roles and a matrilineal kinship system. Women continued to farm, and men often followed their wives to live near the wives' mothers. Among the Choctaws in Indian territory, by the 1840s and 1850s, in contrast, a male-oriented lineage system predominated. Choctaw women who remained in Mississippi, however, also felt the jolt of shifting rules. In 1842, a change in United States law

A watercolor by Alexander Barclay in 1853 depicts a
New Mexico Woman returning from the river with a
tub of washed laundry. It also illustrates Hispanic women's
everyday dress on the southwestern frontier. *("Theresitia*
Suaso of New Mexico, 1853." Watercolor by Alexander
Barclay. Courtesy of the Bancroft Library)

made white men who married into the Choctaw nation ineligible for land claims granted to Choctaws. This meant that women who wed white men found themselves and their children deprived of lands that under traditional Choctaw customs would have been theirs.

For western Indians, who faced the encroachment of settlers, contact with European Americans inevitably meant disruption, and often detriment, as among Native American women of the Pacific Northwest. According to historian Mary C. Wright, these women lost their economic roles in the fur trade and high status in their cultures; new roles in the cash economy failed to take root. But the impact of contact took many forms. After settlers arrived in Sonomo and Mendocino counties, California, at midcentury, the traditional culture of the local Pomo Indians vanished, as did their villages. Men lost their occupational status and avenues to authority, scholar Victoria D. Patterson explains. Pomo women, however, assumed new roles and behavior. Before white settlement, they had rarely headed households; after contact, they became heads of male-absent households, earned wages or goods for their labor as domestics or laundresses, and collected favors or money from white men. Children of mixed race, reminders of these exploitative relationships, became common in their households. In southern Wisconsin, yet another response to contact emerged. As settlers arrived in the late eighteenth and early nineteenth centuries, historian Lucy Eldersveld Murphy shows, Sauk, Mesquakie, and Winnebago women melded old and new economic roles. They produced food for their families and a larger market; retained control over resources and means of production; preserved their status in their communities; and thus adapted traditional gender roles to a new consumer economy. Eventually, however, the Indians of the Fox-Wisconsin Riverway region were either forced west to Indian territory; killed in the Black Hawk War of 1832 or subsequent conflicts; or fell victim to malaria, smallpox, measles, cholera, or starvation.

The impact of westward expansion on Native American women in the early nineteenth century thus varied. Overall, the experience of contact probably reenforced male dominance among European and Native Americans. Clearly, too, for Native Americans, contact brought epidemics, conflict, and often disaster. For survivors, anthropologists suggest, contact usually meant partial assimilation to white culture. It eliminated or diminished native economies, reduced control over resources, and incorporated Native American labor in the margins of white enterprise. It ended tribal autonomy, redefined patterns of authority, and linked status and power to contact with outsiders. Finally, contact tended to alter traditions of sexual propriety, gender hierarchy, and the relations of individual to community. East or west of the Mississippi, Native American women in the nineteenth century confronted these changes and their consequences.

WHITE WOMEN IN THE ANTEBELLUM SOUTH

If the benefits of woman's sphere seemed difficult to retain in the West, the South was even more recalcitrant. Here, as in the North, the feminine ideal—promoted in sermons, speeches, and periodicals—stressed piety, innocence, submissiveness, intuition, compassion, and self-abnegation. But the southern ideal had a regional flavor. Unlike northern celebrations of women's roles, such as Catharine Beecher's *Treatise on Domestic Economy*, the antebellum southern ideal was voiced mainly by men. It did not depend on an exodus of middle-class men from home to workplace, for as historian Elizabeth Fox-Genovese points out, the South escaped the middle-class revolution that transformed northern society. Nor did it reflect a female gain of influence within the home. Instead, the southern ideal was part of the proslavery defense. While northern middle-class women made new claims to influence and authority, the South rejected changes that might challenge existing power relations.

Southern women were affected less by rhetoric than by the region's agrarian lifestyle. During the early nineteenth century, agrarianism became more firmly entrenched, as cotton and slavery expanded into the fertile Southwest. Westward expansion opened up new routes of social mobility, but it did little to alter white women's roles. In Virginia as in Mississippi, most southern women lived in rural areas, where routines resembled those of colonial times.

On small family farms, where a majority of white southerners labored without slaves, women retained traditional roles in farming and in household production: they spun, wove, sewed, made lard, kept gardens, fed poultry, and hoed corn. Male heads of families dominated these antebellum southern farms. In her study of yeoman households in the South Carolina low country, historian Stephanie McCurry finds the power of men rooted in "the inviolability of the household, the command of dependents, and the public prerogatives that manhood conferred." Yeoman wives, in contrast, lacked influence in home, church, and community. "Burdened by children and other household responsibilities," McCurry writes, they "complained of the difficulty of maintainening any kind of social ties, even to beloved kinfolk." Evangelicalism reenforced unspoken assumptions about the gendered nature of authority, and public life belonged solely to men. Yoked to patterns of submission and domination that pervaded southern culture, yeoman wives also faced limitations of class. "In distinct contrast to bourgeois gender ideology, which aspired to obscure class in the claims to universality of womanhood and sisterhood," McCurry contends, "southern gender ideology served, rather, to inscribe class."

On small plantations with slaves, planters' wives were relieved of outdoor work, but household production continued. Southern townswomen, too, engaged in productive labor well into the nineteenth century, historian Suzanne Lebsock reports; city living retained a "barnyard ambiance." Only on substantial plantations with large numbers of slaves did women assume managerial roles. The wife of a big planter might be responsible for the upkeep of a large labor force. She supervised plantation accounts, the distribution of rations, slave health and housing, and a range of productive activities—from the making of clothes to the butchering of hogs. But the grand plantation mistress represented only a tiny proportion, less than 5 percent, of southern white women. Household management, moreover, could be vexing and intimidating, and wives held less than ultimate authority. Plantation mistresses were themselves dependents, as historian Brenda Stevenson points out. Husbands issued critiques and directives, while uncooperative slaves might form "an elusive wall of resistance."

Even for the privileged, the rural nature of southern life limited opportunity for communication, association, and education. Mail arrived infrequently, visiting provided the sole entertainment, social life required special effort and travel, and institutional affiliations often remained limited to church membership. Only daughters of wealthier families had educational options. A southern academy movement had emerged in the Revolution's wake; the more ambitious schools, like the Columbia Female Institute in Tennessee, which opened in 1839, imitated prestigious northern academies. Common school systems barely existed. By midcentury in the Southeast, only 35 percent of school-age white girls (and 40 percent of white boys) attended school. In New England, by contrast, these percentages were doubled. Not surprisingly, almost 25 percent of southern white women over 20 (and almost 15 percent of white men) were illiterate.

To what extent did meager education and the rural environment limit women's participation in public life? Recent research suggests an unexpected degree of involvement in civic affairs and sectional issues. Like the well-to-do Petersburg women who started an orphan asylum, elite and middle-class women in towns might join evangelical societies, benevolent organizations, or temperance groups. Some historians suggest that female-run voluntary associations flourished even beyond towns and cities, and that women's activism extended to facets of political life. Hundreds of Virginia women, for instance, supported the American Colonization Society, formed in 1816, which promoted the emigration of free blacks to Liberia. In this and other circumstances, contends historian Elizabeth R. Varon, women used legislative petitions, political campaigns, and publications to "register their political views." Still, compared to northern counterparts, southern women played a more circumscribed role in public affairs. Female voluntary societies never challenged gender limits but rather reinforced the class prerogatives of elite women. Women who achieved prominence in letters were often transplanted northerners. There were rare exceptions, such as Louisa McCord of Charleston, whose political articles and translations of economic treatises appeared in leading southern journals. But McCord, said *DeBow's Review*, was a "brilliant anomaly." More typically, literate southern women confined their self-expression to correspondence and diaries. Like Mary Chesnut's famous Civil War diary, an artful revision of her wartime records, antebellum women's diaries voiced grievances.

Among the significant motifs in this private literature were women's hostility to slavery and anger at miscegenation—a subject that evoked painful soliloquies. The sexual relations of white men and slave women, diarists contended, ruined marriages and morals and destroyed family harmony. "Southern women are I believe all at heart abolitionists," contended a Georgia matron, Gertrude Ella Thomas, in her journal for 1858, after a long digression on the subject. "I will stand to the opinion that the institution of slavery degrades the white man more than the Negro and exerts a most deleterious effect upon our children. . . . The happiness of homes is destroyed but what is to be done?" Like the planter's wife who told English author Harriet Martineau that she was "the chief slave of the harem," southern diarists also compared their position to that of slaves. Citing the harassment and responsibility that slave management involved, some expressed a desire to free themselves from the institution of slavery, especially from the obligations it entailed. "I believe my servants are going to craze me," wrote Alabama diarist Sarah Gayle in 1835.

But planters' wives' objections to slavery have to be qualified. When southern women complained of slavery, they usually did so on a pragmatic basis rather than a moral one. Calling for reform, not abolition, they rarely opposed slavery in principle or in the abstract, historian Fox-Genovese concludes. Experienced matrons, historian Catherine Clinton points out, "generally groaned over the evils of *slaves* rather than the curse of slavery." Similarly, anger about illicit interracial sex usually targeted women slaves instead of unfaithful husbands. Planters' wives and daughters also knew that their financial security and social status rested upon slave property, which compounded their ambivalence. Most important, whatever their objections toward either slaves or slavery as an institution, they were nonetheless free women in a slave society. Historians differ as to whether southern women colluded in their own oppression because it was in their class interest to preserve hierarchy or whether they lacked weapons to challenge their subordinate status. Still, disadvantages of gender, scholars agree, were far exceeded by the privileges of color and class.

For slave women, the same generalization appeared to apply, though in reverse. In many ways, the woman in slavery had more in common with enslaved men than with free white women. The condition of slavery as a system of labor precluded the kind of distinctions between the sexes so carefully drawn in white society, just as it precluded the social segregation by sex that came to characterize the experience of white women. All slaves worked, and all were property that could be sold, mortgaged, hired out, bequeathed, and inherited. Slave status as property inevitably affected gender roles. It was impossible for slave men to be dominant in the same way that white men were, or for women to assume the same type of subordinate roles that white women did. One result, some historians have suggested, was that there was more sexual equality in slave society, by default, than in free society. Another result, one stressed by northern women reformers, was that gender became yet more of a liability: slave women were deprived of the perquisites of womanhood. After 1830, once women in the North began a spate of activism in benevolence and reform, the plight of the woman in slavery became a prominent concern.

SUGGESTED READINGS AND SOURCES

Historians of the 1960s and 1970s debated whether the early nineteenth-century doctrine of "woman's sphere" represented loss or gain. For a negative view, see Barbara Welter, "The Cult of True Womanhood, 1820–1860," *American Quarterly*, 18 (Summer 1966), 151–175, an analysis of prescriptive literature that identified character traits valued in women; Gerda Lerner, "The Lady and the Mill Girl: Changes in the Status of Women in the Age of Jackson," *Mid-Continental American Studies Journal*, 10 (Spring 1969), 5–15, which stresses the disparity between women's place and opportunities for men; and Mary P. Ryan, "Mothers of Civilization: The Common Woman 1830–1860" in Ryan, *Womanhood in America* (New York, 1975), pp. 137–191. A more positive view is suggested in Nancy F. Cott's pivotal book, *The Bonds of Womanhood: "Woman's Sphere" in New England, 1778–1835* (New Haven, Conn., 1977), which analyzes the liabilities and benefits of sphere; Kathryn Kish Sklar, *Catharine Beecher: A Study in American Domesticity* (New Haven, Conn., 1973), which discusses the development of domestic ideology; Daniel Scott Smith, "Family Limitation, Sexual Control, and Domestic

Feminism in Victorian America," in Mary Hartman and Lois Banner, eds., *Clio's Consciousness Raised* (New York, 1974), pp. 119–136, which posits a female gain of autonomy within the family; and Carroll Smith-Rosenberg, "The Female World of Love and Ritual," *Signs*, 1 (Autumn 1975), 1–29, an exploration of women's relationships in a sexually segregated society. This essay is reprinted in Smith-Rosenberg, *Disorderly Conduct: Visions of Gender in Victorian America* (New York, 1985).

Subsequent works further explore women's domestic lives and social experience. Most of Carl Degler, *At Odds: Women and the Family from the Revolution to the Present* (New York, 1981) concerns women's roles in the nineteenth-century family. Lee Virginia Chambers-Schiller considers the lives of unmarried women in *Liberty, A Better Husband: Single Women in America, The Generations of 1780–1840* (New Haven, Conn., 1984). Ellen K. Rothman examines changing modes of romance in *Hands and Hearts: A History of Courtship in America* (Cambridge, Mass., 1984). Michael K. Grossberg presents the legal history of domestic issues from courtship to custody in *Governing the Hearth: Law and the Family in Nineteenth-Century America* (Chapel Hill, N.C., 1985); on the origins of maternal custody, see Grossberg, *A Judgment for Solomon: The D'Hauteville Case and Legal Experience in Antebellum America* (New York, 1996). For marriage, see Anya Jabour, *Marriage in the Early Republic: Elizabeth and William Wirt and the Companionate Ideal* (Baltimore, Md., 1998); Hendrik Hartog, *Man and Wife: A History* (Cambridge, Mass., 2000); and Nancy F. Cott, *Public Vows: A History of Marriage and the Nation* (Cambridge, Mass., 2000). For divorce, see Norma Basch, *Framing American Divorce; from the Revolutionary Generation to the Victorians* (Berkeley, Calif., 1999). Steven Mintz and Susan Kellogg describe the rise of the middle-class family, 1770–1830, in *Domestic Revolutions: A Social History of American Family Life* (New York, 1988), ch. 3. Christine Stansell examines the experience of urban working-class women in *City of Women: Sex and Class in New York, 1789–1860* (New York, 1986). Mary P. Ryan's local study, *Cradle of the Middle Class: The Family in Oneida County, New York, 1790–1865* (New York, 1981), discusses women's contribution to class identity; see especially chs. 2 and 5. Karen Halttunen, *Confidence Men and Painted Women: A Study of Middle-Class Culture in America, 1830–1870* (New Haven, Conn., 1982), analyzes the rituals, manners, and postures of the upwardly mobile. Jeanne Boydston explores the connection of household labor and industrialization in *Home and Work: Housework, Wages, and the Ideology of Labor in the Early Republic* (New York, 1990). Catherine E. Kelley explores class formation in rural New England in *In the New England Fashion: Reshaping Women's Lives* (Ithaca, N.Y. 1999). For women's roles in public life, see Mary P. Ryan, *Women in Public: Between Banners and Ballots, 1824–1880* (Baltimore, Md., 1990), which discusses New Orleans, San Francisco, and New York, and Catherine Allgor, *Parlor Politics: In Which the Ladies of Washington Help Build a City and a Government* (Charlottesville, Va., 2000), an innovative study of the early republic. Several recent studies consider differences between the experiences of women and men; see Stephen M. Frank, *Life With Father: Parenthood and Masculinity in the Nineteenth Century American North* (Baltimore, Md., 1998); Mark Carnes, ed., *Meanings For Manhood: Constructions of Masculinity in Victorian America* (Chicago, 1990); and Laura McCall and Donald Yacavone, eds., *A Shared Experience: Men, Women, and the History of Gender* (New York, 1998). For an illuminating study of class development in England, see Leonore Davidoff and Catherine Hall, *Family Fortunes: Men and Women of the English Middle Class, 1780–1850* (London, 1987).

Ann Douglas posits an alliance between women and ministers in *The Feminization of American Culture* (New York, 1977). Barbara Leslie Epstein, *The Politics of Domesticity:*

Women, Evangelism, and Temperance in Nineteenth-Century America (Middletown, Conn., 1981), examines the role of religion in the development of feminine consciousness; see ch. 2. Women's religious involvement is further discussed in Barbara M. Welter, "The Feminization of American Religion, 1800–1860," in Mary Hartman and Lois Banner, eds., *Clio's Conscious-ness Raised* (New York, 1974), pp. 137–157; Nancy F. Cott, "Young Women and the Second Great Awakening," *Feminist Studies*, 2 (Fall 1975), 15–29; Mary P. Ryan, "A Woman's Awaken-ing: Evangelical Religion and the Families of Utica, New York, 1800–1840," *American Quar-terly*, 30 (Winter 1978), 602–623; Louis Billington, "Female Laborers in the Church: Women Preachers in the Northeastern United States, 1790–1840," *Journal of American Studies*, 19 (1985), 369–394; Ann M. Boylan, *Sunday School: The Formation of an American Institution, 1790–1880* (New Haven, Conn., 1988); Susan Juster and Lisa McFarlane, eds., *A Mighty Bap-tism: Race, Gender, and the Creation of American Protestantism* (Ithaca, N.Y., 1996), which covers the 1780s to the 1920s; and, for Catholic women, Carol K. Coburn and Martha Smith, *Spir-ited Lives: How Nuns Shaped Catholic Culture and American Life, 1836–1920* (Chapel Hill, N.C. 1999).

For changes in sexual ideology and practice, see in addition to Smith, "Family Limita-tion" and Degler, *At Odds*, above, Nancy F. Cott, "Passionlessness: An Interpretation of Victo-rian Sexual Ideology, 1790–1850," *Signs*, 4 (Winter 1978), 219–236; Linda Gordon, *Woman's Body, Woman's Right: A History of Birth Control in America* (New York, 1976), part I; Janet Farrell Brodie, *Contraception and Abortion in Nineteenth-Century America* (Ithaca, N.Y. 1994); Charles Rosenberg and Carroll Smith-Rosenberg, "The Female Animal: Medical and Biolog-ical Views of Woman and Her Role in Nineteenth-Century America," *Journal of Social History*, 60 (September 1973), 332–356; John S. Haller and Robin Haller, *The Physician and Sexuality in Victorian America* (Urbana, Ill., 1974); Daniel Scott Smith and Michael Hindus, "Premarital Pregnancy in America, 1640–1971: An Overview and Interpretation," *Journal of Interdiscipli-nary History*, 5 (Spring 1975); and G. J. Barker-Benfield, "The Spermatic Economy: A Nineteenth-Century View of Sexuality," *Feminist Studies*, 1 (1972), 45–74. For relationships between women, see, in addition to Smith-Rosenberg, "The Female World of Love and Ritual," William Taylor and Christopher Lasch, "Two 'Kindred Spirits': Sorority and Family in New England, 1839–1846," *New England Quarterly*, 36 (1963), 25–41.

Women's roles as patients and practitioners are examined in Regina Markell Morantz-Sanchez, *Sympathy and Science: Women Physicians in American Medicine* (New York, 1985); Mary Roth Walsh, *"Doctors Wanted: No Women Need Apply": Sexual Barriers in the Medical Professions, 1835–1975* (New Haven, Conn., 1977); Ann Douglas Wood, "The Fashionable Diseases: Women's Complaints and Their Treatment in Nineteenth-Century America," *Journal of Interdisciplinary History*, 4 (Summer 1973), 25–52; Regina Markell Morantz, "The Perils of Feminist History," *Journal of Interdisciplinary History*, 4 (Spring 1974), 649–660; Morantz, "Making Women Modern: Middle-Class Women and Health Reform in Nineteenth-Century America," *Journal of Social History*, 10 (1976–1977), 490–507; and Susan E. Cayleff, *Wash and Be Healed: The Water-Cure Movement and Women's Health* (Philadelphia, 1987). For the begin-ning of the midwife's demise, see Catherine Scholton, *Childbearing in American Society: 1650–1850* (New York, 1985). Judy Barrett Litoff traces the history of midwifery into the twentieth century in *American Midwives: 1860 to the Present* (Westport, Conn., 1978). For a his-tory of childbirth, see Judith Walzer Leavitt, *Brought to Bed: Childbearing in America, 1750–1950* (New York, 1986). Sylvia D. Hoffert explores mothers' leverage in *Private Matters: Attitudes Toward Childbearing and Infant Nurture in the Urban North* (Urbana, Ill., 1989).

On women's education, see Thomas A. Woody, *A History of Women's Education in the United States* (New York, 1929), vol. 1; Barbara M. Cross, ed., *The Educated Woman in America* (New York, 1965); Polly Welts Kaufman, *Women Teachers on the Frontier* (New Haven, Conn., 1984); Anne Firor Scott, "The Ever-Widening Circle: The Diffusing of Feminist Values from the Troy Female Seminary," *History of Education Quarterly*, 19 (Spring 1979), 3–25; Maris A. Vinovskis and Richard M. Bernard, "Beyond Catharine Beecher: Female Education in the Antebellum Period," *Signs*, 3 (Summer 1978), 856–869; Vinovskis and Bernard, "The Female Schoolteacher in Antebellum Massachusetts," *Journal of Social History*, 10 (March 1977), 332–345; Keith Melder, "Woman's High Calling: The Teaching Profession in America, 1830–1860," *American Studies*, 13 (Fall 1972), 19–32; and Amanda Porterfield, *Mary Lyon and the Mount Holyoke Missionaries* (New York, 1997). For the Beecher family, besides Sklar, *Catherine Beecher,* see Jeanne Boydston, Mary Kelley, and Anne Margolis, eds., *The Limits of Sisterhood: The Beecher Sisters on Women's Rights and Women's Sphere* (Chapel Hill, N.C., 1988). For the life of one educated woman, a scholarly clergyman's wife in New England, see Joan W. Goodwin, *The Remarkable Mrs. Ripley: The Life of Sarah Alden Bradford Ripley* (Boston, 1998).

Nina Baym surveys women's literary output in *Women's Fiction: A Guide to Novels By and About Women in America, 1820–1870* (Ithaca, N.Y., 1978). Ann Douglas assesses the influence of literary women and indicts female sentimentalism in *The Feminization of American Culture*, cited previously. Mary Kelley, *Private Women, Public Stage: Literary Domesticity in Nineteenth-Century America* (New York, 1984), studies the careers of women authors. Jane Tomkins, *Sensational Designs: The Cultural Work of American Fiction, 1790–1860* (New York, 1985), defends the sentimental novel. David S. Reynolds discusses the rebellious role of women writers of the 1850s in *Beneath the American Renaissance: The Subversive Imagination in the Age of Emerson and Melville* (New York, 1988), ch. 12. For women writers' interpretations of the past, see Nina Baym, *Women Writers and the Work of History, 1790–1860* (New Brunswick, N.J., 1995). Martha Saxton, *Louisa May: A Modern Biography of Louisa May Alcott* (New York, 1977) leads the field of Alcott biographies; a new edition appeared in 1995. For Sarah Hale's career as editor, see Isabelle Webb Entrikin, *Sarah Josepha Hale and Godey's Lady's Book* (Philadelphia, 1946), and Lawrence Martin, "The Genesis of *Godey's Lady's Book,*" *New England Quarterly*, 1 (January 1928), 41–70. *Godey's Lady's Book* is available on CD-ROM (Scholarly Resources).

Thomas Dublin examines women's experience in the textile mills in *Women at Work: The Transformation of Work and Community in Lowell, Massachusetts, 1826–1860* (New York, 1979), and *Farm and Factory: The Mill Experience and Women's Lives in New England 1830–1860* (New York, 1981). For mill workers' publications, see Benita Eisler, ed., *The Lowell Offering: Writings by New England Mill Women (1840–1845)* (Philadelphia and New York, 1977), and Philip S. Foner, ed., *The Factory Girls: A Collection of Writings on Life and Struggles in the New England Factories of the 1840s* (Urbana, Ill., 1977). Mary H. Blewett explores the sexual division of labor and its ramifications in *Men, Women, and Work: Class, Gender, and Protest in the New England Shoe Industry, 1780–1910* (Urbana, Ill., 1988). Joan M. Jensen examines the work roles of rural Pennsylvania women in *Loosening the Bonds: Mid-Atlantic Farm Women, 1750–1850* (New Haven, Conn., 1986). For paid domestic work, see Faye E. Dudden, *Serving Women: Household Service in Nineteenth-Century America* (Middletown, Conn., 1983). Urban women wage earners are discussed in Stansell, *City of Women,* cited previously; David Montgomery, "The Working Classes of the Pre-Industrial American City, 1780–1830," *Labor History*, 9 (Winter 1968), 3–27; and Sharon Harley, "Northern Black Female Workers: Jacksonian Era," in Sharon Harley and Rosalyn Terborg-Penn, eds., *The Afro-American Woman: Struggles and Images*

(Port Washington, N.Y., 1978, pp. 5–16. Timothy J. Gilfoyle depicts a facet of the urban economy in *City of Eros: New York City, Prostitution, and the Commercialization of Sex, 1790–1920* (New York, 1992). See also Patricia Cline Cohen, *The Murder of Helen Jewett: The Life and Death of a Prostitute in New York City* (New York, 1998), on a murder case of 1836. Alice Kessler Harris integrates labor history with economic and social developments in *Out to Work: A History of Wage-Earning Women in the United States* (New York, 1982). For further sources on women in the labor force, see the suggested readings for chapter 5.

The growing literature on women in the West includes John Mack Faragher, *Women and Men on the Overland Trail* (New Haven, Conn., 1979); Julie Roy Jeffrey, *Frontier Women: "Civilizing" the West? 1840–1880*, rev. ed. (New York, 1998); Glenda Riley, *The Female Frontier: A Comparative View of Women on the Prairie and the Plains* (Lawrence, Kans., 1988); Riley, *Women and Indians on the Frontier, 1825–1915* (Albuquerque, N.M., 1984); Sandra L. Myres, *Westering Women and the Frontier Experience, 1800–1915* (Albuquerque, N. Mex., 1982); and Lillian Schlissel, Byrd Gibbens, and Elizabeth Hampsten, *Far From Home: Families of the Westward Journey* (New York, 1989). An illustrated history is given in Linda Peavy and Ursula Smith's *Pioneer Women: The Lives of Women on the Frontier* (Norman, Okla., 1998). For western women's writing, see Lillian Schlissel, ed., *Women's Diaries of the Westward Journey* (New York, 1982); Lillian Schlissel and Catherine Lavender, eds., *The Western Women's Reader: The Remarkable Writings of Women Who Shaped the American West, Spanning 300 Years* (New York, 2000); Brigette Georgi-Findlay, *The Frontiers of Women's Writing: Women's Narratives and the Rhetoric of Westward Expansion* (Tucson, Ariz., 1996), and Christiane Fischer, ed., *Let Them Speak for Themselves: Women in the American West, 1849–1900* (New York, 1978). Malcolm J. Rohrbough, *Days of Gold: The California Gold Rush and the American Nation* (Berkeley, 1997), ch. 3, considers the impact of separation on families of western migrants. Susan Lee Johnson examines aspects of gender in the Sierra Nevadas in *Roaring Camp: The Social World of the California Gold Rush* (New York, 2000). Judy Yung examines immigration to the nineteenth-century West in *Unbound Feet: A Social History of Chinese Women in San Francisco* (Berkeley, 1995), ch. 1. Sally Zanjani explores the roles of independent women in *A Mine of Her Own: Women Prospectors in the American West, 1850–1950* (Lincoln, Neb., 1997).

For recent essays on the multicultural West, mainly on the postbellum decades and beyond, see Elizabeth Jameson and Susan Armitage, eds., *Writing the Range: Race, Class, and Culture in the Women's West* (Norman, Ok., 1997). Articles of interest include John Mack Faragher and Christine Stansell, "Women and their Families on the Overland Trail to California and Oregon 1842–67," *Feminist Studies*, 2 (1975), 150–166, and Faragher, "History from the Inside Out: Writing the History of Women in Rural America," *American Quarterly*, 33 (Winter 1981), 537–557. Bibliographical articles include Sandra L. Myres, "Women in the West" in Michael Malone, ed., *Historians and the American West* (Lincoln, Neb., 1983), and Elizabeth Jameson, "Toward a Multicultural History of Women in the Western United States," *Signs*, 13 (Summer 1988), 761–791.

The experience of early-nineteenth-century Hispanic women is examined in Janet Lecompte, "The Independent Women of Hispanic New Mexico, 1821–1846," *Western Historical Quarterly*, 12 (January 1981), 17–35; David J. Weber, *The Mexican Frontier, 1821–1846: The American Southwest Under Mexico* (Albuquerque, N.M., 1982); Deena J. González, *Refusing the Favor: The Spanish-Mexican Women of Santa Fe, 1820–1880* (New York, 1999); and Albert L. Hurtado, *Intimate Frontiers: Sex, Gender, and Culture in Old California* (Albuquerque, N.M.,

1999). See also Rosaura Sanchez, *Telling Identities: The California Testimonios* (Minneapolis, Minn., 1995), ch 5.

Studies of Native American Women in the early nineteenth century include Mary C. Wright, "Economic Development and Native American Women in the Early Nineteenth Century," *American Quarterly* 33 (Winter 1981), 525–536, and Joan M. Jensen, "Native American Women and Agriculture: A Seneca Case Study," *Sex Roles* 3 (October 1977), 423–441. For Cherokee women, see Theda Perdue, "Southern Indians and the Cult of True Womanhood," in Walter Frasier, Jr., R. Frank Saunders, and Jon L. Wakelyn, eds., *The Web of Southern Social Relations; Women, Family, and Education* (Athens, Ga., 1985); Perdue, "Cherokee Women and the Trail of Tears," *Journal of Women's History* (1989), 14–30; Theda Perdue and Michael D. Green, eds., *The Cherokee Removal: A Brief History With Documents* (Boston, 1995); and Perdue, *Cherokee Women: Gender and Culture Change, 1700–1835* (Lincoln, Neb., 1998), part 3. The sources used for this chapter include Victoria D. Patterson, "Evolving Gender Roles in Pomo Society," in Laura F. Klein and Lillian A. Ackerman, eds., *Women and Power in Native North America* (Norman, Ok., 1995), pp. 126–145; Daniel Maltz and JoAllyn Archambault, "Gender and Power in Native North America," in Klein and Ackerman, eds., *Women and Power*, pp. 230–250; Lucy Eldersveld Murphy, "Autonomy and the Economic Roles of Indian Women of the Fox-Wisconsin Riverway Region, 1763–1832," in Nancy Shoemaker, ed., *Negotiators of Change: Historical Perspectives on Native American Women* (New York, 1995), pp. 72–89; Clara Sue Kidwell, "Choctaw Women and Cultural Persistance in Mississippi" in Shoemaker, ed., *Negotiators of Change*, pp. 115–134; and Kidwell, *Choctaws and Missionaries in Mississippi, 1818–1918* (Norman, Ok., 1995). For Native American concepts of gender, see Ramona Ford, "Native American Women: Changing Statuses, Changing Interpretations," in Jameson and Armitage, eds., *Writing the Range*, pp. 42–68. An influential interpretation of westward expansion is Patricia Nelson Limerick, *The Legacy of Conquest: The Unbroken Path of the American West* (New York, 1987).

For diverse views of the nature, roots, and impact of southern patriarchy, see Elizabeth Fox-Genovese, *Within the Plantation Household: Black and White Women of the Old South* (Chapel Hill, N.C., 1988) and Catherine Clinton, *The Plantation Mistress* (New York, 1982). An older account of antebellum white southern women is Ann Firor Scott, *The Southern Lady: From Pedestal to Politics, 1830–1930* (Chicago, 1970). Recent scholarship includes Suzanne Lebsock, *The Free Women of Petersburg: Status and Culture in a Southern Town, 1784–1860* (New York, 1985); Jean E. Friedman, *The Enclosed Garden: Women and Community in the Evangelical South, 1830–1900* (Chapel Hill, N.C., 1985); Jane Turner Censer, *North Carolina Planters and their Children, 1800–1860* (Baton Rouge, La., 1984); Sally G. McMillen, *Motherhood in the Old South: Pregnancy, Childbirth, and Infant Rearing* (Baton Rouge, La., 1990); Victoria E. Bynum, *Unruly Women: The Politics of Social and Sexual Control in the Old South* (Chapel Hill, N.C., 1992); Christie Anne Farnham, *The Education of the Southern Belle: Higher Education and Student Socialization in the Antebellum South* (New York, 1994); Stephanie McCurry, *Masters of Small Worlds: Yeoman Households, Gender Relations, and the Political Culture of the Antebellum South Carolina Low Country* (New York, 1995); Margaret Ripley Wolfe, *Daughters of Canaan: A Saga of Southern Women* (Lexington, Ky., 1995); Brenda Stevenson, *Life in Black and White: Family and Community in the Slave South* (New York, 1996), section 1; Martha Hodes, *White Women, Black Men: Illicit Sex in the Nineteenth Century South* (New Haven, Conn., 1997); and Jane H. Pease and William H. Pease, *A Family of Women: The Carolina Petigrus in Peace and War*

(Chapel Hill, N.C., 1999). Peter Bardaglio, *Reconstructing the Household: Families, Sex, and the Law in the Nineteenth-Century South* (Chapel Hill, N.C., 1995) suggests how slavery and then emancipation shaped family relations. Elizabeth R. Varon, *We Mean To Be Counted: White Women in Politics in Antebellum Virginia* (Chapel Hill, N.C., 1998) explores women's activism in public life. For women's impact on small-town life, see Lisa C. Tolbert, *Constructing Town-scapes: Space and Society in Antebellum Tennessee* (Chapel Hill, N.C., 1999), ch. 4.

Useful articles on white southern women appear in Carol Bleser, ed., *In Joy and in Sorrow: Women, Family, and Marriage in the Victorian South* (New York, 1991); Christie Anne Farnham, ed., *Women of the American South: A Multicultural Reader* (New York, 1997); Janet L. Coryell, et al., eds., *Beyond Image and Convention: Explorations in Southern Women's History* (Columbia, Mo., 1998); and Fraser, Saunders, and Wakelyn, eds., *The Web of Southern Social Relations*, cited previously. For primary sources, see Michael O'Brien, ed., *An Evening When Alone: Four Jour-nals of Single Women in the South, 1827–1867* (Charlottesville, Va., 1993); Joan E. Cashin, ed., *Our Common Affairs: Texts from Women in the Old South* (Baltimore, Md., 1996); and Carol Bleser, ed., *Tokens of a Planter's Daughter in the Old South* (Athens, Ga., 1996). For primary sources on microfilm, see "Southern Women and their Families in the Nineteenth-Century: Papers and Diaries" (University Publications of America). A northern counterpart is "New England Women and their Families in the Eighteenth and Nineteenth-Centuries: Personal Papers, Letters, and Diaries" (University Publications of America).

For explorations of southern character and society, see William R. Taylor, *Cavalier and Yankee: The Old South and American National Character* (New York and Evanston, Ill., 1957); Bertram Wyatt-Brown, *Southern Honor: Ethics and Behavior in the Old South* (New York, 1983); and Steven M. Stowe, *Intimacy and Power in the Old South: Rituals in the Lives of the Planters* (Baltimore, Md., 1987). A recent edition of Mary Chesnut's diary, a revised account of her wartime experience, composed in the 1880s, is C. Vann Woodward, ed., *Mary Chesnut's Civil War* (New Haven, Conn., 1981). For the original Civil War diary, see C. Vann Woodward and Elizabeth Muhlenfeld, *The Private Mary Chesnut: The Unpublished Civil War Diaries* (New Haven, Conn., 1984).

For quizzes and additional resources related to American women's history, visit the book's Website at *www.mhhe.com/americanwomen*.

CHAPTER FOUR

Benevolence, Reform, and Slavery, 1800–1860

W HILE POPULAR CULTURE promoted woman's sphere, American women became involved in enterprises beyond the home. In the early nineteenth century, middle-class women in towns and cities formed female societies devoted to charitable and humanitarian ends. Through voluntary associations, women created social and civic networks, developed experience in organization and tactics, and made a distinctive contribution to benevolence and reform. The "female society" provided a stepping-stone from domestic life to public life.

The voluntary associations that women joined between 1800 and 1860 were initially formed to pursue religious goals, with clerical approval. Missionary, charitable, and tract societies, which multiplied in the early 1800s, enabled middle-class women of pious bent to assist and uplift the deprived and depraved. But the habit of association had militant potential. By the 1830s, northern women formed associations not only for benevolent goals but also for broader ones—peace, temperance, abolition, and moral reform. They worked not merely to ameliorate social ills but to eliminate them. Far fewer women were involved in reform than the untold numbers committed to benevolent works. But their activism raised new questions about women's role in public life. By midcentury, the stage had been set for the start of a women's rights movement and a frontal attack on the limitations of sphere.

The tradition of female association reached all regions, though with sectional variations. It began in the urbanizing Northeast and made its way west, but played a more muted role in the South. In the North, a number of circumstances combined to facilitate it. In the early nineteenth century, an era of evangelical fervor, women were prominent, at least by numbers, in Protestant congregations. Ministers depended on their fund raising, support, and good works. Also, the expansion of towns and cities made growing numbers of middle-class women accessible to one another and provided a field for their activism. The poor and impious in urban areas, it seemed, could only profit from women's help and control. As in the churches, these women were filling a social vacuum, not invading a territory occupied by men. After 1830, once the tradition of female association was well established, an outburst of reform opened new options and broadened the arena of women's involvement.

A final contributing factor, throughout the early nineteenth century, was an expanding middle class. Although excluded from business and politics, middle-class women held a positive sense of their roles and responsibilities as women. Benevolence and reform were not merely the most appealing routes to public life for such women but the only ones. Within the female association, they extended the skills they already had, in household management, care for the young, concern for the afflicted. They capitalized on their obligations as bastions of piety and guardians of morals. They also created new roles, parallel or complementary to those of the men in their families—the minister, lawyer, tradesman, and entrepreneur. Excluded from official channels of authority, middle-class women created their own. In so doing, they carved out a public space midway between the realms of domesticity and politics.

ORIGINS OF ASSOCIATION

The founding of female societies for pious purposes in the first three decades of the nineteenth century lay the groundwork for entry into public life. Bible and tract societies, missionary societies, charitable societies, maternal societies, and Sunday school associations—all arose in the wake of religious revivals. The emotional upheavals of the Second Great Awakening and the fervor generated by leading evangelists such as Charles G. Finney left converts with a sense of commitment and mission. Because women were bastions of piety in their congregations and a proven success as domestic evangelists (awakening male relatives to the need for salvation), ministers encouraged their formation of associations. The model for such activism had been established by Englishwomen in the evangelical sects, which lent it a certain legitimacy. Moreover, female societies would extend the Protestant empire and keep the funds flowing. Following the trail of revivals, women's benevolence peppered the East, moved westward with migrants, and spread as far as the territories.

Whatever their titles, early female associations delved into the same type of activities: fund raising, charity, uplift. At one of the first, the Boston Female Society for Missionary Purposes, formed in 1800, members congregated at regular meetings to sew and knit goods for sale. They dispensed the proceeds for a multitude of causes: to prepare young men for the ministry by supporting their education, to fund missionaries to the heathen in the West, and to assist the locally indigent with clothes, food, spiritual inspiration, and donations to their churches. Society members engaged in the vital tactic of "visiting" the poor with such assistance and distributed religious publications along with their charitable contributions. "Visiting" was the crucial word in voluntary benevolence. It led out of the home and into the homes of others. As women's associations multiplied, they developed more specialized goals— such as care for orphans, widows, or destitute mothers. They also created a gamut of institutions, such as schools, asylums, refuges, and workshops, to aid and redeem the worthy poor.

Voluntary benevolence was by no means a female monopoly. Women's societies were often absorbed as "auxiliaries" into large, male-dominated, national, nonsectarian federations—such as the American Bible Society, Tract Society, Home Missionary Society, or Sunday-School Union. On other occasions, female societies spawned auxiliaries and statewide unions of their own. And sometimes they just sprang up independently, as was the case with maternal societies—the most informal of voluntary associations. Members of maternal societies met monthly or biweekly to share methods for raising pious offspring. As the only prerequisites for membership were piety and motherhood, rather than time, funds, or local clout, maternal societies involved a broad social range of women, especially from rural and small-town constituencies. They emerged wherever a few women congregated—in the countryside, in cities, even on the frontier. Their evangelical goals and stress on activism in the home were well within the confines of woman's sphere.

But women's voluntary associations assumed an especially activist role in urban life, primarily in the expanding commercial towns of the Northeast and Midwest and in the older seaports. Growing cities posed challenges because poverty and vice were more proximate. Here women made their most aggressive attempts to assist the indigent, reform the deviant, combat impiety, and provide employment for poor women. Such efforts created a new frontier of social welfare, at first through "visiting" and then through institutions, supported by subscription. Sunday schools, for instance, were formed to impart spiritual values to children of the poor. By the 1820s, hundreds of such schools had been started, enrolling almost 50,000 children and staffed and managed by benevolent women. Female associations also ran charity schools, infant schools, orphan asylums, and a gamut of homes, shelters, and refuges for women in need. Such efforts appeared in southern cities, too, notably those of Virginia, which boasted more urban space than any other southern state and a more diversified economy. In 1812, 46 Petersburg, Virginia, women signed a petition to start a female orphan asylum that would protect the most vulnerable of poor people, parentless girls, "forlorn and helpless," from economic need and sexual hazards. Richmond's Union Benevolent Society, founded by charitable women in 1836, sent "visitors" to aid "worthy females" in poor families around the city and strove "to devise means for the improvement of their situation."

Often the tactic of visiting spawned new goals and institutions. This was the case with one of the earliest charitable associations in New York, formed by 15 women in 1797. Its founder and director, Isabella Graham, a devout Presbyterian widow, and her board of managers provided food and help for worthy widows with families. By 1816, the Society for the Relief of Poor Widows with Small Children supported 202 widows and 500 children. Each manager was responsible for a district, as well as for making sure that the poor widows in her charge did not beg, sell liquor, own property, behave immorally, or have living husbands. The goals of the managers soon expanded. Raising funds by subscription and by lottery, the society turned its attention to the poor widows' children, to prevent them from "growing up in habits of idleness and its native consequence, vice." The society eventually supported three Sunday schools in poor districts, two Sunday schools for adults, and a charity school for poor widows' children. It also ran a tailor shop and a spinning shop, where poor widows made flax. Isabella Graham's daughter, Joanna Bethune, who married a rich merchant and served as a society officer, carried these goals farther and became a dynamo of benevolence. She founded an Orphan Asylum Society, a Female Sabbath School Union, an Infant School Society, and a Society for the Promotion of Industry, which employed 500 women.

As the efforts of Graham and Bethune suggest, female benevolence meant not merely charity but also the start of institutions with distinctly economic goals—to provide both jobs and relief for working women unable to subsist. The Boston Seaman's Aid Society, directed by Sarah Hale, was one example. It began by providing work for women bereft of male support and ended up with a small nonprofit business, a vocational training program, a school, and a residence. Significantly, the Seaman's Aid Society originally had a religious affiliation, but quickly became a secular venture. Another secular model was the Providence Employment Society, which began in the 1830s. Here well-to-do women from prominent families tried to correct the ills of an economic system that victimized poor seamstresses. The society, run by a board of directors and supported by subscription, was in effect a small garment business and model employer. It paid good wages that kept up with inflation. Board members developed a rationale for extending their managerial roles from home to civic work: As women, they understood "what female work is and what female suffering means."

Like the Providence Employment Society and the Seaman's Aid Society, women's benevolent associations usually adopted a corporate structure. They drew up constitutions, elected officers, held formal meetings, and wrote minutes, reports, and tracts. The main business at hand was to solicit, manage, and dispense funds. An unmarried woman might best serve as treasurer, so that no husband could control the money. The association provided a variety of other positions as well—director, board member, manager, corresponding secretary, or the all-important "visitor." Enterprising women often had overlapping memberships, just as the voluntary societies of a locale developed overlapping constituencies. The board of directors who ran such associations were often no strangers to the business world. They came from families of means and were related to men who were active in banking, manufacturing, and commerce.

Whether women managed institutions, taught in Sunday schools, solicited funds from local housewives, or visited in the poorer parts of town, the voluntary association provided an outlet for their skills, a community of peers, and a foothold outside the home. It also provided an avenue for extending female values into the community. Through association, women transformed moral superiority into a social calling. They legitimized the tactics used to achieve benevolent goals—fund raising, tract distributing, and "visiting." Most important, they made the female society acceptable. The tradition of association provided a conduit through which more volatile currents would later flow.

There was of course an ambivalent thrust to voluntary benevolence. The progress it achieved was unconscious and insidious, just as "visiting" was covertly aggressive. Often pious and devout, the thousands of women involved in such societies sought to fulfill a mission rather than to tamper with the boundaries of woman's sphere. Benevolent associations united such women in common cause but never challenged the roles they were assigned by custom, convention, and clergymen. They opened avenues to social activism but were also a means of class identification. Leadership roles in voluntary benevolence were confined to the "haves," who were able to help those with little or nothing.

More liberal, critical spirits, such as Harriet Martineau, Lucy Stone, and Sarah Grimke, decried the defects of benevolent efforts. They cited the inanity of raising funds for male divinity students when women had no access to higher education, or of distributing tracts and Bibles instead of campaigning against slavery. "Men like to see women pick up the drunken and falling," Susan B. Anthony once observed. "That *patching business* is 'woman's proper sphere.'" Lydia Maria Child, however, argued that the evangelical sects, and the female societies they spawned, transformed their participants. They had "urged upon women their prodigious influence and consequent responsibility," said Child in 1841. "They have changed the household utensil into a living energetic being." After 1830, some of the energy unleashed by benevolence was harnessed to humanitarian reform as well.

There were two main links. First, voluntary benevolence promoted the visiting not only of homes but of public institutions—first almshouses, and then asylums, hospitals, jails. By the 1830s, for instance, women were regular presences at prisons where they sought to "commiserate and alleviate the condition of the inmates," as a New York minister proclaimed. Prison reform soon became a female cause. Access to the incarcerated also inspired new callings. When Dorothea Dix discovered her vocation in 1841 she was teaching a Sunday school class for women at the East Cambridge jail. Here she found the insane mixed in with vagrants and prostitutes. For the next two decades, Dix investigated public institutions and deluged state legislatures with "memorials" appealing for funds to expand the care for the insane. Her mission as a reformer rested on the groundwork laid by voluntary benevolence.

Second, voluntary benevolence capitalized on the gender consciousness associated with woman's sphere. It evoked empathy for female victims—the widowed, the abandoned, the "friendless female" destined for prostitution. It spurred disdain for their oppressors—the deserting spouse, the underpaying employer—and for all social evils attributable to men. War, drink, licentiousness, all left in their wake a trail of miserable women—the soldier's widow, the drunkard's wife, the victim of seduction. By the 1830s, when associations were formed to obliterate specific evils, women became involved in female societies for peace, temperance, and antislavery, which were run under the aegis of men's organizations. They also joined societies for moral reform, which were not.

MORAL REFORM

Moral reform, a women's crusade, erupted in the 1830s and early 1840s, with a cast of thousands. Moral reformers intended not only to abate social ills through charitable works but also to make changes in thought and behavior, primarily those of men. The movement was both a benevolent, fund-raising one and a militant pressure group. Within its ranks, urban and rural women united to extend their moral superiority beyond the home with vigor and aggression.

Their platform was to erase the double standard of sexual morality and impose a single standard of moral purity on all Americans, male and female. This involved a gamut of subsidiary planks. Within the home, children were to be given a pious upbringing and moral education. Outside it, moral reformers harbored ambitious goals. They wanted to end prostitution and to punish and ostracize seducers, adulterers, and lechers. They also intended to reform fallen women, to give them support, employment, and moral uplift, and to prevent the downfall of others. Running throughout the moral reformers' aims was a perfectionist streak: to obliterate licentiousness from the minds of men and to drive vice from the face of the earth.

The movement began in New York City in 1834, at a church meeting of middle-class women, following a five-year siege of Finney revivals. It also came on the heels of the Magdalen Society, a brief and abortive attempt by a young divinity student, John McDowell, to reform New York prostitutes and save young men from corruption. The New York Female Moral Reform Society, with Mrs. Finney as its first president, picked up where McDowell had left off. Indeed, the society hired him as an agent. But the female society altered the tenor of his cause. It was now fallen women who were to be saved.

In the 1830s, moral reform expanded geographically at a rapid rate, spawning auxiliaries and attracting large numbers of women. When the Boston Female Moral Reform Society was formed in 1835, 70 women were involved in its founding, and hundreds more soon joined rural auxiliaries. In 1837, the New York society had 250 auxiliaries and 15,000 members. In western New York, local societies gathered as many as 100 to 200 members each. By 1840, the New York society became a national one, the American Female Moral Reform Society, and claimed 555 auxiliaries. The movement had swept through New York and New England and farther west, absorbing local groups, spurring the formation of others, reaching city, town, and rural backwater. The society now held annual conventions and regional meetings; vice-presidents were posted in strategic cities; correspondents among groups addressed one another as "sister." At least two periodicals expounded the cause. The *Advocate of Moral Reform*, begun in New York in 1835, had 20,000 subscribers within a few years. A Boston-based counterpart, the *Friend of Virtue*, filled a similar function.

Although the moral reform movement began with clerical endorsement and help, as did all evangelical groups, this was no ladies' auxiliary. It was a women's campaign. Significantly, by the late 1830s, moral reform societies hired only women as their agents, bookkeepers, and institutional staff. Moral reform was also a specifically female reaction to urbanization and the perils of migration, as historian Mary P. Ryan contends. The mobility of the early nineteenth century brought in its wake a youthful migrant population—apprentices, clerks, seamstresses, factory girls—who left home, boarded out, and moved beyond the reach of parents and ministers. The weakening grip of traditional authority left no one in control in the moral arena and paved the way for manifold abuses, from seduction to prostitution. The vacuum of moral authority was one that women were ready to fill. The cause attracted a range of activists: the well-off, church-going matron who had long resided in a city or town; the migrant mother who had just moved in and feared for the welfare of her children; the rural correspondent of the *Advocate*, ever on the lookout for abuse. Moral reform offered a way to improve the environment, protect the young, help less fortunate women, and exert authority over men—or, as the *Advocate* put it, in a strident moment, "to control masculine behavior as he dictates hers."

Moral reform was distinguished not only by its widespread appeal but by its innovative tactics. At the outset, the New York society hired male agents to proselytize among fallen women in almshouses and jails. But the members of the executive committee soon took over the "visiting" themselves. In New York, in Boston, and wherever they could, moral reformers presented themselves at brothels, where they sang hymns, offered prayers for the fallen, searched out runaway daughters, and noted—and threatened to reveal—the identity of patrons. Moral reformers also assaulted their state legislatures, in Boston and Albany. They petitioned and lobbied for laws that would make seduction a crime; such laws were passed in Massachusetts in 1846 and in New York in 1848. A third battle front was institutional. At first, activists tried to reform prostitutes through prayers, conversion, moral education, and location of alternative employment. Then they founded homes and refuges to redeem the fallen and protect the helpless. The New Yorkers opened a House of Reception, a prostitute's refuge. The ambitious Bostonians founded a Home for Unprotected Girls, a Refuge for Migrant Women, and an Asylum for the Repentant. Both groups set up employment services to place the reformed in domestic jobs, preferably in rural areas where they would be out of harm's way.

Finally, the executive committees of moral reform societies actively investigated alleged instances of immorality, or sought them out. Visiting took on a new and aggressive dimension. In the expanding industrial town of Utica, a fulcrum of revivals and reform in western New York, "visiting committees" went into less prosperous parts of town, where they solicited data on sexual offenses within the home. The Utica reformers also waged a petition campaign against prostitution and urged the prosecution of seducers. Overall, moral reformers battled the enemy on a number of fronts: in brothels, in state legislatures, and in the courts; in their own homes, in other people's homes, and in "homes" they established themselves (although the last had a meager clientele).

The *Advocate*, meanwhile, discussed the dangers of licentiousness and printed letters from rural correspondents exposing seducers and lechers. When called to task for the assertiveness of their campaign, as well as its impropriety, the editors took the offensive: "Why should we be castigated as Amazons . . . when we wish to unite to take measures for the protection of our own sex?" New York reformers, who increasingly empathized with the prostitutes they assisted, became concerned with the low wages paid to working women, the role of poverty as a cause of prostitution, and the plight of women who were destitute or in prison. "The fallen and the falling . . . are our sisters by way of a common humanity," the *Advocate* proclaimed.

But the newspaper's militant stance was short-lived. By 1845, moral reform was retreating from the more aggressive aspects of its campaign. The *Advocate* urged readers to pursue their domestic goal, moral education of the young, and to contain their vigilance within the home. New York reformers gave up their visits to brothels and joined related causes, such as prison reform. Local societies disbanded and ended their far-flung campaigns. Clearly there were limits to the extension of moral superiority beyond the home. These limits were sometimes suggested by the clergy and sometimes established by the reformers themselves. The Boston society, significantly, promised in 1839 to confine its activism to women. The Utica society splintered in 1845 over the issue of whether it was proper to hold a public discussion of sexual matters in a nearby college town. It was difficult, in short, for moral reformers to combat lechery, seduction, and prostitution without violating their own propriety and respectability.

During its decade of activism, however, moral reform involved a broad range of middle-class women. It also served as a link between voluntary benevolence and more radical causes. The Boston society, for instance, was linked to the maternal society movement, which permeated New England. Many of its leaders also belonged to the Boston Female Antislavery Society, founded in 1832. The New York branch drew heavy support from the Tappan brothers, who also financed the early abolitionist campaign. Future women's rights advocates, too, joined moral reform societies. Susan B. Anthony belonged to a society in New York, and Lucretia Mott was an officer of one in Philadelphia. Finally, the moral reformers' demand for a single standard of sexual morality would remain a major plank in women's campaigns for the rest of the century.

But the feminist thrust of moral reform, like the life span of the movement, was limited. This became clear in 1838 when the *Advocate* published a piece by abolitionist Sarah Grimke, the most controversial woman in public life since reformer Frances Wright, who, a decade earlier, had scandalized New York audiences with her public lectures. Like Wright, Sarah Grimke had violated propriety by speaking to "promiscuous" audiences of men and women, and like Wright, she had invoked clerical ire. Her remarks to the moral reformers were much, or too much, to the point. "Men have endeavored to entice, or to drive, women from every sphere of moral action," she declared. Deploring clerical domination, Grimke exhorted *Advocate* readers to "rise from the degradation and bondage to which we have been consigned by men." But moral reformers took offense. They were unwilling to defy ministers and unable, in the end, to defy the limits of sphere. Moral reform illustrated both the radical potential of female association and its limitations. It ended up back in the home.

The abolitionist movement, which emerged at the same time as moral reform, had far different consequences. Abolitionism catapulted women into "politics" and evoked bitter disputes over their role in public life—the very type of controversy the moral reformers tried to avoid. But like moral reform, abolition was an outgrowth of evangelical Protestantism. It evolved in the wake of revivals and employed evangelical techniques. Finally, to women caught up in the cause of the slave, abolition was itself a moral reform and therefore especially appropriate as an arena for female activism.

WOMEN IN SLAVERY

From the 1820s onward, slavery hardened as an institution. The expansion of cotton into the new, fertile lands of the Southwest, the rising value of slaves, the growing fear of rebellion and outside interference, and a universal tightening of the slave codes made slavery at once more permanent and more oppressive. The need for labor in new states—Alabama, Mississippi, Louisiana, and later Texas—increased the likelihood of sale and separation. Sometimes whole plantations were moved to the Southwest. But young adults, in most instances, were more likely to be sold to meet labor demands. Antislavery sentiment began to gain ground, in short, just as slavery became more profitable and entrenched. In all states, emancipation became more difficult, if not impossible. Slave codes, now strictly enforced, prohibited gatherings and curtailed the most minimal of liberties.

Slave women, like slave men, worked mainly in the fields, under the gang system or the task system, usually in all-female groups. They engaged in all types of agricultural work—the sowing, picking, and packing of cotton; the hoeing and milling of corn; even lumbering and construction work. Northern schoolteacher Emily Burke, who taught in Georgia in the 1830s and 1840s and described life on a large plantation near Savannah, observed slave women involved in every facet of labor, from fence building to plowing. "When I beheld such scenes, I felt culpable in living in ease and enjoying the luxuries of life," said Burke, "while so many of my own sex were to drag out such miserable existences merely to procure those luxuries enjoyed by their masters." Middle age brought no relief. Women who performed the most strenuous physical tasks, such as plowing, were probably past their child-bearing years. Untrained in the more skilled and valued crafts (blacksmiths, carpenters, masons),

Under slavery, women typically worked for their owners as field labor. Pictured are slaves picking cotton. (*Schoumburg Center for Research in Black Culture, New York Public Library*)

women might escape field work if assigned to work in the house as cooks, nurses, seamstresses, or maids. But the division between house and field was clear-cut only on the larger plantations; probably no more than 5 percent of slaves attained the status of "house servant", and house service, which involved frequent contact with whites, entailed its own potential for abuse. Women slaves were also hired out. By 1860, about 5,000 worked in cotton and woolen mills, sugar refineries, tobacco plants, and other industries.

Whatever their work, women slaves were valued less as laborers than men; their prices were uniformly lower. But if able to produce more slaves, their value rose. Because slave children, as a Georgia overseer observed, might be considered "part of the crop," the woman who already had one or two children and was assumed to be capable of having more was a profitable investment. Having children was also an advantage to the slave, as it helped to secure her family unit, perhaps even preventing the breakup of her marriage by sale. Slave codes always provided that children of slaves belonged to the mother's master. Although a few states enacted laws to prevent the sale of young children apart from their mothers, such laws were not uniformly or widely enforced. Former slaves who recounted their life stories viewed the separation of mothers and children as a major crime of slavery. "The domestic hearth, with its holy lessons and precious endearments is abolished in the case of a slave mother and her children," wrote Frederick Douglass. Abolitionist women saw the slave as deprived of the right of maternal love. If not thwarted by separation, such love could be used as a weapon against the mother. "You can do anything with a woman when you've got her children," said Cassy, a slave in *Uncle Tom's Cabin* who was driven to immorality and self-mutilation.

Black fertility was high and did not begin to fall until the 1880s. Typically, slave women began having children in their late teens (as did Southern white women). A slave woman was customarily released from field work for a month before and after delivery and was usually allowed to leave the field a few times a day to nurse her infant, who might be left in the care of another child or an aged slave. She also prolonged nursing as long as possible, even for several years. The combination of childbearing and forced labor probably resulted in a high miscarriage and stillbirth rate and in other health problems. The English actress and abolitionist Fanny Kemble, when stranded on her husband's Georgia plantation in the 1830s, investigated the conditions of her women slaves with persistent questions and recorded her findings. "*Sally*, Scipio's wife, has had two miscarriages and three children born, one of whom is dead. She came complaining of incessant pain and weakness in her back," Kemble wrote. "*Charlotte*, Renty's wife, had had two miscarriages, and was with child again. She was almost crippled by rheumatism." Kemble was impressed by the high birth and infant mortality rates, and the serious ailments endured by slave women. Hardly one of these women, wrote Kemble, "might not have been a candidate for a bed in a hospital, and they had come to me after working all day in the field."

Although Kemble recorded attempts to escape, women were less likely than men to become fugitives. Still, there were exceptions. A $40,000 reward was offered for Harriet Tubman, who had escaped from Maryland as a young woman (her husband refused to accompany her) and became the most famous conductor on the underground railroad. She was said to have returned to the South 19 times to lead more than 300 slaves to freedom. If not often fugitives, slave women participated in all forms of resistance. They were as likely as men to join in the sick-outs, slowdowns, theft, and sabotage that were routine forms of protest, as well as in its most dire form, arson. Above all, they strove to preserve the slave family as refuge from the dehumanizing aspects of slavery.

The nature of the slave family has recently been a subject of contention. According to some studies of slavery, notably that of Herbert G. Gutman, the two-parent family was the ideal and the strength of family ties pervasive, as suggested by the tremendous efforts of family members to reunite after emancipation. Even under slavery, separated couples made valiant efforts to keep in touch; escapes were often motivated by a desire to reunite with wives, husbands, or children. Slave marriages were universally respected in the slave community unless a couple was separated, either voluntarily, by "divorce," or involuntarily by sale. Still, under slavery marriage was extralegal and at the owner's discretion. For instance, the success of a "broad" or "abroad" marriage—a union between slaves on different plantations—depended on the cooperation of owners, who often gave it only reluctantly; interplantation visits promoted freedom of movement, desired by slaves but not by masters. Marriage, moreover, might be formal, casual, or nonexistent. Owners usually found it useful— to improve morale, discourage escape, and prevent what appeared to be promiscuity and depravity.

Within marriage, Gutman contends, slave women attempted to assume a supportive role in their relations toward their husbands. If the condition of slavery minimized gender distinctions, slaves tried to restore them in their private lives. Similarly, women also assumed dual work roles, both as plantation workers and as cooks, housekeepers, and caretakers within their own families. Private domestic work represented freedom to slaves, compared to work that was done for their owners. The desire to assume traditional roles within marriage and family would emerge again after emancipation. But again, under slavery, marriage and family life were always precarious. In records of the Union army and the Freedmen's Bureau, former slaves reported that a third of prior marriages had been broken up by "force," that is, by masters. Among Virginia slaves in the late antebellum era, a network of oppressive factors—forced outmigration, involuntary separation, and harsh treatment—took a heavy toll on family life. In all circumstances, family relationships were vulnerable, because they might be abruptly terminated by the death of an owner, the liquidation of an estate, the claims of creditors, or the hiring out or sale of a spouse.

Slaves both accommodated to and resisted the impact of slavery on family life. Not solely dependent on nuclear families, they usually relied on larger kinship networks that included spouses, parents, children, sibling, uncles, aunts, cousins, even distant relatives. According to historian Brenda Stevenson, who examines family life in Loudon County, Virginia, compelling evidence reveals "that many slaves did not have a nuclear structure or 'core' in their families." Slave communities, Stevenson shows, embraced diverse forms of family organization besides monogamous marriage and two-parent families. These included matrifocality, polygamy, single-parent families, abroad spouses, multigenerational households, single-sex and mixed-gender sibling dwellings, and fictive kin. Moreover, in contrast to Gutman, Stevenson finds little evidence to suggest that "a nuclear family structure was the slave's sociocultural ideal." The most discernable ideal of kinship organization, she contends, was "the malleable extended family that, when possible, provided its members with nurture, education, socialization, material support, and recreation in the face of the potential social chaos that the master imposed."

Members of slave families used various tactics to define and maintain the family as an institution, Gutman contends. They managed to perpetuate African customs, such as not marrying their first cousins, a prohibition not observed by their owners. They also used naming practices to preserve kinship ties. Although planters traced slave lineage through mothers and rarely recorded fathers' names in slave registers, slaves strove to perpetuate family ties by naming sons after fathers, though not daughters after mothers. Children of both sexes were often named after other relatives, including deceased siblings (a practice that had faded in white society). Through family networks, kinship customs, naming practices, and sometimes, long-term unions, slaves preserved the family as the primary institution of the slave community.

But undoubtedly the most important efforts at family preservation, research reveals, were those made by women. Because influential studies of slavery underrate the crucial role that women played in family life, historians such as Brenda Stevenson and Deborah Grey White offer correctives. Slave families, they contend, were matrifocal: in their roles as mothers, women were the focus of familial relationships and more central than fathers to the family's continuity and survival. Moreover, White points out, women in slave society "identified and cooperated more with other slave women than with slave men." Citing a number of factors, such as the independence women derived from the absence of property considerations in conjugal relationships, the "abroad" marriage, the ability of female slaves to supplement the diet of family members, the work done by women in groups, the supremacy of the mother–child bond, and the high degree of female cooperation and interdependence, White underlines the distinctive role that women assumed in slave communities: "Slave women did not play the traditional female role as it was defined in nineteenth-century America." Nor did slave families fit into the patterns established by white society.

Some owners ignored the distinctive patterns of slave family life. Others tried to regulate all aspects of slave life, including the realm of moral behavior. Within the slave community, however, a standard of sexual morality different from that of white society prevailed. Extensive sexual freedom was permitted and accepted before marriage. The purity of women, in white terms, was not a major concern. Nor was premarital pregnancy or childbirth seen as irreconcilable with eventual monogamous marriage. No stigma was attached to the "outside child" born before or even outside of marriage. But slaves often regarded adultery, especially female adultery, as a violation of their social code. At the same time, the slave community had a more lenient attitude toward marital breakups. There were no economic reasons under slavery to continue a union that had failed. As a result, "divorce," a rarity in white society, might be commonplace in slave society. When abolitionist editor James Redpath interviewed slaves in the 1850s, he asked one woman why she had left her husband for another man, and she replied, "I didn't like him and I neber did." From a white viewpoint, the customs and morals of the slave community were a world apart.

Women abolitionists, however, cared primarily about one aspect of sexual morality: the exploitation of slave women by white men. Historians suggest that white male sexual license did not exist on the plantation to the extent that it did in antislavery literature. The degree to which white men sexually exploited slave women was limited by slave resistance as well as by a current of white disapproval. But whatever the countervailing pressures, coercive sex was still an integral part of slavery, one that affected slave women far more directly than men. As historian Catherine Clinton points out, "Denial of sex to male slaves cannot be equated with the force of sex to which female slaves were subjected." Under slavery, the threat of sexual exploitation remained a major gender distinction. The impact of such exploitation emerged in a book written by Harriet Jacobs, a fugitive who took the pseudonym of Linda Brent. Jacobs' *Incidents in the Life of a Slave Girl* (1861), edited by abolitionist author Lydia Maria Child, was a saga of brutality and lechery covering, in the author's words, "twenty-one years in that cage of obscene birds." The incidents centered around Jacobs' exploitation by her master, who began to pursue her when she was 15. "The slave girl is reared in an atmosphere of licentiousness and fear," Jacobs explained. "The lash and foul tongue of the master and his sons are her teachers."

> He told me I was his property: that I must be subject to his will in all things. My soul revolted against the mean tyranny. But where could I turn for protection? . . . The mistress, who ought to protect the helpless victim, has no other feelings towards her but jealousy and rage. The degradation, the wrongs, the vices, that grow out of slavery, are more than I can describe. . . .
>
> O virtuous reader, you never knew what it is to be a slave; to be entirely unprotected by law or custom; to have the laws reduce you to the condition of a chattel, entirely subject to the will of another.

Using the language of moral reform, Harriet Jacobs analyzed the evil of slavery as an agent of perversion: "It makes the white fathers cruel and sensual; the sons violent and licentious; it contaminates the daughters, and makes the white women wretched. And as for the colored race, it needs an abler pen than mine to describe the extremity of their sufferings, the depths of their degradation."

To women in the abolitionist movement, such sentiments struck resonant chords. According to their arguments, all slaves were deprived of basic human rights, but women slaves were additionally deprived of the inviolable rights of women. Under slavery, women lacked legal marriage, male protection, and maternal rights and were subject to every type of degradation. "The Negro woman is unprotected by either law or public opinion," wrote Lydia Maria Child in her pioneer antislavery tract of 1833. "She is the property of her master, and her daughters are his property. They are allowed to have no conscientious scruples, no sense of shame, no regard for the feelings of husband, or parent; they must be entirely subservient to the will of their owner, on pain of being beaten as near to death . . . or quite to death, if it suits his pleasure."

Just as southern women objected to the sexual availability of the woman slave, so antislavery women objected to her vulnerability, her powerlessness against male owners. "We should be less than women," asserted members of an Ohio Female

Antislavery Society in a petition to Congress, "if the nameless and unnumbered wrongs of which the slaves of our sex are made the defenceless victims, did not fill us with horror." To abolitionist women, slavery gave licentious men total power to ruin "the sanctity and glory of woman." In addition, as Sarah Grimke pointed out, male power under slavery ruined white women as well as black. The southern white woman, she contended, who "looks upon the crime of seduction and illicit intercourse without horror . . . loses that value for innocence in her own [sex] which is one of the strongest safeguards to virtue."

By voicing such arguments, women in the antislavery movement used gender to justify their antislavery commitment. Their inherent responsibility as women, they insisted, was to rescue women in bondage. "They are our sisters," Angelina Grimke told a women's antislavery convention in 1837, "and to us as women we have a right to look with sympathy for their sorrows, and effort and prayer for their rescue." Again, as women, antislavery activists contended, they had special reason for their activism. "Women can do more than men for the extension of righteousness," exhorted antislavery agent Abby Kelley, "because they have not, from the customs of society, been so much perverted, and hence their moral perception is much clearer." Appealing to the women of Massachusetts, the Boston Female Antislavery Society made the same point. "As *wives* and *mothers*, as *daughters* and *sisters*, we are deeply responsible for the influence we have on the human race," the society declared. "We are bound to urge men to cease to do evil and learn to do good."

Sympathetic toward the woman slave or empathetic toward a subject race, hundreds of northern women supported the antislavery cause. Although the abolitionist movement was dominated by men, the influence that women exerted surpassed their expectations.

ABOLITION AND THE WOMAN QUESTION

As soon as the antislavery crusade began in 1831, when William Lloyd Garrison first published the *Liberator* and founded the New England Antislavery Society, women joined the fold. Female antislavery societies began to form throughout New England in 1832. By 1838, more than 100 such societies had been created. Their spread followed a route familiar to revivals—all over New England, into the major eastern cities, through the towns of western New York, and out to the Midwest, where Ohio became a hotbed of antislavery agitation. Female societies fell at once into the traditional pattern of auxiliaries and devoted their efforts, at first, to fund raising.

But women abolitionists soon engaged in new and more controversial tactics. They spearheaded a militant petition campaign, organized national conventions, and, as antislavery agents, spoke on public platforms, which meant addressing "mixed" or "promiscuous" audiences. Such activism evoked a formidable controversy over woman's proper place, a dispute in which the cause of women and slaves became intertwined. As women defended their roles as abolitionists, they mobilized the conventional rhetoric of benevolence to attack restrictions based on sex. In 1837, a national women's antislavery convention resolved: "The time has come for woman to move in that sphere which providence has assigned her, and no longer remain satisfied in the circumscribed limits which corrupt custom and a perverted application of Scripture have encircled her."

From the outset, this radical cause brought its supporters into the spotlight of public attention and removed the cloak of respectable anonymity that covered women's benevolence. Abolition, to be sure, drew on a narrower constituency. Members of female antislavery societies often came out of reform-minded environments and from families where husbands or fathers were abolitionists as well. Many activists had already liberated themselves from the rigors of orthodox Calvinism and adopted more liberal creeds. Moreover, a significant proportion of abolitionist women were Quakers, with their own long tradition of egalitarianism and a proclivity for relying on conscience, whatever the consequences. Even Quaker meetings, however, castigated women who adopted the cause. Many left their meetings, if only temporarily, to follow "the divine summons" of abolition, as it was described by a Rhode Island Quaker, Elizabeth Buffum Chace. Becoming an abolitionist meant risking social ostracism, loss of reputation, and outright persecution. The rewards were a sense of personal regeneration, the support of new peers in the movement, and an ennobling sense of commitment. According to Chace, "The antislavery spirit grew and prospered in proportion to the difficulties in the way."

The difficulties became clear in 1833 in the cases of Lydia Maria Child and Prudence Crandall. When Child, a successful author, published an *Appeal in Favor of That Class of Americans Called Africans*, which denounced slavery and defended racial equality, she met ostracism, ridicule, and loss of income. Her book sales plummeted. The same year, a young Quaker schoolteacher in Canterbury, Connecticut, admitted a black student into her hitherto successful female academy. After the other students had been withdrawn, Prudence Crandall reopened her academy as a school for black girls, a move that aroused the ire of the citizens of Canterbury. Crandall was arrested three times and eventually convicted under a new state law that prohibited the instruction of out-of-state blacks. Finally the townsfolk vandalized her school. She closed it and vanished into the West. Throughout her ordeal, Prudence Crandall received support and funds from the newly organized abolitionists in New York and Boston, who transformed her isolated instance of defiance into a cause célèbre.

The opprobrium experienced by Child and Crandall was familiar to women who founded female antislavery societies, such as Maria Weston Chapman in Boston and Lucretia Mott in Philadelphia. The Boston society was started in 1832 by Chapman and 12 other women, the Philadelphia society in 1833 by Mott and a few Quaker associates. Like other auxiliary groups, they both profited at first from male assistance (the Philadelphia society was presided over by a man, a black dentist). Both embarked on the spectrum of activities familiar to voluntary benevolence. The women raised funds for the *Liberator* and for the American Antislavery Society. They held "antislavery fairs" where homemade articles were sold. They also distributed tracts, heard lectures on the evils of slavery, supported male agents who spoke for the cause, and pursued charitable works among local blacks—"visiting" black areas and opening black schools.

But in the context of abolition, these once acceptable activities were no longer innocuous. When the Boston Female Antislavery Society invited a prominent

English abolitionist, George Thompson, to address it in 1835, the meeting was disrupted by the threats of a hostile mob and adjourned. Moreover, female antislavery societies soon exceeded their scope as local auxiliaries and united their efforts in a massive petition campaign to Congress, demanding an end to slavery. Not only did women succeed at the arduous door-to-door canvass for signatures, but the petition campaign evoked a sense of shared purpose among female societies. In 1837, abolitionist women organized a national network of volunteers to solicit signatures and set up regional offices in major cities. They also began to hold national conventions, formed an Antislavery Society of American Women, and elected a slate of officers that brought the local leadership to prominence.

The unity evoked by petitioning, however, soon gave way to a controversy that divided the abolitionist crusade. In 1836, the American Antislavery Society proposed that women be hired as antislavery agents. The first women agents, Sarah and Angelina Grimke, were the first southern women to become prominent in public life. Daughters of a prominent, slave-owning South Carolina family (their father and brothers were judges, lawyers, legislators), the sisters had been virtual exiles from the South since 1830, when they settled in Philadelphia. Longtime opponents of slavery, they had passed through a sequence of conversions—from Episcopalianism to Presbyterianism to Quakerism. They then became members of the Philadelphia Female Antislavery Society, a commitment that meant discarding their affiliation with the Friends. The barrage of conversions seemed impelled by its own velocity. For the Grimkes, conscience, like Frances Wright's irrepressible egalitarian streak, knew no bounds, and the outcome was much the same.

The Grimkes began to lecture on abolition in New York in 1836, speaking to women's meetings. But their next lecture tour in New England, sponsored by the Boston Female Antislavery Society, drew men as well. As southerners, members of a slave-owning family, and women, the Grimkes were the most exotic and controversial of antislavery agents. Their engagements attracted crowds in the thousands, made new converts, and spawned new societies. Moreover, as their innovative roles evoked opposition, the Grimke sisters became adept in defending not only the slave but also themselves. Public speaking on behalf of abolition placed them, irrevocably, at a crucial juncture at which demands for racial and sexual equality fused.

The reaction to the Grimkes reached a peak in 1837, when their "obtrusive and ostentatious" behavior drew the wrath of the Massachusetts clergy, who denounced them for assuming "the place and tone of man as public reformer." Such activism was unnatural, the ministers contended; by describing the victimization of slave women, the Grimkes lost "that modesty and delicacy . . . which constitutes the true influence of women in society." The clergy urged the agents to return to "the appropriate duties and influence of women." Sarah Grimke responded with her *Letters on the Condition of Women and the Equality of the Sexes*, a scriptural analysis and a militant response to male domination. Grimke drew a parallel between the condition of women and that of slaves. She also demanded for women equal education, pay, and rights—above all the rights of a "moral being." "Men and women are CREATED EQUAL. They are both moral and accountable beings," said Sarah Grimke. "All I ask our brethren is that they take their feet from off our necks and permit us to stand upright on the ground which God destined for us to occupy."

While Sarah Grimke responded to the clergy, Angelina Grimke took on another formidable adversary, Catherine Beecher. Like the ministers, Beecher objected to the Grimkes' invasion of public life, as she explained in an 1837 tract. Woman held "a subordinate relation in society to the other sex," Beecher declared, and should confine her activities to "the domestic and social circle." In her published reply, Angelina Grimke insisted that female influence should be exerted in the same way as male influence. If ministers could address "promiscuous" audiences, so could women. "It is a woman's right to have a voice in all the laws and regulations by which she is to be governed, whether in church or in state," Angelina Grimke told Catharine Beecher.

The Grimkes' stance offended those abolitionists who felt that the spectacle of women lecturing in public could only damage the cause. This conservative view won favor among many clerically oriented women who were active in organizing and petitioning, such as those in New York and about half the Bostonians. The Grimkes' major defense came from Garrison, who announced in the *Liberator* in 1838: "As our object is *universal* emancipation, to redeem women as well as men from a servile to an equal condition—we shall go for the rights of women to their utmost extent." Garrison, like Sarah Grimke, drew an analogy between women and slaves—it was impossible to advocate the rights of one and deny the rights of the other. For those defending "human rights" there was no other choice.

The controversy over women's roles in antislavery soon caused abolitionists to divide into factions. In 1839, the dominant New England branch cracked into opposing camps, aggravated by a women's petition campaign to permit racial intermarriage in Massachusetts. In 1840, the Boston Female Antislavery Society split, and so did the national organization. The Garrisonians nominated antislavery agent Abby Kelley to the business committee of the American Antislavery Society, imported several hundred New England women to attend the annual convention in New York, and won their point, on women's votes. Conservatives withdrew and formed their own antislavery society. Later that year, the "woman question" crossed the Atlantic and disrupted the World Antislavery Convention in London. After 1840, the abolitionist crusade ran on two tracks.

The divided movement of the next two decades had an important impact on women's history. The Garrisonians provided a setting in which women could participate in all facets of reform, a context in which women's rights as reformers were recognized. By the same token, they severed themselves permanently from politics and from all institutional outlets for effecting emancipation. The Grimkes, meanwhile, had retired in 1838 to work with Angelina's new husband, abolitionist Theodore Weld, on his massive compendium of antislavery testimony. Garrison regarded this retreat from the fray as desertion. But the Grimkes' efforts inspired others. Abby Kelley lectured indefatigably throughout the 1840s and recruited new women agents, including Lucy Stone. Many were soon to throw their energies into women's rights. Confronting hostile audiences and angry mobs, on behalf of the slaves, was a radicalizing experience. "We have good cause to be grateful to the slave," said Abby Kelley. "In striving to strike his irons off, we found most surely, that we were manacled ourselves."

The split within abolition did not prevent more traditional women from continuing their work in the cause. Nor did it have much impact in the West, where female societies spread through the 1840s, fanning outward from Ohio to Illinois, Michigan, Minnesota, and Wisconsin. In St. Cloud, Minnesota, outspoken editor Jane Swisshelm, unable to commit herself to either of the factions in abolition, published an antislavery newspaper, the *Visitor*, that gained, she claimed, thousands of votes for the Free Soil party. In Michigan, Laura Haviland, who formed the first antislavery society in the territory in the 1830s, opened a racially integrated academy, worked as an operative on the underground railroad, and engaged in missionary work among blacks. Like many abolitionist women, including Elizabeth Buffum Chace in Rhode Island and Lucretia Mott in Pennsylvania, Haviland became a professional visitor on behalf of the cause. Working with fugitives, canvassing for signatures, soliciting funds, or addressing conventions, women in antislavery gained training in tactics and a spirit that "grew and prospered in proportion to the difficulties in the way."

Black women too were active in the abolitionist movement. Four black women participated in the founding of the Philadelphia Female Antislavery Society, including three members of the prominent Forten family, one of whom served as an officer. Several black women joined the Boston Female Antislavery Society in the early 1830s. But hostility to slavery did not necessarily mean that whites endorsed association with blacks; racial segregation prevailed throughout the North. When the Fall River (Massachusetts) Female Antislavery Society urged black women to join in 1835, opposition among members was so strong that the society almost disbanded. The 1837 convention of antislavery women condemned "those societies that reject colored members," but black women usually formed their own female antislavery societies.

Nor were African Americans, male or female, at first used as antislavery lecturers. But once they were, women took the lecturn. Bostonian Maria Stewart made several antislavery speeches to mixed audiences as early as the 1830s. Former slave Sojourner Truth proved a popular speaker with antislavery audiences, starting in the 1840s, as did Harriet Tubman in the 1850s. By then, other black women abolitionists had lecturing careers. The best known were relatives of prominent black male abolitionists, such as Sarah Remond of Massachusetts, sister of lecturer Henry Remond, and Frances Ellen Harper, niece of another important abolitionist, who spoke on behalf of the Maine Antislavery Society. Sarah M. Douglas, a noted educator, founding member of the Philadelphia Female Antislavery Society, and frequent participant in women's antislavery conventions, established bonds of affection with leading white women abolitionists. "It rejoices my very heart to meet with an Abolitionist who has turned her back on prejudice," she wrote to her friend Abby Kelley in 1838. Black women outside the abolitionist movement also entered public debate. Teacher and journalist Mary Ann Shadd Cary, a member of a free black family from Delaware, spoke on behalf of African Americans who fled to Canada after the Fugitive Slave Act of 1850. Cary urged African American self-sufficiency and, after the Civil War, promoted women's rights.

Abolitionist women described their commitment and careers as quasi-religious experiences. They recounted conversions to the cause that were often preceded by some inspirational event, such as coming upon a coffle of slaves being sold or hearing a Garrisonian address. The most influential conversion was undoubtedly that of Harriet Beecher Stowe, who first developed antislavery sympathies in Ohio in the 1830s. Attuned to the patriotic and providential, she felt "the heroic element was

I Sell the Shadow to Support the Substance.
SOJOURNER TRUTH.

Born a slave in New York's Hudson River valley around 1797,
Isabella Van Wagner changed her name to Sojourner Truth
in 1843 and began an itinerant ministry. She appeared often
at antislavery and women's rights meetings in the 1840s and
1850s. At her public appearances in the 1860s, she sold copies
of her biography, written by abolitionist Olive Gilbert, and
of her photograph, which she called her "shadow."
(Bentley Historical Library, University of Michigan)

strong in me. . . . It made me want to do something, I know not what . . . to make
some declaration on my own account." Her moment of truth did not occur until
1850 when, while taking communion, the vision of Uncle Tom's death scene came to
her. After much research in antislavery literature, she envisioned the rest of the novel
"with a vividness that could not be denied." Later, Stowe explained that she had
written *Uncle Tom's Cabin* as "an instrument of God." Urging a national conversion in

sentiment, Harriet Beecher Stowe became the most successful antislavery "visitor" of all, reaching more than 300,000 homes.

Unlike Sarah and Angelina Grimke, Harriet Beecher Stowe never joined an antislavery society or spoke on any public platform. She was, on the contrary, a model exerter of "influence." The divided abolitionist movement provided an arena in which women could participate on different levels. By far the greatest number of women who opposed slavery filled the role of "domestic evangelist"; they empathized with Uncle Tom, mourned the death of little Eva, and promoted antislavery views among family members. A more activist group of women joined antislavery societies and, in the context of female associations, became propagandists, fund raisers, petitioners, and visitors. Finally, within the small but embattled Garrisonian faction, women became antislavery agents, public speakers, and converts to the doctrines of "human rights." After 1840, division within the abolitionist ranks neither handicapped the movement nor limited women's attachment to the cause.

The Garrisonians did raise new questions about women's rights in public life. They were not the only reformers concerned about women's rights and roles. During the ferment of the 1840s, even before a formal women's rights movement emerged, women's status in society had become a focus of attention.

COMMUNITARIAN ALTERNATIVES
AND LEGAL RIGHTS

"Many women are considering within themselves what they need and what they have not," wrote Margaret Fuller in her transcendental tract, *Woman in the Nineteenth Century* (1845). A celebration of female potential, Fuller's tract catered to women's rising expectations and captured a sense of impending change. Stressing the imperative to remove "every arbitrary barrier that hindered woman's progress," Fuller asserted that "What woman needs is not as a woman to act or rule but . . . as a soul to live free and unimpeded." The means for attaining such a liberated state were varied, including "a much greater range of occupation than they now have, to raise their latent powers." Above all, Fuller recommended psychological independence from male domination. "I would have Woman lay aside all thought, such as she habitually cherishes, of being taught and led by men," she declared. "Men do not look at both sides, and women must leave off asking them, and being influenced by them, but retire within themselves, and explore the groundwork of life, till they find their peculiar secret. Then, when they come forth again, renovated and baptised, they will know how to turn dross into gold."

Margaret Fuller's tract derived from one of the "conversations" she had held for Boston women in the early 1840s. Here she had sought to fill her listeners with intellectual self-reliance and a sense of possibility. Mystically vague, Margaret Fuller's *Woman* met an appreciative reception. Still, the nineteenth-century reader might well have wondered how she could reach the status of "a being of infinite scope" within traditional marriage, which Fuller described as a flawed institution, or how she could achieve Fuller's goal of a "ravishing harmony of the spheres" in a society split into male and female compartments. But during the 1840s, an era when all institutions were called into question, reformers became absorbed with such problems. One set of answers came from men and women who retreated from the world into the haven of communities.

Since the 1820s, utopian communities had offered models of alternative societies that sought to improve on worldly society. At the thriving New Harmony community in Indiana, founded in 1824, Scottish industrialist and philanthropist Robert Owen established a system of "cooperative labor"; he also tried to erase a trinity of evils that afflicted humanity—private property, organized religion, and marriage. At the short-lived Nashoba community in Tennessee, founded in 1825, reformer Frances Wright engrafted Owenite ideals, including cooperative labor and sexual liberty, onto her ambitious (though unsuccessful) plan for the gradual emancipation of slaves. In the 1840s, utopian ventures proliferated; unlike the anticlerical Owenite models, some were formed by religious sects—such as the Shakers and Mormons. The Oneida community, led by John Humphrey Noyes, was also sectarian in origin. Others were nonsectarian—among them the transcendentalist communities such as Brook Farm and the rash of Fourierist associations that sprang up in the 1840s. Religious or secular, communitarian experiments had two characteristics that linked them to Nashoba and New Harmony. Most rejected, to a greater or lesser extent, the values of capitalist society and attempted to replace them with some variant of socialism. And most attempted to offer alternative ways in which men and women could live together, within or outside the bounds of marriage. As a result, communitarians provided new visions of women's roles.

Shaker communities, for instance, relieved women of sexual oppression by excluding both marriage and sexual relations. These celibate communities, which had existed since the Revolutionary era, experienced their greatest period of growth in the 1840s, when the attraction of communitarian life reached its peak. In particular, the Shakers provided an alternative role for women; the Shaker "families" that peppered the Northeast, encompassing some 6,000 souls, attracted more women than men. Within each Shaker "family," or community, a rigid system of sexual segregation prevailed: Shaker men and women lived, ate, worked, and worshiped separately. To one observer, physician Harriet Hunt, the Shaker "family" offered an asylum from the "perversions of marriage" and "the gross abuses which drag it down." Rejoicing in the role of Shaker women as ministers, elders, and medical practitioners, Hunt concluded that "the equality of women . . . is recognized in every department of Shaker life." But her enthusiasm was not universal. When Abba Alcott, the overworked wife of universal reformer and free spirit Bronson Alcott, inspected a Shaker community, she found that the men had "a fat, sleek, comfortable look," while the women were stiff, awkward, and reserved. "There is servitude somewhere, I have no doubt," Alcott told her journal. "Wherever I turn, I see the yoke on women in some form or other."

Transcendental communities, such as Brook Farm, did not discard marriage as an institution. But they tried to create an atmosphere in which men and women were equal participants in community life. Brook Farm strove to free women from domestic drudgery by dividing menial work, indoors and outdoors, among community members. "Our womenfolk had all the rights of our menfolk," one enthusiastic resident claimed. "They had an equal voice in all our public affairs, voted for our offices,

the separate estate was the trust, in which a third party controlled the wife's estate. While other aspects of equity law fell into disuse, the separate estate rose in popularity. In her study of Petersburg, Virginia, women, historian Suzanne Lebsock notes that instances of separate estates, while rare until 1820, increased markedly thereafter. The object of such devices, she points out, was not to empower women but to keep property in the family—and out of the hands of husbands' creditors.

But separate estates required special arrangements, and affected only a minority of wives. Grievances about their legal status permeated women's writings. "I had lived twenty years without the legal right to be alone one hour, to have exclusive right of one foot of space," complained abolitionist Jane Swisshelm, a supporter of married women's property reform, who sued her husband for property she had inherited. Marriage, claimed Mary Lyndon, the heroine of an autobiographical novel by Mary Gove Nichols, had "turned me into a thing," with no claim over either property or child. When an improvident husband wasted his wife's inheritance, spent her earnings, or sold her furniture, she had no other choice, as author Elizabeth Oakes Smith expressed it, than to "go down with the ship."

In the 1840s, efforts to improve the legal status of married women met with some success. Propertied legislators appreciated measures that would preserve their estates, if inherited by daughters, from disintegration in the hands of sons-in-law. Mississippi enacted the first Married Women's Property Law in 1839. A similar bill had been proposed in 1836 in Albany, where a women's pressure group was formed. Under the leadership of Ernestine Rose, a Polish-born follower of Robert Owen who had just emigrated from England to New York, women petitioned and lobbied for an end to the most blatant disabilities of feme covert status. Married women, they contended, should be allowed to retain ownership of their property, keep their own earnings, and enjoy joint guardianship over their children.

In 1848, the New York legislature passed a minimal bill providing that married women could retain control over their real and personal property, and other states enacted similar measures. An 1860 New York law gave married women the right to their own earnings. By 1865, 29 states had enacted some form of married women's property law, and the process continued for the rest of the century. The passage of such legislation made the equity loophole of "separate estates" available, in theory, to everyone.

Still, the significance of married women's property laws has to be qualified. First, their impact depended on the state courts, where judges often retained an affection for common law. In New York, for instance, where several pioneer statutes were enacted, superior court judges interpreted the new laws conservatively, thus vitiating their intent. A second qualification involves the motives behind the statutes. Their enactment reflected not so much a new respect for wives as a changing economy, one that required investment capital and a spirit of risk. The married women's property acts can be viewed as part of a larger effort to promote commercial ventures by providing buffers against insolvency: Like separate estates, the laws protected property not only from husbands but also from husbands' creditors. Married women's property acts therefore "represented the demands of an acquisitive and propertied middle class," historian Norma Basch contends. But the campaign for marital property reform "also encompassed a constellation of ideas that extended beyond class interest to gender interest," Basch points out. "In the context of the nineteenth century, the right of wives to own property entailed their right not to be property."

The battle against legal inequities continued after 1848 under the banner of the women's rights movement. The new crusade, like the Garrisonian camp of abolition from which it sprang, took on a perfectionist hue. It identified a new, pervasive root evil to be exterminated, and it mobilized a battery of disparate grievances that had been unconnected and diffuse. A combination of multiple inequities, rising expectations, and abolitionist expertise thrust the new movement into existence.

THE WOMEN'S RIGHTS MOVEMENT

When women's rights advocates attempted to draft a manifesto for their first convention at Seneca Falls in 1848, they felt, said Elizabeth Cady Stanton, "as helpless and hopeless as if they had been asked to construct a steam engine." The "Declaration of Sentiments" that resulted mobilized a battery of grievances that women had voiced for two decades and transformed them into a cohesive program of reforms. Identifying the enemy as the "absolute tyranny" of man, the declaration enumerated "his repeated injuries and usurpations." Women had been excluded from higher education, profitable employment, the trades and commerce, the pulpit, the professions, and the franchise. They were deprived of property rights, denied guardianship of their children, and victimized by the double standard. Moreover, their oppression had an insidious psychological dimension. "[Man] has endeavored, in every way that he could, to destroy her confidence in her own power, to lessen her self respect, and to make her willing to lead a dependent and abject life," the declaration stated. After a dozen resolutions demanding redress, the declaration culminated in an assertion of women's right to the vote—an ultimate invasion of the public sphere.

The new call to arms of 1848, and the movement it began, was a direct descendent of the abolitionist crusade, in which most of its leaders had participated. From the abolitionists, the early feminists inherited a geographical circuit, a mode of agitation, a human rights ideology, and even a small constituency. They were also the legatees of decades of activism in benevolence and reform and of female efforts to rescue female victims—of poverty, slavery, prostitution. In this case, to be sure, the agitators and the victims were the same. The women's rights movement was at once an evangelical crusade that aimed at a massive "awakening," a humanitarian rescue mission, and a modern pressure group. Unique in the context of antebellum reform, it challenged the assumptions on which social space was divided. But the women's rights movement was distinguished primarily by its unseverable link with Garrisonian antislavery.

A network of women, formed in the crucible of abolition and joined by other experienced reformers, led the new movement. Elizabeth Cady Stanton, married eight years to a prominent abolitionist, had been thrown into inspirational antislavery circles before moving with her family to Seneca Falls in 1847. She had participated in a local Female Antislavery Society, attended the World Antislavery Convention in London with Lucretia Mott, and campaigned in New York for a Married Women's Property Act. Lucretia Mott, a public Friend since 1817, had a long career as a stalwart of causes—moral reform, temperance, and abolition. An active Garrisonian, she had spent the past decade lecturing on religion and antislavery. Whether fresh from the abolitionist lecture circuit, like Lucy Stone and Abby Kelley; or the property rights campaign, like Pauline Wright Davis and Ernestine Rose; or the temperance crusade, like Susan B. Anthony, women's rights activists were already active in public life in one way or another. "I was a believer and advocate of the doctrine long before I became so publicly," recalled Elizabeth Oakes Smith, a longtime reformer, "for I could not smother aspiration nor could I be a mere household woman."

These advocates brought with them not only experience in reform and an acute sense of "woman's wrongs" but an eagerness to discard the hallmarks of female benevolence. The first to go was the religious impulse that pervaded the majority of women's voluntary associations. Most women's rights advocates had experienced some form of "deconversion" from the rigors of orthodox Protestantism. Converts to the notion of universal salvation, many had moved into more liberal sects or a humanitarian secularism. Others were Friends. Moreover, as Garrisonians, many were skeptical of clerical authority and disdained the "perverse application of the Scriptures" in regard to women. "The pulpit has been prostituted," Lucretia Mott told a women's rights convention in 1854, "the Bible has been ill-used." Elizabeth Cady Stanton, who claimed she had narrowly escaped conversion as a girl, at the hands of Charles G. Finney, eventually became as anticlerical as Frances Wright.

The new movement also discarded formal organization. Although women's rights associations sprang up as far west as Wisconsin, there were no elaborate networks of female societies, no state or national organizations, no battalions of officers, agents, managers, and visitors. Rather, a spontaneous informality prevailed. Individuals or contingents took off on speaking tours or petition campaigns independently, while an informal, shifting series of committees ran conventions. Staged almost annually, along the abolitionist circuit, the conventions passed resolutions, fostered debate with male opponents, and, historian Nancy Isenberg points out, put forth "ingenious arguments for women's full entitlement as citizens." They also drew public attention, which was negative. The new cause encountered hostility and derision. According to Elizabeth Cady Stanton and Susan B. Anthony, women's rights leaders were "wholly unprepared to find themselves the target of the jibes and jeers of the nation." But conventions also provided an opportunity for supporters, drawn mainly from antislavery ranks, to reiterate and refine the sentiments expounded in the 1848 resolutions.

The women's rights convention at Salem, Ohio, in 1850, the only one from which men were excluded, provided one such opportunity. Issuing a call to the women of the state, the Ohio reformers passed 22 resolutions, in which political and economic grievances were reduced, in stages, to psychological dependence and female complicity:

> Resolved, that while we deprecate thus earnestly the political oppression of Woman, we see in her social condition, the regard in which she is held as a moral and intellectual being, the fundamental cause of that oppression.
>
> Resolved, that amongst the causes of such social condition, we regard the public sentiment which withholds from her all, or almost all, lucrative employments, and enlarged spheres of labor.

Resolved, that in the difficulties thus cast in the way of her self-support, and in her consequent *dependence* upon man, we see the greatest influence at work in imparting to her that tone of character which makes her to be regarded as "the weaker vessel." . . .

Resolved, that we regard those women who content themselves with an idle, aimless life, as involved in the guilt as well as the suffering of their own oppression. . . .

The Ohio reformers, like those at other conventions, had two targets. One was the state legislature, which, engaged in rewriting the state constitution, rejected their petition for suffrage. Another was women-at-large, "involved in the guilt as well as the suffering of their own oppression." A basic dilemma of the movement was that women were not aware of the need for rights. Lucretia Mott confronted this problem in an 1849 speech, where she used images of bondage and confinement, inertia and paralysis, to describe the psychological enemy:

[Woman] has been so long subject to the disabilities and restrictions, with which her progress has been embarrassed, that she has become enervated, her mind to some extent paralyzed; and like those still more degraded by personal bondage, she hugs her chains.

The conferring of rights, equal opportunities, and the vote, Mott concluded, "shall raise her from this low, enervated, and paralyzed condition." Women's rights, like abolition, was a humanitarian rescue operation. The vote was a means to emancipation, not an end in itself.

Suffrage, however, proved an unwieldy weapon with which to penetrate the perimeter of sphere, and women's rights activists were ambivalent about it. At Seneca Falls, the demand for the vote was the only resolution that failed to evoke unanimous approval. It was passed, by a small majority, only as a result of the concerted efforts of Elizabeth Cady Stanton and Frederick Douglass. Many women who signed petitions demanding legal rights in the 1840s, as in New York, refused to endorse petitions for suffrage. Most Americans believed that women were not entitled to vote precisely because of their dependent status, a status that women's rights advocates deplored but had to acknowledge. To others, the demand for suffrage symbolized the extreme and unwarranted belligerance of its advocates. "I don't believe woman is groaning under half so heavy a yoke of bondage as you imagine," Lucy Stone's sister wrote to her in 1846. "I am sure I do not feel burdened by anything man has laid upon me, to be sure I can't vote, but what care I for that, I would not if I could." For Garrisonians such as Lucretia Mott, who believed that "political life abounds in outrage," the issue was especially difficult. "Far be it from me to encourage women to vote or take an active part in politics in the present state of the government," she stated. However, Mott also asserted that "[woman's] right to the elective franchise . . . should be yielded to her, whether she exercise that right or not."

The early feminists' dual allegiance—to radical abolition, which rejected the corruption of politics, and women's rights, which demanded access to it—also posed a liability. The women's rights movement was unable to sever itself from the abolitionist crusade because of its leaders' dual commitment, their dependence on other abolitionist women for support, and finally the endorsement of prominent Garrisonian men. While faced with virtually unanimous hostility outside abolitionist circles, women's rights campaigners won unconditional support from the advocates of human rights. Besides Garrison and Frederick Douglass, a loyal spokesman for women's demands, other stalwarts contributed endorsements. Wendell Phillips and Gerrit Smith (Elizabeth Cady Stanton's cousin) supported the cause, as did Samuel May, Thomas Wentworth Higginson, William H. Channing, and Henry Clarke Wright, a staunch backer of the Grimkes. This interesting contingent, composed mainly of liberal ministers, had also escaped from orthodoxy into the more hospitable parlors of Unitarianism and Universalism, antislavery and nonresistance. The women's rights movement's most visible, unified group of backers, significantly, were dissenting clerics within the ranks of radical abolitionism.

What this support was worth, however, is questionable. The mingling of reforms was not necessarily an advantage. On the one hand, it made the cause of women's rights inaccessible to a potential constituency of women who did not share the radical abolitionist stance of its leaders. On the other hand, as historian Ellen Dubois contends, advocates of the cause were restrained by the dual affiliations of their leaders, "which kept them from the mobilization of women around a primary commitment to their own vote." Until the slave was free, the women's rights movement was restricted by its dependence on an antislavery base. Critics were able to attack the movement, as in *Harpers* in 1853, both for its friends (its "intimate connection with all the radical and infidel movements of the day") and for its deviance ("a peculiar enormity of its own . . . a deficit of both nature and revelation").

While women's rights advocates won limited gains in the area of legal rights, they failed to enlarge their tiny constituency. Their tactical successes and failures were best illustrated by the Stanton-Anthony campaigns in New York State in the 1850s. Throughout the decade, activists assaulted the state legislature with an unrelenting petition campaign, demanding further redress in married women's rights (control of their own earnings, joint guardianship rights of children, improved inheritance rights of widows) and suffrage. While Anthony mobilized volunteers and organized the campaign, Stanton, now the wife of a state senator, addressed a joint judiciary committee in Albany to press the case. By 1860, when New York finally passed the most comprehensive married women's property law yet enacted, 14 other states had passed some form of improved legislation as well. Suffrage demands were ignored.

Other tactics backfired. One was an attempt to enlarge the base of support for women's rights by extending it to temperance—a reform movement dominated not only by men but by ministers. Within the crusade against drink, the Daughters of Temperance fulfilled a conventional auxiliary role, unable to participate in conventions or hold office in the male-run national organization. When New York feminists created a State Women's Temperance Association in 1852, 500 women withdrew from the national temperance movement, attended a convention of the new association, and elected Elizabeth Cady Stanton president. But the membership soon splintered and disbanded over Stanton's radical proposal that drunkenness should be cause for divorce. Indeed, Stanton's proposals for liberal divorce laws were unpopular even among advocates of women's rights. A joint feminist-abolitionist invasion of the World Temperance Convention the following year, when activists used the

Garrisonian ploy of nominating a woman to the business committee, resulted in ignominious defeat. The temperance movement remained under ministerial sway. The women within it were unwilling to abandon clerical support in favor of a feminist alliance or to support Stanton's insistence that women had the right "to be present in all Councils of Church and State."

The temperance women's reaction resembled that of the moral reformers in 1838, when Sarah Grimke's remarks in the *Advocate* evoked dismay. The contrast between moral reform and the women's rights movement is significant. While moral reform, balanced on the brink between benevolence and aggression, won the commitment of thousands, it was ultimately hamstrung by its own ideology. Women's rights lacked the widespread support that moral reform had enjoyed. Devoted to stimulating conversions in "sentiment," women's rights advocates were unable to harness such sentiments effectively. They succeeded, however, where the moral reformers had failed, by integrating a barrage of demands and fortifying them with the human rights convictions they brought with them from abolition. Their antebellum triumph was ideological rather than tactical.

The women's rights movement culminated decades of women's encroachment into the public sphere, beginning with the pious, evangelical voluntary societies of the early nineteenth century. As historian Keith Melder has shown, women's benevolence gradually became more independent and innovative, as it veered away from religious goals and began attacking specific evils (prostitution, drink, slavery) that victimized women. The tactics of women's societies similarly shifted from fund raising and visiting to petitions, conventions, and public speaking. The more radical and assertive the cause, the greater the tendency to discard clerical authority and to view the limitations of sphere as illegitimate. In the women's rights movement, attacks on sphere were finally reformulated into a demand for total autonomy. As a women's rights convention resolved in 1851, "the proper sphere for all human beings is the largest and highest to which they are able to attain."

Throughout these decades, the voluntary association provided a framework in which women could function outside the home and collectively exercise what Abbey Kelley called their "clearer moral perception." The Civil War and the vast economic changes that followed wiped out the evangelical and perfectionist impulses that gave antebellum movements their particular character. The heritage that remained was threefold: the tradition of female association, the extension of women's influence through benevolence and reform, and the newborn ideology of women's rights. In the postwar years, all three reemerged—in women's clubs; in temperance work, settlement work, and labor reform; and in the movement for woman suffrage. Between 1800 and 1860, women succeeded in appropriating and feminizing a portion of public space. Their postwar activism in public life was "visiting" writ large.

SUGGESTED READINGS AND SOURCES

Surveys of women's activism in benevolence and reform include Keith Melder, *Beginnings of Sisterhood: The American Women's Rights Movement 1800–1850* (New York, 1977); Ann Firor Scott, *Natural Allies: Women's Associations in American History* (Urbana, Ill., 1991); and

Lori D. Ginzberg, *Women In Antebellum Reform* (Wheeling, Ill., 2000). Deborah Gray White explores the distinctive experience of slave women in *Ar'n't I a Woman? Female Slaves in the Plantation South* 2d. ed. (New York, 1999).

Urban benevolence and social reform are examined in the following works: Barbara J. Berg, *The Remembered Gate: Origins of American Feminism, The Woman and the City 1800–1860* (New York, 1978); Nancy A. Hewitt, *Women's Activism and Social Change: Rochester, New York, 1822–1872* (Ithaca, N.Y., 1984); Lori D. Ginzburg, *Women and the Work of Benevolence: Morality, Politics, and Class in the Nineteenth Century* (New Haven, Conn., 1990); Susan Porter Benson, "Business Heads and Sympathizing Hearts: The Women of the Providence Employment Society, 1837–1858," *Journal of Social History*, 12 (Winter 1978), 301–312; Ann M. Boylan, "Women in Groups: An Analysis of Women's Benevolent Organizations in New York and Boston, 1797–1840," *Journal of American History*, 71 (December 1984), 497–523; and Boylan, "Timid Girls, Venerable Widows, and Dignified Matrons: Life Cycle Patterns Among Organized Women in New York and Boston," 1797–1840," *American Quarterly*, 38 (Winter 1986), 779–797. For southern women's interest in benevolence and voluntary association, see Elizabeth R. Varon, *We Mean to Be Counted: White Women and Politics in Antebellum Virginia* (Chapel Hill, N.C., 1998), ch. 1.

Carroll Smith-Rosenberg assesses the moral reform movement in "Beauty, the Beast, and the Militant Woman: A Case Study in Sex Roles and Social Stress in Jacksonian America," *American Quarterly,* 23 (October 1971), 562–584. Mary P. Ryan explores moral reform in upstate New York in "The Power of Women's Networks: A Case Study of Female Moral Reform in Antebellum America," *Feminist Studies*, 5 (Spring 1979), 66–86. Estelle B. Freedman examines the prison reform movement in *Their Sister's Keepers: Women's Prison Reform in America, 1830–1930* (Ann Arbor, Mich., 1981).

For women in slavery, besides Deborah Gray White, *Ar'n't I a Woman?*, cited previously, see Eugene Genovese, *Roll, Jordan, Roll: The World the Slaves Made* (New York, 1972); Elizabeth Fox-Genovese, *Within the Plantation Household: Black and White Women of the Old South* (Chapel Hill, N.C., 1988), ch. 3; Jacqueline Jones, *Labor of Love, Labor of Sorrow: Black Women, Work, and the Family, from Slavery to the Present* (New York, 1985), ch. 1; Marli F. Weiner, *Mistresses and Slaves: Plantation Women in South Carolina, 1830–1880* (Urbana, Ill., 1997); Angela Davis, "Reflections on the Black Woman's Role in the Community of Slaves," *Black Scholar,* 3 (December 1971), 3–15; and Catherine Clinton, *The Plantation Mistress* (New York, 1983), ch. 11. Herbert Gutman examines slave strategies for family preservation in *The Black Family in Slavery and Freedom, 1750–1925* (New York, 1976), part 1. Brenda Stevenson suggests the negative impact of slavery on family life in *Life in Black and White: Family and Community in the Slave South* (New York, 1996), a study of Loudon County, Virginia, and "Distress and Discord in Virginia Slave Families, 1830–1860," in Carol Bleser, ed., *In Joy and in Sorrow: Women, Family, and Marriage in the Victorian South* (New York, 1991), pp. 103–124. The experience of slave children is examined in Wilma King, *Stolen Childhood: Slave Youth in Nineteenth-Century America* (Bloomington, Ind., 1995) and Marie Jenkins Schwartz, *Born in Bondage: Growing Up Enslaved in the Antebellum South* (Cambridge, Mass., 2000). For recent scholarship on gender and slavery, see David Barry Gaspar and Darlene Clark Hine, eds., *More Than Chattel: Black Women and Slavery in the Americas* (Bloomington, Ind., 1996), which provides a comparative perspective.

For documents, see Dorothy Sterling, ed., *We Are Your Sisters: Black Women in the Nineteenth Century* (New York, 1984), part 1; Gerda Lerner, ed., *Black Women in White America:*

A Documentary History (New York, 1972), parts 1 and 2; Willie Lee Rose, ed., *A Documentary History of Slavery in North America* (New York, 1976); John Blassingame, ed., *Slave Testimony: Two Centuries of Letters, Speeches, Interviews, and Autobiographies* (Baton Rouge, La., 1977); and *Six Women's Slave Narratives*, int. by William L. Andrews (New York, 1988). See also Harriet A. Jacobs, *Incidents in the Life of a Slave Girl, Written by Herself*, ed. by Jean Fagan Yellin, 2nd ed. (Cambridge, Mass., 2000) and Catherine Clinton, ed., *Fanny Kemble's Journals* (Cambridge, Mass., 2000).

For women's roles in the abolitionist movement, see Melder, *Beginnings of Sisterhood*, chs. 5 and 6; Blanche Hersh, *The Slavery of Sex: Feminist Abolitionists in Nineteenth-Century America* (Urbana, Ill., 1978); Jean Fagan Yellin, *Women and Sisters: Antislavery Feminists in American Culture* (New Haven, Conn., 1990); Yellin and John C. Van Horne, eds., *The Abolitionist Sisterhood: Women's Political Culture in Antebellum America* (Ithaca, N.Y., 1994); and Julie Roy Jeffrey, *The Great Silent Army of Abolitionism: Ordinary Women in the Antislavery Movement* (Chapel Hill, N.C., 1998). See also Judith Wellman, "Women and Radical Reform in Upstate New York: A Profile of Grass Roots Abolitionists," in Mabel E. Deutrich and Virginia Purdy, eds., *Clio Was a Woman: Studies in the History of American Women* (Washington, D.C., 1980), pp. 113–127; Gerda Lerner, *The Grimke Sisters from South Carolina: Pioneers for Women's Rights and Abolition* (New York, 1967); Lerner, "The Political Activities of Antislavery Women," in *The Majority Finds Its Past: Placing Women in History* (New York, 1979), pp. 112–144; Elizabeth Ann Bartlett, ed., *Sarah Grimke: Letters on the Equality of the Sexes and Other Essays* (New Haven, Conn., 1988); Dorothy Sterling, *Ahead of Her Time: Abby Kelley and the Politics of Antislavery* (New York, 1992); Edmund Fuller, *Prudence Crandall: An Incident of Racism in Nineteenth-Century America* (Middletown, Conn., 1971); Carolyn L. Karcher, *The First Woman in the Republic: A Cultural Biography of Lydia Maria Child* (Durham, N.C., 1994); and Lucille Salitan and Eve Lewis Perera, eds., *Virtuous Lives: Four Quaker Sisters Remember Family Life, Abolitionism, and Women's Rights* (New York, 1994). Frederick B. Tolles, ed., *Slavery and "The Woman Question"* (London and Haverford, Pa., 1952) contains Lucretia Mott's diary of 1840. The origins of *Uncle Tom's Cabin* are explored in Joan D. Hedrick, *Harriet Beecher Stowe: A Life* (New York, 1994). For divisions in the antislavery movement see Aileen S. Kraditor, *Means and Ends in American Abolition: Garrison and His Critics on Strategy and Tactics* (New York, 1969).

Black women's roles in antislavery are discussed in Shirley Yee, *Black Women Abolitionists: A Study in Activism, 1828–1860* (Knoxville, Tenn., 1992); Rosalyn Terborg-Penn, "Discrimination Against Afro-American Women in the Woman's Movement, 1830–1920" in Sharon Harley and Rosalyn Terborg-Penn, eds., *The Afro-American Woman: Struggles and Images* (Port Washington, N.Y., 1978), pp. 17–27; Janice Sumler Lewis, "The Forten-Purvis Women of Philadelphia and the American Antislavery Crusade," *Journal of Negro History*, 66 (Winter, 1981–1982), 281–288; and Dorothy Sterling, ed., *We Are Your Sisters*, part II. See also Bert Loewenberg and Ruth Bogin, eds., *Black Women in Nineteenth-Century America: Their Words, Their Thoughts, Their Feelings* (University Park, Pa., 1976). Nell Irvin Painter explores Sojourner Truth's celebrated career in antislavery and women's rights in *Sojourner Truth: A Life, A Symbol* (New York, 1996), and Painter, "Representing Truth: Sojourner Truth's Knowing and Becoming Known," *Journal of American History*, 81 (September 1994), 461–492. Jane Rhodes presents a less well-known black woman reformer in *Mary Ann Shadd Cary: The Black Press and Protest in the Nineteenth Century* (Bloomington, Ind., 1988). Angela Davis discusses the antislavery and women's rights campaigns in *Women, Race, and Class* (New York, 1983), chs. 2 and 3.

On transcendentalism, see Paula Blanchard, *Margaret Fuller: From Transcendentalism to Revolution* (Cambridge, Mass., 1978); Charles Capper, *Margaret Fuller: An American Romantic Life*, vol. I (New York, 1992); Anne C. Rose, *Transcendentalism as a Social Movement, 1830–1850* (New Haven, Conn., 1981); Phyllis Cole, *Mary Moody Emerson and the Origins of Transcendentalism: A Family History* (New York, 1998); and Bruce A. Ronda, *Elizabeth Parker Peabody: A Reformer on Her Own Terms* (Cambridge, Mass., 1999). For utopian communities, see Louis J. Kern, *An Ordered Love: Sex Roles and Sexuality in Victorian Utopias—The Shakers, the Mormons, and the Oneida Community* (Chapel Hill, N.C., 1981); Lawrence Foster, *Religion and Sexuality: Three American Communal Experiments of the Nineteenth Century* (New York, 1981); Carol A. Kolmerton, *Women in Utopia: The Ideology of Gender in the American Owenite Communities* (Bloomington, Ind., 1990); and Robert S. Fogarty, ed., *Desire and Duty at Oneida: Tirzah Miller's Intimate Memoir* (Bloomington, Ind., 2000), in which a niece of John Humphrey Noyes discusses sexual issues at the Oneida community in the 1860s and 1870s. For Frances Wright's career in communitarianism and reform, see Celia Morris Ekhardt, *Fanny Wright: Rebel in America* (Cambridge, Mass., 1994), and William Randall Waterman, *Frances Wright* (New York, 1924). The New York State Married Women's Property Acts of 1848 and 1860 are discussed in Norma Basch, *In the Eyes of the Law: Women, Marriage, and Property in Nineteenth-Century New York* (Ithaca, N.Y., 1988), and Carol A. Kolmerton, *The American Life of Ernestine L. Rose* (Syracuse, N.Y., 1999). Lori D. Ginzburg suggests a trend away from evangelism in "'Moral Suasion Is Moral Balderdash': Women, Politics, and Social Activism in the 1850s," *Journal of American History*, 73 (December 1986), 601–622.

The antebellum women's rights movement is assessed by Ellen Dubois in *Feminism and Suffrage: The Emergence of an Independent Women's Movement, 1848–1869* (Ithaca, N.Y., 1978), ch. 1. See also Eleanor Flexner, *Century of Struggle: The Woman's Rights Movement in the United States* (Cambridge, Mass., 1959), chs. 5 and 6; Sylvia D. Hoffert, *When Hens Crow: The Women's Rights Movement in Antebellum America* (Bloomington, Ind., 1995); Virginia Bernhard and Elizabeth Fox-Genovese, eds., *The Birth of American Feminism: The Seneca Falls Convention of 1848* (St. James, N.Y., 1995); Nancy Isenberg, *Sex and Citizenship in Antebellum America* (Chapel Hill, N.C., 1998); Rosalyn Terborg-Penn, *African American Women in the Struggle for the Vote, 1850–1920* (Bloomington, Ind., 1998); and Kathryn Kish Sklar, *Women's Rights Emerges Within the Anti-Slavery Movement, 1830–1870: A Short History with Documents* (Boston, 2000). For international facets of the early women's rights movement, see Margaret H. McFadden, *Golden Cables of Sympathy: The Transatlantic Sources of Nineteenth-Century Feminism* (Lexington, Ky., 1999), and Bonnie S. Anderson, *Joyous Greetings: The First International Women's Movement, 1830–1860* (New York, 2000). Useful document collections include Aileen Kraditor, *Up from the Pedestal: Selected Writings in the History of American Feminism* (Chicago, 1968); and Alice Rossi, ed., *The Feminist Papers* (New York, 1973), part 2.

Women's rights advocates provided their own document collection in Elizabeth Cady Stanton, Susan B. Anthony, and Matilda Joslyn Gage, eds., *History of Woman Suffrage* (New York, 1881); for the antebellum era, see vol. I. For selections from *HWS*, see Mari Jo Buhle and Paul Buhle, eds., *The Concise History of Woman Suffrage: Selections from the Classic Work of Stanton, Anthony, Gage, and Harper* (Urbana, Ill., 1978). The memorial of the Salem, Ohio, women's rights convention of 1850 is reprinted in Gerda Lerner, ed., *The Female Experience: An American Documentary* (Indianapolis, Ind., 1977, and New York, 1992), pp. 342–347. For excerpts from women's rights journals, see Cheris Kramarae and Ann Russo, eds., *The Radical Women's Press of the 1850s* (New York, 1990). The careers of Stanton and Anthony are illuminated in Ellen Carol Dubois, ed., *Elizabeth Cady Stanton/Susan B. Anthony: Correspondence, Writing, Speeches* (New York, 1981). See also the Ken Burns documentary film, "Not For Ourselves Alone" (1999) and Geoffrey C. Ward and Ken Burns, eds., *Not For Ourselves Alone: The Story of Elizabeth Cady Stanton and Susan B. Anthony* (New York, 1999).

Abolitionist and feminist memoirs include Elizabeth Buffum Chace's reminiscences in Malcolm R. Lovell, ed., *Two Quaker Sisters* (New York, 1937), now available in Salitan and Perera, eds., *Virtuous Lives*, cited previously; Maria Weston Chapman, *Ten Years of Experience* (Boston, 1842); Ednah Dow Cheney, *Reminiscences* (Boston, 1902); Lucy Newhall Colman, *Reminiscences* (Boston, 1891); Laura S. Haviland, *A Woman's Life Work, Labors, and Experiences* (Chicago, 1889); Georgiana Bruce Kirby, *Years of Experience* (New York, 1887); Mary Gove Nichols, *Mary Lyndon; or, Revelations of a Life* (New York, 1855), a fictionalized account; Mary Alice Wyman, ed., *Selections from the Autobiography of Elizabeth Oakes Smith* (Lewiston, Maine, 1924); Elizabeth Cady Stanton, *Eighty Years and More* (Boston, 1898); and Jane Swisshelm, *Half a Century* (Chicago, 1880).

For quizzes and additional resources related to American women's history, visit the book's Website at *www.mhhe.com/americanwomen*.

CHAPTER FIVE

Women at Work, 1860–1920

ETWEEN THE CIVIL WAR and World War I, industrialization and urbanization altered the American landscape. Higher rates of immigration, increased internal migration, and westward expansion compounded their impact. These factors shaped women's lives and the work that they did, in the home and outside it. Significantly, many women entered the paid labor force, not only as domestic servants—the largest single category of women workers—but also as factory workers, white-collar workers, and professionals.

The Civil War propelled or accelerated some of the changes in women's work. Far more important were the growing economy, which provided new jobs in factories and offices, and the rise of cities, where they were located. In the late nineteenth century, the quick clip of industrialization shifted ever larger portions of work from farm and household to business and workplace, and in the process, technology opened new options. Better machines reduced the need for skilled labor and increased the need for cheap labor, which women traditionally provided. At the same time, cities expanded. The national population doubled between 1860 and 1910, but the urban population doubled every decade. By 1920, a majority of women lived within range of paying jobs.

Paid employment, of course, did not represent the bulk of women's contributions to the economy. Domestic labor remained women's major occupation. Much of the nondomestic work that women did at home, moreover, was "invisible" because it was unpaid and did not show up on the census rolls, as was the case with female labor on family farms. The farmer's spouse, whether a sharecropper's wife or a pioneer on the Great Plains, labored a lifetime without pay or recognition as a working woman. Other types of work done at home for pay, like taking in sewing, laundry, or boarders, also went unrecorded. Wage labor, however, was in retrospect the wave of the future. In the late nineteenth century, the numbers of wage-earning women rose, the work they did changed, and the nature of the female labor force changed as well.

Statistics tell part of the story. In 1860, women were 10.2 percent of the free labor force. Almost one out of 10 free women over the age of 10 earned wages, in a limited range of jobs such as servant, seamstress, teacher, or mill operative. The slave labor force included about two million women workers. The next census reflected black women's entry into the paid labor force. In 1870, 13.7 percent of women worked for pay, and 14.8 percent of the nation's workers were women. At this point, the numbers of women wage earners started to surge. By 1910, one out of five wage earners was a woman and one out of four women over 14 held jobs. (One out of four children between the ages of 10 and 14 was employed as well.) According to the 1910 census, the numbers of working women had almost tripled since 1870.

The types of work women did also changed. Immediately after the Civil War, as before it, most women wage earners were servants. In 1870, for instance, seven out of 10 women workers were servants. Women continued to dominate domestic work and related types of menial labor. But the proportion of women workers in domestic work fell steadily as other types of jobs opened up—in factories, offices, stores, and classrooms. Most were "new" jobs, that is, jobs provided by the growing economy, not jobs once held by men. Throughout the era, a sexual division of labor curtailed female employment. In industry, women were hired for unskilled or semiskilled work and concentrated in certain industries, such as those that produced cloth, clothing, food products, and tobacco products. In the growing white-collar sector, as in the professions, women entered a small range of jobs, such as teachers, nurses, office workers, or salesclerks. By the turn of the century, teaching and clerical work were clearly feminized—that is, dominated by women. By World War I, more women worked in white-collar jobs than as domestics.

Finally, age as well as occupation defined the woman worker. Typically, she was urban, young, and single. According to a Labor Bureau survey in 1880, for instance, the female work force in cities was 90 percent single, 4.3 percent married, and 5.6 percent widowed; three out of four employed women were age 14 to 24; and nine out of 10 were native-born daughters of immigrants. An exception to this profile was the black woman worker, who was more likely to be older and to work after marriage. Among white women workers, too, thousands of older women—usually single, widowed, deserted, or divorced—entered the labor market. But the typical woman wage earner was now the "working girl." The youth of the female work force meant that the woman worker tended to view wage earning as a temporary phase, as she planned to marry and leave the job market. It meant that she was more apt to contribute to family income than to support her own independence. It also meant that her work experience would differ from that of a male contemporary. Seen as perpetual newcomers to the work force, women were invariably expected to take the lowest-level jobs at the lowest pay.

Women's acceptance of low wages was their special asset on the labor market, and one of many factors that favored their rapid entry into the work force. First, a majority of men could not earn a living wage, which spurred the employment of women family members. Second, employers welcomed low-cost female labor, unless pressured to do otherwise. Third, low-wage, unskilled jobs multiplied as business and industry expanded. Fourth, urban populations bulged with potential women workers, including waves of immigrants and rural migrants, white and black. Finally, throughout the late nineteenth century, the marriage rate dropped and the proportion of single women in the population rose. Family size shrank, the birth rate fell, and educational opportunities increased, especially for middle-class women. The conjunction of these factors created a climate in which women's employment should have increased even more than it did.

But the forces that spurred women's entry into the labor force ran into cultural forces stacked against it. The economic push toward employment was undercut by a middle-class domestic ideal. Most Americans, women included, shared the conviction that a woman's place was at home, supported by men, raising children, keeping house, and bolstering family life. As Theodore Roosevelt wrote around the turn of the century, "If the women do not recognise that the greatest thing for any woman is to be a good wife and mother, why, that nation has cause to be alarmed about its future." Vigorously defended, the domestic ideal affected the experience of women wage earners as much as it did women at home. The story of women who worked for pay concerns mainly those excluded by age, class, race, or need from the domestic ideal, though it still determined their options and expectations. This story began around the era of the Civil War. The war enabled some women to prove their capabilities, opened jobs to others, and forced many more into self-support. It also freed almost two million black women and deposited half their number on the free labor market.

CIVIL WAR AND WOMEN'S WORK

The Civil War affected women's work, in the long run, by spurring productivity and business incorporation, which would later expand the labor market. It had immediate effects as well, though these were different North and South. Among Union women, the war opened up new jobs and new routes to civic involvement, which stimulated the next generation of middle-class reformers and professionals. It also provided models of the large-scale corporate-style associations that women would form in the postwar decades. In wartime, under the aegis of male-run organizations—such as the U.S. Sanitary Commission and freedmen's aid societies—a galaxy of women agents, volunteers, and nurses contributed to the Union effort. Exhilarated by their new roles, women celebrated their contributions for the rest of the century. "At the war's end," nurse Clara Barton claimed in 1888, "woman was at least fifty years in advance of the normal position which continued peace would have assigned her."

Barton's claim was an overstatement; still, many shared her view. Through work with refugees, freedmen, and the wounded, women war workers, paid and unpaid, found a gratifying entry into public service. Ministering to the "boys" in the wards, serving as teachers of former slaves, rolling bandages, or visiting camps, they became participants in national affairs. The Sanitary Commission, which involved thousands of women at the local level, urged a fusion of public service and domestic ideals. According to its literature, which adopted a rhetoric of affection and instruction, the Commission was "a great artery that bears the people's love to the army." Memoirists of war work, too, often viewed the Union, and its army, as an extended family. But their maternal spirit cloaked new aggression.

Western agents of commissions—such as Annie Wittenmyer of Iowa, Laura Haviland of Michigan, Mary Livermore of Illinois, and "Mother" Bickerdyke of Ohio—were good examples. Exceeding their authority, they excelled at manipulating officers and denouncing incompetents. Resigned to such "prima donnas of benevolence," Sanitary Commission officials conceded that women surpassed men as fund raisers and supply collectors. Other women challenged the Sanitary Commission's domestic ideology and stressed their involvement in national affairs. In either case, women war workers took pride in their efforts. The woman in the war, concluded Mary Livermore, "had developed potencies and possibilities of which she had been unaware and which surprised her, as it did those who witnessed her marvelous achievement."

The war era also offered Union women other opportunities. They took over men's jobs in teaching, a field women had already entered, and assumed for the first time positions as clerks in government offices and stores. Such opportunities were born of necessity. Women needed work, and in this instance, employers needed women workers. Nursing was the major occupational battlefront of the war. Like other types of "progress" for women, this too depended on need: Male nurses were in short supply. Nursing also exemplified the back-door approach to a field monopolized by men, medicine. To gain acceptance, nursing pioneers created a domesticated vocation, one that combined menial services with medical ones. The main prerequisite was a capacity for self-sacrifice and solicitude, rather than training or expertise. The highest nursing post of the war, the only major federal appointment won by a woman, went to Dorothea Dix, a leading spirit of benevolence, deemed a more important qualification than experience in medicine. Many women war workers referred to themselves as "nurses," whatever their functions or responsibilities.

Some 3,000 women on both sides of the war served as nurses, most without training, many without pay, and all inspired by the British example set by Florence Nightingale in the Crimean War. Union nurses were more organized than their Confederate counterparts. Originally part of a relief program started by New York women in 1861, the preparation of nurses soon fell to the quasi-official Sanitary Commission, which coordinated relief efforts and staffed hospitals, and to the surgeon general, to whom Dix was responsible. Only a minority of women nurses served as paid appointees under Dix, who, according to her biographer, Thomas J. Brown, failed utterly as a wartime administrator. Most women nurses were unpaid volunteers. All found that wartime nursing fused medical care and domestic service. New York nurse Sophronia Bucklin, former schoolteacher and Dix appointee, wrote an inspired account of her war work, full of mangled limbs and medical crises. Most of her time, however, like that of other nurses, was spent as housekeeper, as she was also expected to cook, clean, and do laundry for her patients.

Despite the fusion of menial and medical, Civil War nursing met resistance from army doctors and officers who disliked the influence of women in the wards and tried to curtail, disparage, or demean it. Women were unfit as nurses, it was argued, because they were variously too weak, annoying, refined, or imprudent, and in any event unsuited to deal with the bodies of strange men. In response, women stressed their traditional roles as caretakers of the sick and feeble at home. "The right of woman to her sphere, which includes housekeeping, cooking, and nursing, has never been disputed," Sanitary Commission agent Jane Hoge argued. The most effective argument in favor of nursing, ultimately, was that women had already done it. After the war, nursing veterans administered hospitals, wrote textbooks, and founded training programs. The 1870 census listed only about 1,000 nurses, including midwives; in 1900, among 12,000 nurses, nine out of 10 were women. Hospital nurses, like household help, commonly worked 12-hour days and lived in the hospitals where they were employed. To compound the fusion of menial and medical, the 1900 census listed nurses in the category of "domestic and personal service."

Like women in the North, Confederate women formed patriotic societies, sent supplies to the front, and nursed the wounded. But their wartime work was often less voluntary and their hardships greater. The South faced higher inflation, more severe shortages, and a far larger loss of manpower: Four out of five eligible southern men served in the Confederate army, as opposed to about half in the Union. With white men away at the front, many women managed farms and plantations, where supplies dwindled, equipment crumbled, and productivity fell. Yeomen's wives met scarcity and deprivation. Plantation mistresses faced other problems: In the absence of husbands and overseers, they had to take charge of slaves—an assignment laden with irony. "The direct exercise of control over slaves was the most fundamental and essential political act in the Old South," historian Drew Gilpin Faust points out. "With the departure of white men this transcendent public duty fell to women." As a Georgia soldier wrote to his wife in 1861, "Go ahead [and] deal with the Negroes [just as if] they were yours and you had to controll them the balance of your life." Such a task proved difficult; slaves grew restive, as evidenced in theft, malingering, sabotage, and mounting audacity. Paradoxically, women confronted slave administration just as the institution of slavery began to crumble. Moreover, historian Clarence L. Mohr contends, southern women had trouble assuming authority, for they were products of a culture that reserved leadership roles for men. Such a heritage, he suggests, "left many women ill-prepared to take control of an isolated enterprise during the prolonged absence of a spouse." In some instances, weary mistresses rebelled. "You may give your Negroes away," one exasperated Texas wife wrote to her husband in 1864. "I cannot live with them another year alone."

The Civil War affected women's work by a final factor, its casualties. Over a million men were killed or wounded, more than in any other American war before or since. These casualties created a generation of widows, spinsters, and wives with disabled husbands, and enlarged the pool of women in dire need of income. Many postwar women, such as those living off meager widow's pensions and those who would never marry, faced the problem of self-support. Most had few skills to market outside the home beyond sewing. So many seamstresses sought work during and right after the war that wages fell for all forms of needlework. The war's demographic impact on women was perhaps the most far-reaching and long-lasting. But the problem of self-support, though national, had its most severe impact on the postwar South. The Confederacy had suffered disproportionate casualties—almost one out of five white men under 44 had died in the war—and the consequences affected women's lives through the turn of the century and beyond.

The southern states after the war were a world in which women were in excess by the thousands, historian Anne Firor Scott points out. In 1870, for instance, women outnumbered men by 36,000 in Georgia and 25,000 in North Carolina. In 1890, the ex-Confederate states claimed more than 60,000 war widows, many of whom had to support themselves. Much of the income-producing work done by women, such as managing farms and plantations, went unrecorded by the census, though Scott assumes it was widespread. White middle-class women who needed income often became teachers; postwar expansion of public education made jobs available, and prerequisites were minimal. Working-class women labored in local factories—binderies, box factories, cigarette factories, and textile mills. In 1890, more than two out of five southern textile workers were women (and almost one out of four was a child). By the end of the century, single women in southern towns and cities, like their counterparts in the North, took work in stores and offices—as typists, bookkeepers, cashiers, and saleswomen. One woman commented in the 1890s that more "well-bred" women were at work in the South than anywhere else in the world.

This entry into the job market, however, was involuntary and unanticipated. Eliza Frances Andrews, author of a famous war memoir and subsequently a newspaper editor and educator, explained that she found it necessary to earn a living in the 1870s "though wholly unprepared either by nature or training for a life of self-dependence." Widows and spinsters seeking work, another woman wrote, had "come to the front, forced there by other movements which they neither anticipated nor are responsible for nor fully comprehend." For postwar southern white women, employment was less a sign of progress than an index of need. An irony of defeat was that southern black women entered the labor force at the same time. The war had freed 1.9 million slave women, and as many as half their number soon became wage earners.

THE BLACK EXPERIENCE

Although many white married women in the late nineteenth century realized the cultural ideal of caring for homes and families, without resort to the paid labor force, a large proportion of black women could not. From emancipation onward, black women worked for pay in disproportionate numbers. At any given time, a far greater proportion of black married women than white married women held jobs. Almost all were hired as agricultural workers or domestic servants. The black working woman, finally, was a symbolic figure. She was part of a syndrome of black life in which shared ideals—of family farms, land ownership, and female domesticity—proved unattainable. These ideals emerged with vigor, however, at the time of emancipation.

During the Civil War and immediately afterward, the freedmen's desire to reconstitute their families was paramount. Newly freed slaves rushed to legalize and sanctify marriages, to locate missing family members, and to establish stable family lives. Some traveled from state to state searching for their husbands or wives or advertised for them in newspapers. The man who walked for more than two months, covering 600 miles, to find his wife and children, the women who broke off relationships with white men, the couples who attempted to resolve marital tangles that had developed under slavery—all illustrated the vulnerability of the family under slavery and its survival despite slavery. So did the huge marriage ceremonies that followed emancipation, sometimes in camps of contrabands and often involving 60 or 70 couples. Former slaves viewed legal marriage and a stable household as the major privileges of freedom. A basic component of the black ideal of family life, significantly, was female domesticity.

"When I married my wife I married her to wait on me," a freedman told his former master, soon after the war, when denying permission for his wife to work in the "big house." "She got all she can do right here for me and the children." This new sense of "woman's place" was widespread. "The women say that they never mean to do any more outdoor work, that white men support their wives, and that they mean that their husbands shall support them," an Alabama planter reported in 1865; some months later he noted that black women still wanted "to play the lady . . . 'like the white folks do.'" Plantation managers voiced similar complaints about black women's refusal to work and the consequent loss of field labor. Clearly, free blacks saw women's work in a white person's house or field as a badge of slavery; many determined that black wives would do neither.

Freedwomen may not have been universally anxious to "play the lady"; as historian Leon Litwack points out, it is not clear that newly freed black women were overly impressed with white women. Still, domesticity had appeal as a perquisite of freedom. The theme emerged on all sides. American Tract Society pamphlets, circulated among southern blacks and aimed at "Young Women," "Young Men," and "Married Folks," reiterated it. Freedman's Bureau literature offered "plain counsels" to becoming a "true woman" and adopting an appropriate role in the home. In Reconstruction, the committed white souls who worked among freedmen, under various auspices, avidly promoted white ideals. Their efforts resembled subsequent ones, in the 1880s and after, to assimilate and Americanize other groups, whether the remnants of Native American tribes or immigrants and their children. But the ideal of female domesticity drew support from blacks as well. Black newspapers urged "development of a womanly nature" as a means of "elevating and refining" the race.

A related perquisite of emancipation may well have been an enhanced sense of male supremacy, or so it seemed to white women teachers who worked with the freedmen. According to Laura Towne, a northern white teacher on the Carolina Sea Islands, black men believed in their right "just found, to have their own way in their families and rule their wives—that is an inestimable privilege." Towne reported that black leaders urged freedmen "to get the women into their proper place," and that "the notion of being bigger than women generally, is just now inflating the conceit of the men to an amazing degree." Massachusetts teacher Elizabeth Botume made the same point in 1869. Male supremacy and female labor, she noted, were not incompatible. "Most of the field-work was done by the women and girls; their lords and masters were much interrupted in agricultural pursuits by their political and religious duties," Botume reported. "When the days of 'Conventions' came the men were rarely at home; but the women kept steadily at work in the fields."

Although the shared ideal of female domesticity outlasted the early days of emancipation, it proved increasingly fragile. Despite the formation of stable two-parent families, southern black men had difficulty earning enough to support them. "My wife takes in washing and goes out to work," said a Richmond working man in 1867, "and so we get by." Reporting on southern black women in 1878, black writer Frances Ellen Harper found rising numbers of wives at work. "In some cases, the Southern woman is the mainstay of the family, and when work fails for men in large cities, the money which the wife can obtain by washing, ironing, and other services, often keeps pauperism at bay." Former antislavery lecturer and clubwoman, Harper liked success stories about black women who owned land, ran businesses, and formed charitable enterprises; but she reserved her greatest praise for those who contributed to family support. In the 1870s, the numbers of black women wage earners rapidly rose. Although most married black women did not work for pay, a black wife was seven times as likely to work as a white one. Female domesticity was not the only black ideal to be endangered or abandoned in the late nineteenth century (widespread landowning never materialized either), but it was a major one.

By the end of Reconstruction, half of black women over 16 were in the paid labor force, and many other black women worked alongside sharecropper husbands or took in work. In 1890, according to the first census that distinguished workers by race, almost a million black women were employed—37.8 percent in agriculture, 30.83 percent as domestic servants, 15.5 percent as laundresses, and a minuscule 2.76 percent in manufacturing. In 1900, about one out of five white women, but more than two out of every five black women, worked for pay. More revealingly, more than a quarter of black married women were wage earners but only 3.26 percent of white married women. Unlike the typical white woman worker, the black woman worker was likely to be married. If rural, she was employed in farm work; if urban, in domestic work or related services. She was rarely able to get work in industry except at the most menial levels. She might be a cleaning woman in the cotton mills, for instance, or a tobacco stripper—labor that involved carrying 30 pounds of the weed in sacks to and from the backless benches where she sat to pull it apart. There were occasions too, as in 1909, when black women were hired as strikebreakers; but this was hardly steady work. As a rule, the work black women *were* able to obtain, whether in field or household, was similar to the work once done by slaves. It was also work that other women attempted to avoid. As social worker Mary White Ovington observed in 1911, the black woman got "the job that the white girl does not want."

The family was the basic work unit for the majority of former slaves who remained in the South as farmers and sharecroppers, as well as for those who migrated west. This Nebraska family poses in front of its sod cabin in 1888. (*Solomon D. Butcher Collection, Nebraska State Historical Society*)

Like the white wage-earning woman, the black woman worker was increasingly likely to live in or move to a city. Most black migrants moved to southern cities. But even before the massive black urban migrations of the World War I era, the lure of jobs drew southern black women to northern cities in greater numbers than black men. Among immigrant groups in northern cities, men were always in a majority, but women predominated among black urban migrants. In New York in 1890, for instance, there were 81 black men for every 100 black women. Such discrepancies in sex ratios could not be explained even by the standard undercount of black men in census reports. Black women dominated the ranks of early urban migrants because they were always able to get jobs, as men could not, in the growing market for domestics—as cooks, laundresses, scrubwomen, and maids. In New York in 1910, for example, four out of five black working women held domestic jobs. By the first decade of the twentieth century, the steady migration of southern blacks to northern cities had already begun to break up black families and communities. A prominent black woman in Chicago, Fannie Barrier Williams, was inundated with supplications from southern mothers, she reported in 1907, begging her to find jobs "domestic or otherwise" for their daughters to save them from becoming servants in the South. In the World War I era, when black migration to northern cities surged, men temporarily outnumbered women among migrants. Still, the black press overflowed with letters from women job applicants anxious to take on work of any sort that would enable them to move north.

In southern cities, a surfeit of female labor was always available for domestic jobs. "We have no labor unions or organizations of any kind," a middle-aged domestic in a southern city reported in 1912. "If some Negroes did here and there refuse to work [for low wages] there would be hundreds of other Negroes right on the spot ready to take their places and do the same work." The glutted southern labor market for black women made their position worse than that of northern counterparts. By the World War I era, domestic jobs in the North paid in a day what was customarily a week's wages in the South. But black women workers in the South, as historian Tera W. Hunter shows, used what resources they had to control their own labor. In late-nineteenth-century Atlanta, where the vast majority of black women wage earners were domestic servants or laundresses, working women developed "survival strategies." Washerwomen profited from relative independence from white supervision, labored in communal spaces in their own neighborhoods, formed community organizations, and even went on strike in 1881. Household workers took unauthorized breaks, feigned illness, "pan-toted" left-overs from their employers' kitchens to compensate for their low pay, and quit their jobs in order to gain respite from their seven-day-a-week obligations. Quitting did not bring higher living standards or improve work environments, Hunter points out, but it was "an effective strategy to deprive employers of complete power over their labor."

Finally, North or South, black women needed to work for the same reason. Throughout the era, prejudice precluded job security for black men. It limited their options for steady employment, excluded them from most types of industrial work, confined them to unskilled work, and often made jobs unavailable, especially in cities. Even employed black men were often unable to support whole families on their low earnings, especially if their employment was seasonal. But black women were usually able to find some sort of menial work, on farms or in households, to supplement or provide family income. According to economist Claudia Goldin, the black working wife "was purchasing a substantial insurance policy against her husband's being unemployed."

The black working woman might also head a male-absent family, although this was not typical. Local studies suggest that between 70 percent and 90 percent of postbellum black families were two-parent families. But the proportion of black families headed by women was always higher in urban areas than in the rural South, and higher in southern cities than in northern ones. In northern cities, there were more female-headed families among blacks than among other ethnic groups, native-born or immigrant. In Philadelphia in 1880, for example, about 25 percent of black families were headed by women, compared to 14 percent of native-born white families and even smaller proportions of Irish or German families. (When only families of equal economic status were considered the differences dwindled or vanished.) In Boston, female-headed households appeared to be more common in the black community than in the Irish community, especially as exposure to urban life increased; city-bred blacks had less stable families than southern migrants. In 1880, among second-generation families with children, 16 percent of Irish families and almost twice that proportion of black families were female-headed. In New York's black neighborhoods in 1905, the proportion of women that headed male-absent families was twice as high as that among women in the Jewish and Italian communities, with all proportions rising as women aged. Historians debate the origins of the black female-headed family; some who work with postbellum data contend that it emerged not as a legacy of slavery but as a response to the conditions of urban life. Among the factors considered are imbalanced sex ratios, high black male mortality, a general level of poverty, black male unemployment or underemployment, and the ability of black women to find work and support themselves. The last factor is of special interest, because in some cases studied, working women appear to have been the "deserters," or instigators of marital breakup, not their husbands.

Although the black working woman was not likely to head a male-absent household, her status differed from that of white counterparts in another way. There was, within black communities, acceptance and support for wives who worked outside the home. This reflected in part the need for and frequency of paid work. Since slavery's end, a majority of black women had contributed to family support—whether or not the census reflected all of their efforts. (That is, the sharecropper's wife and the woman who took in washing or sewing might not be counted as wage earners.) Moreover, women's work was not as strongly opposed by the domestic ideal, as in many black families this ideal had never been realized. Excluded from the benefits of capitalism, the black family in the late nineteenth and early twentieth century could neither indulge in fantasies of domestic femininity as a way of life nor share the confidence in the future held by white families, native-born and immigrant.

Assessing the differences between black and immigrant families around the turn of the century, historian Elizabeth Pleck concludes that black women's paid labor was "a means of coping with long-term income inadequacy." Cultural support for the working mother, she contends, was related to the black family's lack of hope in the future. What hope there was, as Pleck points out, was concentrated in children, and this too spurred the wage earning of married women. Since Reconstruction, black mothers had avidly supported their children's schooling, as Frances Ellen Harper observed, while fathers would have been willing to let the matter drop. Mothers, Harper contended in the 1870s, "are the levers that move in education. The men talk about it, especially about election time . . . but the women work most for it." Such insistence on education persisted through the turn of the century. A distinction between black and immigrant families around 1900 was that black mothers, bent on keeping their children in school, felt obliged to work. In many immigrant families, youngsters were apt to become wage earners and contribute to family income.

By preserving this hope for their children's future, more than a quarter of black mothers sacrificed the domestic ideal and came to represent its antithesis. A majority of black women around 1900, however, provided labor as members of family units on farms. So did most women migrants to the Great Plains.

THE TRANS-MISSISSIPPI WEST

As the nation industrialized, westward expansion drew thousands of settlers, both migrants and immigrants, to the Great Plains and Rocky Mountain regions. Contesting the Indians for desirable land, late-nineteenth-century pioneers filled the farmlands of Wisconsin, Minnesota, Iowa, and the Dakotas; they filed for homesteads, carved out farms, and built mines and ranches. As white settlement encroached, Native American communities on the plains contracted. From the 1860s onward, as their tribes signed treaties with the U.S. government, American Indians were concentrated on federal reservations, mainly in Oklahoma, but also in Arizona, New Mexico, South Dakota, and farther west. Among both western pioneers and plains Indians, women's work roles shifted to meet new circumstances; in both instances, too, federal policies—the Homestead Act of 1863, which granted 160-acre plots of unsettled land to anyone who would cultivate them, and the Dawes Act of 1887, which reorganized life on Indian reservations—helped shape the nature of women's work, though not necessarily in ways that policymakers intended.

For pioneer women in the late nineteenth century, westward expansion imposed frontier conditions, prolonged the family labor system, extended the life of household production, and raised the demand for female labor, paid and unpaid; women remained a minority in the West, especially in remote, rural regions, for many decades. Typically, pioneer women combined housework with farm work and often with income-producing labor, much of which the census ignored. Domestic labor on the plains, well into the twentieth century, was extensive. Women cleaned, cooked, served, baked, and washed; they filled root cellars, turned wild game into meals, made dairy products, soap, and candles, and engaged in all stages of garment production—spinning, weaving, sewing, knitting, dying. Household improvements arrived only gradually, and had far less impact than did mechanization of farming. Technology, historian Glenda Riley points out, "was slower in restructuring labor in the farm home than it was in revolutionizing the work in the barns and fields." Women's labor on farms and ranches included some degree of outdoor work. A western woman had to know how to do "everything that a man does besides her own work, for she has to be ready for any emergency that may occur when men are not around," wrote westerner Susan Laflesche in 1888. Women tended farm animals, raised gardens, and drove reapers, harvesters, and haywagons. Some worked alongside husbands or instead of husbands who were employed elsewhere. In Montana, Texas, and Wyoming, women ran ranches and drove cattle to market. Many women took advantage of the Homestead Act and became homesteaders themselves. In Colorado and Wyoming, between 11 and 18 percent of new homesteaders each year were women, usually single women or widowed heads of household. "I am very enthusiastic about women homesteading," wrote a widow and migrant to Wyoming who filed for land in 1909. "It really requires less strength and labor than it does to go out to wash. . . . whatever is raised is the homesteader's own and there is no house-rent to pay."

Much of women's work in the West fell under a rubric between household work and wage-earning. Families on the labor-scarce plains, for instance, sometimes hired out daughters to work for neighboring households. Farmwives eased their way into the market economy; they made and sold dairy products, beeswax, dried fruit, cloth, and clothing. "Frequently enough, while the men were learning to farm, the women and children actually supported the family," an Iowa woman recalled. "They raised chickens and eggs for the table, raised the vegetables and fruit, and made butter to sell in exchange for things not produced at home." Wage-earning steadily increased. Many single women moved west as missionaries and teachers, in one-room district schools as well as in schools for Mexican Americans and Native Americans. Among immigrants, mainly Germans and Scandinavians, who settled northwest farms, young women became domestic employees and later farm wives. "Have a good home here," a Dakota woman reported. "Have no wish ever to return to Sweden." Some women earned money in mining towns as boardinghouse keepers, cooks, seamstresses, and laundresses, or in the sexual service sector as bar girls, entertainers, or prostitutes. Though the distinctive features of frontier life persisted into the twentieth century, they slowly faded; or as one woman noted, "As time passed, people's circumstances improved." Increasingly, homesteaders depended on store-bought items—cloth, sugar, coffee, and canned goods—and mail-order catalogs; western cities grew. By the turn of the century, wage-earning women entered the industrializing economy, as cannery workers and garment workers, office clerks and telegraph operators.

Among the Indians of the Great Plains—the Blackfoot, Comanche, Sioux, Cheyenne, Navajo, Apache, and other peoples—women were traditionally procurers and producers of food. Their work roles and status varied among the tribes. Some had been liaisons in the fur trade, for instance, and had married non-Indian fur traders. In some tribes, customarily, married women without children accompanied husbands on raids and forays. White encroachment in the nineteenth century, which brought epidemics, wars among tribes, and conflict with settlers, disrupted Indian life as did the consequent concentration of remnants of tribes on federal reservations. The Dawes Act of 1887, which divided reservation lands into family parcels and sold remaining lands to non-Indians, changed life for plains Indians—and remained in effect until the next policy shift, the Indian Reorganization Act of 1934. Under the Dawes Act, the federal government promoted acculturation to white ways of life and imposed new goals—private property, an individualist ethos, and gender hierarchy. For women, such goals meant domesticity, dependence on husbands, and loss of traditional activities. To policymakers, Indian women led lives of drudgery; new rules and roles, they believed, would bring uplift and benefit. Starting in the 1890s, the federal government assigned "field matrons" to help Native American women learn domestic skills.

Native American women responded to pressure to acculturate in conflicting and inconsistent ways. The changes imposed by the Dawes Act coincided with other major changes—with the disintegration of tribal structure, the decline of traditional gender roles, and the shift from a subsistence economy to a market economy. Women thus confronted several changes at once. In some instances, they resisted demands to adopt white lifestyles and created what the Indian Rights Association, a reform organization, called "obstacles to progress." In other instances, they either complied with new demands, picked and chose among them, or adapted new options to suit their own needs. In general, Native American women shaped economic roles that fused elements of their indigenous roles and aspects of the market economy.

Sometimes acculturationist precepts met Native American women's needs. Women of the Pima and Maricopa tribes in Arizona, for instance, converted to Christianity; supported education for their children at government schools, where they learned English; welcomed new food products, clothing, and western medicine; and swiftly adopted new tools such as the sewing machine, which helped reduce their workloads and produce goods for sale. By the early twentieth century, Native American women of various tribes produced many goods to sell outside their communities—moccasins, quilts, pottery, baskets, beads. Other Indian women entered the wage-earning sector; they took low-wage jobs as domestic servants, laundresses, agricultural workers, and seasonal farm labor. Among those who attended government schools, some found employment on reservations with the Indian Bureau. Many women, however, continued traditional forms of agricultural work— that is, gathering and gardening. Sioux women in North Dakota, anthropologist Patricia Albers writes, continued to cultivate crops—to grow root crops, corn, squash, and beans, and to forage for turnips, berries, and plants for food and medicine. In most instances, Native American women defied the expectations of domesticity implicit in the Dawes Act; they found instead roles that combined traditional types of labor with aspects of the commercial system, such as crafts production or wage work. The Sioux women studied by Albers, for example, also entered the cash economy by producing beadwork and quillwork, and by quilting, crocheting, and lacemaking.

In what ways did Native American women's new economic roles affect their status in household and community? Data on the status of plains Indian women in the twentieth century, anthropologist Katherine M. Weist points out, was collected in different eras and by different techniques and defies easy comparison. In some instances, as among the Wichita, scholars found that women's performance of traditional tasks provided stability for households on a disorganized reservation. In other instances, said researchers of the 1950s, women's position was "more important today than that of men." In still other instances, as among the Navaho, according to earlier research in the 1930s, women were too conservative, or rooted to tradition, to capitalize on their new economic roles. Still, Weist concludes, women's roles changed in concrete ways during what anthropologists call "reservation times": "Polygyny [the practice of acquiring multiple wives] was outlawed, neolocal residence [establishment of a new place of residence] and the nuclear family became more prevalent, birth rates increased, subsistence became more precarious, male unemployment became commonplace, and ceremonies changed." Among Sioux women, according to Patricia Albers, despite their rejection of white gender roles, opportunity for autonomy and influence waned. Loss of status resulted from exclusion from diplomacy and trade, which meant from dealings with the federal government. On the other hand, some Sioux women gained status through intermarriage with white men who had bought reservation lands.

The era of plains settlement, though long, was finite. By the start of the twentieth century, cities and industry had begun to transform the trans-Mississippi West, and women were drawn into the labor market. East or West, native-born or foreign born, the wage-earning woman of the turn of the century was likely to be young and single. Expecting to be only a temporary member of the labor force, she retained a grasp on domestic ideals.

IMMIGRANTS, CITIES, AND WORKING GIRLS

By the Civil War, immigrant women were part of the labor force. The largest immigrant group at midcentury, the Irish, had settled in eastern cities. Young Irishwomen entered domestic service, and became a feature of middle-class northeastern homes. In the 1880s, the first waves of new immigrants arrived. Scandinavians customarily migrated to the Great Plains to carve out homesteads on the last frontier; southern and eastern Europeans—Poles, Jews, Slavs, Italians—settled in eastern and midwestern cities and industrial towns. They soon constituted substantial percentages if not majorities of urban populations. Although the new immigrants came from diverse origins, from the Pale of Settlement to the Sicilian village, and although they identified only with members of their own ethnic group, a common cultural tradition united them. The family was the pivot of the new immigration, its cultural center and economic hub. The immigrant family formed a wage-earning unit, and the work of immigrant women was determined by their family roles.

A standard feature of the urban immigrant family was the wife who remained at home. Even in cases where married women had worked outside the home (usually seasonally) in their old countries, new immigrant families often rejected the idea of wage-earning wives and mothers. Married women, therefore, rarely took on full-time jobs, although they often took in piecework or boarders. Italian and Jewish women in New York's immigrant communities, for instance, made artificial flowers, chains, and garments at home, utilizing the hands of available family members. In all immigrant communities, a surplus of single men who boarded with families created a need for paid housekeeping services. By 1900, one out of five urban homes housed boarders. Women at home thus often contributed to family earnings. The income earned by immigrant fathers rarely sufficed to support a family. Employment on railroads, in mines, and in factories was irregular and poorly paid. The immigrant breadwinner never knew when he would next be laid off, which made family support a precarious venture. Unmarried children, therefore, were also expected to contribute to family income.

In Boston, New York, Chicago, and industrial towns across the Northeast, the daughters of immigrant parents sought employment in whatever work was available near their homes—factory work, mill work, domestic work. In Chicago at the turn of the century, for example, half of Italian women aged 15 to 19 worked for pay outside the home. New York's garment industry depended on the low-paid labor of young, single immigrant women. Throughout the late nineteenth century, the majority of women who entered the labor force were young, unmarried immigrants or the daughters of immigrants. "Most immigrant girls worked for about ten years," according to historian Donna Gabaccia, "typically in a variety of short-term, seasonal, and low-paying jobs." Indeed, the typical female factory operative before 1920, writes Gabaccia, was born either "on the other side" or shortly after her parents' arrival in the United States. A bridge between old world patterns and the new environment, the working daughter played a special role in family acculturation and in the economy.

The work patterns of urban immigrant women depended on local opportunities, family traditions, and ethnic attitudes toward women's work. In Pennsylvania steel mill towns, little opportunity existed for female employment outside the home; in cotton mill towns, options rose, and in large urban areas, opportunities were varied. The types of work women did also varied from one ethnic group to another. At mid-century, for instance, in New York's sixth ward, almost half of Irish women under 50 worked outside the home. Most of this group were young, unmarried women who took jobs as domestic servants or in related work. Wives and mothers earned income by caring for boarders. In the Italian community of Buffalo, New York, a half century later, both mothers and daughters avoided work that took them away from home or family. Married or unmarried, women might take in piecework at home or take on seasonal work, on farms or in canneries, but only as members of family groups. Significantly, whatever women did to contribute to family income, even within the tradition-bound Italian family, their work did not necessarily disrupt ethnic patterns, challenge male leadership, or alter the domestic balance of power. Instead, the immigrant family adjusted its economy to the new urban environment.

The ranks of urban women wage earners also included young native-born women who left rural areas and migrated to cities in search of employment. As early as the 1870s, the native-born working girl appeared in fiction, in Louisa May Alcott's *Work* (1873). Alcott's heroine, Christie Devon, a model of pluck and determination, found a series of jobs, as servant, seamstress, hired companion, and, briefly, in the theater, which Alcott viewed as an unwholesome environment. Two decades later, in Theodore Dreiser's controversial novel *Sister Carrie* (1900), Carrie Meeker followed the same episodic trail in search of work, from factory to store to theater, teetering on the line between wage earning and immorality. These fictional experiences reflected fact. For late-nineteenth-century working girls, paid work was irregular and inter-changeable; it shifted from shop to mill to factory to unemployment in rapid succession. Urban migrants who lived apart from their families or employers, like Carrie Meeker, were considered "women adrift." One-fifth of women wage earners in 1900, women adrift sometimes ventured into jobs as chorus girls or dance hall hostesses. This "sexual service sector," historian Joanne Meyerowitz suggests, was part of the urban economy. Whatever her job, the "working girl" became a feature of the city scene, along with its mansions, lodging houses, factories, and tenements. She could be recognized by her outfit, which a turn-of-the-century writer described as "coarse woolen garments, a shabby sailor hat, a cheap piece of fur, a knitted shawl, and gloves."

For Alcott's heroine, as for the next generation of working women, domestic service was often the only job option. In 1900, the million women in domestic service— maids, laundresses, cooks, companions, waitresses, and nurses—were 26 percent native-born, 19 percent daughters of immigrants, 28 percent foreign-born, and 27 percent black. For white workers, servitude was a last resort; the domestic work-week was half again as long as a week of factory work, with irregular hours and rare days off. Young women who had a choice usually preferred factory work to domestic work because of the lack of free time, the drudgery, the boredom, and especially the low status associated with domestic service. A 1902 reporter concluded that Massachusetts women would turn to shoe factories, textile mills, department stores, and restaurants rather than resort to domestic work, even if they earned less. In 1903, a New York settlement worker explained that "only the less desirable girls and new arrivals go willingly into this work." Yet many women had no choice. In midwestern cities, young Scandinavian immigrants often became domestic servants. In the Far West, as cities absorbed Chicano communities, Mexican American women took domestic work to contribute to family income. In the 1880s and 1890s, Mexican

Unlike the antebellum "hired girl," who helped a neighbor's wife with her work, the turn-of-the-century servant performed specialized functions, whether sweeping, scrubbing, baking, serving, preparing food, caring for children, or accepting a calling card. These seven young women posed for a photographer in Black River Falls, Wisconsin, in 1905.
(State Historical Society of Wisconsin)

American women around Los Angeles entered the labor market as domestics and laundresses, as well as fruit canners and farm laborers.

Like the factory girl, the female lodger, and the rural migrant, the prostitute was also a by-product of urbanization—one that generated much anxiety. She appeared wherever men congregated, as in Civil War army camps or western mining towns. In Virginia City, Nevada, a mining town where men outnumbered women three to one in 1875, for instance, one woman in 12 was a prostitute. The prostitute also appeared in cities and metropolises, despite efforts of reformers to lower her numbers and crush her vocation. The urban prostitute had much in common with her wage-earning sisters insofar as she was likely to be young, poor, and often recruited from their ranks. *Why* she had entered prostitution evoked special concern. Surveying the conditions of working women in the 1870s, the Massachusetts Labor Bureau concluded that low pay drove women into vice and that "the root of the evil will not be reached until women's wages will supply them with the necessities of life, elevating them above the clutch of sin." But economic need was not the only cause cited. Sometimes the prostitute appeared to be the victim of a network of villainous seducers and criminal procurers. Sometimes she seemed the victim of unfortunate family circumstances, notably lack of male support. Sometimes, finally, she seemed the victim of her own low threshold of resistance to what was described, variously, as temptation, attraction, and adventure.

Imbalanced sex ratios and greed abetted the growth of Chinese prostitution in San Francisco, where, in 1860, Chinese men outnumbered Chinese women 12 to one; most of these Chinese immigrant women were prostitutes. A decade later, four out of five Chinese women were prostitutes. Their procurement began in China, where agents enticed, bought, or kidnapped young women, transported them to California, and sold them to private owners or tongs (criminal organizations) that profited from their sexual services. Some prostitutes were enslaved; others worked under contracts of indenture of four or five years, without wages, to provide sex for the large Chinese male immigrant population and other customers. If "redeemed" for a fee, as some were, they married Chinese men. In practice, however, according to historian Lucie Cheng Hirata, the contract system offered little advantage over the slave system. The women lacked legal protection; protracted indefinitely, contracts offered only "false hopes." The substantial profits of prostitution, Hirata points out, went to Chinese and Caucasian men, including procurers in China, importers, brothel owners, and San Francisco property owners.

Although the sex ratio among Chinese immigrants grew yet more imbalanced, the proportion of prostitutes among adult Chinese women fell after 1870. In 1880, about 28 percent were prostitutes. By then, according to the manuscript census, a majority of employed Chinese women labored as servants, seamstresses, piece workers, laundresses, and in other occupations. Changing immigration patterns, regulatory laws, and rescue efforts helped to reduce the extent of Chinese prostitution. Local and state regulations impeded but did not end the trade. The Page Law, passed by Congress in 1875, outlawed the entry of contract laborers, prostitutes, and criminals, and the Chinese Exclusion Act of 1882, directed at laborers, vastly reduced Chinese immigration. Chinese women could still legally enter the United States but only as wives of merchants or men in other exempt occupations. Finally, urban

Reformer Donaldina Cameron of San Francisco's Presbyterian Mission Home,
surrounded by some of the residents, in the early twentieth century. Although
the mission won applause for its rescues of Chinese prostitutes, after the
1890s it housed mainly girls removed from abusive homes or "immoral"
circumstances by state agencies and juvenile courts. Cameron's "harvest
of waifs," above, may have included former prostitutes but probably
comprised youngsters who had been taken from their homes.
(California State Library, Sacramento)

rescue missions targeted Chinese prostitution; the Presbyterian Mission Home in
San Francisco, started in the 1870s, was an example. Led after 1900 for four decades
by reformer Donaldina Cameron, the mission staged raids on brothels to save
Chinese women from the sex trade and than retrained the rescued women for domestic or industrial work. Cameron's determination and success won widespread
praise. Former prostitutes, historian Peggy Pascoe shows, used the mission for their
own goals. Some found temporary respite, some chose to return to China, and some
used the mission's services to facilitate marriages with suitors. By the early twentieth
century, Chinese prostitution in San Francisco had been curtailed but not eradicated.

In eastern cities, the young white woman, native-born or immigrant daughter,
seen as the possible victim of the dreaded "white slave trade," became the target of
surveys, investigations, and remedial efforts. One of the first surveys of urban prostitutes was made just before the Civil War at New York's Blackwell Island, the women's
jail. When William Sanger, the prison physician, asked 2,000 women what had led
them into the trade, one out of four answered "inclination." Sanger suspected, however, that "other controlling influences" were at work. Giving more credence to such
answers as "destitution" and "seduced and abandoned," he also cited "the low rate of

wages paid to women." Three out of four prostitutes surveyed had been previously employed, most in domestic work and the rest making such items as clothes, hats, umbrellas, or flowers. Subsequent investigators found that only a narrow line separated the streetwalker from the servant, pieceworker, and factory girl. In 1889, on the basis of a government survey of nearly 4,000 prostitutes in major eastern and midwestern cities, the commissioner of labor, Carroll D. Wright, concluded that prostitutes were often recruited among girls of the "industrious classes." Almost a third of those surveyed had entered the trade directly from home. The rest had been previously employed in a cross section of women's occupations. Half had been domestic servants; the other half were drawn from the ranks of cloakmakers, dressmakers, shirtmakers, boxmakers, milliners, mill girls, salesgirls, cashiers, switchboard operators—indeed, every trade open to urban women.

Women who investigated prostitution in the first decades of the twentieth century stressed the urban evils that led girls astray. Middle-class reformers and professionals, they saw the prostitute as a victim of city life and male predators. Dorothy Richardson, who studied the lot of working women in 1911 by joining them, found factories to be a recruiting ground for the cities' red-light districts. In 1903, New York settlement worker Frances Kellor noted networks of aggressive recruiters ready to prey on newly arrived immigrants. Girls who were "homeless, friendless, penniless," she said, were often unable to "resist temptation . . . attractively presented." In Chicago, Jane Addams cited a combination of urban temptations, female gullibility, and the hazard of seduction. "A surprising number of country girls have been either brought to Chicago under false pretenses or have been decoyed into an evil life very soon after their arrival," she wrote in 1912. City girls too could be "decoyed" by dubious men who took them to disreputable places, such as dance halls, saloons, and vaudeville shows, and supplied them with drink. Rural or urban, said Addams, the girl who loved pleasure and adventure "could be easily recruited to a vicious life."

Yet another cause, the paucity of profitable alternatives, was suggested by a Philadelphia prostitute in the progressive era, in a correspondence she maintained with Boston philanthropist Fanny Howe. Although she had been halfheartedly looking for work, wrote Maimie Pinzer, "I don't propose to get up at 6:30 to be at work at 8 and work in a close stuffy room . . . until dark, for $6 or $7 a week. When I could . . . spend an afternoon with a congenial person and in the end have more than a week's work could pay me." According to historian Ruth Rosen, the progressive era prostitute *could* expect to earn about five times the income of the typical woman wage earner, such as a factory worker. Unlikely to see herself as a passive victim, she often viewed her trade as an avenue to upward mobility. Those prostitutes who responded to investigators' questionnaires also mentioned "bad family conditions" as a motive for entering the trade. Many reported a background of broken, troubled, and estranged families, with a history of incest, alcoholism, and economic crises. "Since prostitutes differed little from other women in the working class, except for a higher incidence of family instability," Rosen concludes, "the lack of family or good family relations may have been an important factor in many women's decision-making. Most women, whatever their class, who lacked the support of a family economy, found survival difficult on the wages paid for 'women's work.'"

By World War I, the campaign against prostitution effectively closed down urban red-light districts, driving prostitutes and the industry that lived off them underground. The prostitute had become more menace than victim. But the woman who became a "factory girl," spending 12 hours a day stitching, packing, or bottling, was often seen as a social hazard as well.

WOMEN IN INDUSTRY

By the turn of the century, five million American women earned wages and one out of five women was employed, a quarter of them in manufacturing. Although women were only 17 percent of the industrial work force, their numbers had vastly increased; there were four times as many women in industry in 1900 as there had been in 1870. This female labor force was mainly white, urban, and young. Three out of four women in industry were under 25, and three out of four were foreign-born or daughters of foreign-born parents. About half worked in the manufacture of cloth and clothing, including shoes, gloves, hats, stockings, and collars. Indeed, women were a majority of garment workers. But large contingents held jobs in other facets of manufacturing—in tobacco factories, where they were 38 percent of the employees, and in canneries, bookbinderies, twine- and box-making factories, packing plants, and commercial laundries.

Unskilled work and low pay distinguished the woman factory worker, as did concentration in a limited segment of industry. In every type of manufacturing that employed them, female workers held "women's jobs," that is, the ones that required the least training. The garment industry was a good example. The most highly skilled work—the cutting of fabric—was reserved for men. Most other work was only semiskilled, and women were easily trained as machine operators, trimmers, and finishers. The same formula applied elsewhere. In breweries, men were brewers and young women were bottle washers. In the preparation of cookies and crackers, men were bakers and women were boxers or "cracker-packers." In bookbinding, men were eligible for four-year apprenticeships to become skilled craftsmen, while women held lower-level jobs. Not surprisingly, unskilled women workers earned less than male workers in the same industries. In 1899, for instance, a man employed in industry could expect to earn $597 a year, and a woman $314. Moreover, the skilled woman worker, one who had learned a trade, earned about half as much as a nonunionized man doing the same work. Finally, women labored mainly in certain industries such as textile and garment manufacturing or food processing. Indeed, women crowded the industries that employed them, which ensured that wages would remain low.

But, as in the early days of the textile industry, the clustering of women workers in industries that were seen as extensions of household production did not mean that women had followed their inclinations for making cloth or food products out of the home and into the factory. On the contrary, by 1900, any form of mechanization that spurred the shift from home to workshop to factory, whether in textile, garment, or food production, tended to open an area of employment to men. The sewing machine, for instance, brought male workers into garment production more than it lured women from hearth to workplace. Clearly, women workers were concentrated in textile mills, hosiery plants, glove factories, and shirtwaist shops because of their exclusion elsewhere. Large numbers of women were not hired in heavy industry, in foundries, mines, or oil rigs, or in the production of machines or shipbuilding or construction. Nor were they welcomed in *any* skilled trade or craft, such as typography, welding, molding, or electrical work, at the insistence of men already employed in such occupations. The prospect of replacement by cheap female labor repelled late-nineteenth-century craftsmen. Nor was it always a viable option for employers. The temporary expectations of young women workers made it expedient for factory owners to hire them to do low-level, unskilled jobs in which one worker could easily replace another. Due to the abundance of young woman applicants, plenty were available for whatever work was open to them.

Once she was hired, whether in garment shop, bottling plant, shoe factory, or laundry, the turn-of-the-century woman worker was likely to confront the same problems that men did—long hours, dismal working conditions, and occupational hazards, which varied according to industry. The 60-hour, five-and-a-half-day

Throughout the early twentieth century, documentary photographer Lewis Hine exposed the evils of industrial life. As a reporter for the National Child Labor Committee, a pressure group founded by settlement leaders and other progressive reformers, Hine investigated working conditions in coal mines and canneries, textile mills and garment factories. His commentary and photographs, many of women and children workers, were published in committee literature and reform-minded journals. Here, garment workers in a sweatshop on New York's Lower East Side in 1908. (*George Eastman House, International Museum of Photography and Film*)

week was commonplace, and every industry had its rush season, which might mean a 14-hour day. When Rose Schneiderman got her first job as a cap maker in the 1890s, doing piecework, she was expected to work from eight until six, stitching linings in golf caps and yachting caps, which brought in, with hard work, about $5 a week. As in other parts of the garment trade, working women had to buy their own machines; they paid them off in installments and lost them entirely if, for instance, a factory burned down. Although a New York law of 1897 limited sweatshop labor, women workers were still subject to the inevitable hazards of factory life—standing, stooping, lifting, and hauling, as well as heat, dust, dampness, noise, monotony, and exhaustion.

Two constant complaints were unsanitary facilities and lack of fresh air. When the Massachusetts Labor Bureau investigated the conditions of needlework employees in the 1890s, it found women stuffed into unventilated attics and basements, "packed like sardines in a box." Women employed in commercial laundries, such as those in San Francisco, worked days and nights in steam-filled rooms, ironing one shirt a minute, dripping with sweat, and breathing ammonia. Investigating the work of bottle washers in a Milwaukee brewery in 1910, Mary Harris ("Mother") Jones reported that they were "condemned to slave daily in the washroom in wet shoes and wet clothes, surrounded with foul-mouthed, brutal foremen. . . . The poor girls work in the vile smell of sour beer, lifting cases of empty and full bottles, weighing from 100 to 150 pounds."

That Mother Jones, celebrated agitator and mine workers organizer, protested the lot of women workers was much in character. Daughter of Irish immigrants, wife of an ironmolder, sometime teacher and seamstress, Mother Jones had entered the labor scene in the 1870s after losing her husband and children to a yellow fever epidemic. In the outspoken role she fashioned for herself—defender of working men, protector of children, and patron saint of the miners—Jones earned her reputation as "mother of the laboring class." "She fights their battles with a Mother's Love," explained a reporter who trailed Mother Jones on a march to protest child labor in 1903. Like the working men she organized, Mother Jones believed that women and children should be protected from the abuses of industrial life. Neither, she contended, should work in mills, mines, and factories.

In the progressive era, several middle-class women investigated the plight of women workers. Some—among them Elizabeth Butler and Mary Van Kleeck—conducted scholarly inquiries into conditions of women's wage earning in various industries. Vassar historian Lucy Maynard Salmon extensively questioned servants and employers for a major study of domestic employment. Others sought to study female labor by joining the work force themselves. These middle-class reporters intended to serve, as one of them put it, as "a mouthpiece for the woman labourer," on the assumption that women workers were unable or unwilling to speak for themselves. They also hoped to discover and reveal the mentality of the woman worker.

Toward this end, in 1903, Bessie Van Vorst and her sister-in-law, Marie Van Vorst, became undercover agents in working-class territory. Marie worked in a Massachusetts shoe factory and then as a spooler in southern cotton mills. Adopting a disguise and an alias, Bessie Van Vorst spent nine months in various factory jobs, and finally worked as a bottler in a Pittsburgh pickle factory. Her job was to stuff the pickles into jars, cork, label, load, and haul. Although critical of working conditions and of discrimination against women workers, Van Vorst also criticized the workers themselves. First, women workers did not seem to be especially ambitious or adept; indeed, Van Vorst herself was immediately recognized by her forewoman as an un- usually bright and able worker. Moreover, she contended, there were significant dif- ferences in motivation between male and female workers, even in the same plant. The men in the pickle factory were "breadwinners," whereas the women were only in part self-supporting. Some contributed to family income, others worked only for "pin money" or to buy themselves clothes. Van Vorst's working girls were hardly committed, whether to pickle bottling, personal advancement, or proletarian causes.

Another undercover woman investigator, Dorothy Richardson, also adopted the role of a "working girl," living in a cheap New York boardinghouse and finding jobs in local factories. Richardson decided that working women would have to unionize before their lot would improve. But like Bessie Van Vorst, she also criticized the working girls' attitudes. The young woman worker, said Richardson, failed as a wage earner because she had "an instinctive antagonism to her task" and was unable to cope with factory life. If she was exploited, it was because she had never learned to "work," only to "be worked," and because of some vital defect in her character. "At the present time," said Richardson, "there is nobody so little concerned about her condition as the working woman herself . . . apathetic, patient, long suffering."

The alleged problem of apathy and passivity to which Richardson pointed had many implications. Because of these qualities, the woman factory worker was seen as both a victim and a menace—to herself, to other workers, and to society at large. As she was easily exploited, she was associated with the lowering of wages in whatever industry she entered and with the consequent demeaning of the work that she did. It was widely suspected that she displaced male workers by her willingness to work for less. New machinery, moreover, seemed to enhance her opportunities. In most in- stances, of course, machinery provided more work for men. But in some trades, such as the shoe industry, mechanization enabled more women to move into factory jobs. Between 1870 and 1910, the proportion of women shoe workers increased fivefold. Shoemaking was, by now, no longer a craft but an assembly-line process, in which machine operators could be quickly trained.

The "progress" of women in industry therefore seemed linked, inexorably, to the degradation of work and the unemployment of men. The woman worker, through no fault of her own, was in a double bind, as government reports made clear. "A gener- ation ago, women were allowed to enter but few occupations," said the commissioner of labor in 1889, "but now there are hundreds of vocations in which they can find employment." Explaining the "vast extension of opportunity," the commissioner pre- sented low wages as a female advantage. "Whenever any industrial occupations are simplified to such an extent that the weaker person can perform what was done of old by the stronger one, the cheaper labor comes in." Women may have lowered wages in the industries they entered, he pointed out, but they earned more than they could before. "In so far as women have displaced men, they have taken advantage of op- portunities which were not open to them before such displacement. . . . They are now earning something where formerly they could earn little or nothing."

A special commission's investigation at the turn of the century also supported the theory that women displaced men in industrial jobs. In her 1910 report on the condition of women and children wage earners for the U.S. Senate, labor historian Helen Sumner assessed the shift of women's work from home to factory with ambivalence. From one point of view, women had advanced by entering industry: "Their unpaid services have been transformed into paid services . . . their ranges of possible employment have increased." From another point of view, the woman wage earner was a liability and a source of problems. "The story of women's work in gainful employments is a story of . . . long hours, low wages, unsanitary conditions, over work, and the want on the part of the woman of training, skill, and vital interest in her work," concluded Sumner. "It is a story, moreover, of underbidding, of strike-breaking, of the lowering of standards for [male] breadwinners."

The working woman had not really displaced men, as government reports contended. Rather, most women wage earners filled gaps in the expanding industrial sector by taking "new" jobs—unskilled jobs that men had never held. Nor is it clear that women wage earners lowered the standards for male "breadwinners," because female labor was concentrated in certain industries and job categories; crowded into the trades that hired them, women tended to lower wages for each other more than for male workers. But the threat posed by the "factory girl" to the male "breadwinner" was still genuine. Not only were women willing to work for low wages, not only were they available in large numbers, but they were usually passive and tractable as employees. Regarding industrial work as a temporary occupation, young women did not seem to see themselves as permanent members of the labor force and were less likely than men to start protests, strikes, or labor organizations. This only increased their threat to the working man. As a result, local and national unions, run by skilled men, tended to view the woman worker with suspicion.

THE UNION EXPERIENCE

Although women workers participated in many labor protests in the post–Civil War era, these strikes—of cigar makers, seamstresses, laundresses, and textile workers—were usually local actions and responses to particular situations, rather than efforts to establish permanent labor organizations. Women textile workers in Fall River, for instance, who protested wage cuts and struck three mills in 1875, mobilized effectively and persuaded men to join them. But eight months later, the starving strikers returned to work, accepted wage cuts, and signed oaths not to join a union; strike leaders were blacklisted. Another factor compounded the impotence of women workers in labor confrontations. National crafts unions, formed by skilled male workers, did not welcome women. In 1890, only two national unions admitted women, and the vast majority of women workers were unorganized. By the turn of the century, only 3.3 percent of women in industry were in unions; and during the next decade, their numbers dropped. A surge of organization among garment workers after 1909 began to turn the tide, but union membership rose slowly. In 1920, women were 20 percent of the work force but under 8 percent of organized workers.

Unions not only lacked interest in organizing women but also consistently tried to exclude them, both from their ranks and from the work force. Unionists had their own rationale. According to male craftsmen, female labor in industry was, variously, a temporary phenomenon, an unfortunate necessity, a capitalist plot, and an insult to women. It was also, explicitly, a threat to themselves. To the skilled male worker, who felt his job endangered by cheap female labor, the woman worker took on an aura of menace. "Wherever she goes," a union leader told a government commission in 1900, "she is reducing [man's] wages, and wherever large numbers of women are employed in any occupation, the point will be reached where woman gets as much as a man by making man's wages as low as a woman's." To the working man, the entry of women would drive down wages for everyone in an industry and even drive men out of the work force. Moreover, craftsmen associated the arrival of women workers with the introduction of machines that foreshadowed their own obsolescence.

As a result of these fears, union men supported the domestic ideal. "Woman was created to be man's companion," argued an official of the National Labor Union in the 1860s, "to be the presiding deity of the home circle . . . to guide the tottering footsteps of tender infancy." The policy of the NLU, made up of skilled craftsmen, set the tone. First, the NLU leaders put the blame for female competition not directly on women but on the employers who hired them—"the worst enemies of our race, the shylocks of the age, the robbers of women's virtue." Second, the Union argued that women should get equal pay for equal work. This was an earnest but double-faced plea. Were women to receive equal pay, there would be less reason to employ them at all. In that event, men—whom employers typically preferred as workers—would get all the jobs, and women would be excluded from the labor force.

Unorganized women workers could not contest this barrage of arguments. But throughout the late nineteenth century, women's rights proponents disputed the reality of the domestic ideal and defended women's need to work. "The old idea, that all men support all women, is an absurd fiction," reformer and writer Caroline Dall claimed in 1860. In 1869, when Susan B. Anthony urged women typographers (who had been excluded from the typographers union) to break strikes, she stressed the right of women to earn wages. "I perfectly agree that women should be married," she answered a unionist who claimed that woman's true role lay outside typography. "The real fact of life is that women have to support themselves." The leading woman organizer of the Knights of Labor, Leonora Barry, echoed the argument. "I believe it was intended that man should be the breadwinner," she wrote in 1889. "But as that is impossible under present conditions, I believe women should have every opportunity to become proficient in whatever vocation they choose."

The Knights of Labor, active in the 1870s and 1880s, was an exception in the unionist crusade against women workers. This national union, with 50,000 women members and 113 all-women locals, tried to organize unskilled women workers, blacks, and immigrants. The Knights' Woman's Bureau was headed by Leonora Barry, an Irish immigrant, widowed mother, and former hosiery worker from upstate New York. When she retired in 1889, Barry recommended the abolition of the bureau she had run. "The time when we should separate the interests of the toiling masses on sex lines is past," she explained. But Barry's hopes for labor unity made little headway. After 1886, the Knights of Labor lost influence, and the American Federation of Labor surged to the forefront of union leadership.

Representing skilled workingmen, native-born and nativist, the AFL grew steadily from the 1890s to the 1920s, when it had more than four million members. An exponent of the domestic ideal, the AFL adopted a position toward women that was, in practice, profoundly ambivalent, as labor historian Alice Kessler-Harris has shown. To the AFL leadership, women were weak, helpless, and easily exploited and therefore a dangerous threat to workingmen. Committed to extracting equal pay for women, the AFL wanted to make them less desirable as employees and get them out of the labor force. The federation hired a few women organizers, such as Mary Kenny in 1892 and Annie Fitzgerald in 1908, but its primary goal was to protect male members. As a result, it urged women to organize, on the one hand, and to stay home, on the other.

AFL leaders waved this "double-edged sword," as Kessler-Harris calls it, with consummate skill. One tactic was to deny the need of women to work. "In our time, and at least in our country, generally speaking," AFL president Samuel Gompers told the *Ladies' Home Journal* in 1905, "there is no necessity of the wife contributing to the support of the family by working." Patently false, such statements also evaded the fact that daughters rather than wives filled the ranks of women in industry. Another tactic was to depict the working class as a huge family. "It is the so-called competition of the unorganized, defenseless woman worker, the girl and the wife, that often tends to reduce the wages of the father and husband," said Gompers. The working woman, as an AFL spokesman told a government commission in 1900, "is competing with the man who is her father and husband, or who is to become her husband." In unionist rhetoric, the working girl became a saboteur of the home. "Is it a pleasing indication of progress to see the father, the brother, and the son displaced as the breadwinner by the mother, sister, and daughter?" asked a craft union leader in the *American Federationist* in 1897. He then answered his own question with a devastating tirade. "The growing demand for female labor is not founded upon philanthropy," he charged. "It does not spring from the milk of human kindness. It is an insidious assault upon the home; it is the knife of the assassin, aimed at the family circle. . . . We can no longer afford to brush away with an impulse of mock gallantry the terrible evil that is threatening the land, the community, the home."

The hostility of male unionists to female labor was effective. Unable either to organize or to stop working, women sometimes formed "protective associations," which were mutual benefit societies rather than unions or bargaining agents. In the 1880s, women reformers created a network of "Working Girls' Clubs," which sought to supply a wholesome environment and foster self-improvement. But these, not unions either, faded away in the 1890s. Meanwhile, women continued to gravitate toward the textile industry and the garment trade. The great shirtwaist strike of 1909 reflected this gravitation and proved that women could organize effectively.

On November 24, 1909, 18,000 garment workers walked off their jobs at 500 of New York's shirtwaist shops. Their grievances included long hours, safety hazards, lack of overtime pay, and the abuses of subcontractors. Throughout the cold winter, as the young strikers, mainly Jewish and Italian, picketed their shops, public attention increased. The New York branch of the Women's Trade Union League (WTUL), formed in 1903 to foster women's unions, offered the services of well-off supporters, who ran a strike center. WTUL activists, like labor leaders Pauline Newman and Rose Schneiderman, galvanized support. Local 25 of the International Ladies Garment Workers Union, whose membership surged to 20,000, held mass protest meetings. In January, the strike spread to Philadelphia, and many of the smaller

During the shirtwaist strike of 1909, the New York Women's Trade Union
League opened a strike headquarters where middle-class "allies" arranged
publicity and raised funds to pay the fines of arrested waistmakers. The
three young women at the left are wearing shirtwaists.
(Museum of the City of New York)

New York manufacturers capitulated to the strikers' demands. But the largest companies, which united in a manufacturers' association, held out. By February, the strikers
drifted back to work. About 300 shops agreed to recognize the union, though not, as
strikers urged, to hire only union workers. Nor did abuses and safety hazards vanish.
When a fire broke out at the Triangle Shirtwaist Company in 1911, 146 women workers burned or plunged to their deaths. "Every year thousands of us are maimed,"
Schneiderman told a mass meeting after the Triangle fire. "We have tried you good
people of the public and we have found you wanting." The public responded with a
state commission to investigate labor abuses in the garment industry.

Several factors made the shirtwaist strike and the organization of garment
workers distinctive. One was the personnel. A large proportion of garment workers
and two-thirds of the shirtwaist strikers were Jewish immigrant women, who drew on
a sense of ethnic solidarity and a tradition of militancy. These pervaded the non-
wage-earning sector as well. For instance, Jewish housewives organized effective
boycotts of kosher meat markets in New York in 1902, in Cleveland in 1906, and in
Detroit in 1910. Another important factor in the strike was the New York branch of
the WTUL, which sought to unite its well-to-do members ("allies") and women
workers in common cause. Eager to demonstrate female solidarity, the league mobilized impressive publicity and support for the waistmakers. Beyond spurring women's
unions, the WTUL also hoped to train working-class women for union leadership.
It made strides on both counts. By 1910, women had been organized in a variety of
trades, including bookbinding, tobacco manufacture, laundries, and some textile
mills, and a dozen national unions admitted women. But the extent of organization

was inadequate. As a result, the WTUL sponsored a combination of vocational training and protective legislation.

Protective laws were intended to ensure the welfare of working women by limiting their hours, raising their wages, and providing improved working conditions. To advocates, such laws would serve as a substitute for unionization, offering women the benefits that unions provided for organized men. Although only nominally supported by male unions, the laws also offered an ideal way to achieve goals long endorsed by the AFL. By limiting working hours and setting minimum wages, protective laws could take away the woman worker's major assets—cheapness and exploitability. Moreover, protective laws could also be used to keep women out of work that might be viewed as injurious to their health, morals, or reproductive capacity. As a craft union leader in the cigar industry observed in 1879, "We cannot drive the female out of the trade but we can restrict [her] through factory laws." Protective laws reflected both the problems of women's unionization and the tenacity of the domestic ideal.

A state supreme court invalidated one of the first such laws, an 1881 statute banning women from working in places that sold alcohol. The law, said the court, violated the state constitution by depriving women of a vocation open to men. But subsequent exclusionary laws were upheld, as were maximum-hour laws. Massachusetts led the way with an 1884 law limiting women's working day to 10 hours, and from the 1890s on, other states followed. By 1914, 27 states regulated women's working hours, and by the 1920s, 15 states had minimum wage laws. Between 1908 and World War I, many states enacted new protective laws or made earlier measures more rigorous. Besides regulating wages or hours or both, such laws might prevent women from working at night, carrying heavy weights, working in dangerous places, such as mines, or in morally hazardous places, such as bars. The growth of protective legislation was propelled by the 1908 Supreme Court case of *Muller* v. *Oregon*, a case concerning a woman laundry worker whose employer was arrested for forcing her to work overtime in violation of the state's 10-hour law. Contending that sex was a valid basis for classification, the Court upheld the Oregon law and thereby endorsed protective legislation. As an AFL columnist contended in 1900, "female labor should be limited so as not to injure the motherhood and family life of a nation."

The enactment of protective legislation had mixed effects. In many cases, the laws *did* protect women's health, improve their working conditions, limit their hours, and raise their wages—the goals of reformers who supported them. Protective laws had long-term benefits, too. They laid a foundation for New Deal wage and hour laws, and after World War I, when the U.S. Women's Bureau was established, gave women activists a foothold in the federal bureaucracy. But there was a downside: Protective laws also narrowed women's employment opportunities. As a result, they provoked an ideological feud among politicized women that continued through the 1920s. Socialists, for instance, who strove for class unity, thought that *all* workers, not just women, should be protected by law. Some feminists, who denied that sex was a valid basis for classification, decried the laws. As Susan B. Anthony had explained early on, they set women apart from men. Social reformers—such as the earnest advocates in the WTUL—devoted to women's welfare, supported the laws in order to protect women workers from exploitation. Women unionists, ever pragmatic, supported them too, though as something of a last resort. Labor leader Fannia Cohen, for instance, who criticized unions for not treating women equally, endorsed protective laws in the 1920s. "Considering that women are not as yet organized into trade unions," she contended, "it would be folly to agitate against such laws."

With or without the laws, male bastions in the industrial work force successfully resisted feminization. This was not the case elsewhere on the labor market. In the late nineteenth century, as business and trade expanded, women moved into other categories of new jobs, in offices and stores. A cut above domestic and factory work, such white-collar jobs drew middle-class women into the labor force. But like her counterpart in industry, the white-collar worker tended to be young, temporary, and crowded into her occupation.

OFFICE, STORE, AND CLASSROOM

The feminization of clerical work and teaching by the turn of the century reflected the growth of business and public education. It also reflected limited opportunities elsewhere. Throughout the nineteenth century, stereotyping of work by sex had restricted women's employment. Job options were limited; any field that admitted women attracted a surplus of applicants willing to work for less pay than men would have received. The entry of women into such fields—whether grammar school teaching or office work—drove down wages. Male workers in turn sought better opportunities elsewhere. The low status of occupations dominated by women resulted from the low pay that accompanied feminization.

The feminization of clerical work and teaching had much in common. Both fields provided new jobs—that is, business and public education were areas of rapid expansion. In private sector or public sector, the cheaper labor of women made them desirable employees. Both fields employed native-born women, not immigrant daughters, especially at the outset. Indeed these new jobs attracted new women into the labor force—middle-class young women with the requisite skills. Those whose accent or appearance might be inappropriate were not hired. In neither field, finally, was there organized opposition to the hiring of women such as that provided in industry by male craft unions. Men did not view grammar school teaching or clerking as desirable, permanent jobs. They were more like *rites de passage*, or first jobs, for young men on their way up to better things. By 1900, expanding opportunities for men reduced their interest in low-paid clerkships or grammar school posts. The combination of better male options elsewhere and the growth of business and education paved a golden path for female employment.

Women first took office jobs during the Civil War, when widows of Union officers received posts in government offices, at lower pay than the men they replaced. Jobs opened up in the private sector, too. In the 1860s, for instance, women bookkeepers were hired at one-third the pay of men. By the 1870s, women *were* competing with men for office jobs in the private sector as clerks and stenographers, with considerable advantages. Not only could they be hired at half men's pay but also they had no expectations of constant promotions and higher salaries, as men did. Office bureaucracies grew rapidly, so few men were deprived of work. Improved technology, meanwhile, created new jobs for women. The introduction of the typewriter, a term also used for the person who typed on it, proved a special boon. By the 1890s, the new machines were widely used. Business schools now trained women as "typewriters," stenographers, and bookkeepers. (The steno-typist had far more skills than the worker she replaced, the copyist.) Half the nation's women high school graduates completed business programs. By 1890, a majority of high school graduates *were* women, which provided a large pool of potential employees.

Women's role in office work rapidly grew. In 1870, women were only about 3 percent of office workers, but by 1890, they were 17 percent. In World War I, women became clerks, stenographers, copyists, typists, and bookkeepers. They also worked as sales clerks in retail stores; between 1870 and 1900 the number of women sales clerks multiplied tenfold. Finally, rising options in commerce and trade were again enhanced by improved technology, namely, the telegraph and the telephone. Although men, or rather boys, were the first phone operators, women who would work for half their pay soon held a share of the jobs. By 1890, all daytime operators were women.

Like other women wage earners, those at typewriters, switchboards, and store counters tended to be young and to view themselves as temporary wage earners. But because they were better educated than women in industry, they considered themselves an elite among women employees. An office worker might earn no more than a skilled garment worker, but the work was more regular, "dignified," and desirable. Women viewed the world of commerce as a new frontier of female employment. As more young women entered office work, the field was reshaped to suit domestic ideals. A sexual division of labor in business transformed office work into service work—or "women's work." A man entering business was expected to be ambitious, aggressive, and competitive, so as to rise in the ranks; but not so the woman office worker. She was expected instead to be neat, clean, agreeable, and useful to others— qualities that would later suit her for home life as well.

In teaching, women had made inroads even earlier. By the Civil War, one out of four teachers was a woman, who earned at most half the salary of a male teacher. When the army advertised for teachers in southern freedmen's schools in 1865, it offered half pay for the same positions as men. Nonetheless, women dominated the ranks of freedmen's teachers and took over many jobs in the common schools as well. After the war, the availability of women candidates and the vast growth of public education ensured rapid feminization of the teaching profession. In 1870, 90 percent of professional women were teachers, and two out of three grammar school teachers were women. The proportion of teachers who were women expanded most rapidly in the 1870s and continued to grow thereafter. By the turn of the century, two out of three professional women were teachers and three out of four teachers were women. In cities this percentage was even higher.

The teacher's status as a "professional" has to be qualified. In the late nineteenth century, the young woman teacher was likely to have no more than a sixth- or eighth-grade education. She taught, as a rule, only at the primary school level; men dominated secondary education. The experience of future suffrage leader Anna Howard Shaw in Michigan during the Civil War illustrates the quality of the teacher's preparation and the nature of her work, especially in rural areas, for the rest of the century.

"When I was fifteen years old I was offered a situation as schoolteacher," Shaw wrote in her memoirs.

> By this time the community was growing around us with the rapidity of these western settlements, and we had nearer neighbors whose children needed instruction. I passed an examination before a school board consisting of three nervous and self-conscious men whose certificate I still hold, and I at once began my professional career on the modest salary of two dollars a week and my board. The school was four miles from my home so I "boarded round" with the families of my pupils. . . . During the first year I had about fourteen pupils, of varying ages, sizes, and temperaments, and there was hardly a book in the schoolroom except those I owned.

As Shaw's experience suggests, even young women of modest means could aspire to teach, because little training was required—but only if they were single. Like other working women, teachers were expected to leave their jobs at marriage, and school boards often mandated that they do so. Beyond spinsterhood, prerequisites were few, at least until the twentieth century, when cities began to require special training and licensing exams. But as teaching was the only profession women could enter in any numbers, college graduates flocked to it also. In the 1880s, teaching absorbed two out of three alumnae who sought employment.

Teaching was also an opportunity for African American women, to whom other white-collar occupations were closed. The establishment of a black public school system in the South drew black women into the classroom. By the turn of the century, they were the mainstays of impoverished rural primary schools throughout the region; black school systems were so underfunded that their teachers received only a fraction of what white teachers earned. The preparation of black teachers was as varied as that of white contemporaries. At one extreme was the example of Susie King Taylor, who had received some rudimentary training as a slave and supported herself through Reconstruction as a teacher. At the other was that of distinguished educators such as Fannie Jackson Coppin, also born a slave, who graduated from Oberlin College in 1865 and went on to head the "female department" of the Philadelphia Institute for Colored Youth. In the progressive era, women teachers, such as Lucy Lainey, Nannie Burroughs, and Mary McLeod Bethune, founded educational institutions, often supported by black and white philanthropy. These schools were a source of pride; the South had few black secondary schools. Finally, teaching provided more black women than men with professional work or at least skilled vocations. As a result, black families went to greater efforts to educate daughters than sons, reversing the priorities of white families.

When suffrage leader Carrie Chapman Catt assessed women's progress in the professions in 1900, she proclaimed that "No occupation illustrates more clearly the immensity of the changes wrought than teaching." Although Catt pointed out that higher positions in the field were reserved for men and that women teachers always received lower pay, her emphasis was on progress—on the "rapidity with which conditions have changed in the last fifty years . . . the constantly increasing demand of women for work, the decrease of prejudice against the woman worker . . . the opening of nearly all occupations to women." In 1903, Charlotte Perkins Gilman similarly celebrated women's vocational advances over the past century as "a phenomenon unparalleled in history." Never before, announced Gilman, "has so large a mass made as much progress in so short a time."

Such celebration, however, ignored the strange ambivalence of women's employment. For most white wage-earning women, "progress" meant movement into new, exploitative types of work, whether in industry, classrooms, or offices. This was work that became underpaid when women assumed it and work that was assumed, for the most part, by the least powerful members of society—young women and poor women. Black women, meanwhile, and white women as well continued to take even less desirable work as domestic servants or in related menial jobs. In either case, the woman wage earner was less liberated by her employment than proletarianized, though reluctant to assume a working-class identity. The pattern of female employment set before 1900, finally, continued to characterize the labor market for decades to come. In the early twentieth century, as in 1860, women's low rank as workers reflected the pervasive belief that their true vocation was at home. A cultural emblem, the domestic ideal relegated women wage earners to second-class status in economic life.

The domestic ideal also affected the roles of middle- and upper-class women, who were better able to capitalize on it. In the late nineteenth century, while thousands of women entered the bottom realms of the labor market, women also entered colleges, the professions, and large, new women's associations. A generation of organizers and institution builders, they expanded the boundaries of "home" to include the nation.

SUGGESTED READINGS AND SOURCES

Alice Kessler-Harris provides an overview of women's roles in the labor force in *Out to Work: A History of Wage-Earning Women in America* (New York, 1982), chs. 4–8. See also Robert Smuts, *Women and Work in America* (New York, 1959); Barbara Meyer Wertheimer, *We Were There: The Story of Working Women in America* (New York, 1977); Julie A. Matthaei, *An Economic History of Women in America* (New York, 1982); Lynn Y. Weiner, *From Working Girl to Working Mother: The Female Labor Force in the United States, 1820–1980* (Chapel Hill, N.C., 1985); Claudia Goldin, *Understanding the Gender Gap: An Economic History of American Women* (New York, 1990); and Kessler-Harris, *A Woman's Wage: Historical Meanings and Social Consequences* (Lexington, Ky., 1990).

For primary sources, see W. Elliott Brownlee and Mary N. Brownlee, eds., *Women and the American Economy: A Documentary History* (New York, 1976), and Rosalyn Baxandall, Linda Gordon, and Susan Reverby, eds., *America's Working Women: A Documentary History*, 2d ed. (New York, 1998). Collections of articles on women and labor include Milton Cantor and Bruce Laurie, eds., *Class, Sex, and the Woman Worker* (Westport, Conn., 1977); Ruth Milkman, ed., *Women, Work, and Protest: A Century of U.S. Labor History* (Boston, 1985); and Ava Baron, ed., *Work Engendered: Toward a New History of American Labor* (Ithaca, N.Y., 1991).

Mary Elizabeth Massey surveys women's roles in the Civil War era in *Bonnet Brigades: American Women and the Civil War* (New York, 1966). For recent research, see Catherine Clinton and Nina Silber, eds., *Divided Houses: Gender and the Civil War* (New York, 1992);

Anne C. Rose, *Victorian America and the Civil War* (New York, 1992); and Elizabeth Young, *Disarming the Nation: Women's Writing and the American Civil War* (Chicago, 2000). The origins of nursing are discussed in Susan M. Reverby, *Ordered to Care: The Dilemma of American Nursing, 1850–1945* (Cambridge, Mass., and New York, 1987); Ann Douglas, "The War Within a War: Women Nurses in the Union Army," *Civil War History*, 18 (1972), 197–212; and Jane E. Schultz, "The Inhospitable Hospital: Gender and Professionalism in Civil War Medicine," *Signs*, 17 (Winter 1992), 363–392. For Union women's activism, see Jeanie Attie, *Patriotic Toil: Northern Women and the American Civil War* (Ithaca, N.Y., 1998) and Judith Ann Giesberg, *Civil War Sisterhood: The United States Sanitary Commission and Women's Politics in Transition* (Boston, 2000). Elizabeth D. Leonard, *Yankee Women: Gender Battles in the Civil War* (New York, 1994), discusses three Union women who participated in the war; in *All the Daring of the Soldier: Women of the Civil War Armies* (New York, 1999), Leonard considers spies and disguised soldiers on both sides. For antislavery women, see Wendy Venet, *Neither Ballots Nor Bullets: Women Abolitionists and the Civil War* (Charlottesville, Va., 1991). Recent biographies of Union activists include Stephen B. Oates, *A Woman of Valor: Clara Barton and the Civil War* (New York, 1994); David L. Gollaher, *Voice for the Mad: The Life of Dorothea Dix* (New York, 1995); and Thomas J. Brown, *Dorothea Dix: New England Reformer* (Cambridge, Mass., 1998), a critical assessment.

The experience of Confederate women is examined in George C. Rable, *Women and the Crisis of Southern Nationalism* (Urbana, Ill., 1989); Drew Gilpin Faust, *Mothers of Invention: Women of the Slaveholding South in the American Civil War* (Chapel Hill, N.C., 1996); and Anne Firor Scott, *The Southern Lady* (Chicago, 1970), chs. 4 and 5. Clarence Mohr discusses women's work on plantations in *On the Threshold of Freedom: Masters and Slaves in Civil War Georgia* (Athens, Ga., 1986), ch. 7. Recent scholarship includes LeeAnn Whites, *The Civil War as a Crisis in Gender, Augusta, Georgia, 1860–1890* (Athens, Ga., 1995); Edward D. C. Campbell, Jr., and Kym S. Rice, eds., *A Woman's War: Southern Women, Civil War, and the Confederate Legacy* (Charlottesville, Va., 1996); Laura F. Edwards, *Scarlett Doesn't Live Here Anymore: Southern Women in the Civil War Era* (Urbana, Ill., 2000); and Edwards, *Gendered Strife and Confusion: The Political Culture of Reconstruction* (Urbana, Ill., 1997), on gender ideology and southern households. Catherine Clinton, *Tara Revisited: Women, War, and the Plantation Legend* (New York, 1995), explores southern myths. Peter W. Bardaglio's study, *Reconstructing the Household: Families, Sex, and the Law in the Nineteenth Century South* (Chapel Hill, N.C., 1995) shows how slavery, war, and emancipation shaped family law and domestic relations. For women's work in the freedmen's schools, see Henry L. Swint, *The Northern Teacher in the South* (Nashville, Tenn., 1941), and Jacqueline Jones, *Soldiers of Light and Love: Northern Teachers and Georgia Blacks, 1865–1873* (Chapel Hill, N.C., 1980).

Jacqueline Jones surveys black women's experience in this era in *Labor of Love, Labor of Sorrow* (New York, 1986), chs. 2–5. For the impact of emancipation, see Leon Litwack, *Been in the Storm So Long: The Aftermath of Slavery* (New York, 1979); Tera W. Hunter, *To 'Joy My Freedom: Southern Black Women's Lives and Labor After the Civil War* (Cambridge, Mass., 1997); Leslie A. Schalm, *A Hard Fight For We: Women's Transition From Slavery to Freedom in South Carolina* (Urbana, Ill., 1997); and Norale Frankel, *Freedom's Women: Black Women and Families in Civil War Era Mississippi* (Bloomington, Ind., 1999). An important war memoir is Susie King Taylor, *A Black Woman's Civil War Memoirs: Reminiscences of My Life in Camp*, ed. by Patricia W. Romero and Willie Lee Rose (Princeton, N.J., 2001). Sociologist Susan A. Mann explores the transition from slave labor to sharecropping in "Slavery, Sharecropping, and Sexual Equality,"

Signs, 14 (Summer 1989), 774–798. For the black family after slavery, see Herbert M. Gutman, *The Black Family in Slavery and Freedom, 1750–1925* (New York, 1977); Gutman, "Persistent Myths About the Afro-American Family," *Journal of Interdisciplinary History*, 6 (Autumn 1975), 181–210; Frank F. Furstenberg, Jr., Theodore Hershberg, and John Modell, "The Origin of the Female-Headed Black Family: The Impact of the Urban Experience," *Journal of Interdisciplinary History*, 6 (Autumn 1975), 211–234; and Elizabeth Pleck, "The Two-Parent Household: Black Family Structure in Late Nineteenth-Century Boston," *Journal of Social History*, 6 (Fall 1972), 1–31.

For urban migration, see Florette Henri, *Black Migration: Movement North, 1900–1920* (New York, 1976); Elizabeth Pleck, *Black Migration and Poverty, Boston, 1865–1900* (New York, 1979); and James Grossman, *Land of Hope: Chicago, Black Southerners, and the Great Migration* (Chicago, 1989). Black women's roles as wage earners are discussed in Claudia Golden, "Female Labor Force Participation: The Origin of Black and White Differences," *Journal of Economic History*, 37 (March 1977), 87–108, and Elizabeth Pleck, "A Mother's Wages: Income Earned Among Married Italian and Black Women, 1896–1914," in Michael Gordon, ed., *The American Family in Social and Historical Perspective*, 2d ed. (New York, 1978), pp. 490–510. For black and white women in poverty, see Jacqueline Jones, *The Dispossessed: America's Underclasses from the Civil War to the Present* (New York, 1992), which focuses on the outmigration of Southerners in the twentieth century.

For women's work on farms and ranches, see Nancy Grey Osterud, *Bonds of Community: The Lives of Farm Women in Nineteenth-Century New York* (Ithaca, N.Y., 1991); Deborah Fink, *Agrarian Women: Wives and Mothers in Rural Nebraska, 1880–1940* (Chapel Hill, N.C., 1992); Sally McMurry, *Transforming Rural Life: Dairying Families and Agricultural Change, 1820–1885* (Baltimore, Md., 1995); Mary Neth, *Preserving the Family Farm: Women, Community, and the Foundations of Agribusiness in the Midwest, 1900–1940* (Baltimore, Md., 1995); Katherine Jellison, *Entitled to Power: Farm Women and Technology, 1913–1963* (Chapel Hill, N.C., 1993); and Dee Garceau, *The Important Things of Life: Women, Work, and Family in Sweetwater County, Wyoming, 1880–1929* (Lincoln, Neb., 1997). Women's work roles in the post–Civil War West are discussed in Sandra L. Myres, *Westering Women and the Frontier Experience, 1800–1915* (Albuquerque, N. Mex., 1982); Lillian Schlissel, ed., *Western Women: Their Land, Their Lives* (Albuquerque, N. Mex., 1988); Glenda Riley, *A Place to Grow: Women in the American West* (Arlington Heights, Ill., 1992), section 4; H. Elaine Lindgren, *Land in Her Own Name: Women as Homesteaders in North Dakota* (Norman, Okla., 1996); and Arlene Scadron, ed., *On Their Own: Widows and Widowhood in the American Southwest, 1848–1939* (Urbana, Ill., 1988). For Mexican American women's labor in the late nineteenth and early twentieth centuries, see Sarah Deutsch, *No Separate Refuge: Culture, Class, and Gender on an Anglo-Hispanic Frontier in the American Southwest, 1880–1940* (New York, 1987); Albert Camarillo, *Chicanos in a Changing Society: From Mexican Pueblos to American Barrios in Santa Barbara and Southern California, 1848–1940* (Cambridge, Mass., 1979); and Mario T. Garcia, "The Chicana in American History: The Mexican Women of El Paso, 1880–1920: A Case Study," *Pacific Historical Review*, 49 (May 1980), 315–337. For the work roles of Native American women on the Great Plains in the late nineteenth and early twentieth centuries, see Nancy Oestrich Lurie, ed., *Mountain Wolf Woman, Sister of Crashing Thunder: The Autobiography of a Winnebago Indian* (Ann Arbor, Mich., 1961); Patricia Albers and Beatrice Medicine, eds., *The Hidden Half: Studies of Plains Indians Women* (Lanham, Md., 1983); Mona Etienne and Eleanor Burke Leacock, eds., *Women and Colonization: Anthropological Perspectives* (New York, 1990); Katherine M.

Wiest, "Plains Indian Women: An Assessment," in W. Raymond Wood and Margot Livesay, eds., *Anthropology on the Great Plains* (Lincoln, Neb., 1980), pp. 225–71; Gretchen M. Bataille and Kathleen Mullen Sands, *American Indian Women Telling their Lives* (Lincoln, Neb., 1994); and Karen Anderson, *Changing Woman: A History of Racial Ethnic Women in Modern America* (New York, 1996), ch. 3.

David M. Katzman examines household servants from 1870 to World War I in *Seven Days a Week: Women and Domestic Service in Industrializing America* (New York, 1978). Studies of prostitution include Ruth Rosen, *The Lost Sisterhood: Prostitution in America 1900–1918* (Baltimore, Md., 1982); Marion S. Goldman, *Gold Diggers and Silver Miners: Prostitution and Social Life on the Comstock Lode* (Ann Arbor, Mich., 1981); Barbara Meil Hobson, *Uneasy Virtue: The Politics of Prostitution and the American Reform Tradition* (New York, 1987); Anne M. Butler, *Daughters of Joy, Sisters of Misery: Prostitutes in the American West, 1865–1890* (Urbana, Ill., 1985); and Timothy Gilfoyle, *City of Eros: New York City, Prostitution, and the Commercialization of Sex, 1790–1920* (New York, 1992). For Chinese prostitutes, see Lucie Cheng Hirata, "Free, Enslaved, and Indentured Workers in Nineteenth Century America: The Case of Chinese Prostitution," *Signs* 5 (Autumn 1979), 3–29, also available in Lucie Cheng and Edna Bonacich, eds., *Labor Immigration Under Capitalism: Asian Workers in the United States before World War II* (Berkeley, Calif., 1984), pp. 402–434; Benson Tong, *Unsubmissive Women: Chinese Prostitutes in Nineteenth-Century San Francisco* (Norman, Okla., 1994); and Judy Yung, *Unbound Feet: A Social History of Chinese Women in San Francisco* (Berkeley, Calif., 1995), ch. 1. For efforts to rescue Chinese prostitutes, see Peggy Pascoe, *Relations of Rescue: The Search for Female Moral Authority in the American West, 1874–1939* (New York, 1990), mainly ch. 3. For prostitution in China, see Sue Gronewold, *Beautiful Merchandise: Prostitution in China, 1860–1936* (New York, 1982). Estelle Freedman discusses the treatment of prostitutes in *Their Sisters' Keepers: Prison Reform in America 1830–1930* (Ann Arbor, Mich., 1981). See also Marc Thomas Connelly, *The Response to Prostitution in the Progressive Era* (Chapel Hill, N.C., 1980), and Ruth Rosen and Sue Davidson, eds., *The Maimie Papers* (Old Westbury, N.Y., 1977).

Donna Gabaccia provides an overview of gender and immigration in *From the Other Side: Women, Gender, and Immigrant Life in the U.S., 1820–1990* (Bloomington, Ind., 1994). Recent studies of immigrant and working-class women include Virginia Yans McLaughlin, *Family and Community: Italian Immigrants in Buffalo, 1880–1930* (Ithaca, N.Y., 1977); Hasia R. Diner, *Erin's Daughters in America: Irish Immigrant Women in the Nineteenth Century* (Baltimore, Md., 1983); Elizabeth Ewen, *Immigrant Women in the Land of Dollars: Life and Culture on the Lower East Side, 1880–1925* (New York, 1985); Judith E. Smith, *Family Connections: A History of Italian and Jewish Immigrant Lives in Providence, Rhode Island, 1900–1940* (Albany, N.Y., 1985); Sydney Stahl Weinberg, *The World of Our Mothers: The Lives of Jewish Immigrant Women* (Chapel Hill, N.C., 1988); Janet Nolan, *Ourselves Alone: Women's Emigration from Ireland, 1885–1920* (Knoxville, Tenn., 1989); Susan A. Glenn, *Daughters of the Shtetl: Life and Labor in the Immigrant Generation* (Ithaca, N.Y., 1990); Miriam Cohen, *Workshop to Office: Two Generations of Italian Women in New York City, 1900–1950* (Ithaca, N.Y., 1992); and Kathie Friedman-Kasaba, *Memories of Migration: Gender, Ethnicity, and Work in the Lives of Jewish and Italian Women in New York, 1870–1924* (Albany, N.Y., 1996). For working women's roles as consumers, see Kathy Peiss, *Cheap Amusements: Working Women and Leisure in Turn-of-the-Century New York* (Philadelphia, 1986) and Nan Enstad, *Ladies of Labor, Girls of Adventure: Working Women, Popular Culture and Labor Politics at the Turn of the Twentieth Century* (New York, 1999). Studies of Chinese women and their roles as immigrants include Judy Yung, *Unbound Feet*, cited previously; Huping Ling, *Surviving on Gold Mountain: A History of Chinese American Women and their Lives* (Albany, N.Y., 1998); and George Anthony Peffer, *If They Don't Bring Their Women Here: Chinese Female Immigration Before Exclusion* (Urbana, Ill., 1999). For the impact of the Chinese Exclusion Act of 1882, see "The Exclusion of Chinese Women, 1870–1943," in Sucheng Chan, ed., *Entry Denied: Exclusion and the Chinese Community in America, 1882–1943* (Philadelphia, 1991). For the Jewish housewives' protest, see Paula E. Hyman, "Immigrant Women and Consumer Protest: The New York Kosher Meat Boycott of 1902," *American Jewish History* 70 (September 1980), 91–105. Articles used in the section on immigration include Daniel Walkowitz, "Working Class Women in the Gilded Age: Factory, Community, and Family Life Among Cohoes, New York, Cotton Factory Workers," *Journal of Social History*, 5 (Summer 1972), 464–490; Carol Groneman, "Working-Class Immigrant Women in Mid-Nineteenth-Century New York: The Irish Woman's Experience," *Journal of Urban History*, 4 (May 1978), 255–274; and Tamara Hareven, "Family Time and Industrial Time: Family and Work in a Planned Corporation Town, 1900–1924," *Journal of Urban History*, 1 (May 1975), 365–389. For documents, see Maxine Seller, ed., *Immigrant Women*, 2d ed. (Albany, N.Y., 1994).

Alexander Keyssar examines women's role in the labor market in *Out of Work: The First Century of Unemployment in Massachusetts* (Cambridge, England, and New York, 1986), ch. 4. Leslie Woodcock Tentler discusses early-twentieth-century working-class women in *Wage-Earning Women: Industrial Work and Family Life in the United States, 1900–1930* (New York, 1979). Joanne J. Meyerowitz explores the lives of urban migrants who lived apart from families and employers in *Women Adrift: Independent Female Wage Earners in Chicago, 1880–1930* (Chicago, 1988). Studies of women industrial workers include Joan M. Jensen and Sue Davidson, eds., *A Needle, a Bobbin, a Strike: Women Needleworkers in America* (Philadelphia, 1984); Carole Turbin, *Working Women of Collar City: Gender, Class, and Community in Troy, New York, 1864–1886* (Urbana, Ill., 1992); Susan Levine, *Labor's True Woman: Carpet Weavers, Industrialization, and Labor Reform in the Gilded Age* (Philadelphia, 1984); Patricia A. Cooper, *Once a Cigar Maker: Men, Women, and Work Culture in American Cigar Factories, 1900–1919* (Urbana, Ill., 1987); and Eileen Boris, *Home to Work: Motherhood and the Politics of Industrial Homework in the United States* (New York, 1994). Mary H. Blewett examines the late-nineteenth-century shoe industry in *We Will Rise in Our Might: Workingwomen's Voices from Nineteenth-Century New England* (Ithaca, N.Y., 1991), part 2.

For the shirtwaist strike of 1909–1910, see Philip S. Foner, *Women and the American Labor Movement* (New York, 1979), ch. 18; Meredith Tax, *The Rising of the Women: Feminist Solidarity and Class Conflict, 1880–1917* (New York, 1980), ch. 8; and Barbara Meyer Wertheimer, *We Were There*, cited above, ch. 16. Contemporary accounts include Helen Marot, "A Women's Strike," *Proceedings of the Academy of Political Science* (New York, 1910), pp. 122–125; "The League and the Strike of the Thirty Thousand," *Annual Report of the Women's Trade Union League of New York, 1909–1910* (New York, 1910); and Theresa S. Malkiel, *Diary of a Shirtwaist Striker* (New York, 1910), a fictional account that assails the WTUL from a socialist perspective; a recent edition (Ithaca, N.Y., 1990) is available. For the history of the garment trade, see Louis Levine, *The Women's Garment Worker* (New York, 1924). Nancy L. Green, *Ready-to-Wear and Ready-to-Work: A Century of Industry in Paris and New York* (Durham, N.C., 1997) offers a comparative perspective on the garment trade. Nancy Shrom Dye examines the New York WTUL in *As Equals and Sisters: The Labor Movement and the Women's Trade Union League of New York* (Columbia, Mo., 1980). An older account is Gladys Boone, *The Women's Trade*

Union League in Great Britain and the United States (New York, 1942). Leon Stein describes the disaster at the Triangle shirtwaist factory in *The Triangle Fire* (New York, 1962). For documents on the shirtwaist strike and the Triangle fire, see John F. McClymer, ed., *The Triangle Strike and Fire* (Fort Worth, Tex., 1998).

Alice Kessler Harris analyzes the obstacles to women's labor organization in "Where Are the Organized Female Workers?" *Feminist Studies*, 3 (Fall 1975), 92–110, and in "Organizing the Unorganizable: Three Jewish Women and Their Unions," *Labor History*, 17 (Winter 1976), 5–23. See also James Kenneally, "Women and Trade Unions, 1870–1920: The Quandary of the Reformer," *Labor History*, 14 (Winter 1973), 42–55; Kenneally, *Women and American Trade Unions* (St. Alban, Vt., 1978); Ann Schofield, *To Do and to Be: Portraits of Four Women Activists, 1893–1886* (Boston, 1997), a comparative biography of labor leaders Gertrude Barnum, Mary Dreier, Pauline Newman, and Rose Pesotta; and Annelise Orleck, *Common Sense and a Little Fire: Women and Working Class Politics in the United States, 1900–1965* (Chapel Hill, N.C., 1995), a study of Rose Schneiderman, Fannia Cohn, Clara Lemlich, and Pauline Newman. For an outstanding study of women's labor organization, see Dorothy Sue Cobble, *Dishing It Out: Waitresses and Their Unions in the Twentieth Century* (Urbana, Ill., 1991). Working girls' clubs are discussed in Joanne Reitano, "Working Girls Unite," *American Quarterly*, 36 (Spring 1984), 112–184; Kathy Peiss, *Cheap Amusements*, cited previously, ch. 7; and Priscilla Murolo, *The Common Ground of Womanhood: Class, Gender, and Working Girls' Clubs, 1884–1928* (Urbana, Ill., 1997). For protective laws, see Susan Lehrer, *Origins of Protective Labor Legislation for Women, 1905–1925* (Albany, N.Y., 1987); Judith A. Baer, *The Chains of Protection: The Judicial Response to Women's Labor Legislation* (Westport, Conn., 1978); Vivien Hart, *Bound by Our Constitution: Women, Workers, and the Minimum Wage* (Princeton, N.J., 1994); and Nancy Woloch, *Muller v. Oregon: A Brief History with Documents* (Boston, 1996). For a comparative perspective, see Ulla Wikander, Alice Kessler-Harris, and Jane Lewis, eds., *Protecting Women: Labor Legislation in Europe, Australia, and the United States, 1880–1920* (Urbana, Ill., 1995); and Kathryn Kish Sklar, Anna Schuler, and Susan Strasser, eds., *Social Justice Feminists in the United States and Germany: A Dialogue in Documents, 1885–1933* (Ithaca, N.Y., 1998).

For women's roles in office work and sales work, see Cindy Sondik Aron, *Ladies and Gentlemen of the Civil Service: Middle-Class Workers in Victorian America* (New York, 1987); Margery W. Davies, *Women's Place Is at the Typewriter: Office Work and Office Workers, 1870–1930* (Philadelphia, 1982); Lisa Fine, *The Souls of the Skyscraper: Female Clerical Workers in Chicago, 1870–1930* (Philadelphia, 1990); Sharon Hartman-Strom, *Beyond the Typewriter: Gender, Class, and the Origins of Modern Office Work* (Urbana, Ill., 1995); and Susan Porter Benson, *Countercultures: Saleswomen, Managers, and Customers in American Department Stores, 1890–1940* (Urbana, Ill., 1986). Stephen H. Norwood examines unionization in *Labor's Flaming Youth: Telephone Operators and Worker Militancy, 1878–1923* (Champaign, Ill., 1991).

The woman worker received much attention from women scholars and reporters of the progressive era. See, for example, Edith Abbott, *Women in Industry: A Study in American Economic History* (New York, 1909); Helen Sumner, *History of Women in Industry in the United States* (Washington, D.C., 1910), part of a massive Bureau of Labor study of women and children in the work force; Alice Henry, *The Trade Union Woman* (New York, 1915); and Theresa Wolfson, *The Woman Worker and the Trade Unions* (New York, 1926). Margaret F. Byington examined women's roles in working-class families in *Homestead: The Households of a Mill Town* (Pittsburgh, Pa., 1910). Foundations and endowments supported studies of wage-earning women, such as Mary Van Kleeck's studies for the Russell Sage Foundation, *Women in the Book*

Binding Trade (New York, 1913) and *Artificial Flower Makers* (New York, 1913); and Elizabeth Butler, *Women and the Trades: Pittsburgh 1907–1908* (New York, 1909). For the accounts of investigators who impersonated working-class women, see Mrs. John Van Vorst and Marie Van Vorst, *The Woman Who Toils* (New York, 1903), and Dorothy Richardson, *The Long Day: The Story of a New York Working Woman* (New York, 1905). Social worker Mary Ovington, a founder of the NAACP, explored black women's experience in *Half a Man: The Status of the Negro in New York* (New York, 1911), ch. 6.

Autobiographies of prominent women in the labor movement include Mary Field Parton, ed., *The Autobiography of Mother Jones* (Chicago, 1925); Rose Schneiderman, *All for One* (New York, 1967); Agnes Nestor, *Woman's Labor Leader: The Autobiography of Agnes Nestor* (Rockford, Ill., 1954); and Mary Anderson, *Woman at Work* (Minneapolis, Minn., 1951). For the immigrant experience, see Mary Anton, *The Promised Land* (New York, 1912); Rose Cohen, *Out of the Shadows* (New York, 1918), now available in an edition with an introduction by Tom Dublin (Ithaca, N.Y., 1995); Elizabeth Hasonovitz, *One of Them* (New York, 1918); and the fiction of Anzia Yezierska, such as *Breadgivers: A Novel* (New York, 1925), now available in an edition with an introduction by Alice Kessler-Harris (New York, 1975), and *Arrogant Beggar* (New York, 1927), now available in an edition with an introduction by Katherine Stubbs (Durham, N.C., 1996).

For quizzes and additional resources related to American women's history, visit the book's Website at *www.mhhe.com/americanwomen*.

CHAPTER SIX

The Rise of the New Woman,
1860–1920

W HEN JANE ADDAMS opened the doors of Hull-House, Chicago's pioneer social settlement, in 1889, she also opened a new era in women's history. Addams exemplified the New Woman of the 1890s, who integrated Victorian virtues with an activist social role. By plunging into what she called a "larger life," she discarded an old persona, that of the dutiful daughter and neurasthenic invalid, and transformed herself into a public figure, admired and emulated. Like Addams, the New Woman had an enhanced sense of self, gender, and mission. Vigorous and energetic, she was involved in institutions beyond the family—in college, club, settlement, or profession. In the last decades of the nineteenth century, women's culture assumed a public shape.

The New Woman reached her stride in the progressive era, although she had antecedents in the 1870s and 1880s. Middle class, if not upper class, she was usually a town or city dweller, the wife or daughter of a business or professional man, and better educated than average. Perhaps she was even a college graduate, a possibility that increased year by year. She was more likely to be single than was any other group of women at any time, before or since, in American history, even more so if she had been to college. If unmarried, she might be employed outside the home, most likely in a profession dominated by women, mainly young women, such as teaching or library work. If she never married, she might maintain her own home, possibly with another woman, rather than live with a relative. If and when she married, she usually gave up salaried work and devoted herself to household and family. Both, however, had been reshaped, much to her advantage.

By the turn of the century, the middle-class home had lost most of its productive functions (no one mourned their passing) and had become a unit of consumption, for which the homemaker was responsible. She also had to meet more stringent standards of housekeeping, though usually with domestic help. But home was emptier, with men at offices and children at school for longer periods of time. At home, the middle-class wife was in firm control, albeit over a diminished domain. She had assumed "all authority and management of home and family," as women's columnist Dorothy Dix told her readers in 1898, because the husband "doesn't want to be bothered about it." If she had fewer children than her mother or grandmother, as was likely to be the case, she was "fully responsible for their mental and physical well-being." Finally, she had come to reign supreme "in the matter of society," Dix emphasized. "She dominates it and runs it." More powerful at home, the New Woman was also more active outside it.

In the late nineteenth century, women used the single-sex association to penetrate public affairs. The middle-class woman was usually connected to some sort of voluntary society, whether a church group, a literary discussion circle, or a welfare project. She might be involved in an alumnae association, a women's club, or the temperance movement. In organization, women assumed a distinctive identity. Unlike men, they entered public life as cooperators, not competitors. Moreover, they took special pride in gender. As temperance leader Frances Willard contended, women were more civilized and refined than men, they stood on a higher step of the evolutionary ladder, and they shared feminine goals and impulses. Her contemporaries agreed. Their special mission in public life was to purify, uplift, control, and reform; to improve men, children, and society; to extend the values of the home. "The home does not stop at the street door," said Marion Talbot, dean of women at the University of Chicago in 1911. "It is as wide as the world into which the individual steps forth. The determination of the character of that world and the preservation of those interests which she has safeguarded in the home, constitute the real duty resting upon women."

The New Woman's ventures beyond the street door evoked controversy. The "woman question" pervaded the late nineteenth century. Should a woman attend college, where she might ruin her health or lose her mind, or enter a profession, where she would risk her feminine identity, or leave the home for innumerable club meetings, or speak in public to groups of strangers? These were vexing questions, to say nothing of whether she should be able to vote. Women responded to such challenges by citing the values of home. A cover for self-assertion and a rubric for a feminine value system, "home" was a code word with many meanings. It was sometimes a euphemism for Anglo-Saxon superiority; foreigners, for instance, had to be taught the values of the middle-class home. It sometimes stood for female control over male sexuality, as in the crusades against drunkenness and prostitution. It was often part of a campaign against business run rampant; many women's groups in the progressive era strove to remedy some evil of industrial capitalism—whether to end child labor, protect women workers, or purify milk.

Despite her assaults on industrial evils, the New Woman was herself the product of industrialization, which removed productive labor from middle-class homes and made her long for something to do. She was the product of urbanization, which brought her into contact with other women and also within range of the "other half" or "submerged tenth." She was a product of prosperity, whether her father's wealth, her husband's income, or the large fortunes that were used to endow private colleges or support settlements. She was the product of an old ideology, which gave her first claim on rectitude, made her a guardian of culture, and legitimized the single-sex association. She was the product of recent history, specifically of the Civil War era, which provided an example of women's talents for public service, whether in local sewing clubs or in the ranks of the Sanitary Commission. Finally, she was a product of the middle-class family, where her "influence" reached an all-time peak.

SHRINKING FAMILIES

While the nation expanded and urbanized, the family became smaller, more companionate, and longer-lived. As life expectancy rose, parents could expect to reach old age, marriages were expected to endure longer, and children were expected to survive to maturity. There were fewer children per home as well. The fertility rate continued its century-long plunge, dropping to 3.56 children per woman in 1900, and kept on falling. These changes contributed to, or were symptoms of, women's changing role at home, especially in the native-born, middle-class home. The late-nineteenth-century American family was a closely knit, highly supportive, and demanding institution. It was also a family in which the wife and mother had gained authority, status, and control.

The link between rising status and falling fertility was hardly a sudden development. The declining birthrate was part of a long-term transformation that had started in the late eighteenth century, when patriarchal power began to be replaced by a new ideal of mutual affection and companionship in marriage. The shift from the traditional family to the modern one meant a rise in the status of women (and children). Over the course of the nineteenth century, historian Daniel Scott Smith hypothesizes, women acquired "an increasing power over sex and reproduction within marriage" and experienced "a great increase of power and autonomy within the family." In the late nineteenth century, women consolidated their gains. If fertility is an index of female status, the companionate family had become much more than an upper-class ideal. Birthrates dropped not only in cities but also in rural areas, not only in the more densely populated Northeast but in all regions, although more slowly in the South. There were some significant variations, however. Black fertility did not begin to decline appreciably until the 1880s. Immigrant families also had more children than native-born Americans, although the disparity decreased in the second generation. Falling fertility was most pronounced in the native-born middle-class white family, especially as women's educational levels rose.

In the last quarter of the nineteenth century, the native-born middle-class white woman could expect to have about three children, to live long past 50, and to survive the departure of the last child from home. A quarter of the women who married between 1880 and 1910 had two children or less, as did 40 percent of those who lived in the middle-Atlantic states or in some midwestern states. The woman who married in the first decade of the twentieth century could expect to spend at least five years less caring for children than had her counterpart a century earlier and to live at least 10 years longer. Such changes had implications for middle-class children and mothers. Child-care standards rose as the number of children per home declined; each child received more attention. In some ways this was a mixed blessing; the middle-class youngster often had less freedom and independence than one who was part of a great brood. But wives and mothers profited. They had less drudgery, better health, more energy, and more free time, which could now be devoted to outside activities.

Most important, the shrinking family was a change to which women contributed. The fall of the nineteenth-century birthrate cannot be correlated with any improvement in birth-control techniques; effective new methods became widespread only in the 1920s. Moreover, throughout the nineteenth century, contraception and abortion were condemned by a wide range of women, from feminists to free love advocates to pious churchgoers; both, critics charged, encouraged the sexual exploitation of women. Continence and abstinence, however, remained effective methods of birth control. Historians suggest that women were able to exert control over men by decreasing the frequency of sexual relations, thereby avoiding pregnancy and increasing their power at home. Nineteenth-century women, historian Carl Degler contends, may well have wanted to "minimize or deny their own sexuality" in order to press for greater autonomy in marriage. Long periods of abstinence were the trade-off for greater individualism. According to this hypothesis, the late-nineteenth-century middle-class wife was both more autonomous and more inviolate than any of her predecessors. The acme of female autonomy and sexual control in marriage was probably in the first two decades of the twentieth century.

If late-nineteenth-century married women gained in autonomy by minimizing sexual "indulgence," this was not because they saw themselves as asexual. Ideas about female sexuality were in transition. The old idea that women were asexual, or markedly less sexual than men, persisted to an extent in medical and popular literature. But there was debate on the subject within the medical profession and in marriage manuals. By the end of the century, female sexuality appears to have been a common assumption. Women, however, were unlikely to view their own sexuality as identical with that of men. This distinction emerged in a pioneer survey of sexual attitudes devised by a woman physician, Clelia Mosher, in the 1890s. The Mosher report surveyed a group of 45 middle-class married women over a 30 year period. These women were hardly typical. Almost two out of three were college educated, as were only 2 percent of all American women in 1890. Their responses, however, may have represented those of the New Woman. Respondents sometimes voiced a high opinion of marital sex—"the most sacred expression of our oneness," one woman commented. But they also voiced a desire for "temperance" and "moderation" in sexual activity. One-third of respondents thought that sexual intercourse was not a "necessity" for either sex, and over half indicated that they engaged in it more than they would have preferred. On an average, the woman surveyed had sexual relations once a week and would have preferred to do so once a month.

The driving theme of women's history in the late nineteenth century was neither to achieve any new type of sexual "freedom" nor to avoid sex, but to assert control over their sexual lives. Historian Linda Gordon uses the term "voluntary motherhood" to describe women's demands for continence and abstinence. In the late nineteenth century, both feminists and advocates of "social purity" voiced such demands. To suffragists of the 1870s, for instance, who defended "enlightened motherhood" or "self-ownership," control of sexual relations within marriage was a vital goal. "Woman must have the courage to assert the right to her own body as the instrument of reason and conscience," wrote suffragist Lucinda Chandler, who published her views in a gamut of women's journals in the 1870s. Proponents of social purity shared such views, and drew a connection between female autonomy and abstinence. "If women had their own way in the matter, this physical intercourse would take place at comparatively rare intervals," wrote social purity advocate Elizabeth Evans in an 1875 tract. "As woman becomes more free and wise and self-sustaining, she will demand the same purity of man that she has always demanded of herself." Physician

Elizabeth Blackwell, who contended in the 1890s that "passion commands" the same "vital force" in women as in men, similarly advocated social purity. Favoring "restraint" over "indulgence," middle-class women strove to exert sexual control and expand their autonomy at home. The late nineteenth century was an era of raised expectations, both of men and of marriage.

One sign of raised expectations in marriage was the divorce rate, which grew to what historian William L. O'Neill calls "critical dimensions." In the 1890s, the divorce rate shot up with unparalleled speed—at a rate three times as great as the rate of population increase. It doubled again in the first two decades of the twentieth century, without any major change in the divorce laws. In 1880, there was one divorce for every 21 marriages; in 1900, one for every 12 marriages; and by 1916, one for every nine marriages. Throughout the era, most demands for divorce came from women, to whom about two-thirds of divorces were granted. Such women rarely rebelled against marriage but rather against mates who failed to meet traditional ideals. In her study of Los Angeles divorces in the 1880s, historian Elaine Tyler May finds that wives applied for divorce if their husbands failed to support them, forced them into the labor force, or violated the purity of domestic life by bringing drinking, gambling, and revelry into the home. (Husbands complained if wives left conjugal, maternal, or domestic obligations unfulfilled; indulged in excessive leisure pursuits outside the home; or admitted to premarital adventures.) Divorce won few public advocates; most contemporaries viewed its increase as a sign of the family's dissolution and of "unwholesome individualism." Historians, however, view the phenomenon as part of the rise of the companionate family and a reflection of higher expectations of marriage, notably among women.

Another sign of raised expectations was that a smaller proportion of Americans married at all. Of women born between 1835 and 1855, between 7 and 8 percent never married. In Jane Addams's generation, born 1860 to 1880, between 10 and 11 percent of women never married, and in the next generation, the percentage was only slightly lower. More important, during the late nineteenth century, the spinster, once a marginal member of society, suddenly moved from the periphery of history to center stage. Single women assumed highly visible leadership roles in the professions, reform, and women's education. Jane Addams was part of a large cohort of never-married women leaders, including Lillian Wald in the settlement movement, Frances Willard in the temperance movement, Anna Howard Shaw in the suffrage movement, and M. Carey Thomas in women's higher education. In the progressive era, when women's impact, on public life reached a new high, more single women were at the peak of their careers, in proportion to all women, than at any other time, before or since.

The decision not to marry reflected a fusion of rising expectations and falling opportunities. Not only did middle-class women expect more of marriage, but they also faced a scarcity of eligible men. Nationwide, the loss or incapacitation of men in the Civil War was eventually mitigated by the rise of a new generation. Increased immigration helped, too; 60 percent of the immigrants arriving between 1880 and 1920 were men. But this did little to enhance the marital options of native-born middle- and upper-class women. The crunch was particularly acute in the East and in cities. In 1880, for instance, there were 50,000 more women than men in bellwether

Massachusetts. That same year in Providence, a typical eastern city, there were 93 men to every 100 women. The greatest scarcity struck at the 20- to 29-year-old group, where there were 86 men to every 100 women. Similar discrepancies in countless eastern towns and cities took their toll on the marriage market. The brunt of the impact fell on young women with the highest status, standards, and educational levels, who were likely to have the fewest options.

In the view of middle-class women, there was a decline not only in the quantity of eligible men but in their quality. Or, as expectations of marriage rose, so did perceptions of male liabilities. A popular speech given by Mary Livermore across the country in the 1870s and 1880s conveyed these liabilities. Livermore advised parents to train their daughters for self-support because chances for good marriages were ebbing. Men who were not killed off by drink, vice, or overwork were not necessarily going to make "good or competent husbands," Livermore warned. They were likely to be invalids or deserters, unambitious or dissolute—in any event, hardly viable candidates for companionate marriage. The protective, close-knit, late-nineteenth-century family itself may have contributed to men's inadequacies. In Jane Addams's family, for instance, none of the young men measured up to her father, John Addams, a self-made man who rose to success in business and in Illinois politics. Both Jane's brother, Weber, and her stepbrother George, the only known applicant for her hand, had nervous breakdowns. One brother-in-law was a professional failure. Similarly, close-knit, protective families may have left young women ill-prepared for the competitive marriage market.

Finally, the single middle-class woman of the late nineteenth century had improved options—for higher education, for professional employment, and for supportive relationships with women outside the family. Such options made spinsterhood not only a viable option but a preferable one. First, an educated woman had to choose between marriage and a career; many chose the latter. Second, many preferred the company of women to that of men. "The loves of women for each other grow more numerous each day, and I have wondered much why such things were," Frances Willard wrote in 1889. "That so little should be said about them surprises me for they are everywhere." Female couples might establish same-sex households or "Boston marriages," based on romantic friendship. Single women in leadership roles often formed long-term relationships with other women, such as that of Jane Addams with two Hull-House residents, first Ellen Gates Starr and then Mary Rozet Smith. Frances Willard, Lillian Wald, and M. Carey Thomas, all heroic figures to their constituencies, had similar relationships with women who contributed either labor or funds to their respective causes. As historian Blanche Wiesen Cook points out, women's institutions, such as the woman's college or the settlement house, could provide life-long support groups for the women who lived in them. In the context of such institutions, some women maintained lesbian ties and many created surrogate families in which they could depend on other women for "emotional sustenance and political support."

One factor that fostered such relationships was that women occupied a separate sphere in public life, a sphere dominated by single women. Another was that women thought themselves morally superior to men, and single women even more so. Their contemporaries agreed. In a 1906 contest run by a local newspaper for "the best woman in Chicago," the competition was limited to single women because, as the editors explained, "Unless the married woman ignores the wishes of her husband, it is difficult for her to achieve the same degree of goodness the unmarried woman does." Demographic liabilities, higher expectations, preferable alternatives, and a personal sense of superiority all contributed to the rise of the single woman in the late nineteenth century. So did the advent of the college-educated woman, who probably had the highest expectations of all.

THE COLLEGE WOMAN

When midwestern land-grant colleges admitted women during the Civil War and when Vassar opened in 1865, they raised the expectations of all American women. Few attended college at the outset, but their proportion of the college population rapidly rose. In 1870, when 1 percent of college-age Americans attended college, 21 percent were women. But by 1910, when about 5 percent of college-age Americans attended college, 40 percent were women. Unanticipated and relatively unhampered, the sudden rise in the number of college women had wide ramifications. Significantly, women made inroads in higher education by cracking the barrier of sphere at one of its weakest links.

The upsurge of women college students in part reflected the rapid growth and feminization of secondary schooling. By 1900, when only 7 percent of Americans went to high school, a large majority were women, as were 60 percent of high school graduates. Boys were more likely to go to work than finish secondary school. A similar phenomenon occurred in higher education. After the Civil War, opportunities for college education grew rapidly, a result of federal largesse and of the large fortunes now available for endowing private institutions. But male interest in college degrees did not keep up with the expansion of college places. Middle-class young men found more opportunity in business than in professions requiring a liberal arts education. As a result, there was a vacuum of space in higher education, which women students surged to fill. "While the education for men has outgrown the old college system," an early president of Vassar explained, "that for women has just grown up to it." According to historian Patricia A. Graham, academia was seen as outside "the mainstream of industrial capitalism" in the late nineteenth century. College education may have been a frontier for women, but for men it was a retreat from the "real" world of business. More of a backwater than a male bastion, the college was therefore vulnerable to an invasion of women students. This development was most visible at coeducational colleges and state universities, where, by 1880, the majority of women students were enrolled.

Higher education for women began in the 1830s at Oberlin where women students followed the "ladies course," received special degrees, and entered men's classes only with special permission. Oberlin admitted women in order to improve education for men—by raising the tone of campus life and preventing the growth of vulgar customs that "so frequently deprave" the all-male college. Oberlin's regard for female influence had little impact on other antebellum schools. But in 1862, when Congress funded higher education through the Morrill Act, a new spurt of coeducation began. By 1870, eight state universities, mainly in the West and Midwest, admitted women, whose tuition fees were more in demand than their influence. Women students were accepted with caution by administrators, and often with hostility by fellow students ("bitter indignation" according to a Wisconsin alumnus). But they formed a pool of ready applicants when men were scarce. Their brothers were either serving in the war or, afterward, bound to farms or entering business. In the 1860s and 1870s, coeducational institutions multiplied. In 1867 there were 22 coeducational colleges and universities and by 1900 almost five times as many.

Although new land-grant colleges welcomed women because doing so cost less than creating separate institutions for them, coeducation also had ideological support. Liberal reformers of the 1860s and 1870s—notably, the small contingent of women suffragists and their male allies—endorsed it with enthusiasm as a route to social equality and an antidote to "sexual polarization." "In a mixed school, as in a family, the fact of sex presents itself as an unconscious healthy stimulus," minister Thomas Wentworth Higginson wrote in the suffragist *Woman's Journal* in 1870. "It is in the separate schools that the healthy relation vanishes and the thought of sex becomes a morbid and diseased thing." Elizabeth Cady Stanton, another avid supporter, told an 1870 suffrage convention that coeducation would lead to "more congenial marriages." Similar idealism pervaded some of the early coeducational schools, such as Cornell and Wesleyan, which saw themselves as egalitarian experiments. But beyond a small group of administrators and reformers, coeducation did not win widespread support. At Wesleyan, for instance, where 8 percent of the students had been women since 1873, a vast majority of male students opposed it. In addition, coeducational colleges were usually of lower quality than elite all-male colleges and later women's colleges. Few could draw on the large private fortunes available to single-sex schools. Finally, women had much to gain from the all-woman institution.

To the new generation of women educators and college founders, the true frontier of women's education was not at the coeducational college, public or private, that needed women to fill up space. It was at the women's college, which, like Vassar, would admit women students through the "front door," not the "side door." At the women's college, said Bryn Mawr's M. Carey Thomas, "everything exists for women students and is theirs by right not by favor." To be sure, at the elite male colleges, on which Vassar and Bryn Mawr were modeled, women were not admitted even through the side door, which was justification enough for establishing women's institutions. Other prominent women's colleges were established in affiliation with leading men's colleges only after the trustees of those schools rejected the admission of women. Though controversial at the outset, the women's college soon won acceptance as the superior institution for women students. At the same time, it enabled women to establish a separate sphere in higher education, one where women were in control and where women could be employed. Finally, it reflected an ambivalence about women's roles that pervaded society at large.

Vassar, the first well-endowed, strongly academic women's college, was followed by sister schools that opened in the 1870s and 1880s—such as Wellesley in 1875, Smith in 1875, and Bryn Mawr in 1884. Coordinate colleges, or women's colleges affiliated with men's universities, included Barnard (1889) and Radcliffe (1894). Mount

Holyoke, accredited in 1888, had already served as a model for a variety of women's schools, some of which also became colleges. Significantly, Vassar saw itself in the early years as an "experiment." This experiment was twofold. First, Vassar had to prove that women ("the daughters of our most affluent and aristocratic families," according to a dean) were capable of undertaking an academic education as stringent as that for elite men. Second, Vassar had to prove that they could do so without ruining their health or going insane. To some, higher education posed even more of a threat to women's health than sweatshops, cotton mills, or canning plants. As Dr. Edward Clarke's influential *Sex in Education* (1873) explained, mental activity drew blood from the nervous system and reproductive organs. Higher education, contended the Boston physician, could cause mental collapse, physical incapacity, infertility, and early death. This line of reasoning continued through the turn of the century in various guises. It was feared, for instance, that college would produce generations of invalids who would never marry or who would have no children or only puny, sickly, nervous children—while immigrant women raised healthy hordes. The women's colleges therefore had a complex mission: not only to educate women but to do so without ruining health, sacrificing femininity, or contributing to "race suicide." The spirit of experiment cultivated at Vassar and its sister schools was both defensive and ambitious, and the institutions it inspired were innovative.

One innovation was an academic curriculum in the arts and sciences similar to that at the best men's schools. Initially, some colleges ran preparatory departments to bring applicants up to par. Administrators also prepared to cover other contingencies. As Vassar stated, the college provided women with a liberal arts education "but one adapted to their needs in life." The most significant special program was a stringent course of physical activity, to ensure health as well as to make college women physically superior to noncollege women. The curriculum also included traditional female courses—such as the arts, music, and in some cases, domestic science (although Bryn Mawr eschewed the last). Finally, the women's college offered a familial environment. College was more than a course of study, it was a surrogate home. Part of the college experience was the common dormitory; the meals in the common dining room; and at some colleges, such as Wellesley and Mount Holyoke, the requirement that students perform domestic tasks, such as serving meals. Besides this multifaceted program—academics, physical education, homelike atmosphere, and domestic service—the women's colleges were, like their male counterparts, exclusionary societies with their own rites and rituals.

The personnel and goals of women's colleges were distinctive, too. Physicians (often women) lived on campus because of the colleges' overriding interest in health. Many if not most professors were women as well, though Wellesley alone established the tradition of a woman college president and an all-female faculty. At first, women professors were supposed to be not so much academic specialists as role models. Always unmarried, they were usually young, as there was not yet an older generation of educated women on whom the colleges could call. One example was Alice Freeman Palmer, a University of Michigan graduate, who became a high school principal at 22, a Wellesley history professor at 24, and president of the college at 26. Palmer looked like one of her students throughout her seven-year reign; she retired to marry in 1888. The desirability of such role models reflected the often ambiguous goals of the women's college. The purpose of college was not primarily advanced learning, as a Smith dean explained, or to produce women who could compete with men, but for "ennobling women as women."

Vagueness of goal enabled college administrators to hedge their bets. The colleges contended, variously, that women were the intellectual equals of men; that they needed special programs to survive the rigors of higher education; and that college prepared them to serve both family and world. Graduates would be able "to fill every womanly duty at home and in society," as at Vassar, or to do the "work of life for which God has made them," as at Smith. Women's colleges shared the assumption that women exerted influence in society and that educated women could do so better than others. It was difficult to explain precisely how academic training would serve such ends, but this was hardly the colleges' fault. It was equally difficult to cite the purpose of a liberal arts education for a business-minded man. There was, however, a residual conflict between femininity and "intellect" that college administrators avoided confronting, except at Bryn Mawr. Here, M. Carey Thomas opted for intellect and refused to offer domestic science, hygiene, child study, or "sanitary drainage." "Of all things, taking care of children seems most utterly unintellectual," she observed in a college speech. But, not completely consistent, Thomas could shift gears to promote Bryn Mawr. In 1901, she contended that college women married better than noncollege women, were healthier, rarely died in childbirth, bore healthy children, and made "efficient housekeepers as well as wives and mothers." Similarly, Thomas proclaimed the superiority of *both* coeducation and single-sex education, depending on the audience she addressed.

If the stated goals of the women's colleges were understandably ambivalent, the college experience was specific. It provided community, sorority, identity, and purpose. It instilled vigor, enthusiasm, and confidence. College, after all, consisted of a group of favored, privileged individuals who devoted themselves to self-improvement. This was an enormous boost to self-esteem. College also provided a new type of socialization, as it was a community beyond the bounds of home—no matter how much the women's colleges made their dormitory common rooms resemble the parlors of upper-class households. M. Carey Thomas recognized this process of socialization when she required that Bryn Mawr students live at the college and avoid frequent visits home, where they would fall under the influence of their mothers. Fathers, who paid the bills, were aware of it too. When Sophonisba Breckinridge of Lexington, Kentucky, entered Wellesley in 1884, her mother wrote her the household news and agonized with concern for her health, but her father, a lawyer and soon-to-be congressman, was full of advice. "It is a double and very hard lesson you are unconsciously learning," he wrote, "the individual insignificance of each of us when put out of our circle . . . and the difference between our home, & any place else." Overflowing with pride in Sophonisba's accomplishments, William Breckinridge urged her, above all, to continue. "If I die, you will have to make your own living," he wrote in 1885, "& if I live you may have to do so anyhow."

What to do after college, however, was a problem. Many alumnae felt alienated when deprived of the identity and community of college—"as if I had been flung out into space," one graduate contended. The college experience was an end in itself, leading nowhere. There seemed to be no purposeful role for college-trained women.

Rigorous science courses distinguished the curriculum of the elite
late-nineteenth-century woman's college from those of its antecedents,
the academy and seminary. Above, a Wellesley class of the 1880s meets
in the physics laboratory, the first to be established in a woman's
college. (*Wellesley College Archives*)

Instead there was something of an abyss between college and "life." Moreover, the
options were loaded. "I hang in a void midway between two spheres," wrote a
Radcliffe alumna of 1900 a decade later. "A professional career . . . puts me beyond
reach of the average woman's duties and pleasures," she said, but "the conventional
limitations of the female lot put me beyond reach of the average man's duties and
pleasures." Left in limbo, few late-nineteenth-century graduates could evade what
Jane Addams called "the family claim." As historian Joyce Antler shows, families
sometimes aided the adjustment after college by supporting career aspirations and
new interests, Emily Talbot, for instance, joined her daughter Marion, a Boston University graduate, in forming the Association of Collegiate Alumnae (ACA) in 1882, so
that the small retinue of women graduates might perpetuate collegial ties and share
common concerns. A thriving organization, the ACA later became the American
Association of University Women. Many families, however, exerted a "claim" as
strong as that of the Addamses. "My life since college has been very quiet at home,"
a Wellesley alumna wrote for the classbook of the class of '97. "At present I am living
with my father and keeping house for him. . . . I have very little strength and haven't
been able to undertake anything beyond my class in Sunday school." "All my plans
for a 'career' have been knocked to atoms," wrote another, who cared for her mother.
"You can put me down as still alive, though."

If alumnae were troubled by postgraduate trauma, society cared more about their low rate of marriage. Although a bare majority of late-nineteenth-century women college graduates married, they married later than noncollege women. Also, fewer married. More than 90 percent of the female population married in the late nineteenth century, but the proportion among college graduates was far lower. Of 8,000 women graduates in the 1880s, only 5,000 were married, and marriage rates were lowest among alumnae of prestigious, single-sex eastern women's colleges, where academic standards were most stringent. By 1890, only 25 percent of Bryn Mawr graduates had married; perhaps they were limited by Thomas's advice to marry college men who were willing to form intellectual rather than sexual alliances. Between then and 1908, 45 percent of Bryn Mawr graduates and 57 percent of Wellesley graduates married. Surveying three decades of Vassar alumnae in 1895, Frances Abbott Sweeney found that among the first four classes, 63 percent had married within 25 years. But less than 38 percent of the 1,085 Vassar women in her survey had married; the rate was lowered by single members of recent classes who were still in the long interim period between graduation and possible alliances. The link between higher education and single status would decline only when the proportion of women attending college vastly increased.

Women's influx into college also affected higher education, where a backlash arose. By 1900, female populations at coeducational institutions had surged. The proportion of women students leapt from 25 percent to 50 percent at the University of Chicago, for instance, in its first decade of life. Some colleges, such as Wesleyan in 1909, ended female admissions. Others, such as Chicago, developed curricula to attract more men. Large state institutions relegated women students to normal schools or home economics programs within the universities. Private colleges that had admitted women or were under pressure to do so formed special women's branches, or coordinate colleges, to segregate their women students and keep them out of the way—as at Tufts, for example. Such measures preserved a college's appeal for male applicants. The specter of encroaching feminization continued to hover over academic life and spurred special tactics to combat it.

Finally, new opportunities drew a small group of African American women into higher education. At least several hundred black women were college graduates by 1910, and many more attended either teacher training schools or vocational institutions. At Alabama's Tuskeegee Institute, for instance, founded in 1881, young women pursued both academic studies at a pre-collegiate level and training in crafts, such as dressmaking, housekeeping, horticulture, upholstery, millinery, and laundry work. Virginia's Hampton institute, founded in 1868, offered a similar program. Segregated state normal schools in the South, mandated by federal law in 1890, enrolled mainly women students. A small number of women students attended the black universities founded since the Civil War, such as Fisk or Atlanta, or other institutions that started out as secondary schools and gradually developed collegiate programs. At Atlanta's all-women Spelman Seminary, founded in the 1880s by Baptist missionaries, most students enrolled in the preparatory division; in the 1920s, Spelman became an accredited college, as did Bennett College in North Carolina. A limited number of young women attended those northern colleges that accepted black students, including Chicago, Cornell, Radcliffe, and Wellesley, as well as Antioch and Oberlin,

Whereas the new women's colleges provided liberal arts curricula, many black educational institutions offered vocational programs. At Tuskegee Institute in Alabama, founded in 1881, women students divided their time between the academic division and the industrial division. Margaret Murray Washington, a Fisk graduate and wife of Tuskegee founder Booker T. Washington, served as director of girls' industries and dean of women. Above, a Tuskegee domestic science class around the turn of the century. *(Library of Congress)*

which had welcomed blacks before the Civil War. Clubwoman and reformer Mary Church Terrell and author and educator Anna Julia Cooper, for instance, were both 1884 graduates of Oberlin. Though one of the only two black women students in her class and sensitive to racial slights, Terrell, who thrived in her studies, reveled in the college environment. "I was accorded the same treatment at Oberlin College at that time as a white girl under similar circumstances," she recalled. "Outward manifestations of prejudice against colored students would not have been tolerated."

The educational experiences of Native Americans differed dramatically from those of non-Indian students. From the 1880s to the 1920s, thousands of American Indian students were sent from western reservations to federally-funded off-reservation boarding schools, which sought to erase their identities as Native Americans and foster acculturation to white ways of life. The best known was the Indian School at Carlisle, Pennsylvania, founded in 1879. Hampton Institute accepted a group of Native American students at the same time. Indian schools multiplied in the 1880s and 1890s; by 1902, there were 25, mainly in the western states, to save on transportation costs. About 3,000 female students were enrolled each year. Few schools offered courses above the eighth or ninth grade level; classes focused on literacy in English (the students spoke many tribal languages, all forbidden) and manual or industrial training. School officials at Carlisle and elsewhere sought to transform young native American girls into models of Victorian womanhood, historians explain. "Don't be discouraged, girls, much more depends upon you than upon the boys," a federal commissioner declared at Hampton in 1898. "[W]e look to you to carry home the refinement that shall really elevate your people." For girls, however, industrial training meant housework—sewing, cooking, canning, ironing, and cleaning. Commonly, female students provided domestic services to their entire schools; a student at the Crow Creek school, Estelle Brown, remembered "small girls from the kindergarten darning stockings for hours on end." After schooling, some young women found lives beyond the reservation. Among those who returned, many encountered problems with readjustment or won little credit for their school-taught domestic skills. The largest employer of female former students was the Indian Bureau, which hired them mainly for menial jobs. Understandably, the Indian schools evoked criticism. Zitkala-Ša (Gertrude Simmons Bonnin), a Yankton Sioux and a prize-winning scholar at Indiana's Earlham College, taught briefly at the Carlisle School, which she assailed for its assimilationist goals. "For the white man's papers I had given up my faith in the Great Spirit," Bonnin declared. Still, as a college graduate (unlike her Carlisle students), Bonnin was poised to enter public life. Lecturer and clubwoman, she became a leader in the Indian Reform movement of the progressive era.

For Gertrude Simmons Bonnin and other women of her generation, higher education had wide ramifications. College women were a new elite, and their advent affected roles on all fronts—home, work, and "world." A major result was the entry of college-trained women into professional work. By the turn of the century, when 17 percent of alumni were women, college graduates dominated the ranks of professional women. This was little threat to the established male professions but led instead to the rapid development of "women's professions," specially suited to the needs and talents of college alumnae.

THE PROFESSIONAL WOMAN

The professional woman was a contradiction in terms, as professions strove to exclude irregular practitioners, notably women. At the turn of the century, experts viewed women and professionalism as if at opposite poles. Professionalism meant specialization, psychologist G. Stanley Hall explained in 1905, which was alien to the female brain. The man, said Hall, tends "by nature to *expertise* and *specialization* without which his individuality would be incomplete." The woman, "less prone to specialization," would clearly make a second-class practitioner, especially if she tried to crack a male bastion such as the ministry or law. In the late nineteenth century, the male bastions remained relatively secure, although women made gains in medicine.

But women professionals surged into teaching, nursing, library work, and social work, and in relatively large numbers entered academic life. These "women's professions" were either old vocations that had already been feminized and were now uplifted to the status of professions, or new vocations shaped and staffed by educated women. Between 1870 and 1930, the proportion of women in professions was twice as high as that in the work force. In 1890, for instance, when women were only about 17 percent of the work force, 36 percent of "professionals" were women.

Women's professions were shaped by the college experience and by the resistance of traditional "male professions" to women. The ministry, for instance, was nearly impenetrable. Pioneers such as Antoinette Brown Blackwell, the first woman ordained as a Congregationalist minister, or Olympia Brown, the first woman Universalist minister, or formidable Anna Howard Shaw, both minister and physician, did not clear paths that others could follow in any numbers. All three, significantly, were more active in the suffrage movement than in the ministry. An extraordinary irregular practitioner, Mary Baker Eddy, however, achieved the clerical influence they sought. Eddy created the new creed of Christian Science, attracted hundreds of thousands of followers, and at her death in 1910 left behind a wealthy, enduring institution. Capitalizing on accepted female virtues (intuition and spirituality), she created a unique way for well-off women, the bulk of her followers, to defeat neurasthenia and physical complaints, the lingering vestiges of Victorian womanhood. Carving out a new terrain in spiritual welfare, Mary Baker Eddy was an astounding success. But as a profession, the ministry rejected women.

There was no hope for irregular practice in law. The legal profession was highly organized and the courtroom, like the saloon, was a male citadel. The first woman lawyer was admitted to the bar in Iowa in 1869, but hardly began a stampede, as each state could decide on its own requirements for bar admission. In Illinois the same year, Myra Bradwell, a lawyer's wife, Sanitary Commission veteran, and suffragist, was denied admission to the bar; the Illinois Supreme Court declared that the "hot strife of the bar, in the presence of the public" would destroy femininity. When Bradwell took her case to the U.S. Supreme Court, it confirmed in 1873 that the delicacy and timidity of the female sex "unfit it for many of the occupations of civil life." Bradwell was not admitted to the Illinois bar until 1890.

Like Myra Bradwell, who read law with her husband, women lawyers were often trained in relatives' offices; law schools began to admit small numbers of women in the 1890s. Once licensed, the woman lawyer, with rare exceptions, was excluded from courtroom practice and limited to office work. Sometimes she found employment with a government agency or women's organization, or else she followed another career. Myra Bradwell, when excluded from the bar, edited a law journal and printed legal forms. Sophonisba Breckinridge, the first woman admitted to the Kentucky bar, in the 1880s, after studying law with her father, moved on to academic life. Other licensed graduates simply gave up: By 1910, there were almost 9,000 licensed women physicians but only 1,500 women lawyers. In 1920, only 3 percent of American lawyers were women.

Medicine, however, was at the lower end of the male professional scale. As its status was most shaky and its organization least rigorous, women's medical colleges blossomed. By the 1890s several major medical schools, public and private, admitted women as well. In 1900, women were 10 percent of medical students, and by 1910, they were 6 percent of the medical profession—a peak figure that soon declined. Unlike women lawyers, women doctors and also women dentists were able to establish practices. Treating mainly women and children, they charged less than male competitors, and often worked out of offices in their homes. Significantly, a high proportion of women physicians in the late nineteenth century combined marriage and career. According to historian Regina Morantz, 30 to 40 percent of women doctors were married, perhaps four times as many as other professional women.

In the late nineteenth century, some women physicians created new institutions, but these were short-lived because, if successful, they were taken over by men. Women's medical colleges were absorbed by men's schools, and women's hospitals, such as Elizabeth Blackwell's New York Infirmary, soon vanished. Nor did women physicians control any medical field; male physicians dominated gynecology and pediatrics. In the early twentieth century, Alice Hamilton created the field of industrial medicine, a field that sprang in large part from her Hull-House residency. The settlement house, and subsequently social welfare work, became havens for women professionals who had few outlets in private practice. Many settlements also ran visiting nurse services to provide medical care for neighborhood residents. Traipsing over the rooftops lugging her medical bag, the visiting nurse was a model practitioner of a women's profession, a vocation that was something of a halfway house between public service and professional expertise.

By the turn of the century, droves of college women became teachers, librarians, settlement workers, and, in smaller numbers, academics. Nurses, still counted as domestics in the census, were not often college women. Still, they could no longer be trained on the job but had to attend special nursing schools and thereby laid claim to professional status. Until 1920, however, hospitals employed only student nurses, at minimal rates, and nursing school graduates competed with untrained nurses for home-care jobs. Teaching, the major outlet for college alumnae, was gradually transformed. The college graduate began to replace the old breed of nineteenth-century teacher—a teenager with a grade school education. College women, boasted M. Carey Thomas in 1907, had driven out women without degrees. With a growing pool of educated women available, states began to impose standards, give licensing exams, and require advanced training. This was a gradual process that went on, state by state, from the 1880s through World War I.

Although women's professions, such as teaching, nursing, library work, and social work, developed in various ways, they had much in common. Each defined itself by extending woman's sphere, that is, by suggesting that women were naturally inclined and equipped to care for the young, sick, or poor, or to serve as guardians of culture, or to guide young women on the path to adulthood. Women's professions were usually practiced in places that could be defined as homelike—whether hospital, schoolroom, library, college, or settlement. They were professions in which the practitioners dealt primarily if not exclusively with other women, with children, and with persons in need. They were also alternatives to marriage, substitute routes for fulfilling female missions. The woman professional was either a young college graduate, filling an interlude between school and marriage, or a lifetime spinster. Most important, she was paid less—both less than a man in the same line of work, who might well rise to an administrative post, and less than a man in a male bastion like law. The most distinguishing mark of the woman professional was that she was almost always a salaried employee, often in the public sector, rather than a free-wheeling entrepreneur. For women, profession meant service not profit.

The librarian, as historian Dee Garrison has shown, typified the woman professional. The public library, funded by taxes and donations, proliferated in the late nineteenth century. It needed low-paid, well-educated workers, and women college graduates needed appropriate work beyond the classroom. Woman's role as guardian of culture easily extended to the library, where she could welcome guests and assist them. The reading public was composed mainly of other women, who had the most time to consume culture, and children. The children's reading room seemed a natural spot for the educated woman. Other library users were at least expected to be quiet and relatively harmless. Under these circumstances, women quickly filled all the lower-level library posts, while men surfaced in the top ones. Women earned half the pay men would have earned. The relatively few men in the field welcomed them. "They soften the atmosphere, they lighten our labor," said a male librarian in 1877, "and . . . they are infinitely better than equivalent salaries will produce of the other sex." By 1880, the profession of librarian was feminized.

Like the librarian, the woman professor was needed at a new institution. She was mainly employed at the women's college, where, in some cases, she competed with men for jobs. She also found work at the coeducational schools, if only "to look after the discipline and home life of women students," as M. Carey Thomas explained in 1901. As the numbers of women students shot up rapidly, a sudden demand for her services emerged. Women were 36 percent of all faculty members in 1880, and about 20 percent from 1890 to 1910. The woman academic usually made a lifetime commitment to spinsterhood. She often found at the women's colleges the same type of surrogate family Jane Addams created at the settlement. If she worked at a coeducational university, she was well advised to carve out a niche in a newly created academic area—such as the indefinite space encompassed by social science, domestic science, and social welfare.

Marion Talbot, for instance, who earned a B.S. degree at MIT in 1888, became an instructor in domestic science at Wellesley but was hired in 1892 by the innovative University of Chicago as a professor of sociology. At Chicago, Talbot strove for women's equality in academe. Her career, however, hung midway between social science and domestic science. Soon dean of women and then head of the department of household administration, Talbot became an officer of the American Home Economics Association and an authority on household management. Her friend Sophonisba Breckinridge, also lured to Chicago, worked as an instructor in her department, while earning a law degree and a Ph.D. in political science. A part-time Hull-House resident, Breckinridge then taught at Chicago's new School of Civics and Philanthropy, where social workers were trained, and became its dean. By creating new disciplines, women academics created space for themselves in academic life.

Few universities were as hospitable as Chicago, but women found academic work in other places as well. Ellen Richards, a Vassar graduate, became the first woman student at MIT, where she earned a B.S. degree in chemistry in 1873. Three years later she established a "woman's laboratory" at MIT, which specialized in applying chemical analyses to the home. Subsequently a professor of "sanitary chemistry," Ellen Richards also became an authority on household management, a leader of the Home Economics Association, and an advocate of scientific careers for women. A model woman professional, although married, Richards was able to fuse woman's special terrain of domesticity with science, and she won the support of male colleagues. "Perhaps the fact that I am not a Radical or a believer in the all powerful ballot for women . . . and that I do not scorn womanly duties, but claim it as a privilege to clean up, is winning me stronger allies than anything else," she contended. The New Woman was least threatening and most welcome if she occupied a sex-specific niche, such as the field of household management, or was contained in a women's profession where she was unlikely to compete with men.

By the turn of the century, women's professions filled an important new space in the nation's occupational hierarchy. Not only did they provide vocations for growing numbers of educated women but, by creating a lower-level professional caste, they helped define the distinctive qualities of male professions: high status, profit, and expertise. But professional work was not the only new space to be filled by women. During the late nineteenth century, middle- and upper-class women also edged into public life in new, large women's associations that defined their own territory.

CLUBWOMEN AND CRUSADERS

The late nineteenth century saw a proliferation of women's associations, which splintered, multiplied, federated, and expanded. The basic units of this outburst, the temperance society and the women's club, arose spontaneously and won adherents rapidly. Temperance gained momentum in the 1880s and the club movement in the 1890s. These associations enabled thousands of conventional middle-class women to learn from others, share female values, and work toward common goals. Combining self-help and social mission, they created an avenue to civic affairs, or what temperance leader Frances Willard called "the home going forth into the world." Winning wide exposure for female "influence," they invigorated their members and politicized their leaders. They also created a separate space for women in public life.

The women's club and temperance movements were reminiscent of the commissions of the Civil War era—those massive federations of volunteer bandage rollers, supply collectors, fund raisers, and organizers. Some commission stalwarts, such as Mary Livermore and Annie Wittenmyer, threw their efforts into the new women's groups. But whereas the U.S. Sanitary Commission had been run by men, the new associations were led by women. Moreover, unlike the majority of antebellum female societies, often formed under clerical auspices, they were secular associations. A separate network of women's charitable and missionary societies continued to maintain religious affiliations. In form, the women's club and temperance movements imitated various male models. Women's clubs, like men's clubs, had formal meetings, followed parliamentary procedures, elected officers, wrote minutes, and read reports. After federation, in 1892, their delegates attended national conventions, debated issues, and passed resolutions. Almost from the outset, the tightly organized temperance movement resembled a women's political party. But like the women's colleges, both movements were also agents of education and socialization. They saw themselves as training grounds for public life. Through association, in the company of peers, homebound matrons could learn to pursue common interests with vitality, enthusiasm, and self-assurance.

Both the women's temperance movement and the first women's clubs sprang up in the decade after the Civil War. The temperance campaign began in Ohio in the early 1870s with a women's crusade to close down saloons through prayers and harassment. Since antebellum days, the saloon had been a powerful symbol, an enemy of women and an insult to the sanctity of the home—because the men who sought companionship in the saloon might spend all their wages, lose their jobs, abuse their wives, victimize their children, or desert their families entirely. The women's crusade of Ohio was quickly successful in small towns, although less so in larger ones, where riots were barely averted. The Ohio saloons that were closed soon reopened, but the revulsion they aroused had long-term repercussions. In 1873, the Women's Christian Temperance Union was formed in Chicago. First led by Annie Wittenmyer, the WCTU surged to prominence after 1879, when Frances Willard took the helm. One-time college president (of the Evanston College for Ladies, a short-lived adjunct of Northwestern) and an organizational genius, Willard dominated the temperance movement for the next two decades and changed its style and direction. She transformed the union from a midwestern prayer group into a militant army of national scope.

A potent politician, Frances Willard attracted converts through nationwide speaking tours. By 1890, the WCTU had 160,000 members, including many in the South, each ready to "bless and brighten every place she enters and enter every place" (the political slogan was one of Willard's fortes). By 1911, with 245,000 members, the WCTU was the largest single women's organization ever. Willard also enlarged the WCTU's single goal of temperance into a plan for reforming the human race, especially the male half of it. As historian Barbara Leslie Epstein has shown, no small degree of sex antagonism spurred much of nineteenth-century female activism, from the early waves of revivalism through the energetic temperance crusade. Under Willard's direction, the WCTU strove to end the production, sale, and consumption of alcohol, and to attain state temperance laws. But the cause now had a larger thrust: to erase all evils for which men were responsible, from prostitution to political corruption. With Frances Willard in charge, the WCTU became a vocal pressure group for the protection of women and the improvement of society.

By 1889, the WCTU was an administrative masterpiece. Willard called it "a branch of social science and religious activity" but it bore more resemblance to a political movement. Her policy of "Do everything" meant that all WCTU members did something—whether in local societies, autonomous state federations, or the huge national federation, which held an annual convention complete with delegates, banners, flags, and music. Wearing her badge, a white ribbon to symbolize the purity of the home, the WCTU member might also work for one of the union's many departments. Each was a propaganda arm for a cause, such as peace, labor reform, social purity, health, or city welfare work. The temperance advocate was likely to find herself opening kindergartens or Sunday schools for the poor, or visiting prisons and asylums, or embarked on some other campaign in which female virtue might prevail over lesser standards. The WCTU member might even be converted to woman suffrage, a cause that Willard endorsed with fervor; she believed that the ballot was "the most potent means of social and moral reform."

A model of the woman politician, like Jane Addams a decade later, Frances Willard excelled at strategy and alliances. She was able to mobilize women to manipulate men, the ultimate target of most WCTU campaigns. The union's success was in its size, stamina, and centrality to women's politics. It established temperance as a cause around which women would rally for decades. It drew middle-class matrons, most of conservative bent, out of their homes into meetings, conventions, and crusades. Providing its members with what Willard called "a nobler form of social interchange" than the visits and calls of a bygone era, it also spurred some of them into the suffrage camp. Though many temperance advocates had little interest in suffrage, others assumed leadership roles, even in the South, where until now women had not been involved in either social reform or public life. To Mississippi suffragist Belle Kearney, in 1900, the WCTU was "the golden key that unlocked the prison door of pent-up possibilities."

Women's clubs similarly drew women into association, at first for cultural purposes, but later to support an agenda of civic reform. Like the WCTU, women's clubs educated their middle- and upper-class members while providing an avenue to public affairs. Less embattled and more exclusive than the WCTU, the clubs had a wide range of potential adherents. At the outset, their goals were vague. The first model for a women's club, Sorosis, established by journalists and other career women in New York in 1868, described itself as "an order which shall render the female sex helpful to each other and actively benevolent in the world." Its organizer was energetic Jane Croly, mother of four, newspaper columnist, and avid exponent of women's involvement in public affairs. The New England Woman's Club, formed the same year, intended to serve as "an organized social center for united thought and action." Its leading spirits were Caroline Severance, wife of a banker, mother of five, and veteran antebellum reformer, and well-known author Julia Ward Howe. Members were Boston professional women and reformers. Significantly, the two pioneer women's clubs were established at the same time and in the same cities as the two pioneer woman suffrage societies. Some women participated in both. The club movement, however, was far more contagious.

In the 1870s, some women's clubs adopted feminist agendas, though most kept their purposes cultural, convivial, and general. But vagueness of goal served the motivating drive behind club formation, the desire to associate. This seemed unquenchable. In the 1880s and 1890s, women's clubs proliferated, some splitting off from larger ones, others arising on their own. By the time the General Federation of Women's Clubs (GFWC) was established in 1890, there were almost 500 affiliate clubs and more than 100,000 members. By the end of the century, women's clubs had 160,000 members; and by World War I, more than a million. Throughout these decades, as historian Karen Blair points out, the women's club movement served a special purpose. It enabled middle-class women to enter public life without abandoning domestic values and without adopting the aggressive stance associated with either the temperance crusade or the politicized woman suffrage movement.

But women's clubs were a step toward politicization as well. The typical women's club of the 1880s began by holding weekly meetings for lectures, discussions, and book reports. Sometimes the group would choose a topic for the week, month, or season, devoting itself to ancient history or contemporary drama. These literary and cultural overtones provided clubwomen with a substitute for the higher education now open to their daughters. Like the college, the club was an exclusionary society, defined as much by who was admitted or left out as by the works of art that were discussed. By the turn of the century, however, the thrust of the clubs had shifted to civic affairs. Clubwomen, explained the president of the General Federation of Women's Clubs in 1904, were abandoning the study of Dante's *Inferno* and beginning to "proceed in earnest to contemplate our own social order."

Clubwomen usually contemplated the social order on a local level in a noncontroversial manner. Women's clubs raised funds for planting trees, establishing libraries, and building hospitals and playgrounds. They supported worthy projects, such as women's colleges, social settlements, and visiting nurse services, and pressured local governments for clean drinking fountains and better school facilities. After women's clubs federated in 1890, delegates to biennial meetings moved on to national issues, passing resolutions on those in which women, home, and family had a stake—such as protective laws, child labor laws, pure food and drug legislation, and finally, in 1914, woman suffrage. That year, GFWC official Mary Woods expressed the tone of the clubs: No cause for social or moral uplift, said Woods, "has not received a helpful hand from the clubwomen."

The influence of women's clubs often depended as much on who their members were as on what they did. In important clubs, such as the exclusive Chicago Woman's Club, which Jane Addams and Ellen Starr approached in 1889 to win support for Hull-House, members were the wives and daughters of wealthy men in prominent positions. Bertha Palmer, for instance, a great patron of Jane Addams and a frequent visitor at Hull-House, was married to a local tycoon who made his fortune during the Civil War, built up much of Chicago, and owned its grand hotel. Club member Louise Bowen, who served as a Hull-House trustee, was able to give the settlement three-quarters of a million dollars. The Chicago Woman's Club was a counterpart of the male power structure. It had access to funds and could generate support for all the projects it undertook, which meant that it could make or break any new venture on its own turf. The GFWC, accordingly, was a superstructure of locally influential women, with outposts in every state.

Whereas early women's clubs had been modeled on men's clubs, black women's clubs were modeled in some ways on white women's clubs, into which some black leaders had been admitted. Josephine Ruffin, wife of a Harvard-trained judge, was a member of the prestigious New England Women's Club. She formed Boston's New Era Club for black women and organized a National Conference of Colored Women in 1895. Fannie Barrier Williams, a lawyer's wife and philanthropist in Chicago, became the first and only black member of the selective Chicago Woman's Club in 1894, after more than a year of debate on the issue. She then turned her attention to the National Association of Colored Women, a federation of clubs established in 1896 after a merger of two earlier federations, the National Federation of Afro-American Women, led by educator Margaret Murray Washington, wife of Tuskegee's founder,

By the turn of the century, women's clubs had shifted their attention from cultural concerns to civic affairs. The delegates to a New York meeting of the General Federation of Women's Clubs around 1900, above, are ready to pass resolutions to protect the home, ensure child welfare, and improve community life. *(Brown Brothers)*

and Mary Church Terrell's National League of Colored Women. But black clubs were not welcomed in the GFWC, as became clear in 1900, when Mary Church Terrell, representing the National Association of Colored Women, was denied seating at a GFWC convention.

Black women's clubs, therefore, occupied a truly separate sphere, rejected by white clubwomen but united by a sense of racial pride. According to Josephine Ruffin, the black women's club movement filled much the same function as the GFWC. Local clubs ran day nurseries, reading rooms, and welfare projects. The national federation, like the WCTU, set up "departments" to deal with major women's issues, such as suffrage, education, and women's employment. It also voiced concern about race-specific causes, such as "railroad conditions" and antilynching. Since the 1890s, pioneer clubwoman and suffragist Ida B. Wells had run her own one-woman crusade against lynching. The black women's club movement, finally, adopted a distinctive mission, which Josephine Ruffin described as "the moral education of the race with which we are identified." By 1900, these upper-rung black club leaders staked out their roles as moral beacons. Through the club movement, they intended to improve "home training" of children, provide racial leadership, and demonstrate that black women could form "an army of organized women for purity and mental worth." The last goal contained a hidden agenda. A driving force behind black club formation, contends historian Gerda Lerner, was to protect black women from charges of moral looseness and from exploitation by white men.

Class formation, too, fueled the growth of black women's clubs in the late nineteenth century. "By embracing a constellation of Victorian middle-class values—temperance, thrift, hard work, piety, learning," historian Glenda Elizabeth Gilmore explains, "African Americans believed that they could carve out space for dignified and successful lives, and that their example would wear away prejudice." Women in particular were agents of mobility and generational change who, Gilmore shows, envisioned three types of advances: in living standards, in opportunities for women of both races, and in white attitudes towards African Americans. At once self-conscious and group-conscious, activist black women had inclusive rather than exclusive goals: they hoped to provide uplift for "the race" as a whole, not to sever themselves from less advantaged parts of it. In the early twentieth century, the activist black women of North Carolina whom Gilmore studies assumed yet another role. Working through their organizations, such as temperance, church, and interdenominational groups, they became "the black community's diplomats to the white community." In the Jim Crow South, Gilmore contends, black women found channels of political activism where black men could not. Gender, she suggests, provided "deep camouflage" and enabled women to "remain invisible as they worked for political ends."

The groundwork of organization laid by the temperance movement and women's clubs bore results in the progressive era. By the end of the century, a vocal and visible woman's movement (or "the woman movement," as it was often called) had developed, with overlapping networks of local, state, and national organizations, united in the conviction that women, as women, had something distinctive and significant to contribute collectively to public life. For many, such social activism symbolized middle-class status. Simultaneously, changes in household technology distinguished the lives of middle-class urban women from those of rural housewives and poorer neighbors.

EDUCATED HOMEMAKERS

By the turn of the century, the middle-class home had been transformed. "The flow of industry has passed and left idle the loom in the attic, the soap kettle in the shed," Ellen Richards wrote in 1908. The urban middle class could now buy a wide array of food products and clothing—baked goods, canned goods, suits, shirts, shoes, dresses. Technological improvements changed the rest of domestic work. Middle-class homes had indoor running water and furnaces, run on oil, coal, or gas, that produced hot water. Stoves were fueled by gas, and delivery services provided ice for refrigerators. Electric power was available for lamps, sewing machines, irons, and even vacuum cleaners. No domestic task was unaffected. Commercial laundries, for instance, had done the wash for urban homes for decades; by the early 1900s, the first electric washing machines were on the market. One innovation after another changed the middle-class homemaker's responsibilities; each removed a different aspect of physical labor and household drudgery.

The new household technology accentuated divisions of class and region. Technological advances always affected the homes of the wealthy first and then filtered downward into the urban middle class; women who lived on farms were only slowly affected by household improvements. Throughout the nineteenth century and well into the twentieth, rural homes lacked running water and electric power. According to a survey of six South Dakota farming counties in 1935, for instance, only one-quarter of homes had indoor plumbing and only one-fifth had electricity. Rural housewives had to haul large quantities of water into the house from wells or pumps. Doing the family laundry, in large vats heated over stoves, remained a full day's work, just as canning and preserving remained seasonal necessities. Heat was provided by wood or coal stoves that left soot and ashes all over the house. The urban poor, similarly, reaped few benefits from household improvements. Urban slum areas such as Chicago's nineteenth ward often had no sewers, garbage collection, or gas or electric lines; tenements lacked both running water and central heating. Nor could poor urban women or rural housewives meet the higher standards of cleanliness that middle-class women adopted. At the turn of the century, variations in the nature of domestic work were probably more marked than at any time before.

As technology invaded middle-class homes, and as the supply of servants shrank, women proposed two strategies, individualist and collective, to enhance the housewife's vocation. A dominant strategy was individualist: to professionalize the homemaker's vocation, to elevate her role to the managerial level, to imbue her calling with value and significance. Housekeeping and child care became specialized missions that required commitment, talent, training, executive abilities, and professional skills. High schools began to teach home economics; college students could study chemistry, hygiene, domestic science, household engineering, and child psychology. Advice books, textbooks, and popular magazines, led by the *Ladies' Home Journal* (an influence since 1889), gave the woman at home some insight into the scope of her obligations. New pressure groups, such as the National Congress of Mothers (1897) and the American Home Economics Association (1908), promoted homes and homemakers. Finally, academics and professionals defined the homemaker's role.

The home had become a center of consumption, Marion Talbot explained in *The Modern Household* (1912), and it needed a trained executive to manage it. Her colleague Alice Norton told a home economics conference that "centrifugal forces" were working against the home, luring its members outside. It was the homemaker's job to make the home "a more interesting place . . . and the possibilities of doing this today are almost endless." If the middle-class homemaker had less menial work than her grandmother, her mental work had increased. Some tasks required special insight into science—such as the job of preventing family members from picking up germs in public places and spreading contagious diseases around the home, or of avoiding items made in contaminated sweatshops. The educated homemaker had to "keep the world clean," a housekeeping text proclaimed. She had to know how to buy appliances to foster efficiency, and to master techniques of scientific management, as explained by expert Christine Frederick in the *Ladies' Home Journal*. In addition to schedules and files of medical records and household expenses, she had to keep

Urban middle-class homemakers were able to
escape the physical labor involved in laundry, first by
hiring laundresses, then by patronizing commercial laundries,
and eventually by buying electric washing machines. But
rural housewives, who lacked indoor plumbing or electricity,
were likely to spend a full day of outside work doing the
laundry. In order to wash, boil, and rinse one load of
clothes, according to historian Susan Strasser, about 50
gallons of water had to be hauled from an outdoor pump
to stoves and tubs. Clothes soaked in caustic substances,
such as lye or lime, had to be scrubbed, rinsed, wrung, and
rinsed again. Until well into the twentieth century, laundry
remained the most strenuous of household jobs, even with
the aid of such devices as the mechanical wringer, shown
here. *(State Historical Society of Wisconsin)*

itemized lists of articles of clothing, birthdays, jokes, and quotations. She also had to adopt a self-critical posture, asking herself the questions proposed by Ellen Richards: "Can I do better than I am doing?" "Is there any device which I might use?" "Is my house right as to its sanitary arrangements?" "Is my food the best possible?" "Can I make the best use of my time?"

The elevation of the homemaker to professional status had allure in many quarters. It catered to the *Ladies' Home Journal* readers for whose patronage advertisers now competed. It appealed to the colleges, which established departments of domestic science and degree programs in home economics, and it won applause in suffragist circles, ready to endorse any enhancement of women's status. The federal government also endorsed home economics as a worthy endeavor. In the Smith-Lever Act of 1914, a follow-up to the Morrill Land Grant Act of 1862, Congress funded educational extension programs in rural areas. The new law supported agricultural programs for men and (in far smaller proportions) home economics programs for women; under its auspices, information on new household technology, home demonstration agents, and home economics curricula reached rural households. To what extend farm wives profited remains unclear. "I must tell you that I, me, myself, *moi*, was able to teach the domestic science lady some things she did not know," a northern Wyoming homesteader wrote to her mother in 1914. Through Smith-Lever, historian Katherine Jellison notes, the government subsidized not only home economics but gender hierarchy, a view that some rural homemakers shared. According to one skeptical Nebraska farm wife, women needed technology tips less than power in the farm family. "On the farm, man's law is supreme," Minnie Boyer Davis told a federal official in 1915. "I see no ray of hope or promise from that Smith-Lever bill. I do not want any visiting nurse of economist from that state university. . . . The greatest thing for the improvement of farm life is to elevate women to an equal status."

As the home economic movement gained momentum, new obligations fell upon mothers. Child care, like housekeeping, had always been a central part of women's culture. But at the turn of the century, the child was "discovered" as the centerpiece of society. Although a large minority of the nation's children in 1900 were employed—in mines, cotton mills, canneries, and other factories—the offspring of middle-class urban families no longer served as either household laborers or family wage earners. Rather, they were the primary products of the home. The decline of the father ("an earning mechanism," said sociologist Arthur Calhoun in the World War I era, "a tame cat") and the rise of the child left the mother in a strong position. The transformation of the child, as Ellen Key explained in her 1909 best seller, *The Century of the Child*, required "an entirely new conception of the vocation of mother."

In the progressive era, motherhood became not only a noble calling but also a learned one. The competent mother, historian Sheila M. Rothman points out, now needed more "insight" than "instinct." She had to acquire expertise and sophisticated skills. The campaign for educated motherhood found an outlet in the 1890s in an outburst of "mothers' clubs" and, in 1897, in the formation of the National Congress of Mothers. By 1910, "mothers' clubs" had 50,000 members, and a decade later, more than three times as many. In 1924, the National Congress of Mothers became the Parents Teachers Association.

The educated mother, like the educated homemaker, won approval from academics and experts, such as psychologist G. Stanley Hall. A regular participant in the National Congress's functions, Hall outlined the prerequisites of scientific motherhood, a status that only an educated woman could attain. The competent mother was a record keeper and rule follower who could learn techniques and instill habits. She had to understand each stage in the child's growth, to gear her responses to the child's changing needs, from infancy to adolescence, and to judge her own self-worth by how well she succeeded. The National Congress of Mothers sought both to perfect middle-class motherhood and also to bring other mothers up to par. Heading the battery of reforms it proposed were kindergartens—to take lower-class children out of less fortunate homes and expose them to educated women who could instill proper values. The congress also supported the mother's right to legal guardianship of children, as well as playgrounds, foster home programs, juvenile courts, child labor laws, compulsory school attendance, and domestic science and child-study courses in the high school and college curricula.

While advocates of home economics and professional motherhood ennobled the homemaker, other women created collective strategies to liberate the woman at home for a larger life outside it. Visions of cooperative housekeeping had a long history, dating back to soon after the Civil War. One early enthusiast, Melusina Fay Peirce, made elaborate plans for producers' cooperatives that would perform domestic work—cooking, baking, sewing, and laundry—collectively. Peirce organized such a cooperative in Cambridge, Massachusetts, in 1869 (the same year she chaired a large "women's parliament" in New York under the auspices of Sorosis, the pioneer women's club). The Cambridge collective fell apart after two years, because husbands, who were assessed for the women's services, objected to the new arrangements. But Melusina Peirce continued to endorse the virtues of "cooperative housekeeping," and other women persevered along similar lines.

Most proponents of collective efforts had experience in the left wing of social reform. In the 1880s, Marie Stevens Howland, former Lowell mill worker and communitarian, became involved in an American experimental community in Mexico and, with the collaboration of an architect and an engineer, drew up plans for community organization that incorporated cooperative housekeeping and child-care schemes. Other advocates of collective arrangements were more in the mainstream of the late-nineteenth-century woman's movement. Reformer Mary Livermore, known for her work in the Sanitary Commission, the temperance crusade, and women's clubs, advocated cooperative laundries, kitchens, and eating facilities that used the services of "professional" household labor. Authorities such as Ellen Richards and Jane Addams endorsed more limited collective schemes, such as public kitchens for working mothers. Finally, at the turn of the century, Charlotte Perkins Gilman became the best-known advocate of collectivist plans. Denouncing the isolated private home and its harmful effects on the human race, Gilman proposed new arrangements for cooperative housekeeping, cooking, and child care, using the services of paid professionals in domestic work. Evoking widespread interest, Gilman's ideas inspired other enthusiasts through the 1920s. Proponents of collective plans disagreed on major issues, such as *who* should do domestic work: housewives, hired help, or paid staffs of domestic specialists. But in all cases, significantly, collectivists viewed domestic work as women's realm. Several themes pervaded their visions of kitchenless homes, communal facilities, and cooperative strategies: Women should be paid for household work, spatial design of home and community should be reorganized to suit women's needs, and divisions between private household space and public space should be revised.

Plans for cooperative housekeeping and other collectivist ventures, however, remained visions more than realities, domestic counterparts to socialist visions that flourished at the same time. At the turn of the century, the middle-class woman, who valued her individualism, was more likely to adopt the role of household executive and professional parent, as touted by the Home Economics Association and the National Congress of Mothers. She also became a vital contributor to the progressive reform agenda. Capitalizing on her domestic expertise, inspired by a sense of shared feminine interests, and supported by a wide range of women's organizations, she was ready to take an active role in public life.

SOCIAL HOUSEKEEPERS

In the progressive era, the ranks of women's organizations exploded. Besides the oldest and largest, the WCTU and the women's club movement, many new associations were formed—by homemakers, mothers, alumnae, professional women, charity workers, and reformers of all stripes. Some new organizations were special interest groups such as the Daughters of the American Revolution (1890) and the National Council of Jewish Women (1893). Others were professional associations—of doctors, nurses, educators, or settlement workers. Yet others carved out new public fiefs, such as the National Congress of Mothers (1897) or the Home Economics Association (1908). Many women's groups specialized in philanthropic works—such as the Young Women's Christian Association, started soon after the Civil War, which aided young women who came to the city alone, or the Junior League (1901), which sponsored civic projects. On the left wing, new coalitions evolved to improve the lot of women workers, such as the National Consumers' League (1899), which sought to improve working conditions in factories and retail sales, and the Women's Trade Union League (1903), which spurred the formation of women's unions. Each club, society, and federation strove for specific goals, but all united to advance women's special interests, which occupied more and more public space.

Here the women's clubs had set the tone. Women were enemies of vice, filth, corruption, ugliness, ignorance, and exploitation. Their special concerns were anything that involved children, home, family, education, health, hygiene, food, sanitation, and other women. However specialized their original goals, most women's associations turned into pressure groups and ended up tackling local officials and state legislators—for playgrounds, kindergartens, compulsory education laws, child labor laws, protective laws, pure food laws, juvenile courts, and other items on the progressive reform agenda. The rationale behind such efforts was so often repeated that it took on the aura of gospel. "The woman's place is in the home," a progressive wrote in a university bulletin in 1915. "But today would she serve the home, she must go beyond the home. No longer is the home encompassed by four walls. Many of its most important duties lie now involved in the bigger family of the city and the state." Capitalizing on a long tradition of female benevolence and combining it with a newfound interest in social science, middle-class women collectively embarked on the solution of urban problems. By the turn of the century, the new woman had become a social housekeeper, an active participant in civic affairs.

The settlement worker, a bridge between traditional philanthropy and progressive reform, served in the front ranks of social housekeeping. The number of settlements multiplied rapidly, along with the number of women college graduates. According to historian Allen Davis, there were six settlements in 1891, 100 in 1900, 200 in 1905, and 400 by 1910. The growth of Hull-House in Chicago suggests the settlement's phenomenal success. When Jane Addams and Ellen Gates Starr moved into an old mansion in the nineteenth ward in 1889, they faced a decaying area full of immigrants, tenements, and saloons. By 1892, Hull-House had absorbed a house next door, formerly a saloon; each week one thousand people of the ward attended 40 settlement programs, run by more than 90 volunteers. In 1895, 20 residents, or live-in volunteers, mainly college graduates from well-off families, worked at the settlement. By 1910, Hull-House had expanded into a large complex of buildings and adjuncts that filled a city block; up to 70 residents offered their services. As Hull-House grew, Jane Addams soared to national prominence. As early as the 1890s, when only in her 30s, she described herself as "the grandmother of American settlements."

Drawing on the talents of college-trained women, the settlement house was more selective than either the women's club or any other voluntary society. It was also an avenue through which the educated women could make a tangible social contribution, by bringing the urban poor and foreign-born in contact with the "best in American life." Although neither settlement work nor settlement programs excluded men, women dominated the ranks of settlement residents and neighborhood participants. The women and children who joined settlement clubs and classes, such as those at Hull-House, were supposed to serve as carriers of values back to their homes. Moreover, most of the men in Chicago's nineteenth ward could not be lured into the Hull-House Men's Club or other settlement functions, whereas the children in the afterschool clubs, the working girls in the Jane Club (a cooperative residence), and the mothers with babies in the day nursery rushed to take advantage of the settlement's services.

The other beneficiaries, as Jane Addams stressed, were the residents themselves. "I can see why life in a settlement seemed so great an adventure," wrote Alice Hamilton, who became a Hull-House resident in 1897. "It was all so new, this exploring of a poor quarter of a big city. The thirst to know how the other half lived had just begun to send people pioneering in the unknown part of American life." Vida Scudder, a settlement pioneer in Boston, had been "aimless and groping" after graduating from Smith in 1884; she felt suffocated by "the customs, the assumptions of my own class." Like Alice Hamilton, Vida Scudder had a "biting curiosity" about the "other half." "Were not the workers, the poor, nearer perhaps than we to the reality I was always seeking?" Few settlement volunteers remained for a lifetime. Allen Davis shows that half of settlement workers married, and most of these spent less than five years in settlement work. But they were replaced by others equally

Even as a young woman, Jane Addams exuded an aura of
authority, one that impressed her college classmates, the
Chicago Woman's Club, and subsequently, the Hull-House
staff. By the 1890s, she was able to describe herself, in
matriarchal terms, as the "grandmother" of American
settlements. (*1896 portrait, Jane Addams Memorial Collection,
University of Illinois Library, Chicago*)

capable of transmitting middle-class values to recent immigrants and the urban
poor. Long-term residents, meanwhile, profited from the settlement's role as surrogate family.

The settlement house resembled not only an upper-class home—with its parlor,
drawing rooms, library, and music room, its fireplaces and stuffed armchairs—but also
the colleges from which most residents had recently graduated. One visitor described
a settlement's atmosphere as that of a "college dormitory in the center of the urban
slums." Like the college, the settlement was an "experiment," but one designed, in
Addams's words, "to aid in the solution of the social and industrial problems which
are engendered by the modern conditions of urban life." In the settlement context,
educated women could preserve a collegial spirit while attempting to solve these

problems. At the same time, settlement work was an opportunity for residents to apply their academic training, using the neighborhood as a social science "laboratory." Hull-House, for instance, became an outpost of the University of Chicago. Searching for the roots of poverty and crime, corruption and labor exploitation, residents collected evidence from daily life and worked it up into generalizations, reform proposals, and legislative remedies.

The settlement worker also had much in common with the educated homemaker because she held the same values. Women and children who participated in settlement programs learned thrift, cleanliness, orderliness, refinement, manners, culture, responsibility, and, above all, citizenship. "Almost daily contact with Jane Addams gave me an abiding faith in the true principles of Americanism," a young working woman at Hull-House recalled. Especially effective were the settlements' clubs, with their rites and rituals, regular meetings, and democratic procedures. Residents also brought the basic lessons of domestic science, or "right living," to the slums. The Italian girl who learned to cook, as Jane Addams explained, could "connect the entire family with American food and household habits." If she learned about child care, she could tell her mother why the baby had to be fed purified milk. The settlement's visiting nurse services meanwhile taught health and hygiene to neighborhood residents; day nurseries and kindergartens exposed infants and toddlers to the best in educated child care, and instilled those habits that the tenement home was unable to provide. Even the Hull-House kitchen reflected Ellen Richards's latest precepts. Residents extended good housekeeping into their community patrols by inspecting water supplies, garbage disposal, and sanitary conditions, reporting violations, and insisting on improved municipal services. The settlement was not only a "big brother" in the playground, as Addams described it, but also a female watchdog that barked whenever male government fell short.

Finally, settlement houses transformed their leading residents into civil servants and politicians. In 1912, for instance, when Jane Addams appeared at the Progressive party convention, Lillian Wald of the Henry Street Settlement served much the same function for the Democrats. Other activists in the settlement movement followed similar paths on the state and local level. As experts in social welfare and spokeswomen for the "other half," settlement workers created a niche for themselves in government service and in political life. Leading spirits ended up as lobbyists who appealed to local governments for improved services and to state legislators for improved laws, especially those that affected women, children, and public welfare. Hull-House alumnae were the prime examples. Florence Kelley, the best known, moved on not only to government appointments, first as an agent for the Illinois Bureau of Labor Statistics and then as a state factory inspector, but also to work as a lobbyist and reformer. The many causes that Kelley promoted included child labor laws, protective laws for women workers, and mothers' pension programs to support children in families that lacked breadwinners. After joining Lillian Wald's Henry Street Settlement in 1899, Kelley took a leading role in the National Consumers' League, another exemplary progressive women's organization.

Like the settlement movement, the Women's Trade Union League and the National Consumers' League attempted to provide a women's bridge between social classes: NCL campaigns sought to benefit middle-class homemakers and women workers. Started in New York in 1891 by Maud Nathan and Josephine Lowell, the Consumers' League became a national organization in 1899. It adopted the settlement technique of thorough investigation, inspecting factories and stores. Its "white label" was awarded only to workplaces with sanitary conditions—to ensure that germ-laden garments and food products would not infiltrate homes. "It is the duty of consumers to find out under what conditions the articles they purchase are produced and to insist that these conditions be at least decent," Maud Nathan said. The league also produced a "white list" of local retail stores, those where the wages, hours, and working conditions of women employees met their standards, and it urged the public to use "selective patronage." Protecting home and housewife, worker and consumer, the NCL, like the WTUL, was a coalition of state branches, each committed to local vigilance. Under Kelley's leadership (1899–1932), it surged to prominence in the crusade for protective labor legislation.

The reform-minded spirit of the New Woman, as embodied in the settlement movement, the NCL, the WTUL, and other women's associations, succeeded on many fronts. One was legislative. In the first decades of the twentieth century, campaigns for child labor laws, protective laws, compulsory education laws, juvenile courts, mothers' pensions, and other causes sponsored by women often prevailed on the state level. Women's campaigns thus affected public policy for decades to come. There were national victories, too, such as the Pure Food and Drug Act of 1908 and the establishment of the Children's Bureau in the Labor Department in 1912. This would be followed, after World War I, by the establishment of the Women's Bureau, intended to guard the interests of women workers. The two bureaus served an important function as permanent female outposts in the federal government. Another success was purely institutional. The progressive era left in its wake hundreds of settlement houses and a spate of national women's organizations, most of them started in the 1890s. This outburst of association was not peculiar to women; many middle-class interest groups coalesced around the turn of the century. But it represented a peak of female activism. By the early twentieth century, the vital, energetic woman's movement had many bases—college, profession, settlement house, and a loose coalition of overlapping interest groups—all committed to women's causes, social service, and civic improvement.

A final success was political. The New Woman of the progressive era, vigorous, confident, and assertive, had left her mark on public life. Her political tendencies varied. Sometimes she tilted to the right, as in the turn-of-the-century WCTU and the women's club movement. Sometimes she tilted to the left, as in the WTUL or among converts to socialism such as Florence Kelley and Ellen Gates Starr. Often she ended up in the progressive camp, as did Jane Addams, and sometimes in the suffrage camp as well. Her ideology centered more around female distinctiveness than sexual equality. But by the 1890s this was the thrust of the suffrage movement, too. By demonstrating her concern for social welfare and her ability to participate in public life, the New Woman contributed to the effectiveness of arguments for woman suffrage. The large, energetic woman's movement, moreover, provided a context in which the suffrage movement could thrive and prosper.

SUGGESTED READINGS AND SOURCES

For an overview of women's new roles in this era, see Sheila M. Rothman, *Woman's Proper Place: A History of Changing Ideals and Practices, 1870 to the Present* (New York, 1978), chs. 1–3.

Changes in family life are examined in Carl Degler, *At Odds: Women and the Family in America from the Revolution to the Present* (New York, 1979), chs. 7–13; Steven Mintz and Susan Kellogg, *Domestic Revolutions: A Social History of American Family Life* (New York, 1988), chs. 4–6; Elaine Tyler May, *Great Expectations: Marriage and Divorce in Post-Victorian America* (Chicago, 1980); and William L. O'Neill, *Divorce in the Progressive Era* (New Haven, Conn., 1967). The concept of family life cycle is explained in Robert V. Wells, "Demographic Change and the Life Cycle of American Families," *Journal of Interdisciplinary History*, 2 (Autumn 1971), 272–282. On "voluntary motherhood," see Linda Gordon, *Woman's Body, Woman's Right: A Social History of Birth Control in America* (New York, 1976), part 2. See also James C. Mohr, *Abortion in America: The Origins and Evolution of National Policy, 1800–1900* (New York, 1978), and John D'Emilio and Estelle Freedman, *Intimate Matters: A History of Sexuality in America* (New York, 1988). For the underside of family life, see Linda Gordon, *Heroes of Their Own Lives: The Politics and History of Family Violence* (New York, 1988), and Elizabeth Pleck, *Domestic Tyranny: The Making of Social Policy Against Domestic Violence* (New York, 1987). For the lives of upper-class urban women, see Maureen E. Montgomery, *Displaying Women: Spectacles of Leisure in Edith Wharton's New York* (New York, 1998). Sarah Deutsch examines new women of varied class backgrounds in *Women and the City: Gender, Space, and Power in Boston, 1870–1940* (New York, 2000).

The social purity movement is examined in David J. Pivar, *Purity Crusade: Sexual Morality and Social Control 1868–1900* (Westport, Conn., 1973). For gender ideology in the late nineteenth and early twentieth centuries, see Cynthia Eagle Russett, *Sexual Science: The Victorian Construction of Womanhood* (Cambridge, Mass., 1989) and Gail Bederman, *Manliness and Civilization: A Cultural History of Gender and Race in the United States, 1880–1917* (Chicago, 1995). Carl Degler, "What Ought to Be and What Was: Women's Sexuality in the Nineteenth Century," *American Historical Review*, 79 (December 1974), 1479–1490, describes the Mosher Report, the earliest survey of female sexuality. Daniel Scott Smith defines "domestic feminism" in "Family Limitation, Sexual Control, and Domestic Feminism in Victorian America," in Mary Hartmann and Lois Banner, eds., *Clio's Consciousness Raised* (New York, 1974), pp. 119–136. Relations between women are explored in Carroll Smith Rosenberg, "The Female World of Love and Ritual," *Signs*, 1 (Autumn 1975), 1–29; Blanche Wiesen Cook, "Female Support Networks and Political Activism: Lillian Wald, Crystal Eastman, and Emma Goldman," *Crysalis*, 1 (1977), 43–61; D'Emilio and Freedman, *Intimate Matters*, cited previously; and Lillian Faderman, *Odd Girls and Twilight Lovers: A History of Lesbian Life in Twentieth-Century America* (New York, 1991), ch. 1. Helen Lefkowitz Horowitz discusses identity and sexuality in "'Nous Autres': Reading, Passion, and the Creation of M. Carey Thomas," *Journal of American History* 79 (June 1992), 68–95. In *Alice James: A Biography* (New York, 1980), Jean Strouse provides insights into female friendship, "Boston marriage," and the dynamics of an unusual late-nineteenth-century family.

The movement of women into higher education is examined in Patricia Albjerg Graham, "Expansion and Exclusion: A History of Women in Higher Education," *Signs*, 3 (Summer 1978), 759–773; Helen Lefkowitz Horowitz, *Alma Mater: Design and Experience in the Women's Colleges from their Nineteenth-Century Beginnings to the 1930s* (New York, 1984); Barbara Miller

Solomon, *In the Company of Educated Women: A History of Women and Higher Education in America* (New Haven, Conn., 1985); and Lynn D. Gordon, *Gender and Higher Education in the Progressive Era* (New Haven, Conn., 1990). Studies of educators include Helen Lefkowitz Horowitz, *The Power and Passion of M. Carey Thomas* (New York; 1994); Ruth Bordin, *Alice Freeman Palmer: The Evolution of a New Woman* (Ann Arbor, Mich., 1993); and Patricia Ann Palmieri, *In Adamless Eden: The Community of Women Faculty at Wellesley* (New Haven, Conn., 1995). For reactions to feminization in higher education, see Rosalind Rosenberg, "The Academic Prism: The New View of American Women," in Carol Ruth Berkin and Mary Beth Norton, eds., *Women of America: A History* (Boston, 1979), pp. 318–341. The roles of women graduates are discussed in Joyce Antler, "After College, What? New Graduates and the Family Claim," *American Quarterly,* 32 (Fall 1980), 409–435; Patricia Palmieri, "Patterns of Achievement of Single Academic Women at Wellesley College 1880–1920," *Frontiers,* 5 (Spring 1980), 63–67; and Roberta Wein, "Women's Colleges and Domesticity, 1875–1918," *History of Education Quarterly,* 14 (Spring 1974), 31–47. Martha H. Verbrugge explores physical education in several women's institutions in *Able-Bodied Womanhood: Personal Health and Social Change in Nineteenth-Century Boston* (New York, 1988). For fiction and the college experience, see Shirley Marchalonis, *College Girls: A Century in Fiction* (New Brunswick, N.J., 1995).

For the development of a black women's college, see Beverly Guy-Sheftall and Jo Moore Stewart, *Spelman: A Centennial Celebration, 1881–1981* (Atlanta, Ga., 1981). The work of black women educators is discussed in Gerda Lerner, "Black Women in the United States: A Problem in Historiography and Interpretation," in Lerner, *The Majority Finds Its Past* (New York; 1979), pp. 63–82, and Evelyn Brooks Barnett, "Nannie Burroughs and the Education of Black Women," in Sharon Harley and Rosalyn Terborg-Penn, eds., *The Afro-American Woman: Struggles and Images* (Port Washington, N.Y., 1978), pp. 97–108. The multivolume *Schomburg Library of Nineteenth-Century Black Women Writers,* ed., Henry Louis Gates, Jr., includes some relevant works. For instance, Anna Julia Cooper, *A Voice from the South,* int. by Mary Helen Washington (New York, 1988), an 1892 book by the pioneer educator, urges black women to assume leadership roles in racial advancement. For instruction in gender roles at schools for Native Americans, see Devon Mihesuah, *Cultivating the Rosebuds: The Education of Women at the Cherokee Female Seminary, 1851–1909* (Urbana, Ill., 1993); David Wallace Adams, *Education for Extinction: American Indians and the Boarding School Experience, 1875–1928* (Lawrence, Ks., 1995), pp. 173–181; Robert A. Trennert, "Educating Indian Girls at Nonreservation Boarding Schools, 1878–1920," *Western Historical Quarterly* 13 (July 1982), 185–201; and Terry P. Wilson, "Osage Indian Women During a Century of Change, 1870–1980," *Prologue* 14 (Winter 1982), 185–201.

For women's efforts to enter traditionally male professions, see D. Kelley Weisberg, "Barred from the Bar: Women and Legal Education in the United States, 1870–1890," *Journal of Legal Education,* 38 (1977), 485–507; Nancy Gilliam, "Myra Bradwell's Fights to Practice Law," *Law and History Review,* 7 (1987), 105–133; Virginia D. Drachman, *Sisters in Law: Women Lawyers in Modern American History* (Cambridge, Mass., 1998); Regina Markell Morantz-Sanchez, *Sympathy and Science: Women Physicians in American Medicine* (New York, 1985); Morantz-Sanchez, *"Conduct Unbecoming of a Woman": Gynecology on Trial in Turn-of-the-Century Brooklyn* (New York, 1999); and Ellen S. More, *Restoring the Balance: Women Physicians and the Profession of Medicine, 1850–1995* (Cambridge, Mass., 2000). See also Morantz, "Feminism, Professionalism, and Germs: The Thought of Mary Putnam Jacobi and Elizabeth Blackwell," *American Quarterly,* 34 (Winter 1982), 459–478. On gender and professionalism, see Elizabeth Lunbeck, *The Psychiatric Persuasion: Knowledge, Gender, and Power in Modern America* (Princeton, N.J., 1994), ch. 2. For nursing see Susan Reverby, *Ordered to Care: The Dilemma of American Nursing, 1850–1945* (Cambridge, England, and New York; 1987). Barbara Melosh discusses the professionalization of nursing since 1920 in *"The Physician's Hand": Work Culture and Conflict in American Nursing* (Philadelphia, 1982). See also Darlene Clark Hine, *Black Women in White: Racial Conflict and Cooperation in the Nursing Profession, 1890–1950* (Bloomington, Ind., 1990). Joan Jacobs Brumberg offers insights into medical practice and women's lives in *Fasting Girls: The Emergence of Anorexia Nervosa as a Modern Disease* (Cambridge, Mass., 1988). For Mary Baker Eddy's unique career as religious leader, see Gillian Gill, *Mary Baker Eddy* (Reading, Mass., 1998).

For women in science, see Sally Kohlstedt, "In from the Periphery: American Women in Science, 1830–1880," *Signs*, 4 (Autumn 1978), 81–96, and Margaret W. Rossiter, *Women Scientists in America: Struggles and Strategies to 1940* (Baltimore, Md., 1982). Sally Kohlstedt, ed., *History of Women in the Sciences* (Chicago, 1999) includes relevant essays. Rosalind Rosenberg examines academic women's careers in social science and psychology in *Beyond Separate Spheres: Intellectual Roots of Modern Feminism* (New Haven, Conn., 1982). Ellen Fitzpatrick explores the impact of social science training in *Endless Crusade: Women Social Scientists and Progressive Reform* (New York, 1990). Joyce Antler presents the innovative career of a married professional pioneer in *Lucy Sprague Mitchell, The Making of a Modern Woman* (New Haven, Conn., 1987). Dee Garrison describes the feminization of library work in *Apostles of Culture: The Public Libraries and American Society, 1876–1920* (New York, 1979). For teaching, see Nancy Hoffman, ed., *Woman's "True" Profession: Voices from the History of Teaching* (Old Westbury, N.Y., 1981). For social work, see Roy Lubove, *The Professional Altruist: The Emergence of Social Work as a Career, 1880–1930* (Cambridge, Mass., 1965). Barbara Harris surveys women's movement into the professions in *Beyond Her Sphere: Women and the Professions in American History* (Westport, Conn., 1978). Joan Jacobs Brumberg and Nancy Tomes assess disparities between professionalism and women's culture in "Women and the Professions: A Research Agenda for American Historians," *Reviews in American History*, 10 (June 1982), 275–296. For the professional man, see Burton J. Bledstein, *The Culture of Professionalism: The Middle Class and the Development of Higher Education in America* (New York, 1976).

The technological changes that transformed domestic labor are examined in Susan Strasser, *Never Done: A History of American Housework* (New York, 1982); Ruth Schwartz Cowan, *More Work for Mother: The Ironies of Household Technology from the Open Hearth to the Microwave* (New York, 1983); and Katherine Jellison, *Entitled To Power: Farm Women and Technology, 1913–1963* (Chapel Hill, N.C., 1993), ch. 1. See also Glenna Matthews, *"Just a Housewife": The Rise and Fall of Domesticity in the United States* (New York, 1987). For the home economics movement and the National Congress of Mothers, see Rothman, *Woman's Proper Place*, ch. 3, and Barbara Ehrenreich and Deirdre English, *For Her Own Good: 150 Years of the Experts' Advice to Women* (New York, 1978), chs. 5 and 6; and Sarah Stage and Virginia B. Vincenti, eds., *Rethinking Home Economics: Women and the History of a Profession* (Ithaca, N.Y., 1997). For the development of a Home Economics department at a leading university, see Maresi Nerad, *The Academic Kitchen: A Social History of Gender Stratification at the University of California, Berkeley* (Albany, N.Y., 1998). Dolores Hayden examines collective housekeeping arrangements in *The Grand Domestic Revolution: A History of Feminist Design for American Homes, Neighborhoods, and Cities* (Cambridge, Mass., and London, 1981). Clifford E. Clark, Jr., *The American Family Home, 1800–1960* (Chapel Hill, N.C., 1986) explores changing vogues of home design. Jennifer Scanlon discusses consumerism in *Inarticulate Longings: The Ladies' Home Journal, Gender, and the Promises of Consumer Culture* (New York, 1995). David M. Katzman discusses the relations of servants and employers in *Seven Days a Week: Women and Domestic Service in Industrializing America, 1865–1895* (New York, 1978). See also Norton Juster, *So Sweet to Labor: Rural Women in America, 1865–1895* (New York, 1979), an evocative collection of primary sources on domestic life.

Some scholars suggest a powerful feminist thrust in both the temperance and women's club movements. For the emergence of the temperance crusade in the early 1870s and the development of the WCTU, see Barbara Leslie Epstein, *The Politics of Domesticity: Women, Evangelism, and Temperance in Nineteenth-Century America* (Middletown, Conn., 1981), chs. 4 and 5; Ruth Bordin, *Women and Temperance: The Quest for Power and Liberty, 1873–1900* (Philadelphia, 1980); Jack Blocker, *"Give Wind to Thy Fears"* (Westport, Conn., 1985); and Blocker, *American Temperance Movements: Cycles of Reform* (Boston, 1989). For an earlier interpretation, see Joseph Gusfield, *Symbolic Crusade: Status Politics and the American Temperance Movement* (Urbana, Ill., 1963). Paula Baker examines WCTU activism on the local level in *The Moral Frameworks of Public Life: Gender, Politics, and the State in Rural New York, 1870–1930* (New York, 1991), ch. 3.

In *The Clubwoman as Feminist: True Womanhood Redefined* (New York, 1980), Karen J. Blair contends that women's clubs promoted autonomy while providing a covert feminist agenda. For the women's city club, see Maureen A. Flanagan, "Gender and Urban Political Reform: The City Club and the Woman's City Club of Chicago in the Progressive Era," *American Historical Review*, 95 (October 1990), 1032–1050. Older histories of the club movement are Jennie C. Croly, *The History of the Women's Club Movement in America* (New York, 1898); Mary I. Woods, *The History of the General Federation of Women's Clubs* (New York, 1912); and Mildred White Wells, *Unity in Diversity: The History of the General Federation of Women's Clubs* (Washington, D.C., 1958).

For the black women's club movement, see Gerda Lerner, "Early Community Work of Black Clubwomen," *Journal of Negro History*, 59 (April 1974), 158–167; Paula Giddings, *Where and When I Enter: The Impact of Black Women on Race and Sex in America* (New York, 1984), ch. 6; Cynthia Neverdon-Morton, *Afro-American Women of the South and the Advancement of the Race, 1895–1925* (Knoxville, Tenn., 1989); Anne Meis Knupfer, *Toward a Tenderer Humanity and a Nobler Womanhood: African American Women's Clubs in Turn-of-the-Century Chicago* (New York, 1996); and Wanda A. Hendricks, *Gender, Race, and Politics in the Midwest: Black Clubwomen in Illinois* (Bloomington, Ind., 1998). A microfilm source is "Records of the National Association of Colored Women's Clubs" (Black Studies Research Sources). Significant recent scholarship examines black women's roles in public life in the late nineteenth and early twentieth centuries. See Evelyn Brooks Higginbotham, *Righteous Discontent: The Women's Movement in the Black Baptist Church, 1880–1920* (Cambridge, Mass., 1993); Stephanie J. Shaw, *What a Woman Ought to Be and Do: Black Professional Women Workers During the Jim Crow Era* (Chicago, 1996); Glenda Elizabeth Gilmore, *Gender and Jim Crow: Women and the Politics of White Supremacy in North Carolina, 1896–1920* (Chapel Hill, N.C., 1996); Judith Weisenfeld, *African American Women and Christian Activism: New York's Black YWCA, 1900–1945* (Cambridge, Mass., 1998); Jacqueline Jones Royster, ed., *Southern Horrors and Other Writings: The Anti-Lynching Campaign of Ida B. Wells, 1892–1900* (Boston, 1997); Linda O. McMurry, *To Keep the Waters Troubled: The Life of Ida B. Wells* (New York, 1999); and Jacqueline M. Moore, *Leading the Race: The Transformation of the Black Elite in the Nation's Capitol, 1880–1920*

(Charlottesville, Va., 1999). Deborah Gray White, *Too Heavy a Load: Black Women in Defense of Themselves, 1898–1994* (New York, 1998) explores the contributions of black women's organizations from the progressive era through the twentieth century.

Marion Talbot and Lois Rosenberry describe the formation of the Association of Collegiate Alumnae in *The History of the American Association of University Women* (Boston, 1931). Susan Levine, *Degrees of Equality: The American Association of University Women and the Challenge of Twentieth-Century Feminism* (Philadelphia, 1995) covers 1929 to the 1980s. Women's philanthropic work is discussed in Josephine Shaw Lowell, *Public Relief and Private Charity* (New York, 1884). For the YWCA, see Elizabeth Wilson, *Fifty Years of Association Work Among Young Women, 1866–1916* (New York, 1916). For the collective endeavors of churchwomen, see Joan Jacobs Brumberg, "Zenanas and Girlless Villages: The Ethnology of American Evangelical Women, 1870–1910," *Journal of American History*, 69 (September 1982), 347–371; Jane Hunter, *The Gospel of Gentility: American Women Missionaries in Turn-of-the-Century China* (New Haven, Conn., 1984); Patricia R. Hill, *The World Their Household: The American Woman's Foreign Mission Movement and Cultural Transformation, 1870–1920* (Ann Arbor, Mich., 1985); and Katherine G. Aiken, *Harnessing the Power of Motherhood: The National Florence Crittenden Mission, 1835–1925* (Knoxville, Tenn., 1998).

Allen F. Davis examines the settlement movement in his pioneer work, *Spearheads for Reform* (New York, 1967). See also Mina Carson, *Settlement Folk: The Evolution of Social Welfare Ideology in the American Settlement Movement, 1883–1930* (Chicago, 1990); and Elisabeth Lasch-Quinn, *Black Neighbors: Race and the Limits of Reform in the American Settlement House Movement, 1890–1945* (Chapel Hill, N.C., 1993). For Hull-House and its personnel, see Allen F. Davis, *American Heroine: The Life and Legend of Jane Addams* (New York, 1973); Christopher Lasch, ed., *The Social Thought of Jane Addams* (Indianapolis, Ind., 1965); Mary L. Bryan and Allen F. Davis, eds., *One Hundred Years at Hull-House* (Bloomington, Ind., 1993); Kathryn Kish Sklar, "Hull-House in the 1890s: A Community of Women Reformers," *Signs*, 10 (Summer 1985), 658–677; Barbara Sicherman, *Edith Hamilton: A Life in Letters* (Cambridge, Mass., 1984); Lela B. Castin, *Two Sisters for Social Justice: A Biography of Grace and Edith Abbott* (Urbana, Ill., 1983); Rivka Shpak Lissak, *Pluralism and Progressives: Hull-House and the New Immigrants, 1890–1919* (Chicago, 1889); Eleanor J. Stebner, *The Women of Hull-House: A Study in Spirituality, Vocation, and Friendship* (Albany, N.Y., 1997); and, for a first-hand account, Hilda Satt Polacheck, *I Came a Stranger: The Story of a Hull-House Girl* (Urbana, Ill., 1989). For the Henry Street Settlement, see Doris Groshen Daniels, *Always a Sister: The Feminism of Lillian D. Wald* (New York, 1995). For the intersection of the settlement impulse and the arts and crafts movement, see Barbara Maysles Kramer, "Saturday Evening Girls and the Paul Revere Pottery," *Style 1900* 8 (1995), 37–40 and Kate Clifford Larson, "The Saturday Evening Girls," M.A. thesis, Simmons College, 1995.

For Florence Kelley's career in the settlement movement and labor reform see Kathryn Kish Sklar, *Florence Kelley and the Nation's Work: The Rise of Women's Political Culture, 1830–1900* (New Haven, Conn., 1995). Helene Silverberg, ed. *Gender and American Social Science: The Formative Years* (Princeton, N.J., 1998) offers insights on women reformers and professionals. An older history of the National Consumers League is Maud Nathan, *The Story of an Epoch-Making Movement* (New York, 1926). For a recent assessment, see Kathryn Kish Sklar, "Two Political Cultures in the Progressive Era: The National Consumers' League and the American Association for Labor Legislation," in Linda K. Kerber, Alice Kessler-Harris, and Kathryn Kish Sklar, eds., *U.S. History as Women's History: New Feminist Essays* (Chapel Hill,

N.C., 1995), pp. 360–62. For the WTUL, see Nancy Shrom Dye, *As Equals and As Sisters: Feminism, Unionism, and the Women's Trade Union League of New York* (Columbia, Mo., 1980); Elizabeth Payne, *Reform, Labor, and Feminism: Margaret Dreier Robins and the Women's Trade Union League* (Urbana, Ill., 1988); Robin Miller Jacoby, *The British and American Women's Trade Union Leagues, 1890–1925: A Case Study of Feminism and Class* (Brooklyn, N.Y., 1994); and Gladys Boone, *The Women's Trade Union League in Great Britain and the United States* (New York, 1942). For women's efforts to build a juvenile justice system, see Elizabeth J. Clapp, *Mothers of All Children: Women Reformers and the Rise of Juvenile Courts in Progressive Era America* (University Park, Pa., 1998). For public policy on child care, see Elizabeth Rose, *A Mother's Job: The History of Day Care, 1890–1960* (New York, 1999), which focuses on Philadelphia, and Sonya Michel, *Children's Interests/Mothers' Rights: The Shaping of America's Child Care Policy* (New Haven, Conn., 1999), especially ch. 2. For the federal Children's Bureau, see Molly Ladd-Taylor, *Raising a Baby the Government Way: Mothers' Letters to the Children's Bureau, 1915–1932* (New Brunswick, N.J., 1984); Ladd-Taylor, *Mother-Work: Women, Child Welfare, and the State, 1890–1930* (Urbana, Ill., 1994); Kriste Lindenmeyer, *"A Right To Childhood": The U.S. Children's Bureau and Child Welfare, 1912–1946* (Chicago, 1997); and Robyn Muncy, *Creating a Female Dominion in American Reform, 1890–1930* (New York, 1991), ch. 2.

The ground swell of association among women is examined by William L. O'Neill in *A History of Feminism in America*, 2d ed., (New Brunswick, N.J., 1989), ch. 3. O'Neill coins the term "social feminist" to describe activists in women's associations and reform movements who might support women's rights but "generally subordinated them to broad social movements they thought more urgent." Nancy F. Cott criticizes this concept in "What's in a Name? The Limits of 'Social Feminism,' or, Expanding the Vocabulary of Women's History," *Journal of American History*, 76 (December 1989), 809–829. In *Womanhood in America* (New York, 1975), Mary P. Ryan uses the term "social housekeeping" to describe women's reform work. Women's activism in reform has recently attracted abundant attention. See, for instance, Robyn Muncy, *Creating a Female Dominion in American Reform*, cited previously; Noralee Frankel and Nancy S. Dye, eds., *Gender, Class, Race and Reform in the Progressive Era* (Lexington, Ky., 1992); Anne Firor Scott, *Natural Allies: Women's Associations in American History* (Urbana, Ill., 1992); and Sklar, *Florence Kelley*, cited previously.

Articles of interest include Marlene Stein Wortman, "Domesticating the Nineteenth-Century City," *Prospects: An Annual of American Cultural Studies*, 3 (1977), 531–572, a study of "municipal housekeeping" in Chicago; Jill Conway, "Women Reformers and American Culture, 1870–1930," *Journal of Social History*, 5 (1971–1972), 164–177; Paula Baker, "The Domestication of Politics: Women and American Political Society, 1780–1920," *American Historical Review* 89 (June 1984), 620–647; and Suzanne Lebsock, "Across the Great Divide: Women and Politics, 1890–1920," in Louise Tilly and Patricia Gurin, eds., *Women, Politics and Change* (New York, 1990). Local studies of women's activism include Anastatia Sims, *The Power of Femininity in the New South: Women's Organizations and Politics in North Carolina, 1880–1930* (Columbia, S.C., 1997); Judith N. MacArthur, *Creating the New Woman: The Rise of Women's Progressive Culture in Texas, 1893–1918* (Urbana, Ill., 1998); Lynne Curry, *Modern Mothers in the Heartland: Gender, Health and Progress in Illinois* (Columbus, Ohio, 1999); and Gayle Gullett, *Becoming Citizens: The Emergence and Development of the California Women's Movement, 1880–1911* (Urbana, Ill., 1999). Estelle Freedman assesses the significance of separate women's institutions—colleges, associations, reform movements—in her important article, "Separatism as Strategy: Female Institution Building and American Feminism, 1870–1930," *Feminist*

Studies, 5 (Fall 1979), 512–549. For primary sources related to women and reform, see "Women and Social Movements in the United States, 1830–1930," co-directed by Kathryn Kish Sklar and Thomas Dublin, at http://womhist.binghamton.edu (as seen on March 1, 2001).

Much recent scholarship explores the intersection of gender, reform, social welfare, and public policy from the progressive era onward. See, for instance, Linda Gordon, ed., *Women, the State, and Welfare* (Madison, Wi., 1990); Gordon, *Pitied But Not Entitled: Single Mothers and the History of Welfare* (New York, 1994); Theda Skocpol, *Protecting Soldiers and Mothers: The Political Origins of Social Policy in the United States* (Cambridge, Mass., 1992); Gwendolyn Mink, *The Wages of Motherhood: Inequality in the Welfare State, 1917–1942* (Ithaca, N.Y., 1995); and Joanne L. Goodwin, *Gender and the Politics of Welfare Reform: Mothers' Pensions in Chicago, 1911–1929* (Chicago, 1997). Studies that focus on young women, social welfare, and public policy include Regina G. Kunzel, *Fallen Women, Problem Girls: Unmarried Mothers and the Professionalization of Social Work, 1890–1945* (New Haven, Conn., 1993); Ruth J. Alexander, *The "Girl Problem": Female Sexual Delinquency in New York, 1900–1930* (Ithaca, N.Y., 1995); and Mary E. Odem, *Delinquent Daughters: Protecting and Policing Adolescent Female Sexuality in the United States, 1885–1920* (Chapel Hill, N.C., 1995). For a comparative perspective on gender and the roots of the welfare state, see Sonya Michel and Seth Koven, "Womanly Duties: Maternalist Policies and the Origins of Welfare States in France, Germany, Great Britain, and the United States, 1880–1920," *American Historical Review,* 95 (October 1990), 1076–1108, and Koven and Michel, eds., *Mothers of a New World: Maternalist Politics and the Origins of Welfare States* (New York and London, 1993).

Memoirs of women reformers include Frances Willard, *Glimpses of Fifty Years: The Autobiography of an American Woman* (Chicago, 1889); Mary Ashton Livermore, *The Story of My Life or the Sunshine and Shadow of Seventy Years* (Hartford, Conn., 1898); Julia Ward Howe, *Reminiscences, 1819–1899* (Boston, 1899); Mary Church Terrell, *A Colored Woman in a White World* (Washington, D.C., 1940); Alfreda Duster, ed., *Crusader for Justice: The Autobiography of Ida B. Wells* (Chicago and London, 1970); Jane Addams, *Twenty Years at Hull-House* (New York, 1910), and *The Second Twenty Years at Hull-House* (New York, 1930); Kathryn Kish Sklar, ed., *Notes of Sixty Years: The Autobiography of Florence Kelley* (Chicago, 1985); Lillian Wald, *The House on Henry Street* (New York, 1915); Vida Scudder, *On Journey* (New York, 1937); Alice Hamilton, *Exploring the Dangerous Trades* (Boston, 1973); and Mary White Ovington, *Black and White Sat Down Together: The Reminiscences of an NAACP Founder,* ed. Ralph Luker; afterward by Carolyn Wedin (New York, 1996). Biographies include Josephine Goldmark, *Impatient Crusader: Florence Kelley's Life Story* (Urbana, Ill., 1953); Ruth Bordin, *Frances Willard: A Biography* (Chapel Hill, N.C., 1986); and Deborah Pickman Clifford, *Mine Eyes Have Seen the Glory: A Biography of Julia Ward Howe* (Boston, 1979). For the careers of Maud Nathan, Lillian Wald, and other reformers, see Ellen Condliffe Lagemann, *A Generation of Women: Education in the Lives of Progressive Reformers* (Cambridge, Mass., 1979).

🌐 For quizzes and additional resources related to American women's history, visit the book's Website at *www.mhhe.com/americanwomen.*

CHAPTER SEVEN

Feminism and Suffrage, 1860–1920

"SO LONG AS woman labors to second man's endeavors and exalt his sex above her own, her virtues pass unquestioned," Elizabeth Cady Stanton reflected in 1898, looking back on the early days of the suffrage campaign. "But where she dares to demand rights and privileges for herself, her motives . . . and character are subjects for ridicule and detraction." In the late 1860s, when the suffrage movement began, it was small in size, divided into factions, and barely able to legitimize its existence, let alone affect public policy. But by World War I, woman suffrage was a mass movement, with membership in the millions and enough support to secure the Nineteenth Amendment in 1920. In the final stage of its 50-year campaign, the suffrage movement became the pivot of women's politics, just as the vote became the symbol of women's rights.

The greatest testimony to the symbolic power of the vote, to both supporters and opponents, was the length of the fight to achieve it, longer than any comparable reform campaign and certainly longer than any other campaign for an electoral reform. But the very length of the suffrage campaign provided a major benefit. For three generations, the suffrage movement gave American women a separate sphere of political life, one with purpose, esprit, and continuity. It politicized existing networks of women, created new ones, and evoked their efforts in common cause—in conventions, addresses, memorials, manifestoes, petitions, resolutions, lobbies, and an endless round of state campaigns. The movement generated both a political context and a feminist community. One consequence was a highly charged sense of feminist unity. "The Woman's Movement," wrote Charlotte Perkins Gilman in 1898, "rests not alone on her larger personality, with its tingling sense of revolt against injustice, but on the wide, deep sympathy of women for each other."

Just as the women involved in other causes were overwhelmingly middle- and upper-class women, so the suffrage movement was a middle-class crusade. "The plutocrats have organized their women," Mother Jones told an astonished gathering of clubwomen who had invited her to speak in the early 1900s. "They keep them busy with suffrage and prohibition and charity." Working-class women, more oppressed by economic inequities than by political exclusion, had little interest in the largely symbolic, remote vote. Nor indeed had most middle-class women, who were more likely to support prohibition or charity than woman suffrage. Suffragists were usually politicized by some special factor, such as advanced education, professional status, or experience in another reform. Not only did the suffrage movement have a singularly middle-class appeal but its arguments began to reflect conventional middle-class values. In the progressive era, the movement adopted such values with a vengeance—to affirm its propriety, enhance its influence, and enlarge its constituency.

As a result, the suffrage campaign became more conservative in tone than its antebellum predecessor. In 1848 the Seneca Falls Declaration of Sentiments had encompassed a broad spectrum of grievances and demands, including the demand for a major shift of attitudes toward women. To antebellum women's rights advocates—a small and marginal group—lack of the vote was part of a complex network of social and institutional oppression, involving marriage, family, employment, education, and religion. Enfranchisement seemed the most farfetched of "women's rights," even to its supporters. After the war, women's rights activists dropped the broad spectrum of grievances to focus on the vote. "Social issues" soon fell by the wayside. By the 1890s, demands for political equality gave way to claims about the good that woman, with her distinctive qualities, could do for society through the ballot. The new tilt of argument reflected the need to attract a broader base. In its final years, woman suffrage was no longer a fringe movement of "wild enthusiasts and visionaries," as women's rights advocates had been called in the 1850s, but a large, legitimate social cause, "bourgeois" (in its own words) and public spirited. As the movement's constituency expanded, in short, its goals contracted and its radicalism diminished.

By the progressive era, the suffrage movement had become a national umbrella for middle-class activists with different priorities. According to historian William L. O'Neill, some suffragists were committed, first and foremost, to gaining equal rights. Others were "social feminists," who turned to suffrage in order to further some other cause to which they were primarily devoted, whether the temperance movement, women's club activities, settlement work, consumer protection, or the organization of women in industry. Though not a term in use at the time, and currently a source of dispute, "social feminist" is a rubric that can be affixed to the majority of women's associations in the late nineteenth and early twentieth centuries and to the women who participated in them, that is, to women committed to public service, civic works, and social reform. It was by coopting such reformers, capitalizing on their achievements, and adopting their outlook and rhetoric that the suffrage movement finally managed to mobilize both feminine and popular support.

The campaign for the vote, however, was still a distinctive phenomenon, apart from the rest of the "woman's movement." All women activists may have challenged male domination, whether they ran colleges, organized temperance societies, or joined women's clubs, but only suffragists did so overtly. Assaulting the main bastion of male power, politics and government, the suffrage movement was a women's crusade to legitimize women's role in public life, a campaign to ensure that women could participate in society as individuals, rather than just as family members. Historian Ellen Dubois suggests that in demanding the vote, early suffragists attempted to "bypass" the family and attain a direct relation to the state. Such a goal proved elusive. Suffragists had to convince male voters, state legislators, and congressmen not only that woman suffrage would benefit society but that women wanted the vote;

indeed, they had to convince women that they wanted the vote. This hurdle, until the very last years of the campaign, remained insurmountable. American women seemed to view woman suffrage as tangential to their interests, irrelevant, useless, or threatening. "In the indifference, the inertia, the apathy of women, lies the greatest obstacle to their enfranchisement," wrote Susan B. Anthony and Ida H. Harper in 1902. In their view, as soon as women showed that they wanted the vote, they would get it—a view that turned out to be correct. The suffrage campaign was therefore a crusade in political education, by women and for women, and for most of its existence, a crusade in search of a constituency.

The search began immediately after the Civil War, when the old women's rights movement—a small battalion of antebellum activists centered around Stanton, Anthony, and Lucy Stone—reassembled itself. In the next decade these veteran crusaders established an independent woman suffrage movement and laid the groundwork for a half-century campaign.

AN INDEPENDENT SUFFRAGE MOVEMENT

Between 1865 and 1869, when the issue of black male suffrage arose, woman suffrage became the focus of women's rights. While the Fourteenth and Fifteenth Amendments were debated and ratified, the small coalition of antebellum women's rights advocates, many of them long immersed in the abolitionist crusade, suddenly had hopes for themselves. Since the freedman's turn, the "Negro's hour," had come, woman suffrage seemed an almost tangible goal.

Women's hopes were also raised, as historian Ellen Dubois points out, because some of their male colleagues in the now victorious abolitionist camp tasted power for the first time and wielded influence in Republican politics. But these old associates, once sympathetic to woman's rights, proved fickle allies. In their view, the fight for black suffrage was enough of a battle and woman suffrage was extra baggage. Prominent abolitionists now turned their efforts to defending the proposed Fourteenth Amendment, which would guarantee black rights—and injected the word "male" into the Constitution. After it was ratified in June 1868, abolitionist politicos began a campaign for the Fifteenth Amendment, to prohibit black disfranchisement. Anxious to preserve their influence among Republicans, they were more reluctant than ever to saddle themselves with feminist demands. "Women's cause is in deep water," Elizabeth Cady Stanton wrote to Susan B. Anthony.

The prospect of black male suffrage both inspired and provoked these veterans of antebellum reform. As Stanton pointed out, any extension of suffrage that excluded women only increased their powerlessness: "In proportion as you multiply the rulers, the condition of the politically ostracized is more hopeless and degraded." Universal manhood suffrage, indeed, brought women "to the lowest depths of political degradation." This nosedive in status caused an outburst of anger against newly enfranchised freedmen as well as against retreating abolitionist allies. First, educated and enlightened women such as those who were prominent in antebellum reform felt more qualified to vote than either newly freed blacks or foreign-born men, "who do not know the difference between the monarchy and the republic," as Stanton wrote in 1869. Women reformers also felt ignored by the nation in general and by abolitionists in particular. During the war, women's rights advocates had supported the Union effort by their patriotic National Women's Loyal League, which had won great praise, as Stanton pointed out, for patience, prudence, loyalty, and ability. But after the war, when these same women began demanding rights for themselves, she contended, they were "uniformly denounced as 'unwise' 'imprudent' 'fanatical' and 'impractical.'" Even old colleagues dismissed their claims. "All their transcendent virtues vanished like dew before the morning sun."

Despite early signs of abolitionist defection, women's rights advocates made one major effort to link their goals with those of their old allies by insisting that the causes of the black vote and the woman's vote went together, hand in hand. Their ploy, the Equal Rights Association of 1866, led by Stanton, Anthony, and Lucy Stone, was dominated by women. It involved at least some abolitionist men; committed Garrisonians such as Parker Pillsbury and Thomas Wentworth Higginson offered support. But those with political influence eschewed it. Petitioning and lobbying through 1866 and 1867, the Equal Rights Association took its major stand in Kansas, an old antislavery battlefield, where it hoped to remove the word "male" from the new state constitution and ensure the vote for women, as well as for blacks. Not only did the Kansas campaign fail (Kansas voters, as it turned out, rejected both woman suffrage *and* black suffrage) but it provoked a split within the Equal Rights Association. During the campaign, abolitionist organizations withdrew funds and support from the cause of the women's vote. At this point, with great resentment, the women activists had autonomy thrust on them. But the abolitionist desertion, to Stanton and Anthony, was not without benefit. "Standing alone, we learned our power," they later concluded. "Woman must lead the way to her own enfranchisement and work out her own salvation."

During the Kansas campaign, Stanton and Anthony reached their summit of unity and friendship. After it, they embarked on a serious search for new allies, including the Democratic party, the newly formed National Labor Union, and, finally, working women. The Working Women's Association of 1868 was the most interesting of all these failed ventures. An attempt to unite women of all classes in common cause, it was part of Stanton's ambitious hope for a liberal, humane "party of reform," one in which feminists could join forces with other reformers. But as women's rights advocates discovered, working women were difficult to organize and generally disinterested in enfranchisement. When the Working Women's Association fell apart, Stanton and Anthony were left floundering, with only one route left: to seek a constituency of middle-class women. As they started to do so, a new conflict emerged, provoking a split in the small but embattled feminist camp.

This was the controversy, during the winter of 1869, over ratification of the Fifteenth Amendment, intended to ensure black male suffrage. The amendment battle divided woman suffragists into factions that lasted for decades. The radical wing—Stanton, Anthony, and their supporters—denounced the amendment. They were now completely disenchanted with the Republican party, which had failed to support woman suffrage. The more moderate faction—led by Lucy Stone, her husband, Henry Blackwell, and a galaxy of former antislavery stalwarts, such as Thomas Wentworth Higginson and Wendell Philips—were willing to support the amendment. They wanted to retain Republican allies, they counted on Republican support in the future, and they felt that universal manhood suffrage was a step in the right direction. Before the year was out, the rival factions, now competing for supporters, split into rival suffrage associations.

The moderates organized first. Their New England Woman Suffrage Association (NEWSA), started in 1868, drew luminaries from the antislavery circuit, including Abby Kelley Foster and Paulina Wright Davis, though Davis subsequently defected to the radicals. It also cornered nationally known Julia Ward Howe. Widely admired, Howe became a pivotal figure in women's politics, a leader of suffrage societies and women's clubs, and an invaluable asset. The NEWSA burst into action all over New England, forming suffrage societies along old antislavery routes. In 1869, it became the American Woman Suffrage Association (AWSA), devoted to pressing on the state level for the removal of the word "male" in the voting provisions of state constitutions (the radicals laid prior claim to the goal of a federal woman suffrage amendment). In 1870, the AWSA began publishing its *Woman's Journal*, an attractive, well-financed publication that lasted for the duration of the suffrage crusade.

The radical faction centered around Stanton and Anthony, who in 1869 founded the National Woman Suffrage Association (NWSA), the fourth association they had started in six years. The radicals were belligerent and outspoken, especially in their opposition to the Fifteenth Amendment. Publicizing their views in *Revolution*, a weekly begun in 1868 and financed by the generous but unreliable George Train, the Stanton-Anthony faction had no hesitancy about denouncing Republicans and their works. The Fifteenth Amendment, said the NWSA, was a step backward for women, one that would only intensify male supremacy and sexual inequality. A *Revolution* reader repudiated the amendment, she claimed, because it asked her to attest to "the inferiority of women." Elizabeth Cady Stanton argued that black men should not be elevated over "women of wealth, education, virtue, and refinement." (This point was made at AWSA meetings too.) She urged *Revolution* readers in 1869 to support woman suffrage "if you do not wish the lower orders of Chinese, Africans, Germans, and Irish, with their low ideals of womanhood, to make laws for you and your daughters." Suffrage, indeed, should be restricted to exclude the "lower orders of men."

But the notion of suffrage restriction was hardly *Revolution*'s only contribution nor was woman suffrage its only cause. Rather, the journal was a hotbed of feminist issues. Decrying unequal pay, unfair divorce laws, and clerical conservatism, *Revolution* pressed for the broad spectrum of goals inherited from the Declaration of Sentiments. The vote was only one part of this spectrum and, in *Revolution*'s view, not the major one. "The ballot is not even half the loaf; it is only a crust, a crumb," wrote Laura Curtis Bullard, a loyal Stantonite, in an 1868 article. "Woman's chief discontent is not with her political, but with her social, and particularly, her marital bondage." Endorsing marriage reform and the principle of "self-ownership," *Revolution* writers agreed with Ballard that "the marriage question reaches down to a deeper depth in woman's heart, and more thoroughly constitutes the core of the woman's movement, than any such superficial and fragmentary question as woman suffrage." Elizabeth Cady Stanton consistently demanded total equality. "The only revolution that we would inaugurate," she told the NWSA in 1870, "is to make woman a self-supporting, dignified, independent, equal partner with man in the state, the church, the home."

Despite the spectrum of goals endorsed by Stantonites and *Revolution*, woman suffrage remained the most viable cause. Once political equality became a major national issue, women's demand for enfranchisement rose from marginality to pre-eminence. Indeed, the vote was now the only issue around which women could mobilize collectively. Like its Boston-based rival, the NWSA did not hesitate to label itself a suffrage association. Like the AWSA, it began actively to seek out middle-class adherents.

NWSA strength began in New York, where it had a strong core group in New York City and a statewide network as well. It also had national ambitions. While the "American" was basically a regional organization, relying on contacts from the old abolitionist network, the "National" began to recruit on a larger scale. In 1868, Stanton and Anthony had gone off on a midwestern campaign tour, spurring the formation of suffrage societies and gaining recruits. These women were usually new-comers to reform, with no abolitionist ties or split loyalties but, rather, with some Civil War experience, often in the Sanitary Commission. Unlike the Stantonites, they tended to view the vote as more important than "social" issues. Also, from the start, the NWSA was clearly an all-woman organization, with all-women officers. To be sure, the AWSA had coopted most of the sympathetic men. But female leadership was also a matter of principle. As Matilda Joslyn Gage later concluded, "Women can work more successfully for their own freedom than anyone else can work for them." Finally, the NWSA announced its intent to push for a federal woman suffrage amendment. The New Englanders, in response, leveled their charges at the states.

The division into rival groups in 1869 was an asset as well as a liability. It enabled the suffrage movement to recruit a wider range of women nationwide than either faction would have reached alone. It also helped the movement survive the NWSA's entanglement with Victoria Woodhull in the early 1870s. A flamboyant personality, originally from backwoods Ohio, Woodhull and her sister, Tennessee Claflin, ran a New York brokerage office and a radical periodical, *Woodhull and Claflin's Weekly*, which endorsed "universal reform" and controversial causes. Woodhull captivated NWSA leaders when she suddenly appeared before the House Judiciary Committee in 1871; there she claimed that women already *had* the right to vote, on the basis of the recently ratified Fourteenth and Fifteenth Amendments. Subsequently an impas-sioned speaker on NWSA podiums, Woodhull won press attention, public applause, and NWSA acclaim. "Go ahead, bright, glorious, young and strong spirit," wrote Susan B. Anthony from a lecture tour. But Victoria Woodhull's reputation soon fell as quickly as it had arisen in a slew of scandals that involved her outspoken support for free love; revelations about the irregular Woodhull-Claflin household, where Victoria's present and former husbands resided; and finally, in 1872, Woodhull's exposé in the *Weekly* of the Beecher-Tilton scandal, soon a notorious divorce case. Injured by its link to Woodhull, the NWSA retreated; so did Stanton, once a sympa-thetic supporter. "We must not let the cause of women go down in the smash," she wrote to Anthony in 1874. "It is innocent."

The Woodhull debacle accentuated the acrimony between the two suffrage as-sociations, increasing antagonisms that took years to heal. It also forced Elizabeth Cady Stanton to tone down her politics, despite her unquenchable radicalism. When Stanton resumed NWSA leadership in 1876, she was willing to adjust to an era of single-issue politics and to steer clear of extraneous issues and risky associates.

The political cartoons of Thomas Nast were a leading
attraction of *Harper's Weekly*, one of the most popular magazines
of the late nineteenth century. This portrayal of Victoria
Woodhull as "Mrs. Satan" appeared on February 17, 1872,
after she had fully expressed her free love philosophy on the
lecture platform and in the press. The woman in the
background, who is carrying the burden of her drunken
husband and children, is saying, "I'd rather travel the hardest
path of matrimony than follow your footsteps."
(New-York Historical Society)

Basically, Stanton was a congenial woman who disliked controversy. Woodhull's third
legacy was the "new departure" she had proposed—for women to assault the polls,
contending that they had been enfranchised by the Fourteenth and Fifteenth
Amendments. The NWSA adopted this strategy in the fall elections of 1872, when
Susan B. Anthony mobilized more than 70 women to vote, nationwide.

"Women are citizens," said Anthony, "and no state has the right to make any new law or enforce any old law, which shall abridge their privileges or immunities." New York State, it turned out, had that right, and indicted Anthony for voting. In 1873, she was tried, convicted, and fined. More important, the Supreme Court soon affirmed, in *Minor* v. *Happersett* (1875), that it was constitutional for a state to deny women the vote. Virginia Minor, a Missouri suffragist who had tried to vote in 1872, had brought suit with her husband (as a married woman she could not bring suit alone) against the registrar who had excluded her from the polls. When the case reached the Supreme Court, the Court declared that the Minors were wrong and that suffrage was not a privilege of citizenship. The Minor decision made it clear that the "new departure" had no future. After its failure, the NWSA once again turned to Congress to lobby for a federal amendment. By 1875, an independent suffrage movement had been established, but it entered the Gilded Age on a note of defeat, with divided ranks, limited adherents, and no leverage over male legislators.

FINDING A CONSTITUENCY

In the 1870s and 1880s, the rival suffrage organizations competed for members; each strove for a larger middle-class base. More regional and parochial, the AWSA sought to excise the word "male" in state suffrage provisions. Better financed, and able to maintain its well-produced *Woman's Journal*, it remained the larger suffrage organization, at least until the mid-1880s. The New York-based NWSA depended on its statewide feminist network but also recruited across the nation. On their far-flung lecture tours, Stanton and Anthony inspired western suffrage networks. Both associations relied on small groups of activists who did all the work: testifying before legislative and platform committees, serving as emissaries to state and national party conventions, and running their own annual conventions. Both adopted a nonpartisan stance in politics, mainly by default, because neither party endorsed woman suffrage or paid much attention to its advocates.

The major feat of the divided suffrage movement in the 1870s and 1880s was survival in the face of almost perpetual rebuff: The rival suffrage associations met with one failure after another. First, neither was able to attract significant numbers of women constituents. The two groups combined had far fewer adherents than newborn reform associations, such as the popular women's temperance movement. Abigail Duniway, an NWSA stalwart in Oregon, summed up some of the problems in recruitment. Inspired by Anthony, Duniway established a state Equal Suffrage Association in the 1870s and traveled widely on behalf of the cause, but her efforts to organize often failed. A group of a dozen or so women might form a suffrage society in one small western town or another. But they would soon spend their dues on some new worthy project and, not long after that, fade into the scenery. Duniway concluded that it was more profitable to agitate for the vote through her own suffragist newspaper, to harangue state legislators, and to convince male voters, than try to organize women.

Inability to attract a large female constituency was compounded by continual failure at both the state and federal levels. Between 1870 and 1890, suffragists convinced eight states to hold referenda on the issue and lost all eight. More often, they were unable to persuade state legislators even to call for a referendum. In Massachusetts, the crucible of AWSA efforts, woman suffrage campaigns were a futile annual ritual. Every year, activists presented petitions to state legislators and testified at public hearings, with no results. And in 1895, when Massachusetts permitted women to vote in a state referendum on woman suffrage (an unusual move), the cause still lost, with far more men than women voting *for* woman suffrage. Agitation on the state level was by no means a total loss, however, as many legislators were willing to vote for a wide array of legal reforms affecting women—indeed, for virtually anything *except* suffrage. By 1890, 33 states had enacted married women's property rights laws, and by the turn of the century, according to Susan B. Anthony, married women could keep their own earnings in two-thirds of the states. In a majority, they could make contracts and bring suit, and in some states they gained equal guardianship rights over children. As in the antebellum era, legal reform proved easier to accept than the highly charged vote. By 1890, 19 states had granted women a limited form of suffrage; that is, the right to vote in school board elections or, in some cases, municipal elections. A modicum of "justice" was not beyond the comprehension of state legislators; it was the prospect of political equality that offended them.

NWSA efforts to make Congress enact, or even consider, a federal woman suffrage amendment were hardly more fruitful. In 1882, NWSA lobbyists convinced each house to create a committee on woman suffrage, and both committees sent bills to the floor. But when the issue finally reached a vote in the Senate in 1886, woman suffrage was defeated. After that, its prospects were even dimmer. Full woman suffrage, to be sure, had been enacted in two territories. In 1869 and 1870, independent of the suffrage movement, women were enfranchised in Wyoming and Utah. Both were special cases. Wyoming was barely settled; it had few women and many mining camps. To improve the area's uncivilized reputation and attract stable settlers, the tiny territorial legislature gave women the vote, which they retained when Wyoming was admitted to statehood in 1890. In Utah, in 1870, Mormon voters enacted woman suffrage in order to outvote non-Mormon settlers, mainly male. Congress revoked woman suffrage in Utah in 1887 in a bill that made polygamy illegal, but when Utah became a state in 1896 it once again enfranchised women. In the 1870s and 1880s Wyoming and Utah remained anomalies. Suffragists had no success elsewhere. Still lacking broad support, they were unable to sway legislators. Moreover, because the vote itself was a prime tool of legislative pressure, scholar Steven M. Buechler points out, "the movement was in the paradoxical position of being denied a major method for seeking legislative change." Finally, Buechler suggests, "the relative exclusion of women from the public realm and existing structures of power meant that women had little institutional power to bring to their movement."

In the 1890s, however, new developments enabled the suffrage movement to expand and legitimize its role. By 1890, the middle-class woman was in motion. The high school population was female-dominated, and women attended many American colleges. They constituted one-third of college students, and more than one-third of professional workers. Most important, middle-class women were creating a large nexus of associations—women's clubs, temperance societies, and charitable and civic organizations of all types. By the 1890s, in short, a new world of organized women had sprung into existence, reflecting a shared desire to participate in public life. The suffrage movement was no longer an isolated island of demanding women but part of a larger phenomenon—one of several national women's groups that held conventions, elected delegates, ran campaigns, and lobbied for causes. Although far outnumbered by women who were active in other reforms and worthy projects, suffragists benefited from the new context. The larger "woman's movement" testified to women's rising social consciousness and made their own efforts more legitimate and respectable.

Encouraged by the new climate, the two wings of the suffrage movement united in 1890. The National American Woman Suffrage Association (NAWSA) was part of a larger trend toward federation in middle-class associations. It was also an attempt to take advantage of women's new social activism and link as many women as possible under a single banner. This goal appealed especially to Susan B. Anthony, the major power of the NWSA, which had grown bigger than the AWSA. To be sure, animosities between the rival suffrage associations had not totally withered. But opposition to the merger came mainly from a minority of dissidents within the NWSA, such as Olympia Brown and Elizabeth Cady Stanton. In Stanton's view, both of the old suffrage groups had grown "political and conservative." Neither Anthony nor Lucy Stone, she felt in 1888, could see anything besides suffrage. "They do not see woman's religious and social bondage, neither do the young women in either organization."

Once the merger had reconciled survivors of the old guard, the new NAWSA streamlined its operations. It ran more formal conventions, attended by delegates from state organizations; it ended internal debate; and it became more professional, especially in tactics and propaganda. Dropping efforts to work for a federal amendment (after 1896, Congress no longer considered such amendments), the NAWSA agreed to direct all its efforts toward the state level. In the 1890s, state campaigns became more numerous and effective, especially as Carrie Chapman Catt, a forceful younger spirit, spearheaded some of NAWSA's major efforts. These campaigns usually failed—between 1896 and 1910 not a single state granted women the vote. But in the same period, the suffrage movement benefited from rising membership, new leadership, and a shift in argument.

Membership rose throughout the progressive era, as the NAWSA became a truly national movement. In the 1890s, it moved into the South, in the wake of the temperance movement and women's clubs. Although never powerful there, the NAWSA acquired a corps of southern leaders, such as Laura Clay of Kentucky, Kate Gordon of Louisiana, Rebecca Felton of Georgia, Belle Kearney of Mississippi, and Sue Shelton White of Virginia. Southern suffragism was always distinctive. Some southern leaders, for instance, imbued with states' rights convictions, opposed enfranchisement by federal amendment, even as suffrage gained momentum in its final decade, and supported state legislation only. Still, in the South as elsewhere, the emergence of other women's groups offered networks on which suffragists could capitalize. Club work and temperance work attracted large numbers of women, and suffragists profited from a coattails effect. In the Midwest and West, for instance, a majority of suffragist leaders were also temperance activists. In the Northwest, as Abigail Duniway testified, the women's club movement provided a "safety valve." It legitimized organized

The International Council of Women, founded in 1888, was
an NWSA ploy to mobilize support for woman suffrage among
delegates of leading women's organizations. Although the ploy
failed, a group portrait of council participants commemorates
the determination with which women entered the public
sphere. Susan B. Anthony is seated in the front row, second
from the left, and Elizabeth Cady Stanton, third from the
right. NWSA activist Matilda Joslyn Gage, second from right,
front row, joined with Stanton and Anthony to edit the *History
of Woman Suffrage*. *(Library of Congress)*

activity for more conservative women who were not politicized enough to support
suffrage and often provided suffragists with an audience—an arena in which they
strove for conversions. Suffragists profited from women's new social activism in other
ways, too, especially when prominent women reformers lent their support.

There had always been a degree of overlapping affiliation among leaders of
women's associations. Since the early postwar days, for instance, Julia Ward Howe
had been a heroine of both the women's club and the suffrage movements. Frances
Willard had converted the conservative Women's Christian Temperance Union to
her own suffragist stance, though after her death it returned to single-interest politics. But in the late nineteenth century, conflict more than affinity defined relations
between suffragists and other women reformers. First, the energies of some suffrage

leaders, such as Howe and Mary Livermore, were diverted into other causes, such as clubs and temperance. Second, suffragists and other women reformers could rarely agree on priorities. When the NWSA invited leaders of many women's groups to attend an International Council of Women in 1888, hoping to gain support for the vote, reformers refused to endorse woman suffrage. And at the World's Columbia Exposition in Chicago in 1893, suffragists and reformers were again at odds, over the highly charged issue of whether to segregate women's achievements in a separate building (the reformers won and a Woman's Building was established). Suffragists hardly dominated the women's movement, nor was woman suffrage a goal to which large numbers of activist women were as yet committed.

In the progressive era, however, differences between suffragists and other reformers became less overt, and a new network of overlapping leadership evolved. The NAWSA now drew support of leaders in the National Consumers' League, the Women's Trade Union League, and the settlement movement—such as Jane Addams and Florence Kelley, both of whom served as NAWSA vice presidents. Indeed, Addams and Kelley held posts in a wide range of women's organizations, including the NCL, WTUL, the General Federation of Women's Clubs (GFWC), and eventually in a new Woman's Peace party. By the twentieth century, the growth of women's organizations and overlapping leadership helped the suffrage movement attract a constituency. In 1893, the new NAWSA had only about 13,000 members—far less than the GFWC or the mammoth WCTU. But in the early twentieth century, the membership rolls began to climb, reaching about 75,000 (these figures were never precise) in 1910.

After 1900, moreover, historians point out, the rise of the progressive movement also favored the suffragist cause. In the context of the progressive reform agenda, woman suffrage was neither outlandish nor bizarre. Progressives endorsed a battery of electoral reforms and believed that all social problems could be solved by legislation. Woman suffrage meshed right into the progressive scheme and promised tactical benefits. Clearly, enfranchising women would double the middle-class, educated electorate who would support other progressive reforms. In addition, suffragists and progressives seemed to share the same vision of society, one run by educated citizens, without poverty, injustice, or corruption. The NAWSA house organ, the *Woman's Journal*, doubled its support for reform legislation, while influential women reformers, such as those at Hull-House, pressured legislators for progressive bills—to clean up slums, sweatshops, sewer systems, food products, and local government. Women reformers declared themselves enemies of party bosses, ward politics, and corruption, thereby enhancing their appeal as potential progressive voters.

Finally, a change of leadership enhanced the NAWSA's new legitimacy. For the first decade of unification, the old guard remained at the helm. Stanton, who presided over the 1890 merger, was never a very popular president. She retired two years later to agitate for divorce reform, resume her role as rebel, and publish her *Woman's Bible* (1895), an attack on organized religion's oppression of women. (The NAWSA, in convention, at once repudiated the *Bible*, by resolution.) Susan B. Anthony, who replaced Stanton, assumed office at age 72 and held it until 1900, when the second generation of suffrage leaders began to move in. Carrie Chapman Catt, who gained notice in the 1890s, was a master strategist of state campaigns. She served as president from 1900 to 1904 and again from 1915 to 1920. Anna Howard Shaw, ordained minister, physician, WCTU lecturer, orator, and protégé of Anthony, held control from 1904 to 1915. Catt and Shaw, both westerners and neither admirers of Elizabeth Cady Stanton, augured a new spirit. Now legitimate, larger, and unified, the suffrage movement shifted its arguments to appeal to its growing constituency.

From 1890 onward, while the suffrage movement gained cohesion and clout, it functioned mainly as an educational crusade, a propaganda machine. Its arguments, presented in resolutions, testimony at hearings, convention speeches, and suffrage publications, took on a new tone. Suffragists put less emphasis on demands for "equal" rights or on the "justice" of enfranchising women, and more stress on the special qualities women would bring to the polls and on the good they could do for the nation. The new arguments presented woman suffrage not as a radical change in women's status but rather as a tool of female benevolence. As a result, movement propaganda reflected traditional ideas about woman's role, in terms that would appeal both to middle-class men's views of women and to women's views about themselves. More of an amalgam of claims than an ideology, suffragist propaganda now sought to attract the largest possible base of female support and to convince the public of the suffrage movement's good intentions. It also responded to arguments against suffrage, which rose in volume as suffragist influence increased.

THE ARGUMENT OVER SUFFRAGE

Antisuffrage sentiment was hardly a novelty, but when the suffrage movement was weak and ineffectual, it emerged only in the occasional congressional debate or state campaign. In the progressive era, however, antisuffragism took on new zest and organizational voice. Associations opposed to woman suffrage began to appear in the 1890s, mainly in states where the suffrage movement was strongest. These "anti" organizations included men but were run and led by women, the same type of women who joined the suffrage campaign—well-off, well-educated, and active in charities, clubs, and reform. Their arguments against the vote emerged in state campaigns, legislative debates, and the press. To antisuffragists, as historian Aileen Kraditor points out, woman suffrage was an attack on traditional beliefs about sex roles and social organization. In defending these beliefs, Kraditor shows, antisuffragists posed the problems that suffragists had to solve.

Opponents of suffrage asserted that the sexes had different functions, that each occupied a separate sphere, and that any perversion of this social division would have dire consequences. According to their arguments, men functioned in society as distinctive individuals, but women were all cut from the same mold—a mold defined by maternity and domesticity. While the state fell into the male realm, the female realm was the home. Suffrage would therefore be an illicit entry into man's province. Moreover, the basic unit of society was not the individual but the family, a unit on which social stability rested. From this premise, antisuffragists drew two contradictory conclusions. One was that women were virtually represented in politics by male family members—by a "household" vote. The other was that if enfranchised, women would vote against their husbands, destroy their homes and families, and bring society to the point of anarchy. Women, therefore, were represented by men but would vote against them if they had the chance.

Despite the inconsistency of these positions, antisuffragists lost no opportunity to stress the damage that woman suffrage would inflict on society. In a congressional debate in 1866, an Oregon senator expressed the classic antisuffragist case. Contending that women could exercise more influence on public affairs by their "elevated social position" than they could "coerce" through the ballot, the senator asserted that with the vote, women would oppose men, turn society "into a state of war, and make every home a hell on earth." This became a staple threat. Leaders of antisuffragist organizations argued that if women were enabled to vote against their husbands, they would "wreck our present domestic institutions." In the 1917 debate on woman suffrage in Congress, a southern representative reiterated that giving the vote to women would "disrupt the family, which is the unit of society, and when you disrupt the family, you destroy the home, which is the foundation of the Republic."

Besides destroying homes, foes of suffrage contended, enfranchised women would harm themselves. A major antisuffragist point was that women were physically, mentally, and emotionally incapable of duties associated with the vote. Lacking rationality and sound judgment, they suffered from "logical infirmity of mind," as a minister argued in 1910. Idealistic and sentimental, they were likely to support wide, sweeping reforms. Unable to withstand the pressure of political life, they would be prone to paroxysms of hysteria. Female character, therefore, with its innate, implicit foolishness or "milder, gentler nature," as a senator put it in the 1860s, disqualified women "for the turmoil and battle of public life." They were not so much excluded from the vote as excused from it: Voting would ruin the purity and moral superiority, they had always claimed. Woman suffrage, as Grover Cleveland explained to *Ladies' Home Journal* readers in 1905, would have "a dangerous, undermining effect on the character of wives and mothers." By the twentieth century, antisuffragists conceded that women *did* have a viable role in public life, but not in what a congressman in 1915 called "the muck and mire of politics." Woman's role was in charity, philanthropy, and indirect influence over male voters.

Toward the end of the suffrage crusade, when the woman's vote loomed far larger as a real possibility, antisuffragists added some pragmatic arguments to their arsenal. These addenda sometimes contradicted other "anti" tenets, but neither suffragists nor their opponents had a monopoly on inconsistency. Woman suffrage, antisuffragists claimed, would double the number of "undesirable" voters, giving the "unfit" a potential majority. (Suffragists went to some pains to answer this argument.) Also, their foes pointed out, suffragists overestimated the impact of the vote. Woman suffrage would not produce any significant reforms because, if enfranchised, women would not vote as a bloc, but as their husbands or class did. Indeed, in states where women already voted, their votes made little difference. Finally (and this was the "anti" trump card), most middle-class women, the ones most qualified to vote, were not interested in their own enfranchisement anyway.

Suffragists sought to answer their opponents by fusing woman suffrage with traditional ideas about woman's role. Since the Civil War, the suffrage argument had blended natural rights and moral superiority. Demands for "justice" (women were entitled to vote) had always mingled with claims of "expediency" (women's votes would benefit the nation). In the progressive era, when the suffrage movement finally gained a constituency, the emphasis shifted to expediency. This was not a sharp break but rather a tilt, a reformulation. The tone of suffrage rhetoric veered away from self-interest to altruism. Significantly, suffrage arguments now stressed not the equality of women, but their difference. "It is because of the difference between men and women that the nineteenth century more than any other demands the enfranchisement of women," Carrie Chapman Catt claimed in 1893. The woman's vote, said suffragists, would accordingly make a difference. It would purify politics, effect reforms, and outweigh the votes of less desirable and less competent voters.

A chasm of "difference" between men and women was only one assumption suffragists shared with antisuffragists. They also assumed that women had special, shared interests and would vote together and that politics was a dirty business. Like antisuffragists, they often contended that the ignorant and foreign-born were unfit voters. But the "anti" argument depicted the woman voter as foolish, hysterical, and destructive. In the suffrage argument, she appeared as a paragon—morally superior, intelligent, educated, competent, humane, and cooperative, with an eye for detail, a skill for management, and a passion for fairness. Suffragists argued that these qualities were needed in government and that the woman's vote would put them there. By such claims they transformed the image of the suffrage movement from a threatening, challenging group into a wise, compassionate, and service-oriented one. The woman voter would not be the destroyer of home, family, and society but their protector. The vote was not a violation of sphere but the consummation of motherhood. The women who asked for it were not a radical fringe but rather models of middle-class virtue. The enemy, significantly, was no longer "man," as in the 1848 Declaration of Sentiments, but, implicitly and explicitly, specific men—lower-class men, the foreign-born, poor, black, and uneducated men, those with links to the saloon, the slums, the party machine, and patriarchal habits.

A major tenet of the suffragist argument was female moral superiority, a claim that had long been present. Elizabeth Cady Stanton, once hesitant about the moral superiority claim, had adopted it in the 1860s (Stanton was a versatile logician). "The male element is a destructive force," she proclaimed in an 1869 speech, "stern, selfish, aggrandizing, loving war, conquest, acquisition, breeding . . . discord, disorder, disease, and death. . . . The need of the hour is . . . a new evangel of womanhood, to exalt purity, virtue, morality, true religion, to lift men into the higher realm of thought and action." Since suffragists asserted that female values would carry over into the polls, uplift was a consistent theme. "Everyone connected with the gambling house, the brothel, and the saloon works and votes solidly against the enfranchisement of women," Susan B. Anthony told the NAWSA convention in 1900, "and I say, if you believe in chastity, if you believe in honesty and integrity, put the ballot in the hands of women." Maternal influence was also cited to reinforce the need for woman's vote. "In so far as motherhood has given to women a distinctive ethical development, it is that of sympathetic personal insight respecting the needs of the weak and helpless, and of quick-witted flexible adjustment of means to ends," declared Anna Garlin Spencer, Unitarian minister and orator, in 1898. "Thus far has motherhood fitted women to give a service to the modern state which men cannot altogether duplicate."

Women's special qualifications for political life, and the consequent good their votes would do, were points picked up by women reformers who added their voices to suffragist claims. Hull-House veterans took the lead, each relying on her own field of expertise. Julia Lathrop, children's advocate, told a NAWSA convention that woman suffrage was "the next great service for the welfare and ennoblement of the home." Florence Kelley, in addresses to the NAWSA from 1898 onward, stressed that woman suffrage was needed to protect the working woman, who, unenfranchised, had lost the respect of the men in her family. Jane Addams emphasized the need for women's contributions to urban government. In a speech to the NAWSA in 1906, she argued that "city housekeeping has failed recently because women, the traditional housekeepers, have not been consulted as to its activities." Men, said Addams, were as indifferent to civic management as they were to housekeeping tasks. "The very multifariousness and complexity of a city government demand the help of minds accustomed to detail and variety of work, to a sense of obligation for the health and welfare of young children and to a responsibility for the cleanliness and comfort of other people." Women had traditionally cared for just such detail,

Fear of role reversal was always an implicit part of the antisuffragist argument. With women in control, literally in the driver's seat, men would be reduced to sewing, laundry, and infant care. Such fear was also a telling comparison between the domestic sphere, limited and confined, and the public sphere. "The Age of Iron," Currier and Ives lithograph, 1869. (*Library of Congress*)

settlem
overlap
"woma
Perkins
identic:
vided a
emotio
left call
    Th
Gilmar
Gilmar
mothei
early li
after a
her wa
speake
activist
NAWS
Her fa
femini:
1915.
debate
    H
econor
most c
rested.
propos
emerg
the N.
oppres
Howe
of fem
terpie
by a w
    B
the ce
neede
"So u
that w
have c
her ab
and ir
behav
any h
her o
femal

Addams explained, before industrialization had transformed the home and society, but now, unable to vote, "they are losing what they always had." This was a powerful argument.

Social reformers also stressed that women's votes were needed to foster legislation to protect the family and to provide progressive reforms. This argument carried considerable weight because many of the women involved in clubs, temperance, and settlements strove to promote such legislation. In a 1910 article in the *Ladies' Home Journal*, Addams reeled off all the problems afflicting modern life that begged for the woman's vote—unsanitary housing, poisonous sewage, contaminated water, adulterated foods, impure milk, infant mortality, smoke-laden air, ill-ventilated factories, juvenile crime, prostitution, and drunkenness. The electorate, Addams concluded, should logically be made up of "those who have in the past at least attempted to care for children, to clean houses, to prepare food, to isolate the family from moral danger." Modern problems, Addams contended, could not be solved by military or business expertise but from "the human welfare point of view."

One more claim bolstered the expediency argument: The votes of middle-class women would outweigh those of the lower classes, foreign-born, and blacks. This response to antisuffragists reformulated an old contention, first voiced at Seneca Falls, that "man" deprived woman of rights "given to the most ignorant, degraded men—both native and foreigner." The old grievance was now adapted to the new argument. The 1893 NAWSA convention resolved that with woman suffrage, literate women could outvote uneducated men and "settle the question of rule by illiteracy." There was an even better solution, as Carrie Chapman Catt told the convention the following year: "Cut off the vote of the slums and give it to women." Franchise restriction, moreover, had long been supported by Elizabeth Cady Stanton, who now advocated "educated suffrage," a proposal to give the vote to all educated citizens, men and women, and take it away from the uneducated.

Other voices joined this chorus. Henry Blackwell, a founder of the AWSA, told the 1895 NAWSA convention that "in every state save one there are more educated women than all the illiterate voters, white and black, native-born and foreign." By outvoting the foreign-born, NWSA's Olympia Brown contended in 1889, women's votes could be used to maintain "our free institutions." And as Mississippi suffragist Belle Kearney told the 1903 New Orleans convention (somewhat to the embarrassment of President Catt), "The enfranchisement of women would insure immediate and durable white supremacy, honestly attained." Because such sentiments were widely voiced, prominent black women expressed reservations about the suffrage movement, even when they supported the cause. "Personally," said Margaret Murray Washington, clubwoman and educator, "woman suffrage has never kept me awake at night."

Black women, indeed, did endorse the suffrage cause, but they were generally excluded from the suffrage crusade, whose leaders feared antagonizing southern members. The NAWSA, for instance, rejected an application for admission from a federation of black women's clubs as late as 1919. On other occasions, suffrage leaders attempted to express unity of interest. In New Orleans in 1903, for instance, after Belle Kearney's speech, Susan B. Anthony paid an expedient visit to a local black women's club, where she was politely received. But this hardly made the NAWSA an

integra
forcefu
NAWS
Terrell
suffrag
argum
torian
dermir

R
They
of sucl
tial fer
enoug
enfran
which
respec
its apo
able t
great

In
any tr
NAW
for Re
mand
sexual
theme
up by
ery, al

The
wome
rathei
suppc
those
after
frage
adhei

I
of its
wome
rian l
loyal
prole

This grotesque creature, with her "feminine tricks and charms," had but a single option—marriage, "the one road to fortune, to life." But as wife, mother, and homemaker, her role had become pathological. First, said Gilman, she had become a nonproductive consumer who "in her unintelligent and ceaseless demands, hinders and perverts the economic development of the whole world." Her economic devastation was exceeded only by the damage she caused as a mother. Motherhood, Gilman contended, was ideally a sacred function; but like woman herself, it had become deformed and perverted. "Human motherhood is more pathological than any other, more morbid, defective, irregular, diseased," as she bluntly put it. "Human childhood is pathological." Children were stunted because mothers manipulated them, interfered with their lives, destroyed their privacy, and, in the end, produced even more monsters: "Idiots, imbeciles, cripples, defectives, and degenerates, the vicious and the criminal, as well as all the vast mass of slow-minded, prejudiced, ordinary people who clog the wheels of progress." Indeed, because woman was defined by "sex-function" and cut off from "all economic use," she became a disaster as both parent and progenitor: "The female segregated to the use of sex alone deteriorates in racial development and naturally transmits that deterioration to her offspring."

Not only did female pathology wreck the economy and future generations, but it was permanently institutionalized in the most deformed of institutions—the home. In a 1903 book entitled *The Home* (as well as in many articles in women's magazines, including the suffragist *Woman's Journal*), Gilman demolished yet another, fundamental female icon.

> The Home, in its arbitrary position of arrested development, does not properly fulfill its own essential function, much less promote social ones. It hinders, by keeping woman a social idiot, by keeping the modern child under the tutelage of the primeval mother. . . . It hinders by its enormous expense; making the physical details of daily life a heavy burden to mankind. . . . They should have long since been reduced to a minor incident.

The home was both an economic disaster and a female prison: "It maintains a low grade of womanhood, overworked or lazy; it checks the social development of men as well as women, and, most of all, children." As the home was not the basis of civilization, but rather its antithesis, the woman who remained in it continued to be thwarted, diseased, and demented. "Only as we live, think, feel and work outside the home," Gilman wrote, "do we become humanly developed, civilized and socialized." Clearly, this assessment contradicted every tenet of nineteenth-century women's culture, which not only sanctified the home but also—according to Frances Willard, for instance—attributed to woman a higher evolutionary status and urged her to civilize and socialize men.

Charlotte Perkins Gilman's remedies for woman's plight were collectivist and futuristic. Economic independence would relieve women of the need to attract men for survival; but to achieve such independence woman had to be emancipated from the tyranny of home. Gilman's proposals included large apartment units, rather than wasteful separate houses, and communal arrangements for housekeeping and child-rearing. Centralized nurseries could replace child care at home, and liberate women for "a far wider sense of love and duty" as well as for better parenthood. The mother would love her child more when not in constant contact with it, when she had her own life and could "give her mind another channel for her own part of the day." Cooperative kitchens, meanwhile, run by specialists, would enable her to fulfill her own specialized, productive role beyond the home. Gilman's remedies, in short, were intended to instill economic independence, redefine femininity, and apply socialist principles to domestic life. They had much in common with the ideas of her fellow socialist Edward Bellamy, whose utopian proposals had won wide popularity. They were also part of the collectivist tradition that can be traced back to Melusina Fay Peirce and her Cambridge cooperative in 1869.

While Charlotte Perkins Gilman had affiliations with the middle-class women's movement, anarchist Emma Goldman agitated outside it, although she too maintained a wide range of contacts with suffragists and reformers. Nor did Goldman express anything like Gilman's visceral animus toward middle-class femininity; though more radical politically, Goldman was a compassionate and sympathetic soul. But like Gilman's, her views were yet another counterpoint to the middle-of-the-road stance represented by NAWSA.

Born in Russia, Emma Goldman emigrated to New York as a teenager in 1885 and began her political career in 1889, when she became involved in anarchist circles. A magnetic personality, Goldman crossed the nation defending anarchism and free speech, throughout the progressive era, and published her views in her magazine *Mother Earth* (1906–1918). To Goldman, as to Gilman, woman suffrage was of little import. As an anarchist, Goldman viewed politics as profane, because they would always be dominated by business interests, whether women voted or not. There was no reason woman should not vote, Goldman said, but "to assume . . . that she would succeed in purifying something which is not susceptible of purification is to credit her with supernatural powers." Central issues of the "woman problem" therefore lay outside the voting booth. Among such issues, Goldman had much to say on the "marriage question" and the nature of woman's "emancipation."

Like Charlotte Perkins Gilman, Emma Goldman rejected woman's role as mere "sex commodity," but she attacked "the conventional lie of marriage" as well. Marriage was primarily "an economic arrangement, an insurance pact," Goldman explained in a 1910 essay. "If, however, a woman's premium is a husband, she pays for it with her name, her privacy, her self-respect, her very life." While Goldman favored mutual affection outside marriage (in her own case, this proved an elusive goal, as she was usually torn between man and cause), she was not surprised that working girls accepted the first offer of marriage, "sick and tired of their 'independence' behind the counter, the sewing or typewriter machine." Never limited by a middle-class perspective, Goldman criticized contemporary feminist notions of "emancipation," in which she found an ascetic, asexual quality: The new, emancipated, independent woman had excluded men from her emotional life. "True emancipation begins neither at the polls nor in court," Goldman wrote. "It begins in a woman's soul."

Emma Goldman's ideal was the woman who could "direct her own destiny" in every way, who could fuse emancipation with romantic attachment. But she felt that contemporary feminists, especially when disdainful of men, had "failed to reach that great end."

The narrowness of the existing conception of woman's independence and emancipation . . . the fear that love will rob her of freedom and independence . . . the horror
that love or the joy of motherhood will only hinder her in the full exercise of her
profession—all these together make of the emancipated modern woman a compulsory vestal, before whom life . . . rolls on without touching or gripping her soul.

No "compulsory vestal" herself, Emma Goldman became an early advocate of birth
control, although arrested for lecturing on the subject in 1916. Her efforts, however,
inspired younger women on the left, such as Elizabeth Gurley Flynn and Margaret
Sanger, who began to crusade for birth control just before World War I and provided
their own counterpoint to middle-of-the-road feminism.

Younger than Gilman and Goldman, socialist lawyer Crystal Eastman represented a new generation of feminists who, at the end of the suffrage crusade, formed
its militant wing. Through her multiple commitments, Eastman linked several aspects of the woman's movement. A Vassar alumna, Crystal Eastman entered public
life through a "social feminist" route, by working at New York settlement houses
while earning a master's degree in sociology and attending law school. She then
moved into the field of industrial safety and in 1909 was appointed to a New York
State commission to draft workmen's compensation laws. In 1912, then married and
living in Wisconsin, Eastman joined that state's woman suffrage campaign. During
the next few years, back in New York, her combination of radical and feminist interests emerged fully.

A member of the feminist group, Heterodoxy, as well as of New York's socialist
circles, Eastman worked with Emma Goldman on causes of mutual interest, such as
birth control and free speech. Committed to women's sexual emancipation, she
shared Goldman's objections to marriage, although she married twice. Unlike Emma
Goldman, Eastman was deeply involved in the suffrage crusade. By 1915, she had become a prominent leader in two new developments. One was the National Woman's
Party, a militant offshoot of the NAWSA, which split apart in 1916 and waged its
own dramatic campaign for the vote. Another was the Woman's Peace Party, formed
in 1915, which involved a broad cross section of feminists, including NAWSA president Carrie Chapman Catt, Charlotte Perkins Gilman, and Jane Addams. Defending
the cause of peace even after the United States entered World War I and most other
suffragists had retreated from pacifism, Crystal Eastman voiced her own brand of
radical feminism. In 1919, she helped to organize a Feminist Congress in New York,
where she advocated the battery of causes that had become important to like-minded
feminists, from economic independence and equal employment opportunities to
birth control.

Crystal Eastman was often trapped between affiliations with different priorities,
such as the conflict between the suffrage movement and the women's peace movement that emerged during World War I. She was also caught up in a conflict of
interest between socialism and feminism, a tension that left many left-wing women
in the lurch. Though sympathetic to woman suffrage, the Socialist party was not
ready to support the type of complete emancipation endorsed by such radicals as
Crystal Eastman. Therefore, though committed to both ideologies, Eastman clung
above all to her feminist vision. "The true feminist, no matter how far to the left she

may be in the revolutionary movement, sees the woman's battle as distinct in its objectives and different in its methods from the worker's battle," Eastman wrote in 1920. "As a feminist she . . . knows that the whole of women's slavery is not summed up in the profit system, nor is her complete emancipation assured by the downfall of capitalism. If we should graduate into communism tomorrow . . . man's attitude to his wife would not be changed."

Crystal Eastman best represents the feminist wave that erupted in the last decade of the suffrage crusade. The onset of "modern feminism," historian Nancy F. Cott contends, was a crucial phenomenon, distinctive from both suffragism and the nineteenth-century woman's movement. Modern feminism embraced a range of goals, for economic, social, and sexual emancipation, or even, in one advocate's words, "complete social revolution." "None of its single tenets was brand new," Cott points out, "Not the claim for full citizenship, nor for equal wages for equal work, nor even for *equal work*, nor for psychic freedom and spiritual autonomy, nor even for sexual liberation, nor for wives' independence." But such demands "assumed intensity in constellation." Significantly, modern feminism embodied paradoxes, Cott points out. Its demands entailed recognition of sexual equality and sexual difference, individual freedom and sex solidarity, unity and diversity, gender consciousness and the elimination of gender roles. The impact of such paradoxes would emerge more fully in women's politics of the 1920s.

The ferment of feminism to which Gilman, Goldman, and Eastman contributed had an important impact on the suffrage crusade. First, these radicals changed the political climate of the woman's movement. By World War I, the cause of woman suffrage truly assumed a centrist stance between more conservative women reformers and left-wing feminists. The feminist left also helped to legitimize NAWSA demands by presenting far more radical ones. "What you ask is so much worse than what we ask," a suffragist once told Charlotte Perkins Gilman, "that they will grant our demands in order to escape yours." Finally, during World War I, when both socialism and pacifism fell into disrepute, woman suffrage was in fact the only major women's cause left. By then, it had come into its own.

PEACE, WAR, AND THE WOMAN'S PARTY

In 1910, the tide began to turn in favor of woman suffrage, slowly at first but then in a mounting crescendo. Signs of progress came in a rush at the outset, when the woman's vote was endorsed by the Progressive party, the General Federation of Women's Clubs, and a string of western states. Progressive endorsement in 1912 was especially gratifying. Although woman suffrage had long won support in progressive circles, the progressives had never been a national party nor mounted a presidential campaign. And neither Republicans nor Democrats had been inclined to support the "non-partisan" suffrage cause. But the national platform at the Progressive party convention of 1912 included a woman suffrage plank. Candidate Theodore Roosevelt, who supported the cause, was "not an enthusiastic advocate of it because I do not regard it as a very important matter," as he had written to a friend four years earlier. Unconvinced that woman suffrage would either improve woman's condition or produce any of the "evils feared," he was certain that women would get the vote whenever "women as a whole show any special interest in the matter."

This special interest emerged in 1914, when the huge General Federation of Women's Clubs finally resolved to support woman suffrage. GFWC approval signified that woman suffrage had at last entered the mainstream—clubwomen were hardly a radical fringe, as their rhetoric confirmed. "Women realize that we are living in an ungoverned world," said the GFWC magazine in 1917. "We know how much we are needed in the world's affairs." Suffragists also won a sudden cascade of western victories between 1910 and 1914. More state campaigns were lost than won during these years, but the rash of success in the West, after over a decade of failure, suggested that the suffrage campaign was finally having an impact.

The western trend had started slowly in the 1890s, when Wyoming, Utah, Colorado, and Idaho enfranchised women. After 1896, western successes came to a halt. But in 1910, when the state of Washington gave women the vote, a major new surge began. A well-mounted, well-publicized California victory in 1911 was crucial. By 1914, Oregon, Arizona, Kansas, Nevada, and Montana had granted women the vote; and in 1913, the Illinois legislature gave women the right to vote in presidential elections. In many states, final victory was hard-won. In Oregon, for instance, woman suffrage had been persistently defeated in five referenda before it was accepted. The western victories enfranchised only a small minority of American women. But they did make western congressmen responsible to women constituents, and they proved that woman suffrage would do little damage. The vote, it was observed, did not destroy the home and family in Colorado. Indeed, according to Helen L. Sumner's pioneer study, it seemed to have little impact there at all, except to suggest that few women would run for public office and that women voters would unite on few issues. But most important, the western victories gave the suffrage movement new impetus. By 1914, the stage was set for a change of leadership and a final surge of agitation.

Anna Howard Shaw, NAWSA president from 1904 to 1915, lacked administrative skill and had never captivated the social feminists—the clubwomen, settlement workers, and labor reformers. She also had the reputation of disliking men. During her reign, massive energies had gone into state campaigns, but no efforts had been made with a federal amendment, which NAWSA had decided to ignore. Congress had considered no such amendment since 1896. Shaw's successor, Carrie Chapman Catt, was a different type of leader. Catt had already led NAWSA at the turn of the century and was by now an experienced politician. Since her rise to influence in the 1890s, as a strategist of state campaigns, Catt had shown great personal charm, political finesse, and organizational zest. As leader of the International Woman Suffrage Alliance, formed in 1902, she presided continually over conferences in European capitals. A well-educated westerner, Catt was the beneficiary of solvent marriages, the last of which included a contract that had given her half the year to work for suffrage and eventually made her a wealthy widow (her husband died in 1905). Like other reform-minded women, to whom she appealed, Catt believed that the vote would be a "first step" toward effecting a range of social reforms. She also maintained a wide range of affiliations among women—from the wealthy contributors who formed her new NAWSA board to Emma Goldman, with whom she discussed anarchism.

By the time Catt again took office in 1915, the NAWSA was shifting its tactics from "education" to more methodical modes of pressure, such as buttonholing legislators. A 1914 handbook for suffragists advised that no political meeting, convention, platform committee, or any appropriate gathering be spared a spate of suffrage demands. In New York, where a crucial victory was anticipated, suffrage clubs were organized on a precinct basis to coerce voters and politicos personally. Leaders mobilized support among working-class women, and spokeswomen for women workers rallied to the cause. "We working women need the ballot for self-protection; that's all there is to it," as labor organizer Leonora O'Reilly told a joint session of Congress in 1912. Carrie Chapman Catt, finally, had a master plan for victory. After converting President Wilson and winning the pivotal New York battle, the NAWSA would overcome congressional lethargy, win a proposed suffrage amendment, and wage state fights to get it ratified. Catt carried her plan into effect even faster than she had anticipated. But she also had to cope with two developments that had not been part of the plan. One was the apostasy of dissident radicals within the NAWSA, which culminated in the formation of a rival suffrage organization, the National Woman's Party (NWP), in 1916. The other was U.S. entry into World War I in 1917, which destroyed an impressive women's peace movement that many suffragists had supported. Both new developments changed the course of the suffrage campaign in its last, crucial years.

Rebellion within the NAWSA had begun before Catt took office. In 1913, a young Quaker activist, Alice Paul, arrived in Washington, fresh from a stint with English suffragists, who were known for their militant tactics. In England, suffragists marched through the streets, chained themselves to lampposts, starved themselves in prison, and attacked the "party in power," whatever it might be, for denying the vote to women. Contending that the Democrats were now responsible for failure to enact a woman suffrage amendment, Alice Paul organized a massive rally to protest President Wilson's inauguration. Such tactics evoked controversy, because the NAWSA prided itself on four decades of nonpartisan politics and less disruptive modes of pressure. But Alice Paul was charismatic, especially among younger women in the suffrage movement—the third generation. She soon had a large, committed following, ranging from radicals such as Crystal Eastman, a pacifist and socialist, to wealthy and imposing Alva Belmont, who committed her funds and energy to the new faction. Forming their own contingent, the Congressional Union, Paul and her followers resurrected the long-dormant campaign for a federal amendment and created a determined congressional lobby.

In 1915, while the NAWSA began its final round of buttonholing, Alice Paul's Congressional Union rebelled. Leaving the NAWSA, the Congressional Union joined forces with western women voters to form the National Woman's Party in 1916. Continuing to attack the Democrats, the NWP resembled the Stanton-Anthony faction of the 1860s, which had attacked the Republicans for failure to support a woman suffrage amendment. Indeed, to some old campaigners, such as Olympia Brown, it seemed to be a rebirth of the old radicalism. This time, however, the radicals attracted supporters in all of the states and mobilized them to oppose the Democrats locally. The Woman's Party also spurred both houses of Congress to consider a federal woman suffrage amendment, which had been shelved since the 1890s.

The Woman's Party proved an embarrassment to the NAWSA, which felt that it would only alienate sympathetic Democrats. The NAWSA also believed that the suffrage movement should be above party politics. But the Woman's Party's dramatic mode of agitation also drew attention to the cause. Attention increased in 1917, when Alice Paul and her supporters began picketing the White House to condemn the "party in power" for failing to produce a woman suffrage amendment. Such militancy aroused both antipathy and interest, especially when the picketers were arrested and went on hunger strikes. Although the jailed suffragists were soon released, their arrests evoked sympathy. All the women had done, as Alva Belmont told the press, was to stand there "quietly, peacefully, lawfully, and gloriously." Despite NAWSA objections to these new rivals, the militants probably had a positive impact. According to historians Ann Firor Scott and Andrew Scott, "nervousness about what the radical women might do next encouraged both Congress and the president to . . . embrace the more conservative suffragists as the lesser evil."

While the National Woman's Party pressured Congress and attracted attention, Carrie Chapman Catt increased the tempo of her master plan. The crucial New York State referendum, won in 1917 (it had failed two years before), suggested that the "slum" vote was not the terror that the NAWSA had once imagined. A new light of tolerance entered the movement, though rather too late to affect its arguments. By now, tactics were more important than argument. In 1917, Catt announced that she did not know whether the vote was a right, a duty, or a privilege, but that "whatever it is, women want it." To ensure that they got it, the NAWSA had to capitalize on all the good works that American women were now contributing to the war effort. It also had to extricate itself from what had become an impressive and powerful women's plea for peace.

In the first two decades of the twentieth century, international peace had become a major theme in women's politics. Since 1869, suffragists had argued that peace-loving women would use the vote to counteract the male martial instinct. At the turn of the century, all major women's organizations had "peace" departments. By 1910, the cause of peace attracted a wide gamut of women leaders and activists, including Catt, Gilman, Addams, and younger radicals such as Eastman. In 1915, 86 delegates from all major women's groups attended the opening meeting of the Woman's Peace Party (WPP) in Washington, chaired by Catt, and drew up a pacifist platform representing the views of "the mother half of humanity." Within a year, the WPP had a membership of 25,000, drawing on the ample membership rolls of other women's groups.

But the WPP's hopeful future capsized almost immediately when the United States entered World War I—a move opposed by the first woman in Congress, Jeanette Rankin, a suffragist who had just been elected from Montana. In wartime, a radical minority continued to agitate for peace. So did Jane Addams, true to her convictions and much to the detriment of her reputation. The National Woman's Party also refused to support U.S. entry into the war. NAWSA, however, unable to oppose the popular tide of patriotism, dropped the cause of peace. Withdrawing from the WPP in 1917, Carrie Chapman Catt brought a large contingent with her. Two years later, the tiny remnant of the WPP became the U.S. section of the Women's International League for Peace and Freedom. NAWSA, meanwhile,

In 1915, the newly formed Woman's Peace Party sent a committee of
delegates to the International Congress of Women in the Hague. The
meeting had been organized by the International Suffrage Alliance, in
which Carrie Chapman Catt was active, to demonstrate female friendship
and solidarity in time of war. "The whole enterprise has about it a certain
aspect of moral adventure," wrote Jane Addams (front row, second from
left) to Lillian Wald. To Alice Hamilton, the mission felt like "a perpetual
meeting of the women's club or the federation of settlements, or something
like that." Although support for the new women's peace movement
dwindled once the United States entered World War I in 1917, the
movement was revived during the 1920s.
(Swarthmore College Peace Collection)

attempted to profit from war. Indeed, its membership doubled, reaching its peak of
two million by 1919.

As historian William L. O'Neill points out, World War I added "a few strings to
the suffrage bow." The war effort won favor among activist middle-class women,
especially clubwomen, who plunged into volunteer war work—selling bonds, saving
food, and organizing benefits for the troops. On the verge of victory, the NAWSA,
with its membership rolls and popular support now at a peak, had too much to lose
by ignoring the war effort or clinging to the cause of peace. Rather, it endorsed the
war, mainly in rhetoric, because Catt did not want her troops to divide their efforts.
During the war, indeed, the suffrage movement's great opportunity finally arrived.
Half a century before, women's rights leaders had complained that all of women's

contributions to the Union cause had gone unheeded and unappreciated. Now Carrie Chapman Catt asked for passage of the woman suffrage amendment as a "war measure." The fight for democracy began at home, Catt argued, in a brief revival of the "justice" argument. The war also presented an additional "expediency" argument: It was unwise to deprive women of the vote just when their war work was needed. Taking the latter position, President Wilson, a convert to woman suffrage since 1916, urged the Senate in 1917 and 1918 to pass a woman suffrage amendment. He contended that such a measure was "vital to the winning of the war." Despite the National Woman's party rebellion and despite, or because of, the interruption of war, Catt's master plan was paying off.

Influenced by the Wilson administration, by NAWSA (which at last showed strength in numbers), and by wartime public opinion, the House of Representatives finally passed a woman suffrage amendment on January 10, 1918. The recalcitrant Senate approved it in June 1919. (A prohibition amendment was ratified that year as well, suggesting that the major causes supported by women would triumph almost simultaneously.) Fourteen months after the Senate suffrage vote, on August 26, 1920, the thirty-sixth state, Tennessee, ratified the woman suffrage amendment, and the woman's vote was finally legal nationwide.

The final months of state suffrage campaigns evoked more female participation, in marches, parades, speeches, and meetings, than had been mobilized for the past 50 years. Indeed, the push for ratification, historian Sara Hunter Graham contends, was the most difficult test NAWSA faced. Obstacles abounded in state politics, and antisuffragists, "sensing Armageddon, redoubled their efforts." Still, once victory was imminent, the woman suffrage movement finally achieved its long-sought momentum. Victory can be attributed to massive participation in the final round of ratification campaigns, to President Catt's organizational skill, to NAWSA's redoubled efforts, and to the fortuitous interruption of the war. Some 26 million women were enfranchised in time for the presidential election of 1920, transformed, as Catt said, from "wards" of the nation into "free and equal citizens." One of the voters was Charlotte Woodward, aged 91, who had ridden with friends to the first women's rights convention in 1848. Then a teenaged farm girl, she had watched the proceedings from a back row and, at the end of the meeting, signed her name to the Declaration of Sentiments. Charlotte Woodward was the sole survivor of Seneca Falls.

WOMEN AND THE VOTE

When Carrie Chapman Catt wrote her "inner story" of the suffrage movement in the 1920s, she itemized the unparalleled string of efforts that had been needed to attain the vote. Over the past half-century, suffragists had waged 56 referenda campaigns and hundreds of assaults on state legislatures, state party conventions, and state constitutional conventions, as well as on Congress. No other electoral reform, said Catt, had ever been so expensive or aroused such antipathy. In the aftermath of their triumph, suffragists awaited the impact of the woman's vote on political life, social reform, and women's status. High expectations prevailed—on the part of both suffrage veterans, who envisioned the vote as a "first step," and the public.

After 1910, the suffrage parade became a leading NAWSA publicity tactic. White-clad suffragists, marching in formation, were an impressive sight on city streets, as in this New York City parade in 1913. Although a major referendum campaign failed in 1915, two years later New York became the first state east of the Mississippi to grant suffrage to women.
(Sophia Smith Collection, Smith College)

Woman suffrage had an immediate impact. Polling places shifted from saloons and barber shops to schools and churches, to accommodate the newly enfranchised. Twenty states passed laws at once to enable women to serve on juries, and some states rushed through protective laws that women reformers had long demanded. Congress too seemed anxious to please women voters, at least for a few years. Its brief spurt of interest began with the Sheppard Towner Act of 1921, a plan to finance maternal education and child health care programs, and ended in 1924 with passage of a federal child labor amendment, which was never ratified. Throughout the decade, however, a Women's Joint Congressional Committee, representing major women's organizations, lobbied for passage of desired bills. Political parties at last began to cater to what was expected to be the "woman's vote." Both major parties welcomed women into their national committees. Finally, in a few localities (Chicago was one) there were signs that women did prefer the least corrupt and most reform-minded candidates and could influence the outcome of elections. But by mid-decade, it seemed that supporters and opponents of woman suffrage alike had overestimated the impact it would have on political life. The onus fell on the supporters. As Mother Jones once observed, suffragists expected that "kingdom come would follow the enfranchisement of women." During the 1920s, such millennial expectations—and even more modest ones—rapidly faded.

A main false assumption apparently shared by suffragists and antisuffragists alike was that women would vote as a bloc. Or at least their rhetoric implied such an assumption. Over the decades, suffragists had often contended that women's votes would purify politics and end war, imperialism, disease, crime, vice, and injustice. According to antisuffragists, women as a group would be carried away by sweeping reforms and wives would vote against husbands, contributing to domestic discord, excessive individualism, social anarchy, and the collapse of the state. But none of the claims had immediate relevance. As the 1920s showed, women voted in smaller proportions than men. There is one significant exception: Isolated data suggest that where blacks were permitted to vote, black women seized the ballot in the same numbers as black men and in greater proportions than white women. Indeed, in northern cities, black women's clubs and their prominent leaders avidly raised votes for Republican candidates. But black women's high turnout at the polls was atypical. Not only did women in general vote in smaller proportions than men, but they voted the same way as male relatives—of course, some antisuffragists had predicted this too. Unable to affect the outcome of elections, women never rallied behind "women's issues"—any more than they rallied behind women candidates, of whom there were few. "I know of no woman today who has any influence or political power because she is a woman," said Emily Blair, a Missouri suffragist who became vice president of the Democratic National Committee in 1924. "I know of no woman who has a following of other women." As politicians soon realized, there would be no great influx of women candidates or officeholders. Women did not seem to share political goals, they were unable to demand an array of reforms, and they voted as individuals, not as a bloc. Moral superiority, in short, had not carried over to the voting booth; the "woman's vote" did not exist.

Suffragists were not the only reformers ever to fall short of their own expectations. Other electoral reforms of the progressive era, such as the referendum, the recall, and direct primaries, historian William E. Chafe points out, also had little impact. Despite progressive efforts to democratize the electoral process, voter turnout in the 1920s fell; only about half of eligible voters participated in presidential elections, for instance, compared to 80 percent in the late nineteenth century. Women alone could not be blamed for the decline, recent studies suggest, for male voter participation dropped as well. Jane Addams made this point at the time: When asked in 1924 by the *Woman Citizen*, "Is woman suffrage failing?" she replied that the question should be, "Is suffrage failing?" Still, women took the blame. By the mid-1920s, articles proclaimed the "failure" of woman suffrage, and veterans of the suffrage movement analyzed what had gone wrong. Women were disappointed in politics, contended Carrie Chapman Catt in 1923, "because they miss the exaltation, the thrill of expectancy, the vision which stimulated them in the suffrage campaign. . . . They find none of these appeals to their aspiration in the party of their choice." Emily Blair, in 1931, found deeper cause for disappointment. Feminism "expressed the desire of women once more to have a part in the making of the world," said Blair. "But it did not work out that way. . . . Women were welcome to come in as workers but not as co-makers of the world. For all their numbers, they seldom rose to positions of responsibility or power. The few who did fitted into the system as they found it. All standards, all methods, all values, continued to be set by men." Historian Chafe concludes that women "faced a no-win situation when it came to electoral politics." First, they had won the vote just when it declined in importance. Second, the two-party system, the lack of single-issue elections, and the varied class and ethnic interests of women voters precluded an independent women's constituency or bloc that could affect the existing parties.

Lack of immediate political clout was only one part of a double blow for suffrage veterans in the 1920s. They also experienced, as Carrie Chapman Catt suggested, the loss of a cause. For decades, suffrage had served as a focus of feminist energies and a source of continuum between generations. "It was a continuous, seemingly endless chain of activity," Catt wrote in 1926. "Young suffragists who helped forge the last links of the chain were not born when it began. Old feminists who forged the first links were dead when it ended." Some women had even personified the generational links—such as Harriot Stanton Blatch and Alice Stone Blackwell, daughters of suffrage leaders who became leaders themselves. But once suffrage was won, the coalition of women that had gathered to fight for it diminished and divided, often in factional disputes over protective laws and a newly proposed equal rights amendment. Indeed, the formation of the Woman's Party in 1916 augured such disputes. Although organized women remained active throughout the 1920s, the inspiration of the suffrage campaign was difficult to recapture—or so its leaders suggested. "I am sorry for you young women who have to carry on the work in the next ten years," Anna Howard Shaw told Emily Blair, "for suffrage was a symbol and you have lost your symbol. There is nothing for women to rally around." Veteran suffragists especially regretted their inability to connect to the "rising generation," the post-World War I cohort of younger women, who took the vote for granted and lacked interest in women's causes. The new generation seemed to be carried away by a new sense of individualism, although not the sort that either suffragists or their foes had envisioned.

Feminist problems in the 1920s, says historian William L. O'Neill, were largely the feminists' fault. They should not have dropped the broad spectrum of demands of the antebellum era, ignored "social" issues, or shifted their arguments toward altruism and expediency. These moves, he contends, contained the seeds of failure, although this was not clear until after the vote was won and suffragist factions fell out of harmony. Mourning the loss of radical ideology, O'Neill also argues that social feminism drained off personnel from the suffrage movement and even prolonged the crusade for the vote. In response, other historians point out that had feminists not narrowed their goals and broadened their constituency, they would have had even less success than they did. Nor is it clear that socialism, as O'Neill suggests, or any other sort of coalition on the left, would have provided solutions to the "woman problem." In the progressive era, many women on the left, whether social reformers like Florence Kelley, ideologists like Charlotte Perkins Gilman, or radical suffragists like Crystal Eastman, were committed to socialism. The Socialist party appreciated the support of its women devotees and voiced concern about the "woman problem," but it had no plans for, nor means of effecting, any substantive changes in women's lives either. Without any broad consensus among women, such as that finally achieved by the suffrage movement, it is unlikely that even a grand coalition of feminists and socialists would have made much headway, had such a coalition been feasible.

Recent studies, moreover, challenge both the negative view of suffragists' achievements and the conclusion that woman suffrage lacked impact in the post-suffrage decade. Historian Nancy F. Cott attacks O'Neill's interpretation by disputing the "failure" of feminism in all its particulars. Starting with electoral politics, Cott denies that suffragists had referred specifically to a future voting "bloc" of women or expected that women would form such a bloc. Nor, she contends, did the "woman's vote" fail. Rather, women's voting participation "varied greatly from place to place, group to group, issue to issue." Minimizing the role of 1920 as a turning point, Cott posits continuity over change in women's political behavior before and after 1920. Most important, she denies that suffragism was "the matrix of women's politics and also a proxy for feminism." Rather, the suffrage crusade and the eruption of modern feminism were separate phenomena. "What historians have seen as the demise of feminism in the 1920s," Cott contends, "was, more accurately, the end of the suffrage movement and the early struggle of modern feminism." Other recent analyses of the aftermath of suffrage refute the notion that woman suffrage made no difference. Historian Kristi Andersen, who analyzes women's political behavior in the 1920s, argues that woman suffrage affected politics in several ways. First, it introduced the *possibility* that the political outcomes of elections would be affected. Second, even if immediate changes were limited, women "renegotiated" the boundary that had previously excluded them entirely from politics. Finally, she argues, women's political participation and voluntary activism after suffrage changed political life; they "served as a bridge between Progressivism and the New Deal and helped to solidify the movement from the highly partisan politics of the nineteenth century to the increasingly non-partisan, candidate-centered group politics of the mid-twentieth century."

Neither miscalculations about the "woman's vote" nor the nature of women's politics after 1920 ultimately suffices to assess the achievement of the suffrage crusade. One question that remains is: What contribution did the achievement of woman suffrage make toward attaining the overhaul of attitudes demanded in 1848 and toward assaulting "aristocracy of sex" or gender hierarchy? Clearly, as Elizabeth Cady Stanton told her friend Theodore Tilton in the 1860s, lack of suffrage was a "symbol" of woman's degradation rather than a cause of it. Clearly, too, the achievement of woman suffrage redressed an inequity more than it bestowed immediate and tangible political power. The most significant impact of woman suffrage may lie in the ways that it assailed male monopoly on power and fostered female autonomy. To journalist Walter Lippmann in 1915, for instance, the suffrage battle represented more than the gain of the vote. Rather it represented "an indefinitely greater change, a change in the initial prejudice with which men and women react towards each other and the world." In Lippmann's view, before the fact, a suffrage victory would inevitably change attitudes. Historian Ellen Dubois stresses the implications of women's involvement in the suffrage movement. Winning the vote, she says, proved that women could unite to affect public policy and change the course of history, to serve as an active agency of change. By acting "deliberately and collectively," in short, suffragists achieved equality and independence. Most important, Dubois points out, the woman suffrage movement successfully challenged "masculine monopoly of the public sphere." The woman suffrage victory thus crushed two fundamental assumptions: that women depended on men and that men held authority over women. As an attack on gender hierarchy, in short, the suffrage movement has no match.

In the 1920s, women's organizations strove to maintain the collective spirit that had won the vote and to continue to act as an agency of change. But after World War, I, new factors came into play. The new era was a politically conservative one, in which enthusiasm for reform dwindled and commitment to cause went out of style. The shift in political climate was accompanied by a shift in social climate, one that had its most profound effect on middle-class women, the constituency of the woman's movement.

SUGGESTED READINGS AND SOURCES

Since the publication of Eleanor Flexner's *Century of Struggle: The Women's Rights Movement in the United States* (Cambridge, Mass., 1959), the history of feminism has enjoyed a revival. Three early studies of the woman suffrage movement have been influential. For the origins of the movement, see Ellen Carol Dubois, *Feminism and Suffrage: The Emergence of an Independent Women's Movement in America 1848–1869* (Ithaca, N.Y., 1978). Aileen Kraditor analyzes the changing suffrage argument in *The Ideas of the Woman Suffrage Movement 1890–1920* (New York, 1965). In *Feminism in America: A History*, 2d rev. ed. (New Brunswick, N.J., 1989), William L. O'Neill provides "an internal study of the woman movement." His account of women's politics in the progressive era is unsurpassed. For the new wave of feminism in the early twentieth century, see Nancy F. Cott, *The Grounding of Modern Feminism* (New Haven, Conn., 1988).

Document collections, or, in some cases, combinations of narrative and documents, include Aileen Kraditor, ed., *Up from the Pedestal: Selected Writings in the History of American Feminism* (Chicago, 1968); William L. O'Neill, *The Woman Movement: Feminism in the United States and England* (New York and London, 1969); Anne F. Scott and Andrew Scott, *One Half the People: The Fight for Woman Suffrage* (Philadelphia, 1975); Marjorie Spruill Wheeler, ed., *Votes for Women! The Woman Suffrage Movement in Tennessee, the South and the Nation* (Knoxville, Tenn., 1995), which includes scholarly articles and documents; and Wheeler, ed., *One Woman, One Vote: Rediscovering the Woman Suffrage Movement* (Troutdale, Ore., 1995), a collection of essays. For the Stanton-Anthony alliance, see Ellen Carol Dubois, ed., *Elizabeth Cady Stanton/Susan B. Anthony: Correspondence, Writings, Speeches* (New York, 1981); Ann D. Gordon, ed., *Selected Papers of Elizabeth Cady Stanton and Susan B. Anthony*, 2 vols. (New Brunswick, N.J., 1997); and Alice Rossi, ed., *The Feminist Papers* (New York, 1973), part 2. An important source book is Mari Jo Buhle and Paul Buhle, eds., *The Concise History of Woman Suffrage: Selections from the Classic Work of Stanton, Anthony, Gage, and Harper* (Urbana, Ill., 1981).

Scholarship on the suffrage movement has gained momentum since the 1960s. Two early studies are Alan P. Grimes, *The Puritan Ethic and Woman Suffrage* (New York, 1967), which examines the early acceptance of woman suffrage in the western states, and David Morgan, *Suffragists and Democrats: The Politics of Woman Suffrage in America* (East Lansing, Mich., 1972), which traces the campaign for suffrage as part of the political process. For state suffrage movements, see Steven M. Buechler, *The Transformation of the Woman Suffrage Movement: The Case of Illinois, 1850–1920* (New Brunswick, N.J., 1986) and Gayle Gullett, *Becoming Citizens: The Emergence and Development of the California Women's Movement, 1880–1911* (Urbana, Ill., 1999).

Significant studies of the 1990s include Suzanne M. Marilley, *Woman Suffrage and the Origins of Liberal Feminism in the United States, 1820–1920* (Cambridge, Mass., 1996); Sara Hunter Graham, *Woman Suffrage and the New Democracy* (New Haven, Conn., 1996); and Ellen Carol Dubois, *Harriot Stanton Blatch and the Winning of Woman Suffrage* (New Haven, Conn., 1997). For Dubois's essays, see Ellen Carol Dubois, *Woman Suffrage and Women's Rights* (New York, 1998). Woman suffrage in the South is examined in Marjorie Spruill Wheeler, *New Women of the New South: The Leaders of the Woman Suffrage Movement in the Southern States* (New York, 1995); and Elna C. Green, *Southern Strategies: Southern Women and the Woman Suffrage Question* (Chapel Hill, N.C., 1997). Jean V. Matthews, *Women's Struggle for Equality: The First Phase, 1828–1876* (Chicago, 1997) covers the origins of the suffrage crusade. For conflict in the final stage of the suffrage movement, see Christine Lunardini, *From Equal Suffrage to Equal Rights: Alice Paul and the National Woman's Party* (New York, 1986), and Linda G. Ford, *Iron-Jawed Angels: The Suffrage Militancy of the National Woman's Party, 1912–1920* (Lanham, Md., 1991). For African American women and the suffrage movement, see Ann D. Gordon et al., eds., *African American Women and the Vote, 1837–1965* (Amherst, Mass., 1997); Rosalyn Terborg-Penn, *African American Women in the Struggle for the Vote, 1850–1920* (Bloomington, Ind., 1998); Glenda Elizabeth Gilmore *Gender and Jim Crow: Women and the Politics of White Supremacy in North Carolina, 1896–1920* (Chapel Hill, N.C., 1996), ch. 8; and Paula Giddings, *When and Where I Enter: The Impact of Black Women on Race and Sex in America* (New York, 1984), ch. 7. See also Angela Y. Davis, "Racism in the Woman Suffrage Movement," in *Women, Race, and Class* (New York, 1983).

For suffragist campaign tactics, see Michael McGerr, "Political Style and Women's Power," *Journal of American History*, 77 (December 1990), 864–885; Linda J. Lumsden, *Rampant Women: Suffragists and the Right of Assembly* (Knoxville, Tenn., 1997); and Margaret Finnegan, *Selling Suffrage: Consumer Culture and Votes for Women* (New York, 1999). Antisuffragism is examined in Aileen Kraditor, *The Ideas of the Woman Suffrage Movement*, cited previously, ch. 2; Jane Camhi, *Women Against Women: American Anti-Suffragism, 1880–1920* (Brooklyn, N.Y., 1974); and Susan E. Marshall, *Splintered Sisterhood: Gender and Class in the Campaign Against Woman Suffrage* (Madison, Wisc., 1997). Two views on the radicalism of the suffrage movement are Ellen Carol Dubois, "The Radicalism of the Woman Suffrage Movement: Notes Toward the Reconstruction of Nineteenth-Century Feminism," *Feminist Studies*, 3 (Fall 1975), 63–71, and William L. O'Neill, "Feminism as a Radical Ideology," in Alfred F. Young, ed., *Dissent: Explorations in the History of American Radicalism* (DeKalb, Ill., 1968), pp. 273–300. For suffragist voices, see Sherna Gluck, ed., *From Parlor to Prison: Five American Suffragists Talk About Their Lives* (New York, 1976).

Several studies consider facets of suffragism and feminism. Late-nineteenth-century suffragists are prominent in William Leach, *True Love and Perfect Union: The Feminist Reform of Sex and Society* (New York, 1980), which links strands of feminist thought to other intellectual currents. Mari Jo Buhle examines the role of socialist women in the suffrage campaign and a variety of women's causes, such as labor organization and sexual reform, in *Women and American Socialism 1870–1920* (Urbana, Ill., 1981). For women on the left, see also Margaret S. Marsh, *Anarchist Women, 1870–1920* (Philadelphia, 1981); June Sochen, *The New Woman: Feminism in Greenwich Village, 1910–1920* (New York, 1969); and Judith Schwartz, *Radical Feminists of Heterodoxy: Greenwich Village, 1912–1940* (Lebanon, N.H., 1982). Conflict between suffragists and other women reformers emerges in Jeanne Madeline Weiman, *The Fair Women: The Story of the Women's Building, World Columbia Exposition, Chicago, 1893* (Chicago,

1981). Lee Ann Banaszak, *Why Movements Succeeded or Fail: Opportunity, Culture, and the Struggle for Woman Suffrage* (Princeton, N.J., 1996) compares suffrage movements in the U.S. and Switzerland. For the peace movement in the progressive era, see Erika A. Kuhlman, *Petticoats and White Feathers: Gender Conformity, Race, the Progressive Peace Movement, and the Debate Over War, 1895–1919* (Westport, Conn., 1997) and the early chapters of Carrie A. Foster, *The Women and the Warriors: The U.S. Section of the Women's International League for Peace and Freedom, 1915–1946* (Syracuse, N.Y., 1995). For international feminism, see Leila J. Rupp, *Worlds of Women: The Making of an International Woman's Movement* (Princeton, N.J., 1997), and Margaret A. McFadden, *Golden Cables of Sympathy: The Transatlantic Sources of Nineteenth Century Feminism* (Lexington, Ky., 1999), ch. 9.

Recent books on women and political life include Rebecca Edwards, *Angels in the Machinery: Gender in American Party Politics from the Civil War to the Progressive Era* (New York, 1997); Michael Lewis Goldberg, *An Army of Women: Gender and Politics in Gilded Age Kansas* (Baltimore, Md., 1997); and Ross Evans Paulson, *Liberty, Equality, and Justice: Civil Rights, Women's Rights, and the Regulation of Business, 1865–1932* (Durham, N.C., 1997). For the political accomplishments of disfranchised women, see Elisabeth S. Clemens, *The People's Lobby: Organizational Innovation and the Rise of Interest Group Politics in the U.S.* (Chicago, 1997), ch. 6. Linda K. Kerber, *No Constitutional Right to Be Ladies: Women and the Obligations of Citizenship* (New York, 1998) includes discussions of jury service and military service; see chs. 4 and 5. Michele Louise Newman, *White Women's Rights: The Racial Origins of Feminism in the United States* (New York, 1999), explores links among imperialism, racism, and feminism in the late nineteenth and early twentieth centuries. Paula Baker considers the long-term process of the politicization of women in "The Domestication of Politics: Women and American Political Society, 1780–1920," *American Historical Review*, 89 (June 1984), 620–647. Louise A. Tilly and Patricia Gurin, eds., *Women, Politics, and Change* (New York, 1990), presents valuable articles on American women's political behavior from the late nineteenth century to the present. Suzanne Lebsock's essay on "Women and Politics, 1880–1920," pp. 35–61, is relevant to this chapter.

The controversial aftermath of the suffrage campaign is discussed in Kristi Andersen, *After Suffrage: Women in Partisan and Electoral Politics before the New Deal* (Chicago, 1996); and Ann L. Harvey, *Voters Without Leverage: Women in Electoral Politics, 1920–1970* (New York, 1998). See also, for a variety of views, William H. Chafe, *The Paradox of Change: American Women in the 20th Century* (New York, 1991), part 1; William L. O'Neill, *Feminism in America*, cited previously, ch. 8; Nancy F. Cott, *The Grounding of Modern Feminism*, cited previously, ch. 3; and Cott, "Across the Great Divide: Women in Politics Before and After 1920," in Tilly and Gurin, eds., *Women, Politics, and Change*, cited previously, pp. 153–176. Evelyn Brooks Higgenbotham discusses the active political roles of black women in the post-suffrage era in "Clubwomen and Electoral Politics in the 1920s," in Ann D. Gordon et al., *African American Women and the Vote, 1837–1965*, cited previously, pp. 134–155. For an astute analysis of the feminist predicament in the 1920s, see Estelle Freedman, "Separatism as Strategy: Female Institution Building and American Feminism, 1870–1930," *Feminist Studies*, 5 (Fall 1979), 512–529.

The suffrage movement is well documented because suffragists wrote their own histories. The major source is the six-volume *History of Woman Suffrage*, eds. Elizabeth Cady Stanton, Susan B. Anthony, et al. (Rochester, N.Y., 1881–1902, vols. 1–4, and New York, 1922, vols. 5 and 6). A massive compilation of speeches, reminiscences, convention reports, and press clippings, the HWS is a memorial to the historical self-consciousness of nineteenth-century suffragists, especially those in the NWSA who started the collection and dominated it until 1890. For highlights of the HWS, see Mari Jo Buhle and Paul Buhle, eds., *The Concise History of Woman Suffrage*, cited previously. A history of NAWSA is Carrie Chapman Catt and Nellie Rogers Shuler, *Woman Suffrage and Politics: The Inner Story of the Suffrage Movement* (New York, 1926). For the National Woman's Party, see Inez Hayes Irwin, *The Story of the Woman's Party* (New York, 1921), and Doris Stevens, *Jailed for Freedom* (New York, 1920). For the women's peace movement, see Mary Louise Degan, *History of the Woman's Peace Party* (Baltimore, Md., 1939). Another useful source for suffragism is "The Significance of the Woman Suffrage Movement," *Annals of the American Academy of Political and Social Science* (May 1910 supplement). Major suffragist publications are available on microfilm, including *Revolution* (New York, 1868–1871); *Woman's Journal* (Boston, 1870–1917); *Woman Citizen* (New York, 1917–1919); and *Suffragist* (Washington, D.C., 1914–1918). Also available on microfilm are the *National Woman's Party Papers*, ed. Anne Firor Scott and William H. Chafe (1989); the *Collected Records of the Woman's Peace Party, 1914–1920*, ed. by the Swarthmore College Peace Collection Staff (1988); and the *Papers of Elizabeth Cady Stanton and Susan B. Anthony*, ed. Patricia G. Holland and Ann D. Gordon (1990).

Feminist autobiography and biography abound. For Stanton, see Lois W. Banner, *Elizabeth Cady Stanton: A Radical for Women's Rights* (Boston and Toronto, 1980); Elizabeth Griffith, *In Her Own Right: The Life of Elizabeth Cady Stanton* (New York, 1984); Ellen Carol Dubois, ed., *Elizabeth Cady Stanton/Susan B. Anthony: Correspondence, Writings, Speeches*, cited previously; Dubois, "On Labor and Free Love: Two Unpublished Speeches of Elizabeth Cady Stanton," *Signs* 1 (Autumn 1975), 257–268; Stanton, *Eighty Years and More: Reminiscences 1815–1897* (New York, 1898); and Theodore Stanton and Harriet Stanton Blatch, eds., *Elizabeth Cady Stanton as Revealed in Her Letters, Diaries, and Reminiscences* (New York, 1922). For Anthony, see Ida Husted Harper, *The Life and Work of Susan B. Anthony*, 2 vols. (Indianapolis, Ind., 1898 and 1908), and Kathleen Barry, *Susan B. Anthony: A Biography of a Singular Feminist* (New York, 1988). See also the Ken Burns documentary "Not for Ourselves Alone" (1999). For Victoria Woodhull, see Barbara Goldsmith, *Other Powers: The Age of Suffrage, Spiritualism, and the Scandalous Victoria Woodhull* (New York, 1998); Mary Gabriel, *Notorious Victoria: The Life of Victoria Woodhull* (Chapel Hill, N.C., 1998); and Richard Fox, *Trials of Intimacy: Love and Loss in the Beecher-Tilton Scandals* (Chicago, 2000).

Feminist memoirs include Harriet Stanton Blatch and Alma Lutz, *Challenging Years: The Memoirs of Harriet Stanton Blatch* (New York, 1940); Olympia Brown, "Autobiography," *Annual Journal of the Universalist Historical Society*, 4 (1973), 1–73; Rheta Child Dorr, *A Woman of Fifty* (New York, 1924); Abigail Scott Duniway, *Pathbreaking: An Autobiographical History of the Equal Suffrage Movement in the Pacific Coast States* (Portland, Ore., 1914); Belle Kearney, *A Slaveholder's Daughter* (New York, 1900); and Anna Howard Shaw. *The Story of a Pioneer* (New York, 1915). For a controversial assessment of Shaw, see James P. McGovern, "Anna Howard Shaw: New Approaches to Feminism," *Journal of Social History*, 3 (1970), 135–153. Ruth Barnes Moynihan examines western suffragism in *Rebel for Rights, Abigail Scott Duniway* (New Haven, Conn., 1983). For Alva Belmont, see Peter Geidel's Ph.D. thesis, "Alva E. Belmont: A Forgotten Feminist," Columbia University, 1993.

For Crystal Eastman, see Blanche Weisen Cook, ed., *Crystal Eastman on Women and Revolution* (New York, 1978). For Charlotte Perkins Gilman, see *The Living of Charlotte Perkins Gilman: An Autobiography* (New York, 1935); Mary A. Hill, *Charlotte Perkins Gilman: The Making of a Radical Feminist, 1860–1896* (Philadelphia, 1980); Carol Ruth Berkin, "Private Woman,

Public Woman: The Contradictions of Charlotte Perkins Gilman," in Carol Ruth Berkin and Mary Beth Norton, eds., *Women of America: A History* (Boston, 1979), pp. 150–176; Carl Degler, "Charlotte Perkins Gilman on the Theory and Practice of Feminism," *American Quarterly*, 8 (Spring, 1956), 21–39; Dolores Hayden, *The Grand Domestic Revolution* (Cambridge, Mass., 1981), ch. 9; Polly Wynn Allen, *Building Domestic Liberty: Charlotte Perkins Gilman's Architectural Feminism* (Amherst, Mass., 1988); and Ann J. Lane, *To Herland and Beyond: The Life and Work of Charlotte Perkins Gilman* (New York, 1990). For Emma Goldman, see Goldman, *Living My Life*, 2 vols. (New York, 1931); Joseph Drinnon, *Rebel in Paradise* (Chicago, 1961); Alix Kates Shulman, ed., *Red Emma Speaks: Selected Writings and Speeches* (New York, 1972); Alice Wexler, *Emma Goldman in America* (Boston, 1984); and Wexler, *Emma Goldman in Exile: From the Russian Revolution to the Spanish Civil War* (Boston, 1989).

For quizzes and additional resources related to American women's history, visit the book's Website at *www.mhhe.com/americanwomen*.

CHAPTER EIGHT

Cross-Currents: The 1920s

HE NEW WOMAN of the progressive era, who had carved out a space in public life, devoted herself to causes, reform, and collective action. Her most visible counterpart in the 1920s was more involved in private life than in public affairs, more attuned to competition than cooperation, more interested in self-fulfillment than in social service. "This new girl, the modern flapper, with her lack of respect for the ideals of her predecessors," had an infectious influence, writer V. F. Calverton proclaimed at mid-decade. She seemed to adopt a provocative, even exhibitionist pose: "Cigarette in hand, shimmying to the music of the masses, the New Woman and the New Morality have made their theatric debut upon the modern scene."

The modern scene was urban, technological, commercial, and conservative. By 1920, half of Americans lived in towns or cities of 2,500 or more, with a growing concentration in large metropolitan areas. New technology and mass communications—telephone, radio, phonograph, movies, and large-circulation magazines—linked middle-class urbanites with one another. The press, the screen, and the world of advertising fostered common values and standards. They spurred the growth of leisure-time interests and generated an air of prosperity and well-being. After World War I, discontent, protest, and even reform became less acceptable. The progressive spirit, with which women's groups had long been allied, wavered and declined. Old political divisions gave way to new generational ones, the sense that old and young, as the *Atlantic* put it in 1922, "were as far apart in point of view, codes, and standards, as if they belonged to different races." The flapper, with her aura of self-indulgence and independence, came to personify the "point of view" of her generation. She signified a demand for equality, because she claimed privileges and liberties once reserved for men. Finally, she represented individualism, the keynote to modernity. Like the heroine of a *McCalls* story in 1925, her philosophy was "To live life in one's own way."

Despite her extensive publicity, the irrepressible flapper was hardly the only New Woman of the 1920s. On the contrary, she was more of a symbol of liberated aspirations, promoted in the movies and the press and vividly imprinted on the popular memory. The decade in fact featured a variety of New Women: the campus coed, now imbued more with hopes of marriage than with a sense of mission; the modern housewife, who adopted the role of companion and consumer; the new professional and businesswoman, who sought to integrate marriage and career; and the post-suffrage feminist, sometimes embroiled in battles over legal and constitutional change and sometimes preoccupied with the new ideal of economic independence. Indisputably, the decade was a crucible of contemporary middle-class roles. It was also a crossroads at which different themes of women's history overlapped and inter-twined. In the 1920s, women embarked on two paths toward equality, though they tended to lead in different directions.

One path was personal. Diffuse, unorganized, and often nonideological, the movement toward individual liberation was overwhelmingly the province of the young—including young women in their twenties and thirties who had participated in or witnessed the last stages of the suffrage campaign. Another path was political. This was the province of organized women, spurred by the achievement of suffrage and full of ambition. The feminist movement of the 1920s entered an intense phase of activism. But it also fought against the tide. Handicapped by the national retreat from reform and caught in a conservative undertow, it was splintered by internal conflict.

FEMINISTS IN CONFLICT

Tensions within the feminist camp arose before the vote was won. At one time, all ac-tivists had been united under the suffrage umbrella; by World War I, the coalition had begun to collapse. Cleavage between more militant feminists and progressive re-formers started in 1915 when Alice Paul's Congressional Union split apart from NAWSA. After 1920, the gulf grew while the ranks of activists shrank. NAWSA, res-urrected after suffrage as the League of Women Voters (LWV), was a fraction of its former size. It had about 100,000 members. Working in tandem with the Women's Joint Congressional Committee, a watchdog agency made up of women's group representatives, and with the new federal Women's Bureau, formed during World War I, the league strove for new goals. It would educate the electorate, democratize political parties (by female infiltration), and support laws to protect women and children. The LWV, in short, represented the reform-minded mainstream of the suf-frage movement.

The new National Woman's Party (NWP), started in 1921, was a more militant but far smaller organization, with only about 8,000 members. Defining itself as a third party, the NWP intended to support women candidates and women's causes, and to work "to remove all the remaining forms of the subjection of women." But one goal became preeminent. In 1923, the NWP proposed an Equal Rights Amend-ment to the Constitution, stating that "Men and women shall have equal rights throughout the United States and every place subject to its jurisdiction." Minimizing the achievement of suffrage, the NWP contended that women were still subordinate to men in all aspects of life; indeed more than 1,000 state laws discriminated against women. The ERA would erase sex as a legal classification and make women equal in every arena, from property rights to divorce rights to employment opportunities. It would also, however, invalidate the barrage of protective laws for which women reformers had long campaigned. Once the NWP goal of equality was posited against the goal of protection, the stage was set for a divisive intramural feud.

The NWP based its arguments on justice. Defending the need for an ERA, it developed two lines of attack on protective laws. These laws, claimed the NWP, were paternalistic, discriminatory, and damaging to women. The landmark *Muller* v. *Oregon* decision, which sanctioned such laws to protect the woman worker's "physical structure and proper discharge of her maternal function," assumed that women had inferior capacities, the NWP charged. Under protective laws, Crystal Eastman argued in 1924, women were classified with children and minors. Moreover, by ensuring different status for women, the laws actually protected men against female competition. Minimum wage laws, for instance, could exclude women from the job market; limits on overtime made them less desirable employees. The eighthour law, Gail Laughlin contended, meant "shutting the doors of opportunity to women." The laws did not protect women, claimed Harriot Stanton Blatch, but "crowded them into lower grades of work." But another facet of the NWP argument sought to distinguish between the laws' protective and exclusionary impact. Denying that they were antilabor or opposed to worker protection, NWP activists contended that protective laws should not be repealed but extended to apply to both sexes. Men deserved protection too, as *Equal Rights*, the NWP journal, argued in 1923. Far from invalidating protective laws, Eastman claimed, the ERA would spur their extension to men. (This was an unlikely outcome in the conservative 1920s, but *Equal Rights* staunchly insisted that "a righteous principle" would bring "good results.") In either event, whether protective laws were dismantled or extended, the ERA would "secure for woman complete equality under the law and in all human relationships."

Most activist women, however, defended protection on the basis of expediency. To the LWV and other women's organizations, an ERA would be a calamity. To Mary Anderson, director of the Women's Bureau, the amendment was diabolical. In fact, said Anderson, militants voiced "a kind of hysterical feminism with a slogan for a program," and as Florence Kelley added, the ERA was a "slogan of the insane." Decrying the prospect of such an amendment, women reformers argued that equality was chimerical, that women were different, that protection was necessary, and that the NWP was an elitist saboteur of working women's interests.

The concept of legal equality, Mary Anderson contended, was a myth. The ERA dealt with "abstract rights, not real rights." Motherhood had indeed given woman a permanent disadvantage, Alice Hamilton argued in the *Woman Citizen* (the LWV journal), and this made protective laws a permanent necessity. "Women cannot be made men" by constitutional amendment, Florence Kelley declared, and would always need laws "different than those needed by men." More women benefited from protective laws than were injured by them, claimed ERA opponents. Moreover, the Women's Bureau confirmed, women were suited to special sorts of work and were therefore restricted in employment opportunity anyway, with or without laws. The ERA would only be used by employers to exploit women workers, as they had before protective legislation was enacted. Finally, reformers charged, the NWP had taken an elitist stance. It represented only the interests of its membership, professional and businesswomen, and had no sympathy for the average woman wage earner.

The type of equality the ERA would impose was appropriate only for competitive professionals seeking career advancement, not for industrial workers. The NWP, in short, represented class interests, not women's interests. By insisting on an ERA, historian Mary Beard wrote to a friend in the NWP, the militants ran the risk of "forsaking humanism in the quest for feminism." And by clinging to the chimera of equality, reformers charged, the NWP rejected the spirit of cooperation that had long characterized the women's movement.

Conflict over equality and protection dominated women's politics throughout the decade. As battle lines hardened, the NWP withdrew its support from *all* women candidates, endorsing only those who supported the ERA. NWP members also campaigned for equal rights measures in state legislatures, though to no avail. By 1930, the only equal rights clause was in Wisconsin's state constitution, and this was a compromise clause, worded to protect protective laws. Meanwhile, conflict among women activists reached international dimensions. In the early 1920s, the NWP and LWV competed fiercely for preeminence within the International Alliance of Women, made up of European and American feminists. ("Feminists intuitively understand that they are citizens of the world," as *Equal Rights* declared.) In 1926, NWP rejection by the alliance created a major schism, causing the withdrawal of European "equal rights" advocates and seriously weakening the international woman's movement. The two American factions, however, continued to vie for influence on the international front. While the LWV maintained its status within the alliance, the NWP campaigned for an international equal rights treaty. By the end of the decade, conflict between feminist factions had alienated many women's leaders from one another. Although the battle over the ERA continued into the 1930s, it reached a peak in the mid-1920s, when feminist fortunes began to falter. The year 1925 was a turning point.

Equality may have been a chimera, but so by now was the "woman's vote." Women had never formed a voting bloc to support either women candidates or "women's issues." By mid-decade, political parties, which had at the outset wooed women voters, began to drop women from party committees. Congress, which never considered an ERA, became unresponsive to the demands of *all* women's groups. Retaining the allegiance of women constituents no longer seemed to involve an obligation to support women's causes. Moreover, progressive reforms fell out of favor. This meant in effect that protective legislation now had as dim a future as the ERA. A major obstacle was the Supreme Court. In 1923, in *Adkins* v. *Children's Hospital*, the Court declared a federal minimum wage law for women unconstitutional, and thereby undermined a major goal of women reformers. Such a law, said the Court, deprived a woman of the liberty to bargain directly with her employer, a position endorsed by the NWP. (In Florence Kelley's view, the Court had affirmed only "the inalienable right of women to starve.") Another blow to reformers was failure to attain a federal child labor law. Congress passed child labor laws in 1918 and 1922, but in both instances the Supreme Court declared the laws unconstitutional. A final tactic was to strive for a child labor amendment, which Congress approved in 1924. But this too failed; by 1930, only six states had ratified it. In addition to such rebuffs, reform-minded feminists met defeat even in victory, as the strange fate of the Sheppard-Towner Act was to prove.

Right after suffrage was won, Congress made a few gallant bows to what it expected to be the "woman's vote." The most important gesture was the Sheppard-Towner Act of 1921, a measure to reduce infant and maternal mortality. The first federally funded health care act, it provided states with matching federal funds to establish prenatal and child health centers, where expectant mothers could receive advice and where preventive health checkups would be provided for women and children. The centers would also send public health nurses out into homes. The act focused on rural areas, as urbanites were more likely to have the services of city welfare agencies or settlements.

From the woman reformer's viewpoint, Sheppard-Towner was a major triumph. An expensive measure, it had been enacted by an overwhelming majority of congressmen, all anxious to curry favor with women constituents. Even southern legislators, never known for feminist sympathies, voted heavily in its favor. Moreover, the passage of Sheppard-Towner suggested that woman suffrage had opened a new era of humane, benevolent legislation. Not only would the law protect maternal and child health, but it would enlarge women's roles in the public sector. The centers, staffed by physicians (mainly women) and public health nurses, would be overseen not merely by the states but by the federal Women's Bureau. After passage of the law, indeed, Sheppard-Towner centers provided classes, literature, and health services, and reached thousands of pregnant women and millions of infants and children.

But Sheppard-Towner aroused opposition. The NWP disliked it, since it classified all women as "mothers." Birth control-advocate Margaret Sanger disliked it, too. She contended that Sheppard-Towner's "benevolence" was superficial, nearsighted, and "dysgenic." Women wanted to have fewer children, Sanger claimed, but the Sheppard-Towner centers "would teach them to have more." (Birth control was not one of the preventive health measures the centers espoused.) Most important, from the outset, the American Medical Association (AMA) opposed the law and campaigned against it. Physicians objected to the interference of outsiders, such as federal officials and women reformers, in the health care business. Moreover, preventive health care, such as checkups of pregnant women and well children, was a potentially lucrative field. In the 1920s, preventive care was absorbed into private practice; the doctor's domain expanded to include the office visit for well patients. In 1929, capitulating to the AMA, Congress terminated the Sheppard-Towner program. The short-lived act did have an impact, although not the impact its supporters had envisioned: It forced physicians to take a stand on preventive health and enlarged the scope of medical practice.

Although the fate of Sheppard-Towner was unknown at mid-decade, women's reform organizations faced other setbacks. Like all progressive groups, they suffered from diminished size and influence, a part of the postwar retreat from reform. There were some new ventures. In the South, a new women's movement for interracial cooperation developed, followed in 1930 by the Association of Southern Women for the Prevention of Lynching. Founded by Texas suffragist Jessie Daniel Ames, the anti-lynching group, which drew on women's church networks, responded to a major concern of black women—one that had been voiced since the days of Ida B. Wells. But some important older women's institutions had passed their prime. The National Consumers' League, still ambitious, grew smaller. The Women's Trade Union League, which had working-class leadership by 1919, still depended on upper-class funds, which waned. Efforts to organize women workers faded, although replaced by educational projects. The settlement movement also suffered. Many settlements had financial problems and could not recruit new residents; "social work" was now a career more than a cause. Other women's organizations gained members but lost their reform thrust. The huge General Federation of Women's Clubs, for instance, promoted home economics and the use of electric appliances. Finally, the LWV joined the retreat from reform by concentrating on child welfare measures rather than on women's issues. "We are not feminists primarily," a league officer would declare in 1933. "We are citizens." The shifts in women's reform bastions reflected the "New Era's" conservative swing. They also reflected feminist inability to appeal to the next generation.

"My generation didn't think much about the place or the problem of women," playwright Lillian Hellman recounted in her autobiography. "[We] were not conscious that the designs we saw around us had so recently been formed that we were still part of the formation." By mid-decade, the alienation of the young was clear. Young middle-class women appeared to have little interest in organized feminism, either in its militant egalitarian wing or in its social reform one. Moreover, they tended to associate feminism with "sex antagonism" or hostility to men. In 1927, psychologist Lorine Pruette suggested that women under 50 could be divided into three groups: those who had "struggled for independence of action . . . and never quite [lost] their bitterness towards men"; younger women who were less familiar with either bitterness or struggle; and still younger ones who were "likely to be bored" when feminism was mentioned. Women of the new generation took feminist gains for granted, an LWV member wrote in 1928. The rights won by the "old feministic movement" were accepted by the young as a matter of course. "'Feminism' has become a term of opprobrium to the modern young woman," writer Dorothy Dunbar Bromley confirmed in *Harper's* in 1927. Young women had contempt for those "who antagonize men with their constant clamor about maiden names, equal rights, woman's place in the world, and many another cause." And the youngest women, those growing up in the 1920s, said psychologist Phyllis Blanchard, equated feminism with being lonely and unmarried. Each year the generation gap among women seemed to take a harsher toll.

This toll was compounded by a drop in commitment even among women who had recently been active in the last stages of the suffrage campaign. The NAWSA's two million members were not expected to continue the fight for women's causes once the vote was won; suffrage had generated singular momentum. But now even highly committed, militant young women withdrew—from feuds, politics, and collective action. Their withdrawal was reflected in the *Nation's* "Modern Women" series in 1926–1927—a group of anonymous essays by independent, self-supporting, career-minded feminists. Most of the authors had, as one put it, "lost faith in the righteous cause of women." "I no longer work in movements," wrote a second, a former militant suffragist and demonstrator. "My energies are bent on achieving an income." Since the vote had been won, wrote a third, who had once been arrested in suffrage marches, her interests had become "broader and more human . . . especially in my belated recognition of the vital importance of economic independence for women."

Founded in 1920, the League of Women Voters (LWV) represented the mainstream of postsuffrage feminism. Determined to promote child welfare, protect women workers, and educate the female electorate, it also attempted to shape the planks of party platforms. But to younger women of the 1920s, the LWV conveyed a staid, old-fashioned image. The long tradition of female association was losing its appeal. *(Library of Congress)*

Economic independence was in fact the new frontier of feminism in the 1920s. A change of direction from the service-oriented, progressive goals of the presuffrage era, it was also a shift of emphasis from public cause to private career, from society to self.

ASPIRATION AND CAREER

In *Concerning Women*, a feminist primer of 1926, Suzanne LaFollette argued that sexual equality could be based only on economic independence. Women's main achievement had been their entry into the labor force—into factories, shops, schools, and professions, "invading every field that had been held the special province of men," LaFollette wrote. "This is the great unconscious and unorganized women's movement." After World War I, the aspiration for economic independence grew.

The proportion of women in the labor force remained unchanged, about 25 percent. But the numbers of working women increased, more middle-class women became wage earners, and the types of work women did changed. Characteristically, change led in two directions at once.

On the one hand, fewer women worked at the rock bottom of the vocational ladder, as domestics, and more entered white-collar jobs, such as clerical and sales work. New vocations opened up in the business and professional worlds. Educated women, whose numbers continually rose, surged into professional work. Many of these women strove to combine careers and marriage, another major innovation. In the 1920s the proportion of women wage earners who were married rose 25 percent, with the greatest increase among women in their twenties and thirties. On the other hand, the decade's aspirations collided with its limitations. Traditional male professions closed ranks against female entry. Most women were confined to "women's professions," and in the business world, to lower-level job categories. Disparities in pay between men and women rose as more women entered the labor market. Finally, the gains of the decade were all middle-class gains. In industry, where women faced protective laws and weakened unions, the situation was especially bleak.

World War I created no enduring jobs for women. Some 16,000 women served overseas under the auspices of the American Expeditionary Force, mainly though not exclusively as nurses, clerical workers, canteen workers, and telephone operators. At home, more than 12,000 women enlisted in the Navy and Marine Corps, a major innovation; tens of thousands civilian women worked in army offices and hospitals; and many others found posts in industry. They worked in iron, steel, and munitions plants, as well as in other traditionally male jobs, such as those of streetcar conductors and railroad workers. Overall, women's wartime labor challenged conventional gender roles; but new opportunities soon vanished. At the war's end, most emergency appointees were forced to retire, and new options in industry ended. In the 1920s, the woman worker's plight was dismal. Despite the decade's aura of prosperity, some industries—such as textiles, in which many women worked—suffered setbacks, and unemployment rose. Women's unionization fell to a new low of 3 percent. Although the labor movement as a whole lost ground, only one working woman in 34 was a union member, as opposed to one man in nine. Because the WTUL shifted its efforts from organization to education, and because the AFL, much weakened, had always been indifferent if not hostile to women workers, hopes for organization were slim. Efforts to form industrial unions faded when the left was demolished, and skilled workers of the AFL were concentrated in industries from which women were excluded. For most working-class women, work experience in a sex-segregated labor force remained less a source of economic "independence" than a confirmation of second-class status.

Not surprisingly, the exclusionary facet of protective laws abetted the income gap between men and women. Such laws did protect women in fields where they were already in a majority, such as in the garment industry, by regulating hours and improving working conditions. But they had an adverse impact in fields where fewer women worked, since limits on women's hours and functions made men more desirable employees. Moreover, they often excluded women completely, not only from heavy industry but also from the new leisure industries, such as bowling alleys, that required night work. Women reformers, meanwhile, concentrated their efforts on women who were already active unionists. One ambitious project was the summer school for women workers, started at Bryn Mawr in 1921 by M. Carey Thomas and WTUL member Hilda Smith, a social welfare professor. Intended to train working women for union leadership roles, the summer school inspired its participants and spurred similar programs at other colleges. But it had little impact on the average woman industrial worker who was unlikely to be a union member.

Compared to the woman factory worker, the white-collar worker had many more opportunities. The expanding business world of the 1920s needed clerks, stenographers, typists, switchboard operators, and saleswomen. By 1930, two million women office workers—secretaries, typists, and file clerks—constituted one-fifth of the female labor force. Women's roles in the lower realms of the business world won acclaim; the working girl had found her place at desk, counter, and switchboard. Even the *Ladies' Home Journal,* which had once condemned the exodus of young women from home to office, discovered by 1916 that the secretary "radiated the office with sunshine and sympathetic interest." Female office help became part of the businessman's perquisites. "The businessman begins to feel himself a success when he has a secretary," Lorine Pruette wrote in 1931. "A girl feeds his vanity. . . . The stenographer is wife and mother, child and mistress."

New vocational options included the cosmetics counter and beauty parlor—a bonanza for hairdressers, manicurists, cosmeticians, and the vocational schools that trained them. By 1930, more than 40,000 beauty parlors were open for business in towns and cities across the nation. The expanding market for beauty products fueled the success of such entrepreneurs as rival cosmetic tycoons Elizabeth Arden and Helena Rubinstein, both immigrants, and of Madame C. J. Walker (Sarah Breedlove), a daughter of former slaves, whose 500-agent company sold millions of dollars worth of hair and skin products to a black clientele. After her death in 1919, Madame Walker's thriving enterprise, based in Indianapolis, amassed profits until the depression. Women also entered real estate, retailing, and banking, although they rarely rose beyond the rank of buyer, cashier, or supervisor of other women. Still, a spirit of adventure pervaded the business world, as in advertising. At J. Walter Thompson, the innovative Women's Editorial department, run and staffed by women copywriters, brought in half the agency's earnings. Throughout the decade, moreover, novel vocations for women won applause. The press celebrated such advents as the nation's first woman kettle-drummer (1922) or deep-sea diver (1924), suggesting new heights of female emancipation. The most exciting frontier of the era, aviation, also attracted women, who joined in stunt flying and barnstorming. Young Amelia Earhart, briefly a teacher and settlement worker, gained acclaim, as Charles Lindbergh did, first as a barnstormer and then, in 1927, by flying across the Atlantic as part of a crew of three. But neither "firsts" nor press coverage created vocations. Every business had special service jobs intended for women, that is, for short-term employees receiving lower pay and doing lower levels of work.

The vanguard of vocational progress was the professions. In the 1920s, the number of women professionals increased by 50 percent and the percentage of women workers in professions rose from 11.9 percent to 14.2 percent. As historian Frank Stricker points out, the proportion of adult women who pursued careers in

Summer schools for women industrial workers were one of the WTUL's most
idealistic enterprises. Under the pioneer Bryn Mawr program, financed by union
funds, 60 or more women wage earners were brought to the campus for six to eight
weeks of academic courses—economics, history, politics, or even creative writing.
Although some participants resented the contrast between campus privilege and
working-class lives, and others demanded courses that were critical of capitalism, the
response was usually enthusiastic. "I believe that worker education will lead to a new
social order," one student declared. The Bryn Mawr summer school ran from 1921
until 1938, when financial support dwindled. The wage earners
above were part of a class in American civilization in 1929.
(Schlesinger Library, Radcliffe College)

professions and business rose during the 1920s and would continue to rise after the
Great Depression. Three out of four professional women entered "women's fields"—
the space in the public sector that progressive women had carved out. And this space
expanded too, especially in education and social welfare. By the 1920s, the upper-
class settlement resident had been replaced by a trained, licensed, salaried social
worker, usually a woman, although men held managerial posts, as they did in library
work and education. Mass communications, another rapidly growing field, also provided new jobs. In the 1920s, the number of women editors, reporters, and journalists doubled. But in most competitive fields, women had to fight a rising tide of professionalism.

Professional men hoped both to increase their own status and to preserve traditional divisions of sphere; even in the progressive era, few doors opened more than a
crack except in medicine and academic life. Medicine, which had started out with
lower status than law or the ministry, rose rapidly. Since 1910, the medical profession
had extended its influence, limited its practitioners ("fewer and better doctors" became AMA policy), and shut women out. Foundations poured money into prestigious medical schools, while lesser schools closed. As prestigious schools kept strict

quotas on women entrants and 90 percent of hospitals refused to appoint women interns, the proportion of doctors who were women began to decline—from 6 percent in 1910 to 5 percent in 1920 and 4.4 percent in 1930. And as the profession itself grew smaller, the number of women physicians dropped by a third. Medical rebuff was not caused by feminist decline; it had started when the suffrage movement was at its peak. Still, as Alice Hamilton pointed out in the 1920s, it was easier for women physicians when they could "count on the loyalty" of devoted feminists who would choose a doctor because she was a woman.

While medicine shrank, higher education expanded. In academic life, slower to curtail female presence, women capitalized briefly on progressive gains. Since 1910, the proportion of doctorates earned by women rose—from 10 percent that year to 15.1 percent in 1920 to 15.4 percent in 1930. The proportion of women in college teaching faculties rose too—from 18.9 percent in 1910 to 30.1 percent in 1920 to 32.5 percent in 1930. Clearly, women's advances had been most substantial in the decade 1910 to 1920, when the feminist movement gained momentum. "I find myself wondering whether our generation was not the only generation of women which ever found itself," wrote Marjorie Nicolson, a college graduate in 1914 and much later Columbia's first tenured woman professor. "We came late enough to escape the self-consciousness and belligerence of the pioneers, to take education and training for granted. We came early enough to take equally for granted professional positions in which we could make full use of our training." Here too the tide began to turn around 1920, when the proportion of women graduate students started to decline, in part a response to universities' tightened quotas. But in the 1920s, when women earned one-third of all graduate degrees, their numbers constantly rose. Significantly, many academic women of the decade made their mark in the behavioral sciences, fields to which progressive era women had been attracted.

Some of these anthropologists, psychologists, and social scientists were linked to pioneers of earlier generations, just as they became involved in the careers of woman scholars of the next one. Social scientist Katherine Bement Davis, whose survey of sexual attitudes was published in the 1920s, had once studied with Marion Talbot at the University of Chicago. In the prewar era she supervised the work of such Chicago graduate students as psychologist Jessie Taft, who became a leading figure in child welfare and social work education. Ruth Benedict began work in anthropology at the New School in 1919 with ethnologist Elsie Clews Parsons. In the 1920s, as a lecturer at Columbia, Benedict helped inspire a new generation of graduate students, including Margaret Mead. Historian Rosalind Rosenberg has shown that these women scholars were part of a special tradition in social science that began in the 1890s. Encouraged and supported by a coterie of prominent academic men, from John Dewey to Franz Boas, they questioned traditional assumptions about sex differences, stressed the impact of cultural conditioning, and "formulated theories about intelligence, personality development and sex roles that . . . affected the whole course of American social science."

As social scientists, women scholars often saw themselves as participants in two cultures—a male culture of academic research and scientific rigor, and women's culture; as women, indeed, they were often relegated to the very periphery of academic life. But their vocations held great allure. New behavioral scientists described their choice of field as a way to resolve quandaries about their roles or to understand women's place in society. For psychologist Phyllis Blanchard, a student of G. Stanley Hall, "the necessity of solving my own problems developed into a desire to understand all problems, and I turned to the social sciences." For Ruth Benedict, the discipline itself provided a mode of accommodation to her culture. Dissatisfied with conventional role limitations but unable to discard expected patterns of behavior, Benedict found in anthropology a reconciliation between scientific and humanistic inclinations, a resolution of what she viewed as a male/female dichotomy. Psychologist Lorine Pruette, another Hall student, found a different kind of accommodation through her career. "In general," she wrote, "all my old feministic revolt has been transferred from men to the condition of human existence."

Young anthropologist Zora Neale Hurston, a leading figure in the 1920s Harlem Renaissance, was more involved in black culture than in women's culture. In 1927, as a Boas graduate student at Columbia, she embarked on a field trip to southern Florida to collect black folklore, a project intended to invalidate racial stereotypes. In her novels, Hurston dealt with the intersection of race and gender, as did other authors of the Harlem Renaissance, such as Jessie Fauset and Nella Larsen. Another Boas student, Ella Deloria, a Dakota Sioux, used her skill at ethnography to collect Sioux narratives, which she began to publish in the 1930s. In a novel written in the 1940s, Deloria sought to convey a woman's perspective of Sioux life in the nineteenth century. Yet another Boas student at Columbia, Margaret Mead, was, like her cohort, informed by a feminist consciousness. In 1925 she persuaded Boas to support her plans for field work outside North America, despite the objections of prominent men in the field who thought her sex a handicap. "Margaret's mother passed on to her the ideal of women's rights, and in the difficult process of persuading her father to let her go to college she learned who the 'enemy' was," Mead's first husband, anthropologist Luther Cressman, recalled a half-century later. "She had the firm conviction that she could establish and hold her place in the profession with men." A similar conviction inspired other ambitious young women of Mead's generation. But, as women seeking careers in competitive fields, they had to confront a new array of problems.

The loss of a cohesive woman's movement deprived professionals of a united body of support. Professional situations were competitive, not cooperative; aspiring career women were more likely to join professional societies than women's societies, to strive for advancement rather than pave the way for others. "As soon as a woman has it for herself," Anna Howard Shaw told Emily Blair, "she will have entered a man's world and cease to fight as a woman for other women." Professional success was also apt to require accommodation more than militancy. "Any weakness is likely to be considered feminine," warned Elizabeth Kemper Adams in a 1921 study of professional women. The woman professional, Adams explained, worked not for profit but out of "intellectual and moral devotion." Still, she could expect to be judged more rigorously than a man and to "breathe an atmosphere of being on trial." In addition, the professional woman of the 1920s often tried to combine career and marriage, a novel, modern goal.

The married career woman represented a shift from the progressive era, when marriage and career had been viewed as mutually exclusive. Since 1910, the proportion of professional women who married had steadily increased—from 12.2 percent in 1910 to 19.3 percent in 1920 to 24.7 percent in 1930. In the 1920s, even the proportion of teachers who married doubled, despite the refusal of most school boards to hire married women. The new trend reflected not only the rapid increase of college-educated women and the rising rate of marriage among them but a shift in goals. The modern young woman as Dorothy Dunbar Bromley explained in her *Harper's* article, "Feminist—New Style," in 1927, believed that "a full life calls for marriage and children as well as a career." Freda Kirchwey, who edited the *Nation's* series on "modern women" claimed that the New Woman of the 1920s was "not altogether satisfied with love, marriage, and a purely domestic career." A Barnard graduate, former suffragist, and active supporter of birth control, Kirchwey enumerated the New Woman's goals. "She wants money of her own. She wants work of her own. She wants some means of self-expression, perhaps, some way of satisfying her personal ambition. But she wants a home, husband, and children, too."

The problem of fusing marriage and career emerged as a theme in the *Nation* essays, whose authors, all working professionals, were mainly married—although few had children. "Marriage is too much of a compromise," wrote Sue Shelton White, NWP leader, lawyer, and Democratic politician. "It lops off a woman's life as an individual." But renouncing marriage was also a "lopping off," White wrote. "We choose between the Frying Pan and the Fire." Psychologist Phyllis Blanchard described a long struggle "between my own two greatest needs—the need for love and the need for independence." At first unable to reconcile the two or to abandon her "desire for personal autonomy," she eventually found, in marriage at 30, both "love and freedom, which once seemed to me such incompatible bedfellows." But the *Nation* essayists' desire for autonomy and their low rate of childbearing did not impress the experts whose critiques were appended to the series of articles. Only Beatrice Hinkle, psychoanalyst and feminist, commended their struggles with "convention and inertia" and felt they signified "the birth of a new woman."

Reconciling marriage and career called for further measures. Another goal was to reshape the home to suit women's needs, along the lines suggested by Charlotte Perkins Gilman. A pioneer attempt had been made in 1915 by Greenwich Village feminist Henrietta Rodman. Rodman planned an apartment house with communal nursery, cooking, laundry, and housework, to free married women for productive work. A decade later, Smith College opened an Institute for Coordination of Women's Interests, directed by Ellen Puffer Howe, another *Nation* essayist. Its purpose was to resolve the "intolerable choice between career and home," to integrate family life with women's "continuous intellectual interest," and to provide models for combining marriage and career—through cooperative nursery, kitchen, laundry, and shopping arrangements. Neither project succeeded; Rodman's building was never built, and the Smith institute lasted only six years. But both were attempts to adjust the home to accommodate women, rather than the reverse.

Some feminists of the 1920s went even further by advocating a readjustment of the workplace, economy, and society. The Smith attempt to "modernize" the home was only a "temporary expedient," wrote Alice Beal Parsons in *Women's Dilemma* (1926). Parsons proposed part-time jobs, payments to mothers for child care, crèches (infant care centers), and day-care centers run by professionals. Suzanne LaFollette, similarly critical of the Smith institute, contended that sexual equality required "profound psychic and material readjustment" so that women could be equal participants in the economy. LaFollette insisted that woman was primarily an individual, not a wife or a mother. She denied "the assumption that marriage is the special concern of woman" or "that marriage and motherhood constitute her normal life and her other interests are extra-normal." Individualism, as LaFollette defined it, had a vocal, optimistic coterie of support, though primarily middle-class support. African American and ethnic working women often had other priorities.

MIGRANTS AND IMMIGRANTS

In the first three decades of the twentieth century, about two million African Americans left the South and the number of blacks in the North rose three times over. Some 454,000 blacks moved north or west between 1910 and 1920, and 749,000 in the 1920s. Unlike earlier waves of black migrants, newcomers in the World War I era came from the deep South and a greater proportion moved to the Midwest. By 1920, the nation's largest black communities were in New York, Philadelphia, and Chicago. A combination of perils spurred the exodus: sharecropping, crop failures, disfranchisement, and Jim Crow laws urged migrants out of the South. Employment opportunities, especially in wartime, brought them north. So did the desire for personal liberty. "The lure of high wages and a freer life proved irresistible to a people limited to agriculture and domestic service," observes historian Jacqueline Jones. Still, migration meant facing difficult circumstances—a discriminatory job market, run-down housing, and increasingly segregated neighborhoods.

Black women migrants of the early twentieth century, who tended to be younger and better educated than those left behind, eagerly sought factory jobs. "I'll never work in nobody's kitchen but my own," a box factory worker in Chicago declared in 1920. By 1920, a small proportion of black women wage-earners in urban areas had moved away from domestic work to industrial work or other service jobs, such as operating elevators. But in industry, as Jones shows, black women were a reserve labor force. If employed in manufacturing, typically when the supply of new immigrants diminished or became unavailable, they usually worked in menial or undesirable jobs—as hog killers in meatpacking plants, or in commercial laundries, or as strikebreakers. The new opportunities of the 1920s, in clerical and sales work, remained closed to black women, who, if hired at all, worked in store basements or back rooms. Domestic labor was frequently the only option, even for the educated. In the 1920s, almost three out of four employed black women were domestic servants or laundresses. After World War I, black women constituted one-fifth of domestics in New York City and Chicago, one-half in Philadelphia, and 90 percent in Pittsburgh. Black workers of the 1920s changed the nature of domestic work by refusing to "live in" and by taking only "day work," which insured more autonomy. City life in the 1920s, finally, offered a small group of black women work in commercial entertainment—as dancers, performers, hostesses, and waitresses in cabarets. Harlem's famous "Cotton Club," patronized by downtown whites, featured a chorus line of light-skinned young women, billed as "tall, tan, and terrific." Another Harlem club, "The Brown Skin Models Review" catered to an African American audience.

The great migration of the World War I era brought thousands of African Americans from the rural South to northern and western cities. Above, a black family arrives in Chicago in 1916. *(Schomburg Library)*

Imbalanced sex ratios in northern cities limited marriage options: except during war, women were a majority of black migrants. In New York City in the mid-1920s, there were about 85 men to every 100 women; nearly three out of ten black women lived alone or as lodgers. Some cities, like Chicago, attracted single women, Jacqueline Jones notes. Others, such as Pittsburgh or Detroit, which offered men industrial jobs, drew larger proportions of families. Among black urban families, a high proportion of wives worked for wages. In Detroit, one out of four black married women worked outside the home, and in New York, 46.4 percent. Overall, however, young women 16–24 remained the largest contingent of black women workers. Black women's branches of the Young Women's Christian Association, founded in major cities since the 1890s, focused on the needs of young working women, especially migrants who came to the city alone. New York's black YWCA, founded in 1905, moved to Harlem in 1913, became a fulcrum of activism in World War I, and increased its range in the 1920s. Future lawyer and minister Pauli Murray, then a college student from Durham, North Carolina, remembered the summer of 1928, when she worked as a part-time switchboard operator at the YWCA's residence on 137th Street, as "a heady experience for an eighteen-year old." To Murray, the women staffers at the Y were "role models in the pursuit of excellence."

The surge of black migration broadened the options of middle-class African American women, who pursued racial uplift through work with the National Association of Colored Women (NACW), the YWCA, or politicized groups like the NAACP or the Urban League. Heavy black migration, historian Evelyn Brooks Higgenbotham points out, also increased black women's role in electoral politics. "The conflation of woman's suffrage and black urban migration made possible greater political opportunity and leverage for blacks as a group," she writes. "It also served to broaden black women's perceptions of their own influence and activism." The NACW, which had led the suffrage cause among black women, "became the springboard for future political work." Through NACW clubs in 41 states, black women leaders of the 1920s mobilized support for the Republican party, with which the African American community had been allied since Reconstruction, and worked especially hard for the election of Calvin Coolidge in 1924. "How little have we realized in our club work for the last twenty-five years that it was God's way of preparing us to assume this greater task of citizenship," an activist declared. By 1931, as the depression took hold, the affinity between black women and the Republican party waned, Higgenbotham notes, and by the election of 1936 it had ended. The shift of allegiance to the Democratic party among black leaders such as Mary McLeod Bethune, prominent educator and women's club leader, "symbolized the changed mood of the black electorate."

Mexican population movement to the United States, growing since the 1880s, reached new highs in the 1920s. After revolution in Mexico in 1910, which generated violence, economic distress, and political disorder, migration increased. The spread of commercial farming in the Southwest, meanwhile, increased employers' demand for cheap labor. More than a million Mexicans, about 10 percent of Mexico's population, entered the United States between 1910 and 1930. At the end of the 1920s, almost two-thirds of foreign-born Mexicans in the U.S. had entered since 1915. The Mexican population of Los Angeles more than tripled in the 1920s; the numbers of Mexicans in Texas cities like San Antonio rose by half or more; and Mexican communities mushroomed in the Midwest, especially in Chicago and Detroit. But the concentration remained southwestern; in 1930, 80 percent of the Mexican American population lived in Texas, California, New Mexico, Arizona, and Colorado. Migration from Mexico occurred mainly in family groups. Men, who outnumbered women as migrants, often arrived first, and later sent for extended families. Some single women, however, migrated alone. Mexican immigrant women of the 1920s experienced a tension "between role expectations of Mexican society and their new American circumstances," historian Karen Anderson writes. "Men's low wages meant they had to assume responsibility for family support, yet cultural norms prescribed a domestic and familial role for women." Mexican women, in short, had to confront not only "a hostile Anglo world and an exploitative market economy," but, in addition, "their problematical gender status within their own and the larger culture."

Mexican migrant women of the 1920s had limited employment options. Most worked in agricultural labor, as pickers of beets, onions, or cotton. Others held domestic jobs or found work in the garment industry or in food processing; these jobs were labor-intensive, seasonal, insecure, and low-paid. But employer demand remained high. Employers encouraged the migration of families, with many working members, to secure a tractable labor force that could survive on low wages. When families labored together in field work or food processing, the head of the family was paid; women earned less than men and lacked leverage as family members and workers. The family, Anderson notes, served as both a "buffer against the vicissitudes of American life" and a curb on autonomy. At the end of the 1920s, among Mexican American women workers, 38 percent held service jobs, 25 percent blue-collar jobs, and 21 percent agricultural jobs; 3 percent worked in clerical or sales jobs; and 3 percent were professionals.

California reformers and social workers of the 1920s targeted Mexican American women through "Americanization" programs that sought to change their cultural values and promote conformity to American ways. When homemakers proved resistant to Americanization, historian George J. Sanchez shows, reformers refocused their efforts on daughters, who, in the tradition of immigrant daughters elsewhere, strove to emancipate themselves. "The freedom and independence in this country bring the children into conflict with their parents," one Mexican mother told a UCLA sociologist. "They learn nicer ways, learn about the outside world, learn how to speak English, and then they become ashamed of their parents who brought them here that they might have better advantages." Young women adapted most readily to the American market economy and to American culture, specifically, consumer culture. In Mexican communities, historian Vicki L. Ruiz points out, the ethic of consumption reached immigrants through English-language and Spanish-language publications. The Los Angeles-based publication, *La Opinion*, for instance, started in 1926, offered advice columns, celebrity gossip, advertisements for clothes and cosmetics, and tips on behavior, such as the 1927 article titled "How Do You Kiss?" Teenagers shared "cultural messages they gleaned from English and Spanish-language publications, afternoon matinées, and popular radio programs," including the desire to "date." A handful of Latina actresses, such as Dolores Del Rio and Lupe Velez, served as role models of the American dream. Consumer culture especially affected young women factory workers, who, overworked and underpaid, strove to control their leisure time. As the ethic of consumption encroached, young women's earning power, small as it was, could be a "bargaining chip." Consumerism, according to Ruiz, challenged the ideology of control that Mexican families exerted over daughters.

For European immigrants of the progressive years and especially for their daughters, the postwar decade was an era of acculturation. The National Origins Act of 1924 curtailed the flow of immigrants, especially those from southern and eastern Europe who had dominated the ranks of newcomers since the 1880s. Curbs on immigration and changes in the labor market affected women's employment. As state laws gradually barred child labor, the number of working wives in immigrant families rose, especially after World War I. More markedly, daughters of European immigrants moved upward into white-collar work and women's professions. Mainly, they abandoned factory work for jobs in department stores and offices. Even between 1910 and 1920, according to historian Donna Gabaccia, the number of foreign-born sales clerks had increased by more than 200 percent and of foreign-born typists by 100 percent. Commercial high school and business colleges prepared immigrant daughters for English-speaking jobs; daughters of artisans, skilled workers, and widows, Gabaccia notes, sought training for office work with special frequency. Some daughters of immigrant families became professionals, too. By the early 1930s, Jewish women constituted almost half of New York City teachers.

The ethic of consumption affected women of new immigrant background who grew up exposed to the American marketplace. In the 1920s, many immigrant families sought middle-class status. Some women used volunteerism as a stepping-stone, and devoted time to women's ethnic organizations. Many relied on American women's publications for clues to genteel manners and values. Author Philip Roth remembers how his mother, Bess Finkel, the first-generation offspring of poor immigrants from eastern Europe, a high school graduate of 1922, and a former secretary, was, as a New Jersey housewife, faithful to women's magazines such as the *Ladies' Home Journal, Redbook,* and the *Women's Home Companion:* "In their pages, she confirmed her sense of how to dress and to furnish a home, found the recipes that she clipped and filed in her recipe box, and received instruction in the current conventions of child-rearing and marriage." Possessions, too, played a role in acculturation. Immigrant housewives, Donna Gabaccia notes, "quickly became avid consumers of American products." According to historian Jenna Weissman Joselit, among Jewish immigrant women, "shopping became a tangible instrument of integration and Americanization." More radical spirits mocked the corrupting influence of consumption, but without impact. The marketplace, in short, became an effective "Americanizer."

The marketplace of the 1920s had special salience for the young. Since the progressive era, as historian Kathy Peiss reveals, young working women of urban immigrant communities had learned how to spend money on themselves and to enjoy their leisure time. In the 1920s, as mass culture—radio, movies, advertisements, the popular press—gained ground, these trends became more widespread. For second-generation young women, education, employment, and mass culture served as a trio of Americanizing influences. These influences spurred generational conflict, and as the second generation matured, divisions peaked. The individualism of American society, for instance, challenged the family-centered culture of southern Europeans, Donna Gabaccia observes, especially as the second generation dressed and behaved in American ways. The messages of mass culture, however, were at once liberating and conservative: overall, they fostered domestic ideals. Young women of immigrant families "committed themselves almost universally to marriage, motherhood, and American-style domesticity," Gabaccia contends. "The daughters of the peak pre-World War I migrations pioneered in creating domesticity as a female right rather than a class privilege." Mass culture of the 1920s also brought exposure to the "new morality," the upshot of a long-term change in sexual attitudes and behavior.

THE NEW MORALITY

The sexual revolution of the early twentieth century was not an overnight change but rather an evolutionary change in attitudes and practices that had been building since at least the 1890s. Its hallmarks were a positive view of human sexuality, acceptance of female sexuality, freedom in the discussion of sexual issues, looser moral standards, and new norms of sexual behavior. Shifts in all areas were well underway before the 1920s; some symptoms of change can be traced back to the last third of the nineteenth century. By the pre-World War I period, middle-class mores were in transition. The flapper had made her first appearance; dance crazes caught popular attention; the press mentioned sexual issues such as venereal disease and prostitution; and readers besieged popular columnists with questions about the behavior of well-bred daughters. Beatrice Fairfax responded, with regret, that "Making love lightly, boldly, and promiscuously seems to be part of our social structure." ("Making love," in this context, meant some form of affectionate display, or what came to be labeled petting.) Dorothy Dix observed in 1913 that "the social position of women has been revolutionized since mother was a girl."

But changing sexual attitudes had greatest impact in the 1920s. Before the war, liberated behavior, notably among young women, was regarded as a hazard. In the 1920s, while still controversial, the same behavior became a given rather than an omen. In the prewar era, sexual emancipation had had a narrow base of urban sophisticates. In the 1920s, it became a national concern, dividing the generations in small-town America as well as in the metropolis. In the prewar era, sexual revolutionaries such as Margaret Sanger and her Greenwich Village cohort were usually affiliated with the left. Their rebellion was fueled by political fervor and linked to rejection of all middle-class values. After World War I, the new mood of sexual emancipation veered off from its radical origins and became itself a middle-class attribute. The new morality now received a label. Defended by enthusiasts, celebrated in the media, and immortalized by youth, it was absorbed into popular culture.

The ideology of sexual revolution arrived full force in the prewar era, with the writings of Sigmund Freud, Ellen Key, and Havelock Ellis, but it had at that time a limited audience, such as the radical New York vanguard. By the 1920s, "sexual enthusiasm," once a left-wing perquisite, had permeated the mainstream. Freud stressed the centrality of sex in human experience; his popularizers in the 1920s stressed the hazards of sexual repression. The "id" and "libido" became a part of common lingo. Key advocated free sexual expression for women, including "free motherhood" (without marriage). "The most sacred thing in life is individual desire," she wrote, "with special emphasis on sex-desire." Key contended, too, that every woman should set aside a decade for having three or four children. Havelock Ellis's philosophy received wide attention at Margaret Sanger's instigation in the 1920s. Ellis had long been a herald of female sexuality. In 1905, he had proclaimed that the "sexual impulse in women" existed apart from the "reproductive instinct." Presenting sexuality as ennobling, not destructive, and "restraint" as more dangerous than "excess," Ellis had urged a new morality based on greater freedom and self-expression.

In the 1920s, the ideology of sexual emancipation helped to sweep away old rules and introduce new ones. Now, sex was central to life, repression damaging to health and psyche. Lending support to changes in attitudes and practices already underway, the new morality legitimized a role reversal for women. Men had always been assumed to have sexual natures, even if "restraint" had once been thought preferable to "indulgence." But the new morality proclaimed equality of desire. Discarding purity for sexuality, women could now claim a facet of male privilege. "The myth of the pure woman is almost at an end," one enthusiast, V. F. Calverton, proclaimed in 1928. "Women's demands for equal rights have extended to the sexual sphere as well as the social." Equal rights in the sexual sphere remained as elusive as they were undefinable. Nonetheless, two important, overlapping types of sexual revolution occurred at various points after 1910, both based on shifting attitudes toward female sexuality.

One was a sexual revolution within middle-class marriage. Indeed, middle-class married women were the unsung sexual revolutionaries of the early twentieth century. This gradual revolution had long-term repercussions, starting in the 1920s when marriage was redefined as a sexual institution. The other sexual revolution was the new behavior of "youth," especially of middle-class daughters. The revolution of youth took the form of revamped courtship customs, a modest but significant increase in premarital affairs, and a far larger increase in premarital sexual contact. Youthful rebellion affected the older generation, first, because it was widely publicized (as the revolution within marriage was not) and second, because youth was brief, and the young, single generation that seemed to dominate the decade quickly became an older, married one.

A major symptom of change in the 1920s was that middle-class women adopted a positive view of sexuality; this change had been in progress over the first two decades of the century. Its impact was revealed in 1929 when Katherine Bement Davis published her pioneer sexual survey. Carried out in 1918, Davis's survey reflected the responses of 2,200 middle-class women, married and unmarried, mainly college graduates, whose names came from women's club membership rolls and alumnae files—indeed, it was quite an elite, upper-crust sample. Undertaken to further the cause of social hygiene and the social purity movement, the survey ultimately served another purpose: to document the importance of sexual experience in women's lives. The Davis survey actually caught women at an important *pre*-1920s junction in the shift of sexual attitudes and practices. More than half of the unmarried women, for instance, and three out of ten of the married women, had intense emotional relationships with women. One out of five respondents had homosexual experiences, though few had premarital heterosexual relations. This aspect of the survey reflected the old morality. The married women Davis surveyed, however, most of whom used contraceptives, described sexual relations in positive, receptive terms—"as an expression of love," "because it is a natural, normal relation," "for pleasure, satisfaction, development," "for mental and physical health." As the average respondent was born around 1880, the Davis survey suggested that changes in middle-class women's attitudes toward sexual experience were well underway before the 1920s. Moreover, Davis was forced to conclude (contrary to her expectations) that frequency of intercourse could not be correlated with poor health or sterility, thereby supporting the sexual revolution within marriage.

Katherine Bement Davis's study, the first national survey of its type and the most comprehensive until the Kinsey report, was significant in another way, too. Earlier sexual surveys were usually carried out among prostitutes and delinquents to analyze "deviance." Davis was herself trained in such research. Only in the 1920s did researchers turn their attention to what was "normal." While Davis was interested in all facets of female sexual life, as well as in women's attitudes toward sexual experience (her respondents provided reams of commentary), most researchers were bent on tabulating loss of purity. Rising rates of (middle-class) premarital and extramarital intercourse were seen as the hallmark of sexual revolution, and surveys and studies of the 1920s and 1930s pointed to the decade after 1910 as a watershed of moral change. Later, using broader samples that more accurately measured the repercussions of changing mores (beyond the urban middle-class), Kinsey found that twice as many women born after 1900 had premarital experience as those born before 1900, putting the brunt of change in the 1920s. The gist of the research, during the 1920s and after, was that around the time suffrage was won, traditional morality had started to crack. Using premarital sex as a touchstone, male and female "morals" were starting to become more alike. The "single standard" of morality had materialized, said Beatrice Hinkle, and it was "nearer the standard associated with men."

The death of the double standard was wildly exaggerated. But even shifts toward a single standard bewildered women who had grown up with the old morality. "We were reared, educated, and married for one sort of life, and precipitated before we had a chance to get our bearings into another," Frances Woodward Prentiss wrote in *Scribners*. "Perhaps we cannot take sex as lightly as the young nor as calmly as the old." Nor were women who defended the new morality unaware of its liabilities. "Far more will be expected of sex when it is left free to express itself than under any repressive system," Elsie Clews Parsons had predicted in 1914. The interest of the 1920s, however, was neither in the reaction of women past youth nor in the rising expectations Parsons anticipated. Rather, it was in the newly emancipated young, especially young women, who seemed to be the prime movers in moral change.

To some observers, the sexual emancipation of young women was linked to economic independence. "In the great cities . . . where women can control their own purse strings, many of them are able to drift into casual or steady relationships which may or may not end in marriage," Alyse Gregory wrote in *Current History* in 1923. The self-supporting young woman "has her own salary at the end of the month and asks no other recompense from her lover but his love and companionship." Other observers agreed that once young women supported themselves, they were likely to develop behavior patterns more like those of men. The liberation of the young working woman had been in progress in urban areas for several decades. Self-consciously "modern" middle-class women of the 1920s began to adopt the lifestyle developed by working-class women around the turn of the century. But neither economic independence nor the emancipation of city life were seen as the main spurs of the new morality of the 1920s. "Youth" as a whole, even youth supported by their parents, seemed to be shifting moral gears, as reflected in endless articles with such titles as "These Wild Young People" and "The Uprising of Youth."

The phenomenon evoked alarm, concern, and, among its best-known analysts, acclaim. Enthusiasts were notably middle-aged men. One, for example, was Denver judge Ben Lindsey, who, at 54, defended *The Revolt of Modern Youth* in 1925. Youth of the decade had been transformed, Lindsey wrote, by the modern environment—by its economy and culture, by science and technology; by the car, movies, and radio; and by the very speed of change. The world of the young was so different from that of their parents that old morals and standards had no significance. "Youth has always been rebellious; youth has always shocked the older generation," Lindsey said. "But this is different. It has the whole weight and momentum of a new scientific and economic order behind it. . . . These boys and girls can do what boys and girls were never able to do in the past." Lindsey was referring mainly to "tentative excursions into sex experience" and "sexual liberties," although he pegged the premarital sexual intercourse rate between 15 and 20 percent. Emancipated behavior, he felt, was preferable to outworn values, "the ragtag and bobtail of adult puritanism." Especially commendable was the modern young woman, "who makes her own living, votes, holds her own in competition with men [and] is capable of doing things her mother couldn't come within sight of." To defenders of the new morality, suffrage, self-support, self-assertion, and sexual emancipation were linked together in a modern package.

To traditionalists, the rebellion of youth was a danger signal, and on this issue, feminists aligned with the traditionalists. Veterans of the last generation such as Jane Addams objected to the "astounding emphasis upon sex," and Charlotte Perkins Gilman opened fire on "selfish and fruitless indulgence." "It is sickening to see so many of the newly freed abusing that freedom in a mere imitation of masculine weakness and vice," she wrote in *Century Magazine* in 1923. Gilman was repelled by young women who gave way to "appetite and impulse," who adopted "a coarseness and looseness in speech, dress, manners, and habits of life," and who, instead of preparing for motherhood, were "enjoying preliminaries" or even "mastering birth control and acquiring experience." Clearly, progressive era feminism and sexual emancipation did not necessarily lead in the same direction; rather, they seemed at cross-purposes. Gilman made a political as well as a personal critique. As historian Lindia Gordon points out, feminist suspicions of sexual permissiveness were well-founded. Assertion of female sexuality did not of itself raise woman's status, nor did the new legitimacy of "indulgence" ensure women freedom, independence, or power. Rather, women had lost bargaining power, or the right of refusal, a crucial weapon in nineteenth-century sexual politics.

Traditionalists, however, including the older generation of feminists, lost ground in the 1920s. Not only did the new morality enjoy extensive publicity, but its very emblem was the young woman, customarily one of society's most powerless and least influential members. Now, significantly, she became a cultural symbol. From the outset, she was anonymous. "This nameless one, the American flapper," H. L. Mencken had labeled her in 1915. Urban and upper middle class, the prewar flapper had had a superficial sophistication. She had "forgotten how to simper," Mencken wrote. "She seldom blushes; it is impossible to shock her." She opposed the double standard, favored a law prohibiting it, and planned to read Havelock Ellis over the summer. Columnist Dorothy Dix confirmed that the prewar flapper was "a girl in good position in society" and defined her by her energy, spunk, and sportive esprit. She could "play golf all day, drive a car, offer first aid, and . . . is in no more danger of swooning than a man would be." Before the war, there was a certain looseness in flapper definition. After, the role became a mold, a style, a stereotype. "The flapper of fiction, plays, movies, and newspapers," said the *New Republic* in 1922, "offers a vivid pattern of modern young life and creates a certain bravado . . . the necessity for living up to current opinion."

The flapper of the 1920s, still distinguished by youth and class, was at once "boyish" and provocative. In dress, habits, and mannerisms, she assumed a dual role. On the one hand, she was a temptress, an aspect emphasized in movie stars who exuded sexual power and appeal, whether Gloria Swanson's upper-class heroines or Clara Bow's lingerie salesgirl in *It* (1927). On the other hand, the 1920s flapper was a pal and a sport, a challenger and competitor. This facet was revealed in other heroines of the decade such as Amelia Earhart and Gertrude Eberle, who broke boundaries and set records. In both cases, the flapper was characterized by assertion and defiance—of rules, traditions, and conventions, although defiance itself became a convention. Winning contests or smoking in public, she claimed privileges reserved for men, including that of sexuality. According to the tabloids, she might even assume the role of sexual aggressor, as demonstrated by 16-year-old Peaches Browning, who ensnared her millionaire sugar daddy. The heroine of *Flaming Youth* (1923), a sensational best-seller soon made into a movie, was equally aggressive. Willful and capricious, this "dangerously inflammable" 18-year-old seduces a friend of the family, a married man of 40, who at last discards his wife to reward her efforts—with marriage. A new type of heroine, the fictional flapper had novel tactics but traditional goals.

The flapper was a vital economic symbol too. She was defined by the goods and services she was able to buy, whether silk stockings, bobbed hair, jazz records, or rouge compacts. Her attributes symbolized, at once, freedom, availability, and purchasing power. Clothes, the great liberator of the decade, were her major hallmark. While the styles of the 1890s had enabled women to ride bicycles and work in offices, the flapper's clothes advertised both equality and sexuality. The ready-made women's clothing industry of the 1920s began to surpass "cloakmaking" as the mainstay of the garment trade. The flapper's cigarette was also a loaded symbol. It proclaimed equality with men, who conventionally smoked in public, while conveying an aura of suggestion and bravado. Between 1918 and 1928, production of cigarettes more than doubled. By the end of the decade, cigarette ads showed women, sometimes movie starlets, smoking or having their cigarettes lit by men. Cosmetics were another suggestive accoutrement. A generation earlier, makeup was associated mainly with prostitutes. It now conveyed the intent to be provocative. By 1929, the flapper could choose from a grand array of cosmetics, another multimillion-dollar business. Temptress and challenger, she was also a consumer, an advertisement for the clothing, tobacco, and beauty products industries.

Finally, the flapper was a great competitor. Her styles and affectations represented not only new freedoms—to wear, to do, to buy—but also new criteria for success. "Youth in this day and age," wrote sociologist Ernest Burgess, "are rated in terms of sex appeal," and the flapper sought a high score. Sometimes she competed with men, though only in a pallish, sportive, companionate way. More often, flappers competed with one another, and not only in dance contests and beauty pageants. Even Dorothy Dunbar Bromley's "feminist—new style" did not identify with other women or profess any "loyalty to women en masse." Rather, she was "a good dresser, a good sport, a good pal," who dealt with men on a basis of "frank comradeship." Dropping "sex-antagonism," she also discarded older traditions of female friendship, fellowship, and association. Once sexual expression was viewed as central to life,

Since the late nineteenth century, carnivals and mass circulation newspapers had used beauty contests as publicity devices, but the formal beach beauty contest came to characterize the 1920s. Like the winner and runners-up in this California contest in 1920, contestants were valued for their natural, unsophisticated qualities. They also personified the spirit of exhibitionism, competition, and novelty so prized in the flapper. Beginning in 1921, the Miss America contest in Atlantic City made the beauty contest a national ritual. *(UPI/Bettmann)*

opportunities for same-sex relationships among women decreased, a change that did not escape notice. During the 1920s, men and women, husbands and wives, became "more than before . . . friends," wrote Floyd Dell, editor of the *Masses*, the vanguard magazine read by modern radical urbanites in the prewar era. "At the same time the intensity of friendship between people of the same sex seems to be diminishing." As romance was eroticized, the intense friendships between women that had character-ized the Victorian era appeared to fade.

What happened to same-sex relationships in the 1920s? Again, the currents of change flowed both ways, for as historian Lillian Faderman points out, elements of liberation and repression coexisted. New York sophisticates, for instance, attended drag balls as spectators; Greenwich Village bohemians, who embraced the uncon-ventional, defended homosexuality and experimented with bisexuality; a working-class lesbian subculture began to evolve in big cities. Concurrently, among middle-class Americans, the pendulum swung in another direction. As sex became more legitimate, same-sex relationships became less so. Once love between women was *seen* as sexual, such relationships no longer seemed harmless, but rather a hazard—a barrier to heterosexual happiness. With its promise of sexual equality, the new moral-ity erased a facet of women's culture.

The young woman growing up in the 1920s was more likely to be influenced by national culture, by the media, and by her peers. Two particular influences, the campus and the movies, helped her to fuse the new morality with traditional roles.

"PALS" AND "PARTNERS"

In the 1920s, for the first time, more than half of young people were enrolled in some sort of educational institution. The numbers of high school and college students surged upward. By 1930, more than half of Americans of high school age attended high school, 12 percent of the college-aged went to colleges and universities, and many others were at "junior colleges" and teacher-training schools. Although the proportion of women in the college population declined slightly during the decade, from a high of 47.3 percent in 1920 to 43.7 percent in 1930, women flocked to college at almost the same rate as men. The pacesetting college woman of the 1920s was not the student at an elite woman's college, as had been the case in the 1880s and 1890s, but the coed at a large state college or university. In the college setting, where the authority of peers replaced that once held by parents and community, her role was shaped by the campus itself.

The campus context, as historian Paula Fass explains, provided "informal access" between the sexes. Such access promoted a new sense of equality and also encouraged "pronounced attention to sexual attractiveness." The coed of the 1920s assumed the roles of "pal" and "partner," both defined in terms of her relationship to men. Her dual role rested on the assumption that equality meant assuming the privileges and mannerisms once monopolized by men. It carried an aura of experimentation and innovation, adventure and bravado. Men on campus defended such bravado, especially in the pages of college newspapers (men tended to dominate extracurricular activities while women students engineered social events). "The flapper is the girl who is responsible for the advancement of women's condition in the world," announced an Illinois editor in 1922, citing her "independent" and "pally" qualities. The coed was not inferior, claimed an Ohio editor, and therefore did not need special rules and regulations, "as if she were feeble-minded or insane." But there were new rules and regulations on campus, determined by the students themselves. The social rites and rituals that began in the 1920s were extremely important for the coed, whose marital future might well be decided in the campus arena (a "glorified playground" one educator called it). Moreover, college students were innovators and pacesetters. Their customs and manners affected the roles of women attending single-sex colleges, primarily on weekends, when they came in contact with men. Simultaneously, collegiate manners spread to students in high school, and thereby became staples of national youth culture.

"Dating" was a major innovation. Going out on dates was a marked change from the calls paid at home by suitors of an earlier generation, and suggested a more assertive, independent role for middle-class daughters; adult supervision had been banished. The main architects of the dating system, historian John Modell contends, were middle-class girls. They had more to gain, he suggests, because the new version of the double standard that dating put in place "was considerably less restrictive than

Gender roles were of prime concern to coeds of the 1920s. Sorority sisters at the University of Kansas surround the "Most Perfect Man," a title given annually to the coed judged most capable of "dressing and acting like a gentleman." *(Bettmann)*

the one it replaced." On the other hand, historian Beth Bailey points out, dating shifted power *from* women *to* men; courtship no longer took place in the home, a female domain, but in the world beyond. The dating phenomenon clearly invites varied interpretations. Still, dating had indisputable influence on women's roles. It provided practice in the paired activities that would later be a way of life—basic training in the roles of "pal" and "partner." Also, the coed who went out on dates four nights a week had less opportunity for the single-sex fellowship of an earlier day. The sense of sisterhood shared by the previous generation now gave way to competition for dates. By the mid-1920s, Bailey explains, dating had almost completely replaced the system of "calling," and in so doing, had transformed American courtship. The rite of dating was abetted by the automobile, which replaced the front porch—although it was hardly a "house of prostitution on wheels," as labeled by a juvenile court judge in Middletown (Muncie, Indiana, whose residents were studied in the 1920s by sociologists Helen and Robert Lynd). Still, the car served as a vehicle of liberty, both for campus couples already removed from the authority of home and for small-town couples who, the Lynds reported, could now drive off to the next town.

The custom of dating contributed to a second innovation in social rituals—"petting," another rehearsal for future roles. Like dating, petting was a significant change but not a total rejection of custom and convention. It was linked to the old framework of courtship; marriage was still the ultimate goal. In a survey of young women's attitudes, Phyllis Blanchard and Carolyn Manasses reported that their subjects viewed petting as "a substitute for more advanced sexual activity." Moreover, campus surveys suggested, students' attitudes were more liberal than their practices. The "wild and reckless and radical" aspect of youth was exaggerated, a campus editor at Duke University observed in 1927, "a lot of lashing and lather on the surface with miles of unmoved depths below." But early training in paired relationships, Blanchard and Manasses suggested, could be an advantage. "The girl who makes use of the new opportunity for freedom is likely to find her experiences have been wholesome," they wrote in 1931. "She may be better prepared for marriage by her playful activities than if she had just clung to a passive role." Like campus editors, the surveyors contrasted the "active" role of the 1920s girl with the "passive" role of her grandmother. They also added that in young men's views, purity was not as important in a potential wife as were compatible qualities, such as "congenial tastes" and "ability to take an interest in the husband's work."

The coed's preparation for her future included not only social but extracurricular activities. These centered around the sorority—a popular college institution of the 1920s modeled on the fraternity, which had appeared in the mid-nineteenth century. The first sororities, founded in the late nineteenth century, had served a special function at coeducational schools by providing a separate space for women students as well as practice in the types of social service work appropriate for middle-class women. In the 1920s, fraternities and sororities served to impose social order on a rapidly expanding, heterogeneous college population. Sororities proliferated so rapidly that most big coed colleges had about 15 or 20, and they spread to the high school level, where they affected an even larger student population. For the coed of the 1920s, historian Sheila Rothman points out, the sorority replaced the social service club and college suffrage league of the last generation. It also served a different purpose than its nineteenth-century antecedent. An exclusionary institution, the sorority now fostered a competitive spirit more than a sororal one. The qualities it favored for admission were the same as those appreciated by men in dating relationships: attractiveness, amiability, and compatibility. By cultivating such attributes, and by setting standards on appearance, social behavior, and even sexual conduct, the sorority promoted the role of "pal" and "partner."

Finally, the college itself also took a hand in preparing women students for future roles. As college populations grew, luring thousands of middle-class students who would not have been there a decade earlier, business and home economics provided new arenas for male and female specialization. In the 1920s, men and women were educated together in larger numbers, but they were expected to follow different paths after graduation. Home economics, which pervaded both high school and college curriculums, had been financed at state colleges and universities by the federal Smith-Lever Act of 1914. Unlike women's schools of the 1890s, the colleges now produced housewives rather than moral leaders, and the trend influenced women's colleges too. Vassar, for instance, in 1925, introduced its interdisciplinary School of Euthenics, devoted to the development and care of the family. Here again, a contrast with the previous generation emerged. When Marion Talbot began her department of "sanitary science" at the University of Chicago in the 1890s, the curriculum included physics, chemistry, physiology, political science, and modern languages. The goal was to prepare experts in modern urban life. But the new school at Vassar carried such courses as "Husband and Wife," "Motherhood," and "The Family as an Economic Unit." Like the expanding home economics programs in state colleges, it fostered accommodation to traditional roles.

While campus activities, curricular and extracurricular, shaped women's goals, the new era of mass communications also had an influence. A major influence, setting standards and ideals, molding dreams and fantasies, was the movies. Few could attend Vassar's School of Euthenics, but the impact of the screen was universal, affecting the small-town girl and immigrant daughter as well as the college student. By the end of the 1920s, 115 million Americans each week viewed the wiles of a gallery of movie heroines. Since 1910, the innocence and purity of Mary Pickford had been succeeded by Theda Bara's dangerous vamp, who in turn gave way to such sex symbols as Clara Bow, the "slam-bang kid" of 1927, full of vitality and appeal. Movies also gave graphic lessons in social behavior. They taught how to look, talk, and behave, and how to compete in the marital marketplace. As one college woman observed, the movies provided "a liberal education in the art of making love."

Movies of the decade, historian Mary P. Ryan points out, conveyed advice on sexual tactics. Film heroines, significantly, preserved their virginity until marriage, whatever their allure, dazzle, and sex appeal. Screen women also knew where to be—in places where the sexes were in close proximity. They knew how to assert themselves, as captivating a man was no longer a passive proposition. Alarmingly, considerable animosity arose between the sexes on screen; plot construction often made heroes and heroines adversaries. But women in the movies had even more animosity toward one another. Because relations with men were central, female friendships were casual and insubstantial; interchanges between women tended to be snide. Sexual conquest, the movies suggested, was a competitive vocation—whether for the well-off heroine or for the humble white-collar worker, the salesgirl or secretary who escaped her job (so much for economic independence) by finding a man. The arch success was that of the gold digger, like Anita Loos's Lorelei Lee, who captured the richest bachelor in America. With pluck, daring, and know-how, a girl might marry a millionaire.

At the same time, the movies offered lessons in consumption. They showed what merchandise to buy, from makeup and lingerie to bathtubs and furniture. Clothes were the screen star's forte. In a 1920 film, Gloria Swanson retained her husband's affection by buying an exotic flapper wardrobe and revamping her image. Movies also revealed the latest in household technology and home decor. They enabled the viewer, as one woman wrote to a fan magazine, "to observe the better way of living." "Here [at the movies]" wrote another, "I learn what to wear, how to dress, how a refined home should look." A third fan revealed that she returned from the theater and rearranged her home "like I have seen at the movies." The woman of Chicago's nineteenth ward in 1900 might have learned "right living" from the settlement, but her daughter saw it on the screen. Like the campus, the movies steered a young woman toward traditional goals—man, marriage, and domestic life.

After the turn of the century, more women married and at younger ages. Even women college graduates, by the 1920s, wed at near the rate of the general female population. This was not a sudden shift but one that had been building, with a turning point around 1910. In the latter part of the nineteenth century, about half the graduates of women's colleges had remained single (coeds were always more likely to marry). By the 1920s, the pattern had changed. Of those who graduated between 1919 and 1923, 80 percent married. In 1923, a survey of Vassar graduates revealed that 90 percent wanted to marry, and an even higher percentage shared that ambition in other schools surveyed.

Younger women were similarly inclined, especially as the decade wore on. When Lorine Pruette surveyed the ambitions of teenage girls in the early 1920s, the results were mixed. Of her sample of young women aged between 15 and 17, 35 percent wanted careers and were willing to give up marriage and family for them. Pruette found their goals unrealistic because they tended to envision glamorous jobs. Even more teenagers wanted to combine career and marriage, perhaps an equally unrealistic goal. By the end of the decade, Blanchard and Manasses found that among young women 18 to 26 years old, few were willing to forgo marriage for a career. Their survey revealed that young women of the 1920s, at least those in their middle-class sample, had fused liberal attitudes with traditional goals. Almost all favored divorce, for instance, if marriage failed; and more than half expected marriage to provide sexual satisfaction even more than economic security. Most important, young women of the 1920s had high expectations tinged with egalitarian hopes. They envisioned marriage as "a perfect consummation of both personalities that would involve all phases of mutual living."

COMPANIONS AND CONSUMERS

In the prewar decade, radical spirits proposed all sorts of marriage reform. Greenwich Village sophisticates often rejected matrimony, along with other middle-class values. Left-wing figures who congregated at Mabel Dodge Luhan's Fifth Avenue salon were influenced by the sexual radicals whose books they read. Havelock Ellis contended that the "artificial restraints of marriage" should be replaced by "natural monogamy." His wife, Edith Ellis, during an American tour of 1914, explained the virtues of "semi-detached" marriage, like her own. Ellen Key, whose tributes to Havelock Ellis were published in the *Birth Control Review*, recommended "free motherhood." The 1920s provided innovative ideas too. In 1927, Judge Lindsey proposed a form of trial marriage, based on contraception. "Companionate marriage" could be easily dissolved at the initiative of either spouse if no children had been born. But marriage was neither discarded nor legally reformed during the 1920s, along Lindsey's lines or any other. Rather, it was redefined.

The new ideal of marriage in the 1920s was a romantic-sexual union. The role of the wife was that of sexual partner and agreeable companion, an extension of the qualities valued in dating relationships. Contemporaries described the new ideal in egalitarian terms—compatibility, reciprocity, and mutuality—that reflected women's raised expectations. The New Woman of the 1920s expected more of marriage, Dorothy Dunbar Bromley wrote in 1927. She wanted to be satisfied in her role "as a lover and companion" and expected *"more freedom and honesty within the marriage."* Elsie Clews Parsons confirmed that women demanded "more of marriage than in the days when they had little to expect but marriage." Young middle-class women, according to Blanchard and Manasses, expected to attain through marriage "a fuller and richer life." They envisioned "sharing joys and sorrows with a mate who will be not merely a protector and provider but an all round companion." Companionate qualities were now defined by experts—sociologists, psychologists, psychiatrists, and physicians. Their views appeared in college texts, marriage manuals, advice columns, and mass-circulation magazines. Reflecting changes that had already occurred, at least within the middle class, descriptions of marriage now fused egalitarian hopes with a new set of prescriptions.

Sexuality was primary to companionate marriage of the 1920s. Sociology texts explained that women were sexual beings and that marriage was both a romantic and sexual institution. Ernest Burgess declared that the "highest personal happiness comes from marriage based on romantic love." Ernest Groves and William Ogburn, in their textbook on marriage and the family, confirmed that modern matrimony was a "fellowship of love." Birth control advocates added their own message to the marriage literature. Physician Ira Wile posited a new criterion for the success of marriage: the sexual satisfaction of the partners. In a text on the family in the early 1930s, sociologist and birth control advocate Joseph K. Folsom contended that sex served to "intensify, beautify, and sanctify love." Margaret Sanger, who in 1926 published a marriage manual, *Happiness in Marriage*, revealed that marital sex was elevating, romantic, and pivotal. Both partners must realize "the importance of complete fulfillment of love through the expression of sex," Sanger wrote. "Sex expression, rightly understood, is the consummation of love, its completion and consecration."

Although the literature presented sexual-romantic marriage as a medley of passion, friendship, and equality, the role of "companion" assumed the same ambivalence it had had in the late eighteenth century. This became clear in the popular press, where companionship, realistically, involved unequal obligations. The responsibility of amiable companionship fell on the wife, who had to keep romance and friendship alive. From metropolis to Middletown, women received the same message: To "keep the thrill in marriage," wives had to maintain a high level of sex appeal. They also had to "keep up"—their appearance, interests, and contacts. The successful wife was no longer primarily industrious or thrifty; rather, she had to be able to propose enjoyable joint activities, and to be attractive, agreeable, and available. Even the birth of a child could imperil a marriage. It could drain a woman's energy, make her less interesting, and sabotage sexual mutuality. (The white fertility rate, which had steadily declined since 1800, plunged in the 1920s.) Other women were also a hazard. The married woman needed survival tactics to meet the competition—whether from the next generation of flirts and flappers, with access to offices and husbands; from family friends, as in *Flaming Youth*; or from married peers. Almost

300 movies in the 1920s dealt with the theme of infidelity, and their lessons were obvious. The companionate wife would have to work at it.

Companionate marriage took another toll too, belying the egalitarian rhetoric used to describe it. As Suzanne LaFollette explained in *Concerning Women*, marriage was still a "state" for men, but for women it was a "vocation," a calling. The dictum of the 1920s, contrary to the aspirations of the "feminist—new style," was that marriage was a woman's primary role. Work or career, if she had any, would be confined to the interval, if there was one, between school and marriage. This axiom had a new corollary: Marriage alone could satisfy all needs; outside activities were secondary, if not perilous, to the health of the union. Women had to be willing, as was one Vassar student in a survey of goals, "to pay whatever price the companionship costs." Surveys among college students reflected division of opinion over what companionate marriage meant. One issue was whether wives should work, even in the early (childless) years of marriage. Men rejected the idea; women supported it. The "abyss of disagreement," as one researcher called it, extended to decision-making within marriage. Male students expected their future wives to contribute only to certain types of decisions, those affecting "the family as a whole," while women nurtured more egalitarian expectations. But equality and companionship were not necessarily compatible. Sexual-romantic marriage, according to the surveys, seemed most viable if the wife lacked individual goals or forceful opinions. Companionate potential could best be realized if she was willing to assume a subordinate role, preferably a domestic one.

The lure of domesticity emerged in the press, especially in such mass-circulation magazines as the *Ladies' Home Journal* and *McCalls*. Since 1889, editor Edward Bok had steered the *Journal*, which led the field, to unparalleled success. Sometimes adopting a muckraker role, as in its campaigns against adulterated food and venereal disease, the *Journal* maintained a conservative stance. After opposing woman suffrage, it began the 1920s by condemning jazz and all it represented ("a bolshevik element of license"). In 1923, Bok revealed in his autobiography that he neither liked women nor understood them. Still, the *Journal* and its competitors understood what women at home liked to read, and articulated what historian William H. Chafe calls "an elaborate ideology in favor of home and marriage." Positing the fulfilled homemaker against the unfeminine, sex-deprived career woman, women's magazines urged their readers to renounce careers and strive for "an executive position in the home."

A major part of this position was as purchaser. "Where income permits," wrote Elsie Clews Parsons, "the wife continues to be the consumer." Since 1910 the magazines women read had become heavy with ads for devices that would save time and energy—for cleaners, polishers, refrigerators, sewing machines, washing machines, stoves—and products such as canned soup that would liberate wives from "constant drudgery." In the 1920s, the volume of advertising doubled, the range of household products increased, and the electric appliance industry boomed. Helen and Robert Lynd reported from Middletown that household appliances had invaded middle-class homes and that the physical labor of housework had decreased, although rising standards kept housewives just as busy. (Poorer families also invested in household improvements—such as linoleum and running water.) Some professional women, like the copywriters at J. Walter Thompson, used the growth of the female market to build careers. Efficiency expert Lillian Gilbreth, a "household engineer," for instance, served as a conduit between the business world and middle-class women. Manufacturers targeted women purchasers. Electrical companies urged women to give up sweeping, buy a vacuum cleaner, and "delegate to electricity all that electricity can do." Time-saving new products, such as electric toasters and irons, were necessary to keep up with the social whirl and retain attractiveness. "Time for Youth and Beauty! Time for Books and Plays!" a Middletown laundry advertised. Shopping could even be an enjoyable companionate activity. The cover of the Sears Roebuck catalog of 1927 depicted an attractive, well-dressed young couple, intertwined on a settee, making mail-order selections. While the wife takes the lead in pointing out items, the attentive, affectionate husband looks on, engrossed. Modernity was translated into romance, home and consumption.

The Sears Roebuck catalog cover of 1927, by Norman Rockwell, promoted both the joy of consumerism and the ideal of romantic marriage. The modern, companionate, middle-class couple is absorbed in a future of prospective purchases. The leading illustrator of the *Saturday Evening Post* since 1916, Rockwell was able to capture the way a large audience of Americans wish to see themselves.

(Sears, Roebuck and Company)

The final message received by the middle-class wife of the 1920s was the need for adjustment. Women's magazines advised her not to reject femininity but to enjoy it, to approach domesticity with a positive outlook. Articulate feminists waged a counterattack. Suzanne LaFollette, for instance, assaulted the consumer mentality. Influenced by advertising, leisure, and luxury, she claimed, women were living "without ideas, without ideals." Alice Beal Parsons contended that Havelock Ellis had pointed the way to "limitations" not liberation. Sex was not a panacea, she insisted; productive work was preferable to "getting everything out of some man that one can." By 1931, Lorine Pruette, a consistent critic, sounded a note of desperation. Most women, she wrote, led "contingent lives." They preferred "to work through another person and to find their own joys and compensation in the success of another. This is not so self-sacrificing; generally, it appears to be the easier way."

Some psychological advisers of the 1920s also took issue with the glorification of domesticity in the popular press. The "nervous housewife," wrote Abraham Myerson, a prominent neurologist, suffered from an increasing desire "for a more varied life than that afforded . . . by a life of housework." To career-minded feminists, the solution lay in employment, aspiration, and individualism. To Myerson, the cure was "adjustment . . . fortitude . . . patience . . . fidelity to duty," and community activities. Still, he identified a real discrepancy: The "modern" housewife played a premodern role. But this was a minority view. Freudianism, parceled out into popular advice, had a double-barreled message for women of the 1920s. One part was that sexual repression was harmful. The other was that it was healthy to adjust to familial roles and domestic vocations.

By providing the latest in science, psychological advisers supported the message of advertisers who displayed the latest in technology. Modern women were to find fulfillment in traditional roles, now enlivened by a sexual dimension. Eschewing maladjustment and neurosis, aspiration and ambition, they were to seek satisfaction in romance, marriage, and sexual expression. Significantly, contraception underlay the new ideal of sexual-romantic marriage. Throughout the decade, birth control changed middle-class moral standards, courtship customs, and marital ideals while these very changes simultaneously made birth control all the more imperative. Contraception had created its own dynamic.

CONTRACEPTIVE POLITICS

The twentieth-century battle for birth control arose in the cauldron of the pre–World War I left, among circles of socialists and anarchists, rebels and radicals. Emma Goldman, for instance, endorsed contraception in her speeches as early as 1910 and even dispensed contraceptive devices. Such actions were illegal; Congress in 1873 had passed the Comstock law, which classified contraceptive information and devices as obscenity and made it illegal to send either through the mail. Another federal law of 1873 barred the importation of contraceptive information or devices, and supportive state laws, which varied from state to state, imposed yet further restrictions on their manufacture, sale, or distribution. Birth-controllers sought to change the law, and to make contraception available to women, especially working-class women, who had least access to it.

In the context of the left, Margaret Sanger sought a leadership role. In 1911, when she was in the her early thirties, Sanger entered Greenwich Village social life and left-wing politics, and, within the left, moved swiftly *to* the left. First an organizer for the Socialist party, she soon joined the International Workingmen of the World (IWW). Trained as a nurse, she also worked briefly as a visiting nurse for the Henry Street Settlement. In 1912, Sanger began writing articles on sex-related topics ("What Every Girl Should Know") for the Socialist weekly, the *Call*, and in 1914, published her own radical monthly, the *Woman Rebel*. The *Rebel* sought to combat women's enslavement by "machinery, by wage slavery, by bourgeois morality, by customs, laws, and superstitions." It also promoted "birth control," a term Sanger coined. "A Woman's body belongs to herself alone," the *Rebel* declared. "Enforced motherhood is the most complete denial of a woman's right to life and liberty."

In the next few years, as the birth-control movement took shape, Sanger went through a series of formative experiences. After the U.S. Post Office declared the *Woman Rebel* unmailable, she fled the country to avoid a federal trial—but left behind a pamphlet, "Family Limitation," that explained contraceptive methods, as the *Rebel* had not. Her colleagues on the left, such as Emma Goldman and Elizabeth Gurley Flynn, distributed it. In England, meanwhile, Sanger absorbed the eugenic views and sexual romanticism of a new mentor, Havelock Ellis, who urged her to focus on a single cause. In Holland, next, she learned more about contraceptive devices. When Sanger returned to New York in 1915, a birth-control campaign was in full swing, due in part to the arrest and trial of her first husband, William Sanger, whom she would soon leave. Her pace now increased. In the fall of 1916, Margaret Sanger opened the first birth-control clinic, in Brownsville, Brooklyn, a working-class area. Ten days later, she was arrested, along with two colleagues. Tried and convicted, she was jailed for 30 days. But the left-wing tactic of "direct action" (breaking a law and gaining publicity for the cause) had results. When the New York Court of Appeals reviewed Sanger's case in 1918, it paved the way for a broader interpretation of the state law that barred dissemination of contraceptive devices. Physicians, said the court, could provide "help or advice to a married person to cure or prevent disease." Doctors would thereafter be pivotal to the birth-control campaign. So would well-off women, who had supported Sanger at her 1916 trial and provided funding for her next endeavor, the *Birth Control Review*, started in 1917.

World War I demolished the left-wing context in which the birth-control battle arose; waves of repression during and after the war put socialists and radicals in jail or in exile, or silenced them. As the 1920s began, Sanger salvaged the birth-control campaign by severing it from its radical base. In the *Birth Control Review*, and through a new organization, the American Birth Control League, formed in 1921, she shifted her arguments to suit the new era. Birth control was no longer a radical cause but an educational campaign to turn the tide of popular opinion and especially to solicit the support of the medical profession. Contraception was no longer a form of "direct action," an anticapitalist weapon, or a mode of self-help among working-class women. Now it was a tool of eugenics to "discourage the overfertility of the mentally and physically defective." Birth control, Sanger claimed, would liberate women from

MOTHERS!

Can you afford to have a large family?
Do you want any more children?
If not, why do you have them?
DO NOT KILL, DO NOT TAKE LIFE, BUT PREVENT
Safe, Harmless Information can be obtained of trained
Nurses at

46 AMBOY STREET
NEAR PITKIN AVE. — BROOKLYN.

Tell Your Friends and Neighbors.   All Mothers Welcome
A registration fee of 10 cents entitles any mother to this information.

מומערס!

זיים איהר פערמעגליך צו האבען א גרויסע פאמיליע?
ווילם איהר האבען נאך קינדער?
אויב נים, ווארום האם איהר זיי?
מערדערם נים, נעהמם נים קיין לעבען, נור פערהים זיך.
זיכערע, אונשעדליכע אויסקינפטען קענם איהר בעקומען פון ערפארענע נורסעס אין

46 אמבאי סטרים נעער פיטקין עוועניו **ברוקלין**

מאכם דאם בעקאנם צו אייערע פריינד און שכנות.   יעדער מוטער איז ווילקאמען
פיר 10 סענם איינשרייב־געלד זיינם איהר בערעכטיגם צו דיעזע אינפארמיישאן.

MADRI!

Potete permettervi il lusso d'avere altri bambini?
Ne volete ancora?
Se non ne volete piu', perche' continuate a metterli
al mondo?

NON UCCIDETE MA PREVENITE!

Informazioni sicure ed innocue saranno fornite da infermiere autorizzate a
46 AMBOY STREET   Near Pitkin Ave. Brooklyn
a cominciare dal 12 Ottobre.   Avvertite le vostre amiche e vicine.
Tutte le madri sono ben accette.   La tassa d'iscrizione di 10 cents da diritto
a qualunque madre di ricevere consigli ed informazioni gratis.

A 1916 handbill advertising the services of the Brownsville clinic in English, Yiddish, and Italian. As providing information about contraception violated New York law, Margaret Sanger and her two colleagues at the clinic were quickly arrested. (*Library of Congress*)

repression ("loathing, disgust, or indifference") and promote new ideals of sex, "sex as a psychic and spiritual avenue of expression." Finally, it would enable women to be full participants in life. With birth control, Sanger wrote, the "moral force of woman's nature will be unchained." Before World War I, Margaret Sanger had taken direct action to liberate working-class women from "enforced motherhood." In the 1920s, she espoused the new ideal of sexual emancipation, just as it reached a nationwide middle-class audience.

In the 1920s, the impact of contraception became visible. It legitimized female sexuality, as no tract or argument could do. It contributed to new sexual norms. Without contraception, the dictum that repression was unhealthy would hardly have been viable. It promoted premarital experimentation, although not to the extent that traditionalists feared. It enabled couples to marry earlier, since the economic burden of children could be postponed. Most decidedly, contraception transformed marital ideals. Separating sex from procreation, it released the companionate potential of marriage. Liberating women from "involuntary motherhood," it transformed marital sex from "obligation" to "communication." At the same time, contraception facilitated the new desire to merge marriage and career. It is fair to say that throughout the 1920s, contraception was at once the crux of the new morality, the opening wedge of "economic independence," and the most crucial change in women's lives.

The brunt of its impact of course fell on middle-class women. Contraception had long been a common middle-class goal, but in the 1920s it received mounting approval and acceptance. Widespread use of the pessary (or diaphragm), meanwhile, made it even more effective. Middle-class women, who favored this method, were able to obtain the device from private physicians, although doctors were legally required to look for "indications" and prescribe contraceptives only to "cure or prevent disease." But indications were broadened in private practice, just as birth-control advocates argued that they should be broadened in law. Meanwhile, illegal importation of contraceptive devices expanded, creating a lively underground traffic. At mid-decade, one researcher estimated that up to six out of ten American women used contraceptives. Surveys of middle-class women supported such claims. Blanchard and Manasses found that 80 percent of their sample of young women planned to use contraception when they married. Of the unmarried women interviewed by Katherine Bement Davis, 85 percent believed contraception should be practiced in marriage and less than 8 percent disapproved. About 75 percent of the married women in Davis's sample avowed belief in the principle of contraception, and almost all of this group practiced it.

Although contraception remained a middle-class perquisite, there were some ramifications beyond. In the prewar years, birth-control activists had sometimes expressed the fear that they would never convert the working class. After Sanger published *Women and the New Race* in 1920, she received thousands of letters from working-class women expressing resentment that contraception was a class privilege. "The rich don't seem to have so many children, why should the poor who can't afford to?" asked one correspondent. "I cannot see why it's always the poor that's got to suffer," wrote another. In the 1920s, contraceptive use was broadened, as much as a result of the World War I campaign against venereal disease as of the birth-control crusade. Working-class use, according to contemporaries, never reached the middle-class high. For instance, one research project in 1925 suggested that among young married women aged 25 to 29 with one child, about 80 percent of the well-off but only 36 percent of poorer women used contraception. In Middletown, the Lynds reported, contraceptive use presented "the appearance of a pyramid." "Relatively efficacious" methods were in almost universal use at the top, among the "business group," but then declined as one descended the social scale. Among African Americans, however, whose fertility fell rapidly between the late nineteenth century and World War II, extensive support for birth control prevailed. Black migrants to cities deliberately limited families, recent research suggests: blacks participated in the founding of birth-control clinics; the black press covered birth-control issues; and leaders such as W.E.B. Dubois linked woman's progress and independence to "motherhood at her own discretion."

Still, the birth-control crusade of the 1920s never became either a working-class movement or a feminist movement. Both wings of organized feminism, in fact, ignored the issue of contraception. Before the war, when Margaret Sanger had tried to drum up suffragist support, she was told to wait until the vote was won. But after 1920, there was no support in the feminist camp. In 1927, the NWP rejected a birth-control plank, and three years later the LWV refused to study the issue. There were of course supportive individuals. Physician Alice Hamilton, for instance, endorsed birth control as a cure for poverty. As she wrote in the *Birth Control Review* in 1925, the poor should have "the knowledge and power which has long been in possession of those who need it least." But leading feminists remained suspicious or ambivalent. When Sanger appealed to Carrie Chapman Catt in 1920 to support the cause, Catt's reply epitomized feminist equivocation. "Please be assured that I am no opponent even though I do not stand by your side," she wrote.

> In my judgment you claim too much as the result of one thing. Most reformers do that. Your reform is too narrow to appeal to me and too sordid. When the advocacy of contraception is combined with as strong a propaganda for continence (not to prevent conception but in the interest of common decency), it will find me a more willing sponsor. . . . There will come some gains even from the program you advocate— and some increase in immorality through safety. The gains will slightly overtop the losses however, so I am no enemy of you and yours.

Charlotte Perkins Gilman would later endorse birth control too, but in the 1920s she was a formidable critic. Gilman voiced her objections in the *Birth Control Review*, where she attacked Sanger's defense point by point. She denied that sex was the ultimate in spiritual communion or self-expression, that "indulgence" was necessarily an improvement over "repression," and that new prescriptions were better than old ones. Birth control, Gilman contended, would not improve marriage but transform it into "unromantic, dutiful submission to male indulgence." Finally, she pinpointed a double standard of expectations. "When men talk of sex, they mean only intercourse," Gilman wrote. "For women it means the whole process of reproduction, love, and mating." Both Gilman and Catt suspected that birth control would bolster an old form of male tyranny, forcing women into male-ordained sexual roles. Significantly, neither viewed contraception as an individual "right" or a form of "protection," but, rather, as a new factor in sexual politics.

Without a feminist base, a working-class base, or a left-wing base, the birth-control movement of the 1920s created its own constituency. Margaret Sanger had embarked on this effort during the war when she began to win the allegiance of well-off women. In the 1920s she turned to professional men. To alter both medical opinion and popular opinion, the American Birth Control League sought to win the endorsement of influential opinion-makers—especially physicians, but also academics, eugenicists, and other experts. A related thrust was the ABCL campaign for "doctors only" bills. For the first half of the decade, this policy was controversial. Former suffragist Mary Ware Dennett founded the Voluntary Parenthood League, which fought to repeal obscenity laws. The "doctors only" policy, it contended, meant "special privilege class legislation," as only the well-off had access to doctors. But by mid-decade, the Dennett faction had capsized and disbanded. "Doctors only" was now the thrust of the birth-control movement. The ABCL strove to broaden, not repeal, the obscenity laws so that physicians could legally prescribe contraception for healthy women. The physician became the key to contraceptive progress.

This policy of course affected birth-control clinics, which the ABCL now established. Here physicians took charge, as had not been the case at the Brownsville clinic in 1916. In the 1920s, clinic doctors could prescribe contraceptives either by stretching "indications" or by sending healthy patients to private physicians who would do so. Birth control was still a precarious business. Clinics appeared in 23 cities in 12 states, but many were short-lived. At the decade's end, some 30 to 50 were in operation, though their numbers would increase rapidly during the depression. Significantly, the clinics had more of a eugenicist goal than a feminist one. In 1919, Margaret Sanger argued that birth control would produce "more children from the fit, less from the unfit," and this theme became a dominant one. In the 1920s, Sanger stressed the movement's mission to eliminate the illiterate and degenerate. Birth control would not only protect women from pregnancy, it would also protect society from decay. "A high rate of fecundity," Sanger wrote in 1922, "is always associated with the direst poverty, mental defects, feeble-mindedness, and other transmissible traits." Eugenic arguments helped to win support from doctors, professionals, and well-off contributors. The last was vital, as clinics were expensive. They needed salaried doctors, salaried staff, medical backing, community backing, and operating funds. A new branch of philanthropy, the clinics were also a eugenic mission of social control.

While organizing the clinic movement, the ABCL turned much of its attention to physicians, seeking their support for contraception. Medical views of the 1920s were in transition. Doctors had already sanctioned a first wave of sexual revolution, or evolution, by rejecting continence as a moral and medical ideal. Support had shifted to moderate "indulgence." Sanction of birth control was a next logical step. Moreover, physicians were suspicious of "indiscriminate" distribution of contraceptives by outsiders, just as they were hostile to the encroachment of Sheppard-Towner outsiders on medical turf. By mid-decade, the medical profession had begun to shift ground; physicians preferred to control birth control themselves. "Conjugal hygiene" now became a part of the medical curriculum, a topic at professional conferences, and the province of an AMA committee. Margaret Sanger's pragmatic campaign for medical support was proving effective.

Though gaining influence in the AMA, the ABCL had far less impact on the law. In the 1920s, obscenity laws were neither broadened nor repealed. Contraception for the healthy remained precarious until federal court decisions of the 1930s. A 1930 decision opened the mails to contraceptive information and devices and in 1936, in *United States* v. *One Package*, a suit brought by physician and birth-controller Hannah Stone won for doctors the right to import contraceptive devices. In the 1920s, however, the law had not caught up to the new morality. This was evident in the case of birth-controller Mary Ware Dennett, still an opponent of the obscenity laws and a crusader for "free speech." Dennett advocated free dispersal of sex education material and contraceptive information without interference. But in 1929 she was arrested and convicted under the obscenity laws for mailing out copies of a published sex education essay, describing reproduction. Upholding her conviction, a federal court of appeals contended that Dennett's motive, an educational one, was irrelevant, as the information conveyed was "clearly indecent." Unlike Mary Ware Dennett, Margaret Sanger profited from whatever controversy she created. When her prize New York City birth-control clinic, run by physician Hannah Stone, was raided by the police in 1929, Sanger's courting of the medical profession paid off. Physicians now supported her cause. The birth-control movement of the 1920s succeeded not only in converting physicians but in converting itself—into a respectable middle-class reform movement.

Whereas organized feminism, diminished in strength and divided in policy, had difficulty adapting to the New Era, the birth-control movement had done so with finesse. The ABCL quickly became a centralized, professional organization. With its appeal to doctors, its eugenic thrust, and its aura of science and technology, it was able to survive and prosper in an apolitical, antireform, and increasingly antifeminist era. Although Sanger remained dominant, the birth-control movement was guided by professional men. In 1926, the ABCL reached a peak membership of 37,000 native-born, well-off supporters, mainly from the North and Midwest. Almost nine out of ten were women volunteers who devoted their time to the league's multifaceted campaigns. But professional men assumed the managerial, influential roles. Margaret Sanger, meanwhile, recruited among the prominent, speaking to women's clubs and social service groups, which she had once denounced as capitalist tools. While paid field workers organized local leagues and health professionals ran clinics, Sanger, using extensive private funds obtained through her second marriage, hired a physician to address medical societies. The one-time radicalism of the birth-control movement had been modernized, professionalized, and mainstreamed.

In the 1914 *Woman Rebel*, Margaret Sanger had declared that "Women cannot be on an equal footing with men until they have full and complete control over their reproductive function." In the 1920s, equal footing emerged as an ideal—for supporters of the ERA, for women striving for "economic independence," for women combining careers and marriage, and for "pals" and "partners" with romantic hopes of companionate relationships. New aspirations, from individualism to equal rights in the "sexual sphere," permeated the middle class. Throughout the decade, sexual rules were changing, but social, economic, and political rules remained much the same. Neither the vote nor contraception, alone or together, ensured equal footing. In the 1930s and 1940s, two national emergencies, depression and war, provided a new combination of liabilities and opportunities.

SUGGESTED READINGS AND SOURCES

Surveys of twentieth-century women's history discuss women's roles in the 1920s. See, for instance, William H. Chafe, *The Paradox of Change: American Women in the 20th Century* (New York, 1991), chs. 1–5; Lois W. Banner, *Women in Modern America: A Brief History*, 2d ed. (New York, 1984), ch. 4; Peter Gabriel Filene, *Him/Her/Self: Gender Identities in Modern America*, 3d ed. (Baltimore, Md., 1998), ch. 5; Sheila M. Rothman, *Woman's Proper Place: A History of Changing Ideals and Practices, 1870 to the Present* (New York, 1978), chs. 4 and 5; and

Rosalind Rosenberg, *Divided Lives: American Women in the Twentieth Century* (New York, 1992), ch. 3. Dorothy M. Brown surveys the decade in *Setting a Course: American Women in the 1920s* (Boston, 1987).

Feminism in the 1920s is examined in Nancy F. Cott, *The Grounding of Modern Feminism* (New Haven, Conn., 1987); William L. O'Neill, *Feminism in America*, rev. ed. (New Brunswick, N.J., 1989), chs. 7 and 8; Susan D. Becker, *The Origins of the Equal Rights Amendment: Feminism Between the Wars* (Westport, Conn., 1981); J. Stanley Lemons, *The Woman Citizen: Social Feminism in the 1920s*, 2d ed., (Charlottesville, Va., 1990); Lois Scharf and Joan M. Jensen, eds., *Decades of Discontent: The Women's Movement, 1920–1940* (Boston, 1987); Christine A. Lunardini, *From Equal Suffrage to Equal Rights* (New York, 1986); and Wendy Sarvasy, "Beyond the Difference versus Equality Policy Debate," *Signs* 17 (Winter 1992), 329–362. Elaine Showalter, ed., *These Modern Women: Autobiographical Essays from the 1920s* (Old Westbury, N.Y., 1978) contains the series of articles by feminists published in the *Nation* in 1926–1927. For the intersection of women's politics and constitutional law, see Joan G. Zimmerman, "The Jurisprudence of Equality: The Women's Minimum Wage, the First Equal Rights Amendment, and *Adkins v. Children's Hospital*, 1905–1923," *Journal of American History*, 78 (June 1991), 188–225, and Vivien Hart, *Bound By Our Constitution: Women, Workers, and the Minimum Wage* (Princeton, N.J., 1994). For the impact of the Sheppard-Towner Act, see Lynn Curry, *Gender, Health, and Progress in Illinois, 1900–1930* (Columbus, Ohio, 1999), ch. 5. An important article on the fate of feminism in the 1920s is Estelle B. Freedman, "Separatism as Strategy: Female Institution Building and American Feminism, 1870–1930," *Feminist Studies*, 5 (Fall 1979), 512–529. See also Freedman, "The New Woman: Changing Views of Women in the 1920s," *Journal of American History*, 61 (September 1974), 372–393.

The impact of woman suffrage is explored in Felice D. Gordon, *After Winning: The Legacy of the New Jersey Suffragists, 1920–1947* (New Brunswick, N.J., 1986); Kristi Andersen, *After Suffrage: Women in Partisan and Electoral Politics Before the New Deal* (Chicago, 1996); and Anna L. Harvey, *Votes Without Leverage: Women in American Electoral Politics, 1920–1970* (New York, 1998), chs. 4 and 5. See also Nancy F. Cott, "Across the Great Divide: Women in Politics Before and After 1920" in Louise A. Tilly and Patricia Gurin, eds., *Women, Politics, and Change* (New York, 1990), pp. 153–176. Elizabeth Israels Perry examines a unique political figure in *Belle Moscowitz: Feminine Politics and the Exercise of Power in the Age of Alfred E. Smith* (New York, 1987). For women's roles in politics, see Melanie Gustafson, Kristie Miller, and Elisabeth Israels Perry, eds., *We Have Come to Stay: American Women and Political Parties, 1880–1960* (Albuquerque, N.M., 1999), which includes essays on the 1920s. For the politics of peace, see Carrie A. Foster, *The Women and the Warriors: The U.S. section of the Women's International League for Peace and Freedom, 1915–1946* (Syracuse, N.Y., 1995), chs. 4–7. Joyce L. Kornbluh and Mary Frederickson present the workers' education movement in *Sisterhood and Solidarity: Workers' Education for Women, 1914–1984* (Philadelphia, 1984). For the Bryn Mawr summer school, see the film *The Women of Summer* (1984), by Suzanne Bauman and Rita Heller, in which former students tell how the school affected their lives.

Anne Firor Scott discusses the activism of southern women in "After Suffrage: Southern Women in the 1920s," *Journal of Southern History*, 30 (August 1964), 298–315, and Scott, *The Southern Lady: From Pedestal to Politics, 1830–1930* (Chicago, 1970), ch. 8. See also Marjorie Spruill Wheeler, *New Women of the New South: The Leaders of the Woman Suffrage Movement in the Southern States* (New York, 1993), ch. 6. For the women's interracial movement and the development of the ASWPL, see Jacqueline Dowd Hall, *Revolt Against Chivalry: Jessie Daniel*

Aymes and the Women's Campaign Against Lynching (New York, 1979). Kathleen M. Bree provides a counterpoint in *Women of the Klan: Racism and Gender in the 1920s* (Berkeley, Calif., 1991).

Maureen Weiner Greenwald discusses women's wartime employment in *Women, War, and Work: The Impact of World War I* (Westport, Conn., 1980). For women's roles in World War I, see also Susan Zeiger, *In Uncle Sam's Service: Women Workers with the American Expeditionary Force, 1917–1919* (Ithaca, N.Y., 1999), and Kathleen Kennedy, *Disloyal Mothers and Scurrilous Citizens: Women and Subversion during World War I* (Bloomington, Ind., 1999), which focuses on women of the left. For African American women, see William J. Breen, "Black Women and the Great War: Mobilization and Reform in the South," *Journal of Southern History*, 44 (1978), 421–440. For women in the labor force, see Leslie Woodcock Tentler, *Wage-Earning Women: Industrial Work and Family in the United States, 1900–1930* (New York, 1979); Alice Kessler-Harris, *Out to Work: A History of Wage-Earning Women in the United States* (New York, 1982), ch. 8; Claudia Goldin, *Understanding the Gender Gap: An Economic History of American Women* (New York, 1990); Julia Kirk Blackwelder, *Now Hiring: The Feminization of Work in the United States, 1900–1995* (College Station, Tex., 1997); and Kessler-Harris, *In Pursuit of Equity: Women, Men, and the Quest for Economic Citizenship in Twentieth Century America* (New York, 2001). For the federal Women's Bureau, see Judith Sealander, *As Minority Becomes Majority: Federal Reaction to the Phenomenon of Women in the Work Force, 1920–1963* (Westport, Conn., 1983). For the beauty industry, see Kathy Peiss, *Hope in a Jar: The Making of America's Beauty Culture* (New York, 1998); Julie A. Willett, *Permanent Waves: The Making of the American Beauty Shop* (New York, 2000); and Philip Scranton, ed., *Beauty and Business: Commerce, Gender, and Culture in Modern America* (New York, 2001). For the career of Madam C. J. Walker, see A'Lelia Bundles, *On Her Own Ground: The Life and Times of Madam C. J. Walker* (New York, 2001).

Frank Stricker assesses women's advances in the professions and business in "Cookbooks and Lawbooks: The Hidden History of Career Women in Twentieth-Century America," *Journal of Social History*, 10 (Fall 1976), 1–19. See also Barbara Harris, *Beyond Her Sphere: Women and the Professions in American History* (Westport, Conn., 1978), ch. 5. For the development of the social work profession, see Daniel J. Walkowitz, *Working With Class: Social Workers and the Politics of Middle-Class Identity* (Chapel Hill, N.C., 1999), and Karen W. Tice, *Tales of Wayward Girls and Immoral Women: Case Records and the Professionalization of Social Work* (Urbana, Ill., 1998). Studies of professional women include Joyce Antler, *Lucy Sprague Mitchell: The Making of a Modern Woman* (New Haven, Conn., 1987); Sara Alpern, *Freda Kirchwey: A Woman of "The Nation"* (Cambridge, Mass., 1987); Judith Schachter Modell, *Ruth Benedict: Patterns of a Life* (Philadelphia, 1983); Margaret M. Caffrey, *Ruth Benedict: Stranger in This Land* (Austin, Tex., 1989); Robert C. Bannister, *Jessie Bernard: The Making of a Feminist* (New Brunswick, N.J., 1991); Desley Deacon, *Elsie Clews Parsons: Inventing Modern Life* (Chicago, 1997); and Jane Howard, *Margaret Mead: A Life* (New York, 1984). For Mead's memoir, see *Blackberry Winter: My Earlier Years* (New York, 1972). "Margaret Mead: An Observer Observed," a film by Virginia Yans-McLaughlin, starts out with Mead's career in the 1920s and 1930s. Laurel D. Graham examines the contributions of a pioneer efficiency expert in "Domesticating Efficiency: Lillian Gilbreth's Scientific Management of Homemaking, 1924–1930," *Signs* 24 (Spring 1999), 633–675. Susan Ware explores the life of a culture heroine in *Still Missing: Amelia Earhart and the Search for Modern Feminism* (New York, 1993).

For the Harlem Renaissance, see Robert E. Hemenway, *Zora Neale Hurston: A Literary Biography* (Urbana, Ill., 1977); Thadious M. Davis, *Nella Larsen, Novelist of the Harlem*

Renaissance: A Woman's Life Unveiled (Baton Rouge, La., 1994); Cheryl A. Wall, *Women of the Harlem Renaissance* (Bloomington, Ind., 1995); Marcy Knopf, ed., *The Sleeper Wakes: Harlem Renaissance Stories By Women* (New Brunswick, N.J., 1993); and Ann Douglas, *Terrible Honesty: Mongrel Manhattan in the 1920s* (New York, 1995). Jacqueline Jones discusses outmigration from the South in the early twentieth century in *Labor of Love, Labor of Sorrow: Black Women, Work, and the Family From Slavery to the Present* (New York, 1985), ch. 5, and *The Dispossessed: America's Underclass from the Civil War to the Present* (New York, 1992), part 3. For activist black women, see Judith Weisenfeld, *African American Women and Christian Activism: New York's Black YWCA, 1905–1947* (Cambridge, Mass., 1997); Evelyn Brooks Higgenbotham, "Club-women and Electoral Politics in the 1920s," in Ann D. Gordon et al., eds., *African American Women and the Vote, 1837–1965* (Amherst, Mass., 1997), pp. 134–155; and Paula Giddings, *When and Where I Enter: The Impact of Black Women on Race and Sex in America* (New York, 1984), chs. 8–12. For African American women's roles as consumers in the 1920s, see Kathy Peiss, *Hope in a Jar*, cited previously, ch. 7. For the works of Ella Deloria, see *Dakota Texts* (New York, 1932); *Deer Women and Elk Men*, ed. Julian Rice (Albuquerque, N.M., 1992); and *Buffalo People*, ed. Julian Rice (Albuquerque, N.M., 1994). For Native American women in the 1920s, see Margaret D. Jacobs, *Engendered Encounters: Feminism and Pueblo Cultures, 1879–1934* (Lincoln, Neb., 1999), chs. 5 and 6.

For Mexican American women, see Rosalind Gonzalez, "Chicanas and Mexican Immigrant Families, 1920–1940: Women's Subordination and Family Exploitation," in Lois Scharf and Joan M. Jensen, eds., *Decades of Discontent: The Woman's Movement, 1920–1940* (Boston, 1987), pp. 59–84; George Sanchez, "'Go After the Women': Americanization and the Mexican Immigrant Woman, 1915–1929," in Ellen Carol Dubois and Vicki L. Ruiz, eds., *Unequal Sisters: A Multicultural Reader in U.S. Women's History* (New York, 1990), pp. 252–263; Sanchez, *Becoming American: Ethnicity, Culture, and Identity in Chicano Los Angeles, 1900–1945* (New York, 1993); and Vicki L. Ruiz, *From Out of the Shadows: Mexican American Women in Twentieth-Century American* (New York, 1998). Sarah Deutsch discusses changes in women's work roles in the Southwest in *No Separate Refuge: Culture, Class, and Gender on an Anglo Hispanic Frontier* (New York, 1987), ch. 6. Studies of race, ethnicity, and gender include Karen Anderson, *Changing Woman: A History of Racial Ethnic Women in Modern America* (New York, 1996) and Donna Gabaccia, *From the Other Side: Women, Gender, and Immigrant Life in the U.S., 1820–1990* (Bloomington, Ind., 1994).

For recent work on Jewish women's roles in the early twentieth century, see Jenna Weissman Joselit, *The Wonders of America: Reinventing Jewish Culture, 1880–1950* (New York, 1994), which discusses material culture, acculturation, and ethnicity; Joselit, *New York's Jewish Jews: The Orthodox Community in the Interwar Years* (Bloomington, Ind., 1990), especially ch. 4; Paula E. Hyman, *Gender and Assimilation in Modern Jewish History: The Roles and Representation of Women* (Seattle, 1995), ch. 3; Ruth Gay's insightful personal history, *An Unfinished Journey: Eastern European Jews Encounter America* (New York, 1996), especially ch. 10; and Joyce Antler, *The Journey Home: Jewish Women and the American Century* (New York, 1997). An excellent reference book is Paula E. Hyman and Deborah Dash Moore, eds., *Jewish Women in America: A Historical Encyclopedia*, 2 vols. (New York, 1998).

A valuable source for the 1920s is Paula S. Fass, *The Damned and the Beautiful: American Youth in the 1920s* (New York, 1977). Fass assesses changes in the family as well as the values, mores, and behavior of middle-class collegiate youth. The problem of finding the origin of changes in sexual behavior is suggested in Daniel Scott Smith, "The Dating of the American

Sexual Revolution," in Michael Gordon, ed., *The American Family in Social and Historical Perspective*, 2d ed. (New York, 1978), pp. 426–438. James P. McGovern offers evidence of a new morality in the prewar era in "The American Woman's Pre–World War I Freedom in Manners and Morals," *Journal of American History*, 55 (September 1968), 315–333. Kenneth A. Yellis considers aspects of the flapper in "Prosperity's Child: Some Thoughts on the Flapper," *American Quarterly*, 21 (Spring 1969), 44–64. For the dating system that flourished from the 1920s through the 1950s, see Beth L. Bailey, *From Front Porch to Back Seat: Courtship in Twentieth-Century America* (Baltimore, Md., 1988), and John L. Modell, *Into One's Own: From Youth to Adulthood in the United States, 1920–1975* (Berkeley, Calif., 1989). Lillian Faderman describes currents of sexual experimentation and repression in *Odd Girls and Twilight Lovers: A History of Lesbian Life in Twentieth-Century America* (New York, 1991), ch. 3. Joanne Meyerowitz discusses the emancipation of young middle-class wage earners in the 1920s in *Women Adrift: Independent Wage-Earners in Chicago, 1880–1930* (Chicago, 1988), ch. 6. For young women, see Sherrie A. Inness, *Delinquents and Debutantes: Twentieth Century American Girls' Cultures* (New York, 1998).

Rosalind Rosenberg examines the pioneer work of women social scientists as surveyors of sexual behavior in *Beyond Separate Spheres: Intellectual Roots of Modern Feminism* (New Haven, Conn., 1982), ch. 7. Mary P. Ryan suggests the impact of the movies in "The Projection of a New Womanhood: The Movie Moderns in the 1920s," in Jean E. Friedman and William G. Shade, eds., *Our American Sisters: Women in American Life and Thought*, 2d ed. (Boston, 1976), pp. 366–383; see also Lary May, *Screening Out the Past: The Birth of Mass Culture and the Motion Picture Industry* (Chicago, 1980); Cari Beauchamp, *Without Lying Down: Frances Marion and the Powerful Women of Early Hollywood* (Berkeley, Calif., 1997); and Linda Mizejewski, *Ziegfeld Girl: Image and Icon in Culture and Cinema* (Durham, N.C., 1999). For women entertainers through the 1920s, see Susan A. Glenn, *Female Spectacle: The Theatrical Roots of Modern Feminism* (Cambridge, Mass., 2000). For beauty contests, see Lois W. Banner, *American Beauty* (New York, 1983), ch. 12. Virginia Scharff explores technology's impact in *Taking the Wheel: Women and the Coming of the Motor Age* (New York, 1991). Jennifer Scanlon examines magazine readers, women's fiction, and women advertising executives of the 1920s in *Inarticulate Longings: The Ladies' Home Journal, Gender, and the Promises of Consumer Culture* (New York, 1995). For the impact of Freudianism and its clash with feminism, see Mary Jo Buhle, *Feminism and its Discontents: A Century of Struggle with Psychoanalysis* (Cambridge, Mass., 1998).

For the birth-control movement, see Ellen Chesler, *Woman of Valor: Margaret Sanger and the Birth Control Movement in America* (New York, 1992); Linda Gordon, *Woman's Body, Woman's Right: A Social History of Birth Control in America* (New York, 1976), chs. 9 and 10; David M. Kennedy, *Birth Control in America: The Career of Margaret Sanger* (New Haven, Conn., 1970); James Reed, *From Private Vice to Public Virtue: The Birth Control Movement and American Society Since 1930* (New York, 1977); Carole R. McCann, *Birth Control Politics in the United States, 1916–1945* (Ithaca, N.Y., 1994); Joan M. Jensen, "The Evolution of Margaret Sanger's 'Family Limitation' Pamphlet, 1914–1921," *Signs* 6 (Spring 1981), 548–557; and Alex Baskin, ed., *The Woman Rebel* (New York, 1976). Margaret Sanger's relationship with Havelock Ellis is discussed in Phyllis Grosskurth, *Havelock Ellis: A Biography* (New York, 1980). Sources on Sanger from the Library of Congress are available in microfilm in "The Papers of Margaret Sanger" (Scholarly Resources). For sources in the Smith College archive, see "The Margaret Sanger Papers: The Smith Collection," ed. Esther Katz (University Publications of America). For Sanger's competitor in birth control politics, see Constance M. Chen, *The Sex Side of Life: Mary Ware Dennett's Pioneering Battle for Birth Control and Sex Education* (New York, 1996), and, on microfilm, "The Papers of Mary Ware Dennett and the Voluntary Parenthood League" (University Publications of America). For African Americans and birth control, see Jessie M. Rodrique, "The Black Community and the Birth Control Movement," in Judith Walzer Leavitt, ed., *Women and Health in America: Historical Readings* (Madison, Wisc., 1999), pp. 293–305. For the eugenics movement, see Daniel Kevles, *In the Name of Eugenics: Genetics and the Uses of Human Heredity* (New York, 1985). Judith Walzer Leavitt discusses changes in childbirth practices in the 1920s in *Brought to Bed: Childbearing in America, 1750–1950* (New York, 1986), ch. 10. For the Greenwich Villagers of the 1910s and 1920s, see June Sochen, *The New Woman in Greenwich Village, 1910–1920* (New York, 1972); Caroline F. Ware's book of 1935, *Greenwich Village, 1920–1930*, ed. Deborah Dash Moore (Berkeley, Calif., 1994); and Christine Stansell, *American Moderns: Bohemian New York and the Creation of a New Century* (New York, 2000).

Women of the 1920s, a self-conscious decade, provide an abundance of commentary. For feminism, see Suzanne LaFollette, *Concerning Women* (New York, 1926); Lorine Pruette, *Women and Leisure: A Study of Social Waste* (New York, 1924); Pruette, *Why Women Fail* (New York, 1931); Charlotte Perkins Gilman, "The New Generation of Women," *Current History*, 18 (August 1923), 735–736; Gilman, "Van Guard, Rear-Guard, and Mud-Guard," *Century Magazine*, 104 (1922), 349–350; and Nancy F. Cott, ed., *A Woman Making History: Mary Ritter Beard Through Her Letters* (New Haven, Conn., 1991). Of special interest is Dorothy Dunbar Bromley, "Feminist—New Style," *Harper's*, 155 (October 1927), 552–560. Women's status is examined in Elizabeth Kemper Adams, *Women Professional Workers* (New York, 1921); Sophonisba P. Breckinridge, *Women in the Twentieth Century: A Study of Their Political, Social, and Economic Activities* (New York, 1933); and *Annals of the American Academy of Political and Social Science*, 142 (May 1929), on "Women in the Modern World."

A classic of the decade is Helen Merrill Lynd and Robert S. Lynd, *Middletown: A Study of Contemporary American Culture* (New York, 1929). See also the textbook by Ernest R. Groves and William F. Ogburn, *American Marriage and Family Relationships* (New York, 1928). For the new morality, see V. F. Calverton, *The Bankruptcy of Marriage* (New York, 1928); Freda Kirchwey, ed., *Our Changing Morality* (New York, 1930); Phyllis Blanchard and Carolyn Manasses, *New Girls for Old* (New York, 1930); Floyd Dell, *Love in the Machine Age: A Psychological Study of the Transition from Patriarchal Society* (New York, 1930); Ben Lindsey and Wainright Evans, *The Revolt of Modern Youth* (New York, 1925); Lindsey and Evans, *The Companionate Marriage* (New York, 1927); and Katherine Bement Davis's 1918 survey, *The Sex Life of Twenty-Two Hundred Women* (New York, 1929). Two popular contemporary novels are Warner Fabian, *Flaming Youth* (New York, 1923), and Percy Marks, *The Plastic Age* (New York, 1924). The classic novel about a woman's experience in small-town America is Sinclair Lewis, *Main Street* (New York, 1920). See also Dorothy Parker's short stories of the 1920s and 1930s, available in *The Collected Dorothy Parker* (New York, 1973), and Marion Meade's biography, *Dorothy Parker: What Fresh Hell Is This?* (New York, 1988). For magazine fiction of the 1920s, see Maureen Honey, ed., *Breaking the Ties That Bind: Popular Stories of the New Woman* (Norman, Okla., 1992). Martha Banta discusses the aesthetic antecedents of the 1920s "New Woman," in *Imaging American Women: Ideas and Ideals in Cultural History* (New York, 1987), ch. 1.

🌐 For quizzes and additional resources related to American women's history, visit the book's Website at *www.mhhe.com/americanwomen*.

CHAPTER NINE
Emergencies: The 1930s and 1940s

*I*N THE 1930s and 1940s, national events reshaped women's history. The Great Depression and World War II were disruptive "emergencies" that changed women's roles, at home, at work, and in public life.

The emergencies affected, first, women's participation in the labor force. In both the 1930s and the 1940s, women were advised to adapt their roles to suit the nation's economic needs. When depression struck, they were urged to remain at home and leave what jobs there were for male "breadwinners." In World War II, they were exhorted to assume paid jobs, especially in war industry, to relieve the nation's manpower shortage. In both emergencies, however, women's participation in the work force rose, slowly during the 1930s and rapidly during World War II. Both emergencies, moreover, drew married women into the labor market. The new opportunities provided by war were temporary; at demobilization, women's jobs in the millions were lost. But by the end of the 1940s, when the female segment of the labor force began again to expand, its composition had changed. Unlike wartime welders and riveters, the average new worker in the postwar era was likely to enter a traditional "woman's field," not heavy industry. But like the war worker, and indeed like many new wage earners of the 1930s, she was apt to be married and middle-aged. She was also more likely to be middle class than the average working woman before the depression. The emergencies set the stage for the contemporary female labor force.

The long-range change in women's work patterns was not connected to a national shift in ideas about woman's role in society. On the contrary, the emergencies confirmed a shared conviction that in the best of times as in the worst of times woman's place was in the home. Two decades of crises only underlined a desire for stable, secure American families, with paychecked fathers and homebound mothers. Throughout the 1930s and 1940s, domestic ideals showed resilience. Vindicated in depression and retained through the war, they emerged stronger than ever in the postwar era. World War II, which disrupted family life, was a turning point. By the end of the 1940s, a vigorous cult of domesticity had gained ground. The emergencies of the 1930s and 1940s did not pave a path to sexual equality, at least ideologically. Rather, they laid the groundwork for a conservative division of gender roles, an apparent retreat from public affairs, and a pronounced antifeminist mood.

Feminist decline was another theme of the 1930s and 1940s. In the 1920s, the woman's movement had been beset by strains, internal and external, but full of fight as it reorganized for the postsuffrage era. The sequence of emergencies, however, did not provide a favorable climate. Egalitarian hopes were an early casualty. New aspirations of the expansive 1920s, for economic independence and individualism, were quenched by depression, which made them, quite quickly, irrelevant luxuries. The minority National Woman's party, committed to egalitarian goals, soon assumed a marginal role. "Social feminism," a larger and more hardy specimen, faded away gradually. In the early New Deal, veterans of progressive reform affected federal policy. But women's activism in politics and government in the New Deal was more a last gasp of progressive energy than an omen of future trends.

By the late 1930s, all varieties of postsuffrage feminism declined and world war, once again, was a turning point. By the end of World War II, the social reform wing of the woman's movement was almost gone. Its functions had been supplanted by New Deal welfare policies, labor laws, and the emergence of a strong labor movement. The government social worker had long since replaced the settlement-house reformer. Large surviving groups such as the General Federation of Women's Clubs, now apolitical, and the civic-minded League of Women Voters had melted into the suburban scenery. Although the battle over an Equal Rights Amendment continued into the early 1950s, feminism was now a fading force. By the postwar era, the energetic world of women's politics no longer existed. A major blow came at the outset, when the Great Depression began.

DEPRESSION FAMILIES

"I have watched fear grip the people in our neighborhood around Hull-House," Jane Addams wrote in 1931, "men and women who have seen their small margin of savings disappear; heads of families who see and anticipate hunger for their children before it occurs. That clutch of cold fear is one of the most hideous aspects." In the 1930s, the clutch of cold fear transformed family life, not only for the families of the 25 percent of workers who were unemployed by 1933, such as West Virginia miners, but also for those middle-class families whose incomes were so drastically reduced that they fell from a state of relative security into a limbo of uncertainty and panic. For the family as for the economy, the depression interrupted the rapid movement toward modernity of the 1920s, with its upwardly mobile, individualistic, and consumerist thrust. The retreat from modernity affected many aspects of American life. Migration to cities, for instance, halted or even reversed itself, as urban areas became pits of unemployment rather than centers of opportunity. For women, the depression brought a sudden end to the aspirations of the 1920s. Sometimes it reinforced traditional roles. More often it demanded new emergency roles, appropriate to the dire situation.

Ideologically, the depression gave new currency to the dogma that woman's place was at home, that women who worked did so mainly for "pin money," and that jobs should be reserved for male "breadwinners." In 1930, when Frances Perkins, the future secretary of labor, denounced the "pin-money worker" as a "menace to society, a selfish and short-sighted creature who ought to be ashamed of herself," she expressed a widely held view. The wage-earning wife, it appeared, took away a man's salary and, implicitly, deprived another family of income. As unemployment rose and family income sank, government, business, labor, and public opinion reinforced the need to exclude married women from the work force.

Federal law, from 1932 to 1937, prohibited more than one family member from working in the federal civil service. Although women's groups, including both the LWV and especially the NWP, mobilized to repeal Section 213 of the National Economy Act, they had no success. Women were three-quarters of those federal workers forced to resign. States, too, rejected married women from government posts, and local governments instituted similar policies. In half the states, bills arose to bar the hiring of married women in *any* job, but a women's lobby led by the LWV defeated these measures. Still, bias against wives was extensive. In 1931, three out of four school boards surveyed by the National Educational Association would not hire married women teachers, and most dismissed women teachers who married. Private businesses discouraged women from competing with men for jobs, while women's colleges urged their graduates to avoid paid work. Organized labor joined the campaign as well. Married women workers with employed husbands, said the executive council of the AFL, "should be discriminated against in the hiring of employees."

Public opinion reinforced antipathy to the working wife, and in the 1930s public opinion became a tangible entity; the public opinion poll was the latest contribution to social science. In 1936, when the Gallup poll asked whether wives should work if their husbands had jobs, a resounding 82 percent of all respondents (and 75 percent of women respondents) said no. The same year, *Fortune* revealed that 85 percent of male readers and 79 percent of female readers thought that *no* wife should work outside the home; in 1937, more than half of all Gallup respondents (and 42 percent of female respondents) agreed. In 1938, the *Ladies' Home Journal* reported that although 75 percent of its readers believed that husbands and wives should make decisions together, 90 percent thought that the wife should give up work if the husband wished her to remain at home. Despite the consistent differential between male and female views, the weight of the polls opposed the working wife.

But public animosity to married women wage earners clashed with family need. During the depression the proportion of married women in the work force rose. Indeed, most new workers were married women—precisely those who were urged to remain at home. (The proportion of single women who worked declined.) The wife whose wages went to family support had little link with those hopes for individualism and economic independence that had been voiced in the expansive 1920s. "Feminists—new style" of the 1930s who sought to merge marriage and career did not publicize their endeavors; aspiration had gone out of vogue. Now wage work could be defended only as a means of family sustenance. Historian Lois Scharf contends that the depression caused "an erosion of feminist rhetoric and thought," one that would long outlive the 1930s. This erosion damaged the credentials of the NWP, which steadfastly championed women's right to work outside the home. If the 1920s had proved unsympathetic to "equal rights," Scharf points out, the 1930s provided an even more hostile climate.

While many married women assumed new roles as wage earners, often in temporary or part-time work, most retained traditional roles as homemakers. But their contributions to the household economy became more significant: home management assumed new importance as family resources dwindled. The thrifty, inventive housekeeper—one who could "make ends a meet"—was crucial to family survival. As household budgets fell, women began to sew their own clothes and can their own food, reversing the trend of the 1920s toward ever more consumer goods. Housewives also took in paid work, such as laundry, boarders, or dressmaking, and started small household businesses—whether running kitchen beauty parlors or selling baked goods or clothes items. "In the South, if you were a lady, you sewed," recalled a Chicago widow, southern-born and once well-off, who had gone into the negligee business with a friend.

Home industry was not the only retreat to traditionalism. The family of the 1930s often expanded to include marginal members, old or young, who sometimes doubled up with another generation. New York public health nurses sometimes found 12 people in three rooms. At the bottom of the depression, in fact, family life seemed to disintegrate. While divorce declined, due to the expense, desertion increased and marriage was postponed. After 1929, the marriage rate plunged, and it did not start to rise again until 1934. "Do you realize how many people in my generation are not married?" a Chicago educator asked Studs Terkel in *Hard Times*, his oral history of the depression. "There were young men around when we were young but they were all supporting mothers." Available men were likely to disappear, as her own prospect did when he lost his job: "It hit him like a ton of bricks and he just vanished."

While the marriage rate took a sudden fall, the birthrate continued its long-term decline. Births per 1,000 women of child-bearing age plunged from 97.4 to 75.7 in the nadir of 1933. "The drop has been precipitous," *Harper's* announced in 1935. Overall, the birthrate fell less in the 1930s than it had in the 1920s. Still, contraception gained new popularity, especially among men. "Before the depression I never gave a thought to birth control," one father told sociologist Mirra Komarovsky. "Had we been able to foresee the depression, we would have felt differently about it." Birth-control clinics, which had dwindled in number by 1929, suddenly boomed. In 1931, 85 clinics gave out advice to alleviate "mental and physical suffering." Birth-control clinics also provided counseling for married and engaged couples, and the *Birth Control Review* shifted its stress from eugenic arguments to "marriage and family guidance." Birth-control proponents, meanwhile, attempted to incorporate contraception into New Deal programs. By the end of the decade, the birth-control movement had won major victories. Federal court decisions of 1930 and 1936 opened the mails to contraceptive information and devices and enabled physicians to import such devices. Doctors could now make contraception available except where prohibited by state law, as in Massachusetts and Connecticut.

While the marriage rate fell and the birthrate dropped, the depression family withdrew into itself, as reported by the small army of sociologists that examined it. Study after study showed that husbands and wives tended to drop social friendships and outside connections because of fear of snubs, suspicion of others, or inability to meet the expenses of socializing. Family members now relied on one another for company. "The unemployed man and his wife have no social life," Mirra

Komarovsky wrote in 1934, and for months at a time the family had no social contacts with outsiders. "The only visitors that they have are their married children with their families." In some cases, sexual withdrawal accompanied social withdrawal, as in Komarovsky's sample of depression-stricken lower-middle-class families, where sexual activity often came to a halt. In only one of 59 cases was increased activity reported. When a husband proved unable to provide for the family, sociologist Eli Ginzburg observed, "his wife frequently lost her balance." Such lack of balance was exemplified by Mrs. Wolfe, who revealed "a changed attitude toward intercourse." When her husband supported her, "she supposed it was his right to have sexual relations and she therefore acquiesced," Ginzburg wrote. "Now she avoids it. She has limited sexual relations to once a week and even tried to get out of this. . . . She saw no reason [to use] contraception just to give her husband pleasure."

If Mrs. Wolfe appeared unbalanced, or at least a poor sport, this was because woman's traditional role was to provide psychological sustenance, especially for men who were humiliated by loss of work. As the obligation of "breadwinner" fell on men, they became desperate when jobs vanished. "Like searing irons, the degradation, the sheer terror and panic which loss of job brings, the deprivation and the bitterness have eaten into men's souls," an officer of a District of Columbia welfare agency wrote in 1931. In some cases women shared this despair; they withdrew from life and retreated into "dreary little worlds of their own," psychologist Lorine Pruette reported in 1934. More often, she found, they "triumphed over their difficulties." Protected by gender roles, women did not suffer the same humiliation from loss of work that afflicted men. Married women, moreover, who were less likely to have jobs to lose, continued in their usual routines and often took on expanded responsibilities. They also assumed increased authority, while husbands' wages and power declined. "When Mr. Raparka lost his job in the fall of 1933, he dominated the family," Wight Bakke observed in *Citizens Without Work*. "Two years later it was Mrs. Raparka who was the center of authority."

Not all households studied were transformed by the depression. In the mid-1930s, sociologist Margaret Hagood traveled through the Southeast, interviewing the wives of tenant farmers, whose lives remained much the same. Caring for large families, doing field work, farm work, and housework, in dire circumstances, poor rural women retained traditional and subordinate roles. But most researchers focused attention not on the families of migrant workers nor on families that had always been poor but rather on middle-class families that had suffered a sudden decline in status. In such families, wives often filled a power vacuum. The Burtons, described in a University of Michigan study, were a good example. The father, once a successful wholesale merchant in Saginaw, lost his business and took a salesman's job in Ann Arbor. This meant a loss of community ties and far lower pay. His income dropped from $10,000 to $3,000 a year. After the move, Mr. Burton lost energy, became nervous, and suffered from strain. But Mrs. Burton, once a conventional housewife whose outside affiliations extended only to the wives of her husband's associates and a church auxiliary, catapulted into the ascendancy. In Ann Arbor, she earned most of the family's income by taking in boarders. Although she never made any new outside connections, she quickly became, in the case analyst's words, "the family heroine."

While sociologists of the 1930s focused on urban families, photographer
Dorothea Lange, who worked for the Farm Security Administration,
documented the Great Depression's impact on rural Americans. In the years
1936–1938, working with sociologist Margaret Hagood, she traveled through
the South and the Dust Bowl, where bad weather and crop failures had forced
farmers off the land. This picture of a migrant mother and her children was
taken on a Texas roadside in 1936. *(Dorothea Lange, Library of Congress)*

She remains healthy, ambitious, vivacious, while doing all the housework for her own
family and looking after the rooms for eight students, as well as doing their washing
and ironing. . . . She has given up all her former activities. She finds her life completely within the home. Now and then she wishes for her old life but is on the whole
contented.

Families that were well-adjusted, like the Burtons, sociologists stressed, were
able to survive the depression in better shape than those that were not. In fact, in less
well-integrated families, children rather than mothers moved into control, an even

more drastic form of role reversal. This was the case with the Riley family in the Michigan study. Mr. Riley, a never-too-successful lawyer but a big spender, neglected his practice and slid swiftly downhill in the early 1930s, taking to the local poolroom where he played cards with "riff-raff" and became very nervous. His wife cared little about his mental decline or financial problems. But 24-year-old Winifred, a musical performer, took charge. "As her father's income went steadily down, that of his daughter went steadily up, so that she became the chief breadwinner," the case analyst reported. "Winifred became a family leader."

Young people such as Winifred often resented being put into "breadwinner" positions, according to *The Survey*, a publication for social workers, in 1935. Once the "emergency" became a "permanency," employed offspring, especially working teenagers, protested against "the hardships of supporting unemployed fathers, brothers, sisters, and others living in the home." Depression role reversals, whether parent/child or husband/wife, came to be associated with negative causes—poverty, misfortune, and downward mobility. Underlining the depression's impact, such role reversals only enhanced a desire for the traditional family of more prosperous times, where authority rested with the male "breadwinner." Still, once crisis struck, women's significance at home seemed to increase (relative to that of men), transforming even inconspicuous housewives like Mrs. Burton into "heroines." Ironically, women sometimes fared better than men as wage earners as well. For despite injunctions to remain at home, the depression actually had a dual message for women workers.

WORKING WOMEN

Contradictory pressures affected women in the 1930s: Public attitudes urged them not to work for pay, but economic circumstances both spurred wage labor and in some instances made jobs available. Not surprisingly, public policy and public opinion took a toll on female employment. Women professionals were especially hard hit. By the end of the 1930s, the proportion of women in professional work had dropped, as men sought jobs in such fields as social work and education. The teaching force, which had been 85 percent female in 1920, was only 78 percent female in 1940. Other women lost jobs in business, as bookkeepers and insurance agents, for instance, and descended in the occupational scale. By 1938, one-fifth of the female work force was unemployed. But wage-earning women were still less likely than men to be forced out of the work force entirely. Throughout the depression, women's overall participation in the labor force increased, to a higher level than ever before. Women entered the labor force at twice the rate of men, the number of women workers rose 25 percent, and the proportion of married women who worked rose as well. In 1930, only 29 percent of women wage earners were married, but in 1940, 35 percent. Even in some professions, the numbers of women grew.

The increase of women in the work force was not due solely to a rise in "need"—though as the Women's Bureau claimed in a stream of publications, women *did* work out of need and not for "pin money." Rather, the depression's impact on women workers was minimized because sexual segregation in the labor force provided some insulation. Women workers were concentrated in "women's fields," such as sales, clerical, and service occupations, and these were less hard hit than the areas of heavy industry—autos, steel, construction—where few women held jobs. In some states, at the depths of the depression, male unemployment was as much as four times as great as female unemployment. Similarly, the sectors that employed the most women tended to recover most rapidly. Moreover, government measures to revive the economy created more women's jobs, especially in clerical and sales work.

Finally, segregated occupational patterns held fast. Beyond some encroachment into "women's professions," men did not seek "women's work." In theory, as sociologist Ruth Milkman points out, women were a reserve labor force to be pushed out of the labor market when times were bad. In practice, however, they were protected to an extent by division of labor within the work force. In addition, while all wages fell, women's wages actually rose proportionally to 63 percent of men's wages. (Ordinarily, any increase of women workers causes this percentage to drop.) In many ways, therefore, women wage earners were relative beneficiaries of economic crisis, or at least some of their disadvantages became assets. A major beneficiary was the woman worker in industry, whose status at the outset was desperate.

The end of European immigration in the 1920s should have gradually expanded opportunities for women in industry, but the onset of depression wiped out or at least postponed any hope of such expansion. By the early 1930s, the status of the woman industrial worker had reached a nadir. If still employed, she was likely to work for reduced pay, which sometimes dropped yet lower. Southern textile workers, for instance, earned less than five cents an hour, and in some garment shops, the Massachusetts Consumers' League reported, women were hired as "apprentices" for no pay only to be fired when their "apprenticeship" ended. Like all factory labor, a woman worker faced layoffs or speed-ups as companies reduced production or cut back on costs, but she was less likely to be organized, except in a company union. The mid-1930s, however, brought the beginnings of change. New Deal policies were prolabor, prounion, and geared toward protection. And women workers, worst off to begin with, had the most to gain.

From the outset, the Roosevelt administration sought labor support and strove to improve the worker's status, especially through wage and hour regulation, a cause for which women reformers had campaigned in the 1920s. First, the National Industrial Recovery Act (1933) gave the government the power to establish industrywide codes that included wage and hour provisions. (The Supreme Court had rejected a federal minimum wage law in 1923 and continued to do so until 1937, when it reversed itself.) After the Court invalidated the NIRA in 1935, Congress passed the Fair Labor Standards Act of 1938, which established maximum hours and minimum wages, starting at 25 cents an hour, in industries involved in interstate commerce. "Everyone claimed credit for it," said Labor Secretary Frances Perkins, though in her view credit belonged to FDR and herself. The FLSA also helped to improve sweatshop working conditions, provided minimum wages for women doing piecework at home, and, like the defunct National Recovery Administration codes, prohibited child labor in factories. (The child labor amendment never made any progress.) During the New Deal, in short, the federal government began to fulfill both women reformers' goals and those endorsed by the NWP in the 1920s—extending "protection" to both male and female workers.

This protection was not always extended in an egalitarian way. Recovery, not equality, was the major New Deal aim. Just as federal work-relief programs either excluded women, as in the case of the Civilian Conservation Corps, or gave men preference and paid them more, as in the case of CWA and the Public Works Administration, labor regulations too reflected sexual preference. While work relief programs focused on heads of household, usually men, labor regulations excluded women in other ways. The NRA codes covered only certain industries, and excluded some with large proportions of women workers, like the textile industry. Of the short-lived codes, 75 percent included provisions for equal pay to women workers, which Mary Anderson, head of the Women's Bureau, claimed as a victory of her agency. But the 25 percent that set lower minimum wages for women than for men covered industries with large proportions of women workers, such as cloakmaking, electronics, and commercial laundries. Ten women's organizations, led by the WTUL and NCL, protested the discriminatory aspects of the NRA codes but to no avail. The Fair Labor Standards Act was more effective than the poorly enforced NRA codes and did affect most women in factory work, although clearly it had no impact on other large categories of women wage earners, such as those in sales, service, domestic, or agricultural work.

Whenever protection was provided and enforced in laws or codes, however, women tended to benefit more than men because they were concentrated in unorganized industries and in the lowest paid work. Even the minimum wage often meant a hefty salary hike for women workers, though not enough to make men seek their jobs. New Deal laws offered other benefits, too. Owners of some types of factories, such as cigar factories, were able to receive government assistance for technological improvements to transform their plants to assembly-line production, which created more low-paid work for women (indeed, this was the very sort of transformation skilled craftsmen had always feared). Finally, in a major shift from policies of the 1920s, the New Deal spurred the formation of labor unions, which benefited all industrial workers.

Depression had weakened the union movement, and women's union membership had dropped, but an upswing began in 1933. Section 7A of the NIRA protected the right of unions to organize and required employers to bargain with union representatives. As soon as the law went into effect, union membership rose. The ILGWU, which had hit a low point, increased its size four times over in 1934 alone. After the Supreme Court invalidated the NIRA, the National Labor Relations Act of 1935 again protected the right of labor to organize and, because it included provisions for enforcement and barred company unions, served as an even more effective spur to union growth. The most important advance for the woman worker, usually neither in skilled crafts nor organized, was the industrial union. These began to form in 1935, first under the industrial union committee of the AFL and then, after 1937, under the new Congress of Industrial Organizations. Although the main focus of the CIO in the late 1930s was in heavy industry with predominantly male employees—such as mining, steel, and automobiles—it also moved into factories where many women worked, such as northern textile plants, and the West Coast canning industry. Between 1930 and 1940, women's union membership tripled, reaching 800,000 by the end of the decade.

Like the NRA codes and the FLSA, the union movement of the late 1930s had no impact on the majority of women in the labor force who were outside of factory work. "In the thirties, there was no union," a former salesclerk told interviewer Jeane Westin. "Any woman lucky enough to have a job better not complain about conditions." Nor did the union movement ensure equality to the woman industrial worker. In industries where the majority of workers were men, unions approved contracts with unequal pay for women and men doing the same jobs and also created separate seniority lists for women, which perpetuated inequality in union ranks. Women were poorly represented in union leadership, for reasons that had long been recognized by the WTUL. "Women had an awfully tough time in the union because the men brought their prejudices there," remembered Stella Nowicki, an organizer in the Chicago meat-packing plants in the 1930s and also a "colonizer" for the Communist party, which sent its emissaries into the shops to organize. "The fellows couldn't believe that women in the union were there for the union's sake," Nowicki recalled in Staughton and Alice Lynd's oral history, *Rank and File:*

> The women felt the union was a man's thing because once they got through the day's work they had to take care of their one to fifteen children and the meals and the house and all the rest. . . . The union didn't encourage women to come to meetings. They didn't actually want to take up the problems that women had. . . . The union had so many things to work for—the shorter work day, improved conditions—so many things that they couldn't worry about these things in relation to women.

The great surge in women's organization and CIO growth was yet to come, during World War II, when women constituted more than a third of the work force and when the meat-packing industry and others were at last successfully organized. Still, the 1930s marked the start of a new era for the woman factory worker. At the same time, the major gains of the New Deal era—such as minimum wage laws, maximum hour laws, child labor prohibitions, and the spurt of unionization—also marked the beginning of the end of the women's movement to protect women workers. In the 1930s, the WTUL was active but waning. Its budget shrank and the last of its Washington lobbyists resigned. In World War II, when the numbers of women in unions shot upward, the WTUL began to fold its wings, and it finally dissolved in 1950. The National Consumer's League, similarly active in the 1930s, hung on until around 1970.

While the women's movement role in labor organization faded, that of the Communist party grew. Party membership doubled in the early 1930s and continued to grow; in 1933, one out of every six members was a woman and by the end of the decade, more than one out of three. Although Communist women never organized autonomously, as socialist women had before World War I, and relatively few assumed key roles on party committees, mere involvement held attraction. For some women on the left, communism seemed to exert the same appeal that feminism had a generation earlier. The party, moreover, made efforts to engage women members. Through a staffed women's commission, women's publications, and a *Daily Worker* column, it addressed "women's issues." It also provided political space for long-time radicals like Elizabeth Gurley Flynn, once Margaret Sanger's colleague in the IWW, or Ella Reeve Bloor, another veteran of prewar socialism, labor organization, and the birth-control crusade. Throughout the decade, women members were active in party campaigns, whether sit-ins, protest marches, industrial organizing, or mobilizing the relatives of male workers, as at the Flint, Michigan, Auto Strike of 1937.

The woman factory worker of the 1930s was typically white and native-born, or of European extraction. Mexican American women, who had recently found work in western food-processing plants and urban garment industries, saw their options shrink. CIO organizing in the West Coast canning industry, where many young Mexican American women worked, brought benefits. Entering the union was "like joining a great big family," one worker recalled. "I loved it." More often, when depression struck, industrial work meant piecework at home at the lowest pay. Encouraged to migrate during prosperous times, low-wage Mexican labor was now urged to return to Mexico. Under a federal "repatriation" policy, some returned voluntarily and others were coerced. By the end of the 1930s, more than 400,000 Mexican Americans, many of them U.S. citizens, had left the country. The combination of depression and repatriation adversely affected Mexican American women, as historian Karen Anderson explains. In some instances, as in San Antonio, women lost their low-paid jobs when FLSA minimum wage requirements closed down industries. In other instances, the threat of expulsion kept women from applying for welfare benefits, which at best were minimally available. "A Mexican family of the low class . . . in any event live on about half what would an American family," an Arizona relief official declared. Finally, repatriation removed a disproportionate number of men of wage-earning age, which skewed sex ratios, disrupted family life, and increased women's problems of self-support. By the end of the 1930s, among Mexican Americans in their thirties, there were 87.7 men to every 100 women. According to the census a decade later, 38 percent of Mexican American women over 14 were unmarried.

For Native American women, the depression years brought increased contact with mainstream America through schools, jobs, the market, and government agencies. The Indian Organization Act of 1934 sliced federal expenses; it ended assimilationist policies, cut back boarding schools, stopped the division of Native American lands into individual plots, and established tribal governments, run by Native American men, on reservations. As in white communities, however, women's labor became more important to family sustenance. When New Deal work relief programs favored men, as among Florida Seminoles on federal reservations, women found jobs nearby picking crops or in the commercial tourist trade. Acquiring sewing machines, they produced dolls and clothing, sold these items to visitors, and contributed to family income. Seminole women's status may have improved, even as the traditional tribal economy collapsed. In the San Francisco Bay area, young Pomo women in their teens and twenties left impoverished *rancherios*, or groups of cabins in the countryside, to take jobs as domestics in Oakland and San Francisco. "We have jobs only for girls," an Oakland YWCA administrator said. "The boys can't get jobs down here." Almost all of the young Pomo women eventually returned to the countryside, but only after exploiting the city environment for income, novelty, and a "good time." Finally, a small group of schooled women on reservations took jobs in federal employ, as clerical workers, nurses, and teachers. World War II increased the pace of assimilation, and one-fifth of Native American women found paid work off the reservation.

The black working woman was unlikely to benefit from either the growth of unions or New Deal labor laws. Women in general faced discrimination in the labor market, the Women's Bureau contended in 1938, but "such hardships have fallen upon Negro women with double harshness." Married or unmarried, black women had long worked for family support, a position new to many white middle-class women in the 1930s. The black woman worker had never been accused of working for "pin money." More important, she was customarily excluded from most occupations open to white women, such as white-collar work or industrial work, and relegated to the lowest-paid and most menial jobs, a situation that remained unchanged by the depression. In 1930, according to the Women's Bureau, 90 percent of black women workers were domestics or farm laborers, occupations uncovered by either the NRA codes or the FLSA. In 1938, only 10 percent of black women workers held jobs in industry and mainly in such bottom-level categories as laundry work (under the NRA, the 30,000 black women working in power laundries were granted a 14-cent minimum wage, but it was never enforced). Finally, in the North or the South, married or single, the black woman worker was more likely than a white woman to be unemployed and less likely to be included in a federal work-relief program.

Throughout the depression, black women suffered a disproportionately high unemployment rate. More than half lost their jobs, compared to three out of ten working white women. The depression severely cut into domestic employment, especially in the South. A Kentucky study of 1933 noted that more than half of black women in domestic service were unemployed, and federal data confirmed such reports. In 1934, Federal Emergency Relief Administration surveys of persons on relief in urban centers showed that two-thirds of women once employed as domestics were out of work, with the greatest concentrations in southern cities. In large cities such as New York, black women would congregate at streetcorner "slave markets" early in the morning, seeking a day's work and bargaining with customers for rates as low as 10 cents an hour. While blacks of both sexes had higher unemployment rates than whites in the 1930s, the differences were pronounced between men and women as well as between blacks and whites. In Chicago in 1931, for instance, 43.5 percent of black men were unemployed and 29.7 percent of white men; 58.5 percent of black women were unemployed and 19.4 percent of white women. (Unemployment rates, of course, covered only persons who had once been in the labor force, a category that included a far larger proportion of black women than white women.) Clearly, occupational segregation by sex, which provided something of a cushion against job loss for white women in white-collar work, was of no benefit to black women.

Relief rolls reflected the high unemployment figures. Between 1930 and 1935, the proportion of the black population on relief doubled. Although a higher percentage of blacks than whites received federal aid, a smaller percentage of unemployed blacks benefited from work-relief programs, which tended to aid the "temporary" poor, those who had recently fallen in status. The National Youth Administration (NYA) had a relatively good record in warding off discrimination, but blacks often faced disadvantage in other New Deal work-relief agencies, and black women were likely to be excluded entirely, especially in the South. Women's greatest complaints were about programs administered by state personnel, such as the PWA and WPA. They voiced their grievances in a trail of letters to FDR, Eleanor Roosevelt, and the heads of federal agencies. "Mr. Hopkins, colored women have been turned out of different job projects to take us other jobs and white women were hired & sent for and given places that colored women was made to leave or quit," wrote a North Carolina woman in 1937 in a letter indicting the WPA. Other correspondents echoed these grievances. "I has no mule, no wagon, no feed, no grocery," a Georgia widow with seven children told the secretary of agriculture, "and these women and men that is controlling the civil work for the government won't help me."

On the eve of World War II, black women retained their disproportionate share of the female work force. Thirty-eight percent of black women and 24 percent of white women were employed, while the proportion of black married women that worked was more than double the proportion of white married women. But the decade of the 1930s had provided little to improve the black woman's status as a wage earner. The white woman worker, however, survived the crisis in better shape than her male counterpart. Although the depression limited options, sanctioned demotions, and quenched aspiration, it also provided hidden advantages and drew even more women into the work force. At the same time, what seemed like throngs of women assumed administrative posts on the federal level. During the early 1930s, when the New Deal was in its experimental phase, an experienced group of women reformers had an impact on politics and government.

WOMEN'S NEW DEAL

In the 1920s, to many observers, women's political clout had contracted, not expanded. At mid-decade, once the "woman's vote" had failed to materialize, women's welcome in political parties flagged and women's groups' proposals for reform stagnated. But the early New Deal brought a rise of women in Democratic ranks, an influx of women into New Deal posts, and a brief revival of female "influence." To social reformers especially, the New Deal seemed a major triumph, even a vindication of the now defunct Sheppard-Towner Act, as New Deal legislation incorporated measures for which women activists had long campaigned. Child labor, for instance, was banned under the NRA codes in 1933; the Social Security Act of 1935 provided maternal and child welfare benefits; and the Fair Labor Standards Act of 1938 ensured minimum wages and maximum hours. The New Deal proved that the federal government could act to promote human welfare, aid homes and families, protect women workers, and take responsibility for what Jane Addams called "our unfortunate fellow citizens." Above all, once Eleanor Roosevelt entered the White House, the social reform wing of the woman's movement gained an advocate and exemplar.

Two personal tragedies spurred Eleanor Roosevelt's involvement in public life. In 1920, when she was around 40, she discovered her husband's affair with Lucy Mercer, her social secretary; and in 1921, when FDR was stricken with polio, she was further impelled to seek an independent life. The women's movement of the 1920s provided a route. Eleanor became active in the new League of Women Voters and the Women's Trade Union League. She also found a role in New York state politics; by 1924, she had an office at the Women's Division of the Democratic State Committee. When FDR served as governor from 1928 to 1932, Eleanor Roosevelt increased her commitments. She taught history at a progressive school in New York, began a series of radio talks, and edited a magazine about babies, as well as a party publication, the Women's Division's *Democratic News*. What she wanted most out of life, Eleanor Roosevelt told *Success* magazine, was "the opportunity of doing something useful." She also expounded a social philosophy. In a 1932 radio speech, she voiced her hope that hard times would teach Americans the lessons of "interdependence"—of community, cooperation, and mutual obligation. "If we can get back to the spirit that we are responsible for each other, these years of depression would have been worthwhile."

In the White House, Eleanor Roosevelt played an unprecedented role, as evident in the single year of 1933. As soon as FDR took office, she made contact with the press—through a interview with a favored friend, AP reporter Lorena Hickok, and two days later, held her first press conference, open only to women reporters. The Monday-morning press conferences were a brilliant device. Eleanor began by talking about household, family, and daily life but was quickly drawn into issues of public policy; the press was ecstatic. Bylines assured, reporters covered Eleanor Roosevelt's many causes. She pressed for government posts for women, urged relief programs for unemployed women, ran a White House conference on women's "Emergency Needs," campaigned to end Washington's alley slums, sang songs with jobless bonus marchers, promoted the federal homestead program, and took part in a planned community for unemployed miners near Morgantown, West Virginia. The public responded; in 1933, the First Lady received 301,000 letters, and answered 50 a day. "You are the center of it all," wrote Carrie Chapman Catt, "the beginning of a grand display of stateswomen we are going to have."

By the end of the decade, Eleanor Roosevelt had assumed an array of strategic functions. As presidential assistant, she traveled around the country, a visible spokeswoman who reported to the White House. As political strategist, she ran the 1936 campaign, acting as an intermediary between FDR in the White House and James Farley and Molly Dewson at Democratic headquarters. As resident guardian of "human values," she served as an ombudsman for the disadvantaged, a link between depression victims and the administration. As outspoken liberal, she steadily took stands to the left of FDR, especially in her contacts with the National Association for the Advancement of Colored People, pacifist groups, and the American Youth Congress. Such liberalism not only captivated her own constituency but spared the President, who was uninvolved, some assaults from the left. As a public figure or as a "private citizen," Eleanor Roosevelt never ceased her campaigns. She persistently defended the homestead program; she testified before legislative committees on migratory workers and on discrimination in the armed forces; and she became entrenched in the administration of relief agencies, notably the NYA and WPA.

Some of her causes had only "token" success, like the resident camps for women; others became controversial; and others failed completely, such as her demands for compulsory health insurance, a child labor amendment, and an anti-lynching law. But Eleanor Roosevelt succeeded as a political presence. She increased her influence not by evading traditional roles but by extending them. Officials vied for her attention, pressure groups besieged her, newswomen trailed her, and voters admired her. "I am sure, Eleanor dear, that millions of people voted with you in their minds also,"

Eleanor Roosevelt surrounded by reporters at one of her Monday-morning press conferences. *(Franklin D. Roosevelt Library Collection)*

Rose Schneiderman of the WTUL wrote after the 1936 election. In 1939, 67 percent of a Gallup poll approved her conduct as First Lady, with more support among women than men. In the 1940 campaign, Republican women confirmed her impact with large campaign buttons that read: "We Don't Want Eleanor Either."

Eleanor Roosevelt was also central to a female upsurge in politics and government. A publicist for women's projects, she served as a White House liaison for women's groups and a lobbyist for women reformers' causes. In 1939, for instance, when the LWV urged Children's Bureau head Katherine Lenroot to pressure the House Appropriations Committee to fund improved social services for the District of Columbia, Lenroot asked the president's wife to hold a White House conference. When this proved impossible, Eleanor Roosevelt waged a personal campaign. She addressed the House committee, conferred with its chairman, and even after victory continued to pressure members of Congress with letters demanding the appointment of a district coordinator of child care—adding that she was acting "simply as a private citizen." Not surprisingly, women in government such as Katherine Lenroot and Mary Anderson relied on Eleanor Roosevelt as an advocate. So did the LWV and the WTUL.

While Eleanor Roosevelt capitalized on her personal influence, Mary W. Dewson mobilized women within the Democratic party. A superb administrator, Molly Dewson won impressive victories. At the Democratic national convention of 1936, there were 219 women delegates, compared to 60 at the Republican convention, and 302 alternates; women made eight seconding speeches. Dewson also gained for women equal representation on the platform committee, and, under her leadership, the Women's Division played a crucial role in Democratic campaigns. In 1936, Dewson's troops of Democratic women explained New Deal policies door-to-door, a tactic she called "mouth to mouth" campaigning. The Women's Division's *Democratic News*, meanwhile, vastly expanded its audience. By the start of FDR's second term, when the administration rewarded Molly Dewson with an appointment to the Social Security Board, women were seen as part of the new Democratic coalition.

Finally, in the New Deal, women made unprecedented inroads on appointive offices, a triumph symbolized by Frances Perkins's appointment as labor secretary. Women appointees were concentrated in the Labor Department, where Anderson and Lenroot headed the Women's and Children's Bureaus, and in newly created federal agencies and advisory boards, where they would not encroach on traditional male fiefs. New Deal agencies, in short, provided new space for women in the federal bureaucracy. Emily Blair, Mary Harriman Rumsey, and suffragist lawyer Sue Shelton White, for instance, served on the NRA consumers' advisory board (Frances Perkins's "afterthought"); Rose Schneiderman served on the NRA labor advisory board; Ellen Woodward and Hilda Smith held administrative posts under FERA and WPA; Mary McLeod Bethune, a leading black educator, was chosen at Eleanor Roosevelt's instigation to head black programs at NYA; and after 1935, White, Woodward, and Dewson were appointed to the Social Security Board. A smaller group of women appointees moved into other areas. Nellie Tayloe Ross was appointed to the Treasury Department; Florence Jaffrey Harriman and Ruth Bryan Owen became the first women diplomats; and Ohio judge Florence Allen, who had headed the list of nominees drawn up by Molly Dewson and Eleanor Roosevelt, became the first woman appointed to a federal court of appeals.

Most of the New Deal's high-level women appointees, like their sponsors, Dewson and Roosevelt, shared backgrounds in women's organizations and social welfare. Frances Perkins's career was significant. A Mount Holyoke graduate, Perkins had been drawn to social service after hearing Florence Kelley give a college talk. She then worked in settlement houses and in the New York Consumers' League before becoming New York State's industrial commissioner under FDR in 1928. Other women installed in federal posts in 1933 had similar backgrounds, as did later appointees. Florence Allen had left law school midway through to work for the New York League for the Protection of Immigrants and the College Equal Suffrage League, while living at the Henry Street Settlement. Florence Harriman, a founder of New York's Colony Club, had served on President Wilson's Federal Industrial Relations Committee and, during the 1920s, had led NCL opposition to the ERA.

Long-time Democratic activist Emily Blair found it "enlightening" that the first woman cabinet member achieved her position "by way of social welfare work" rather than through traditional routes of party service. A leadership role in social welfare, she contended in 1933, did not offend men's prejudices "as to the proper sphere of women." Rather it seemed "merely an extension of woman's traditional job of helping the unfortunate." The type of affiliations shared by women in New Deal posts had further significance. Historian Susan Ware has identified a network of 28 women, linked by a history of "personal friendship and professional interaction," who moved into jobs in politics and national government in the 1930s. The network included not only federal appointees but activists in the Democratic party's Women's Division, such as Emma Guffey Miller, and elected officials, such as representatives Mary T. Norton of New Jersey and Caroline O'Day of New York. Long in existence, the network had roots in suffrage, progressivism, and social reform. Born around 1880, network members were usually well-off and well educated; two-thirds were married. They knew each other from the WTUL, the NCL, and politics. During the 1920s most had been active in Democratic campaigns. Significantly, about half of network members were, like Eleanor Roosevelt, daughters, sisters, or wives of male politicians. Ellen Woodward and Katherine Lenroot, for instance, were senators' daughters; Emma Guffey Miller was a senator's sister; and Ruth Bryan Owen was the daughter of William Jennings Bryan.

In the New Deal, Ware contends, women officeholders used their longtime network to "maximize their influence in politics and government." Though committed to the advancement of women, most network members avoided the label of "feminist," which was now reserved for National Woman's party members. They identified themselves as social reformers. Like Molly Dewson, network members believed that women's goals in politics differed from men's, and that women's special role in office was to "humanize" government policy. They also felt that women in office had special interests to protect. As Ellen Woodward stated in a 1939 speech, "Whether we are actively engaged in homemaking or not, we are family conscious." The New Deal network was not completely monolithic. Two of its members, Sue Shelton White and Emma Guffey Miller, supported the ERA. But despite such internal disagreements, network members consistently provided one another with help and support. "Those of us who worked to put together the New Deal," Frances Perkins later told Molly Dewson, "are bound by spiritual ties that no one else can understand."

Within the women's network, Frances Perkins was the most powerful figure, next to Eleanor Roosevelt. Her Labor Department, moreover, was active in the creation of the Social Security Act of 1935 and the Fair Labor Standards Act of 1938—enduring laws that incorporated a raft of protective measures long endorsed by women reformers. The Social Security Act, for instance, provided unemployment compensation, old age pensions, and care for the disabled. It also included many measures prepared by Grace Abbott and Katherine Lenroot of the Children's Bureau such as grants to the states for the care of homeless, destitute, delinquent, or crippled children, as well as for public health services, maternal care, and infant care. Aid to Dependent Children (ADC), though a minor part of the 1935 law, has special significance. Replacing the mothers' pension programs that had been enacted by some forty state legislatures in the progressive era, ADC provided funds to families in which male breadwinners were dead, absent, or incapacitated. Under ADC, as under the pension plans, states could judge the "suitability" or "propriety" of the recipient parent (most of the aid went to widows). In 1950, ADC became Aid to Families with Dependent Children (AFDC), the crux of the welfare system until the 1990s. In retrospect, a combination of progressive measures, promoted by women reformers and etched into New Deal legislation, provided the core of the modern welfare state.

Always held up by Eleanor Roosevelt as an exemplary public servant, Frances Perkins also exemplified the tenets of the reform-minded branch of the woman's movement, as opposed to the egalitarian National Woman's party. Since the days of the crusade for woman suffrage, which she never viewed as of major importance, Perkins had always been "more deeply touched by the problems of poverty, the sorrows of the world, the neglected individual." She defined feminism as "the movement of women to participate in service to society" and clung to the goal of service to others. When accepting her cabinet appointment, she had "more of a sense of obligation to do it for the sake of other women than I did for any other thing."

But Frances Perkins's post was the New Deal's hot seat. Labor bills were always controversial, and as the first woman cabinet member, Frances Perkins was suspect from the outset. When she arrived in Washington, no one save Grace Abbott and Mary Anderson sent welcome notes; the newsmen's annual rite excluded her; and on formal occasions, when cabinet members were seated by rank, Perkins was usually placed with their wives. Congress called on her endlessly to testify, far more so than any man in the executive branch. Organized labor suspected her, as she had never been a union leader or even a union member. Mary Anderson criticized her for lack of partiality to working women. (During Perkins's tenure, the Women's Bureau remained small, while the Children's Bureau grew.) According to Anderson, Perkins "leaned over backwards" not to favor women and "did not want to be thought of as a woman too closely identified with women's problems." Setting a precedent for women officeholders under such circumstances was a major achievement.

Another precedent setter was Mary McLeod Bethune, head of "Negro affairs" at NYA from 1935 to 1943 and a leader of FDR's shifting "black cabinet." Bethune envisioned "dozens of Negro women coming after me, filling positions of high trust and strategic importance," as she told *Ebony* magazine in 1949. Though not a member of the women's network identified by Susan Ware, Bethune was closely connected to Eleanor Roosevelt, who urged her appointment and found in her a kindred spirit. An educator and women's club leader, Bethune had been president of Bethune-Cookman College, a Florida vocational school she founded herself, and an officer of the National Association of Colored Women. In 1935, she became the first president of the National Council of Negro Women, a coalition of black women's organizations. Bethune saw herself as a black advocate rather than a woman's advocate. As an administrator, however, she was often unable to take stands on racial equality as strong as those of such pressure groups as the NAACP and the Urban League.

Her tiny office, staffed by an aide and a few secretaries, was hardly a power base. Lines of authority had never been firmly established, so it was unclear whether Bethune or state NYA directors would shape black programs, just as it was unclear whether state NYA advisory boards would be segregated or integrated. Bethune pressed for integrated boards, for black training projects in skilled work, for black project supervisors, and for black participation in NYA policymaking. Effective with both black and white audiences, she urged black appointments to other high-level jobs. "It is impossible for you to enter sympathetically and understandingly into the program of the Negro, as the Negro can do," she told the mainly white national advisory committee of the NYA in 1939.

The mood of reform that brought women such as Perkins and Bethune into New Deal posts had peaked by 1936. Once the climate of experiment cooled, women's influence began to wane and access to important jobs diminished. But the New Deal still had a permanent impact on women's role in public service: As federal and state agencies expanded, so did opportunities for social workers. After the federal government initiated welfare and relief measures, the social work profession, two-thirds female throughout the decade, grew by leaps and bounds. Not only did social welfare leaders permeate New Deal agencies, where they served on advisory boards and helped to draft legislation, but jobs also opened up down the line—on the federal, state, and county levels.

Social work was already in transition. In the early twentieth century, as graduate programs emerged, the social worker gained a professional identity. In the 1920s, when the casework method became popular, her attention shifted from social reform to individual "adjustment." Finally, in the depression, the social worker changed from an agent of assimilation, who helped immigrants adapt to American life, to a middlewoman between the depression family and the public purse. "My studies at school didn't prepare me for this," recalled a new county caseworker who had graduated from college in 1933, in Studs Terkel's *Hard Times*. "We were still studying about immigrant families. Not about mass unemployment." In her research trips for Harry Hopkins, Lorena Hickok found that social workers had been trained to deal with "problem families," not with "respectable citizens, who, through no fault of their own, were obliged to have some help from the federal government." Carrying large caseloads and adapting to the welfare bureaucracy, new social workers often resented the insensitivity their roles demanded. "We're under pressure to give as little help as possible," a caseworker complained in 1934.

But the New Deal era also brought the social worker rewards. In Eleanor Roosevelt's view, she gained "the satisfaction of feeling that she has entered the lives of innumerable families and left them better off than she found them." A more tangible reward was that she was able to get a job, at a time when others were losing them. The start of large-scale federal relief programs had another impact too. Once the volunteer settlement worker was permanently replaced by the trained, salaried government employee, another rung of the woman's movement broke. This process was under way in the 1920s, but the New Deal was a turning point. Afterward, social welfare was a government function and no longer an extension of "woman's sphere," as it had been for more than a century. The social worker, however, was not the career woman most in the public eye during the 1930s. This was probably the woman reporter, suddenly elevated to the status of culture heroine.

"FRONT PAGE WOMAN"

Mass culture had become an important force in the 1920s. In the 1930s, despite the depression, the power of the media dramatically increased. Drops in film attendance only spurred new ingenuity from the movie industry; huge newspaper chains competed for readers; and the number of radio sets doubled. In the media blitz of the 1930s, women emerged in assertive roles—the ambitious career girl, the gutsy entertainer, the sophisticated socialite, the blond seductress, and, leading the list, the worldly wise reporter. Though hardly cut from a single mold, women in mass culture exuded vitality. Dynamic, aggressive, even flamboyant, they provided a respite from the apathy or panic that seemed to characterize real life. The new publicity for female assertiveness was not always favorable; the depression was not a feminist era. But the headstrong heroines of the 1930s, real and invented, provided a repository for some of the lost aspirations of the 1920s.

During the depression, misery loved company. The universality of domestic woes was explicit in the new radio soap opera. Daytime serials (38 of them by 1938) revealed predicaments with which entire homebound families, but mainly homebound women, could identify. Indeed, the formula for serials required that each episode begin and end with severe troubles. Soap operas also provided a mode of escape. The most popular centered around women who had recently moved, upward or downward, to a new status, whether *Backstage Wife*, *Our Gal Sunday*, or *The Romance of Helen Trent*. Surveys concluded that the more complex a listener's problems the more serials she followed. Escape literature served a similar function. The fatter the novel, the bigger the bargain—whether the beleaguered protagonists were Chinese peasants or antebellum aristocrats. Pearl Buck's *The Good Earth*, a novel about the rise of a Chinese family from peasantry to wealth, was the most widely read book of 1932; Margaret Mitchell's *Gone With the Wind* (more than a thousand pages) sold a million and a half copies by 1937 and became a movie in 1939. Social causes also played a role in depression culture, as in Hallie Flanagan's Federal Theatre Project, under the WPA, which ran from 1935 to 1939. But escapism was the dominant mode in entertainment.

Seekers of adventure and excitement could also turn to real life as depicted in the daily press. Newspapers flaunted sensational stories about disasters—such as the Lindbergh kidnapping or Amelia Earhart's disappearance in flight—as distractions from private problems. As ballast, the press also presented comic diversion, such as Chic Young's *Blondie*, who in 1930 began maneuvering the inept Dagwood through domestic and vocational crises. At the outset, Blondie had been a gold-digging flapper and Dagwood a millionaire's son. But the Bumsteads adapted to changing times and became an everyday troubled family, like everyone else. By 1940, Brenda Starr, girl reporter, joined Dagwood and Blondie in popularity. Her vocation was significant. For women readers, the press provided a new type of role model.

The woman reporter surged to prominence in the 1930s, whether Anne McCormick and Dorothy Thompson reporting from Europe or Ruby Black and Bess Furman covering the White House. The great rise in the number of women journalists had in fact occurred in the 1920s; in the depression, however, their number continued to increase. And for those who had already gained a foothold, in major chains or press associations—like Lorena Hickok, Emma Bugbee, Bess Furman, and Ruby Black—the syndicated column and national byline were major boons. Eleanor Roosevelt's press conferences, meanwhile, gave Washington newswomen excellent publicity. Significantly, the First Lady joined them herself, by becoming a member of the Newspaper Guild, the journalists' union, and starting a media blitz of her own. Before her first term in the White House ended, Eleanor Roosevelt had become a radio personality in major-network, commercially sponsored talks. She had also embarked on well-paid lecture tours, continued her articles for women's magazines, and in December 1935, started "My Day," a syndicated column for United Features. In 1936, the column appeared in 62 newspapers, reaching an audience of up to 4 million. By the end of the decade, 136 papers printed it.

As a journalist, Eleanor Roosevelt faced competition. Dorothy Thompson's syndicated column, "On the Record," appeared in 140 papers in 1936 and even more at the decade's end. Since 1920, Thompson had climbed from unpaid correspondent to European bureau chief for the Curtis chain, which included the *Philadelphia Inquirer* and the *New York Evening Post*. In the 1930s, unhampered by her failing marriage to Sinclair Lewis, Thompson won a national reputation. She reported from Europe, lectured frequently, broadcast over NBC as a regular commentator, reached millions of readers through "On the Record," and in 1937 began a monthly column for the *Ladies' Home Journal*. An exemplar of the ambitious, successful career woman, Thompson embodied the aspirations of the 1920s. Once depression struck, few could follow Thompson's example—or that of Bugbee, Black, Furman, and Craig. But aspiration was not yet quenched. The enterprising career woman of the 1930s was alive and well on the movie screen.

The woman reporter, in particular, cut a wide swath through a succession of celluloid city rooms. As film historian Marjorie Rosen has shown, the movie stars of the early 1930s often portrayed working women who survived by their wits in assertive and competitive roles. While female unemployment rates rose, Bette Davis appeared as a stenographer and political campaigner in 1932, as a copywriter, insurance probator, and government agent in 1934, and as a reporter *(Front Page Woman)* in 1935. Joan Crawford, Loretta Young, and Jean Arthur were similarly at home in the working world. Resourceful go-getters, the movie careerists competed with men, stole their stories, met their deadlines, and hogged the screen. The clothes they popularized—man-tailored suits with broad, padded shoulders—signified their competitive intent. Though competent, confident, and full of ambition, the movie career women had their limits; they were willing to give up their jobs for the right man. Jean Arthur's reporter married the boss, while Bette Davis in *Front Page Woman* ensnared a competitor from a rival paper. (In real life, Bess Furman married a fellow journalist and kept on working for the AP. In the 1940s, she ran an independent news service, worked for the Office of War Information, and replaced Eleanor Darnton as the Washington "woman interest" reporter for the *New York Times*.)

Cleverness and assertiveness spread beyond the city room in the 1930s films. The woman reporter was only one of a gallery of enterprising heroines. Moviegoers could also watch Greta Garbo as a spy, Myrna Loy as an amateur detective, or Joan Blondell as an ambitious chorus girl in *Gold Diggers of 1933*. Throughout the depression, high society held great fascination. Sophisticated comedies in upper-class settings provided a vehicle for Katherine Hepburn, who radiated intelligence and independence. (A Bryn Mawr graduate, Hepburn was indeed upper class. Her mother, moreover, was one of Margaret Sanger's lieutenants in the birth-control crusade.) Low society had equal appeal. Mae West provided a powerful aggressor who controlled her own plots and manipulated men. "It's not the men in my life but the life in my men that counts," said Mae, who described herself as "the woman's ego."

But Mae West's movies, usually period pieces, were set in a personal fantasy land; West was a joke more than a threat. The movies of the 1930s also revealed a harsh, mean antiwoman streak. Headstrong heroines who dominated the screen were often meddlesome, manipulative, selfish, or dangerous. Jean Harlow's characters, low-life or high-life, were faithless, immoral, conniving, and scheming. In a steady spate of underworld movies, gun molls and girlfriends were mauled, discarded, and pushed in the face. Other inauspicious signs emerged as well. The malicious gossip of spoiled socialites in Clare Boothe Luce's *The Women* (1939) conveyed disgust with the entire sex. By the end of the 1930s, the ambitious career woman faded. "Men demand and need in marriage the full emotional power of the women they love," Dorothy Thompson told *Ladies' Home Journal* readers in 1939. "I should hate to see most women exteriorize their lives as I have," she exhorted in 1940. Thompson reflected the tone of the times. The working woman of 1940s movies sometimes retained her zest, competitiveness, and career. Katherine Hepburn, for instance, in her movies with Spencer Tracy, was, successively, an athlete, lawyer, and reporter. But in World War II, a new type of wage-earning heroine appeared. Though embarked on a job for the course of the war, she was usually waiting for a man to come home.

Like the depression, the war had a dual message for women. A sudden demand for female labor vastly expanded women's economic options, as the depression era had not. But the woman war worker was also a hazard. Lured into factories and praised for her patriotism, she inspired a backlash that hit full stride at demobilization.

THE IMPACT OF WORLD WAR II

In the depression, the federal government joined with local government, school boards, and private business to exclude married women from the work force. A decade later the policy was reversed. By 1942, the War Department was inviting women into defense plants, urging women to enter government offices, and pressuring employers to utilize "the vast resource of womanpower." War created a tremendous labor shortage, both in the rapidly expanding defense industry and in the private sector, as millions of men (seven times as many as in World War I) joined the armed services. The national work force was quickly transformed. During World War II, more than 6 million women took jobs for the first time, and the number of working women rose by 57 percent. In 1940, women were under 25 percent of the labor force; by July 1944, 35 percent. The number of married women holding jobs doubled, the age of the female labor force rose, and the number of unionized women surged from 800,000 in 1940 (9.4 percent of unionized workers) to 3 million in 1944 (21.8 percent of unionized workers.) "Almost overnight," wrote Mary Anderson, "women were reclassified from a marginal to a basic labor supply."

The greatest need for "womanpower," as government propaganda made clear, was in war industry. At defense plants, which absorbed 2 million female workers, women made airplane frames, engines, propellers, parachutes, gas masks, life rafts, artillery, munitions, and electrical equipment. They loaded shells, assembled machine guns, cleaned spark plugs, wired instrument panels, and operated hand drills, turret lathes, rivet guns, and band saws, and learned their jobs in two to six months. The aircraft industry, a prime example, quickly adapted to female labor. By 1943, at major factories like Boeing's huge Seattle plant, half the workers were women. The aircraft worker was joined by the woman keel binder, toolmaker, foundry worker, stevedore, and die cutter; bans against women in heavy industry were discarded. Many states modified their protective laws or temporarily removed restrictions on night work or overtime, or lifting heavy weights. As publicity features and personal testimonials suggested, there was no job a woman could not fill. "Today I had a good job," wrote Nell Giles, a Boston reporter who went to work in a defense plant. "It was to bore twenty holes in an aluminum disk, which is part of one of the instruments we make."

While the number of women employed in defense industry rose 460 percent, the number of women in other manufacturing rose too. By the war's end, it had doubled. Government bureaucracy expanded as well. More than 2 million new women workers found jobs in offices, half of them in the federal government. By 1945, the nation's clerical work force had doubled. There was spillover into the professions, as ranks of male competitors were depleted. In Washington, D.C., for instance, the number of women journalists tripled. Finally, after a major shift of government policy, thousands of women joined the armed services, filling the ranks of the Women's Army Auxiliary Corps (WAAC), quickly formed after Pearl Harbor. By 1943, women pilots, or WASPs, tested planes, ferried them from base to base, and flew other noncombat missions. Women volunteers, meanwhile staffed the Red Cross, ran bond drives, served on ration boards, and worked on civil defense. Eleanor Roosevelt and WPA administrator Florence Kerr worked out a plan to use volunteer "woman-power" in civil defense. Once the program was approved, Eleanor Roosevelt, after some wavering, took a place at its helm. But the formal appointment exposed her to criticism, and she soon resigned.

During the war, the woman worker gained not only a new range of job possibilities but a chance to move up the vocational ladder, or at least off its bottom rungs. Defense work was the most attractive option, as pay was 40 percent higher in war plants than in factories making consumer goods. Many women migrated to such war production centers as Detroit, Seattle, and Baltimore in order to take these well-paid jobs. High wages, moreover, easily lured working women away from jobs as waitresses and laundry workers, which now went begging. Significantly, in wartime, the number of women in domestic service fell rapidly. By the war's end, the proportion of black women workers in domestic jobs had dropped to 48 percent, while 18 percent worked in industry—about twice as many as before the war. But as in the depression, when they were the first to be fired, black women were the last line of emergency workers, hired for nondomestic jobs only when both white workers and black men were unavailable. Although their options rose, few black women could get more than low-level jobs in manufacturing, while entry into white-collar fields was still limited. Only a tiny proportion were accepted either in the Women's Army Corps (in 1943, WAAC became WAC) or as army nurses. For black women, racial barriers remained in effect more than they were discarded. Many, however, joined a new wave of migration from the rural South to northern cities, one that would continue through the 1950s.

Still, the need for women workers in wartime dramatically changed the female labor force. For the first time, most women workers were married, as were three out of four new women workers. The proportion of wives who held jobs, which had risen from 12 percent to 15 percent in the 1930s, now shot upward. By 1945, one out of four married women worked. The age of the female labor force rose; three out of five new workers were former housewives over 35. Not only were new woman workers

In August 1943, a corps of Women Airforce Service Pilots (WASPs) was formed to meet the wartime pilot shortage. Until then, women pilots with civilian status had provided aircraft ferrying services. WASPs, too, did noncombat jobs, mainly ferrying bomber and fighter planes from factories to airbases and embarkation points. They also towed targets for anti-aircraft gunnery practice and flew engineering missions, did instrument flight checks, and flew test flights of modified plane models. Although the presence of WASPs often evoked antagonism from male pilots on army bases, the women pilots captured the imagination of press and public. By the end of 1944, when the critical shortage of male pilots ended, the House of Representatives narrowly defeated a proposal to make the WASPs part of the Army Air Forces. The corps of women pilots was disbanded without military status or veterans' benefits, an injustice not remedied until 1979. *(Smithsonian Institution)*

likely to be older and married, but one-third had children under 14 at home. Objections to working wives and mothers temporarily faded. The war era thus accelerated a trend toward wage-earning wives that had begun before the depression, continued throughout it, and would pick up again in the 1950s. According to historian William H. Chafe, World War II was a "watershed in the history of women at work."

Rapid absorption of women into the work force, however, testified to the extent of the emergency rather than to any sudden shift in opinion about gender roles; behavior changed more than convictions. Indeed, as historian Karen Anderson has shown, World War II reinforced traditional beliefs about family life and woman's place. First, the war enhanced the significance of men while diminishing their supply, especially for women in their early twenties. The sex ratio for those aged 20 to 24, for instance, plummeted; there were two women for every man. But scarcity of men appeared to increase male value rather than female autonomy. Young women felt a

By the end of World War II, more than 4,000 black women had enlisted in
the Women's Army Corps, other were admitted to the WAVEs, and a small
number served as officers, in both army and navy. But racially segregated
units were the rule, for women as for men. The 500 black nurses who
served in the Army Nurse Corps were assigned to hospitals serving
only black men. Above, newly trained army nurses await disembarkment
in Scotland. *(UPI/Bettrnann)*

"sense of urgency regarding marital prospects," and early marriages abounded.
Meanwhile, stresses on family life such as wartime separations spurred concern. Rising divorce rates were often attributed to new work options for women. Anxiety rose
about women deserting domestic life, rejecting their families, neglecting their children, and fostering juvenile delinquency. Finally, fearful that wartime breakdowns of
authority would encourage promiscuity, the government waged a special campaign
to end "sex delinquency" among young women in war production areas. Such responses to wartime changes, Karen Anderson contends, "were important in shaping
Americans' values and behavior in the postwar era."

Nor did temporary acceptance of Rosie the Riveter reflect a change of view about
"woman's place" in the work force. Although 60 percent of Gallup poll respondents
during the war believed wives should work in war industry, sexual equality was never
an issue for workers, employers, or the federal government. At the war's start, government and industry hesitated to hire women workers, especially married ones. By
1942, once men were scarce, reluctance diminished, but hostility to women in policy-
making continued. The Women's Bureau, Mary Anderson complained, was never
consulted about women's employment policies. A Women's Advisory Commission
was finally created, under pressure, as a counterpart to the War Manpower Commission, but the advisory board, a New Deal tactic, now wore thin. Advisory committees,
said Mary Anderson, were "not really allowed to have a voice in formulating policy."
Resentment about wartime inequity, however, was muted. Women war workers

appreciated their options for better jobs and higher pay though men earned more. The National War Labor Board stipulated equal pay for equal work, but it also provided loopholes by which women workers could be placed in separate job categories and paid less for the same work—both in war industry and in the private sector.

One issue that illustrated the government's attachment to traditional ideas was its resistance to creating child-care centers for women in defense work, despite an absentee problem among working women with young children at home. War-torn England, with an even larger percentage of women in the work force, provided a rash of special services, such as hot meals to take home after work and child-care facilities. But the American government was reluctant to enter the child-care arena, and Perkins, Anderson, and Lenroot at the Labor Department agreed. "A mother's primary duty is to her home and children," the Children's Bureau said. "This duty is one she cannot lay aside, no matter what the emergency." Women wage earners, significantly, also suspected institutionalized child care. They associated it with public welfare and preferred to leave children with friends or relatives. "I guess I'm not the only woman who's raising a second batch of children, now that the country needs the young women to make munitions," said a grandmother in *McCalls* in 1942. In 1943, funds were finally allotted to establish federal child-care centers, under the Lanham Act, but as these centers fell under the auspices of seven agencies, their administration was inefficient. Only 10 percent of defense workers' children were enrolled, and by 1946 federal funding for the centers had ended.

Traditional convictions about woman's place also emerged in the government's campaign to lure women into the work force. At the head of this effort was the Office of War Information, run by advertising men. Throughout the war, the OWI, the War Manpower Commission, and the War Advertising Council gave guidelines and suggestions for the press, radio networks, and advertisers. Newsreels, posters, billboards, feature articles, and such radio shows as "Commando Mary" reflected their efforts. The propaganda campaign was a hard sell. Whenever reporter Bess Furman, now a disgruntled employee of OWI, opened the newspaper, read a magazine, or listened to the radio, she heard "the pitch." Wartime propaganda, as historian Leila M. Rupp has shown, sought to ensure that women's war work would be only a temporary response to an emergency, with no permanent effects on either the work force or women's status. By portraying the woman war worker as an attractive wife and mother who sacrificed home life to patriotism, wartime propaganda minimized the war worker's challenge to traditional roles. Changes in behavior, propaganda suggested, reflected only the "emergency," not any basic change in attitudes.

Attempts to attract women into defense work therefore appealed to such qualities as altruism and affection, rather than the base motive of high pay. Contributing to the war effort, propaganda suggested, would shorten the war and protect family members from death on the battlefield. Each bullet that the war worker produced, said a National Association of Manufacturers pamphlet, might "avenge her son." War work was also shown to be glamorous, sometimes by featuring movie stars in the propaganda campaign. Hollywood, too, depicted heroines in an array of wartime jobs—Ann Sothern as an aircraft worker, Lucille Ball in a defense plant, Claudette Colbert as a welder, Jennifer Jones as a nurse's aid, and Lana Turner, variously, as a war correspondent and a WAAC. An army photographer discovered Marilyn

Her Man is "Out There!"

Her Uniform—and His—Come First
Nothing Else Matters

SHE HASN'T heard from him. The day after he went away she put on a work uniform and went to work in a cotton mill. An 8-hour stretch, so she can put their boy through school. If she's worried, she doesn't let anybody see it. Nothing at Pepperell is so vital as seeing that her man gets his fighting clothes—and that she and her millions of sisters in other plants throughout America get theirs. Every Pepperell worker wants war-orders to come first. Arm in arm with the textile industry we're filling them fast and asking for every new challenge. If you find fewer Pepperell Sheets and Blankets in the stores, you know that more Pepperell Fabrics are working for her and her man. Nothing else counts.

Victory is *Everybody's* Business

PEPPERELL MANUFACTURING COMPANY, BOSTON, MASSACHUSETTS

Following Office of War Information guidelines, advertisers
attempted to spur women into the civilian labor force
while reinforcing sex-role stereotypes. Typically, as above,
wartime ads appealed to traditional female qualities, and
emphasized women's loyalty to home, men, and nation.
(*Life*, January 18, 1943.) Fear of role reversal, however,
lurked beneath the surface. Usually a subliminal theme, it
emerged in one of Norman Rockwell's most impressive covers
for the *Saturday Evening Post* on May 29, 1943. Opposite, a
muscle-bound Rosie the Riveter, wearing her propaganda
buttons like medals and her mask tilted back like aviator
glasses, is armed with a pneumatic riveting machine.
Proud, self-contained, and self-satisfied, this young amazon
appears immovable, especially from her well-paid wartime job.
(*Curtis Publishing Company*)

Monroe, then 18-year-old Norma Jean Dougherty, assembling target airplanes in a
California factory. The picture appeared in a feature on women war workers in *Yank*
magazine.

Propaganda often stressed the similarity between industrial work and "women's
work." Munitions making, for instance, was compared to running a sewing machine
or a vacuum cleaner. "If you've used an electric mixer in your kitchen, you can learn
to run a drill press," read a billboard sign in 1943. Advertisers assumed that women

had a special proclivity for tedious, repetitive work, whether on the assembly line or in the household. So did business magazines, which praised women's ability to work in small spaces and adapt to factory life. The female personality, *Nation's Business* confirmed in 1942, was ideally suited to industrial work, because women had less initiative, were "creatures of habit," and "don't get bored as easily." But the letters women war workers wrote to the OWI suggested different motives. "The major inducement is money!" one woman wrote. Women also reported other benefits, such as getting out in the world and away from the home, as well as personal satisfaction.

A major government goal, however, even before the end of the war was in sight, was to ensure that women would not replace men in the postwar labor force, crowd the market, force wages down, and destroy family life. Like role reversals in the depression family, the new role represented by the woman welder caused mounting anxiety and underscored a desire to return to traditional arrangements where the economy did not depend on women. "What About Women After the War?" the *New York Times Magazine* asked as early as 1943. Answers varied. Women war workers, the Women's Bureau found, had originally intended to take jobs only for the "emergency" but by the end of the war, in a survey of major defense industry areas, three out of four women workers who had held jobs for the first time wished to remain at them. This sentiment, however, was strongest among older, married war workers who had already raised families. It did not seem to be shared by all women workers, many of whom viewed their war jobs as temporary and identified with the domestic images prevalent in wartime propaganda. ("I think a woman's place is in the home—except when there's a war on," a discharged war worker in Detroit was quoted in the press in 1945.) Nor was it shared by public opinion, employers, or the Labor Department.

"We should immediately start planning to get these women back where they belong," a correspondent wrote to OWI in 1943, "amid the environment of home life." "Too many women should not stay in the labor force," the head of the National Association of Manufacturers confirmed in 1945. "The Home is the basic American institution." Before the war ended, the Labor Department issued recommendations to sever women from wartime jobs, provide work for returning veterans, and ensure a smooth transition. The Women's Bureau faced a predicament. Frieda Miller, who replaced Mary Anderson in 1944, voiced resentment that public opinion was tilting against the woman worker. The war, she contended, had proved women's capacities; they should not be forced to "return to their proper sphere—the kitchen." Still, Miller also sought to assuage public opinion. "Women workers do not want to get ahead at the expense of the veterans," she said in 1944. "In fact, they have never regarded their own work as a substitute for that of men." The ambivalent stand of the Women's Bureau seemed to reflect the mixed views of women war workers.

When millions of veterans were demobilized in 1945, women were again called upon to alter their roles to suit the nation's economic needs. As war production plants closed and large industries like aircraft and shipbuilding laid off workers, the number of women in heavy industry dropped. In the auto industry, which had made tanks, jeeps, and trucks during the war, women's share of the work force plunged from 24 percent in 1944 to 7.5 percent in mid-1946. Layoffs were greatest in the high-paid industries that had customarily employed men, but spread further as well. Comparing women's experiences in auto production and the electric industry, traditionally a big employer of women, sociologist Ruth Milkman finds similarities. In both cases, a prewar pattern of sexual division of labor was disrupted by war but not eliminated. During the war, most women worked in predominantly female departments or job classifications; boundaries changed but did not vanish. After the war, management revived prewar sex-typing of jobs, laid off women, and took on men, both veterans and others—though hiring experienced women and new women workers would have cost less, Milkman contends. Labor efforts helped reinforce old patterns. In auto plants, male unionists supported sex discrimination in seniority to preserve men's monopoly of jobs; in the electric industry, men endorsed elimination of sex discrimination in wages to reduce the prospect of female competition and replacement. Distinctions arose among types of women employees. "Let's keep the single girl on the job and put the married woman back in the kitchen," declared the leaflet of an electrical workers' local.

By the end of 1946, 2 million women had left the labor force and another million were laid off. Black women, the last line of emergency workers, were among the hardest hit by the postwar loss of jobs. So were workers in heavy industry and older women whom the war had drawn into the labor force. Although other women moved into jobs at the same time, the proportion of women who worked plummeted from 36 percent at the war's end to 28 percent in 1947. Moreover, the high pay and new options that had once attracted women to wage earning vanished, as did the public approval the war had briefly engendered.

To focus on war workers obscures the diverse effects of World War II on American women: pacifists, protesters, volunteers, homemakers, and soldiers' relatives—all had distinct experiences. A unique experience was that of Japanese American women. In February 1942, the federal government ordered the evacuation of Japanese Americans from the West Coast and their removal to internment camps in desolate areas of the West. Under the War Relocation Authority, more than 110,000 Japanese Americans, two-thirds of them native-born U.S. citizens, or Nisei, were sent to relocation centers, guarded by military police. A majority were youngsters—infants, school-age children, and young people under 21. Motives for internment included a half-century of anti-Japanese sentiment in the West and fear of Japanese sabotage after Pearl Harbor. "I don't think you can tell people how awful it was at that time, how terrible it was," Lili Sasaki, the Los Angeles wife of a medical intern in the 1940s, told interviewers in the 1980s. "And how embarassing because we thought we were being such good citizens. . . . And I didn't want the Japanese to win. None of us did. We didn't want to be under Japanese rule, no." Miné Okubo, an artist from Riverside, California, had been evacuated with her brother to Tanforan racetrack, an assembly center, for six months and then to a relocation camp in Topaz, Utah, for one and a half years. "We were suddenly uprooted—lost everything and treated like a prisoner with soldier guard, dumped behind barbed wire," she remembered. "We were in shock. . . . You can't believe it is happening to you. . . . After being uprooted, everything seemed ridiculous, insane, and stupid. . . . I tried to make the best of it, just adapt and adjust." The Supreme Court upheld facets of relocation in several cases of 1944, by which time a program of gradual release began. In 1988 Congress voted to pay compensation to 62,000 living interns.

Of the four legal challenges to relocation policy to eventually reach the Supreme Court, the last, and most successful, came from a young California Nisei, a civil servant with brothers overseas in the U.S. armed forces. Evacuated from Sacramento in 1942, Mitsuye Endo began the internment process with the intent of bringing suit. Her lawyer had to visit her, first, in a horse stall at Tanforan, where the army had placed her, and then at the Tule Lake camp in California, one of ten major internment centers. There, Mitsuye Endo applied for a writ of habeas corpus; she asked the WRA for discharge and restoration of liberty. In 1944 her case reached the Supreme

Forced to sell their property and homes, 112,000 Japanese Americans
faced life behind barbed wire during World War II. Here, a mother
and child on the way to a West Coast internment camp. The tags
announce the family's number. *(Museum of History and Industry, Seattle)*

Court, which, in *Ex Parte Endo*, unanimously reversed an earlier decision against her.
Mitsuye Endo successfully challenged the legality of detaining loyal citizens without
due process of law as a violation of the Fifth Amendment. Unlike the complainants
in three earlier cases, which involved curfews and evacuation procedures, Mitsuye
Endo won a decision that upset relocation policy and helped end internment camps.

World War II's impact on American women, historian Susan M. Hartmann suggests, was a mixed one that precludes sweeping generalizations about war and social
change. On the one hand, Hartmann points out, the war provided unprecedented
employment opportunities, higher wages, public recognition of the woman worker,
and an easing of restrictions in some areas. On the other hand, it also contained
"powerful forces which put checks upon women's aspirations and options." Indeed,

as traditional attitudes about gender roles were sustained throughout the war, some historians contend that continuity was a more important theme than change. The attitudes that seemed least changed by war, in the end, were those toward the married wage earner. Once the war was over, the woman worker was no longer a symbol of patriotic ardor but rather a threat to social and economic security. The Gallup poll now found that 86 percent of Americans opposed the employment of married women. But the anxiety created by the woman war worker remained. It soon emerged in a new barrage of propaganda extolling the virtues of traditional roles.

POSTWAR PROSPECTS

"What's Become of Rosie the Riveter?" asked the *New York Times Magazine* in May 1946. By now she had lost her well-paid job in war industry and was, presumably, readjusting to life at home; the postwar era brought a swing back to private life. In 1946, more marriages occurred than in any other year, and in 1947, the birthrate accelerated. This extended a trend of the war years and reversed the trend of more than a century to smaller and smaller families. The postwar era also brought inflation ("a spend-thrift masculine-looking spiral," Bess Furman wrote), economic expansion, and new hopes of social mobility. The end of the 1940s revealed, finally, the distinctive themes of women's history in the coming decade: a growing number of women wage earners, an orchestrated outburst of domestic ideology, and a large space where the woman's movement once had been.

American feminism had not survived the emergencies intact. Since suffrage was won, feminists had been battered by a series of blows; but in the 1930s and 1940s, the organizations that once had made up the woman's movement fell by the wayside—by shrinking, folding, or losing their feminist thrust. In the early New Deal, women's pressure groups had warily monitored government policy. The NWP, the LWV, and the dwindling WTUL joined forces to combat Section 213 and other offensive developments, such as sex discrimination in federal relief projects. But the tone of reform changed in the 1930s. As historian Lois Scharf points out, idealists were more interested in revising the economic system than in enhancing individual rights. The cause of women's rights, in particular, became peripheral. In World War II, women's pressure groups were pushed even farther toward the edge of public life, and after the war, their marginality increased. Feminism, traditionally, was a middle-class movement with upper-class leadership. By the postwar era, a growing middle class no longer shared those common class interests that had propelled the suffrage and progressive movements. No umbrella issue, like the vote, could now unite a range of middle-class women for whom, on the whole, family mobility mattered more than women's causes.

Feminists lacked leadership as well. Most New Deal survivors, who had entered public life early in the century, had now retired or been absorbed into the recesses of the federal bureaucracy. More important, no major women's institutions had been formed since the vote was won and the old ones no longer served as training grounds for public life; the generation gap of the 1920s was now a chasm. Once the woman's movement faded, the media took over as women's representatives in public life. In the media, serious statements about women took on an underground quality, appropriate to a hostile environment. "Women must become more conscious of themselves as women and of their ability to function as a group," Eleanor Roosevelt wrote in *Good Housekeeping* in 1940. "At the same time they must try to wipe from men's consciousness the need to consider them as a group, or as women, in their everyday activities, especially as workers in industry or the professions." This indeed was an archetypical feminist dilemma. It was also a double bind.

The most visible tension between "women as individuals" and "women as a group" was the prolonged conflict over the Equal Rights Amendment that accompanied feminist decline in the 1930s and 1940s. In the New Deal years, social reformers had trounced the NWP, which also endured internal schisms. Most women prominent in political life, such as Frances Perkins and Eleanor Roosevelt, viewed the ERA as anathema. Still, the amendment made progress. In the late 1920s it had won approval from women's business and professional groups, and in the 1930s it gained support among male politicians. No man in public office wanted to be considered an opponent of "equal rights," Mary Anderson complained. In 1936, a House subcommittee endorsed the ERA; in 1938, the Senate Judiciary Committee reported it to the floor. In 1940, the Republican party endorsed the amendment, as did the General Federation of Women's Clubs. In 1944, the amendment finally won the support of the Democratic party, after a vigorous campaign by Emma Guffey Miller, a member of the platform committee, who then assumed a leading role in what remained of the NWP.

ERA opponents now mobilized. In 1945, the Women's Bureau described National Woman's party members as aging suffrage veterans, militant and leisure class, who resented "not having been born men." Legal change could only harm women, the bureau claimed, by depriving them of such benefits as alimony. "This doctrinaire position," Frances Perkins told Florence Armstrong, head of the NWP, would make it difficult to pass laws to aid "working sisters." Trade unions joined the opposition as well. In 1945, a coalition of 43 organizations united to defeat the "Unequal Rights Amendment," including the League of Women Voters, the American Association of University Women, the Young Women's Christian Association, the New York branch of the Women's Trade Union League, the National Congresses of Catholic and Jewish Women, and 25 trade union groups. ERA opponents included Carrie Chapman Catt, Alice Hamilton, Mary McLeod Bethune, Freda Kirchwey, Frances Perkins, and Frieda Miller; Eleanor Roosevelt had avoided taking a stand on the issue at the time of the 1944 Democratic party convention. When the ERA reached the Senate in July 1946, it did not win the needed two-thirds majority; 38 senators were in favor and 35 opposed. "Motherhood cannot be amended," said the *New York Times*. In 1950, the Senate approved an ERA with a rider excluding protective laws from its impact, and it repeated this effort in 1953. But by now the issue seemed dead. And so, by and large, did the woman's movement, which had argued about it since the 1920s. Pockets remained in the LWV, which monitored the electoral process; the remnant of the NWP; and the Women's Bureau, a small bastion in the federal bureaucracy.

By the time the ERA finally capsized, the female work force was changing. The postwar economy provided new space for women wage earners, and in 1947, the number of working women began to climb. By the end of the decade, the proportion of women in the work force had risen to 31 percent and kept rising; this quickly made up the losses of the immediate postwar slump. Women no longer entered heavy industry, as they had done during the war, nor did they surge into the professions. Rather, they took jobs in traditional "women's fields"—office work, sales, and services—which rapidly expanded. The postwar female work force, however, retained important wartime characteristics. It was predominantly married, older, and middle class, a trend that had started in the 1920s but was not noticeable until World War II. The postwar era even provided a new justification for the middle-class working wife. As historian William H. Chafe points out, a second income was needed to maintain a middle-class lifestyle. Inflation, not "individualism," spurred the married wage earner. In the 1930s, depression had served the same purpose.

Wage earning in the late 1940s did not necessarily provide a rise in status, either outside the family or within it. First, in 1946, Congress failed to act on an Equal Pay bill, one supported by women's organizations and labor unions (which feared the replacement of male wage earners by cheap female labor). Second, in the view of sociologists, the postwar family was settling into a staunchly traditional shape. According to the *American Journal of Sociology* in 1947, the modal type of family was now the "semi-patriarchal form in which a dominant husband 'brings in the bacon' and a submissive woman plays a traditional wife-and-mother role." Not only had the companionate model of marriage waned, but men sought spouses who had less education than they did and were less qualified to make decisions. Even if both spouses worked, the wife's wages, which were less than the husband's, were regarded as minor. A similar trend toward hierarchy within the family had been noticed even earlier in the decade. Changing attitudes threatened sexual equality, as sociologist Joseph K. Folsom had warned in 1943, when he prophesied a "resubjection of women." Moreover, he contended, younger women were urged into traditional domestic roles, as opposed to careers, by a barrage of "adroit publicity."

The full-scale revival of domestic ideology in the postwar era hardly materialized out of the blue. Rather, it reflected currents that were present in the depression, when wage-earning women seemed to threaten "breadwinners," and throughout the war, when working women loomed as a threat to social stability. After the war, the press reduced the threat of the married wage earner to a personal problem. Conflict between traditional roles and outside involvements was the "American woman's dilemma," said *Life* magazine in 1947. Should she work outside the home or should she devote her time and energy solely to household and family?

The issue arose that year in the prestigious *Annals of Social and Political Science* in a special issue, "Women's Opportunities and Responsibilities," which revealed the anxiety that was brewing over women's roles. Clearly, there were two sides. Frieda Miller of the Women's Bureau rose to the defense of women's work and aspiration. "Intermingled . . . with the necessity for self-support is the desire for self-expression, the need to make a contribution to society in a field adapted to one's individual personality," said Miller. Some women, she contended, found work in office, store, factory, school, or hospital more satisfying than work at home. Pursuing a career, she suggested, was no longer an "act of heroism," nor restricted solely to single women. "It may very well be that we are approaching a period when for women to work is an act of conformism." But by 1947, Miller's view was out of date. A WTUL activist since World War I and a protégé of Frances Perkins, Miller represented the old guard. The latest insights into women's needs came from psychiatry, a profession that had made strides during World War II. Conflict between home and career, psychoanalyst Marynia Farnham pointed out in the 1947 *Annals*, could lead a woman into psychological purgatory. She might want a career as "a source of prestige," but this required "a great deal of drive, self-assertion, competition, and aggression," while fulfillment of her biological function through marriage and childbearing called for qualities "that can best be classified as protective or nurturing, passive and receptive." The disparity between such contradictory demands made women harassed and even psychologically ill, "hostile, aggressive, and perpetually at odds with their environment."

The popular press of the late 1940s often dealt with the "dilemma" by favoring domesticity. Articles with such titles as "Isn't a Woman's Place in the Home?" accompanied fiction extolling the advantages of romance over career. Prominent journalists contributed to the vogue. "Women Aren't Men," Journalist Agnes Meyer told *Atlantic* readers. "God protect us from the efficient, go-getter business woman whose feminine instincts have been completely stifled." *Redbook* in 1947 contended that divorce was "less an expression of our freedom than a new indication of failure to adjust." Not surprisingly, as an article in the 1947 *Annals* confirmed, "Girls of today apparently accept the feminine role with less rebellion than their mothers did." Such acceptance appeared in the questions submitted to Eleanor Roosevelt's question-and-answer column—first in the *Ladies' Home Journal* and then, after 1949, in *McCall's*. "I am a rather young housewife who for four years has been working to help my husband make a down payment on a little home," wrote a reader. "Do you think I could safely quit my job now and keep house as I have wanted to do all my life?" A youngster was more to the point. "Do you agree that a girl should hide her intellectual side if she's going to be popular with boys?"

The new propaganda for domesticity probably made little impression on women who had embarked on careers in the 1920s and 1930s and advanced in them in World War II. But it seemed to affect young middle-class women who were planning their futures. Betty Friedan remembered 1949 as "the year the feminine mystique really hit us." Recently out of college, Friedan was part of the cohort most severely hit. "In 1949, nobody had to tell a woman that she wanted a man, but the message certainly began bombarding us from all sides; domestic bliss had suddenly become chic, sophisticated.... It almost didn't matter who the man was who became the instrument of your feminine fulfillment." Injunctions to reject masculine values and to find "domestic bliss" had insidious appeal. "The feminine mystique," said Friedan, "made it easier for a woman to retire smugly, avoiding conformity and competition as men could not."

Although the postwar version of domestic ideology had ample precedents, starting in the 1920s, there was one important difference. Now, in the late 1940s, since feminist pressure groups had faded or folded, countervailing arguments won little attention. Domestic ideology, however, enjoyed ample publicity. In *Modern Woman: The Lost Sex*, a best-seller of 1947 written by psychoanalyst Farnham and sociologist Ferdinand Lundberg, the "independent woman" was labeled a contradiction in terms. An extremist tract, *Modern Woman* drew critical scorn ("dogmatic and sensational") but reached a wide audience. Feminism, said Farnham and Lundberg, was a neurotic reaction to natural male dominance. The true woman, on the other hand, revealed self-acceptance, dependence on men, and passive fulfillment in sex and motherhood. Proposing government measures to spur such fulfillment, such as subsidies for childbearing, Farnham and Lundberg demanded that feminine women "reclaim the home as their proper domain."

Modern Woman was a legacy of World War II and of the resistance toward women wage earners that had built up during depression and war. But the war left other legacies too: economic recovery, higher wages, higher living standards, a market bulging with goods and services, and a national rise in expectations. In the 1950s, more Americans had access to middle-class status than ever before. Within the growing middle class, women were impelled by two forces, not unlike those that pervaded the "emergencies." One was a search for domestic security, a goal that had intensified in the 1930s and 1940s. Another was a thrust toward wage earning, once again fostered by family need and expanding employment opportunities. The emergencies left a legacy of apparent contradictions.

SUGGESTED READINGS AND SOURCES

For overviews, see William H. Chafe, *The Paradox of Change: American Women in the 20th Century* (New York, 1991); Lois W. Banner, *Women in Modern America: A Brief History*, 2d ed. (New York, 1984), ch. 5; Peter Gabriel Filene, *Him/Her/Self: Gender Identities in Modern America*, 3d ed. (Baltimore, Md., 1998), ch. 6; and Rosalind Rosenberg, *Divided Lives: American Women in the Twentieth Century* (New York, 1992), ch. 4. Two cogent surveys are Susan Ware, *Holding Their Own: American Women in the 1930s* (Boston, 1982), and Susan M. Hartmann, *The Home Front and Beyond: American Women in the 1940s* (Boston, 1982).

Sociologists of the 1930s and 1940s provide a wealth of studies on the depression's impact on family life. See, for instance, Ruth S. Cavan and Katherine H. Ranck, *The Family and the Depression: A Study of One Hundred Chicago Families* (Chicago, 1938); Mirra Komarovsky, *The Unemployed Man and His Family: The Effects of Underemployment upon the Status of Men in Fifty-Nine Families* (New York, 1940); Winona L. Morgan, *The Family Meets the Depression: A Study of a Group of Highly Selected Families* (Minneapolis, Minn., 1939); Robert S. Lynd and Helen Merrill Lynd, *Middletown in Transition: A Study in Cultural Conflict* (New York, 1937); Wight Bakke, *Citizens Without Work* (New Haven, Conn., 1940); and Eli Ginzburg, *The Unemployed* (New York, 1943). The case studies of the Burtons and the Rileys are in Robert Cooley Angell, *The Family Encounters the Depression* (New York, 1936). "The Modern American Family," an issue of *Annals of the American Academy of Social and Political Science*, 160 (March 1932), includes articles on homemaking and welfare services. For contemporary sources on women wage earners, see Lorine Pruette, *Women Workers Through the Depression* (New York, 1934), a study of white-collar employment, and the steady stream of publications from the Women's Bureau (Washington, D.C.) in the 1930s. Margaret J. Hapgood, *Mothers of the South: Portraiture of the White Tenant Farm Woman* (Chapel Hill, N.C., 1939), describes women's work and family roles in the rural South.

Lois Scharf, *To Work or to Wed: Female Employment, Feminism, and the Great Depression* (Westport, Conn., 1980), examines women's roles in the labor force and family, with attention to the experience of married working women. Ruth M. Milkman, "Women's Work and the Economic Crisis: Some Lessons from the Great Depression," in Nancy Cott and Elizabeth Pleck, eds., *A Heritage of Her Own* (New York, 1979), pp. 507–541, suggests the effect of sexual segregation in the workplace on women's employment. Winifred D. Wandersee Bolin, "The Economics of Middle-Income Family Life: Working Women During the Great Depression," *Journal of American History*, 65 (June 1978), 60–74, examines the increase of married women in the 1930s labor force. See also Wandersee, *Women's Work and Family Values, 1920–1940* (Cambridge, Mass., 1981), and Alice Kessler-Harris, *Out to Work: A History of Wage-Earning Women in the United States* (New York, 1982), chs. 9 and 10. Wandersee and Kessler-Harris show that significant changes in married women's employment patterns began before the 1940s. Staughton Lynd and Alice Lynd examine labor organization in *Rank and File: Personal Histories of Working Class Organizers* (Boston, 1973). For recent essays on women's labor history, see Ava Baron, ed. *Work Engendered: Toward a New History of American Labor* (Ithaca, N.Y., 1991), chs. 12 and 13. Two films on women and the labor movement in the 1930s are "Union Maids," by Julia Reichert, Jim Klein, and Miles Mogulescu, which focuses on three women workers, and "With Babies and Banners," by Lorraine Gray, on the Women's Emergency Brigade in the General Motors Sit-Down Strike of 1937 (both from New Day Films).

For the problems of black women wage earners, see Jean Collier Brown, *The Negro Woman Worker*, Bulletin 165 of the Women's Bureau (Washington, D.C., 1938), and Jacqueline Jones, *Labor of Love, Labor of Sorrow* (New York, 1985), ch. 6. Letters of protest about racial discrimination appear in Rosalyn Baxandall, Linda Gordon, and Susan Reverby, eds., *America's Working Women* (New York, 1976), pp. 248–251, and Gerda Lerner, ed., *Black Women in White America: A Documentary History* (New York, 1976), pp. 398–405. For southern migrants, black and white, of the 1920s and 1930s, see Jacqueline Jones, *The Dispossessed: America's Underclasses from the Civil War to the Present* (New York, 1992), chs. 7 and 8. Evelyn Nakamo Glenn examines work roles in the 1930s and after in *Issei, Nisei, Warbride: Three Generations of Japanese American Women in Domestic Service* (Philadelphia, 1976). For the experience of Latina women in the depression and after, see Julia Kirk Blackwelder, *Women of the Depression: Caste and Culture in San Antonio, 1929–1939* (College Station, Tex., 1984); Rosalinda M. Gonzolez, "Chicanas and Mexican Immigrant Families 1920–1940: Women's Subordination and Family Exploitation," in Lois Scharf and Joan M. Jensen, eds., *Decades of Discontent: The Women's Movement, 1920–1940* (Boston, 1987), pp. 59–84; Virginia E. Sanchez Korrol, *From Colonia to Community: The History of Puerto Ricans in New York City, 1917–1948* (Westport, Conn., 1983); Vicki L. Ruiz, *Cannery Women, Cannery Lives: Mexican Women, Unionization, and the California Food Processing Industry, 1930–1950* (Albuquerque, N.M., 1987); Ruiz, *From Out of the Shadows: Mexican American Women in the Twentieth Century* (New York, 1998), ch. 4; and Karen Anderson, *Changing Woman: A History of Racial Ethnic Women in Modern America* (New York, 1996), ch. 5. Sources on Native American women in the depression include Anderson, *Changing Woman*, ch. 4; Victoria D. Patterson, "Indian Life in the City: A Glimpse of the Urban Experience of Pomo Women in the 1930s," *California History* 71 (Fall 1992), 402–411; and Harry A. Kersey, Jr. and Helen M. Banner, "Patchwork and Politics: The Evolving Role of Florida Seneca Women in the Twentieth Century," in Nancy Shoemaker, ed., *Negotiators of Change: Historical Perspectives on Native American Women* (New York, 1995), pp. 193–212.

Social histories of the depression include Caroline Byrd, *The Invisible Scar: The Great Depression and What It Did to American Life, from Then Until Now* (New York, 1966); Studs Terkel, *Hard Times: An Oral History of the Great Depression* (New York, 1970), a collection of reminiscences from a broad cross section of Americans; and David H. Kennedy, ed., *The American People in the Depression* (West Haven, Conn., 1973), a short sourcebook. Jeane Westin, *Making Do: How Women Survived the 30s* (Chicago, 1976), is a lively collection of interviews. For rural women, see Mary Neth, *Preserving the Family Farm: Women, Community, and the Foundation of Agribusiness in the Midwest, 1900–1940* (Baltimore, Md., 1993); Katherine Jellison, *Entitled to Power: Farm Women and Technology, 1913–1963* (Chapel Hill, N.C., 1993), chs. 3–5, which cover the 1930s and 1940s; Pamela Riney Kehrberg, ed., *Waiting on the Bounty: The Dust Bowl Diary of Mary Knackstadt Dyck* (Iowa City, Iowa, 1999); and Melissa Walker, *All We Knew Was To Farm: Rural Women and the Upcountry South, 1919–1941* (Baltimore, Md., 2000).

For Eleanor Roosevelt's life, see Blanche Wiesen Cook, *Eleanor Roosevelt: Volume One, 1884–1933* (New York, 1992), and Cook, *Eleanor Roosevelt: Volume Two, 1933–1938* (New York, 1999); Joseph P. Lash, *Eleanor and Franklin* (New York, 1971); Tamara K. Hareven, *Eleanor Roosevelt: An American Conscience* (Chicago, 1968); Lois Scharf, *Eleanor Roosevelt: First Lady of American Liberalism* (Boston, 1987); and Joan Hoff-Wilson and Marjorie Lightman, eds., *Without Precedent: The Life and Career of Eleanor Roosevelt* (Bloomington, Ind., 1984). The relationship between Eleanor Roosevelt and Lorena Hickok is discussed in Doris Faber, *The Life of Lorena Hickok: Eleanor Roosevelt's Friend* (New York, 1980); and Lorena Hickok, *Reluctant First Lady* (New York, 1962). Eleanor Roosevelt's relations with the Washington press corps are conveyed in Bess Furman, *Washington By-Line* (New York, 1949), and Maureen Beasley, ed., *The White House Press Conferences of Eleanor Roosevelt* (New York, 1933). For the 1940s, see Doris Kearns Goodwin, *No Ordinary Time, Franklin and Eleanor Roosevelt: The Home Front in World War II* (New York, 1994). For the postwar era, see Allida M. Black, *Casting Her Own Shadow: Eleanor Roosevelt and the Shaping of Postwar Liberalism* (New York, 1995).

Susan Ware, *Beyond Suffrage: Women in the New Deal* (Cambridge, Mass., 1981), examines the women's "network" that moved into posts in the federal government and Democratic party in 1933. For some network members' comments on women's political roles, see Mary T. Norton, "What Politics Has Meant to Me," *Democratic Digest* (February 6, 1938), 18; Emily Newell Blair, "Women and Political Jobs," *New York Herald Tribune Magazine*, April 23, 1933, p. 4; and Eleanor Roosevelt, "Women in Politics," *Good Housekeeping*, 110 (March 1940), 45. Women's careers in major New Deal posts are described in Mary Anderson, *Woman at Work* (Minneapolis, Minn., 1951); George F. Martin, *Madame Secretary: Frances Perkins* (Boston, 1976); Frances Perkins, *The Roosevelt I Knew* (New York, 1946); Susan Ware, *Partner and I: Molly Dewson, Feminism, and New Deal Politics* (New Haven, Conn., 1987); James T. Patterson, "Mary Dewson and the American Minimum Wage Movement," *Labor History*, 5 (Spring 1964), 135–152; Rackham Holt, *Mary McLeod Bethune: A Biography* (New York, 1964); B. Joyce Ross, "Mary McLeod Bethune and the National Youth Administration: A Case Study of Power Relationships," *Journal of Negro History* 60 (January 1975), 1–28; and Audrey Thomas McCluskey and Elaine M. Smith, eds., *Mary McLeod Bethune: Building a Better World* (Bloomington, Ind., 1999), which includes essays and documents. For archival sources on microfilm, see "Mary McLeod Bethune: The Bethune-Cookman Collection, 1922–1955" and "Mary McLeod Bethune: The Bethune Foundation Collection," three parts, which include NYA papers (all from University Publications of America). For the origins of the welfare state, see Linda Gordon, ed., *Women, the State, and Welfare* (Madison, Wisc., 1990); Theda Skocpol, *Protecting Soldiers and Mothers: Political Origins of Social Policy in the United States* (Cambridge, Mass., 1992); and Landon R. Y. Storrs, *Civilizing Capitalism: The National Consumers' League and New Deal Wage-Hour Policy* (Chapel Hill, N.C., 2000). For the background of Aid to Dependent Children, see Linda Gordon, *Pitied but Not Entitled: Single Mothers and the History of Welfare, 1890–1935* (New York, 1994); Blanche D. Coll, *Safety Net: Welfare and Social Security, 1929–1979* (New Brunswick, N.J., 1995); and Gwendolyn Mink, *The Wages of Motherhood: Inequality in the Welfare State, 1917–1942* (Ithaca, N.Y., 1995). For gender differences in New Deal regulations, see Suzanne Mettler, *Dividing Citizens: Gender and Federalism in New Deal Public Life* (Ithaca, N.Y. 1998).

Feminism in the 1930s is explored in Susan D. Becker, *The Origins of the Equal Rights Amendment: American Feminism Between the Wars* (Westport, Conn., 1981), a study of the National Woman's party; Lois Scharf and Joan M. Jensen, eds., *Decades of Discontent: The Women's Movement, 1920–1940* (Boston, 1987); Susan Ware, *Beyond Suffrage*; and Lois Scharf, *To Work or to Wed*. For social work, see Clarke A. Chambers, *Seedtime of Reform: American Social Service and Social Action, 1918–1933* (Minneapolis, Minn., 1972), and Grace Abbott, *From Relief to Social Security: The Development of the New Public Welfare Services and Their Administration* (Chicago, 1941). Women's activism in the Communist party is discussed in Susan Ware, *Holding Their Own*, ch. 5. See also the reminiscences collected by Vivian Gornick in *The Romance of American Communism* (New York, 1977).

Many works of scholarship explore women's roles in 1930s culture and society. Susan Ware, *Letters to the World: Seven Women Who Shaped the American Century* (New York,1998) contains illuminating portraits of achievers in several fields. For women's careers in journalism, see Agnes E. Meyer, *Out of These Roots: The Autobiography of an American Woman* (Boston, 1953); George Martin, *Cissy: The Extraordinary Life of Eleanor Medill Patterson* (New York, 1979); Peter Kurth, *American Cassandra: The Life of Dorothy Thompson* (Boston, 1990); Richard Lowitt and Maurine Beasley, eds., *One Third of a Nation: Lorena Hickok Reports on the Great Depression* (Urbana, Ill., 1983); and Ishbel Ross, *Ladies of the Press: The Story of Women in Journalism by an Insider* (New York, 1936). For the career of a radical journalist and novelist, see Elinor Langer, *Josephine Herbst: The Story She Could Never Tell* (Boston, 1983). Women's roles in 1930s movies are described in Marjorie Rosen, *Popcorn Venus: Women, Movies, and the American Dream* (New York, 1971); June Sochen, "Mildred Pierce and Women in Film," *American Quarterly*, 30 (Spring 1978), 3–20; Andrew Bergman, *We're in the Money: Depression America and Its Films* (New York, 1971); Jeanine Basinger, *A Woman's View: How Hollywood Spoke to Women, 1930–1960* (New York, 1993); Emily Wortis Leider, *Becoming Mae West* (New York, 1997); and Mary Beth Hamilton, *When I'm Bad, I'm Better: Mae West, Sex, and American Entertainment* (Berkeley, Calif., 1999). See also Maureen Harvey, "Images of Women in the *Saturday Evening Post*, 1931–1936," *Journal of Popular Culture*, 10 (1976), 352–358. For Margaret Mitchell's career, see Claudia Roth Pierpont, "A Study in Scarlett," *New Yorker* 68 (August 31, 1992), 87–103, and Darden Asbury Pyron, *Southern Daughter: The Life of Margaret Mitchell* (New York 1991).

For fictional renditions of the 1930s, see Tess Slesinger, *The Unpossessed* (New York, 1934), a novel about the left; Mary McCarthy's short stories in *The Company She Keeps* (New York, 1942); and McCarthy, *The Group* (New York, 1963), a novel about the Vassar class of 1933. Also of interest are Mary McCarthy, *Intellectual Memoirs: New York, 1936–1938* (New York, 1992); recent biographies of McCarthy, such as Carol Gelderman, *Mary McCarthy: A Life* (New York, 1988), and Carol Brightman, *Writing Dangerously: A Critical Biography of Mary McCarthy* (New York, 1992); and Paula Rabinowitz, *Labor and Desire: Women's Revolutionary Fiction in Depression America* (Chapel Hill, N.C., 1991). For murals and plays of the 1930s, see

Barbara Melosh, *Engendering Culture: Manhood and Womanhood in New Deal Public Art and Theater* (Washington, D.C., 1991). For depression-era photography, see *The Photographs of Dorothea Lange*, text by Keith F. Davis (New York, 1996). For the career of a champion athlete and popular figure of the 1930s and 1940s, see Susan E. Cayleff, *Babe: The Life and Legend of Babe Didrickson Zacharias* (Champaign, Ill., 1995).

William H. Chafe presents World War II as a watershed in the history of women's employment in *Paradox of Change*, chs. 7–9. Chafe's interpretation has been challenged or modified by other studies, such as Karen Anderson, *Wartime Women: Sex Roles, Family Relations, and the Status of Women During World War II* (Westport, Conn., 1981), an examination of the war's impact on women's lives in three major defense production areas; Ruth Milkman, *Gender at Work: The Dynamics of Job Segregation During World War II* (Urbana, Ill., 1987), which explores the experience of women workers in the electrical and auto industries; and Amy Kesselman, *Fleeting Opportunities: Women Shipyard Workers in Portland and Vancouver During World War II and Reconversion* (Albany, N.Y., 1990). Sherna Berger Gluck, ed., *Rosie the Riveter Revisited: Women, the War, and Social Change* (Boston, 1987), presents ten oral histories of war workers.

For studies of women's war work from the 1940s, see Laura N. Baker, *Wanted: Women in War Industry* (New York, 1943); Helen Baker, *Women in War Industries* (Princeton, N.J., 1942); Eva Lapin, *Mothers in Overalls* (New York, 1943); and Katherine Glover, *Women at Work in Wartime* (New York, 1943). For demobilization, see Frieda S. Miller, "What's Become of Rosie the Riveter?" *New York Times Magazine*, May 3, 1946, pp. 21ff. Among Women's Bureau publications, see *When You Hire Women*, Special Bulletin no. 14 (Washington, D.C., 1944), a list of suggestions to employers; *Changes in Women's Employment During the War*, Special Bulletin no. 20 (Washington, D.C., 1944), and *Women Workers in Ten Production Areas and Their Post-War Employment Plans*, Bulletin no. 209 (Washington, D.C., 1946). Available on microfilm are Anne Firor Scott and William H. Chafe, eds., *Records of the Women's Bureau of the U.S. Department of Labor, 1918–1965, Part II: Women in World War II*. Elizabeth Faulkner Baker describes the labor that women performed in war industry in *Technology and Women's Work* (New York, 1974).

D'Ann Campbell surveys women's wartime experiences in *Women at War with America: Private Lives in a Patriotic Era* (Cambridge, Mass., 1984). For aspects of women's lives during the war, see Leila M. Rupp. *Mobilizing Women for War: German and American Propaganda, 1939–1945* (Princeton, N.J., 1978); Sheila Tobias and Lisa Anderson, "What Really Happened to Rosie the Riveter?" *Ms*, 1 (June 1973), 92–94; and Susan M. Hartmann, "Prescriptions for Penelope: Literature on Women's Obligations to Returning World War II Veterans," *Women's Studies*, 5 (1978), 223–239. For African American women, see Karen Anderson, "Last Hired, First Fired: Black Women Workers During World War II," *Journal of American History* 69 (June, 1982), 82–97; Martha S. Putney, *When the Nation Was in Need: Blacks in the Women's Army Corps During World War II* (Metuchen, N.J., 1992); Gretchen Lemke Santangelo, *Abiding Courage: African American Migrant Women and the East Bay Community* (Chapel Hill, N.C., 1996); and Maureen Honey, ed., *Bitter Fruit: African American Women in World War II* (Columbia, Miss., 1999). For Native American women, see Alison R. Bernstein, *American Indians and World War II: Toward a New Era in Indian Affairs* (Norman, Okla., 1991), pp. 73–74. For wartime homemakers, see Amy Bentley, *Eating For Victory: Food Rationing and the Politics of Domesticity* (Urbana, Ill., 1998). Eleanor Straub assesses the problems of the Women's Advisory Committee in influencing policy in "United States Government Policy Toward Civilian Women During World War II," *Prologue* 5 (Winter, 1973), 240–254. For the Japanese-

American woman's wartime experience, see Deborah Genensway and Mindy Roseman, *Beyond Words: Images from America's Concentration Camps* (Ithaca, N.Y., 1987); Ronald Takaki, *Strangers from a Different Shore: A History of Asian Americans* (Boston, 1989); and Valerie Matsumoto, "Japanese American Women During World War II," *Frontiers*, 8 (1984), 6–14, which is reprinted in Ellen Carol DuBois and Vicki L. Ruiz, eds., *Unequal Sisters* (New York, 1990), pp. 373–386. A brief survey of Japanese internment in Roger Daniels, *Prisoners Without Trial: Japanese Americans in World War II* (New York, 1993).

For women's military roles, see Hartmann, *The Home Front and Beyond*, ch. 3; D'Ann Campbell, "Women in Uniform: The World War II Experiment," *Military Affairs*, 51 (July 1987), 137ff; Leisa D. Meyer, *Creating G. I. Jane: Sexuality and Power in the Women's Army Corps During World War II* (New York, 1996); Judy Barett Litoff and David C. Smith, *We're in This War, Too: World War II Letters from Women in Uniform* (New York, 1994); Martha S. Putney, *When the Nation Was in Need*, cited previously; and Paula Nassen Poulos, ed., *A Woman's War Too: U.S. Women in the Military in World War II* (Washington, D.C., 1996). For civilian women in the Pacific theater, see Theresa Kaminski, *Prisoners in Paradise: American Women in the Wartime South Pacific* (Lawrence, Ks., 2000). Nancy Caldwell Sorel examines women war correspondents in *The Women Who Wrote the War* (New York, 2000). Interpretations of the war experience include John Costello, *Virtue Under Fire: How World War II Changed Our Social and Sexual Attitudes* (Boston, 1985), and Alan Berube, *Coming Out Under Fire: The History of Gay Men and Women in World War II* (New York, 1990). See also Lillian Faderman, *Odd Girls and Twilight Lovers: A History of Lesbian Life in Twentieth-Century America* (New York, 1991), ch. 5. The impact of war on gender roles is explored in Margaret Randolph Higgonet, Jane Jensen, Sonya Michel, and Margaret Collins Weitz, eds., *Behind the Lines: Gender and the Two World Wars* (New Haven, Conn., 1987). Beth Bailey and David Farber reveal a cauldron of cultural change in *The First Strange Place: The Alchemy of Race and Sex in World War II Hawaii* (New York, 1992).

For peace movements of the 1930s and 1940s, see Linda K. Schott, *Reconstructing Women's Thoughts: The Women's International League for Peace and Freedom Before World War II* (Stanford, Calif., 1997); Carrie A. Foster, *The Women and the Warriors: The U.S. Section of the Women's International League for Peace and Freedom, 1915–1946* (Syracuse, N.Y., 1995), chs. 7–14; Rachel Waltner Goossen, *Women Against the Good War: Conscientious Objection and Gender on the Home Front, 1941–1947* (Chapel Hill, N.C., 1997); and, for women and isolationism, Glen Jeansonne, *Women of the Far Right: The Mother's Movement and World War II* (Chicago, 1998). For women and world affairs, see Edward P. Crapol, ed., *Women and Foreign Policy: Lobbyists, Critics, and Insiders* (Westport, Conn., 1987), chs. 5 and 6.

Attitudes toward women in the late 1940s are discussed in Chafe, *Paradox of Change*, ch. 9, and Betty Friedan, *It Changed My Life* (New York, 1977), pp. 26–37. See also *Annals of the American Academy of Political and Social Science*, 251 (May 1947), on "Women's Opportunities and Responsibilities"; Ferdinand Lundberg and Marynia Farnham, *Modern Women: The Lost Sex* (New York, 1947); Agnes Meyer, "Women Aren't Men," *Atlantic*, 186 (August 1950), 32–36; Joseph K. Folsom, *The Family and Democratic Society* (New York, 1943); and Reuben Hill, "The American Family: Problem or Solution," *American Journal of Sociology*, 53 (September 1947), 125–130. Mari Jo Buhle, *Feminism and Its Discontents: A Century of Struggle With Psychoanalysis* (Cambridge, Mass., 1998), chs. 4 and 5, discusses the postwar clash of Freudianism and feminism. For the equal pay campaign of the late 1940s, see Cynthia E.

Harrison, *On Account of Sex: The Politics of Women's Issues, 1945–1968* (Berkeley, Calif., 1988), ch. 3; Alice Kessler-Harris, *A Woman's Wage: Historical Meanings and Social Consequences* (Lexington, Ky., 1990), ch. 4; and Dennis A. Deslippe, *"Rights, Not Roses": Unions and the Rise of Working-Class Feminism, 1945–1980* (Urbana, Ill., 2000), ch. 2. For the political mood at mid-century, see Elaine Tyler May, *Homeward Bound: American Families in the Cold War Era* (New York, 1988), and Leila Rupp and Verta Taylor, *Survival in the Doldrums: The American Women's Rights Movement, 1945 to the 1960s* (New York, 1987), ch. 7. Studies of women in politics include Ralph G. Martin, *Henry and Clare: An Intimate Portrait of the Luces* (New York, 1991); Sylvia Jukes Morris, *Rage For Fame: The Ascent of Clare Boothe Luce* (New York, 1997); and Ingrid Winther Scobie, *Center Stage: Helen Gahagan Douglas, A Life* (New York, 1992).

For quizzes and additional resources related to American women's history, visit the book's Website at *www.mhhe.com/americanwomen*.

CHAPTER TEN

High Expectations: 1950–1975

HE DECADE OF the 1950s is remembered as a conventional and complacent one. But in women's history it was also a decade of significant change. Postwar America boasted an expanding economy, a growing middle class, and an abnormally high birthrate that rose for about a decade. A new outburst of domestic ideology accompanied this demographic reversal. At the same time, the postwar economy provided vocational space for women workers, who entered the labor force in record numbers. In the 1950s, women's expectations shifted in two directions, simultaneously.

As a result, the decade had an overt agenda, the return to domesticity, and a hidden one, a massive movement into the labor market. The first, though temporary, was more visible. The 1950s were an affluent era, when upward mobility seemed within reach; a consumerist era, when goods and services flooded the market; a conservative era, when voices of protest were muted or silent; and a period of consensus, when goals and aspirations were widely shared. The much-publicized domestic ideal of the decade appeared to be the most widely shared goal of all. "The suburban housewife was the dream image of the young American woman," Betty Friedan wrote in 1963. "She was healthy, beautiful, educated, concerned only about her husband, her children, her home. She had found feminine fulfillment."

SUBURBAN HOUSEWIVES

In *Life*'s special issue "The American Woman" in 1956, the largest amount of picture space was devoted to a suburban housewife, aged 32 and mother of four. A high school graduate who had married as a teenager, *Life*'s major subject, described as "pretty and popular," was a hostess, volunteer, and "home manager," who sewed her own clothes, entertained 1,500 guests a year, and was supported by a husband whose annual income was $25,000. "In her daily round she attends club or charity meetings, drives the children to school, does the weekly grocery shopping, makes ceramics, and is planning to learn French," *Life* revealed, as it followed the housewife from domestic chores to social gala. "A conscientious mother, she spends lots of time with her children, helping with their homework . . . listening to their stories or problems." That *Life*, which monitored the national pulse, chose the housewife as woman of the hour in 1956 was no surprise. In the 1950s, woman's sphere received extensive publicity.

The domestic ideology of the 1950s, hardly new, had been popular for more than a century. Though challenged by a feminist gust in the early twentieth century, the domestic ideal had gained ground since the 1920s. After World War II, it was cloaked in modern garb, bolstered by experts, and widely promoted. In part antifeminist, domestic ideology incorporated the backlash against women and fear of female competition that had followed the war. In part anti-elitist, it posited fulfillment at home as a goal to which women of all classes and backgrounds might aspire. Most important, in the 1950s, the domestic ideal won a fresh constituency: women who had grown up during depression and war and looked forward to stable, traditional roles in secure, prosperous environments. Domestic ideology did not reign unquestioned; mass culture in fact reflected a variety of views. Still, the domestic ideal drew support from the dominant trends of postwar life—a consumer economy, an expanding middle class, a great spurt of suburban growth, and a 15-year baby boom.

Early marriages and young families prevailed in the 1950s. After the war, the average marriage age for women dropped to 20. By 1951, one woman in three was married by 19, and in 1958, more women married between 15 and 19 than in any comparable age span. The postwar rush to matrimony accompanied a surge in the birthrate that continued for a decade, far longer than minor postwar baby booms in other modern nations. The American birthrate did not peak until 1957, when it reached a high of 25.3 per thousand people. The birthrate among college-educated women, moreover, was only slightly lower than that of the general female population. As more young women were taking care of more young children than at any time in recent memory, domestic ideology had a captive audience. But that ideology rested on a built-in demographic flaw. Postwar childbearing was usually compressed into the teens and twenties; the average mother might expect to have her last child by the age of 30. Within a decade after that, all her children would be in school if not starting to go off on their own. More than half her adult life would be spent neither having children nor caring for them. The discrepancy between domestic ideology and the female life cycle was obscured, however, by the appeal and demands of suburban life.

The domestic passion of the 1950s coincided with a massive exodus to the suburbs, the ideal place for raising families. Suburbs had evolved in the 1890s and had grown again in the 1920s, but their rapid expansion was a post-World War II phenomenon: Many Americans could now afford homes, cars, and early marriage. In the 1950s alone, two-thirds of American population growth occurred in suburbs. Federal policy supported such growth. Young couples in search of suburban havens benefited from low-interest mortgages, veterans benefits, and federal support for highway construction. The same policies promoted domestic ideals, since suburban life, for women, meant commitment to home and family, to house care and child care. For the college-educated housewife later described by Betty Friedan, this commitment was a "mistaken choice," a step backward into traditional roles. But for the typical new postwar housewife, it was a step upward into the middle class, into normalcy,

A baby shower in the 1950s. Abetted by suburbanization, the
total fertility rate of American women soared to more than 3.6,
higher than that of 1910. In tune with the times, Planned
Parenthood clinics adapted to the baby boom. They developed
sex counseling programs and stressed the value of birth
control as a tool to create enduring sexual
relationships in marriage. (*Suzanne Szasz*)

though it was a "normalcy" that had never existed before. After World War II, the
proportion of Americans who were middle class approximately doubled. The postwar middle class, wrote journalist Agnes Meyer at midcentury, had been "augmented
by seepage from above due to the decline of big fortunes and by seepage from below,
due to the rise in wages, the improvement of educational opportunities, and technological progress."

Born in the depression, the new homemaker appreciated her security, lifestyle,
and rising standard of living. Sociologist Herbert Gans, who lived in a New Jersey
Levittown in the early 1960s, recorded a high level of satisfaction among his subur-
banites, male and female, who came from lower-middle- or working-class origins.
For Levittowners, suburban life was not a "retreat into localism and familialism" but
rather a continuation of it. "Most Levittowners grew up in the depression and re-
membering the hard times of their childhood, they wanted to protect themselves and
their children from stress," Gans wrote. So did the new suburban housewife of the
1950s. Neither a college graduate nor a career woman manqué, she was a survivor.

The new suburban housewife of the 1950s rarely assumed a leadership role in
community affairs. She might serve as a volunteer, but she avoided policymaking positions, which were filled by men. On a national level, women in public affairs received little publicity—with such notable exceptions as Margaret Chase Smith, who
entered the Senate in 1948. Women in fact remained active as volunteers in political
campaigns, in unions, and in the movement against nuclear armament. Women

Strike For Peace, formed in 1961, would soon mobilize thousands to support the ban of nuclear tests and to oppose the Vietnam War. But major women's organizations of the 1950s, like the League of Women Voters, receded to the background. They opposed an Equal Rights Amendment, supported child welfare, and avoided controversy. By 1960, the LWV was half the size it had been in the 1920s. Feminism was mocked in the press if mentioned at all. However, the housewife was not excluded from the nation's economic life. In an era of mass consumerism, she became once again an important consumer.

After World War II, items that had once been relative luxuries were, like the suburban home, now within reach for cash or credit. More than a million new homes a year needed appliances, decoration, and upkeep, creating a huge new household market. Housewives, who made 75 percent of family purchases, bought electric mixers and sewing machines, chose among floor waxes and detergents, and selected food and clothes for five or six people. The power of a woman, never undervalued by the *Ladies' Home Journal* or its competitors, was not moral power but purchasing power. "The buying of things," as an advertising expert told Betty Friedan, could provide a "sense of identity, purpose, creativity . . . self-realization." Aspiration assumed material shape. A Gallup poll run for the *Journal* in 1961 revealed that most young women could define their goals, beyond four children, with graphic precision—built-in ovens, formica counters, finished woodwork, and "a split-level brick with four bedrooms with French provincial furniture." Tupperware parties, at which women viewed demonstrations of household products in the home of a "hostess," became a hallmark of the 1950s. This novel marketing strategy shrewdly blended domesticity, consumerism, and homemakers' need for extra income.

Advertisers were not the only promoters of domestic ideals after World War II. So were the experts, who offered scientific, medical, and psychological counsel. In postwar America professionals assumed new authority. Femininity was now defined by specialists whose messages filtered into magazines, movies, and marriage manuals. Women, said the experts, found fulfillment in passive roles. The basic tenets emerged right after the war. The feminine woman, psychoanalyst Helene Deutsch had written in 1946, "leaves the initiative to the man and out of her own needs, renounces originality, experiences her own self through identification." Unlike the "masculine" woman—intelligent, aggressive, and bent on achievement, due to some mishap in her psychological development—Deutsch's "ideal life companion" abandoned ambition, avoided competition, and relied on intuition, "God's gift to the feminine woman." Women's needs, Marynia Farnham and Ferdinand Lundberg confirmed in their 1947 best-seller, were "a wish for dependence, inwardness, a wish to be protected and made secure, a strong desire for passivity and compliance." Clearly the experts supported traditional roles; their warnings posited two alternatives, femininity or disaster. "Psychiatrists who studied the causes of our disturbing divorce rate," according to *Life* in 1956, "note wives who are not feminine enough."

Another type of passivity was urged on mothers. In the 1950s, child-rearing manuals catered to a huge market of middle-class mothers. Dr. Spock, the most popular manual writer, reached one million readers a year between 1946 and 1960. But the mother's authority as guardian of youth had diminished. She was expected, instead, to act as a conduit between expert and child. Above all, she was exhorted to avoid two assertive attitudes that the experts deplored: rejection and overprotection. The working mother, for instance, escaped responsibility, leaving behind an abandoned, deprived, and potentially delinquent child. In his early editions, Dr. Spock cautioned mothers who wanted to leave young children for paid work to seek psychological or social counseling; it was best to leave home only for a trip to the beauty parlor, to see a movie, buy a new hat or dress, or visit a good friend. The overprotective mother, recently discovered, was another hazard. During the war, many army recruits had received psychiatric discharges due to maladies doctors attributed to overdependence on their mothers. Powerful and grasping, the overprotective mother was now described as a saboteur, who attempted to keep her children emotionally immature and bound to her forever, thereby ruining their lives. Aware of the dangers of both rejection and overprotection, the postwar mother was supposed to be primarily a constant presence—nonassertive, available, and able to follow professional advice. If she had a problem, as did the thousands of mothers who wrote to Dr. Spock each year, she was likely to attribute it to her personal defects—in one mother's words, "my own emotionalism and lack of control."

The passivity urged on wives and mothers affected younger women too. The college woman, always a useful barometer, was hardly immune to domestic ideals. Indeed, the rush to matrimony took on new urgency. "Girls feel hopeless if they haven't a marriage at least in sight by commencement time," the *New York Times* reported in 1955. The Vassar woman no longer expected to make "an enduring contribution to society," a visitor observed in 1962. "Her future identity is largely encompassed by the projected role of wife and mother." Authorities and educators sometimes reinforced the college woman's new traditionalism. Colleges should not treat women as "men in disguise," the president of Mills urged in 1950, but rather provide a "distinctively feminine curriculum," centered around a course in the family, that would not cut women off from their domestic destinies. Even in traditional courses, social science students were likely to learn that current ideals of gender roles served a functional purpose in society. Not surprisingly, college women adjusted their sights to cultural demands. In *Women and the Modern World* (1952), Barnard sociologist Mirra Komarovsky analyzed their modes of adjustment.

Komarovsky had a bias. She labeled demands for feminine curricula as "neo-antifeminist," linked such demands to the baneful rise of psychoanalytic influence, and even found fault with the ideal feminine woman Deutsch had described. ("At her worst, she risks a self-abased subjection to tyranny and a deterioration of personality.") The students she had surveyed in the past decade, however, favored traditional goals. All but a handful anticipated marriage and motherhood, although most intended to work between graduation and marriage. "Work experience is beneficial because it gives some insight into the husband's world," a student observed. Beyond these areas of consensus, aspirations were divided. Twenty percent of the college women were determined careerists who hoped to marry and have families as well; 30 percent were "middle-of-the-road" types who anticipated employment after ten or 15 years of homemaking and child-rearing. But half looked forward to lifelong domestic careers after marriage, contending "that it is natural for a woman to be satisfied with her husband's success and not crave personal achievement"; "that a woman who worked cannot possibly be as good a mother as one who stays home"; and "that a husband is naturally superior in certain spheres but that he requires constant and watchful encouragement on the part of the wife to maintain his superiority."

Komarovsky contended that students defended traditional roles "all the more passionately" because they felt tempted by "other goals." Conflict between individual inclinations and traditional roles emerged in some of the seniors' responses. "I am a natural leader," one student wrote. "But I know that men fear bossy women, and I always have to watch myself on dates not to assume 'the executive role.'" "Quite frankly, I am afraid to go into some kind of business career because I have a feeling that I would cheat myself out of marriage," said another senior. "I may be wrong, but I am just old-fashioned enough to believe that men (at least the type I want to marry) still want their wives to be feminine, domestic, dependent, and just a little inferior mentally."

The domestic ideology that Komarovsky's college students revealed remained alive and well for a decade after her book was published. Its impact emerged again in 1962 in responses to a massive 209-question Gallup poll, as reported in the *Saturday Evening Post*. "Our study shows that few people are as happy as a housewife," the pollsters, George Gallup and Evan Hill, concluded after interviewing 2,300 women. "Apparently the American woman has all the rights she wants." Supporting this assertion, 96 percent of those surveyed declared themselves extremely happy or very happy. "Being subordinate to men is part of being feminine," an Arizona mother volunteered. "A woman's prestige comes from her husband's opinion of her," a Portland housewife declared. "Women who ask for equality fight nature," said a New Jersey mother of three, formerly a career woman. Asked to identify the "most satisfying moments" of their lives, nine out of ten women voted for childbirth. "The most thrilling moment of Eleanor's life came when she watched her children being born, and being a good mother is the goal she considers most important," Gallup and Hill reported. "I want to be the kind of woman who gives her children emotional security," Eleanor explained. "That's one of the reasons why I don't think a mother should work." She was also bent on "broadening my interests so I won't bore Jim." Interviewing thousands of women offered lighter moments, though these too revealed a facet of traditional roles ("Why, you talk to my wife as if you thought she knew what she was talking about," a husband told the researchers). But the Gallup poll also provided a few downbeat notes. Most women interviewed wanted their daughters to have more education and marry later, and 90 percent hoped that their daughters would not "lead the same kind of life they did."

Gallup and Hill's testimonial to the 1950s domestic ideology was, ironically, one of its first obituaries. A second and more important one appeared in 1963. In *The Feminine Mystique*, journalist Betty Friedan revealed the hazards of a popular ideology that limited women's aspirations, deprived them of self-esteem, and presented them with a "problem that has no name." Since the end of the war, Friedan contended, women had been "told that they could desire no greater destiny than to glory in their own femininity," to find fulfillment as wives and mothers. Urged homeward by experts and educators, advertisers and women's magazines, psychologists and social scientists, women had become the victims of the feminine mystique. It confined them to the home, "a comfortable concentration camp"; it barred them from assuming adult roles, as independent individuals; and it deprived them of a sense of self.

"Encouraged by the mystique to evade their identity crisis, permitted to escape identity altogether in the name of sexual fulfillment, women once again are living with their feet bound in the old image of glorified femininity," Friedan declared. "And it is the same old image, despite its shiny new clothes, that trapped women for centuries and made the feminists rebel."

Devoid of purpose and laden with problems, Friedan insisted, the postwar housewife was neither a good wife nor a good mother; nor was she a fulfilled human being, as documented by an array of personal testimony. "I've tried everything women are supposed to do," one of the mystique's victims revealed, "but I'm desperate. I begin to feel that I have no personality." "By noon I'm ready for a padded cell," said another homemaker. The feminine mystique, Friedan concluded, had "succeeded in burying millions of women alive." And women themselves were in part responsible for their own predicament. After World War II, "the American woman made her mistaken choice," Friedan accused. "She ran back home to live by sex alone, trading in her individuality for security." Security had temptations, she conceded (and these seemed to resemble the lures of "contingent living" revealed by psychologist Lorine Pruette three decades before). "It is easier to live through husband and child," Betty Friedan wrote, "than to make a road of her own in the world."

A revivalist tract, crammed with telling anecdotes and references to personal experience, *The Feminine Mystique* proposed some remedies. Education and employment, Betty Friedan contended, would liberate the housewife from the suburban home and enable her "to find herself, to know herself as a person by creative work of her own." Revised educational policies would steer her toward a career; a "new life plan" would enable her to mesh family role and vocational goals; a national education program similar to the GI Bill would allow women to resume their education and "commit themselves to professions." But the power of *The Feminine Mystique* was not in its remedies, which seemed quite meager compared to the imposing conspiracy against women that Friedan described. Rather, it was in the revelation of the "mystique" itself.

Readers of *The Feminine Mystique* responded immediately to Betty Friedan. The flood of correspondence she received expressed both gratitude and antagonism. Few critical letters came from men; many wrote to say that they had bought the book for their wives. But among women, a chasm divided the negative and positive reactions, both of which, curiously, substantiated the impact of the "feminine mystique." "I happen to love the rewards of being completely passive," wrote a California housewife. "I don't want to compete with my husband. I want to respect and admire him." Other negative responses, from similarly angry women, contended that Betty Friedan needed psychiatric help. There were also, overwhelmingly, positive responses. "It struck at the center of my being," wrote an Iowa woman. "I feel like I am on the threshold of a new life." Significantly, many of the appreciative letters, which confirmed Freidan's thesis, overflowed with negative feelings—guilt, shame, resentment, despair—and low self-images. Women described themselves variously as mops, zombies, sissies, drudges, and freaks. "I have been trying for years to tell my husband of my need to do something to find myself—to have a purpose," wrote a Florida mother of four. "All I've ever achieved was to end up feeling guilty about wanting to be more than a housewife and mother." Younger women expressed a different kind of guilt. "I feel like an appliance," wrote a young Michigan mother of three. "My brain seems dead and I am nothing but a parasite."

The impact of the book was unanticipated. Friedan was able to transform a personal problem first into a social problem, then into a public cause, and ultimately into political capital. Clearly, her message of 1963 was geared to educated women like herself, capable of "creative work" and "professional achievements," who appeared to be the mystique's major victims. Her interpretation of women's experience in the postwar era was similarly skewed by middle-class bias; it was both limited and exaggerated. Friedan insisted on a hegemony of experience that did not exist, except perhaps in women's magazines, whose rhetoric she adopted and whose stereotypes she reenforced. In fact, Friedan's self-portrait of a woman entrapped by the feminist mystique was in part a "reinvention," historian Daniel Horowitz reveals. As a college student and labor journalist in the 1940s and 1950s, Friedan had extensive experience with unions, radicalism, and left-wing causes, aspects of her past that she chose to downplay or ignore. A long-time critic of consumerism and corporate capitalism, Friedan was a political sophisticate, not a typical suburban housewife. But she was also an ambitious professional, for whom middle-class women provided a sphere of influence—as her working-class sympathies and left-wing politics had not. Significantly, the remedies she proposed, such as the "new life plan," were individual solutions, not collective solutions. Friedan did not urge or envision the birth of a new women's movement. Still, the "problem that has no name" was one that women readers recognized. From the outset, Friedan's polemics had more impact than her proposals. Her revelations, finally, were extremely well-timed.

By 1963, when *The Feminine Mystique* appeared, the phenomenon it assaulted had started to lose its foundations. The birthrate was dropping, the marriage age was rising, and the conservative social climate was starting to change. Moreover, since the late 1940s, when (according to Friedan) the "feminine mystique" struck, middle-class women had been moving steadily into paid employment.

WORKING MOTHERS

When Gallup and Hill surveyed the views of "the American woman" in 1962, they paid scant attention to working wives. But after World War II, the female work force dramatically increased and the woman wage earner became a standard part of middle-class life. Before the war, only one out of four women over 16 years old worked. But in 1960, two out of five held jobs, twice as many in number as in 1940. Women's proportion of the work force continued to grow. In the 1960s, two-thirds of new employees were women; and by the end of the decade, almost half of adult women earned wages. The new woman worker of the 1950s and 1960s, moreover, was likely to be married, middle-class, and middle-aged. And with each year that passed, she was more likely to be a mother with children under 17 at home.

The advent of the working wife was the first major structural change of the postwar era. By 1950, married women made up more than half the female work force, and each year their proportion rose. In 1940, only 15 percent of wives worked; in 1950, 21 percent; in 1960, 30 percent; in 1970, over 40 percent; and by 1980, over

50 percent. The age of the female work force also rose. The largest segment of new women workers in the 1950s were those in their forties or older; by 1960, the median age of the working woman was 41. Throughout the 1950s, the social status of the woman worker also rose; women from middle-class families entered the labor force faster than any other group. The new woman worker was also more likely to be a parent. In 1948, when the postwar female work force was just starting to expand, only one out of four women with school-age children, between six and 17 years old, held jobs, but by 1960, two out of five of such women were at work. By the end of the 1960s, over half of all mothers of school-age children were in the labor force. Unlike the baby boom, which hit its peak in 1957 and then declined, the movement of wives and then mothers into paid employment steadily gathered momentum. The greatest increases, ironically, were during the 1950s, when domestic ideals held sway.

The figures cited here are somewhat overblown, as they include women who took on temporary, part-time, or seasonal work, as well as full-time wage earners. Moreover, the female work force continued to include a large proportion of "traditional" wage earners—women supporting themselves and their families, such as single women, widows, a growing number of separated and divorced women, and women married to low-income men. In the 1950s, two out of five women wage earners came from low-income families. Still, it can be fairly said that the "New Women" of the postwar era were middle-class working wives and, in ever growing numbers, working mothers.

The working wife had been denounced as anathema in the 1930s when jobs were scarce (though her numbers increased), and she was only reluctantly and temporarily accepted during World War II, when men were scarce. But in the 1950s a new set of circumstances not only spurred her entry into the labor force but quietly legitimized it. As the economy rapidly expanded, demand for low-paid qualified workers in sales, service, and office work grew. Clerical jobs multiplied so quickly that by 1960, one of three women wage earners held one. Elementary school teachers were needed as well, as school systems started to expand to accommodate the baby boom. At the same time, the pool of available young, single women diminished. Birthrates had been low in the 1920s and 1930s and now, in the 1950s, young women married earlier and had children. The short supply of young women workers created vocational space for older, married women, whom employers welcomed. The married woman's family, meanwhile, welcomed her wages. Since inflation was constant, a second income served to maintain a family's middle-class status and higher living standards, as well as to pay for college education that would ensure the prospects of children. The decade of the "feminine mystique," therefore, was also one in which married women workers were much in demand and when their income (on the average about one-quarter of family income) was needed in middle-class homes.

The types of jobs women took also legitimized wage earning for middle-class women. The new woman worker of the 1950s and 1960s was likely to enter a sex-typed occupation. "Most of the jobs women hold are still in traditional fields," *Life* announced in 1956. "Household skills take her into the garment trades; neat and personable, she becomes office worker and sales lady; patient and dexterous, she does well on repetitive, detailed factory work; compassionate, she becomes teacher and nurse." *Life* did not ignore professional women, such as the "homemaker-lawmaker" and "housewife-architect." But these were rare compared to the anonymous hordes of middle-aged office workers, garment workers, and saleswomen captured by the *Life* photographer. Women workers of the 1950s did not surge into prestigious professions. After World War II, professional, technical, and managerial fields expanded so rapidly that the proportion of women in them steadily fell. In the 1950s, the proportion of women dropped even in the "women's professions," such as grade school teaching, and social work. But the *number* of women in the professions steadily rose.

Because working women moved mainly into traditional types of white-collar work, they received traditional low rates of pay. Therefore, as the female work force grew, so did the disparity between male and female wages. In 1955, the median income of full-time workers was 63.9 percent that of men; but by 1963, it had dropped to 60 percent, and continued to fall thereafter. The disparity was even larger in fields that absorbed large numbers of women, such as sales work, where in 1960, for instance, the median wage of women was only 40 percent that of male workers. Postwar women, in short, provided an expanding pool of inexpensive labor.

This pool of female labor quickly became an essential part of the economy. In the 1950s, the Labor Department, especially the Women's Bureau, sought to increase it. No longer devoted solely to protective laws, though of course in favor of them, the Women's Bureau urged employers to take advantage of "womanpower" and encouraged women to enter the worker-hungry labor market. Significantly, the Women's Bureau, a vestige of the old "woman's movement," was the only agency inside or outside government to represent the interests of working women, a group that now included a hefty segment of middle-class women. In this capacity, the bureau collected complaints of sex discrimination in employment, though little could be done about them. It also called for policies to aid working women, such as paid maternity leaves, day-care facilities, and equal pay legislation. While *McCall's* promoted family "togetherness," a speaker at the 1955 White House conference on "Womanpower," sponsored by the Women's Bureau, defended women's "rights as achievement-oriented individuals."

Despite the factors that favored women's entry into the work force, the postwar working wife received mixed signals about her legitimacy as a wage earner. Although she could easily find a job in a traditional field, her role as a worker remained suspect. Domestic ideals, moreover, affected her attitudes and expectations. She was likely to defend paid work in terms of family need, not personal aspiration or individualism. (This was one of the depression's lasting legacies.) She was unlikely to plan ahead, seek special training, or expect vocational advancement. She rarely objected to sex-typing of occupations or wage discrimination, which were seen as part of the rules of the game. She was especially apt to feel guilty if she had children at home; the largest segment of new workers in the 1950s, accordingly, were older women with presumably less child-care responsibility or none at all. By shaping her work role around the family, often by entering the work force in middle age, the new working wife of the postwar era adjusted her goals to cultural demands.

Working mothers were nonetheless a major concern. Their absence from home, critics alleged, led to child neglect, emotional ailments, and juvenile delinquency. Researchers of the 1950s voiced surprise that such ill effects were not borne out in their surveys. "Broken homes" more than working mothers seemed to injure children's

During the 1950s, an expanding economy and a rapidly
growing service sector provided a vast increase of jobs for
women in traditional fields, such as office work and retail sales.
Like these Macy's saleswomen in 1956, preparing for the
Christmas rush, new women workers tended to be middle-class
and middle-aged. Although sales work may not have provided
a sense of identity, as later recommended in *The Feminine
Mystique*, it was often part-time or seasonal and easily fused
with family roles. And it did provide a second income, which in
turn provided household appliances, automobiles, television
sets, and middle-class status. *(Eliot Elisofon, Life Magazine)*

prospects; the only significant differences between working and nonworking mothers seemed to be that the former lived in cities, were better educated, and had more
anxiety because of their dual roles. In the early 1960s, the working mother rose into
even greater favor with sociologists. She did have an impact on family structure and
child-rearing, they said: Work outside the home increased her influence within it.
She was likely to assume a greater role in decision-making and to encourage self-
reliance and independence in her children. "Employment emancipates women from
domination by their husbands, and secondarily, raises their daughters from inferiority to their brothers," wrote sociologist Robert O. Blood in 1965. As a result, "the
male-dominated, female-serviced family is being replaced by a new symmetry."

The prospect of such symmetry had most appeal to the college-educated middle-
class woman of the 1950s and 1960s, who, if unemployed, was apt to feel overtrained

and undervalued. "Certainly today's homemaking chores are no great challenge to such a woman," said Women's Bureau head Esther Peterson in the early 1960s. "Her sense of frustration is likely to heighten as her children go to school and there is even less need for her in the home." Working-class and lower-middle-class wives did not share this discontent with domestic roles. Among blue-collar wives in the 1950s, Mirra Komarovsky found "little evidence of status frustration." Lower-middle-class wives, Herbert Gans reported from Levittown in the 1960s, were not so sure as upper-middle-class women "that life ought to be more than raising a family." But educated women, who measured themselves against educated men, were more likely to feel deprived of status, a deprivation for which domestic ideology did not compensate. Still, because they accepted the primacy of their roles as child rearers, their options for achieving vocational status were limited. While the New Women of the 1920s had been preoccupied with fusing marriage and career, the preoccupation of educated women of the 1960s was how to combine children and career.

This theme surfaced in a special issue of *Daedalus* in 1964, most of which concerned the problems of the educated woman and her need to mesh traditional and modern roles. As women would probably continue to be primarily responsible for child-rearing, sociologist Alice Rossi pointed out, ways must be devised "to ease the combination of home and work responsibility." Unlike Betty Friedan's *Feminine Mystique*, which urged women to liberate themselves from "occupation: housewife" through private routes, Rossi began with the premise that sexual equality was a positive good and that social measures were needed to effect it. Training a corps of wage-earning substitute mothers, she contended, would enable women to pursue careers; so would a national network of day-care centers. A new type of quasi-urban residence, between suburb and city, Rossi proposed, would facilitate employment for married women. Most important, she stressed, was the need to avoid sex-typing, both in educational institutions, where children were socialized, and in occupations. Sexual equality would not exist, she posited, "until women participate on an equal basis with men, in politics, occupations, and the family."

In the early 1960s, finally, public policy recognized the working woman. In 1961, President Kennedy created a President's Commission on the Status of Women, a gesture to compensate for the paucity of women's appointments to high-level posts in the new administration. The new commission had links to the past: The last project ever headed by Eleanor Roosevelt, it was instigated and dominated by the Women's Bureau, which had its own motives. The WB wanted to promote women's role in the work force, attain equal pay legislation, maintain protective laws, and end what WB head Esther Peterson called "futile agitation" about an Equal Rights Amendment. The commission fulfilled the Women's Bureau goals and at the same time, in unforeseen ways, built a bridge to the future.

When the Commission on the Status of Women (comprising 13 women and 11 men, five of them cabinet members) presented its report in October 1963, it rejected, as expected, the prospect of an ERA. "A Constitutional Amendment need not now be sought in order to promote equal rights," the commission concluded. The report endorsed an alternative method, proposed by Yale law school fellow Pauli Murray, to attain equal rights: Equality, Murray contended, was guaranteed under the equal protection clause of the Fourteenth Amendment. The report asserted that women had primary responsibility for family life just as men had primary responsibility for family support. It also cited a wide range of injustices that impeded sexual equality and proposed a slew of remedies, including day-care programs, tax deductions for the child-care expenses of working mothers, continuing education programs, vocational training, equal opportunity in employment, more part-time jobs, paid maternity leaves, equal pay laws, and promotion of women to upper-level federal jobs. "Aspiration must be fostered," the report declared.

Like World War II advisory commissions, the new commission was not expected to accomplish much; its report received scant attention. But the commission was not without impact. First, when it disbanded, it spawned both a permanent Citizens' Advisory Council on the Status of Women and many state commissions on women's status—32 within a year and 50 by 1969. The state commissions began to compile data on sexual inequities, and their members met with one another, thus creating a new communications network on women's issues. Almost inadvertently, the federal government had helped lay the groundwork for both a feminist agenda and, before long, a new women's movement. Second, the Kennedy administration took the lead in initiating a federal policy against sexual discrimination: The Equal Pay Act of 1963, which required equal pay for equal work, was enacted while the commission was in progress. First proposed in 1945, the new law had long been urged by the Women's Bureau. Like the Fair Labor Standards Act, which it amended, the Equal Pay Act left large categories of women workers, such as domestic workers and farm workers, unaffected. Nor did it oblige employers to hire women workers in the first place. Finally, at the last minute, the "equal work" provision replaced a stronger one that had provided equal pay for comparable work. Still, the Equal Pay Act was the first federal law against sex discrimination. Its passage was also the first occasion since World War II on which Congress recognized women's status as wage earners.

In retrospect, the Equal Pay Act of 1963 and the publication of Betty Friedan's *Feminine Mystique* that year represented the tension that had developed since the end of the war between domestic ideals and the actual context of women's lives, which were now more likely to include some combination of domestic role and paid employment. The two events also marked a hiatus between the reign of domestic ideology and the rise of the women's movement, which would soon challenge it. But the decade of the 1960s itself set the scene for feminist revival. The 1960s provided an enlarged supply of educated women; a liberated social climate; a growing emphasis on personal fulfillment; and finally, a new political climate, characterized by protest, activism, and militancy.

MIXED SIGNALS

In the 1960s, women's roles reached a point of precarious balance. At the decade's end, about half of American women held jobs, as did almost half of mothers of school-age children and a quarter of the mothers of preschoolers. The steady surge into the work force was accompanied by a drop in the birthrate, which had been falling since 1957; a slight rise in the marriage age; and a new fragility in the institution of marriage—the divorce rate increased by 80 percent. As the proportion of young adults in the population started to bulge, college enrollments grew, the number of single persons almost doubled, and a new wave of sexual revolution rolled in. The decade in which feminism reappeared was also one in which a modern aura of individualism and competition undercut the traditional expectations of the 1950s.

If the working mother was a major New Woman of the 1960s, so was the educated daughter. In the 1960s, the number of women college students doubled. The rise in college attendance was part of a long-term development. Right after World War II, women's proportion of the college population took a nose dive. In 1940, women were 40 percent of college students, but by 1950, they had dropped to 31 percent and earned only 25 percent of bachelor's degrees. The relative decline of women graduates came at a time when overall college attendance vastly increased. Between 1940 and 1950, a decade of great social mobility, the proportion of the college-age population attending college leapt from 14 percent to 27 percent; between 1945 and 1950 alone, college enrollment doubled. Most new students were men, and many were veterans (98 percent male) who entered college under the GI Bill. The immediate postwar education gap between men and women was only temporary, however. In the 1950s, when college enrollment continued to expand, the proportion of women students grew as well. By 1960, women earned 35 percent of college degrees; and by 1970, when almost 44 percent of the college-age population went to school, one-third of college-age women were enrolled and women students earned 41 percent of degrees.

As college attendance became an increasingly "average" part of life, the aspirations of college women tended to become average as well. But college was still a community of experience, one that extended individualism through the late teens. It was also a singularly egalitarian experience, as college made approximately the same demands on men and women, provided both with the same sort of lifestyle, and conferred on both, at graduation, the same reward—certification of middle-class status. Despite calls in the 1950s for distinctively "feminine" curricula, such changes made few inroads; coeducational universities and major women's colleges continued to provide academic programs, not preparation for domesticity. College, in short, remained a world apart, where men and women were more equal than elsewhere. In 1961, collegiate equality even carried over to a new federal agency, the Peace Corps, which drew on recent college graduates and accepted women volunteers on an equal basis with men. Not surprisingly, the college community provided a breeding ground for social activism in the 1960s and a constituency for the new feminism—a core of young women with egalitarian ideals, high expectations, and little investment in traditional roles.

The woman college student of the 1960s, however, received mixed signals. Her academic experience might be relatively egalitarian, but the social cues she absorbed were not. One type of cue made it difficult for her to plan ahead. The average college girl viewed her future "through a wedding band," *New York Times* reporter Marilyn Bender observed in 1962. "Despite compelling evidence that she will be working by 35, today's 21-year-old has difficulty looking beyond [the ceremony of] her own marriage." Even if she harbored what Mirra Komarovsky had labeled "middle-of-the-road" goals—to join the work force after a hiatus for child-rearing—it was difficult to be either ambitious or specific about such goals. As writer Caroline Bird pointed out

Recent college graduates of the 1960s, women and men, served
in forty third-world nations under the auspices of the Peace
Corps, an agency created by President Kennedy. Here,
members of the first group of Peace Corps volunteers depart
for Ghana in 1961. (*Associated Press*)

in 1968, "Most girls find it hard to plan what they are going to do when they have
reared children whose fathers they have not yet met."

A related handicap was the tendency to discard ambition, avoid competition, and
minimize achievement, so as to keep the field clear for an appropriate marriage. In
1972, psychologist Matina Horner described a "fear of success" revealed by 80 percent of the college women in her samples of the late 1960s, who felt that any kind of
achievement, in college or career, would undercut their attractiveness and limit their
options. Young women, said Horner, had incorporated society's attitudes "that competition, success, competence, and intellectual achievements are basically inconsistent with femininity." Such internalized cues, feminists of the late 1960s contended,
were reinforced by external ones. Caroline Bird pointed to an "invisible bar that
keeps women down." It started early in life and continued at home and school, as well
as in graduate school, professional school, job interviews, first jobs, and lost chances
for promotions or administrative positions. "Fear of looking aggressive" could be as
great a handicap for the employed woman as "fear of success" was for the college
student.

Another source of mixed signals in the 1960s was a newly liberal social climate
and, especially, the latest blast of sexual revolution—well underway by mid-decade.
The rules of the game had been shifting throughout the twentieth century, but in the

1960s, as in the 1920s, the pace of change seemed to accelerate. A new enthusiasm for casual "relationships," uninhibitedness, open discussion, and self-fulfillment came into vogue, both among the large cohort of youth and among adults seeking a second youth in the sexual marketplace. The origins of the new vogue of self-indulgence remain elusive. According to writer Barbara Ehrenreich, a "male revolt" against domestic ideology had been building since the 1950s, characterized by a flight from commitment, responsibility, and breadwinner roles. Men, in short, were the first to demand "liberation." The media of the 1960s, however, depicted freedom from traditional values and behavior as a universal desire. By the end of the decade, surveys among college students revealed a pronounced rise in premarital sex, notably among women, along with widespread acceptance of liberal sexual attitudes. National magazines, movies, surveys, and exposés proclaimed extramarital sex a national pastime, and a new array of advice literature spouted a lingo of personal fulfillment. *Open Marriage: A New Life Style for Couples*, by Nena and George O'Neill, for instance, endorsed equal-opportunity infidelity as the modern route to intimacy, trust, and "identity."

Sexual liberation of the 1960s had its own landmarks. The Supreme Court sanctioned contraception for married women in *Griswold* v. *Connecticut* (1965), and subsequently, in *Eisenstadt* v. *Baird* (1972), gave all women the right to privacy, which included the right to use contraception. Just as important was the marketing of birth-control pills in the early 1960s. William Masters and Virginia Johnson's *Human Sexual Response* (1966) was another significant landmark. If Alfred C. Kinsey (1948 and 1953) had confirmed the existence of female sexuality, Masters and Johnson testified to the equality, or even superiority, of female sexual responsiveness and invalidated long-held convictions about female sexual passivity. Masters and Johnson, moreover, surpassed all previous sex researchers by relying not on questionnaires but on scientific observation. Performance now took priority over "attitudes."

The celebration of female sexuality coincided with a new wave of sexual availability. The 1960s saw the influx of a generation of "singles," their ranks soon swollen by the first of the baby boom cohort. As in the 1920s, "economic independence" also played a role. The decade began with a rash of publicity for the Single Girl, as advertised by editor Helen Gurley Brown, first in *Sex and the Single Girl* (1962), which Brown called an "upward and onward" book, and subsequently in the pages of *Cosmopolitan*, destined for the young singles market. Not unlike one of the New Women described in the 1920s, the Single Girl supported herself in an urban environment, worked in an office ("A job gives a single woman something to be," said Helen Gurley Brown), and moved in the realm of men. The Single Girl also had "relationships," and challenged the homebound housewife as a boring antique. "Her world is a far more colorful world than the one of P.T.A., Dr. Spock and the jammed clothes dryer," Brown wrote. "She is engaging because she lives by her wits." To be sure, the Single Girl wanted above all to get married—no simple assignment, as single women far outnumbered eligible men in the office world. Many "possibles" might turn out to be weird, dull, undesirable, or vocational failures. However, all men had their uses, Brown advised, including the occasional married man ("While they are using you to varnish their egos, you're using *them* to add spice to your life"). Finally, with determination and "quiet, private, personal aggression," the Single Girl could reach her goal of marriage. But in the interim, which might be a long one, she was both engaging and available.

The Single Girl and a well-publicized single standard of morality had a dual impact. By the late 1960s, confusion arose between the new vogues of sexual liberation and women's liberation, which were often assumed to be the same thing. Liberated sexual attitudes played a major role in the feminist movement; sexual grievances were openly discussed and sexual orientation became an allied cause. But the new vogue of license, feminists revealed, was a mixed blessing. By the end of the 1960s, women's role as what feminists called a "sexual object" had increased. The new premium on availability also changed the tone of the sexual marketplace. For young activists who joined the civil rights and New Left campaigns of the early 1960s, as described by historian Sara Evans, "the double standard collapsed into a void." Striving for autonomy while seeking stable "relationships" with male counterparts often proved a source of frustration. Expanded options for sexual encounters, young women discovered, were not in the end egalitarian. Moreover, men had a built-in demographic advantage. Not only were marriageable men outnumbered by available women in all age brackets, but male leverage increased with age. Once liberated from marriage, men were better able to dive downward into the pool of young singles, where available women were now in abundant supply. The latest blast of sexual revolution created a new atmosphere of lifelong sexual competition, with more liabilities for women than for men, as feminists observed. "The Sexual Revolution and the Women's Movement are at polar opposites," a *Ms.* article declared in 1972. "Women [have] been liberated only from the right to say 'no.'"

Finally, in the 1960s, the political climate changed. Change had been simmering since the mid-1950s. After the *Brown* v. *Board of Education* decision of 1954, a new civil rights movement emerged and set the tone for the next decade. From the Montgomery bus boycott and battles over school integration through the "freedom summer" of 1964, civil rights activists created a mood of protest and a new receptivity to social change. By the mid-1960s, student rebellion and protests against the Vietnam War fostered escalation of unrest. Once American policies at home and abroad came under assault, the stage was set for yet other reforms. Feminist revival in the mid-1960s began in the wake of freedom rides, voter registration drives, campus upheavals, teach-ins, sit-ins, and antidraft demonstrations. But it was the civil rights movement, above all, that paved the way for feminist resurgence.

BLACK WOMEN IN POSTWAR AMERICA

While suburbanization and its ramifications affected much of postwar history, black history followed another trajectory. The mechanical cotton picker reduced the need for southern field labor, sharecropping ended as a way of life, and waves of black migrants, mainly young, left the rural South for northern cities. The exodus began around 1940 and continued into the 1960s; by midcentury, one-third of blacks lived outside the South. Simultaneously, black population movement changed the South. By 1960, almost three out of five southern blacks lived in towns and cities, with a concentration in metropolitan areas. Large-scale urban migration spurred rising aspirations and often promoted social mobility. It also magnified the problems associated with urban ghetto life. In all instances, it affected the experience of black women, which in significant respects differed from that of the white majority.

Elements of continuity characterized the black female labor force. One was limited opportunity. Demobilization after World War II afflicted black women workers more severely than white counterparts, for wartime jobs were not quickly replaced by new ones in industry or offices. Mechanized farming, meanwhile, cut the proportion of black women who worked in agriculture to one in ten. At midcentury, 60 percent of black working women held service jobs, either in private households or in restaurants or offices. Young women who migrated to cities might find work on the margins of the urban economy. Ruby Daniels Haynes, featured in Nicholas Lemann's study of postwar migration, moved from Clarksville, Mississippi, to Chicago in the late 1940s. Over the next two decades, she worked variously in a janitorial job, a laundry, an awning factory, and as a barmaid, hotel maid, and office cleaner. During these years she raised eight children, sometimes with the aid of welfare payments.

Throughout the postwar era, the heyday of the "feminine mystique," black women remained major contributors to family support. They sought employment in higher proportions than did women as a whole, worked more continuously through the life cycle, and often combined paid employment with child-rearing. As among white women, the role of wives and mothers in the work force increased. In 1950, three out of ten black married women worked, compared with 19 percent of white wives. A decade later, more than 40 percent of nonwhite women living with husbands worked, and in the 35- to 44-year-old age bracket, about half. The black female labor force changed in other ways, too: The proportion of black women in professional and white-collar work kept rising. At midcentury, black women constituted well over half of black college graduates and 58 percent of all black professionals. In 1960, more than a third of black women workers held professional, sales, or clerical jobs, compared with less than a fifth in 1940. Indeed, in 1960, more black women than black men held college degrees, advanced degrees, and professional status, mainly because women constituted the bulk of black teachers. Black women's incomes bolstered the growth of the black middle class. Between 1947 and the late 1960s, the income of black households more than doubled. Only 10 to 15 percent of the black population was considered middle class before 1960, but up to one-third had that status two decades later.

The prominent role of black women in the work force, however, drew negative attention from postwar sociologists. Reviewing the literature of the field in 1966, sociologist Jessie Bernard referred to the "superiority" of black women—compared with black men—as measured by education, ability to find work, and familiarity with white society. In 1960, for instance, black women had an average of 8.5 years of schooling as against 7.9 years for black men; typically they could expect to marry less-educated men. They could usually find employment, as black men could not, "even a higher kind of work than that available to Negro men; if not, [their] services were always wanted in the home." Black women also had superior "contacts with the white world," Bernard contended. "More doors—back doors to be sure, but doors, have opened for them. . . . Even in their contact with social work agencies, and the world of bureaucracy, they have known their way around." Summarizing the researchers' conclusions, Bernard observed that black men and women "tended to live in some-what [different] worlds," that "Negro women fell into a higher class," and that the disparity between the sexes "may be destructive to both."

When the Kennedy Commission on the Status of Women met in the early 1960s, the group that discussed the problems of black women, led by National Coun-cil of Negro Women president Dorothy Height, reiterated such conclusions in its re-marks about "matriarchy." According to the commission report, the black woman had been "forced" into the labor market, "where she often earns more than her hus-band and sometimes seems the only earner for the family." The black periodical press, which catered to a middle-class audience, occasionally echoed this concern. *Ebony*, points out historian Jacqueline Jones, applauded the postwar return to black homes (as opposed to white ones). At the same time, it "presented working wives and mothers in a positive and frequently heroic light," and championed black women who entered male occupations. In other instances, however, the black press voiced anxiety about wage-earning women by linking their "independence" to the mount-ing rates of divorce and separation. Historian Paula Giddings cites two apposite arti-cles. In one, on "Why Men Leave Home," Roosevelt University social scientist St. Clair Drake asserted, "When they [black men] have a chance to become solidly middle class, desertion rates will stop." A *Negro Digest* article on "Why Women Leave Home," by author Gwendolyn Brooks, contended that "Some working women leave home when they discover their husbands are gold-diggers."

The black press mentioned another factor of concern: an imbalanced black sex ratio in cities. Since 1910, the urban black sex ratio hovered around 90 men to every 100 women. In 1962, for the 25- to 44-year-old age group, this ratio was 88. Attrib-uted in part to the traditional undercount of urban black men, the disparity now seemed linked to their dangerous, marginal, or shortened lives. Attorney Pauli Murray, who played a pivotal role in the Kennedy Commission on the Status of Women, discussed the problem of sexual disparity in a 1963 speech to an NCNW conference. More than 600,000 "excess" black women might never marry, Murray said; the black woman could not necessarily "look to marriage for either economic or emotional support," and this deprivation injured her. "As long as . . . she must com-pete fiercely for a mate, she remains the object of sexual exploitation, and the victim of all the social evils which such exploitation involves," Murray observed. In *Black Metropolis*, a 1945 study of Chicago's black community, St. Clair Drake and Horace Cayton also cited a lack of leverage. "Most lower-class [black] women have to take love on male terms," they commented. "The men . . . are strongly tempted to take advantage of such a situation and to trade love for a living."

Growing black communities in northern cities, characterized by public housing, underemployment, and active street life, now absorbed researchers' attention. How were families affected? A few black migrant families, contends historian Jacqueline Jones, "managed to parley the slimmest of means into a stable and relatively privi-leged existence." Sociologists of the 1960s focused on less auspicious trends. In 1960, studies suggested, instability among black families in urban areas, especially central cities, exceeded that in rural areas. The hallmarks of such instability were rising numbers of female-headed households and mounting illegitimacy rates. By the end of the 1950s, 25 percent of black families were headed by women. In the 1950s, female-headed black families declined by 48 percent on farms but rose 58 percent in urban areas. In 1960, one out of three black adult women was divorced or separated. Simultaneously, the numbers of out-of-wedlock births surged, mainly among women who were already mothers. Between 1947 and 1962, the black illegitimacy rate doubled. The strain on the black urban family emerged in Daniel P. Moynihan's 1965 report on *The Negro Family*. Moynihan's remarks about "pathology" and "instability" in the black family evoked fury from black opponents and liberal critics—a response that silenced discussion of the subject for almost two decades—and continues to stir controversy.

Rapid urbanization of postwar blacks, finally, affected political life: It fostered the eruption of the civil rights movement, in which black women played a major role. The movement began in 1955, a year after the *Brown* v. *Board of Education* decision, when Rosa Parks, a seamstress in a Montgomery, Alabama, department store, refused to cede her seat on a bus to a white passenger. A longtime NAACP member and local activist, Parks had just attended a summer program at the Highlander School in Tennessee, a unique adult education venture and a training ground in protest tactics. She seized the chance to take a political stand. The Montgomery Improvement Association, an organization of local ministers, soon led by Martin Luther King, generated a new protest movement, to which women made vital contributions. Household servants who boycotted the buses, for instance, disrupted employers' lives. Analyzing the reasons for black women's extensive participation in the new movement, historian Jacqueline Jones points out that women had a long-time custom of informal leadership in southern black communities. They also formed the bulk of congregations in Baptist and Methodist churches, whose religious rhetoric suffused the campaign.

Black women had long been active in such organizations as the NAACP, and from the outset the new civil rights movement welcomed their support. Over the next decade, they participated in boycotts, demonstrations, acts of civil disobedience, sit-ins, and voter registration drives. According to civil rights leader Ella Baker, "The movement of the fifties and sixties was carried out largely by women." Some were already prominent in black organizations. Daisy Bates, president of the NAACP chapter in Little Rock, Arkansas, for instance, took a leading role in the school integration struggle of 1957. After the freedom rides of the early 1960s, the newly militant southern civil rights movement made increasing use of women. Students like Anne Moody in Mississippi served as field workers, canvassers, and demonstrators. At the time of the freedom summers, 1964-1965, many black women activists were young, like Rubye Doris Robinson, a Spelman College student and former freedom rider, who assumed a prominent role as SNCC's executive secretary. Some were older women, such as Fannie Lou Hamer, a former sharecropper who lost her job and home when she attempted to vote. Hamer became active in the SCLC citizenship program, served as SNCC field secretary, and in 1964 helped form and lead the Mississippi Freedom Democratic party, made up of blacks who were barred from the Mississippi delegation at the Democratic Party Convention. A charismatic figure and gifted public speaker, Fannie Lou Hamer was always able to arouse passion, loyalty, and commitment. "Her speeches had themes. They had lessons. They had principles," recalled civil rights activist and lawyer Eleanor Holmes Norton. "You never needed to hear anybody else speak again."

Rosa Parks being fingerprinted in Montgomery in 1956. *(AP/Wide World Photos)*

Ella Baker, who exemplified women's leadership role in civil rights organizing, linked the pre-1960s and post-1960s civil rights movements. Born in Norfolk, Virginia, in 1903, Baker grew up in rural North Carolina, the granddaughter of slaves. In 1927, after graduating from Shaw University in Raleigh, North Carolina, she moved to New York City and organized consumer cooperatives. In the 1930s, she worked in consumer affairs for the Federal Works Project Administration and began 20 years of work for the NAACP, where she became national director of local branches. During World War II, she directed the New York City branch, served as an adviser for the office of Price Administration, and ran unsuccessfully for the New York State Assembly on the Liberal party line. In the mid-1950s, Baker worked in the South as a field organizer for the NAACP, and after the founding of the SCLC in 1957, served as its national director. In 1960 she organized a conference that created the Student Nonviolent Coordinating Committee, and in 1964, with Fannie Lou Hamer, founded the Mississippi Freedom Democratic party.

What kind of leadership roles did black women assume in the civil rights movement? Some scholars have categorized movement men as "leaders" and women as "organizers." Sociologist Belinda Robnett, in contrast, posits that black women provided a particular *type* of leadership that was "critical for the civil rights movement's

Fannie Lou Hamer addresses the credentials committee at the Democratic National Convention in Atlantic City in August, 1964. A former sharecropper and prominent civil rights leader, Hamer told how she lost her job and home when she registered to vote two years earlier. Her testimony supported the efforts of the Mississippi Freedom Democratic Party, which sought to unseat the all-white regular Mississippi delegation. (*AP/Wide World Photos*)

successful mobilization of rural communities and small cities." Not necessarily formal or titled leaders, though some were, women, Robnett argues, were typically "indigenous bridge leaders"—grassroots activists, door-to-door recruiters, and agile networkers—who fostered ties between the movement and community residents. Such bridge leaders were not exclusively women, Robnett notes, but women constituted a large proportion of this leadership group. Capitalizing on their local ties and ability to elicit loyalty, bridge leaders "enabled constituents to cross formidable barriers between their personal lives and the political life of civil rights organizations."

The civil rights movement led to the Civil Rights acts of 1964 and 1965 to integrate the workplace and protect voting rights, and played a vital role in women's history. Besides creating a climate of protest, it provided a model for feminist activists. Challenging racist ideas and segregationist practices, the civil rights movement posited equality as a positive good. It provided new types of militant, effective pressure groups such as CORE and SNCC, whose activities were well publicized. Through confrontation tactics like sit-ins and public events like the 1963 March on Washington, it captured the attention of the media and the sympathy of the public. Most of all, it established a precedent for ending discrimination under law. Civil rights goals, tactics, and rhetoric were soon adapted to new purposes by activist women. By the end of the 1960s, feminists had created a two-pronged movement, calling both for legal equity and for the restructuring of gender roles and social institutions.

CIVIL RIGHTS AND WOMEN'S LIBERATION

Like the civil rights movement that preceded it, the feminist outburst was spurred by a specific federal act. In the case of civil rights, that act had been the Supreme Court's 1954 decision declaring segregation of schools by race unconstitutional. In the feminists' case, the spur was the Civil Rights Act of 1964, Title VII of which prohibited discrimination in employment on the basis of race. In an apparent effort to defeat the bill, 81-year-old Virginia representative Howard W. Smith proposed an amendment to Title VII that would prohibit discrimination in employment on the basis of sex. Smith's motives were in fact complex. To be sure, he opposed civil rights; thus, to many, his proposal seemed facetious. Still, a long-time ally of Alice Paul and of the National Woman's party, Smith had sponsored an ERA in Congress for many years. In late 1963, expecting debate on the civil rights bill, NWP leaders decided to push for an amendment to end sex discrimination; two Virginia members of NWP had urged Smith to propose it. Whether the congressman intended to defeat civil rights or to fight sex discrimination, or both at once, remains a moot point. Several women involved in the battle that ensued felt that his act was a gesture of southern chivalry to white women.

Whatever Smith's motives, his maneuver caused havoc. The proposed amendment delayed passage of the bill and evoked great controversy. Liberal groups opposed it, as did Esther Peterson at the Department of Labor and women's organizations such as the LWV. These critics did not want to endanger the cause of black civil rights by adding a new one. In addition, as Brooklyn Congressman Emmanuel Celler contended in a speech in the House, equality of the type the amendment presaged might "endanger traditional family relationships" and even deprive women of such hard-won privileges as alimony and child custody. Celler's line of argument would often be repeated in the decade ahead, as other sex-equity measures arose. But the Johnson Administration mobilized support for the civil rights bill, as did Democratic Congresswoman Martha Griffiths, another NWP member, and Republican Senator Margaret Chase Smith. Historians differ as to whether the success of the Smith amendment was an accident or an orchestrated effort. In any case, Congress enacted the Civil Rights bill in the summer of 1964, its provision against sex discrimination in employment intact; the law went into effect one year later.

The new law provided that employment discrimination complaints could be sent for investigation to the Equal Employment Opportunities Commission (EEOC), which was soon besieged with women's grievances. Viewing sex discrimination as less serious than race discrimination, the overworked commission followed up only class action complaints. It ignored individual complaints and in general paid little attention to women's grievances. Indeed, the commission saw little cause to pursue such grievances without the insistence of public pressure groups such as those that de-manded civil rights. Unequal treatment at the EEOC soon spurred the rudiments of feminist organization. While Representative Martha Griffiths charged in the House that the EEOC deprived women of legal rights, a core of activist women tried to press the commission into action. But this feminist nucleus, in which Betty Friedan was prominent, was unable to evoke support from existing women's groups, such as the LWV, the American Association of University Women, or even the Citizens' Advisory Council on the Status of Women, which had been set up at the request of the Kennedy commission. Thus rebuffed, the new feminist nucleus felt compelled to create a civil rights organization for women. The National Organization for Women (NOW) was formed by 28 women in 1966 "to take action to bring American women into full participation in the mainstream of American society *now*."

Unlike the group of New Deal women that coalesced around Eleanor Roosevelt in 1933, the founders of NOW had no longtime network of communication and cooperation. Nor did they have much connection with survivors of the last feminist wave. "Most of us were the kind of women who never had any patience with League of Women Voters teas," Friedan later told a NOW conference. Rather, the NOW founders were politicized, professional women, some of them veterans of state com-missions on the status of women or the Kennedy commission, others union leaders from the United Auto Workers. The tone they adopted in the NOW "statement of purpose" of 1966 was that of the civil rights movement. Decrying "tokenism," NOW demanded "a fully equal partnership of the sexes, as part of the worldwide revolution of human rights." It demanded remedies for professional inequities, disparity of pay, and educational discrimination. It called also for a new concept of marriage, integra-tion of women into political life, and changes in "the false image of women now prevalent in the media."

Like Seneca Falls feminists, NOW founders pointed to the psychological impact of sex discrimination by opposing "all policies and practices [that] not only deny opportunities but also foster in women self-denigration, dependence, and evasion of responsibility, undermine their confidence in their own abilities and foster contempt for women." NOW denied enmity to men, who were also victims of "half-equality" and would benefit from complete equality. Unlike the supporters of woman suffrage, NOW denied that men and women had different roles or responsibilities in society. "We reject the current assumption that a man must carry the sole burden of sup-porting himself, his wife, and family . . . or that marriage, home and family are pri-marily woman's world and responsibility," NOW declared. "We do not accept the traditional assumption that a woman has to choose between marriage and mother-hood, on the one hand, and serious participation in industry or the professions on the other." Finally, presenting self-interest as human interest, NOW contended that women's problems were society's problems. "Above all, we reject the assumption that these problems are the unique responsibility of each individual woman, rather than a basic social dilemma which society must solve."

A political pressure group, NOW was from the outset a formal organization with elected officers (Betty Friedan was its first president), dues-paying members, and state branches. Its resolutions demanded changes in public policy, such as equal opportunity legislation, a national network of day-care centers, and retraining programs for women who had retired from the work force to care for children; the voice of Friedan ran through NOW proposals. But as NOW's membership expanded, rising from about 1,000 in 1967 to 15,000 in 1971, so did its reform agenda. NOW's goals were soon affected by the emergence of a younger, more feminist wing, which, with singular zest and originality, launched its own assault in 1967–1968. Another by-product of the 1960s, radical feminism arose out of contradictions faced by young women who were active in New Left groups and in the civil rights movement. Within the context of these campaigns, devoted to ending social, economic, and racial discrimination, women had developed a new consciousness of sexual inequity.

In the early 1960s, hundreds of college-age women activists had participated in voter registration drives in the South, under the aegis of SNCC, and in community organizing projects in the North run by Students for a Democratic Society (SDS), the central organization of the New Left. Their experiences on the "cutting edge" of social protest, as described by historian Sara Evans, were expansive and exhilarating, especially in the South. During the "freedom summers" of 1964 and 1965, women made up almost half of the contingent of northern civil rights volunteers. Running freedom schools and libraries, canvassing for voters, living with violence, risk, and fear, and sharing in egalitarian goals, they grew in self-confidence and political awareness. College student Heather Booth, who joined the Mississippi Freedom Summer Project in 1964 and later crossed the nation addressing campus audiences on civil rights, felt that she "began to identify a whole new world of meaningful concerns and actions." In addition, white women civil rights workers were exposed to role models of black women activists. "Black women seemed different from white women," recalled civil rights worker Jo Freeman. "They seemed stronger. . . . They occupied more social space than white women, played more roles, were a bigger presence in their communities." For a brief interlude, the civil rights movement provided both a new arena for integrated effort and a new space for female activism, though not without cross-currents of racial and sexual tensions.

But by 1965, the space on the left created by white activist students was contracting. When SNCC turned its focus from civil rights to black power and excluded white participants, the "movement" turned its energies toward antidraft protests, in which, inevitably, men were pivotal and women marginal. "Girls say yes to guys who say no," read a movement slogan. More important, throughout the civil rights and SDS campaigns, women claimed, they were customarily excluded from decision-making roles and expected to assume traditional ones—as typists, clerical workers, and sexual companions to male activists. According to Evans, the movement played a dual role for the young women involved in it. It "provided women with a particular kind of social space within which they could grow in self-confidence," but at the same time it "exhibited the same sexism characteristic of American society."

Resentment over sexual inequality began to simmer in civil rights circles in the early 1960s, spurring analogies between racial and sexual discrimination. In a SNCC "position paper" of 1964, activist Casey Hayden contended that "assumptions of male superiority are as widespread and deeply rooted and every much as crippling to the woman as the assumptions of white superiority are to the Negro." Antipathy to male dominance within the movement finally erupted at a Chicago Conference for

New Politics in 1967, when dissatisfied women, whose grievances had been ignored, announced their intent "to organize a movement for women's liberation." Politicized by their recent personal experience, the New Left feminists soon unleashed a torrent of activism. Because radical protest was at its apogee, movement networks provided a ready-made constituency for feminist discussion groups. By 1968, the small contingent of Chicago dissenters had counterparts in other cities and college communities across the nation. Adapting New Left techniques to feminist ends, radical women's groups now embarked on the novel mission of "consciousness raising."

Consciousness raising was at once a recruitment device, an initiation rite, and a resocialization process aimed at transforming group members' perceptions of themselves and society. Originally intended to raise the political consciousness of oppressed communities such as ghetto blacks, the technique proved more successful with middle-class women. By sharing personal experiences, Jo Freeman explained, a group would learn to regard personal problems as "common problems with social causes and political solutions." In consciousness raising, said Susan Brownmiller, "a woman's experience at the hands of men was analyzed as a *political* phenomenon." While engaged in self-discovery and social analysis, group members would also gain in self-esteem and, ideally, benefit from mutual support and group solidarity. Usually, a series of questions helped to elicit shared experiences. ("Discuss your relationships with men. Have you noticed any recurring patterns?" was part of a list of consciousness-raising topics proposed by the Radical Feminists, a New York group. "Discuss your relationships with other women. Do you compete with women for men? Growing up as a girl, were you treated differently from your brother?") "Three months of this sort of thing," said feminist Shulamith Firestone, "is enough to make a feminist of any woman." Moreover, a raised consciousness, group members found, permanently altered their social vision. "It makes you very sensitive—raw, even—this consciousness," wrote Robin Morgan in *Sisterhood Is Powerful* (1970). "You begin to see how all-pervasive a thing is sexism—the definition of and discrimination against half the human species by the other half."

Once the conversion process was complete, a group might move to some form of action, such as organizing a women's health collective or a day-care center, forming an abortion counseling center or a theater troupe, making a film or publishing a newsletter. Group projects reflected the range of topics that had contributed to consciousness raising—from sexual relationships and reproduction to child care and housework. ("[Men] recognize the essential fact of housework right from the beginning," wrote Pat Mainardi in a widely distributed position paper. "Which is that it stinks.") Sexual reform projects also became part of the feminist agenda. Rape, wife battery, sexual harassment, and child abuse, feminists claimed, were feminist issues and political ones. By the mid-1970s, alumnae of the discussion groups were running rape crisis centers, shelters for battered women, and vigorous campaigns against pornography and sexual violence. But women's liberation's greatest contribution to the new feminism, beyond its new issues and projects, was a critique of sexism that quickly infiltrated less radical feminist groups and rhetoric as well.

Discrimination against women, feminists postulated, permeated society. Sexism was institutionalized in the family and in government, in the schools and in law. It pervaded religion, the economy, and social life. It assigned to men and women

A new left technique, consciousness raising contributed to a revival of the tradition
of female association, which had been fading since the 1920s. During the early 1970s,
when widely publicized in the media, it created hundreds of pockets of feminism
across the nation. Here, a consciousness-raising group meets for the first time in
New York City's Women's Liberation Center, December 5, 1970. *(Bettye Lane)*

different character traits, personalities, and social roles, which were methodically
instilled from infancy. Sexism ensured that men would be the primary, most valuable
members of society, and that women would assume a secondary, subordinate
place. They would depend on men, define themselves in relation to men, have poor
self-images and low self-confidence, and devalue other women as well. The elimination of sexism, like the elimination of racism, therefore called for a drastic transformation—a change in values, attitudes, behavior, and institutions. Getting rid of
sexism, according to the ideology of women's liberation, meant both a massive awakening and fundamental social change or "revolution." Such goals and rhetoric might
not have surprised some activists of the early National Woman Suffrage Association.
The women's movement, Paulina Wright Davis had declared in 1870, "was intended
from its inception to change the structure, the central organization of society."

Women's liberation groups often disagreed on how to combat the oppression of
sexism. Some groups maintained New Left affiliations, others discarded them; some
attempted to transform relations with men, while others contended that heterosexual
relationships locked women into second-class status. "It is the primacy of women's
relations to women . . . which is at the heart of women's liberation and the basis of
cultural revolution," wrote the Radicalesbians. But despite the variety of political and
sexual stances, divisions among groups did not hamper the growth of the movement.
A structureless phenomenon, women's liberation had no formal organization, policy,
headquarters, elections, officers, or, ideally, leaders. Lack of structure, at the outset,
promoted diffusion. Between 1968 and 1970, feminist discussion groups splintered

and multiplied, permeating city, campus, and suburb. "It's not a movement, it's a State of Mind," writer Sally Kempton was quoted in the *New York Times* in 1970.

Consciousness raising, moreover, had enormous appeal, well beyond radical circles. NOW, which organized nationwide networks of feminist discussion groups, adopted and promoted it. Radical feminists, meanwhile, evoked media attention by staging happenings—crowning a sheep at the Miss America Pageant of 1968, putting a hex on Wall Street, or invading an all-male New York bar. (Such public theater was more reminiscent of the tactics used by moral reformers of the 1830s than of civil rights sit-ins; feminist demonstrators expected neither violence nor arrests.) In 1970, women journalists staged their own rebellion at such major publications as *Time*, *Newsweek*, and the *Ladies' Home Journal*. By August 26, 1970, when thousands of women mobilized for a march to commemorate the suffrage victory of 1920, members of diverse women's liberation groups mingled with the more "moderate" feminists of NOW.

Considerable friction existed, however, between the two distinctive feminist wings. Some NOW founders considered the radicals a "lunatic fringe" whose "antics" would only injure the cause. Many radical feminists of New Left origins viewed Betty Friedan as a bourgeois conservative and NOW's equity goals as minor and meliorist, in view of the enormity of sexism. Others conceded similarities. Both factions of feminists were "achievement-oriented," radical feminist Anne Koedt contended, one in the professions, the other in the radical movement. "From both ends we were fighting a male power structure that prevented us from achieving." Friedan, too, avowed mutual interests, explaining to NOW that younger women from the ranks of women's liberation could provide feminist "troops." Since 1966, moreover, NOW had been transformed by its growing membership and, accordingly, had enlarged its demands to suit its constituency. Whereas the progressive era suffrage movement had moved to the right to secure a following, NOW shifted to the left.

In 1967, NOW resurrected the Equal Rights Amendment, shelved by Congress since the early 1950s and ostensibly put to rest by the Kennedy commission. The ERA drew support from National Woman's Party veterans, although labor representatives in NOW at first objected to it. NOW also demanded the repeal of abortion laws—a popular cause within radical ranks, a controversial one outside them, and one that perplexed NWP veterans. "As far as I can see, ERA has nothing whatsoever to do with abortion," 87-year-old Alice Paul told an interviewer. Finally, in 1971, NOW again catered to radical views by acknowledging "the oppression of lesbians as a legitimate concern of feminism." NOW's shift to the left evoked controversy. Some founding members departed, only to form new women's rights organizations. Feminist politics were pervaded by disagreements, both within and between the two wings. But diversity of views served to enlarge the feminist constituency. By the start of the 1970s, the two wings of feminism had assumed a complementary posture. Neither the "egalitarian ethic" nor the "liberation ethic," Jo Freeman declared in 1971, could succeed without the other. Indeed, liberation voices seemed to fulfill the traditional role of left-wing reform—making the centrist position more acceptable.

The women's movement that emerged in the 1960s had much in common with earlier outbursts of feminism. Like the antebellum women's rights movement and the

While sit-ins and street actions brought women's liberation to national attention, the Women's Strike for Equality on August 26, 1970, suggested a unity of feminist interests. Commemorating the victory of woman suffrage in 1920, the Strike for Equality was the largest women's rights demonstration ever. Organized mainly by local chapters of NOW, the strike stressed the issues of day-care, abortion rights, and equal employment opportunity. But feminist solidarity was the major theme. Divisions among activists were temporarily suspended, as thousands of women across the nation joined marches and demonstrations. Above, New York women march down Fifth Avenue. *(Bettye Lane)*

progressive era suffrage crusade, the new feminism of the 1960s arose in and profited from an era of reform. Like earlier feminist movements, too, it reflected the goals of ambitious, educated, middle-class women, those with the highest expectations. At the outset, neither minority nor working-class women of the 1960s viewed the feminist campaign with much enthusiasm. For many black women of the early 1960s, race remained a greater source of oppression than sex. As civil rights activist, feminist lawyer, and Kennedy commission contributor Pauli Murray explained, black women were "made to feel disloyal to racial interests if they insisted on women's rights." Nor did black women feel that they had a "feminine mystique" to combat; rather, they had a reputation for female dominance. "If the Negro woman has a major underlying concern, it is the status of the Negro man," National Council of Negro Women head Dorothy Height had stated when the Kennedy commission met in 1963, and civil rights activists of the 1960s reiterated this view. "We don't want anything to do with that feminist bag," a young woman in SNCC told Betty Friedan in 1966. The important thing for black women, Friedan was informed, was "for black men to get ahead." Reluctance to enter feminist ranks was part of a long tradition; black women had often viewed race discrimination as more oppressive than sex discrimination. Convictions that racism and sexism were inextricably entwined gained ground as feminism developed. Still, as Aileen Fernandez, the president of NOW in 1974, herself black, told an annual conference, "Some black sisters are not sure that the feminist movement will meet their current needs."

Other minority women in the late 1960s were distant from the feminist uprising because other causes took precedence. Mexican American women who had mobilized to support the United Farm Workers, like Jessie Lopez de la Cruz, an organizer recruited by Cesar Chavez in 1962, gave that cause priority. "I felt I had to get other women involved," de la Cruz recalled. Native American women had joined the American Indian Movement (AIM), a group devoted to American Indian identity formed in 1968, and other Native American organizations. But assertions of equal rights met rebuff in the Supreme Court case of *Martinez* v. *Santa Clara Pueblo* (1978), a case that began in the early 1970s. Julia Martinez sued so that the children of women who married outside the tribe could retain full rights as members, as could the children of men in the same position. The case, historian Karen Anderson shows, posed the right of Native American tribes to define their own memberships against the right of Native American women to seek redress against sex discrimination under the Indian Civil Rights Act of 1968; the women lost. The discrepancy between tribal sovereignty and women's rights, Anderson points out, raised complex issues.

White working-class homemakers were also alienated from the feminist crusade. According to historian Susan Estabrook Kennedy, the white working-class housewife of the 1960s felt threatened by "the independent, assertive, self-determined, equal role put forward for the liberated woman." She valued her domestic role, a role that women's liberation rhetoric devalued; she viewed this role as more liberating than the alternatives, factory work or service work; and she had little interest in entering either all-male bars or men's jobs. "If your husband is a factory worker or a tugboat operator, you don't want his job," explained Congresswoman Barbara Mikulski. Attracted to, not repelled by, domestic ideals, the white working-class housewife saw feminist attacks on sexism as an assault on her lifestyle. Women's liberation seemed an elitist, self-interested, and suspiciously radical cause. Moreover, it seemed allied to other suspicious causes, such as school integration, civil rights militance, and antiwar protest.

The stance of working-class women toward the new feminism has to be qualified, however. As historians such as Nancy Gavin and Dennis Deslippes have shown, union women in the 1960s helped shape the debate over gender equality. Catalyzed by the passage of Title VII in 1964, union women—auto workers, packinghouse workers, electrical workers—became engaged in the debate over equal rights and equal roles. Wage-earning women of the 1960s were not always in agreement among themselves; many supported protective labor laws which had long provided a tool to control employers. Nor did union women necessarily share middle-class women's enthusiasm for passage of an ERA. Still, throughout the 1960s, working-class women helped shape the content of the debate. They supported the passage of the Equal Pay Act of 1963, challenged labor market segregation and inequities, testified before Congressional committees, filed Title VII-based charges of sex discrimination, and eventually pressured their unions to support an ERA. "Rank and file women were central to the story of the emergence of gender equality in the 1960s and 1970s," Deslippes contends. Union leaders, meanwhile, participated in the start of NOW in 1966. "We do not want separate little unequal unfair laws and separate little unequal low-paid jobs," a member of the Chemical Workers Union told a Congressional Committee in 1970. "We want full equality."

The involvement of unionized women made second-wave feminism different from previous feminist movements. Other aspects of the new feminism also were distinctive. First, unlike suffragist predecessors in the 1860s, new feminists were immediately free to find a middle-class following. They had no male allies, or former allies, to break away from, as neither the civil rights movement nor the New Left had ever been committed to feminist concerns. New feminists were independent from the outset, and they had a large potential constituency. Second, they were not bound to a single goal, like the vote, on which the fate of the entire movement rested. The new feminism was characterized by an amalgam of goals, a gamut of grievances, and an extremely diffuse structure. Third, and perhaps most important, new feminists abdicated the traditional domestic power base and rejected all claims to special character traits and the perquisites that went with them. NOW, for instance, spurned "the idea that mothers have a special child-care role that is not to be equally shared by fathers," while radical feminists seemed to find anything connected with home, child care, or conventional roles demeaning. Finally, unlike the earlier woman's movement, the new feminism of the 1960s depended on a large core of highly educated young women with political experience, well-developed faculties of social criticism, and zealous attachment to ideology. Usually the least powerful members of society, young women now assumed a pivotal role. Their influence was felt through the 1970s, when feminism caused significant shifts in attitudes and opportunities.

LEGITIMIZING FEMINISM

By the early 1970s, the feminist movement had generated both an ideology and an agenda, embracing a spectrum of issues and goals. As commonly perceived, feminist demands fell between two poles, a "moderate" call for equity laws and a "radical" cry for abolishing gender roles. "The aims of the movement range from the modest, sensible amelioration of the female condition to extreme and revolutionary visions," *Time* announced in 1972. But antipathy to sexism pervaded both moderate and radical demands. It emerged in the agenda endorsed by NOW—calling for an ERA, a national child-care system, abortion law repeal, and equal opportunity legislation— just as it permeated radical feminist ideology. "Revolutionary visions" were a vital part of the feminist campaign, if only because they made more moderate demands seem reasonable and legitimate by comparison. The feminist agenda was further legitimized in the early 1970s by an outburst of organization, by media dissemination of feminist issues, and by a new direction in public policy.

A sign of momentum was the proliferation of feminist groups. By 1973, a national women's newsletter provided a directory of several thousand. While NOW's membership tripled between 1971 and 1975, new national groups joined the equity campaign. The Women's Equity Action League (WEAL), a 1968 split-off from NOW, pressed for ending discrimination in employment and education; the National Women's Political Caucus, started in 1971, supported women candidates and raised "women's issues at all levels of government and in campaigns"; the Women's Action Alliance created *Ms.* magazine; the Women's Lobby campaigned for ERA; Human Rights for Women pursued sex discrimination and abortion cases; a Professional Women's Caucus began in 1970; and by 1973, a National Black Feminist Organization had been founded. To these new pressure groups, which often had overlapping directorates, were added hundreds of projects and collectives that had been started by women's liberation cadres. New feminist alliances, simultaneously, emerged within church associations and professional associations, among airline stewardesses, secretaries, and federally employed women. The vast spurt of organization in the early 1970s created a ferment of activism and provided varied routes to participation in the feminist movement, thereby broadening the cause's constituency and generating support for feminist goals.

Consciousness raising, meanwhile, became a public undertaking, through an inundation of books, articles, and media attention. Although hostile to the initial rounds of women's liberation, the media by the early 1970s found the subject irresistible. Between 1970 and 1972, every national network and major publication devoted time and space to the women's movement, and made the new vocabulary of feminism—"sexism," "male chauvinism," "sisterhood," "sexual object"—a part of common parlance. National magazines published special issues on women's status, such as the *Ladies' Home Journal* supplement of August 1970 and *Time*'s edition of March 10, 1972; *Ms.* magazine, edited by Gloria Steinem, provided an ongoing forum for feminist issues. With a subscription of nearly 200,000 by 1973 and many advertisers, *Ms.* was a novel propaganda organ. The name itself was significant. A major feminist goal was to erase sexual discrimination from language, and "Ms.," which made no distinction between married and unmarried women, quickly gained wide currency. The publication was significant, too. Unlike women's liberation newsletters, which were limited to a readership of insiders, *Ms.* extended the movement's message to a wider audience of unaffiliated sympathizers. A 1973 poll of subscribers revealed that almost three-quarters of the respondents were not members of feminist organizations. Still, the *Ms.* audience suggested an identifiable feminist constituency. Almost 90 percent were college-educated; 75 percent worked part-time or full-time, and two-thirds of these were in professional, technical, or managerial occupations; half were married, and 72 percent were under 35.

Public consciousness raising in the early 1970s did not depend solely on the media. Feminist authors also provided a steady stream of propaganda, polemical and fictional. "Our society, like all other historical civilizations, is a patriarchy," wrote Kate Millett in *Sexual Politics* (1969). "The fact is evident at once if one recalls that the military, industry, technology, universities, science, political office, and finance—in short, every avenue of power within the society, is entirely within male hands." In *The Dialectic of Sex: The Case for Feminist Revolution* (1970), Shulamith Firestone presented the ultimate of "revolutionary visions"—a society in which gender, class, and family would play no role, in which women would be freed from "the tyranny of their reproductive biology by every means available," and in which "humanity could finally revert to its naturally 'polymorphously perverse' sexuality." Radical feminism might alarm the faint-hearted, but feminist fiction had insidious appeal. Starting with Sue Kaufman's *Diary of a Mad Housewife* in 1967 and continuing through the 1970s with the novels of Alix Kates Shulman, Marge Piercy, and Marilyn French, among others, the case against male chauvinism reached ever-widening circles of readers. Poetry too was mobilized in the cause, as suggested by the attention paid to Sylvia Plath, a suicide in 1962, and to feminist poet Adrienne Rich. The new feminism became a literary crusade as well as a political one.

Changes in federal policy also helped to legitimize feminism. Between 1970 and 1975, a spate of congressional laws, court decisions, executive orders, and Labor Department directives gave official sanction to feminist demands. Once again, the civil rights movement had paved the way. In many cases, the federal policy of nondiscrimination on the basis of race was simply extended to include sex. In 1967, for instance, President Johnson extended an executive order prohibiting racial discrimination by federal contractors to prohibit sex discrimination as well; by the end of 1970, the Labor Department had issued "affirmative action" guidelines to all federal contractors in order to ensure nondiscriminatory hiring. Enforcing directives for affirmative action proved more difficult than issuing them. Still, the federal government in a few years made more efforts to end sex discrimination than in all the nation's history. The new thrust of federal policy was accompanied by a surge of women candidates for political office; by massive pressure from feminist interest groups; and by a burst of feminization in the Democratic party. At the 1972 national convention, where the delegates were 40 percent women, the party platform endorsed federally funded day-care and an ERA. The shift in federal policy also drew support from women in government—such as representatives Bella Abzug and Martha Griffiths, who sought to attach amendments against sex discrimination to federal bills at every opportunity. Congressional passage of the ERA in 1972 symbolized the impact of feminist political clout.

Since 1964, the Senate Judiciary Committee had reported the amendment favorably, but trade unions and the Women's Bureau viewed it as a threat to protective laws. Once a feminist movement emerged, the tide turned dramatically. By 1970, state and federal courts had started to void protective laws as sexually discriminatory, and thus swept away historic objections to an ERA. In 1969, the Women's Bureau switched its stance, followed in short order by the labor movement, the Citizens' Advisory Council on the Status of Women, and finally the LWV. "The President has publicly supported this amendment," Nixon adviser Chuck Colson wrote to another White House staff member in early 1970. "Fortunately the good sense and ultimate wisdom of Congress has always kept this ridiculous proposal from being enacted." But Congress soon changed its mind. Approved by the House in 1970 and 1971, the ERA became the leading feminist cause. In 1972, both houses of Congress passed the ERA by huge majorities, 354 to 23 in the House and 84 to 8 in the Senate. The amendment stated that "Equality of Rights under the Law shall not be denied or abridged by the United States or any State on the basis of sex," which meant that it would preclude sex discrimination on the part of the government, its agencies and officials, or any institutions closely tied to the government. By 1972, 16 states had their own equal rights provisions, 14 of them enacted since 1969. After the amendment was sent to the states for ratification, 28 approved it within a year. Generating interest in feminist issues, the ERA created what Martha Griffiths called "a moral climate for reform."

This climate reached its peak in the early 1970s in Congress and in the courts. Between 1971 and 1974, Congress enacted an unparalleled barrage of equity laws. It prohibited sex discrimination in medical training programs, enabled middle-income families to claim income tax deductions for child care if both spouses worked; extended employment benefits for married women in federal government jobs; prohibited creditors from discriminating on the basis of sex or marital status; extended coverage of the 1963 Equal Pay Act by an Education Amendments Act; and passed a Women's Equity Act, which supported training and counseling programs for women. Such equity statutes usually required only minimal federal funding. Federal court decisions complemented congressional concern for equity. While lower courts voided protective laws, challenged sex labeling of jobs, and reaffirmed the principle of equal pay for equal work, equity cases began to appear on the Supreme Court calendar. In the early 1970s, for instance, the Court invalidated a state law giving preference to men as executors, banned the press from referring to sex in "help wanted" ads, and upset an armed forces regulation denying dependents of women members the same benefits as those of male members. Finally, in *Roe* v. *Wade* (1973), the Court upheld women's constitutional right to abortion—a major feminist triumph, coming close on the heels of congressional passage of the ERA.

Since the 1960s, the right to abortion had proved the most controversial cause in the feminist arsenal. Like contraception in the early twentieth century, it seemed to involve a battery of complex legal, medical, and moral issues. State antiabortion statutes in effect in the 1960s had been enacted at the end of the nineteenth century, in the wake of the 1873 Comstock law. Most state laws prohibited abortion except for preservation of the mother's life, and it could be obtained only with medical certification of a life-threatening situation and with the approval of a board of doctors. Illegal abortion, as a result, was a thriving business. In 1972, according to one estimate, more than 2,500 such abortions were performed every day. But in the 1960s, a movement to liberalize abortion laws evolved. In 1962, the American Law Institute recommended revised abortion laws, to cover cases of rape and incest and those where fetal deformity was suspected, and in 1967, the American Medical Association endorsed such proposals. By 1972, 16 states and the District of Columbia had liberalized their abortion laws.

Once feminists organized, however, their cause was abortion law repeal, not reform. Abortion on demand, they contended, was a woman's right—the same claim Margaret Sanger had made for birth control in 1914. The decision to abort was a woman's alone, not that of the AMA or the state. In 1970, three states repealed their abortion laws, and in 1973, in *Roe* v. *Wade* the Supreme Court confirmed the feminist stance by invalidating a state antiabortion law. For most of the nineteenth century, Justice Blackmun pointed out in the majority decision, "Woman enjoyed a substantially broader right to terminate a pregnancy than she does in most states today." *Roe* v. *Wade* immediately affected the lives of millions of women. Maternal deaths from illegal abortions dropped. Abortion now became an option open to all women; before it became legal in New York State in 1970, for instance, therapeutic abortions had been granted almost exclusively to white women. *Roe* v. *Wade* had swift political repercussions, too. Opponents at once proposed a "right-to-life" amendment and started an antiabortion campaign that burgeoned for the rest of the decade. As of 1973, however, the Supreme Court's decision helped to legitimize feminism: The federal government had endorsed a large chunk of the feminist agenda.

In only one instance did feminists meet a monumental roadblock. A Comprehensive Child Development Bill, which would have provided a nationwide network of day-care centers, was vetoed in 1972 by President Nixon, who denounced the "communal approach to child-rearing" and the "family-weakening implications" of the bill. Day care was hardly a simple equity measure. It required extensive federal funding, and it hit an invisible boundary, where women's aspirations appeared to take precedence over child welfare. The prospect of day care evoked considerable opposition within the child-guidance community, indeed within the middle-class community. The major postwar precedent for day care was the Johnson administration's Head Start program, intended to provide remedial training for very young children from culturally deprived homes. But Head Start was child-centered, whereas day care was clearly mother-centered. "It's Fine for Mother, but What About the Child?" asked the *New York Times* in 1973. Nixon's veto sabotaged the feminist agenda at its weakest link, where family role and vocational role intersected.

Despite the day-care setback, feminist momentum of the early 1970s seemed unimpaired. Feminism finally won legitimacy by its own success, especially by its impact on education and employment. By 1975, for instance, textbooks were scanned to eliminate sexist stereotypes; primary and secondary schools revised their curricula so that boys and girls were not segregated into shop or cooking classes; athletic allotments started to be channeled into girls' sports as well as boys' sports. Opportunities for higher education grew as women were admitted to all-male schools, among them the U.S. Military Academy and Ivy League strongholds. Several women's colleges, however, followed a different route, and found new pride in single-sex status. Women's studies courses, which began in the late 1960s, became permanent institutions on college campuses. By 1974, 500 colleges offered an array of 2,000 such courses; a decade later, there were 30,000. Academic disciplines, meanwhile, were revised to include female experience—whether in history, psychology, religion, literature, or the social sciences. By creating new areas of expertise and women's studies programs, feminists carved out separate space for women on campuses. (In the progressive era, home economics programs had served a similar function.) Finally, in the 1970s, the number of women students rose by more than 60 percent; in 1979, more women were enrolled in college than men.

By the mid-1970s, the feminist movement also made a major impact on women's employment. Some changes reflected feminist pressure and federal policy. After a WEAL class action complaint in 1970, for instance, colleges and universities, threatened with loss of federal contracts, had to turn personnel files over to the Department of Health, Education, and Welfare for judgments as to whether affirmative action or sex discrimination was in effect. In 1972, a sex discrimination suit against American Telephone and Telegraph was settled out of court, with a multimillion-dollar payment to women workers and a plan to use both men and women in such formerly sex-typed job categories as linemen and operators. The AT&T decision suggested that equity measures would benefit the average woman worker, not merely the college graduates and professionals who appeared to dominate the feminist movement. Federal enthusiasm for utilizing "womanpower" exceeded the feminist agenda. By 1979, the armed forces, which had been racially integrated under President Truman, were once again integrated, this time with women. The Women's Army Corps, created during World War II, was abolished. Though expediency spurred sexual integration (once the draft ended in 1973, the all-volunteer army faced manpower problems), acceptance of women suddenly transformed the military into an equal opportunity employer and forced it to confront an unending list of equity problems.

The mounting number of equity suits, class action complaints, and sex discrimination charges, and the new shift in federal policy, did not end the concentration of women workers in women's fields or decrease income disparities between women and men. Nor was feminism alone responsible for the vast rise in female labor force participation of the 1970s, when the numbers of women who worked or sought work rose 47 percent—compared to 21 percent for men. Women had been entering the work force in steadily growing numbers since the late 1940s. But in the 1970s, economic and cultural factors seemed to reinforce one another: Feminism legitimized female wage earning in a way that family need had not. And as the new women's movement gained momentum, significant changes pervaded the prestigious professions—a major focus of feminist energy.

Between 1971 and 1981, for instance, according to the Labor Department, the proportion of lawyers and judges who were women rose from 4 percent to 14 percent; of doctors, from 9 percent to 22 percent; and of engineers, from 1 percent to 4 percent. The proportion of professional students who were women rose even more. In the first half of the 1970s alone, the proportion of Ph.D.s awarded to women almost doubled; by 1977, women students earned one out of five law degrees and one out of six medical degrees. Radio and television networks rushed to hire women as anchor persons and news reporters; women seminary graduates, ordained as ministers, took over congregations; and women executives entered high-level jobs in banking, finance, and government. Women's new mobility in business and the professions had widespread consequences. The nation's teaching force, for instance, began to lose a captive labor pool of educated women on which it had drawn for over a century; equal opportunity had hidden costs that were not always evident in the 1970s, when employment patterns began to change. Equally important, career women established footholds for feminism in business and professional associations, as well as in male-controlled interest groups such as the ACLU, the National Council of Churches, foundations, and unions.

Public opinion polls of the early 1970s suggested that the feminist movement caused a shift in women's attitudes, most clearly among the educated, employed, and young. By 1975, 63 percent of women respondents on a Harris poll, for instance, supported "efforts to strengthen and change women's status in society"; a majority had disapproved of such efforts four years earlier. Gallup polls in the early 1970s showed a similar tilt toward approval of the feminist agenda—day care, abortion rights, and equal employment opportunity. Young women seemed especially receptive to feminist goals. According to Yankelovitch surveys among college students in the early 1970s, a large majority endorsed the ideas of the women's movement. Polls that included men also reflected an egalitarian turn, especially among the young. A 1973 poll, for instance, revealed that 65 percent of respondents approved a wife's working even if her husband's income was "sufficient," a view shared by 80 percent of respondents under 30. The feminist "state of mind," polls suggested, had made an impact.

Newly liberalized attitudes did not always reflect a willingness to change behavior. As Alice Rossi had observed in 1964, "Many people . . . espouse belief in sex equality but resist its manifestations in their personal lives." Male Ivy League students, Mirra Komarovsky discovered in the early 1970s, often accepted the intellectual equality of women but clung nonetheless to traditional expectations. ("It is only fair to let a woman do her own thing if she wants a career," one student said. "Personally, though, I would want my wife at home.") Nor did feminist visions win universal acclaim. In the early 1970s, when feminism made rapid legislative gains, "women's liberation" evoked powerful attacks from conservative critics, such as Midge Decter's *The New Chastity* (1972) and George Gilder's *Sexual Suicide* (1973). By the end of the decade, the term "liberation" had faded from the vocabulary of the women's movement, as it was now called, while more tangible equity goals took precedence. But it was also clear that a decade of feminism had evoked a hostile reaction among a vocal contingent of American women.

Although all major women's organizations had endorsed the ERA, and although national polls showed that most Americans approved the amendment, many women remained suspicious of it; others opposed both the ERA and the thrust of the new feminist movement. Some distrusted feminist rhetoric, which seemed both to urge gender pride and to deny it. "Without saying so, most feminists have accepted the male model of the good life in sex, work, marriage, and parenthood," psychologist Judith Bardwick pointed out. "The most visible goals of mainstream feminists are status, power, money, and autonomy—all historically associated with men." Other women objected to the feminist movement's apparent rejection of *them*—by devaluing their contribution to family life, or scorning them for not having careers, or demeaning them as oppressed victims. Others were wary of the androgynous ideals that had emerged in feminist literature. And some suspected that feminist goals, like the ERA, would undercut women's traditional role in the family and thereby bring more losses than gains. In the late 1970s, conflict between traditional family values and feminist values became more visible. Not only did foes of feminism coalesce under a "pro-family" banner, but a conservative shift in political mood appeared to threaten feminist plans. After a decade of extraordinary achievement, the women's movement entered an era of consolidation and contention.

SUGGESTED READINGS AND SOURCES

For a brief view of women's experience from World War II to the 1970s, see William H. Chafe, *Women and Equality: Changing Patterns in American Culture* (New York, 1977).

An influential interpretation of the postwar era is Betty Friedan's exposé, *The Feminine Mystique* (New York, 1963). Friedan describes reactions to the book in *It Changed My Life* (New York, 1976), pp. 21–51. Pillars of the feminine mystique include Marynia Farnham and

Ferdinand Lundberg, *Modern Woman: The Lost Sex* (New York, 1947); Lynn White, Jr., *Educating Our Daughters* (New York, 1950); and Helene Deutsch, *The Psychology of Women*, 2 vols. (New York, 1944). The impact of domestic ideology is suggested in Ashley Montagu, "The Triumph and Tragedy of the American Woman," *Saturday Evening Post*, 231 (September 27, 1958), 13–15; "The American Woman," a special issue of *Life*, 41 (December 24, 1956); and George Gallup and Evan Hill, "The American Woman," *Saturday Evening Post*, 235 (December 22, 1962), 15–32. Mirra Komarovsky discusses the attitudes and goals of college women in *Women and the Modern World* (New York, 1952). Joanne Meyerowitz challenges Friedan's interpretation in "Beyond the Feminine Mystique: A Reassessment of Postwar Mass Culture, 1946–1958," *Journal of American History* 79 (March 1993), 1455–1482, and in Meyerowitz, ed., *Not June Cleaver: Women and Gender in Postwar America* (Philadelphia, 1994). For Betty Friedan's self-image, see her memoir *Life So Far* (New York, 2000). For insights on Friedan's career, see Daniel Horowitz, *Betty Freidan and the Making of the Feminist Mystique: The American Left, the Cold War, and Modern Feminism* (Amherst, Mass., 1998) and Horowitz, "Rethinking Betty Friedan and the Feminine Mystique: Labor Union Radicalism and Feminism in Cold War America," *American Quarterly*, 48 (March 1996), 1–42, which illuminate a link between the old left and modern feminism. For Friedan's private life, see Judith Hennessee, *Betty Friedan: A Life* (New York, 1999).

For postwar domestic life, see Elaine Tyler May, *Homeward Bound: American Families in the Cold War Era*, 2d ed. (New York, 2000), and Stephanie Coontz, *The Way We Never Were: American Families and the Nostalgia Trap* (New York, 1992). Eugenia Kaledin surveys women's roles in *Mothers and More: American Women in the 1950s* (Boston, 1984). For suburbanization and its history, see Herbert Gans, *The Levittowners* (New York, 1967); John Modell, "Suburbanization and Change in the American Family," *Journal of Interdisciplinary History*, 8 (Spring 1977), 621–646; Kenneth T. Jackson, *Crabgrass Frontier: The Suburbanization of the United States* (New York, 1985); Margaret Marsh, *Suburban Lives* (New Brunswick, N.J., 1990); and Rosalyn Baxandall and Elizabeth Ewen, *Picture Windows: How the Suburbs Happened* (New York, 2000). For the baby boom, see Jessica Weiss, *To Have and to Hold: Marriage, the Baby Boom, and Social Change* (Chicago, 2000). Nancy Pottishman Weiss discusses changes in childcare manuals and the responses they evoked from readers in "Mother, the Invention of Necessity: Dr. Benjamin Spock's 'Baby and Child Care,'" *American Quarterly*, 29 (Winter 1977), 519–546. See also Barbara Ehrenreich and Deirdre English, *For Her Own Good: 150 Years of the Experts' Advice to Women* (New York, 1977), ch. 7; Sheila M. Rothman, *Woman's Proper Place* (New York, 1978), ch. 6; and Sonya Michel, *Children's Interests/Mother's Rights: The Shaping of America's Childcare Policy* (New Haven, Conn., 1999), ch. 5. For women and the postwar marketplace, see Alison J. Clarke, *Tupperware: The Promises of Plastic in 1950s America* (Washington, D.C., 1999).

Memoirs of the 1950s include Joyce Johnson, *Minor Characters: A Beat Memoir* (Boston, 1983), available in a 2d. ed., introduction by Ann Douglas (New York, 1999); Sally Belfrage, *Un-American Activities: A Memoir of the Fifties* (New York, 1994); Mary Cantwell, *Manhattan, When I Was Young* (Boston, 1995); and Nora Sayre, *Previous Convictions: A Journey Through the 1950s* (New Brunswick, N.J., 1995). Katherine Graham's autobiography, *Personal History* (New York, 1997), also offers reflections on the 1950s. Wini Breines, *Young, White, and Miserable: Growing Up Female in the Fifties* (Boston, 1992) focuses on cultural discontent among middle-class girls. For personal stories of women growing up in the 1950s, see Brett Harvey, ed., *The Fifties: A Woman's Oral History* (New York, 1993). Martha Saxton, *Jayne Mansfield and the American Fifties* (New York, 1975) provides insightful commentary on the decade. For the gender politics of the Communist Party in the 1940s and 1950s, see Kathleen Anne Weigand, *Red Feminism: American Communism and the Making of Women's Liberation* (Baltimore, Md., 2000).

For the sexual revolution of the 1960s, see *Annals of the American Academy of Political and Social Science*, 376 (March 1968), issue entitled "Sex and the Contemporary American Scene;" William H. Masters and Virginia Johnson, *Human Sexual Response* (New York, 1966); Mary Jane Sherfey, *The Nature and Evolution of Female Sexuality* (New York, 1966); Paul A. Robinson, *The Modernization of Sex: Havelock Ellis, Alfred Kinsey, William Masters, and Virginia Johnson* (New York, 1966); Elizabeth Siegel Watkins, *On the Pill: A Social History of Contraception, 1950–1970* (Baltimore, Md., 1998); and Beth Bailey, *Sex in the Heartland* (Cambridge, Mass., 1999). For sex surveys and their impact on behavior, see Julia A. Erickson with Sally A. Steffen, *Kiss and Tell: Surveying Sex in the Twentieth Century* (Cambridge, Mass., 1999). The mood of the 1960s is conveyed in William L. O'Neill, ed., *Coming Apart: An Informal History of America in the 1960s* (New York, 1971); Sara Davidson, *Loose Change* (New York, 1979); Nena O'Neill and George O'Neill, *Open Marriage: A New Life Style for Couples* (New York, 1972); and Helen Gurley Brown, *Sex and the Single Girl* (New York, 1962). Barbara Ehrenreich posits a "male revolt" against 1950s ideology in *The Hearts of Men: American Dreams and the Flight from Commitment* (New York, 1983). John D'Emilio and Estelle B. Freedman assess the sexual revolution and its impact in *Intimate Matters: A History of Sexuality in America* (New York, 1988), chs. 13 and 14. Rickie Solinger, *Wake Up Little Susie: Single Pregnancy and Race Before Roe v. Wade* (New York, 1992) examines attitudes toward unwed mothers, black and white, in the postwar era. For 1960s popular culture, see Susan J. Douglas, *Where the Girls Are: Growing Up Female with the Mass Media* (New York, 1994), and Alice Echols, *Scars of Sweet Paradise: The Life and Times of Janis Joplin* (New York, 1999).

The roles of educated women in the 1960s are examined in Robert J. Lifton, ed., *The Woman in America* (Boston, 1965), and Eli Ginzburg and Alice M. Yohalem, *Educated Women: Life-Styles and Self-Portraits* (New York, 1966). Alice Rossi's 1964 article, "Equality Between the Sexes: An Immodest Proposal," is reprinted in the Lifton volume. The Kennedy commission's report appears in *Report of the President's Commission on the Status of Women* (New York, 1965). The commission's formation and impact is discussed in Cynthia E. Harrison, "A 'New Frontier' for Women: The Public Policy of the Kennedy Administration," *Journal of American History*, 67 (December, 1980), 630–646, and in Harrison, *On Account of Sex: The Politics of Women's Issues, 1945–1968* (Berkeley, Calif., 1988). For the role of the federal Women's Bureau from World War II through the 1960s, see Kathleen A. Laughlin, *Women's Work and Public Policy: A History of the Women's Bureau, U.S. Department of Labor, 1945–1970* (Boston, 2000). Leila J. Rupp and Verta Taylor, *Surviving the Doldrums: The American Women's Rights Movement, 1945 to the 1960s* (New York, 1987), focuses on the NWP. Susan M. Hartmann examines political behavior in *From Margin to Mainstream: American Women and Politics Since 1960* (New York, 1989). Amy Swerdlow explores the roles of activist women in *Women Strike for Peace: Radical Politics in the 1960s* (Chicago, 1993). Susan Lynn, *Progressive Women in Conservative Times: Racial Justice, Peace, and Feminism, 1940 to the 1960s* (New Brunswick, N.J., 1992) looks at the YWCA and the American Friends Service Committee. For women in Congress, see Emily George, *Martha W. Griffiths* (Washington D.C., 1982); Patricia Ward Wallace, *Politics of Conscience: A Biography of Margaret Chase Smith* (Westport, Conn., 1995); and Janann Sherman, *No Place For a Woman: A Life of Margaret Chase Smith* (New Brunswick, N.J., 1999).

Allida Black discusses Eleanor Roosevelt's later career in *Casting Her Own Shadow: Eleanor Roosevelt and the Shaping of Postwar Liberalism* (New York, 1995). See also Allida M. Black, ed., *Courage in a Dangerous World: The Political Writings of Eleanor Roosevelt* (New York, 1999), parts 4–6. Blanche Linden-Ward and Carol Hurd Green survey politics, education, and other topics in *American Women in the 1960s: Changing the Future* (New York, 1993).

For women's entry into the labor force after World War II, see Alice Kessler-Harris, *Out to Work* (New York, 1982), ch. 11, and Claudia Goldin, *Understanding the Gender Gap: An Economic History of American Women* (New York, 1990). Valerie Kincaid Oppenheimer assesses the causes of change in the postwar female work force, in *The Female Labor Force in the United States: Demographic and Economic Factors Governing Its Growth and Changing Composition* (Berkeley, Calif., 1970). Victor R. Fuchs examines married women's motives for entering the labor force in *How We Live: An Economic Perspective on Americans from Birth to Death* (Cambridge, Mass., 1983), ch. 5. See also Lois Waldis Hoffman and Ivan Nye, *Working Mothers* (San Francisco, 1975), and Robert O. Blood, "Employment of Married Women," *Journal of Marriage and the Family*, 27 (February 1965), 43–47. Studies of women's vocations include Louise Kapp Howe, *Pink Collar Workers: Inside the World of Women's Work* (New York, 1977); Rosabeth Moss Kanter, *Men and Women of the Corporation* (New York, 1979); Cynthia F. Epstein, *Woman's Place: Options and Limits in Professional Careers* (Boston, 1970); and Barbara Melosh, *"The Physician's Hand": Work Culture and Conflict in American Nursing* (Philadelphia, 1982). For housewives, see Helen Z. Lopata, *Occupation: Housewife* (New York, 1971), a study of urban homemakers, and Rae Andre, *Homemakers: The Forgotten Workers* (Chicago, 1981).

The experience of working-class women since World War II is examined in Lee Rainwater, Richard P. Coleman, and Gerald Handel, *Workingman's Wife: Her Personality, World, and Lifestyle* (New York, 1959); Mirra Komarovsky, *Blue Collar Marriage* (New York, 1964); Lillian Rubin, *Worlds of Pain: Life in the Working-Class Family* (New York, 1976); and Nancy Seifer, *Nobody Speaks for Me: Self-Portraits of American Working-Class Women* (New York, 1976). For a historical perspective, see Susan Estabrook Kennedy, *If All We Did Was to Weep at Home: A History of White Working-Class Women in America* (Bloomington, Ind., 1979). Elizabeth Laporsky Kennedy and Madeline D. Davis explore the lives of working-class women in Buffalo, New York, in the 1940s and 1950s in *Boots of Leather, Slippers of Gold: The History of a Lesbian Community* (New York, 1993). For a novel about lesbian experience in the postwar era, see Patricia Highsmith, *The Price of Salt* (Tallahassee, Fla., 1993), first published under the pseudonym Claire Morgan in 1952. Studies of ethnicity among postwar women include Bonnie J. Morris, *Labavitcher Women in America: Identity and Activism in the Postwar Era* (Albany, N.Y., 1998) and Carole Bell Ford, *The Girls: Jewish Women of Brownsville, Brooklyn, 1940–1995* (Albany, N.Y., 2000).

Black women's roles in the 1950s and 1960s are discussed in Jacqueline Jones, *Labor of Love, Labor of Sorrow* (New York, 1985), chs. 7 and 8, and Paula Giddings, *When and Where I Enter* (New York, 1984), part 3. See also *Ebony*, 21 (August 1966). For higher education, see Jeanne L. Noble, *The Negro Woman's College Education* (New York, 1956). The impact of postwar population movement is discussed in Nicholas Lemann, *The Promised Land: The Great Black Migration and How It Changed America* (New York, 1991); Jacqueline Jones, *The Dispossessed: America's Underclasses from the Civil War to the Present* (New York, 1992), chs. 7 and 8; and Gretchen Lemke Santangelo, *Abiding Courage: African American Migrant Women and the East Bay Community* (Chapel Hill, N.C., 1996). Jessie Bernard surveys the sociology of black family life as of the early 1960s in *Marriage and Family Among Negroes* (Englewood Cliffs, N.J.,

1966). See also St. Clair Drake, "Folkways and Classways Within the Black Ghetto" *Daedalus*, 94 (Fall 1965), 771–814, and Lee Rainwater, "Crucible of Identity: The Negro Lower-Class Family," *Daedalus*, 95 (Winter 1966), 172–216. The classic study of Chicago by St. Clair Drake and Horace Cayton, *Black Metropolis* (New York, 1945), was enlarged and reissued in the 1960s (New York, 1963). LaFrances Rodgers-Rose describes demographic trends in "Some Demographic Characteristics of the Black Woman, 1940–1975," in Rodgers-Rose, ed., *The Black Woman* (Beverly Hills, Calif., 1980). For the "Moynihan Report," see Daniel P. Moynihan, *The Negro Family: The Case for National Action* (Washington, D.C., 1965). For response to the report, see Lee Rainwater and William L. Yancey, *The Moynihan Report and the Politics of Controversy* (Cambridge, Mass., 1967). William H. Chafe draws an analogy between the experience of women and blacks since World War II in *Women and Equality* (New York, 1977), chs. 3 and 4. Major themes in black women's history are discussed in Gerda Lerner, *The Majority Finds Its Past* (New York, 1979), chs. 5–7, and Angela Y. Davis, *Women, Race, and Class* (New York, 1983). Archival sources of microfilm include "The Records of the National Association of Colored Women's Clubs," part 2, 1958–1968 (University Publications of America).

For the postwar civil rights movement and women's part in it, see Sara Evans, *Personal Politics: The Roots of Women's Liberation in the Civil Rights Movement and the New Left* (New York, 1979); Jo Ann Gibson Robinson, *The Montgomery Boycott and the Women Who Started It* (Knoxville, Tenn., 1987); Vicki Crawford, Jacqueline Ann Rouse, and Barbara Woods, eds., *Women in the Civil Rights Movement: Trailblazers and Torchbearers, 1941–1965* (New York, 1990); Belinda Robnett, *How Long? How Long? African-American Women in the Struggle for Civil Rights* (New York, 1997); Darlene Clark Hine and Kathleen Thompson, *A Shining Thread of Hope: The History of Black Women in America* (New York, 1998), chs. 11 and 12; and the acclaimed television series *Eyes on the Prize*. Clayborne Carson, ed., *The Eyes on the Prize Civil Rights Reader* (New York, 1991) includes short pieces by, or interviews with, Rosa Parks, Ella Baker, Daisy Bates, Fannie Lou Hamer, and others. Autobiographies include Daisy Bates, *The Long Shadow of Little Rock: A Memoir* (New York, 1962); Anne Moody, *Coming of Age in Mississippi* (New York, 1968); Mary King, *Freedom Song: A Personal Story of the 1960s Civil Rights Movement* (New York, 1987); Pauli Murray, *Pauli Murray: The Autobiography of a Black Activist, Feminist, Lawyer, Priest, and Poet* (Knoxville, Tenn., 1987). Charlayne Hunter-Gault, *In My Place* (New York, 1992); Melba Pattillo Beals, *Warriors Don't Cry: A Searing Memoir of the Battle to Integrate Little Rock's Central High* (New York, 1994); and, for a prominent figure in law, Constance Baker Motley, *Equal Justice—Under Law: An Autobiography* (New York, 1998). See also Pauli Murray's family memoir, *Proud Shoes: Story of an American Family* (New York, 1956) and Rosalind Rosenberg, "Pauli Murray and Killing of Jane Crow," in Susan Ware, ed., *Forgotten Heroes from America's Past* (New York, 1998), pp. 279–287. Biographies include Kay Mills, *This Little Light of Mine: The Life of Fannie Lou Hamer* (New York, 1993); Chana Kai Lee, *for Freedom's Sake: The Life of Fannie Lou Hamer* (Urbana, Ill., 1999); Joanne Grant, *Ella Baker: Freedom Bound* (New York, 1998); and Cynthia Griggs Fleming, *Soon We Will Not Cry: The Liberation of Ruby Doris Smith Robinson* (New York, 1998). Mary Aicken Rothschild discusses the experience of civil rights workers in "White Women Volunteers in the Freedom Summers," *Feminist Studies*, 5 (Fall 1979), 466–494. Donald Allen Robinson examines conflict and cooperation between activists in the civil rights and feminist movements in the 1960s and 1970s in "Two Movements in Pursuit of Equal Opportunity," *Signs* 3 (Spring 1979), 413–433. Doug McAdam follows women civil rights volunteers into the 1970s in *Freedom Summer* (New York, 1988). See also Constance Curry et al., *Deep in Our Hearts: Nine White Women in the Freedom*

Movement (Athens, Ga., 2000). For discussions of the origins of the amendment to the Civil Rights Act of 1964, see Carl M. Brauer, "Women Activists, Southern Conservatives, and the Prohibition of Sex Discrimination in Title VII of the 1964 Civil Rights Act," *Journal of Southern History* 49 (1983), 37–56; Michael Evan Gold, "A Tale of Two Amendments: The Reasons Congress Added Sex To Title VII . . ." *Duquesne Law Review* 19 (Spring 1981), 453–477; and Hugh Graham Davis, *The Civil Rights Era: Origins and Development of National Policy, 1960–1972* (New York, 1990), ch. 8.

For the development and ideology of the new feminism, see Sara Evans, *Personal Politics*, cited previously; Jo Freeman, *The Politics of Women's Liberation: A Case of an Emerging Social Movement and Its Relation to the Public Policy Process* (New York, 1975); Judith Hole and Ellen Levine, *Rebirth of Feminism* (New York, 1971); Barbara Sinclair Deckard, *The Women's Movement: Political, Socioeconomic, and Psychological Issues* (New York, 1975); Anne Koedt, Ellen Levine, and Anita Rapone, eds., *Radical Feminism* (New York, 1973); Gayle Graham Yates, *What Women Want: The Ideas of the Movement* (Cambridge, Mass., 1971); Marcia Cohen, *The Sisterhood: The True Story of the Women Who Changed the World* (New York, 1988); Alice Echols, *Daring to Be Bad: Radical Feminism in America, 1967–1975* (Minneapolis, Minn., 1989); Flora Davis, *Moving and Mountain: The Women's Movement in America since 1960* (Urbana, Ill., 1991); and Ruth Rosen, *The World Split Open: How the Modern Women's Movement Changed America* (New York, 2000). For the role of unions in feminist resurgence, see Nancy Gabin, *Feminism in the Labor Movement: Women and the United Auto Workers, 1935–1975* (Ithaca, N.Y., 1990), ch. 5; Dorothy Sue Cobble, "Recapturing Working-Class Feminism: Union Women in the Postwar Era," in Joanne Meyerowitz, ed., *Not June Cleaver*, cited previously, pp. 57–83; and Dennis A. Deslippe, *"Rights, Not Roses": Unions and the Rise of Working-Class Feminism, 1945–80* (Urbana, Ill., 2000). The documentary film, "Step by Step: Building a Feminist Movement," directed by Joyce Follett, examines links between labor activists of the 1940s and 1950s and second-wave feminism. For women's involvement in the United Farm Workers, see Ellen Cantarow, *Moving the Mountain: Women Working for Social Change* (New York, 1980), part 3 on Jessie Lopez de la Cruz, and Margaret Rose, "From the Fields to the Picket Line: Huelga Women and the Boycott, 1965–1975," *Labor History* 31 (Summer 1990).

Some of the classics of the new feminism, besides Friedan's *Feminine Mystique*, are Alice Rossi, "Equality Between the Sexes: An Immodest Proposal," in Lifton, *Woman in America*, pp. 98–143; Caroline Bird, *Born Female: The High Cost of Keeping Women Down* (New York, 1969); Kate Millett, *Sexual Politics* (New York, 1969); Shulamith Firestone, *The Dialectic of Sex: The Case for Feminist Revolution* (New York, 1970); Robin Morgan, ed., *Sisterhood Is Powerful: An Anthology* (New York, 1970); Vivian Gornick and Barbara K. Moran, eds., *Women in Sexist Society: Studies in Power and Powerlessness* (New York, 1971); Shulamith Firestone and Anne Koedt, eds., *Notes from the Second Year: Major Writings of the Radical Feminists* (New York, 1970); Boston Women's Health Collective, *Our Bodies, Ourselves* (New York, 1971); Germaine Greer, *The Female Eunuch* (New York, 1972); and Susan Brownmiller, *Against Our Will: Men, Women, and Rape* (New York, 1975). See also Jane Howard, *A Different Woman* (New York, 1973), and Elizabeth Janeway, *Man's World, Woman's Place: A Study in Social Mythology* (New York, 1970). For Gloria Steinem's articles since the 1960s, see *Outrageous Acts and Everyday Rebellions* (New York, 1983). For documents of postwar feminism, see Miriam Schneir, ed., *Feminism in Our Time: The Essential Writings, World War II to the Present* (New York, 1994) and Rosalyn Bakundall and Linda Gordon, eds., *Dear Sister: Dispatches From the Women's Liberation Movement* (New York, 2000). For activists' accounts of the movement they shaped, see Rachel Blau

DuPlessix and Ann Snitow, eds., *The Feminist Memoir Project: Voices From Women's Liberation* (New York, 1999); and Susan Brownmiller, *In Our Time: Memoir of a Revolution* (New York, 1999).

Articles about the new feminism in the 1970s include Jane Kramer, "Founding Cadre," *New Yorker*, 46 (November 28, 1970), 51–139, on the formation of a women's liberation group; Susan Brownmiller, "Sisterhood Is Powerful," *New York Times Magazine* (March 15, 1970), 27; Sally Kempton, "Cutting Loose: A Private View of the Women's Uprising," *Esquire*, 74 (July 1970), 54–57; Gerda Lerner, "The Feminists: A Second Look," *Columbia Forum* (Fall 1970), 24–30; Jane O'Reilly, "Click! The Housewife's Moment of Truth," *The Girl I Left Behind* (New York, 1980), pp. 23–58; and Joseph Adelson, "Is Women's Lib a Passing Fad?" *New York Times Magazine* (March 19, 1972), 26, a thoughtful, critical assessment. For opinion polls, see Louis Harris, "Changing Views on the Role of Women," *The Harris Survey* (May 20, 1971, and December 11, 1975). Mirra Komarovsky examines the reactions of college students to changing social norms in "Cultural Contradictions and Sex Roles," *American Journal of Sociology*, 52 (November 1946), 164–189, and 78 (January 1973), 873–884. For feminist fiction of the 1970s, see, for example, Alix Kates Shulman, *Memoirs of an Ex-Prom Queen* (New York, 1972); Marge Piercy, *Small Changes* (New York, 1973); and Marilyn French, *The Women's Room* (New York, 1977). Two early critiques of radical feminism are Midge Decter, *The New Chastity and Other Arguments Against Women's Liberation* (New York, 1972), and George Gilder, *Sexual Suicide* (New York, 1973).

The impact of the new feminism is discussed in Cynthia Fuchs Epstein, "Ten Years Later: Perspectives on the Women's Movement," *Dissent*, 22 (Spring 1975), 169–176; Judith M. Bardwick, *In Transition: How Feminism, Sexual Liberation and the Search for Self-Fulfillment Have Altered America* (New York, 1979); Elizabeth Janeway, *Cross Sections from a Decade of Change* (New York, 1983); Janet Giele, *Women and the Future: Changing Sex Roles in Modern America* (New York and London, 1978); and Winifred D. Wandersee, *On the Move: American Women in the 1970s* (Boston, 1988). Amy Erdman Farrell, *Yours in Sisterhood: Ms. Magazine and the Promise of Popular Feminism* (Chapel Hill, N.C., 1998) assesses an innovative publication. Marian Faux examines the Supreme Court's pivotal 1973 decision in *Roe v. Wade: The Untold Story of the Landmark Supreme Court Decision That Made Abortion Legal* (New York, 1988). See also Sarah Weddington, *A Question of Choice* (New York, 1992) and Rickie Solinger, ed., *Abortion Wars: A Half-Century of Struggle* (Berkeley, Calif., 1998), which explores pro-choice campaigns before and after 1973. David J. Garrow provides a constitutional history of reproductive rights in *Liberty and Sexuality: The Right to Privacy and the Making of Roe v. Wade* (New York, 1994). For the feminist attack on Freudianism in the 1960s, see Mari Jo Buhle, *Feminism and its Discontents* (Cambridge, Mass., 1998), ch. 6. Susan M. Hartmann shows how women unconnected to organized feminism promoted feminist ideas and practices in the 1960s and 1970s in *The Other Feminists: Activists in the Liberal Establishment* (New Haven, Conn., 1998).

For black women's response to feminism in the 1970s, see Pauli Murray, "The Liberation of Black Women," in Mary Lou Thompson, ed., *Voices of the New Feminism* (Boston, 1970), pp. 87–102; Gerda Lerner, ed., *Black Women in White America: A Documentary History* (New York, 1972), pp. 585–614; Toni Cade, ed., *The Black Woman: An Anthology* (New York, 1970); and Gloria T. Hull, Patricia Bell Scott, and Barbara Smith, *But Some of Us Are Brave: Black Women's Studies* (Old Westbury, N.Y., 1982). Diane K. Lewis assesses educational and occupational changes of the 1960s and 1970s in "A Response to Inequality: Black Women, Racism, and Sexism," *Signs*, 3 (Winter 1977), 339–361. Cynthia Fuchs Epstein examines the status of black professional women in "Positive Effects of the Multiple Negative: Explaining the Success of Black Professional Women," *American Journal of Sociology*, 78 (January 1973), 912–935. Carol B. Stack discusses black ghetto women's kinship and friendship networks in *All Our Kin: Strategies for Survival in a Black Community* (New York, 1974). Bonnie Thornton Dill posits a distinctive historical model of black womanhood in "The Dialectics of Black Womanhood," *Signs*, 4 (Spring 1979), 543–555. For black women's concerns in the 1970s, see *The Black Scholar*, 6 (March 1975).

For feminist impact on the social and behavioral sciences in the 1970s and early 1980s, see, for instance, Michelle Zimbalist Rosaldo and Louise Lamphere, eds., *Women, Culture and Society* (Stanford, Calif., 1974); Bernice A. Carroll, ed., *Liberating Women's History: Theoretical and Critical Essays* (Urbana, Ill., 1976); Nancy Chodorow, *The Reproduction of Mothering: Psychoanalysis and the Sociology of Gender* (Berkeley, Calif., 1978); and Carol Gilligan, *In a Different Voice: Psychological Theory and Women's Development* (Cambridge, Mass., 1982). The development of feminist scholarship also spurred new work on sex, sexuality, and same-sex relationships. For an example of multidisciplinary effort, see *Signs*, 5 (Summer 1980), and *Signs*, 6 (Autumn 1980), two issues devoted to "Women—Sex and Sexuality." Lillian Faderman examines declining acceptance of same-sex relationships in *Surpassing the Love of Men: Romantic Friendship and Love Between Women from the Renaissance to the Present* (New York, 1981). John D'Emilio traces the evolution of the contemporary gay subculture in *Sexual Politics, Sexual Communities: The Making of a Homosexual Minority in the United States, 1940–1970* (Chicago, 1983).

For quizzes and additional resources related to American women's history, visit the book's Website at *www.mhhe.com/americanwomen.*

CHAPTER ELEVEN

In Search of Equality: Since 1975

B Y THE START of the 1980s, the women's movement had made a significant impact on American life. Laws, aspirations, and institutions had been transformed. Federal policy had been revised, new coalitions of women's organizations had been formed, and women's issues became national issues. But women's changing status in society brought with it new conflicts—between political factions, between women and men, and, indeed, among women with competing interests. It also raised new questions about public policy. Could legislation ensure sexual equality, for instance, when structural inequality persisted? Were policies that addressed sexual difference needed to provide equal opportunity? To what extent, moreover, could the state regulate the workplace and family? At issue in the 1980s and 1990s was the elusive goal of "gender justice," and the challenge of how to achieve it.

FEMINISM AT STALEMATE

"It was not the cause, or its rhetoric, or any single issue that emboldened or exhilarated us," Betty Friedan wrote in 1982. "It was the movement itself, the process, the activity of taking control of one's own destiny." By the 1980s, however, the conjunction of reform mood and feminist ground swell that had characterized the late 1960s had vanished. In the 1970s, an antifeminist backlash erupted, as evidenced in the "Stop ERA" campaign, led by Phyllis Schlafly, an experienced right-wing activist, and the "right-to-life" movement, which sought to reverse federal abortion policy. The role of women became a major issue in national politics, one around which the conservative right could organize. Antipathy to feminism now evoked the commitment of thousands of women, to whom the women's movement represented an assault on women's interests and traditional values. With the same zeal as that shown by feminists, their foes assaulted state legislatures, ran for public office, and mobilized support for "pro-family" policies.

The defeat of the ERA in June 1982, only three states short of ratification, was less a tribute to "Stop ERA" efforts than to the solid South, as no southern state legislature ratified the amendment. Southern hostility represented a long tradition; the

South had never favored either feminist demands or federal encroachment on states' rights. The ERA defeat exemplified as well the difficulty of the amending process, especially the ratification procedure. The decade-long battle over ERA, however, was a revealing one. On both sides, women measured the perils of legal equality, such as increased liability to the draft, against the benefits; they weighed the threatened loss of now traditional rights, whether to support in marriage or to child custody and alimony in divorce, against the gain of relatively unknown rights. The ERA was once again a stacked deck, as it had been at the Kennedy commission meetings in the 1960s. It forced women to balance hypothetical gains against hypothetical losses, and roles as individuals against roles as family members.

Like woman suffrage, the ERA became a highly charged symbolic issue. Some experts contended that the amendment would make little difference to women's lives or women's rights; even some sympathizers conceded doubts about ERA's potential for ensuring an egalitarian society. To foes, however, it represented an assault on womanhood and family life. An ERA, wrote Phyllis Schlafly, would free men from family support obligations, force women into the labor market, and cause "radical loosening of the legal bonds that tend to keep the family together." To ERA defenders, the battle over the amendment became a referendum on feminism. Defeat, said Eleanor Smeal, NOW president, in 1978, "might give a false message to the courts and state legislatures that the country does not want to have a policy on sex discrimination." After the ERA capsized in 1982, the next Congress reconsidered it. In November 1983 the House rejected the ERA by six votes.

The cumbersome process of constitutional amendment, while a handicap in the ERA campaign, turned to feminists' advantage in the case of abortion. Opponents of *Roe* v. *Wade* had proposed a "right-to-life" amendment that would prevent the federal government and the states from "depriving any human being of life." Contending that life began at conception, the right-to-life movement began a massive antiabortion campaign that burgeoned in the late 1970s. When Congress held hearings on when life began, women assumed leading roles on both sides of the issue. Right-to-life advocates contended that abortion should not be allowed under any circumstances. Feminists, Planned Parenthood, and liberal pressure groups defended the option of abortion as a woman's constitutional right. By the start of the 1980s, an antiabortion amendment seemed stymied. In June 1983, the Supreme Court reconfirmed women's constitutional right to abortion by upsetting an array of city ordinances that limited access to it. A few weeks later, the Senate defeated the Hatch amendment, intended to make abortion unconstitutional.

But the battle had only begun. In the 1980s, well-organized right-to-life groups picketed abortion clinics, intimidated doctors who performed abortions, and, in some areas, ensured that "choice" was virtually unavailable. By the end of the decade, the Supreme Court had assumed a more conservative cast. President Reagan had added three new appointees: Sandra Day O'Connor, the first woman to sit on the Court, in 1981; Antonin Scalia in 1986; and Anthony Kennedy in 1988. In *Webster* v. *Reproductive Health Care Services* (1989), by a five to four majority, the Court upheld a Missouri statute that contained 20 provisions designed to limit a woman's right to choice. Before approving abortions, for example, physicians were supposed to perform tests to determine whether a fetus estimated at more than 20 weeks was "viable"; no such fetus could be aborted except to preserve a woman's life or health. Nor could public facilities or employees be used to perform abortions except under the same circumstances. Four justices indicated that they were ready to overturn *Roe v. Wade*, but Justice O'Connor, who had voted with the majority to uphold the Missouri law, contended that the *Webster* case did not require a reconsideration of the 1973 decision. In his majority opinion, Chief Justice Rehnquist stated that "politically divisive" issues should be decided by state legislatures.

This possibility seemed imminent in the spring of 1992, when the Court began consideration of a Pennsylvania law that regulated access to abortion. The conservatives now had a firm majority; many expected the justices to take the next opportunity to overturn *Roe v. Wade*, and turn the abortion battle back to the states. Instead, in June 1992, in a five to four ruling, the justices upheld the 1973 decision. In *Planned Parenthood* v. *Casey*, the Court allowed most of the limits on abortion that the Pennsylvania law imposed. Such restrictions as a 24-hour waiting period or the requirement that a teenager gain the consent of a parent or judge did not impose an "undue burden" on a woman seeking an abortion, the decision stated. At the same time, the Court upheld the constitutional right to abortion. According to the majority opinion, "The essential holding of *Roe* v. *Wade* should be retained and again affirmed." Although further state limitations on abortion were anticipated, *Roe v. Wade* now seemed likely to endure. Still, challenges to abortion law filled court calendars.

Supporters and opponents of abortion gather outside the United States Supreme Court building on July 3, 1989, to await the decision on the *Webster* case. (*Jose R. Lopez/NYT Pictures*)

In *Steinberg* v. *Carhart* (2000), the Supreme Court ruled five to four that states could not ban the procedure that foes called partial-birth abortion, because it was the most medically appropriate way to terminate some pregnancies. The same year, in *Hill* v. *Colorado*, the Court upheld by a vote of six to three a state law creating a "no ap-proach" zone outside medical offices; such a zone, said the justices, did not violate the free speech rights of abortion protesters who sought to convince women not to proceed with abortions.

What was public opinion on this controversial issue? A 1991 poll found that 40 percent of Americans believed "abortion should be generally available to those who want it"; 19 percent thought "it should not be permitted"; and 39 percent felt it should be "available but under stricter limits than it is now." Excepting a technolog-ical breakthrough, the fight over abortion seemed destined to continue. Such a breakthrough was perhaps in the offing. The mislabeled "day after" pill, RU-486, developed by a French physician, if taken within around six weeks of conception, could create the condition of a miscarriage by preventing an egg's implantation in the uterine wall. Barred from the United States by the Bush administration, RU-486 was in use in France, England, and China. At the start of 1993, President Clinton lifted the ban on importing RU-486, though delay at the Food and Drug Administration (FDA) kept the drug off the market for the rest of the decade. In September 2000, RU-486 finally won FDA approval.

If the dispute between "choice" and "life" seemed insoluble, so did a concurrent conflict: the battle over pornography. As in the cases of ERA and abortion, women campaigned on both sides, but in this instance, feminists broke ranks. Ironically, since the start of the women's movement, pornography production had mush-roomed; new technology—the VCR—and liberalization of obscenity laws abetted its growth. By the late 1980s, pornography was a $7-billion-a-year industry; profits rolled in from videotapes, X-rated cable stations, phone services, and numerous pub-lications. Lawyer Catharine MacKinnon and writer Andrea Dworkin, who joined forces at a law school seminar in 1983, spearheaded a feminist antipornography cru-sade. Adhering to feminist Robin Morgan's dictum, "Pornography is the theory; rape is the practice," MacKinnon and Dworkin argued that pornography involved vio-lence against women. Moreover, they stated, pornography was not a free speech issue but a civil rights issue; it was a form of sex discrimination that violated the Civil Rights Act of 1964. The two women sponsored a Minneapolis ordinance that classi-fied pornography as sex discrimination and gave victims a chance to complain at the local civil rights commission. Approved by the city council, the ordinance was vetoed by the mayor. A similar law, enacted in Indianapolis the following year, was struck down by a federal judge. When a panel of judges of the U.S. Court of Appeals re-viewed the ordinance in 1985, they found that it violated freedom of speech but accepted MacKinnon's premise that pornography was "central to creating and main-taining sex as a basis of discrimination."

The feminist crusade against pornography, however, allied the crusaders with conservative foes of pornography. Other feminists objected to this odd alliance. Some questioned the thesis that pornography "inspires negative attitudes and actions to-ward women" as unproven. Some stressed a civil libertarian approach: Objectionable as it might be, they argued, pornography was protected by the First Amendment and had to be tolerated. "Without free speech we can have no feminist movement," two leaders of NOW responded to MacKinnon in 1991. Others defended women's right to freedom of sexual expression, decried the posture of victim that the antipornography campaign imposed, and claimed that the campaign reinforced sexual stereotypes. Still others sought to distinguish between pornography and erotica. The irresolvable pornography conflict seemed destined for longevity.

Catharine MacKinnon was also pivotal in the campaign to criminalize sexual harassment, a form of aggression that victimized women. The author of *Sexual Harassment of Working Women* (1979), MacKinnon began to bring harassment cases to the federal courts in the late 1970s. As in the case of pornography, she sought to classify sexual harassment as a form of sex discrimination that violated civil rights law. A practice was discriminatory, she contended, if it "participates in the systemic social deprivation of one sex because of sex." In this instance, MacKinnon won some crucial victories. The Equal Employment Opportunities Commission (EEOC) in 1980 adopted three tests for deciding whether "unwelcome verbal or physical conduct" in the workplace violated Title VII of the Civil Rights Act. Under EEOC guidelines, the conduct had to be (1) "quid pro quo" behavior that made submission to sex an explicit or implicit condition of advancement, (2) behavior that "unreasonably interferes with an individual's job performance," or (3) behavior that creates an "intimidating, hostile, or offensive working environment."

The Supreme Court endorsed both the concept of sexual harassment as sex discrimination and the "hostile environment" test in *Meritor Savings Bank* v. *Vinson* (1986), a landmark case brought by a bank employee, Mechelle Vinson, against a supervisor. Still, sexual harassment remained a problematic crime. First, the "hostile environment" claim evoked controversy. An employee, for instance, might find it difficult to work because of a pattern of sexual overtures or remarks, or even the display of pornographic pictures in the workplace. EEOC guidelines, however, drew no firm line between allowable and illegal behavior, because what constituted harassment depended upon what a particular individual found offensive. Men and women might interpret a specific type of conduct—a risqué joke, for instance—in different ways; indeed, one woman might interpret it in a different way than another. The crime was defined neither by the perpetrator's intent nor by the conduct per se, but by the victim's response to it. In another landmark case, *Ellison* v. *Brady* (1991), the Ninth Circuit Court of Appeals set a slightly tighter standard: how a "reasonable woman" would have responded.

A second peculiarity of sexual harassment, researchers of the 1980s revealed, was that it involved power more than sex. In MacKinnon's words, sexual harassment referred to an "unwanted imposition of sexual requirements in a relationship of unequal power." It was an abuse of power, a way to make women employees feel vulnerable, and a tactic to devalue their role in the workplace. Less than 5 percent of harassment cases involved a bribe or threat for sex. Most were attempts to control or intimidate victims. Significantly, some studies suggested, sexual harassment occurred most frequently in occupations or workplaces where women were new or in a minority and where they filled jobs that men had traditionally held. Other studies, however, suggested that women in white-collar work, such as office employees, were the most common targets. Government surveys in the 1980s found that 42 percent of

Using demonstrations, boycotts, petitions, and propaganda,
the antipornography campaign protested "writing or
imagery that objectifies, degrades, and brutalizes a person,
usually a woman or girl, in the name of sexual stimulation
or entertainment." This photo shows "tabling," or petition-
signing, on a New York street corner during the summer of
1983. A cover of *Hustler* magazine
is tacked to the poster. *(Leonard Speier)*

women employed in federal agencies had experienced harassment, mainly unwelcome sexual remarks, leers, suggestive looks, and pressure for dates. (So had 14 percent of men in the agencies.)

Few of these employees complained of the offensive conduct—a third peculiarity of sexual harassment. Researchers indicated that only 3 percent of those who felt
victimized complained or pressed charges. Some blamed themselves, or feared that
they would not be believed, that retaliation would follow, or that they would lose

their jobs, foreclose their options, or ruin their careers. Such caution seemed in some ways warranted, lawyers explained, for those who brought sexual harassment charges were likely to endure yet a second bout of humiliation, including queries into their private lives and social habits. Harassment charges, moreover, were difficult to substantiate, especially if a long period of time had passed since the alleged incidents or if there were few corroborating witnesses. All aspects of sexual harassment would receive publicity in 1991, when lawyer Anita Hill accused Supreme Court nominee Clarence Thomas of offensive conduct a decade earlier when she had been his aide at the Department of Education and at the EEOC. The Hill-Thomas hearings before the Senate Judiciary Committee would provide a national seminar on sexual harassment, spur an increase in harassment charges, and indeed affect national politics.

Concern over legal issues such as pornography and sexual harassment represented a surge of attention among feminists to forms of aggression that victimized women, such as sexual abuse in the home, wife battery, and rape. In 1994, Congress passed the Violence Against Women Act to protect women from domestic violence and sexual assault. In *United States* v. *Morrison* (2000), the Supreme Court invalidated five to four the law's civil damages provision, which permitted suits in federal court by victims of crime motivated by gender. Concern over such issues, finally, fueled another feud among 1980s feminists over "cultural feminism" or relational, transformative, or essentialist feminism—all rubrics for lines of thought that acknowledged and celebrated gender difference.

A trend within feminism since the early 1970s, cultural feminism championed women's unique nature and qualities. It challenged the women's movement's current emphasis on equal rights; stressed women's links to one another, and their differences from men; and argued for distinctive female perceptions and abilities. Cultural feminists protested not the existence of gender roles, but the negative connotations of those roles and their devaluation in a male-dominated culture. They capitalized, for instance, on psychologist Carol Gilligan's influential book, *In a Different Voice* (1982), which argued that men and women had different moral sensibilities; agreed with Catharine MacKinnon's assertion that "the engendered nature of law privileges men"; and appreciated linguist Deborah Tannen's best-seller *You Just Don't Understand* (1990), which analyzed gender differences in communication. "Pretending that men and women are the same hurts women, because the ways they are treated are based on the norms for men," Tannen contended. Opponents, however, charged cultural feminists with withdrawing into female culture or returning to a Victorian value system. "The question of whether feminism entails the transcendence of gender or the affirmation of femaleness has become the new feminist faultline," historian Alice Echols observed in 1988.

As the 1990s began, feminism remained a powerful force in public life, but as a political movement it clearly faced obstacles. Young, educated, professional women of the so-called "postfeminist" generation, for instance, sometimes took the achievements of the women's movement for granted, resented the status of oppression that it seemed to confer, or voiced disinterest in affiliation with a militant crusade—as young women had done in the 1920s. "Feminists are losing the second generation because of this incredible bitterness we can't identify with," a young woman told a reporter in 1982. To some, emancipation meant independence from feminism and the ability to get ahead on one's own. Other women claimed "feminist fatigue" after years of striving for feminist ideals that seemed elusive, if not unobtainable. Critiques from within also generated debate. In *The Second Stage* (1982), Betty Friedan urged the women's movement to pay more attention to issues involving the family. In *A Lesser Life* (1986), economist Sylvia Ann Hewlett assailed the feminist preoccupation with equal rights; feminism had failed, she argued, because of its reluctance to consider women's continuing child-care concerns. Perhaps most important, the political climate took a toll. The Reagan-Bush years saw massive cuts in social programs, a verbal emphasis on "family values" without any legislation to support such values, and official hostility to feminist messages. In 1991, journalist Susan Faludi issued a broadside, *Backlash*, that cited the many ways in which movies, the media, industry, the government, the right wing, and assorted revisionists had undercut or sabotaged feminist gains in the 1980s.

At the same time, the goals of the women's movement seemed to have been widely diffused. Many women, for instance, participated in vocational associations that promoted women's issues or grassroots efforts to protect women's rights. In other instances, the goals of the women's movement were privatized. "The people I hang out with or socialize with aren't hard-core card-carrying feminists," a woman police detective in Raleigh, North Carolina, told a *New York Times* reporter in 1987. "But there are women's issues they take sides with." Achieving equality after 1975 became as much an individual battle as an organizational crusade. Several preoccupations of the 1980s—achieving vocational success, weighing career against motherhood, coping with the dual stress of child-rearing and employment—suggested that the search for equality had shifted to a specific arena, the workplace.

WOMEN IN THE WORKPLACE

An influx of new women workers since the 1960s transformed the workplace and the labor force. Women had penetrated prestigious occupations, entered new semiprofessional fields, and moved into the growing service industries, as well as into jobs once dominated by men. By 1980, for instance, women were the majority of insurance adjusters, bill collectors, and real estate agents, and almost half of all bus drivers and bartenders. By 1990, 58 percent of women were in the labor force, where they held about 45 percent of all jobs. In the 1980s, women filled four out of five new jobs. As the female work force grew, its nature changed. By the end of the 1980s, about two-thirds of married women held jobs, as did 68 percent of women with children. The working wife—indeed the working mother—became the norm.

Concerns of women workers reflected both the impact of the women's movement and the changing composition of the female labor force. A major change since the 1960s was the increase of employment among mothers of preschoolers. In 1991, almost 60 percent of mothers with children under six held jobs, compared with 20 percent in 1960. Many working parents left their very young children with relatives or in informal, unlicensed child-care arrangements. Others hired private caretakers, often recent immigrants, legal or illegal. One facet of the child-care problem received publicity at the start of the Clinton administration when the president's first nominee for attorney general was forced to withdraw because she had hired an illegal alien to care for her child and failed to pay the employee's social security. At the end of the 1980s, one-quarter of young children attended day-care centers. Still, day care remained a minimum-wage industry, with low-paid personnel and high turnover. "Quality care," if available, meant substantial expense. Surveys reported that working women's major goals were "helping balance work and family" and "getting government funding for programs such as child care and maternity leave." Among industrialized nations, the United States remained one of the few without subsidized day care and the only one with no statutory maternity leave.

The latter seemed elusive. The Federal Disability Law of 1978 barred discrimination against prospective mothers, and a California law went further. It required unpaid leave of several months for pregnant women, who would be guaranteed their original jobs when they returned. In 1987, the Supreme Court upheld the measure in *California Federal Savings and Loan Association* v. *Guerra*. But the case evoked a dispute about "preferential treatment." NOW, for instance, attacked the California law. To regard women under law as a different class of workers, NOW asserted, would foster sexist stereotypes and increase discrimination against women; the only nonsexist leave policy was one available to all workers. In 1990, President Bush vetoed a

By the mid-1980s more than 150 day-care chains ran centers around the country.
Typically, they paid employees the minimum wage. Pictured is a day-care center in
Montgomery, Alabama, in 1984. *(Mark Chesnutt/NYT Pictures)*

"family leave" bill that would have provided unpaid leave to workers with family obligations. Although he favored the policy, the president contended, it should be voluntary and not obligatory on the part of employers. In early 1993, President Clinton signed a family leave bill that offered workers 12 weeks of unpaid leave, with job retention and continuation of health benefits, for pregnancy, temporary disability, or to care for family members.

Wage differentials between male and female workers also remained a major concern. By the end of the 1980s, the average earnings of full-time women workers were 70 percent those of men, and young women earned yet higher proportions of male wages. In occupations traditionally dominated by men, such as professional, managerial, and technical jobs, a federal spokesman explained, "the male-female wage gap . . . is narrowing." Overall, however, the wage gap continued. Women were predominant among newcomers to the job market, and the lower wages earned by new women workers lowered the average for all women employees. Experts offered other explanations, too: Women were less likely than men to work in unionized occupations; if they had families, they might prefer convenient or flexible work to higher pay; or they may have met discriminatory treatment. A lobbyist for the Women's Equity Action League blamed wage differentials on "sex discrimination, the old boys' network, and massive stereotyping of women's work."

To combat sex discrimination in employment, women relied on the government and the courts, and specifically on Title VII of the 1964 Civil Rights Act, an antidiscrimination policy enforced by the Equal Employment Opportunity Commission. In 1987, in *Johnson* v. *Transportation Agency*, the Court extended its affirmative action thrust by ruling six to three that employers might sometimes favor women and minorities over better-qualified men and whites to correct "a conspicuous imbalance in traditionally segregated job categories" and to bring its work force into line with the makeup of the labor market. The decision enlarged an earlier one: In 1978, in *Steelworkers* v. *Weber*, the Court had ruled that private employers might sometimes give job preference under voluntary affirmative action plans "to break down old patterns of race segregation and hierarchy." In the *Johnson* case, the Court rejected a suit by a man whom the Santa Clara, California, County Transportation Agency had passed over in promotion to the job of dispatching road crews in favor of a woman with a slightly lower score in a competitive interviewing process. Supporters of the decision predicted an increase of women in jobs historically held by men. Opponents charged that the ruling would encourage employers to discount merit and reduce their risk of "reverse discrimination" suits.

Not all affirmative action suits succeeded, as illustrated by the drawn-out Sears case. In 1979, the EEOC sued Sears Roebuck and Co., the first major retail chain to adopt an affirmative action plan, for sex discrimination in hiring, promotion, and pay. Not enough women had been given jobs in commission sales—the vending of such big-ticket items as automotive parts and aluminum siding—the EEOC charged. Sears claimed that it had met reasonable standards for hiring women, that it had a commendable record on affirmative action, and that women had been less interested in and less qualified for commission sales. In 1987, a federal judge supported Sears's claim that it lacked discriminatory intent and criticized the statistical evidence presented by the EEOC, which had never produced a witness to testify to discrimination.

The case was less important for its results, as the EEOC case was faulty, than for the testimony of two expert witnesses, both prominent historians, who debated whether factors other than sex discrimination were likely to have limited women's aspirations to big-ticket sales positions. Alice Kessler Harris claimed that women workers strove for the highest wages and that only employer discrimination barred them from non-traditional jobs. Rosalind Rosenberg contended that historically men and women had different job preferences and that women's cultural conditioning could have led them to avoid competitive sales jobs at Sears.

Affirmative action cases such as the *Johnson* and *Sears* cases affected only women who entered, or sought to enter, fields dominated by men or nontraditional jobs. But despite the inroads that women had made in higher-paid and nontraditional occupations, most women of the 1980s and 1990s, as before, faced a segregated job market, or "massive stereotyping of women's work." Three out of five women workers in the 1980s held pink-collar jobs, and, as a census department official explained, "Working in an occupation that has a high proportion of women has a negative effect on earnings." The segregated job market fostered a demand for "pay equity" or "comparable worth," a campaign to raise pay levels in occupations in which women predominated. A clerical worker, for instance, pay equity advocates claimed, should receive the same pay as a truck driver working for the same employer.

After the United States armed forces turned from conscription to a volunteer force in 1973, the number of women recruits mushroomed. By 1987, more than 225,000 women served in the armed forces. They constituted 10.2 percent of military personnel, compared to 1 percent 20 years earlier. *(J. P. Laffont/Sygma)*

The premise of pay equity was that the "worth" of a job could be reasonably determined, based on such factors as skill, training, effort, and responsibility. Critics contended that the concept took no notice of "market forces," or the demand for a certain type of worker. Supporters, too, voiced qualifications. A study in the *Harvard Law Review* argued that comparable worth, though desirable, defied implementation by the courts and would have only a negligible impact on women's wages. A study of pay equity among public employees in Minnesota, which adopted the policy in the mid-1980s, suggested that it remedied low wages but increased managerial power. For many feminists, still, pay equity remained an attractive cause. If implemented, it would affect large numbers of ordinary wage earners rather than those professionals who had thus far reaped the profits of feminist breakthroughs.

Pay equity, however, was unlikely to alter the structure of the economy, which itself posed problems for women workers in traditional fields. Since 1970, the rise of service industries and of new technology had created many new jobs that women now held. But new options often entailed new liabilities. Computers, for instance, which had transformed office work, may have also devalued the labor of clerical employees, to whom repetitive data-processing tasks resembled piecework. "Automation is producing the sweatshops of the 1980s," an official of Nine To Five, a secretarial union, declared. Part-time work presented problems, too. As women surged into the labor market, employers increasingly relied on temporary or part-time workers. In the mid-1980s, more than half of women wage earners worked part-time or for only part of the year. Less costly to employers, such "contingent" workers lacked the benefits available to full-time employees, such as health care insurance or pension plans. Women's need for "flexible" jobs—plus their massive entry into paid work and employers' desire for cheap labor—could create a class of second-class workers.

Upscale employees in the business world voiced other grievances. One was a "glass ceiling" that barred advancement beyond middle management. Another was the sacrifice that the fast track, or even the middle management track, imposed. By the mid-1980s, 30 percent of managerial personnel were women. A slew of advice books on "The Right Moves" and "Feminine Leadership" offered strategies for success in business circles. But studies of women executives revealed "ambivalence," "burnout," and a feeling that "something's missing." Success in the higher ranks of business or the professions, the press suggested, seemed to exact a toll in personal life. In 1989, Felice Schwartz, president of a research group that focused on women in business, proposed in the *Harvard Business Review* that employers avoid the cost of high turnover among women executives by creating a two-track plan. "Career-primary" women managers, said Schwartz, needed an unimpeded "path to the top." However, "career-and-family" managers would benefit from a different track, one that involved maternity leave, flexible scheduling, part-time work, job-sharing, lower pay, and slower advancement. Such a plan would accommodate both women managers and business, said Schwartz, which "needs all the talented women it can get." The "mommy track," a term coined by foes of the plan, evoked a storm of protest. One critic charged that it would "perpetuate a cycle in which generations of women have been depreciated, divided, and weakened." Schwartz replied that she urged employers to "create policies that help mothers balance career and family responsibilities" and "eliminate barriers to productivity and advancement."

The debate over the "mommy track" in part reflected Schwartz's assertion that "The cost of employing women in management is greater than the cost of employing men." It also illuminated some disparities that had increased since 1970. As women's rates of job holding rose, economist Juliet B. Schor, points out, men's fell. Moreover, among employees, the numbers of hours worked annually increased for men by 98 and for women by 305. Those most affected by "elastic" working hours were salaried—managerial and professional—workers, among whom women's numbers had steadily risen. Employers, however, enjoyed a structural advantage in the labor market, Schor points out, as more candidates existed for managerial and professional jobs—those that provided "job satisfaction"—than there were openings. With candidates competing for high-status employment, employers gained advantages. Typically, they favored cost-cutting measures, disliked work-sharing or part-time arrangements among managers, and preferred to extract longer hours. Employers, apparently, did not yet share Felice Schwartz's contention that measures to retain trained women managers would lower costs. In 1992, only 10 percent of large companies had adopted flexible scheduling or other programs to aid workers with families. Even if employees wanted more time for themselves, as many claimed they did, Schor suggests, few could "reconcile the conflicting demands of employer and family." Women with families who entered competitive occupations were likely to be caught in a crunch between employer demands and private lives.

Advocates of equity for women workers therefore faced a variety of considerations, under less than favorable circumstances. Would demands concerning "family" issues, such as day care or parental leave, dilute demands for equal rights in the workplace? Would any acceptance in law or custom of gender distinctions foster discrimination against women workers and leave them at a competitive disadvantage? Would insistence on absolute equality limit the options for "flexible work" and "balance" that many women workers demanded, and also leave them at a competitive disadvantage? Would sex-neutral policies always work in women's interests? Or would they help some women and harm others? The search for equality in the workplace seemed to revive the issue of "difference" versus "equality" that had plagued the women's movement in the 1920s. It also involved another set of factors—changing expectations about family life.

FAMILIES IN TRANSITION

While politicians relentlessly endorsed "family values," the "traditional" family of postwar America faded. In the 1980s, the Census Bureau and social scientists issued a rash of messages about delayed marriage, unwed cohabitation, single parenthood, and mounting illegitimacy. Ironically, the impact of feminism coincided with significant shifts in domestic life, whose beneficiaries did not appear to be women or children. The new woman of the "postfeminist" generation might well be the working wife in an upwardly mobile two-career family. But she might also be a single mother, deserted spouse, impoverished family head, or, by choice or circumstance, a woman living alone.

An acceleration of change began in the 1970s, when the marriage age started to climb. In 1960, the average marriage age for men was 22.8 and for women 20.3; 30 years later, it was 26.1 for men and 23.9 for women, about the same as in the

1890s. In 1960, again, only 28 percent of women aged 20 to 24 were single; in 1985, over 58 percent. Part of the increase of young single women reflected an increase of cohabiting unwed couples, whose numbers surged in the 1970s and rose again, by 80 percent, in the 1980s. Not all such couples were heterosexual. Quasi-legitimization of gay and lesbian lifestyles spurred an increase in the households of same-sex couples in the 1970s and 1980s, especially in urban areas.

"Living together"—a relationship that resembled Ben Lindsey's plan for "companionate marriage" in the 1920s—had tentative connotations. But when a woman married legally, her security as family member became more tentative, too. In the 1950s, the divorce rate declined slightly, but between 1960 and 1980 it more than doubled. In the 1980s, almost one out of two first marriages ended in divorce; by 1990, the divorce rate had tripled since 1970. If separated or divorced when young, a woman was as likely as a man to remarry, but as she aged, her odds for remarriage dwindled. A census study in the mid-1980s revealed that among those aged 35 to 44, there were 84 eligible men to every 100 eligible women. For older women, the odds dropped even more. In her late forties, a woman was only half as likely as a man to marry again. The 1980 census reported 50 percent more separated or divorced women than men, as well as a 90 percent rise, since 1970, in the number of women living alone. The trend continued into the 1990s.

Interpretation of trends in the marriage market offered fuel for conflict. In 1986 a team of social scientists from Harvard and Yale released dire predictions about educated women's options for marriage based on a study of census data. College-trained women who had not married by 25 had only a 50 percent chance of doing so, the study said. At age 30, the odds dropped to 20 percent, at 35 to 5 percent, and at 40, to 1 percent. According to the social scientists, "marriage deferred is translating into marriage forgone." Census Bureau figures, cited previously, mitigated the scope of decline in marriage odds for women in the population at large, and for educated women as well. Still, to many women, the warnings reflected experience. When asked about the Harvard-Yale study, young professional women suggested that diminished options reflected heightened selectivity more than male scarcity. "If you're college-educated and pursuing a career and trying to achieve something . . . half the men in the world are no longer interesting to you," a Yale graduate told a reporter. "I think women are much less frightened of going out and being alone," a young stockbroker added. "They get so much satisfaction from other parts of their lives that they don't rely so heavily anymore on the man in their life."

Another controversy involved the impact of "no-fault" divorce laws, enacted in 43 states by the mid-1980s. Under no-fault divorce, a court held neither party responsible for the breakup of the marriage or subject to punitive charges; rather, the court divided a couple's property equitably between the parties. In *The Divorce Revolution* (1985), sociologist Lenore Weitzman argued that divorce impoverished ex-wives, especially older wives, and their children. Using a small sample of divorces in Los Angeles County, Weitzman contended that in the first year after divorce, ex-wives experienced a 73-percent drop in their standard of living, and husbands experienced a 42-percent rise. Other studies reported a less dire differential. In 1996, reevaluation of the data by another sociologist suggested a 27-percent drop in women's standard of living and a 10-percent rise for men. Still, the upshot of the studies on divorce and the marriage market was that women faced structural disadvantages; notably, as they aged, their options and leverage shrank, as men's did not. A built-in, and quite traditional, gender gap affected social life.

If marriage options had changed since the 1960s, so had expectations of motherhood. In 1981 the birth rate was 15.7 per thousand people compared with 18 in 1970 and 25.3 at the height of the baby boom in 1957. One census study in 1980 predicted a total fertility rate of 2.06 children per woman, under the 2.2 needed for a no-growth population birthrate. Among young single women, one-fifth expected to have no children at all. If she had children, the young woman of the 1970s and after was likely to have them later than her mother had done. In the 1970s, fertility dropped precipitously among women in their early twenties, although it increased among women a decade older. At the start of the 1990s, some experts suggested that the birthrate had bottomed out and would shortly rise. Still, the era of the baby boom and "togetherness" seemed ancient history.

Women of the 1990s, however, were likely to be the primary caretakers of children, despite NOW's 1966 contention that child care should be "shared equally by fathers." In the 1970s and 1980s, to be sure, as women surged into the labor force, the fraction of married women who were full-time housewives fell from 30 to 15 percent of the adult female population. Men with families, meanwhile, spent increased hours at domestic tasks, including child care. Men's annual hours of household labor, economist Juliet B. Schor estimates, rose by 151, while women's fell. ("The more work women do for pay, the less they do without it.") By 1990, men did almost 60 percent as much domestic work as women. Still, women shouldered the bulk of home-care–child-care responsibilities. Similarly, they bore most of the burden of caring for the aged. Finally, they were increasingly likely to face these responsibilities alone. In the 1970s, when the women's movement had its greatest surge, the number of one-parent families doubled, and most such families were headed by women— divorced women, separated women, and unmarried women. Between 1970 and 1981, the number of families headed by never-married women increased four times over, and in the 1980s, births to single mothers leapt by 70 percent. By the late 1990s, the rate of increase in births to single women began to fall; still, more than one-third of children born in the 1990s had single mothers.

The rise of the female-headed family generated a "feminization" of poverty. In 1980, two-thirds of female-headed families received child welfare and two-thirds of the long-term poor were women. No doubt poverty had always been feminized, but its new visibility invited analysis. The rising failure rate of marriages and the low income of many women who were separated or divorced contributed to the "feminization" trend. Even more so did the massive rise in the number of babies born to single mothers, especially teenagers. In the 1970s, half of all births to single women involved teenagers, and 16 percent of all births were to teenage women. If uneducated, unskilled, and unfinanced, the single mother was likely to turn to public support. The Aid to Families with Dependent Children (AFDC) program, which had begun in the 1930s as a temporary pension for mothers who were widowed or married to unemployed or disabled men, reflected the rise of the single mother and the female-headed household. Between 1955 and 1987, the number of women receiving AFDC benefits rose 600 percent. In 1994, the number of welfare recipients peaked at nearly 14 million, almost all of them women and children.

In August 1996, President Clinton and Congress ended what the president called "welfare as we know it." The Personal Responsibility and Work Opportunity Act of 1996 cut $55 billion in welfare spending over six years, capped welfare payments, and cut benefits to recipients who had not found work in two years. The shift from welfare to "workfare" meant an abandonment of the federal welfare system that had been in place since the New Deal and a shift of authority to the states, each of which now set its own welfare policies. Within a year two million women and children left the welfare rolls. Even modest work requirements produced huge declines in caseloads, the states reported. About half the women who left the rolls found jobs, some relied more heavily on family members, and some sank more deeply into poverty. Almost all the burdens of child support fell on mothers. Finally, states with large welfare populations reported that shrinking welfare rolls left record proportions of minorities. Officials surmised that minority recipients were more severely disadvantaged, less likely to have finished school, and more likely to live in job-scarce central cities.

A disproportionate number of poor black women and children characterized the feminization of poverty from the outset. By the start of the 1980s, over half of all black children were born to unmarried mothers, compared with 15 percent in 1940; 85 percent of black teenage mothers were unmarried; and 47 percent of black families were female-headed, compared with 8 percent in 1950. As the decade progressed, the trend continued. Among all women who had children in 1991, the Census Bureau reported, nearly one out of four and 57 percent of all black women were unmarried; two-thirds of teenage mothers and 90 percent of black teenage mothers were single. By the early 1990s, 26 percent of children under 18 lived with a single parent, as did more than 60 percent of black children. According to Marian Wright Edelman, founder of the Children's Defense Fund, the high black illegitimacy rate "practically guarantees the poverty of the next generation of black children." The escalating rate of births to black single mothers and the rise of the female-headed household precipitated discussion of a "crisis" in the black family. "With the exception of drugs and crime, the biggest crisis facing the black community today is the plight of the single mother," declared an article in *The Crisis*, an NAACP publication, in 1988.

Why were female-headed households increasing in the black community? Some answers focused on dwindling numbers of eligible black men and rising unemployment among black men. An Urban League study in 1984 attributed the black family's problem to "steady attrition in the numbers of black men who can support a wife and children." The Labor Department confirmed that black male employment had steadily dropped from 74 percent in 1960 to 55 percent at the start of the 1980s. At an NAACP Civil Rights Institute in 1985, one panel revealed that among blacks aged 20 to 24, there were only 45 eligible men for every 100 women, due to the impact of such factors as unemployment and incarceration. Among black men in the next age category, 25 to 34, in 1987, only 39 percent were married and living with wives (as were 62 percent of white men, whose commitment to marriage had also fallen off). Women's responses to scarcity received less attention. "It is the news but no one with clout will explain it," wrote a journalism professor who regretted her daughter's dwindling options. "It is better to have no man than a no-good man," a Chicago divorcee told a reporter for *The Crisis*.

Several analysts sought long-term causes. "At the heart of the crisis lies the self-perpetuating culture of the ghetto," contended Eleanor Holmes Norton, Georgetown law professor and former EEOC head, in 1985. "This destructive ethos began to surface 40 years ago with the appearance of permanent joblessness and the devaluation of working-class men." As the postwar economy had helped to produce a black middle class, Norton concluded, it had also destroyed "the black working class and its family structure." The source of the black family crisis, she said, lay not with women and children, but "with working-class black men whose loss of function in the post-World War II economy has led directly to their loss of function in the family." In *The Truly Disadvantaged* (1987), scholar William Julius Wilson argued that deindustrialization, which started in the early 1970s, and the movement of jobs to the suburbs left unskilled young men increasingly unemployable and undesirable as marriage prospects. The exodus of middle- and working-class blacks from the inner cities, meanwhile, left ghettos filled with the poor and unemployed, plagued by joblessness and lawlessness. Neither of these answers of the 1980s escaped challenge; scholars continue to debate the nature and roots of the feminization of poverty and the factors that affect black family formation.

Scarcity of men, however, affected black communities beyond the inner city as well. Among educated black women, for instance, a marriage crisis loomed in proportions similar to that experienced by white college graduates a century earlier. By the end of the 1980s, studies reported, an educational gender gap emerged: 60 percent of black college students were women (as opposed to about half of all students), and the numbers of black women exceeded black men in most forms of professional training. Black women, the American Council on Education predicted, would be better educated, have more prestigious jobs and higher incomes than black men, and hold more leadership positions. The president of the United Negro College Fund pointed out that there had always been more black women than men in college because there was more family pressure to save themselves from careers as maids. Joyce Ladner, sociology professor at Howard, said that the message of the educational gender gap for black women was "that the pool of eligible black men for them gets smaller and smaller the further they go up the educational and career ladder."

Since the start of the civil rights and feminist movements, many reports suggested, black women had made impressive and indeed disproportionate strides. In 1987, for instance, black women who completed college earned slightly more than white college-trained women; black college men, however, earned 78 percent of white men's incomes; among all workers that year, black median income was 57 percent that of whites. Black women held two-thirds of all professional jobs held by blacks (and white women 48 percent of white professional jobs). The proportion of black professionals that was female seemed destined to increase. The number of black men entering medical school, for instance, dropped 23 percent in the 1970s and 1980s, while the number of black women increased. As black women's vocational status rose, their likelihood of marriage fell. In 1987, only 48 percent of black professional women were married, compared with 62 percent of white professional women.

The gender gap among blacks—educational, vocational, social—might be viewed as an extension of trends that pervaded relations between the sexes in the population at large. Illegitimacy, rising divorce, the female-headed family, and the scarcity of eligible men were not solely black developments. Social scientist Andrew Hacker, for instance, finds a convergence of trends and experiences among blacks and whites. Other scholars find in trends among black women predictors of trends among all women. Still, black women's lives after 1975 reflected circumstances that affected blacks in particular. One notable circumstance was the apparent split among blacks between an upwardly mobile middle class and a downtrodden urban "underclass," a term whose pervasive use itself incurred criticism.

Not surprisingly, black women sought a distinctive stance as feminists. "Black feminist thought," according to sociologist Patricia Collins, "sees three distinctive systems of oppression as being part of an overarching structure of domination . . . a system of interlocking race, class, and gender oppression." Nor was white feminism necessarily an appropriate model. "One of the problems with white feminism is that it is not a tradition that teaches white women that they are capable," author Alice Walker told a reporter in 1984. "Whereas my tradition *assumes* that I'm capable. . . . I have cleared fields, I have lifted whatever, I have *done* it." In the 1980s, Walker coined the term "Womanism" to represent black feminism. Womanism was "a word that is organic, that really comes out of the culture, that really expresses the spirit we see in black women," she said. "You know, the posture with the hand on the hip, 'Honey, don't you get in my way.'" Black feminist commentary reflected a growing emphasis on diversity. To consider women's status in the 1980s and 1990s meant paying attention to differences of race, class, and ethnicity—and in view of rising immigration since the 1960s, to the roles of women in the fastest-growing ethnic groups.

IMMIGRATION, ETHNICITY, AND DIVERSITY

The new immigration that followed the Immigration Act of 1965 rapidly increased the numbers of foreign-born Americans, especially those of non-European origin. Between 1960 and 1990, 45 percent of immigrants came from the Western Hemisphere and 30 percent from Asia. Several features marked the new immigration. First, women migrants outnumbered men, an uncommon pattern in recent international migration. In 1979, the sex ratio among adult migrants to the United States was 87 men to every 100 women, and among those of certain groups, such as Filipinos, Koreans, and non-Communist Chinese, far lower. Second, immigrant women typically joined the labor force. Many single women came to the United States, as men had in the past, to seek employment; others, who arrived as family members, did the same. New York City demographers found that many women preceded their families because it was easier for them than for men to find work. Active labor force participation affected women's experience as immigrants and increased their importance in the economic life of their ethnic groups.

Working immigrant women were especially visible on the East and West Coasts, where they often congregated in distinct sectors according to ethnicity—many Filipino and Korean women, for instance, became medical personnel; Latin American, Mexican, and Asian women found jobs in the garment industry; and women from many nations took work in private households, thus expediting the exodus of other women to the job market. For some women, immigration entailed downward occupational mobility, as was the case for many white-collar workers from Cuba in the 1960s who took blue-collar jobs. Among Soviet emigrés of the 1970s and later, many former professionals faced similar downgrading. For most women, however, immigration provided vocational opportunity. A skilled nurse, for instance, might earn more by working one day with overtime in an American city than she would in a month in Manila. Trained or untrained, women immigrants expected better options, higher pay, and higher living standards than in their countries of origin.

Women's work roles were significant among the largest groups of newcomers, those of Latino and Asian descent. Each contingent represented numerous nations; each encompassed its own diversity of class, education, and wealth. New arrivals in both groups often joined ethnic communities that had been established for decades or generations. In both cases, women might experience tension between their traditional roles in ethnic families and contemporary American women's roles, and often viewed their achievements as wage earners as contributions to the family economy.

Asian Americans, a rapidly expanding group, accounted for more than 40 percent of total immigrants since 1975. In the 1980s, the Asian American population grew by 80 percent. Arriving from China, Taiwan, Hong Kong, Vietnam, Cambodia, Japan, the Philippines, and South Korea, newcomers valued their national identities over their common Asian heritage. Disproportionately professional, Asian immigrants and their children proved upwardly mobile. Immigration law favored relatives of U.S. citizens and "persons with professional skills needed in the U.S. economy"; well trained in their countries of origin, many Asians arrived ready to compete for middle-class careers. Still, class distinctions provided varied experiences.

Japanese Americans, less affected than other groups by the new immigration, set a standard of economic achievement. By the 1990s, Japanese income exceeded the national per capita income, and women's occupations reflected the upward trend. Before the new immigration, women of Japanese origin had been employed mainly in craft, factory, and service jobs; in the 1970s and 1980s, their daughters became technicians, professionals, and managers. But not all new immigrants arrived prepared for upward mobility. Among Chinese immigrants, historian Ronald Takaki shows, different class backgrounds led to the formation of a "bi-polar Chinese American community—a colonized working class and an entrepreneurial middle class." Nearly half of Chinese immigrants between 1966 and 1975, mainly newcomers from Taiwan and Hong Kong, had professional and technical occupations. But 80 percent of New York's Chinatown at the end of the 1980s—often immigrants from mainland China—were low-wage laborers, either service workers or factory workers. These included many women seamstresses in garment shops, whose experience resembled that of women garment workers at the turn of the century.

The "bi-polar" quality pervaded the new Asian immigrant community. Like the professionals from Taiwan and Hong Kong, many Asian American women arrived with extensive education. Among Filipino immigrants, predominantly female, 65 percent had professional and technical occupations. Overproduction of doctors and nurses in Korea also sent an influx of women professionals to the United States. Immigrants from Southeast Asia, less exposed to educational opportunities at home, fell into the lower-paid ranges of occupations. Still, as among other Asian immigrants, a high proportion of women entered the labor force. Among Vietnamese refugees in the late 1970s, one study suggests, 42 percent of women found work, as did 64 percent of men. "Some women can get jobs in factories, and those with a high school education can go for vocational training," a resettlement worker among Southeast Asians explained. "So in many families, the woman has become the breadwinner. They not only make more money than the husband, they often have better jobs."

Asian American women's reflections on ethnic identity, typically written by second- or third-generation women of Chinese or Japanese origin, describe strong family traditions, intergenerational tension, and conflict between ethnic and American culture. In her memoir, *The Woman Warrior* (1976), Maxine Hong Kingston gives an example of cultural conflict from her American childhood. "Normal Chinese women's voices are strong and bossy," she wrote. "We American-Chinese girls had to whisper to make ourselves American-feminine." In a 1970s essay, Magoda Marayoma, a third-generation Japanese American from California, cited a contrary example. "My parents urged me, unconsciously I am sure, to perpetuate the stereotype of the quiet, polite, unassuming Asian," she wrote. "But survival in American society requires one to speak up vociferously to defend one's rights and gain recognition." Recognition of cultural differences, however, impeded neither ethnic pride nor upward mobility. Nor did it impede intermarriage, a trend first noted among Japanese American women and subsequently among other Asian American women. "In general in the American culture, if you're a professional Asian woman . . . you're extremely acceptable," a third-generation Korean American woman from Hawaii commented. "In fact, I think it has become fashionable for white men to marry Asian women. Chinese American women married to white men are really pervasive. You don't see the reverse as much . . . for Asian men, it is more difficult."

Americans of Latino origin, the fastest-growing ethnic group, similarly encompassed people of varied nations and backgrounds. In 1960, before the new immigration, 85 percent were American-born; some traced their American ancestry back to the seventeenth century. By the end of the 1980s, however, more than half of Latino Americans were foreign-born or children of immigrants. As immigration from the western hemisphere grew, so did the proportion of women among migrants. Among entrants from Mexico, men had traditionally predominated; by the early 1990s, half of Mexican immigrants who settled in the United States were women. Many families headed by women arrived from Mexico as well as from war-torn Central American or Latin American countries. Spanish-speaking Americans usually followed the assimilation patterns of other immigrant groups. However, 20 percent of Mexicans and 30 percent of Puerto Ricans remained below the poverty line. At the end of the 1980s, 74 percent of Latino families were two-parent families, as were 80 percent of white families. Out-of-wedlock births constituted 29 percent of Latino births, compared with 17 percent of white births and 62 percent of black births.

Latino women's work roles might reflect their immigrant status. A study of Mexican women migrants in Los Angeles County in the early 1980s shows that undocumented women found work in factories, restaurants, and private homes; legal immigrants were more likely to take white-collar jobs in offices and public institutions. The higher women's skills and knowledge of English, the more easily they could transfer their skills to the new economy. Their attitudes toward work might reflect both class differences and a tradition of male domination, as seen in Yolanda

Prieto's study of Cuban women in New Jersey. Among these immigrants of the 1960s, mainly middle class, more than half of women joined the work force. Although they considered work necessary for family mobility, they voiced other motives as well. "I work to help my family," one woman said. "But besides that I couldn't stand the loneliness if I stayed home." One university graduate, formerly a professor in Cuba and now a teacher, merged her work role with her traditional family role: "I have always been very independent, that is why I have always worked," she stated. "Of course, I think that a woman should *never compete* with her husband. Women's role is fundamentally the family. But if a woman is intelligent and knows how to combine work and family she shouldn't have any problems."

Sociologist Norma Williams, who studied second- and third-generation Mexican American families in Austin and Corpus Christi, Texas, in the 1980s, elicited similar responses from "professional-class" working women. Although male domination was "modified" among her urban respondents, she notes, it persisted, and women had to deal with it. One way for women to minimize the role strain between demands of job and family, Williams notes, was "to 'compartmentalize' their lives and give priority to motherhood over their careers." One respondent, for instance, "reshaped her role to minimize conflict with her husband and the threat to his identity." "I started to work and get involved with civic issues," the woman said. "His pride began to show, and we started to argue. I guess he was jealous because I really enjoy my work. It wasn't easy for me, and I don't want you to think that it was." Williams cites a difference, however, between women in professional families and those in working-class families. Professional-class women were likely to take an "independent" identity for granted, whereas working-class women sought it. Although both groups saw themselves as "twice a minority," Williams concludes, socioeconomic status affected their attitudes. "Working class women conceive of ethnicity as a more compelling issue than gender; professional women typically perceive gender issues as more salient than ethnicity."

Do gender issues become more salient for most women as social class rises? Significantly, Williams challenges assumptions of hegemony, specifically "the assimilationist model that has been so prevalent among social scientists." Noting that "generalizations about family life and women's gender roles have often been based on the white middle class" and that "the assimilationist world view looks on the social order from the top down," she observes that "certain role-making patterns among Mexican-American working-class and professional women do not conform to those in the privileged sector of Anglo society." Do women share commonalities that transcend ethnic boundaries? Williams, uncertain, concludes that "differences between privileged Anglo women and women of color may be greater than the similarities."

The attitude of new immigrants and other ethnic Americans to diversity was complex. Most new immigrants looked forward to assimilation and upward mobility. They had less impulse to define themselves as oppressed minorities than did native-born blacks, and less affinity to the 1960s mode of political pressure that spawned the civil rights movement and the women's movement. Women of ethnic groups also faced particular tensions. Historian Maxine Seller points to "apparent contradictions between the traditional, submissive sex roles dictated by their ethnic cultures, and the assertive, egalitarian behavior dictated by the women's movement." Many felt "that their first loyalty should be to their ethnic group." One representative of Native American women, Paula Gunn Allen, a writer of Pueblo and Sioux descent, presents a contrasting point. "Rejection of tradition constitutes one of the major features of an American life," Gunn contends. But in her view, rejection of Native American tradition resulted from white colonial oppression, patriarchal values, and forced acculturation, developments that demeaned the "sacred ways of women." Contemporary American Indian communities, she argues, "value members who are deeply connected to the traditional ways of their people." Current research suggests that generalizations about women's roles are subject to class and ethnic variations and need to be qualified. Generalizations about women in politics demand revision as well.

THE GENDER GAP

In the early 1980s, an unexpected trend developed. A "women's vote" had appeared— or at least a "gender gap" in political views, as revealed in election data and political polls. As suffragists had once contended, the "women's vote" seemed to be a reform-minded vote that defied conservative trends in national politics. According to the polls, more women than men opposed Republican policies, high unemployment, ending federal funds for human services, and large expenditures on nuclear weapons.

Until the late 1970s, polls showed that political opinions were undifferentiated by sex except on questions involving the use of force, which women tended to oppose more than men. In the 1980 presidential election, however, differences began to appear. Women provided far larger proportions of the vote for Democrat Jimmy Carter (58 percent), who lost the election, than of the vote for victor Ronald Reagan (49 percent). Moreover, as subsequent polls confirmed, women, who now voted for the first time in the same proportion as men, differed from men on major issues. In mid-1982, polls showed that greater proportions of women than men favored Democratic policies on employment, inflation control, and avoiding war. Curiously, views remained similar on the major women's issues, the ERA and abortion; indeed, men were slightly more favorable to both.

Significantly, wage-earning women contributed more to the gender gap than women who were not employed. According to some analysts, women's precarious vocational status and concentration in lower-income jobs were major determinants of their political values. As women under 45, who were rapidly entering the labor force, now voted in higher proportions than men, the gender gap could be expected to continue and increase.

In 1984 Democrats sought to capitalize on the new development. Democratic presidential nominee Walter Mondale chose New York representative Geraldine Ferraro as his running mate at the 1984 convention. Describing herself as a "housewife from Queens," Ferraro had spent three terms in Congress and had headed the 1984 Democratic Platform committee. Several circumstances led to her candidacy. First, there were no self-evident competing choices for the nomination. Second, NOW applied pressure by threatening withdrawal of support for the Democrats if a woman was not chosen. Third, as Betty Friedan suggested, selecting a woman represented a commitment to expansion of opportunity for all, a theme that the Democrats wished to emphasize. Fourth, among the possible women candidates, Ferraro seemed the most promising because of her potential appeal to an ethnic, working-class vote, as well as to other traditional Democrats. The daughter of Italian immigrants, Ferraro had worked her way up in the world as a teacher, lawyer, and public prosecutor. Finally, the Mondale camp felt the need of a bold, unconventional step, both to energize the campaign and to prove that the candidate could take strong, decisive action.

Ferraro's nomination generated widespread excitement, drew an outpouring of volunteers, and represented a triumph to feminists. Republicans criticized the nomination as tokenism. "I would like it better if she were a candidate, and not a woman candidate," said former senator Margaret Chase Smith of Maine, the first woman to serve in both houses of Congress, when interviewed in retirement. "Now, I was never a woman candidate." As soon as the campaign began, a furor erupted over whether Ferraro would reveal all of her family finances beyond the income tax statements required by law. To do so, as the press demanded, meant exposure not only of her own finances but those of her husband, a possible source of irregularities (as later turned out to be the case). No comparable concern over a spouse's finances had arisen before a woman ran for vice president. Ferraro finally released the information that the press demanded, but the controversy jarred the Democratic campaign.

On election day, President Reagan, who won 59 percent of the popular vote, garnered 57 percent of the women's vote as opposed to 42 percent for Mondale. (The men's vote was 61 percent for Reagan to 37 percent for Mondale.) All nine women challengers for Senate seats lost, as did 39 of 41 women challengers for House seats. "I think we can consider the gender gap closed," said Reagan's new Secretary of Transportation, Elizabeth Dole. Recriminations abounded in the Democratic camp. Feminists were "remote from the women's vote," a Democratic consultant charged. "These people can't deliver their sisters." With an 18-point chasm between the candidates, Democratic women pointed out, the gender gap could not be expected to provide a victory. Defeating Reagan at the height of his popularity, Ferraro observed four years later, "would have required God on the ticket." Had she not been a woman, she conceded, she would not have been the vice presidential nominee. "Cynics will say it was strictly a political move playing to the gender gap. I agree," Ferraro declared. "But . . . it was equally important to [Mondale] to right a wrong; he removed gender as a disqualification for national office."

The gender gap survived 1984 and played a major role in 1986, when women's votes enabled Democrats to recapture a majority of Senate seats after six years of Republican control. In seven states, where a majority of men supported the Republicans, only the Democratic women's vote ensured victory. In two other states, where men were equally divided, women again provided the margin of victory. Women were now over half of voters. In a 1987 article, analysts suggested that peace was the crucial women's issue. Compared to men, women were more opposed to military involvement, military spending, capital punishment, and nuclear power, and more supportive of arms control and gun control. One pundit noted that the ideal Republican candidate would be a woman and the ideal Democratic candidate a general. The presidential victory of George Bush in 1988, like the Reagan victory of 1984, underlined another facet of the gender gap: a greater proportion of men than of women now

New York Representative Geraldine Ferraro, just selected as the Democratic nominee for Vice President, and presidential candidate Walter Mondale greet crowds in July 1984. (*AP/Wide World Photos*)

voted Republican. In the 1994 races, 62 percent of white men (and 56 percent of white women) would do so. This pattern persisted for the rest of the century.

As evidence about a gender gap accumulated, women who ran for elective office made major strides, especially on the local level. By the mid-1980s, 15 percent of state and local officials were women. In 1991, state legislatures were 18.2 percent female, compared to 4.8 percent in 1971. Bipartisan women's fund-raising groups, such as the Women's Campaign Fund and the National Women's Political Caucus, aided women candidates, as did EMILY's List ("Early Money Is Like Yeast"), which supported pro-choice Democratic women candidates in the early stages of their campaigns. As the 1990s began, an unexpected sequence of events suddenly fused gender issues, national politics, and the prospects of women candidates.

In October, 1991, Anita Hill, a law school professor at the University of Oklahoma, appeared before the Senate Judiciary Committee to accuse Supreme Court nominee Clarence Thomas, a judge on the federal Court of Appeals, of sexual harassment a decade earlier when she was his aide, first at the Department of Education and then at the EEOC, which he had headed from 1982 to 1990. After Thomas vigorously denied the charges, the senators, eight Democrats and six Republicans, interrogated Thomas, Hill, and panels of witnesses, who testified to either Hill's veracity or Thomas's good character. Three days later, the committee chair, Senator Joseph Biden of Maryland, suddenly halted the tumultuous proceedings. The Thomas nomination, controversial even before Hill's accusations, moved to the floor of the Senate, where it was confirmed by a bare majority of 52 to 48.

Anita Hill at a news conference in Norman, Oklahoma, on
October 7, 1991, four days before her testimony to the Senate
Judiciary Committee. *(Scott Anderson/NYT Pictures)*

The Thomas-Hill hearings riveted public attention on sexual harassment in the
workplace and evoked divergent responses to Anita Hill's charges. "If Professor Hill's
account is true, it's certainly sexual harassment, in that it created a hostile environment for her to work in," said Catharine MacKinnon, now a law professor at the
University of Michigan. But were the charges true? Public opinion research at the
time of the hearings suggested that Thomas's denial carried more weight than Hill's
allegations; national polls reported that 55 percent of men and 49 percent of women
found Thomas more believable. According to a *New York Times*–CBS poll, which reported support for the Thomas confirmation by a two-to-one margin, among both
women and men, 40 percent of respondents believed that neither Thomas nor Hill
told "the entire truth." Black public opinion, previously divided on the nomination
of a black conservative, also tilted toward Thomas; among blacks, his support leapt
from about half, before Hill's testimony, to 70 percent. Among women, too, reporters and pollsters found divisions. Professionals and managers tended to believe
Hill's charges, but office workers expressed skepticism. A vocal portion of Anita
Hill's sympathizers, however, pointed to the all-male panel that had questioned her
and to the almost all-male Senate that had confirmed Clarence Thomas, and saw an

opportunity. "Sisterhood may not be powerful now," an official of the Women's Campaign Fund told *Wall Street Journal* reporter Jane Mayer, "but it's going to be a hell of a lot more powerful soon."

Prospective women candidates tended to agree: When the nation watched the Thomas-Hill hearings, many women complained that there were no women on the Judiciary Committee and only two in the Senate: Nancy Kassebaum of Kansas, a member of the pro-choice faction of Republican women, and Democrat Barbara Mikulski of Maryland, a longtime women's rights advocate who had been elected in the Democratic sweep of 1986. Angered by the treatment of Anita Hill in the Thomas hearings, a record number of women decided to run for office in 1992. By the spring of that year, twice as many women had entered congressional contests as had done so in 1990. Women's political fund-raising groups reported that contributions had doubled over those of two years earlier. The Thomas-Hill hearings and the performance of the Judiciary Committee, wrote columnist Elizabeth Drew, turned out to have been "radicalizing events that galvanized women to run for office." Women's roles also rose into view as a campaign issue. Republican strategists

California representative Barbara Boxer leads women members of Congress to the Senate side of the Capitol on October 8, 1991, to demand a delay in the vote on the Thomas nomination. *(Paul Hosefros/NYT Pictures)*

By the end of the 1990s, women constituted 22.3 percent of state legislators,
compared to 10.3 percent in 1979 and 4 percent in 1969. In the Washington State
legislature in 1999, above, women were 40.8 percent of the members, the highest
percentage in the nation. *(Larry Davis for the New York Times)*

targeted Hillary Clinton, wife of the Democratic nominee, as a liability. A corporate
lawyer in Little Rock, Hillary Rodham Clinton had long been active in public life.
She had proposed educational reforms in Arkansas, worked on the Children's Defense Fund, and led the American Bar Association's commission on women. Under
media scrutiny, Hillary Clinton modified her campaign style. The Democratic nominee sought the votes of working women. Bill Clinton presented himself as "the
grandson of a working woman, the son of a single mother, the husband of a working
wife," and told the voters, "I have learned that building up women does not diminish
men." The campaign, wrote columnist Anna Quindlen, showed "how we feel about
smart women, professional women, new women."

A three-way race, the 1992 presidential contest was the first in which suburban-ites and baby-boomers constituted a majority of voters. So did women, now 54 percent of the electorate. The gender gap persisted: Clinton won 41 percent of white women voters (and 37 percent of men) and 86 percent of black women voters (compared with 77 percent of men). Women candidates, who attracted increased funding, notably from women's political fund-raising groups, profited from a predicted rise in support: the number of women doubled in the House, tripled in the Senate, and rose in state and local office. Two new women senators quickly won seats on the Senate Judiciary Committee, whose former all-male membership had angered viewers of the Thomas-Hill hearings. The new administration appointed a record number of women to high-level advisory offices and Cabinet posts, among them the first woman attorney general, Janet Reno, and subsequently, in Clinton's second term, the first woman secretary of state, Madeline Albright. The new administration also resolved some longstanding issues. Within a few weeks of assuming office, for instance, the president signed a family leave bill. In June, 1993, after Justice Byron White's retirement, Clinton named to the Supreme Court federal judge Ruth Bader Ginsburg, who had argued landmark sexual equality cases in the 1970s. A generation after the start of a new women's movement, the "women's vote" seemed to carry political weight.

The two-term Clinton administration brought surprises to the women's groups that endorsed its policies and the rest of the nation. A major surprise was the prominent role that First Lady Hillary Rodham Clinton assumed in policy-making and public life. In the fall of 2000, just before her husband's second term expired, the First Lady won election as a senator from New York. When she took office in 2001, a record-breaking 13 women served in the Senate. Another surprise of the Clinton era was the president's legal entanglements. Significantly, as the century entered its last decade, the women's movement had a significant impact on the law.

WOMEN AND THE LAW

By the 1990s, the law had long been a focus of feminist effort. Many advances of the women's movement—in reproductive rights, employment opportunity, and other areas—depended on changes in law. Above all, feminists strove to terminate laws that treated women differently than men. Progress began in the 1970s when law professor Ruth Bader Ginsburg argued a series of cases before the Supreme Court. Ginsburg sought equal treatment for women and men under the equal protection clause of the Fourteenth Amendment. *Reed* v. *Reed* (1971), for instance, invalidated an Idaho law that preferred men to women as administrators of decedents' estates; neither sex, said the Court, deserved preference. *Frontiero* v. *Richardson* (1973) upset a federal law that denied benefits to spouses of women in military service. In this case and others Ginsburg's tactic was to remedy laws that disadvantaged men. In each of her victories, the Court rejected the assumption that men would be breadwinners and women dependents.

By the mid-1970s, Ginsburg's strategy of Fourteenth Amendment litigation plus Title VII of the 1964 Civil Rights Act served in lieu of an ERA as instruments to achieve sexual equality. Important gender cases of the 1980s reflected the massive increase in women's employment: issues such as maternity leave and affirmative action came to the fore. The controversial decision of *California Federal Savings and Loan Association* v. *Guerra* (1987), handed down by a divided Court, discussed earlier, led to a federal law providing "family leave" in 1993. In *Johnson* v. *Transportation Agency* (1987), another split decision upheld a voluntary affirmative action program. It was permissible to consider sex as a factor when choosing among qualified job candidates, said the Court. In the 1990s, three issues—fetal protection, single-sex education, and sexual harassment—proved contested areas. In each instance, the Supreme Court took steps to promote equal rights; in each case as well issues of difference versus equality arose.

In *UAW* v. *Johnson Controls* (1991), workers at a battery-manufacturing company and their union challenged the company's fetal protection policy, adopted in 1982, which excluded women capable of childbearing (but not fertile men) from jobs that required exposure to lead in quantities that exceeded federal standards. This policy, the company claimed, was legal because lead exposure entailed risk to the health of fetuses. Accepting the company's argument, a federal Circuit Court of Appeals found that a "real physical difference" between men and women justified the company policy; as potential mothers, women workers might risk the health of unborn children. The potential motherhood argument had been a convincing one in *Muller* v. *Oregon* (1908), which upheld a ten-hour law for women employed in factories and laundries. The Supreme Court in 1991, however, reversed the Court of Appeals ruling. The justices unanimously found the fetal protection policy discriminatory under Title VII of the 1964 Civil Rights Act because women who are pregnant or potentially pregnant must be treated like others. "Concern for a woman's existing or potential offspring has historically been the excuse for denying women equal employment opportunity," Justice Blackmun wrote. Neither the courts nor employers could "decide whether a woman's reproductive role is more important to herself and her family than her economic role. Congress has left this choice to the woman as hers to make."

Widely hailed as a feminist triumph, the *Johnson Controls* decision still posed problems. Did gender neutrality always ensure justice? Did equal opportunity in the workplace subject women workers to risk? Or did it simply remove employers from liability for risk—for either women or men? In a sense, women had sued not only for equal opportunity but for the right to be subject to the same hazards as men (or "Women are Now Free to Choose Dangerous Jobs," as a headline proclaimed). The *Johnson Controls* decision provided no guidelines for situations in which women *might* be at higher risk than men nor did it address the dangers of exposure to industrial toxins for both women and men. Moreover, as scholar Cynthia R. Daniels points out, the controversy over fetal protection presented feminists with a paradox: "To ignore difference is to risk placing women in a workplace designed by and for men, with all of its hazards and lack of concern for the preservation of health and life," Daniels points out. "On the other hand, to treat women differently from men in the workplace is to reinforce those assumptions and economic structures which form the foundation of women's inequality."

In *United States* v. *Virginia* (1996), the difference versus equality issue emerged in another arena. Here, the Court faced the question of whether the Virginia Military

Institute, a state-supported college, might remain a single-sex men's school. VMI contended that it offered an "adversative method" of "rigorous military training" (one designed to induce stress) that was intended solely for men. A federal district court agreed that "substantial educational benefits flow from a single-gender environment, be it male or female, that cannot be replicated in co-educational setting." To satisfy an appellate court's demand for equal opportunity and to preserve VMI's single-sex status, Virginia had created a women-only program, the Virginia Women's Institute for Leadership, at nearby Mary Baldwin College. But did this separate program provide equality opportunity? The Fourth Circuit Court of Appeals said yes, but the Supreme Court disagreed. In a 7:1 vote (Clarence Thomas was exempt because his son attended the school and Justice Antonin Scalia dissented), the court rejected Virginia's argument. "Women seeking and fit for VMI-quality education cannot be offered anything less under the State's obligation to afford them genuinely equal protection," declared Justice Ginsburg in the majority opinion. The women-only program at Mary Baldwin College was not a valid alternative, but only a "pale shadow" of what VMI offered to male students. Moreover, "[e]stimates of what is appropriate for *most women* no longer justify denying opportunity to women whose talents and capacity place them outside the average description." Finally, Ginsburg cited a 1982 case, *Mississippi University for Women* v. *Hogan*, with an opinion written by Sandra Day O'Connor, that held unconstitutional the exclusion of men from a state supported nursing school. Under Title VII, said the Court, the state had to provide an "exceedingly persuasive justification" for any official action that treats men and women differently.

Justice Scalia argued in his dissent that the VMI decision did not interpret the Constitution but created it; that it threatened private single-sex colleges that received various forms of federal aid including tax-exempt status; and that it reduced educational diversity (the opportunity of students to choose among diverse educational experiences). The majority opinion in the VMI case, however, provided equality without completely discarding difference. It contended that "'inherent differences'" between men and women "remain cause for celebration"; recognized no stigma in gender separatism or single-sex education; and in a footnote left open the possibility that single-sex education might provide equal educational opportunity: "Indeed, it is the mission of some single-sex schools 'to dissipate, rather than perpetuate, traditional gender classification.'" Moreover, according to the majority opinion, even state-run single-sex programs were not invariably unconstitutional; an "exceeding persuasive justification" might exist to support public single-sex education. But Virginia had not provided one. The VMI decision also affected the Citadel in South Carolina, where a similar men-only policy had come under attack. In 1992, Shannon Faulkner, a South Carolina high school student and rejected applicant, sued the Citadel. Faulkner won her case, was accepted, and dropped out after five days, citing stress and isolation. By the century's end both schools had small groups of women students.

While the VMI decision provoked conflict, it was sexual harassment that became the most controversial gender issue of the 1990s. Anita Hill's testimony in 1991 unleashed a torrent of complaints. In September 1992, the EEOC reported a 50-percent surge in harassment complaints since the Hill-Thomas hearings. Reported incidents of harassment filled the press. Assaults on women at a 1991 convention of the Tailhook Association, a group of naval aviators, led to the resignation of the Secretary of the Navy and the reassignment of an admiral. A series of sexual harassment accusations again descended on public officials, including two senators. A professor of neurosurgery at Stanford resigned to protest decades of harassment and sexism in academic medicine. A new rash of books explained how to file sexual harassment complaints, and as the century closed, the U.S. Army's highest-ranking woman launched a sexual harassment charge against another Army general. Meanwhile "sensitivity" became the catchword of response. Women executives demanded sensitivity training for their colleagues. Employers, now liable for damages of up to $300,000 to victims of job discrimination, including sexual harassment, under the 1991 Civil Rights Act, began to hire such sensitivity trainers. Network television raised viewer sensitivity by explaining the hazards of a "hostile environment" in the workplace. Finally, as a series of cases made their way through the courts, federal judges modified and refined the concept of sexual harassment.

In *Meritor Savings Bank* v. *Vinson* (1986), the Supreme Court had endorsed the concept of sexual harassment and the "hostile environment" test. But who would determine whether offensive behavior was "severe or pervasive" enough to create a hostile environment in the workplace? In *Ellison* v. *Brady* (1991), the Ninth Circuit Court of Appeals held that sexual harassment should be evaluated from the perspective of a "reasonable woman." In *Harris* v. *Forklift Systems* (1993), the Supreme Court redefined a "hostile environment" as one that a "reasonable person" would find hostile or abusive or detrimental to performance. But were the reasonable woman and the reasonable person one and the same? Did men and women interpret sexual harassment in different ways? Could gender neutrality apply to this issue? Or was the "reasonable person" in effect the "reasonable man," who was less likely to find sexual harassment a problem in the first place? Feminists took conflicting positions in this debate. Meanwhile, a series of decisions in 1998 further clarified sexual harassment law.

In *Faragher* v. *City of Boca Raton* and *Burlington Industries* v. *Ellerth*, by votes of 7:2 (with Scalia and Thomas dissenting), the Court defined the obligations of employers and workers. In *Faragher*, in an opinion by Justice David Souter, the Court held employers responsible for preventing and eliminating sexual harassment in the workplace and made employers liable even for harassing acts of supervisory employees of which top managers had no knowledge. In *Burlington*, the Court considered whether a woman was entitled to damages if she quit a company after a supervisor made advances but before she either submitted to them or suffered consequences for refusing to do so. In the majority opinion, written by Justice Anthony Kennedy, the Court said an employee could sue even without showing job-related harm. She must, however, have availed herself of effective complaint policies and other protection offered by the company. In a third case of 1998, *Oncale* v. *Sundowner Offshore Services*, a unanimous opinion, written by Justice Scalia, protected employees from sexual harassment in the workplace by others of the same sex. In a fourth case of 1998, *Gebser* v. *Lago Vista Independent School District*, the Court voted 5:4 that school districts are not liable for a teacher's sexual harassment of a student unless officials knew of the problem, refused to intervene, and, acting with "deliberate indifference," failed to stop the harassment. Finally, in 1999, in another 5:4 decision that affected schools, the

Court extended the responsibility of school administrators. In *Davis* v. *Monroe County Board of Education*, the Court held school districts liable for damages under federal law for failing to stop a student from subjecting another student to severe and pervasive sexual harassment.

Yet another sexual harassment case usurped the headlines. In *Paula Corbin Jones* v. *William Jefferson Clinton*, an Arkansas state employee sued the president for an alleged incident of harassment that had occured in a room of a Little Rock hotel on May 8, 1991, when Clinton had been governor of Arkansas. In May 1997, the Supreme Court turned down Clinton's request to postpone the suit. The president's lead lawyer stressed first that Jones' claims were false and next, that even if Clinton had behaved inappropriately, Jones suffered no legal harm and could prove no sexual harassment. The federal district judge agreed (the *Burlington* decision concerning an unfulfilled threat had not yet been handed down). When a federal district court dismissed the case in April 1998, Paula Jones at first filed an appeal and then settled for $850,000. While the case was in progress, however, Jones lawyers had called for testimony from the president and from women reported to have had relationships with him. This category included a White House intern, Monica Lewinsky. The Jones case eventually led to revelations of what Clinton called an "inappropriate relationship" between the intern and the president, extended an investigation of presidential misconduct by special prosecutor Kenneth Starr, and inspired charges of lying under oath and impeachment hearings in the House. Sexual harassment charges by an obscure state employee thus led indirectly to impeachment of the president, though not to conviction.

Sexual harassment remained, however, a confusing area of law, or as legal journalist Jeffrey Toobin contended, "mired in murk." Was it intended to protect women from sexual impropriety (as Paula Jones' lawyers assumed) or from job discrimination? Did women need special "protection" on the job that men did not? Did the law blur (as some charged) the difference between consensual sex and harassment? Finally, did job discrimination against women have to involve sexual harassment? In many instances, claimed law professor Vicki Schultz, judges had ruled against women who endured job discrimination that was not overtly sexual. The courts, she asserted, had subscribed to an overly narrow conception of the hostile work environment, one that centered on sexual abuse, primarily on a male supervisor's advances to a less powerful female subordinate, thus ignoring an equally injurious, nonsexual form of gender-based discrimination in the workplace. "But the real issue isn't sex, it's sexism on the job," Schultz argued. In articles in the *Yale Law Journal* and the *Nation*, Schultz sought to return sexual harassment law to it roots as antidiscrimination law. Most harassment cases were about "protecting work—especially the most favored lines of work—as preserves of male competence and authority," she claimed. "Sex harassment is a means for men to claim work as masculine turf. That's why women who work in jobs traditionally held by men are more likely than other women to experience hostility and harassment at work." According to Schultz, the law should prevent not sex but discrimination. The law must be true to Title VII's intent "to provide people the chance to pursue their life's work on equal terms."

Supreme Court cases of the 1990s thus dealt with questions of gender neutrality and gender justice, and brought up difficult questions of difference and equality with which women were concerned. For more than a decade, contemporary feminism had wrestled with contradictions. Some feminists gave priority to securing equality between men and women; others celebrated differences between men and women. This tension had pervaded feminism since its origins. Women politicians of the 1990s often capitalized on one or the other strands of the feminist debate. In some instances, they contended that they filled the same roles as men. As Senator Nancy Kassebaum, a Republican, explained in 1991 before the Senate vote on Clarence Thomas, she rejected the suggestion that she "vote not as a Senator but as a woman." In other instances, they cited the theme of difference. Men could not "hear with a woman's ear or process information through a woman's experience," said Democrat Ann Richards, who served as governor of Texas in the early 1990s. "We pick up different nuances and bring valuable skills to the process." As the twenty-first century began, tensions inherent in feminism and conflict over women's rights and roles remained prominent features of political debate and public life.

SUGGESTED READINGS AND SOURCES

For surveys of recent women's history, see William H. Chafe, *The Paradox of Change: American Women in the 20th Century* (New York, 1991), ch. 12, and Rosalind Rosenberg, *Divided Lives: American Women in the 20th Century* (New York, 1992), ch. 7.

For feminism in the 1980s and 1990s, see Betty Freidan, *The Second Stage* (New York, 1982); Sylvia Ann Hewlett, *A Lesser Life: The Myth of Women's Liberation in America* (New York, 1986); Elizabeth Fox-Genovese, *Feminism Without Illusions: A Critique of Individualism* (Chapel Hill, N.C., 1991); Naomi Wolf, *The Beauty Myth* (New York, 1991); Susan Faludi, *Backlash: The Undeclared War Against American Women* (New York, 1991); Carol Tavris, *The Mismeasure of Woman* (New York, 1992); Katha Politt, *Reasonable Creatures: Essays on Women and Feminism* (New York, 1994); Nancy Whittier, *Feminist Generations: The Persistence of the Radical Women's Movement* (Philadelphia, 1995); Deborah L. Rhode, *Speaking of Sex: The Denial of Gender Inequality* (Cambridge, Mass., 1997); Linda Nicholson, ed., *Second Wave* (New York, 1997); and Barbara Johnson, *The Feminist Difference: Literature, Psychoanalysis, Race, and Gender* (Cambridge, Mass., 1998). Robert Max Johnson explores the waning of gender inequality in *Destined for Equality: The Inevitable Rise of Women's Status* (Cambridge, Mass., 1998). Discussions of feminist ideas include Hester Eisenstein, *Contemporary Feminist Thought* (Boston, 1983); Elizabeth V. Spelman, *Inessential Women: Problems of Exclusion in Feminist Thought* (Boston, 1989); and Jean Bethke Elshtain, *Power Trips and Other Journeys: Essays in Feminism as Civic Discourse* (Madison, Wisc., 1990). See also Susan Bolotin, "Voices from the Post-Feminist Generation," *New York Times Magazine* (October 11, 1982), 28ff. Betty Friedan comments on feminist history at intervals in the *New York Times Magazine* articles, including "Feminism Takes a New Turn" (November 18, 1979); "Twenty Years After the Feminine Mystique" (February 27, 1983); and "How to Get the Women's Movement Moving Again" (November 3, 1985). Vivian Gornick reflects on the 1960s generation of feminists in "Who Says We Haven't Made a Revolution: A Feminist Takes Stock," *New York Times Magazine* (April 15, 1990).

For women's opposition to feminism, see Phyllis Schlafly, *The Power of the Positive Woman* (New York, 1978); Andrea Dworkin, *Right Wing Women* (New York, 1983); Susan Harding, "Family Reform Movements: Recent Feminism and Its Opposition," *Feminist Studies*, 7

(Spring 1981), 57–75; Rebecca Klatch, *Women of the New Right* (Philadelphia, 1987); and Elinor Burkett, *The Right Women: A Journey through the Heart of Conservative America* (New York, 1998), For the ERA, see Jane J. Mansbridge, *Why We Lost the ERA* (Chicago, 1986); Mary Frances Berry, *Why ERA Failed: Politics, Women's Rights, and the Amending Process of the Constitution* (Bloomington, Ind., 1986); Joan Hoff-Wilson, ed., *Rights of Passage: The Past and Future of the ERA* (Bloomington, Ind., 1986); and Donald G. Mathews and Jane Sherron De Hart, *Sex, Gender, and the Politics of ERA: A State and the Nation* (New York, 1990), which focuses on the conflict over ERA in North Carolina. For the abortion controversy, see Kristin Luker, *Abortion and the Politics of Motherhood* (Berkeley, Calif., 1984), and Faye D. Ginsburg, *Contested Lives: The Abortion Debate in an American Community* (Berkeley, Calif., 1989).

Positions on pornography are presented in Laura Lederer, ed., *Take Back the Night: Women on Pornography* (New York, 1980); Susan Griffeth, *Pornography and Silence: Culture's Revenge Against Nature* (New York, 1981); Linda Williams, *Hard Core: Power, Pleasure, and the "Frenzy of the Visible"* (Berkeley, Calif., 1989); Dorchen Leidholdt and Janice G. Raymond, eds., *The Sexual Liberals and the Attack on Feminism* (New York, 1990); and Catharine A. MacKinnon, *Only Words* (Cambridge, Mass., 1994). Joan Hoff discusses the pornography controversy and other contemporary legal issues in *Law, Gender, and Injustice: A Legal History of U.S. Women* (New York, 1991). For feminist essays on sexuality, see Christine Stansell, Ann Snitow, et al., *Powers of Desire: The Politics of Sexuality* (New York, 1983). Issues of sex, power, and victimization are discussed in Katie Roiphe, *The Morning After: Sex, Fear, and Feminism on the American Campus* (Boston, 1993); Linda A. Fairstein, *Sexual Violence: The War Against Rape* (New York, 1993); Adele M. Stan, *Debating Sexual Correctness: Pornography, Sexual Harassment, Date Rape, and the Politics of Sexual Equality* (New York, 1995); and Pamela Susan Haag, *Consent: Sexual Rights and the Transformation of American Liberalism* (Ithaca, N.Y., 1999). For the roots of sexual harassment law, see Catharine MacKinnon, *Sexual Harassment of Working Women: A Case Study of Discrimination* (New Haven, Conn., 1979). Studies that convey the theme of sexual difference include Carol Gilligan, *In a Different Voice: Women's Conception of the Self and Morality* (New York, 1982); Carroll Smith-Rosenberg, *Disorderly Conduct: Visions of Gender in Victorian America* (New York, 1985); Suzanne Gordon, *Prisoners of Men's Dreams* (Boston, 1991); and Deborah Tannen, *You Just Don't Understand* (New York, 1990). See also Deborah L. Rhode, ed., *Theoretical Perspectives on Sexual Difference* (New Haven, Conn., 1990); and Eleanor E. Maccoby, *The Two Sexes: Growing Up Apart, Coming Together* (Cambridge, Mass., 1998). Catharine MacKinnon's books include *Towards a Feminist Theory of the State* (New York, 1989), and *Feminism Unmodified: Discourses on Life and Law* (Cambridge, Mass., 1987). For a discussion of MacKinnon's work, see Fred Strebeigh, "Defining Law on the Feminist Frontier," *The New York Times Magazine* (October 6, 1991), 28ff. Studies of same-sex relationships include Lillian Faderman, *To Believe in Women: What Lesbians Have Done for America, A History* (Boston, 1999) and Leila J. Rupp, *A Desired Past: A Short History of Same Sex Love in America* (Chicago, 1999).

For issues in women's higher education, see Mirra Komarovsky, *Women in College: Shaping New Feminine Identities* (New York, 1985); Nadya Aisenberg and Mona Harrington, *Women of Academe: Outsiders in the Sacred Grove* (Amherst, Mass., 1988); Dorothy Holland and Margaret A. Eisenhart, *Educated in Romance: Women, Achievement, and College Culture* (Chicago, 1990); and Michelle M. Tokarczyk and Elizabeth A. Fay, *Working-Class Women in the Academy: Laborers in the Knowledge Factory* (Amherst, Mass., 1993). For the impact of Women's Studies, see Elizabeth Minnich, Jean O'Barr, and Rachel Rosenfeld, eds., *Reconstructing the*

Academy: Women's Education and Women's Studies (Chicago, 1988); Jean F. O'Barr, *Feminism in Action: Building Institutions and Community through Women's Studies* (Chapel Hill, N.C., 1994); Daphne Patai and Noretta Koertge, *Professing Feminism: Cautionary Tales from the Strange World of Women's Studies* (New York, 1994); Patricia McDermott, *Politics and Scholarship: Feminist Academic Journals and the Production of Knowledge* (Urbana, Ill., 1994); Marilyn Jacoby Boxer, *When Women Ask the Questions: Creating Women's Studies in America* (Baltimore, Md., 1998); and Joan Wallach Scott, ed., *Women's Studies on the Edge* (Bloomington, Ind., 2000). The link between single-sex colleges and female achievement is discussed in M. Elizabeth Tindall, "Perspectives on Academic Women and Affirmative Action," *Educational Record*, 54 (Spring 1973), 130–135, and Joy K. Rice and Annette Hemmigs, "Women's Colleges and Women Achievers: An Update," *Signs*, 13 (Spring 1988), 546–559. Discussions of gender bias in schools include Peggy Orenstein, *Schoolgirls: Young Women, Self-Esteem, and the Confidence Gap* (New York, 1993), and Myra and David Sadker, *Failing in Fairness: How America's Schools Shortchange Girls* (New York, 1994). For the contemporary debate on coeducation, see David Tyack and Elisabeth Hansot, *Learning Together: A History of Coeducation in American Public Schools* (New York, 1992), ch. 9.

Much recent literature illuminates feminism's impact on academic disciplines and the history of ideas. See, for instance, for gender's role in shaping scientific knowledge, Londa Scheibinger, *Has Feminism Changed Science?* (Cambridge, Mass., 1999). For women and evolutionary theory, see Natalie Angier, *Woman: An Intimate Geography* (Boston, 1999) and Helen Fisher, *The First Sex: The Natural Talents of Women and How They are Changing the World* (New York, 1999). For psychoanalysis and feminism, see Mari Jo Buhle, *Feminism and its Discontents: A Century of Struggle with Psychoanalysis* (Cambridge, Mass., 1998) and Judith M. Hughes, *Freudian Analysts/Feminist Issues* (New Haven, Conn., 1999). For history, see Bonnie G. Smith, *The Gender of History: Men, Women, and Historical Practice* (Cambridge, Mass., 1998); Joan Wallach Scott, *Gender and the Politics of History* (2d. ed.) (New York, 1999); and Eileen Boris and Nupur Chaudhuri, eds., *Voices of Women Historians: The Personal, the Political, and the Professional* (Bloomington, Ind., 1999).

Victor Fuchs examines the development of the female work force since the 1960s in *Women's Quest for Equality* (Cambridge, Mass., 1988). Andrew Hacker surveys issues connected with female employment in the 1980s in "Women vs. Men in the Work Force," *New York Times Magazine* (December 9, 1984), 124ff, and "Women at Work," *New York Review of Books*, (August 14, 1986), 26–32. Felice Schwartz's controversial proposal, "Management Women and the New Facts of Life," appeared in the *Harvard Business Review* 67 (January–February 1989), 65–82. For a defense of the proposal, see Felice N. Schwartz with Jean Zimmerman, *Breaking with Tradition: Women and Work, The New Facts of Life* (New York, 1992). For the *Johnson* v. *Santa Clara County* case of 1987, see Melvin I. Urofsky, *A Conflict of Rights: The Supreme Court and Affirmative Action* (New York, 1991). For affirmative action, see also Susan D. Clayton and Faye J. Crosby, *Justice, Gender, and Affirmative Action* (Ann Arbor, Mich., 1992). For *EEOC* v. *Sears* (1987), see Alice Kessler-Harris, "EEOC v. Sears, Roebuck & Co.: A Personal Account," *Radical History Review*, 35 (Spring 1986), and Thomas Haskell and Sanford Levinson, "Academic Freedom and Expert Witnessing: Historians and the Sears Case," *Texas Law Review*, 66 (1989), 1629–1659.

For the impact of pay equity, see Paul Weiler, "The Wages of Sex: The Uses and Limits of Comparable Worth," *Harvard Law Review* 99 (June 1986), 1728–1807; Sara M. Evans and Barbara J. Nelson, *Wage Justice: Comparable Worth and the Paradox of Technocratic Reform* (Chicago,

1989), a study of Minnesota employees; and Linda M. Blum, *Between Feminism and Labor: The Significance of the Comparable Worth Movement* (Berkeley, Calif., 1991). Recent studies of women at work include Rosanna Hertz, *More Equal Than Others: Women and Men in Dual Career Marriages* (Berkeley, Calif., 1986); Sarah Hardesty and Nehama Jacobs, *Success and Betrayal: The Crisis of Women in Corporate America* (New York, 1986); Arlie Hochschild, *The Second Shift: Working Parents and the Revolution at Home* (New York, 1989); and Hochschild, *The Time Bind: When Work Becomes Home and Home Becomes Work* (New York, 1997); Faye J. Crosby, *Juggling: The Unexpected Advantage of Balancing Career, and Home for Women and Their Families* (New York, 1993); Virginia Valian, *Why So Slow? The Advancement of Women* (Cambridge, Mass., 1998), on bias against women in employment; Susan Chira, *A Mother's Place: Taking the Debate About Working Mothers Beyond Guilt and Blame* (New York, 1998); and Rosalind C. Barnett and Caryl Rivers, *She Works/He Works: How Two-Income Families are Happy, Healthy, and Thriving* (Cambridge, Mass., 1999). For child care, see Sonya Michel, *Children's Interests/Mothers/Rights: The Shaping of America's Child Care Policy* (New Haven, Conn., 1999). A lucid analysis of pregnancy and the law is Lise Vogel, *Mothers on the Job: Maternity Policy in the U.S. Workplace* (New Brunswick, N.J., 1993), which includes a discussion of *California Savings and Loan Association* v. *Guerra* (1987).

For women's roles in the armed services, see Helen Bogan, *Mixed Company: Women in the Modern Army* (Boston, 1981); Judith Hicks Stiehm, *Arms and the Enlisted Woman* (Philadelphia, 1989); Jeanne Holm, *Women in the Military: An Unfinished Revolution* (2d ed.) (Novato, Calif., 1992); Linda Byrd Francke, *Ground Zero: The Gender Wars in the Military* (New York, 1997); and *Gender Issues*, 16 (Summer 1998), which is devoted to gender and the military. Stephanie Gutman challenges sexual integration in the armed forces in *The Kinder, Gentler Military: Can America's Gender Neutral Fighting Force Still Win Wars?* (New York, 2000). Sexual harassment in the military is discussed in Jean Zimmerman, *Tailspin: Women at War in the Wake of Tailhook* (New York, 1995). Useful surveys of women's work roles include Ruth Milkman, ed., *Women, Work, and Protest: A Century of U.S. Women's Labor History* (New York, 1985), and Claudia Goldin, *Understanding the Gender Gap: An Economic History of American Women* (New York, 1990). Juliet B. Schor offers insights on the past two decades of economic change in *The Overworked American: The Unexpected Decline of Leisure* (New York, 1991). For interpretations of women's economic roles, see Nancy Folbre, *The Invisible Heart: Economics and Family Values* (New York, 2001) and Alice Kessler-Harris, *In Pursuit of Equity: Women, Men, and the Quest for Economic Citizenship in Twentieth Century America* (New York, 2001). For women's changing role in the economy and many other developments, see Sandra Opdycke, *The Routledge Historical Atlas of Women in America* (New York, 2000).

Discussions of the contemporary family include Mary Jo Bane, *Here to Stay: Families in the Twentieth Century* (New York, 1976); Christopher Lasch, *Haven in a Heartless World* (New York, 1979); Brigette Berger and Peter L. Berger, *The War Over the Family: Capturing the Middle Ground* (New York, 1983); Andrew Hacker, "Farewell to the Family?" *New York Review of Books*, 29 (March 18, 1982), 37–44; Philip Blumstein and Pepper Schwartz, *American Couples: Money, Work, Sex* (New York, 1983); and Stephanie Coontz, *The Way We Really Are: Coming to Terms with America's Changing Families* (New York, 1997). Barbara Katz Rothman examines medical, legal, and social issues in *Recreating Motherhood: Ideology and Technology in a Patriarchal Society* (New York, 1989). Leonore J. Weitzman assesses the impact of no-fault divorce in *The Divorce Revolution: The Unexpected Social and Economic Consequences for Women and Children in America* (New York, 1985). For a critique of Weitzman's thesis, see Susan Faludi, *Backlash*, cited previously, pp. 19–25.

For the feminization of poverty, see Ken Auletta, *The Underclass* (New York, 1982), and Ruth Sidel, *Women and Children Last: The Plight of Poor Women in Affluent America* (New York, 1986). See also Elliot Lebow, *Tell Them Who I Am: The Lives of Homeless Women* (New York, 1993), and Susan Sheehan, *Life For Me Ain't Been No Crystal Stair* (New York, 1994). For women's relation to the welfare state, see Linda Gordon, ed., *Women, the State, and Welfare* (Madison, Wis., 1990), and Gordon, *Pitied But Not Entitled: Single Mothers and the History of Welfare* (New York, 1994). For the replacement of welfare with workfare in 1996, see Gwendolyn Mink, *Welfare's End* (Ithaca, N.Y., 1998). Discussions of changes in black family life include Norman Riley, "Single Motherhood," *The Crisis* (November 1988), 18–22ff., and Eleanor Holmes Norton, "Restoring the Black Family," *New York Times Magazine* (June 2, 1985), 43ff. Discussions of race with attention to women's changing roles include Andrew Hacker, *Two Nations: Black and White, Separate, Hostile, Unequal* (New York, 1992), and Christopher Jencks, *Rethinking Social Policy: Race, Poverty, and the Underclass* (Cambridge, Mass., 1992). For a critical analysis of scholarship on the feminization of poverty, see Susan L. Thomas, "From the Culture of Poverty to the Culture of Single Motherhood: The New Poverty Paradigm," *Women and Politics* 14, no. 2 (1994), 65–97. For analysis of the determinants of African American family formation and family structure, see Mark A. Fossett and K. Jill Kiecolt, "Mate Availability and Family Structure Among African Americans in U.S. Metropolitan Areas," *Journal of Marriage and the Family* 55 (May, 1993), 288–302 and Donna L. Franklin, *Ensuring Inequality: The Structural Transformation of the African American Family* (New York, 1997). For the role of African American women as trendsetters, see Bart Landry, *Black Working Wives: Pioneers of the American Family Revolution* (Berkeley, Calif., 2000). For the perspective of black feminists, see bell hooks, *Ain't I a Women: Black Women and Feminism* (Boston, 1981), and *Talking Back: Thinking Feminist, Thinking Black* (Boston, 1989); Alice Walker, *In Search of Our Mothers' Gardens* (San Diego, Calif., 1983); Patricia Collins, *Black Feminist Thought: Knowledge, Consciousness, and the Politics of Empowerment* (Boston, 1989); and Barbara Smith, ed., *Home Girls: A Black Feminist Anthology* (New Brunswick, N.J., 2000).

Women's experience as immigrants in the 1970s and 1980s is discussed in "Women in Migration," a special issue of *International Migration Review*, 18 (Winter 1984); a special issue of *Migration World*, 14(1/2) (1986); Rita James Simon and Caroline Betrell, *International Migration: The Female Experience* (Totowa, N.J., 1986); and Maxine Schwartz Seller, ed., *Immigrant Women*, 2d ed. (Albany, N.Y., 1994). For an overview of women's experiences as immigrants, see Donna Gabaccia, *From the Other Side: Women, Gender, & Immigrant Life in the U.S., 1820–1990* (Bloomington, Ind., 1994). For the impact of ethnic diversity on women's history, see Ellen Carol Dubois and Vicki L. Ruiz, eds., *Unequal Sisters: A Multicultural Reader* (3d. ed.) (New York, 2000). Recent considerations of immigration and ethnicity include David Reimers, *Still the Golden Door: The Third World Comes to America* (New York, 1985); Lawrence H. Fuchs, *The American Kaleidoscope: Race, Ethnicity and the Civil Culture* (Middletown, Conn., 1990); and Ronald Takaki, *A Different Mirror: A History of Multicultural America* (Boston, 1993).

The experience of Mexican American women is examined in Norma Williams's sociological study, *The Mexican American Family: Tradition and Change* (Dix Hills, N.Y., 1990) and Vicki L. Ruiz, *From Out of the Shadows: Mexican Women in Twentieth-Century America* (New York, 1998). See also Alfredo Mirandé and Evangelina Enríquez, *La Chicana: The Mexican American Woman* (Chicago, 1979). For Puerto Rican women, see Altagracia Ortiz, ed., *Puerto Rican Women and Work: Bridges in Transnational Labor* (Philadelphia, 1996), and Felix V. Matos-Rogrigues and Linda C. Delgado, eds., *Puerto Rican Women's History: New Perspectives*

(Armonk, N.Y., 1998). Aspects of women's immigration from the Philippines are discussed in Raquel Z. Ordonez, "Mail-Order Brides: An Emerging Community" in Maria P.P. Root, ed., *Filipino Americans: Transformation and Identity* (Thousands Oaks, Calif., 1997), pp. 121–142. For the East Asian immigration, see Takaki, *Strangers from a Different Shore* (Boston, 1989); Joann Faung Jean Lee, ed., *Asian American Experiences in the United States* (Jefferson, N.C., 1991); Mei T. Nakano, *Japanese American Women: Three Generations, 1890–1990* (San Francisco, 1990); Elaine H. Kim and Eui-Young Yu, *East to America: Korean American Life Stories* (New York, 1996); Ai Ra Kim, *Women Struggling for a New Life* (Albany, N.Y., 1996); Young I. Song and Ailee Moon, eds, *Korean American Women: From Tradition to Modern Feminism* (Westport, Conn., 1998); Lisa Lowe, *Immigrant Acts: On Asian American Cultural Politics* (Durham, N.C., 1996); and Huping Ling, *Surviving on Gold Mountain: A History of Chinese American Women and Their Lives* (Albany, N.Y., 1998), part 3. See also Asian Women United of California, ed., *Making Waves: An Anthology of Writings By and About Asian-American Women* (Boston, 1989). Fiction by Asian-American women includes Jade Snow Wong's classic, *Fifth Chinese Daughter* (New York, 1950); Maxine Hong Kingston, *The Woman Warrior: Memoirs of a Girlhood Among Ghosts* (1976); Amy Tan, *The Joy Luck Club* (1989); Gish Jen, *Mona in the Promised Land* (New York, 1996); and Mei Ng, *Eating Chinese Food Naked* (New York, 1998). For voices of immigrant women from Asia, India, Africa, and elsewhere, see Meri Nana-Ama Danquah, ed., *Becoming American: Personal Essays by First Generation Immigrant Women* (New York, 2000). For Native American Women, see Paula Gunn Allen, *The Sacred Hoop: Recovering the Feminine in American Indian Tradition* (Boston, 1986); Mary Crow Dog, *Lakota Woman* (New York, 1990); Wilma Mankiller, *Mankiller: A Chief and Her People* (New York, 1993); and Karen Anderson, *Changing Woman: A History of Racial Ethnic Women in Modern America* (New York, 1996), ch. 4.

Discussions of the Hill-Thomas hearings of 1991 include Timothy M. Phelps and Helen Winternitz, *Capitol Games: Clarence Thomas, Anita Hill, and the Story of a Supreme Court Nomination* (New York, 1992); Paul Simon, *Advice and Consent: Clarence Thomas, Robert Bork, and the Intriguing History of the Supreme Court's Nomination Battles* (Washington, D.C., 1992); Toni Morrison, ed., *Race-ing Justice, En-gendering Power: Essays on Anita Hill, Clarence Thomas, and the Construction of Social Reality* (New York, 1992); Robert Chrisman and Robert L. Allen, eds., *Court of Appeal: The Black Community Speaks Out on the Racial and Sexual Politics of Clarence Thomas vs. Anita Hill* (New York 1992); John C. Danforth, *Resurrection: The Confirmation of Clarence Thomas* (New York, 1994); and Jane Mayer and Jill Abramson, *Strange Justice: The Selling of Clarence Thomas* (Boston and New York, 1994). See also Mayer and Abramson in "The Surreal Anita Hill," *New Yorker* 69 (May 24, 1993), 90–97. Anita Hill's publications of the 1990s are Anita Faye Hill and Emma Coleman Jordan, eds., *Race, Gender, and Power in America: The Legacy of the Hill-Thomas Hearings* (New York, 1995); and Anita Hill, *Speaking Truth to Power* (New York, 1997).

Women's political roles are explored in Susan M. Hartmann, *From Margin to Mainstream: American Women and Politics Since 1960* (New York, 1989); Ethel Klein, *Gender Politics: From Consciousness to Mass Politics* (Cambridge, Mass., 1985); Linda Witt, Karen M. Paget, and Glenna Matthews, *Running as a Woman: Gender and Power in American Politics* (New York, 1993); and Kathleen Hall Jamieson, *Beyond the Double Bind; Women and Leadership* (New York, 1995). For the 1984 election, see Geraldine A. Ferraro with Linda Bird Franke, *Ferraro: My Story* (New York, 1985); Jane Perlez, "Women, Power, and Politics," *New York Times Magazine* (July 24, 1984), 23ff; Elizabeth Drew, "A Political Journal," *New Yorker*, 60 (August 13, 1984),

34–44; and Maureen Dowd, "Reassessing Women's Political Role: The Lasting Impact of Geraldine Ferraro," *New York Times Magazine* (December 30, 1984), 18ff. Interpretations of Hillary Rodham Clinton's role in public affairs include Connie Bruck, "Hillary the Pol," *New Yorker* 70 (May 30, 1994) 58–96; Henry Louis Gates, Jr., "Hating Hillary," *New Yorker* 72 (February 26 and March 4, 1996), 116–121; and Joyce Milton, *The First Partner, Hillary Rodham Clinton* (New York, 1999). For EMILY's List, see Jon Freedman, "The Founding Mother," *New York Times Magazine* (May 2, 1993), 50ff. The issue of coeducation at military schools is presented in Catherine S. Manegold, *In Glory's Shadow: Shannon Faulkner, the Citadel, and a Changing America* (New York, 2000). For Ruth Bader Ginsburg's career, see Jeffrey Rosen, "The New Look of Liberalism on the Court," *New York Times Magazine* (October 5, 1997), 60ff.

The issue of sexual harassment in the workplace is discussed in Catharine MacKinnon, *Sexual Harassment of Working Women*, cited previously; Amber Coverdale Sumrall and Dena Taylor, eds., *Sexual Harassment: Women Speak Out* (Freedom, Calif., 1992); Celia Morris, *Bearing Witness and Beyond—Every Woman's Story* (Boston, 1994); Alison M. Thomas and Celia Kitzinger, eds., *Sexual Harassment: Contemporary Feminist Perspectives* (Bristol, Pa., 1997); Linda Lemoncheck and Mane Hajdin, *Sexual Harassment: A Debate* (Lanham, Md., 1997); *NWSA Journal* 9 (Summer 1997), an issue on sexual harassment; Daphne Patai, *Heterophobia: Sexual Harassment and the Future of Feminism* (Lanham, Md., 1998); Laura W. Stein, ed., *Sexual Harassment in America: A Documentary History* (Westport, Conn., 1999); and Gwendolyn Mink, *Hostile Environment: The Political Betrayal of Sexually Harassed Women* (Ithaca, N.Y., 2000). See also Kathryn Abrams, "The Reasonable Woman: Sense and Sensibility in Sexual Harassment Law," *Dissent* 42 (Winter 1995), 48–54, and Vicki Schultz, "Reconceptualizing Sexual Harassment," *Yale Law Journal* 107 (April 98), 1635–1805. On Clinton's impeachment, see Richard A. Posner, *An Affair of State: The Investigation, Impeachment, and Trial of President Clinton* (Cambridge, Mass., 1999) and Jeffrey Toobin, *A Vast Conspiracy* (New York, 2000).

For the concept of gender justice, see David L. Kirp, Mark G. Yadof, and Marlene Strong Franks, *Gender Justice* (Chicago, 1986); Susan Moller Okin, *Justice, Gender, and the Family* (New York, 1989); and "Women and Rights," *Dissent*, 38 (Summer 1991), 369–405. Legal issues are discussed further in Joan Hoff-Wilson, *Law, Gender, and Injustice*, cited previously; Deborah L. Rhode, *Justice and Gender: Sex Discrimination and the Law* (Cambridge, Mass., 1989); Susan Gluck Mezey, *In Pursuit of Equality: Women, Policy, and the Federal Courts* (New York, 1992); D. Kelley Weisberg, ed. *Feminist Legal Theory: Foundations* (Philadelphia, 1993); Patricia Smith, ed., *Feminist Jurisprudence* (New York, 1993); Cynthia R. Daniels, *At Women's Expense: State Power and the Politics of Fetal Rights* (Cambridge, Mass., 1993); Lani Guinier, Michelle Fine, and Jane Balin, *Becoming Gentlemen: Women, Law School, and Institutional Change* (Boston, 1997); Nancy Levit, *The Gender Line: Men, Women, and the Law* (New York, 1998); and Sandra F. VanBurkleo, *"Belonging to the World:" Women's Rights and American Constitutional Culture* (New York, 2001).

For quizzes and additional resources related to American women's history, visit the book's Website at *www.mhhe.com/americanwomen*.

Index

Note: Italic pages indicate illustrations.